Coastal California

John A Vlahides, Alex Hershey

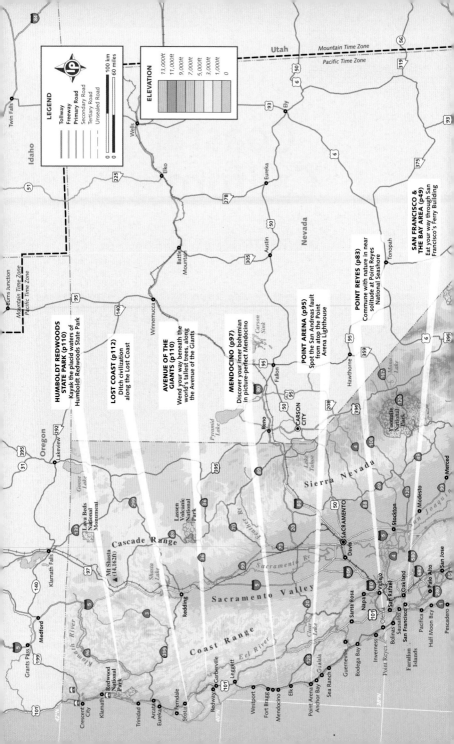

LEGEND

Tollway
Freeway
Primary Road
Secondary Road
Tertiary Road
Unsealed Road

ELEVATION

13,000ft
11,000ft
9,000ft
7,000ft
5,000ft
3,000ft
1,000ft
0

100 km
60 miles

HUMBOLDT REDWOODS STATE PARK (p110)
Kayak the placid waters of Humboldt Redwoods State Park

LOST COAST (p112)
Ditch civilization along the Lost Coast

AVENUE OF THE GIANTS (p110)
Wend your way beneath the world's tallest trees, along the Avenue of the Giants

MENDOCINO (p97)
Discover your inner bohemian in picture-perfect Mendocino

POINT ARENA (p95)
Spot the San Andreas fault from atop the Point Arena Lighthouse

POINT REYES (p83)
Commune with nature in near solitude at Point Reyes National Seashore

SAN FRANCISCO & THE BAY AREA (p49)
Eat your way through San Francisco's Ferry Building

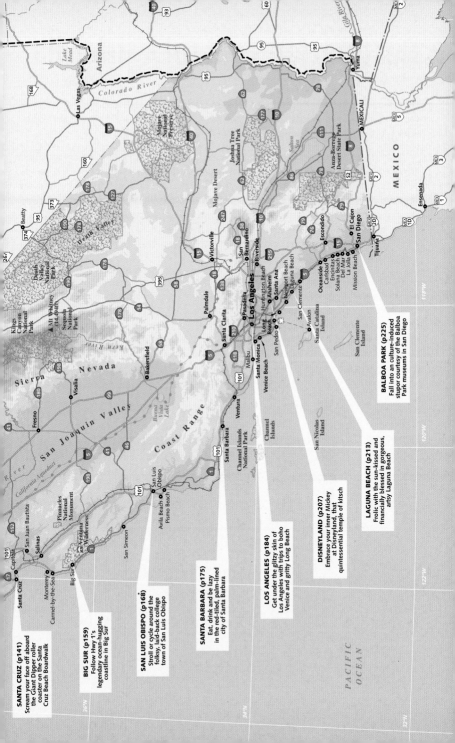

SANTA CRUZ (p141)
Scream your face off aboard the Giant Dipper roller coaster on the Santa Cruz Beach Boardwalk

BIG SUR (p159)
Follow Hwy 1's legendary ocean-hugging coastline in Big Sur

SAN LUIS OBISPO (p168)
Stroll or cycle around the folksy, laid-back college town of San Luis Obispo

SANTA BARBARA (p175)
Eat, drink and be lazy in the red-tiled, palm-lined city of Santa Barbara

LOS ANGELES (p184)
Get under the glitzy skin of Los Angeles with trips to boho Venice and gritty Long Beach

DISNEYLAND (p207)
Embrace your inner Mickey at Disneyland, that quintessential temple of kitsch

LAGUNA BEACH (p213)
Frolic with the sun-kissed and financially blessed in gorgeous, artsy Laguna Beach

BALBOA PARK (p225)
Fall into an culture-induced stupor courtesy of the Balboa Park museums in San Diego

Destination Coastal California

Welcome to the westernmost edge of Western civilization. Coastal California has a way of capturing the imagination unlike any other place in the US, thanks in part to the comic-book proportions of the culture.

Go-go Los Angeles really is just like in the movies, with palm–tree–lined boulevards, Rolls Royce convertibles and Botoxed blondes awaiting their big breaks. Check out the parade of hotties on Orange County's sandy beaches, where too-cool dudes and bikinied babes strut and preen as if auditioning for spots on *Baywatch*. If you prefer goofy grins to chiseled chests, head to Northern California, land of free love, go-it-alone politics and cannabis-buyers' clubs. Frolic au naturel in the crashing surf of a nude beach. Scream your face off aboard a rickety wooden roller coaster on the boardwalk in Santa Cruz. Or head to San Francisco and eat like a prince on a pauper's budget.

But the biggest wow in Coastal California is the spectacular scenery – thousand-foot cliffs plunging into the sea, the world's tallest trees clinging precipitously to almost-vertical hill-sides, lonely lighthouses standing sentinel as giant gray whales breach offshore. This is where America ends and the vast blue Pacific begins. There's something magical about being on the shore of the largest body of water on Earth, hypnotized by the play of color and light, your view restricted only by the curvature of the planet. And that's the one thing that Californians agree on: all stand in awe of the coast's limitlessness and mystery. You will too.

DAVID RYA

Highlights

JOHN ELK III

Stand in awe where the sea meets the sky at Drakes Bay, Point Reyes National Seashore (p83)

Surfing USA! Santa Cruz (p141) is a perfect place in Coastal California to take off, drop in and hang ten

RICK GERHARTER

ANTHONY PIDGE

Feast on a stellar range of local, sustainable and regional foods at the Ferry Building (p49) in San Francisco

Make a pit stop at quirky Redwood Trails general store (p130) in Humboldt County for horseback rides and kitschy souvenirs

RICHARD CUMM

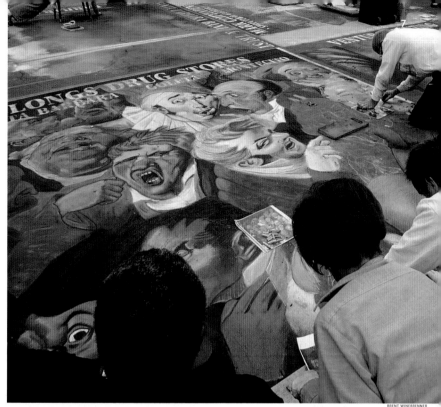

BRENT WINEBRENNER

A riot of color and artistic talent is a hallmark of the Madonnari Italian Street Painting Festival (p177) at the Mission Santa Barbara, Santa Barbara

It's worth rising early for a picture-postcard view of dawn fog as it rolls across the Golden Gate Bridge (p50) in San Francisco

RICHARD CUMMINS

RICHARD CUMMINS

MICHAEL

Tune in to the vibe in Venice (p196) and
be entertained by local icons such as
Harry Perry Kama Kosmick Krusader

Put the top down and roar over the Bixby Bridge
(p160), along the Big Sur coastline

Kids (and those who are long in the tooth, too) will be delighted by new friends at San Diego's
SeaWorld (p230)

EDDIE BRA

Contents

Regional Map Contents

North Coast (p87)

San Francisco & the Bay Area (p48)

Central Coast (p140)

Los Angeles & Orange County (p188)

San Diego Area (p218)

The Authors

JOHN A VLAHIDES
**Coordinating author,
San Francisco Bay Area, North Coast**

Native New Yorker John A Vlahides lives in San Francisco. He is a French-trained chef, former luxury-hotel concierge and member of *Les Clefs d'Or*, the Paris-based union of the world's elite concierges.

John is the executive editor and cofounder of 71miles.com, an insider's guide to local travel. He coproduces a monthly TV travel segment and has appeared as a travel expert on national and local TV networks and contributed articles to Condé Nast, *Sunset,* the *San Francisco Chronicle, Out Traveler* and others. John spends free time downhill skiing in the Sierra Nevada, touring California by motorcycle, singing tenor for the SF Symphony and sunning on the beach beneath the Golden Gate Bridge.

My Favorite Trip

While I dig LA's go-go-vibe and San Diego's perfect weather, my favorite spots lie further north. There the land is undeveloped, cell phones don't work, and you're free to trip out, on the play of light over the land and sea. March is the 'emerald month' and my fave time for travel in California because the hills turn electric green. I'd start in magical Big Sur (p159), which remains true to its boho roots. I never grow bored with San Francisco (p47), but when I need a break I hide out in Anchor Bay (p94). No matter how many times I see them, giant redwoods always blow me away, especially in Klamath (p132). When it's time to rejoin civilization, there's no place like Sonoma (p90) with its fabulous food and wine.

ALEX HERSHEY
**Coastal California Outdoors, Central Coast,
Los Angeles & Orange County, San Diego Area**

Perhaps sensing Alex's total lack of direction after graduating from Smith College with degrees in philosophy and Russian, her friend Julia tossed Alex into the car and the two were soon Kerouacing westward…destination Seattle, via Baja. Alex soon became a Californian in spirit if not yet in body. After two years traveling and teaching in Asia, she found herself working at Lonely Planet in Oakland, escaping down Hwy 1 as frequently as possible. Alex is currently working toward her master of science in information studies at the University of Texas at Austin, and is trying to forget how far away she is from the ocean (and In-N-Out Burger).

LONELY PLANET AUTHORS

Why is our travel information the best in the world? It's simple: our authors are independent, dedicated travelers. They don't research using just the internet or phone, and they don't take freebies in exchange for positive coverage. They travel widely, to all the popular spots and off the beaten track. They personally visit thousands of hotels, restaurants, cafés, bars, galleries, palaces, museums and more – and they take pride in getting all the details right, and telling it how it is. For more, see the authors section on www.lonelyplanet.com.

Getting Started

California is huge, and it takes time to get around. You can take the train or bus between cities and some towns, but you'll need a car to reach the coast's many remote sights. Once outside of major metropolitan areas it's easy to navigate, and your biggest problem will be keeping your eyes focused on the road and not on the beautiful scenery. If you've got kids with you, fret not: there's plenty for them to do. And despite the proliferation of high-cost lodging along the coast, budget travelers will find deals along the way.

WHEN TO GO

Most visitors arrive in summer, between June and September, crowding major tourist attractions and causing significant spikes in room rates, even at motels. If you come in summer, try to travel midweek, when crowds are thinner and rates cheaper. Urban and suburban traffic is worst on Fridays and Sundays. If you must travel then, avoid driving between 3pm and 7pm.

See Climate Charts (p250) for more information.

Expect summertime fog anywhere north of Santa Barbara, from late May through September. It gets chilly and gloomy, but never cold. (However, if you crave July heat, you'll have to head inland to escape the fog.) Though it rains in winter, the coast never freezes, and the hills turn green; March through May, they're dotted with wildflowers before summertime droughts turn them golden-brown again. March may be the prettiest month of all; it's nicknamed the 'emerald month' because the entire state turns green – great for pictures, bad for allergies. During the spring and fall, the ubiquitous coastal fog clears, providing the best opportunity to see the famous coastal vistas. Indian summer stretches from September through October. Visiting in winter is iffy, since rain may ruin the views, but you can get great rates on some lodging.

You can enjoy hiking, canoeing, rafting and other warm-weather outdoor activities in summer, spring and fall; swimming is only comfortable at the height of summer in Northern California and from around May to October in Southern California, though surfers and divers hit the waters year-round in wet suits. Winter is whale-watching season when gray whales migrate down the coast from Alaska.

COSTS & MONEY

Coastal California is pricey. The biggest costs are transportation, accommodations, food, drink and sightseeing. If you're traveling with children or want to keep your costs down, always ask about discounts.

The easiest, most comfortable way to see California is by car. Car-hire rates range from $160 to $300 a week; insurance costs $15 to $35 depending

---

DON'T LEAVE HOME WITHOUT...

- A good playlist for your iPod.
- Games for long car rides, especially if you have kids; Yahtzee is always good and takes little space.
- A sweater in summer, a raincoat in winter.
- Hotel or camping reservations for the places where you *really* want to stay. Don't settle for second best during the peak summer period.
- Mood lighting for ugly motel rooms; a colored light bulb and votive candles do wonders!

on the coverage selected. Gasoline is expensive in remote areas such as Big Sur – as much as a dollar per gallon more than in metropolitan regions. For more information on transportation, see p259.

Lodging costs run highest between Memorial Day (late May) and Labor Day (early September). Basic motels start at $50 a night and top out at $130. Midrange accommodations cost $100 to $200, and up to $900 for luxurious top-end resorts. B&Bs range from $100 to $300 (see also Accommodations, p247). To save cash, head inland and choose motels near freeways as accommodations along the coast cost up to 30% more.

If you don't insist on sit-down meals, you need not spend much money on food. Eat at simple, hole-in-the-wall restaurants or *taquerias* (taco shops; burritos are the California survival food). For more substantial meals, lunch is cheaper than dinner. Remember to add tax and a 15% to 20% tip. Plan on $10 to $30 per meal; ask for childrens menus too.

Many museums have an admission-free day or evening once a month. Entrance to national parks and historic sites costs $4 to $20 per vehicle and is valid for multiple entries over seven days.

TRAVEL LITERATURE

Southern California would not exist as it does today without water. Marc Reisner's must-read *Cadillac Desert: The American West and Its Disappearing Water* examines, in dynamic prose, the contentious, sometimes violent, water wars that gave rise to modern California.

In *Where I Was From,* Joan Didion dissects the mythology of life in California, from the early pioneers, of whom she is a descendant, to the new arrivals and their shut-the-door-behind-me mentality; the latter chapters examine a Southern California suburb gone haywire following the demise of the local aerospace industry.

For a frothy taste of San Francisco in 1978, the serial-style *Tales of the City,* by Armistead Maupin, collars the reader as the author follows the lives of several colorful, fictional characters, gay and straight. Its short chapters make it ideal for reading on the plane, and you'll want to rush to the sights mentioned in the text.

If you've never read any novels by John Steinbeck, you must do so before visiting Coastal California. Pick up *Cannery Row,* particularly if you plan to visit Monterey. Travel back to a time when California's first capital was populated by adventurers and hooligans, heroes and whores. In Steinbeck's classic tale, you'll come to appreciate the humanity and holiness in all of them. *East of Eden* takes place in nearby Salinas, and is an epic family drama as well as a study of archetypes and opposites. Best of all, when you arrive in the area, you'll immediately recognize the landscape and sites Steinbeck so deftly describes in both texts.

INTERNET RESOURCES

Hunt down bargain airfares, book hotels, check on weather conditions or chat with locals and other travelers about the best places to visit – or avoid – on the internet.

Start with the Lonely Planet website (www.lonelyplanet.com). You'll find succinct summaries and the Thorn Tree forum, where you can post questions before you go or dispense advice when you get back.

Other recommendations:

California Department of Tourism (www.gocalif.com) Links to all visitors bureaus throughout the state.

California State Government (www.ca.gov) Links to general information, history, culture, doing business and environmental protection.

HOW MUCH?

Motel room in Northern California $50-110

Dinner for two in Los Angeles $35-60+

Movie ticket to feature film $10

Local phone call 35-50¢

Small cup of coffee $1.50

TOP TENS

Party Time

Californians love a good party. From street fairs to regattas, there are festivals all year long. Here are some of our favorites, but check the destination chapters for more ideas.

- Festival of Swallows (San Juan Capistrano; p216) March 19
- Bay to Breakers (San Francisco; p59) May
- Kinetic Sculpture Race (Arcata; p125) May
- Midnight Mass (San Francisco; p59) June through August
- San Francisco Gay Pride (p59) June
- Amtrak Mooning (Laguna Niguel; p214) July
- Pageant of the Masters (Laguna Beach; p215) July
- US Open Sandcastle Competition (Imperial Beach; p235) July
- Reggae on the River (Garberville; p109) August
- Monterey Jazz Festival (Monterey; p153) September

Now Playing

Crank up the tunes, dude. Create a California playlist for your iPod, starting with the following songs.

- 'California Waiting' – Kings of Leon
- 'California Bound' – Frank Black
- 'California' – Rogue Wave
- 'Californication' – Red Hot Chili Peppers
- 'California Love' – 2Pac
- 'California' – Tom Petty & the Heartbreakers
- 'California Dreamin'' – The Mamas & the Papas
- 'It Never Rains in California' – Albert Hammond
- 'California Girls' – Beach Boys
- 'Back to California' – Sugar Cult

Top Reads

Want a book to read at the beach? Consider any of the following, all of which lend cool insights into the Golden State.

- *My California: Journeys by Great Writers* (2004)
  Donna Wares and Mark Arax
- *A Heartbreaking Work of Staggering Genius* (2001)
  Dave Eggers
- *The Woman Warrior* (1998)
  Maxine Hong Kingston
- *The Electric Kool-Aid Acid Test* (1968)
  Ken Kesey
- *Dharma Bums* (1958)
  Jack Kerouac
- *The Maltese Falcon* (1930)
  Dashiell Hammett
- *The Joy Luck Club* (1989)
  Amy Tan
- *Baghdad by the Bay* (1949)
  Herb Caen
- *Cannery Row* (1945)
  John Steinbeck
- *Less than Zero* (1985)
  Bret Easton Ellis

California State Parks (www.parks.ca.gov) Indispensable site for history, information and reservations at all state parks.

Caltrans (www.dot.ca.gov) For questions about driving in California including trip planning, map assistance and highway and weather conditions.

National Park Service (www.nps.gov) Provides information on every national park, historic site and monument.

National Weather Service (www.wrh.noaa.gov) Extensive climate data including forecasts, radar, weather records and satellite images.

Itineraries
CLASSIC ROUTES

A TALE OF TWO STATES   San Francisco to San Diego / Two to Three Weeks

Northern and Southern California couldn't be more different. Observe the increasing cultural divide as you work your way south. Get a primer on the NorCal food scene in **San Francisco** (p47), before driving down Hwy 1 along the edge of the continent. Consider the merits of socialism on the beach in **Santa Cruz** (p141) before donning hiking boots and going off the grid in **Big Sur** (p159). Once you've dropped your jaw at **Hearst Castle** (p164), pull yourself together in oh-so-civilized **Santa Barbara** (p175) and taste why Miles in *Sideways* refused to drink merlot in the **Santa Barbara Wine Country** (see boxed text, p178). Shop for strappy sandals and trip on the star-maker machinery in **Los Angeles** (p185), then question the nature of happiness at the 'happiest place on Earth,' **Disneyland** (p207). Ditch the car and dig the arts in picture-perfect **Laguna Beach** (p213), the OC's prettiest town, then settle in **San Diego** (p218), home to the US Naval fleet. It's America's best-looking city where nothing ever happens. Finish with a day trip to dusty **Tijuana** (p244) – aka Mexico-light – where Northern California feels *really* far away.

It's not just the land that changes as you zip down the coast from Northern to Southern California; the culture also changes greatly. Two weeks is enough to get a sense of place, but if you want to take sides in the culture wars, you'll need at least three weeks to start forming your own opinions.

A NORCAL FORTNIGHT   San Francisco to Crescent City / One to Two Weeks

If you've dreamed of discovering the Northern California coast, two weeks provide just enough time to get a sense of place. Start in San Francisco, but once you're out of the city, trade your Italian-leather shoes for a pair of Timberland boots and blend right in.

Spend a few days exploring the tapestry of neighborhoods in **San Francisco** (p47). On your way out of town, snap killer pictures of the Golden Gate Bridge from the **Marin Headlands** (p72). Spend a few nights near **Point Reyes National Seashore** (p83), where you can trek among herds of elk and watch whales breach offshore. Very cool. Next, set up house around **Anchor Bay** (p94) and climb **Point Arena Lighthouse** (p95) to scout a hike on the coastal bluffs. Take your inner artist on a retreat to moody **Mendocino** (p97), and learn to see beauty in the fog. Next say hello to redwood country, where you can wander in the cathedral of trees in the world's largest contiguous redwood forest at **Humboldt Redwoods State Park** (p110). Ditch civilization as you hike the **Lost Coast** (p112), then reemerge into a time warp in Victorian **Ferndale** (p115). Argue politics in **Arcata** (p122), where the Green Party is considered moderate. Ogle critter-packed tide pools at **Patrick's Point State Park** (p129) before disappearing beneath the canopy of 1500-year-old trees in **Redwood National Park** (p130). Spot eagle and osprey vying for salmon over the river at **Klamath** (p132), then stock up on provisions in **Crescent City** (p135) before exploring the river canyons along the state's last-remaining undammed waterway in the **Smith River National Recreation Area** (see boxed text, p138). Leave time to get lost!

The moody, fog-shrouded North Coast extends northward from San Francisco in a patchwork of misty coves, giant forests and tiny little towns straight out of a Hitchcock movie. Two weeks are ideal, but one gives a good taste of the NorCal boho life.

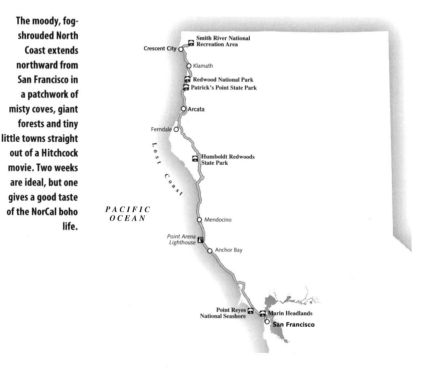

BEYOND THE REDWOOD CURTAIN   One to Two Weeks

The world's tallest trees tower over the North Coast of California. The lush forest beneath the canopy – carpeted with spiky ferns, giant rhododendrons and purple-and-green clover patches – is a magical world found nowhere else on Earth. To groove on the mighty giants and the mysterious fog-shrouded world beneath, start in **San Francisco** (p47) and make a loop. Head north on Hwy 101, the Redwood Hwy, all the way to the far north on day one, then slowly work your way back along the Pacific. Alternatively do this in reverse and make the return trip in one day.

Cross the **Golden Gate Bridge** (p50) and drive eight hours to the nothing-special town of **Crescent City** (p135), which nonetheless makes a good base for exploring the big trees in **Jedediah Smith Redwoods State Park** (p137). Better yet, camp in the park beside the Smith River. Head south to **Redwood National Park** (p130) and stay in **Klamath** (p132), capital of the Middle of Nowhere. After a few nights in the woods, city folks appreciate a fancy meal with a good bottle of wine in **Eureka** (p117), or a hot bath in a claw-foot tub in a B&B in Victorian **Ferndale** (p115). Feel dwarfed, as if driving a Matchbox car, along the **Avenue of the Giants** (p110), the perfect backdrop for a homemade suspense movie. Make a beaded necklace in boho-chic **Mendocino** (p97), then set up in a seaside housekeeping cottage in **Anchor Bay** (p94). Before heading back to the city, make a detour to **Sonoma Wine Country** (see boxed text, p90) to sample the local vintages. Spend an extra day or two in **San Francisco**. Celebrate your return to civilization with a fabulous dinner.

Crescent City
Jedediah Smith
Redwoods State Park
Klamath
Redwood National Park
Eureka
Ferndale
Avenue of the Giants

PACIFIC
OCEAN

Mendocino

Anchor Bay

Sonoma Wine Country

San Francisco
Golden Gate Bridge

Strolling beneath California's famous redwoods is a knockout experience that everyone should do at least once in their lives. This one- to two-week trip up the North Coast provides lots of opportunities to crane your neck and stare slack-jawed at these mighty giants.

CENTRAL COAST CLIMBS & SEASIDE JAUNTS   One to Two Weeks

Along the Central Coast, the Coastal Range lords over sophisticated seaside towns. If you like a mix of outdoor activities and in-town culture, use the following outline to find some primo spots for your fave activities.

Start your week in **San Luis Obispo** (p168), where you can wonder who in the hell thought chewing gum made good wall art. Pull on your hiking boots and summit beautiful Bishop's Peak; scramble to the top for the spectacular vista and a strenuous hike. Rest your muscles and recuperate on the sand at **Avila Beach** (p171) or **Pismo Beach** (p173), where you can indulge in the tasty-fun local specialty: clam chowder in a bread bowl. Barge the dunes on the massive shifting sands of **Guadalupe Dunes Preserve** (p173), and see where Cecil B DeMille buried his enormous *Ten Commandments* movie set. Shop for a sexy black dress on Sate St in **Santa Barbara** (p175) and climb to the top of the courthouse for bird's-eye views over town. Sample the juice in pastoral **Santa Barbara Wine Country** (see boxed text, p178), where you can get lost on winding back roads. Go for a thigh-busting hike up the giant Santa Ynez Mountains, the giant peaks above Santa Barbara. Back on the coast, meet local hotties in a pickup game of volleyball on East Beach (p179), or take your sweetheart to Butterfly Beach (p179) and play Great Gatsby. If you can deal with isolation, board the boat for **Channel Islands National Park** (p182), and devote several days to exploring the 'American Galapagos.' Back on dry land, make a detour to **Malibu** (p195) to check out the amazing antiquities of the Getty Villa and speculate about how they procured them.

The Central Coast has a perfect blend of outdoor sports and sybaritic pleasures. If you like to spend your days hiking, but never want to be too far from a good bottle of pinot noir, you'll do well on this itinerary.

TAILORED TRIPS

FREAKS & WEIRDOS UNITE

While researching the North Coast, we encountered an ultraconservative innkeeper who told us, 'I run a safe place. I don't allow any gays, freaks or troublemakers.' Hmmm. Doesn't sound too safe to us. This got us thinking, What about the leftie-liberal freaks? Nobody writes for them. This *is* California after all; if you can't be freaky here, where can you be? So instead of going on the defensive, unfurl your dreadlocks and head for the epicenter of freakdom: Northern California. Safe space, we promise.

In **Santa Cruz** (p141) bumper stickers read, 'Keep Santa Cruz Weird.' Indeed. Meet like-minded freaks at **UC Santa Cruz** (p141). Hear conspiracy theories at **Cafe Pergolesi** (p147). In **San Francisco** (p47), America's most liberal city, visit **Haight Street** (see boxed text, p62) to see who's trapped in 1968. Meet gay boys in the **Castro** (see boxed text, p62). Join a drumming circle on Hippie Hill in **Golden Gate Park** (p56). The **Mission District** (see boxed text, p62) is San Francisco's new melting pot; everyone fits in, even you. For all its gift shops **Mendocino** (p97) is remarkably broad minded; visit **Mendocino Coast Environmental Center** (p102) to hear the latest ecocontroversies. **Garberville** (p109) is pot-growing country, and where there's pot, there are weirdos. 'Nuf said. But no place embraces freaks like **Arcata** (p122); head directly to **Humboldt State University** (p124) to find your tribe.

AMERICANA KITSCH

Way back when, before Disney corporatized the theme park, quirky roadside attractions were everywhere in California. Most have long since disappeared, but you'd be surprised how many wacky spots remain. Where else could you drive through a carved-out redwood or stroll through an ersatz Danish village, complete with faux windmills?

On the North Coast, squeeze your Buick through the **Shrine Tree** (p111) and spot animatronic hobbits in the woods at **Hobbiton** (p111). Get to the **Chandelier Drive-thru Tree** (p107) and play tricks on gravity at **Confusion Hill** (p107). Look for **chainsaw burl carvers** along Hwy 1 (one claims to be 'carving for Christ'). In San Francisco, shove quarters in the opium den at the **Musée Mécanique** (p57) and wow at Leonardo da Vinci's invention, the **Camera Obscura** (p59). On the Central Coast, spin a compass in Santa Cruz at the **Mystery Spot** (p141), check out the fake waterfall in the mens room of the **Madonna Inn** (p170), and chase windmills in compulsively cute **Solvang** (p174). In LA, shop at **Skeletons in the Closet** (see boxed text, p198), the LA County Morgue's gift shop, then blur the edges of reality at the **Museum of Jurassic Technology** (p196). And what could be more Americana than America's first theme park? Head to **Knott's Berry Farm** (see boxed text, p210) and fatten up on Mrs Knott's fried chicken.

THIS LAND IS YOUR LAND

Two of California's six national parks are on the coast. In the north, crane your neck at the world's tallest trees in **Redwood National Park** (p130). Tip: get the lock combination to the gate to **Tall Trees Grove** (p130). Take a boat to reach **Channel Islands National Park** (p182); for a $125 splurge, fly there. Wintertime whale-watching is fantastic at **Cabrillo National Monument** (p229) in San Diego; and up north at **Point Reyes National Seashore** (p83). In Santa Barbara, hike the **Santa Ynez Mountains**, which lord over town like enormous curtains.

State beaches dot the coast, even amid SoCal's sprawl. Some have hiking up the cliffs, like Orange County's **Crystal Cove State Park** (see boxed text, p212). On the Central Coast, meander amid shoulder-high spring flowers

at **Montaña de Oro** (p167). For kick-ass hiking with drop-dead views, head to Big Sur's **Ventana Wilderness** (p183).

The picture-postcard views of the craggy North Coast are great at **Sonoma Coast State Beach** (p89) and from the rocky promontories of **Mendocino Headlands** (p99). Canoe up the tidal estuary of **Big River** (p99), or scuba dive in the underwater reserve at **Salt Point** (p92). Disappear from civilization along the **Lost Coast** (p112). Bring a kayak to the calm waters of **Humboldt Lagoons** (p129). Every naturalist should see the **Smith River** (see boxed text, p138), the state's last-remaining undammed river.

FOR THE WEE ONES

Coastal California is chockablock full of old-fashioned boardwalks and family-friendly attractions sure to keep little ones jazzed – and as every parent knows, when the kids are happy, everyone's happy.

You gotta see **Disneyland** (p207), but **Knott's Berry Farm** (see boxed text, p210) also merits a visit for its thrill rides and Gold Rush–era buildings. In San Diego, visit the **San Diego Zoo** (p227) and the just-out-of-town **Wild Animal Park** (see boxed text, p227), where giraffes and zebras roam free. Check out puppet shows and the model-train museum at **Balboa Park** (p225). If you have preteens, make a beeline for **Legoland** (p242) in Carlsbad. In LA, go around on a solar-powered Ferris wheel on the **Santa Monica Pier** (p196). Ride a vintage-1924 wooden roller

coaster at the **Santa Cruz Beach Boardwalk** (p141), then ride the **Roaring Camp Railroad** (see boxed text, p144). Press your nose against a million-gallon glass tank at **Monterey Bay Aquarium** (p151).

Hop aboard a San Francisco **cable car** (see boxed text, p58), en route to **Alcatraz** (p50), then push buttons at the **Exploratorium** (p57), an interactive science museum; reserve tickets for the way-cool Tactile Dome. Pump quarters into century-old arcade games at the **Musée Mécanique** (p57).

On the moody North Coast, the fun is self-made: ascend the **Point Arena Lighthouse** (p95); hunt for agate at **Patrick's Point State Park** (p129); and play make-believe in the prehistoric-looking world of **Fern Canyon** (p130).

Snapshot

California leads America in environmental policy. While the rest of the country consumes more and more energy every year, California's annual consumption has remained relatively steady since the mid-1970s, despite significant growth over the past 30 years. And ever since *An Inconvenient Truth,* the feature film by politician-turned-movie-star Al Gore, hit theatres in 2006, everyone has been talking about global warming – especially movie-star-turned-politician Governor Arnold Schwarzenegger. In 2006 the Governator signed into law legislation capping greenhouse gas emissions, the first law of its kind in the US; the goal is to reduce such emissions by 25% before the year 2020.

Critics call the Republican governor's move an election-year maneuver to curry favor with Democrats, who had largely been disappointed by the former action-hero's record on environmental legislation. Regardless, the law has had a major impact on energy companies, who had been constructing coal-fired electric plants, scheduled to go on-line in a few years. But if California, the largest-single-western-state customer of the utilities, won't buy the electricity, then the future of these carbon-producing plants in Nevada and other neighboring states is uncertain. The policy is a gamble, but with California's financial clout – remember, the state has the world's fifth-largest economy – the gamble may pay off.

California has a lot at stake in the unfolding global-warming crisis. Its water comes from snowfall in the Sierra Nevada Mountains, where storms are never that cold to begin with. If warming continues unchecked, snow will fall as rain, undermining the state's natural water-storage system. Nothing has shaped California like the ongoing water wars: if the supply were to diminish, there's no telling what would happen. Southern California has money and political power; Northern California has water and timber. For years, Southern California's (SoCal) insatiable thirst has emptied ancient lakes and diverted major waterways as far north as the Oregon border, but Northern Californians are fed up. There's even talk of decommissioning dams on the Klamath River, the state's second-largest river (see p134). Though this wouldn't directly affect SoCal, it doesn't bode well for the region's growth: if there's no water, you can't build new houses. Southern California has never prescribed to a slow-growth political ideology, but soon it may have to. Or at least it will have to give up green lawns, which would go a long way toward reducing consumption.

Meanwhile, gasoline prices are on everyone's mind, and more and more Californians are trading in their SUVs for fuel-efficient hybrids. (One third of all hybrids in the US are driven in California.) The website for CBS 2 in Los Angeles even has a tab in its navigation bar on gas prices, listing the latest news on the subject as well as the 10 cheapest places to find gasoline in LA. Articles and a blog declare, 'Pain at the Pump.' But prices in LA aren't nearly as painful as in the Bay Area, which is usually at the top of the list of most expensive gasoline sold in America.

The most exciting, progressive solutions to the mounting energy problems come not from LA, but from San Francisco (surprise, surprise), where Mayor Gavin Newsom is looking into harnessing the powerful tidewater moving through the Golden Gate to generate electricity. Now *that* is innovation, just what you'd expect from California.

FAST FACTS

Total length of California's coast: 1100 miles

California's population: 35.6 million

Projected population, 2025: 50 million

Median age, California: 33.3 years

Median age, US: 35.3 years

Median household income, California: $49,300

Median household income, US: $43,318

Total percentage of Americans who live in California: 12%

Average rush-hour speed on LA freeways: 17mph

Fine for molesting butterflies in Pacific Grove: $500

History

PREHISTORIC TIMES

People have been migrating to California for thousands of years. Archaeological sites indicate the state was inhabited soon after people came across the long-gone land bridge from Asia during an ice age as long as 25,000 years ago. Stone tools found in the Bakersfield area have been dated to around 8000 to 12,000 years ago. Many other sites across the state have yielded evidence, from large middens of sea shells along the coast to campfire sites in the mountains, of people from around 4000 to 8000 years ago.

The most spectacular artifact left behind by California's early inhabitants is their rock art, dating from 500 to 3000 years ago. Many of the sites are closed to the public in the interest of preservation, but you can visit Chumash Painted Cave State Historic Park (p178), near Santa Barbara.

NATIVE CALIFORNIANS

To delve into local history, start at the websites of the California Historical Society (www.californiahistory.net), the San Francisco Historical Society (www.sfhistory.org) and the San Diego Historical Society (www.sandiegohistory.org).

Archaeological evidence paints a clear picture of the Native Americans at the time of European contact. The indigenous peoples of California belonged to more than 20 language groups with around 100 dialects. They lived in small groups, often migrating with the seasons from the coast up to the mountains.

Acorn meal was their dietary staple, supplemented by small game and fish and shellfish along the coast. Plants were used for food and the fiber used for making baskets and clothing. They used earthenware pots, fish nets, bows, arrows and spears with chipped-stone points, but their most developed craft was basket weaving. Their baskets were decorated with attractive geometric designs. Some were so tightly woven that they would hold water. You can see some of the native plants used in basket weaving at Sumêg, the authentic reproduction of a Yurok village at Patrick's Point State Park (p129).

Coastal and inland peoples traded, but they generally didn't interact much, partly because they spoke different languages. Conflict was almost nonexistent. California Native Americans had neither a warrior class nor a tradition of warfare – at least not until the Europeans arrived.

EUROPEAN DISCOVERY

Following the conquest of Mexico in the early 16th century, the Spanish turned their attention toward exploring the edges of their new empire. In 1542 the Spanish crown engaged Juan Rodríguez Cabrillo, a Portuguese explorer and retired conquistador, to lead an expedition up the West Coast to find the fabled golden land beyond Mexico's western coast. He was also charged with finding the equally mythical Strait of Anian, an imagined sea route between the Pacific and the Atlantic.

When Cabrillo sailed into San Diego, he and his crew became the first Europeans to see mainland California. (The precise etymology of the name 'California' has never been convincingly established, though there is now wide consensus that it derives from 'Calafia,' a Spanish novel's heroine queen, who ruled a race of gold-rich black Amazons.) Cabrillo's ships sat out a storm in the harbor, then sailed northward. They made a stop at the Channel Islands where, in 1543, Cabrillo fell ill, died and was buried. The expedition continued

20,000–15,000 BC	AD 1542
The Americas' early inhabitants arrive from Asia and groups eventually settle in California	Spanish navigator Juan Rodríguez Cabrillo and his crew are the first Europeans to sight mainland California

as far as Oregon, but returned with no evidence of a sea route to the Atlantic, a city of gold or islands of spice. The unimpressed Spanish authorities forgot about California for the next 50 years.

The English pirate Sir Francis Drake sailed up the California coast in 1579. He missed the entrance to San Francisco Bay, but pulled in near Point Reyes – at what is now Drakes Bay – to repair his ship, which was bursting with the weight of plundered Spanish silver. He claimed the land for Queen Elizabeth, named it Nova Albion (New England) and left for other adventures.

THE MISSION PERIOD

Around the 1760s, as Russian ships came to California's coast in search of sea-otter pelts, and British trappers and explorers were spreading throughout the West, the Spanish king Carlos III grew worried that they might pose a threat to Spain's claim. Conveniently for the king, the Catholic Church was anxious to start missionary work among the native peoples, so the Church and State combined forces and developed Catholic missions inside presidios (military forts). The Native American converts would live in the missions, learn trade and agricultural skills, and ultimately establish pueblos (small Spanish towns).

Ostensibly, the purpose of the presidios was to protect the missions and deter foreign intruders. In fact, these garrisons created more threats than they deterred, as the soldiers aroused hostility by raiding the Native American camps to rape and kidnap women. Not only were the presidios militarily weak, but their weakness was well known to Russia and Britain, and did nothing to strengthen Spain's claims to California.

The mission period was an abject failure. The Spanish population remained small; the missions achieved little more than mere survival; foreign intruders were not greatly deterred; and more Indians died than were converted. For a glimpse back in time, head to Mission Santa Barbara (p177).

THE 19TH CENTURY

Mexico gained independence from Spain in 1821, and many of the new nation's people looked to California to satisfy their thirst for private land. By the mid-1830s the missions had been secularized, with a series of governors doling out hundreds of free land grants. This process gave birth to the rancho system. The new landowners were called rancheros or Californios; they prospered quickly and became the social, cultural and political fulcrums of California. The average rancho was 16,000 acres in size and largely given over to livestock to supply the trade in hide and tallow.

American explorers, trappers, traders, whalers, settlers and opportunists showed increasing interest in California, seizing on prospects that the Californios ignored. Some of the Americans who started businesses converted to Catholicism, married locals and assimilated into Californio society. One American, Richard Henry Dana, author of *Two Years Before the Mast* (1840), worked on a ship in the hide trade in the 1830s and wrote disparagingly of Californians as 'an idle and thriftless people who can make nothing for themselves.'

Impressed by California's potential wealth and hoping to fulfill the promise of Manifest Destiny (the imperialist doctrine to extend US borders from coast to coast), US president Andrew Jackson sent an emissary to offer the financially strapped Mexican government $500,000 for California. Though

Though some are in ruins, most of California's missions are still standing. To learn more about their cultural influence and historical significance, log on to the California Missions website, www.california missions.com.

1769	1821
Spain attempts to settle California by establishing the first Catholic mission, Mission San Diego de Alcalá	Mexico gains independence from Spain, and California falls under Mexican rule

American settlers were by then showing up by the hundreds, especially in Northern California, Jackson's emissary was tersely rejected.

In 1836 Texas had seceded from Mexico and declared itself an independent republic. When the US annexed Texas in 1845, Mexico broke off diplomatic relations and ordered all foreigners without proper papers to be deported from California. Outraged Northern California settlers revolted, captured the nearest Mexican official and, supported by a company of US soldiers led by Captain John C Frémont, declared California's independence from Mexico in June 1846 by raising their 'Bear Flag' over the town of Sonoma. The Bear Flag Republic existed for all of one month. The banner lives on, however, as the California state flag.

Meanwhile, the US had declared war on Mexico following the dispute over Texas, which provided the US all the justification it needed to invade Mexico. By July, US naval units occupied every port on the California coast, including the then-capital, Monterey.

When US troops captured Mexico City in September 1847, putting an end to the war, the Mexican government had little choice but to cede much of its northern territory to the US. The Treaty of Guadalupe Hidalgo, signed on February 2, 1848, turned over California, Arizona and New Mexico to the US. Two years later, California was admitted as the 31st state of the United States. (An interesting detail of this treaty guarantees the rights of Mexican citizens living in areas taken over by the US. Many Mexicans feel that this provision still entitles them to live and work in those states, regardless of their country of birth.)

> 'Gold was discovered and quickly transformed the newest American outpost. The population surged from 15,000 to 90,000 from 1848 to 1849.'

THE GOLD RUSH

By an amazing coincidence, gold was discovered several days before the signing of the treaty and quickly transformed the newest American outpost. The population surged from 15,000 to 90,000 over the course of a year from 1848 to 1849.

The growth and wealth stimulated every aspect of life, from agriculture and banking to construction and journalism. But mining ruined the land. Hills were stripped bare, erosion wiped out vegetation, streams silted up and mercury washed down rivers into San Francisco Bay. San Francisco itself became a hotbed of gambling, prostitution, drink and chicanery, giving rise to the title, the Barbary Coast, whose last vestiges live today in the strip joints along Broadway in North Beach.

In 1860, California experienced a second boom with the discovery of the Comstock silver lode, though the lode was actually beyond the Sierra Crest in what would soon become Nevada. Exploiting it required deep-mining techniques, which necessitated companies, stocks, trading and speculation. San Francisco made more money speculating on silver than Nevada did mining it: huge mansions sprouted on Nob Hill (p62), and California businessmen became renowned for their unscrupulous audacity.

THE RAILROAD & AGRICULTURE

The transcontinental railroad shortened the trip from New York to San Francisco from two months to five days, opening up markets on both coasts. Tracks were laid simultaneously from the east and the west, converging in Utah in 1869.

1848	1850
Gold is discovered in California and the population jumps from 15,000 to 90,000	California becomes the 31st state of the United States of America

By the 1870s speculation had raised land prices to levels no farmer or immigrant could afford; the railroad brought in products that undersold the goods made in California; and some 15,000 Chinese laborers – no longer needed for rail construction – flooded the labor market. A period of unrest ensued, which culminated in anti-Chinese laws and a reformed state constitution in 1879.

Los Angeles was not connected to the transcontinental railroad until 1876, when the Southern Pacific Railroad (SP) laid tracks from San Francisco to the fledgling city. The SP monopoly was broken in 1887, when the Atchinson, Topeka & Santa Fe Railroad Company (AT&SF) laid tracks linking LA across the Arizona desert to the East Coast. The competition greatly reduced the cost of transport and led to more diverse development across the state, particularly in Southern California and the San Joaquin Valley. The lower fares spurred the so-called 'boom of the '80s, a major real-estate boom lasting from 1886 to 1888. More than 120,000 migrants, mostly from the Midwest, came to Southern California, settling in the 25 new towns laid out by AT&SF in the eastern part of Los Angeles County.

Much of the land granted to the railroads was sold in big lots to speculators who also acquired, with the help of corrupt politicians and administrators, a lot of the farm land that was released for new settlement. A major share of the state's agricultural land thus became consolidated as large holdings in the hands of a few city-based landlords, establishing the pattern (which continues to this day) of industrial-scale 'agribusiness' rather than small family farms. These big businesses were well placed to provide the substantial investment and the political connections required to bring irrigation water to the farmland. They also established an ongoing need for cheap farm labor.

In the absence of coal, iron ore or abundant water, heavy industry developed slowly, although the 1892 discovery of oil in the LA area stimulated the development of petroleum processing and chemical industries.

THE 20TH CENTURY

The population, wealth and importance of California increased dramatically throughout the 20th century. The great San Francisco earthquake and fire of 1906 decimated the city, but it was barely a hiccup in the state's development. The revolutionary years in Mexico, from 1910 to 1921, caused a huge influx of immigrants from south of the border, reestablishing Latino communities that had been smothered by American dominance. The Panama Canal, completed in 1914, made shipping feasible between the East Coast and West Coast.

The Great Depression saw another wave of immigrants, this time from the impoverished prairie states of the Dust Bowl. Outbreaks of social and labor unrest led to a rapid growth of the Democratic party in California. Some of the Depression-era public works projects had lasting benefits, from San Francisco's Bay Bridge to the restoration of mission buildings.

WWII had a major impact on California. Women were coopted into war work and proved themselves in a range of traditionally male jobs. Anti-Asian sentiments resurfaced, many Japanese-Americans were interned, and more Mexicans crossed the border to fill labor shortages. Many of the service people who passed through California liked the place so much that they returned to settle after the war. In the 1940s the population grew by 53% (reaching 10.6 million in 1950), and during the 1950s by 49% (reaching 15.9 million in 1960).

San Francisco's first cable car started running along Clay St on August 1, 1873.

Los Angeles once had a wonderfully efficient system of streetcars, until General Motors allegedly conspired to destroy it: search Google for 'General Motors streetcar conspiracy' and make up your own mind.

Five days a week for half a century, Herb Caen wrote a column in the *San Francisco Chronicle*. Read his collected musings in *Baghdad by the Bay*. He paints a portrait of everyday San Francisco during the second half of the 20th century with pith and panache.

1873	1908
Levi Strauss & Co receives a patent for its hard-wearing denim pants – the first blue jeans	Los Angeles produces its first narrative film and 'the Industry' is born

SOCIAL CHANGE

Unconstrained by tradition, California has long been a leader in new attitudes and social movements. As early as the 1930s, Hollywood was promoting fashions and fads for the middle classes, even as strikes and social unrest rocked San Francisco, and author John Steinbeck articulated a new concern for the welfare and worth of working-class people.

Jack Kerouac's autobiographical *Dharma Bums* explores the transformative power of relationships, and the paradoxes of spiritual awakening and middle-class values in late-'50s California.

During the affluent postwar years of the 1950s, the Beat movement in San Francisco's North Beach railed against the banality and conformity of suburban life, instead choosing North Beach coffeehouses for jazz, poetry and pot. When the postwar baby boomers hit their late teens, many took up where the Beat generation left off, heeding Tim Leary's counsel to 'turn on, tune in, drop out.' Their revolt climaxed in San Francisco's Haight district (p62) during the 1967 'Summer of Love.' Sex, drugs and rock-and-roll ruled the day.

Laying the foundation for social revolution, the '60s yielded gay liberation, which started in New York in 1969, but exploded in San Francisco in the '70s. Today San Francisco remains the most exuberantly gay city in the world. To visit the thriving community, stroll through the Castro district (p62).

In the late 1980s and '90s, California catapulted to the forefront of the healthy lifestyle, with more aerobics classes and self-actualization workshops than you could shake a totem at. In-line skating, snowboarding and mountain biking rose to fame in California. Be careful what you laugh at: from pet rocks to soy burgers, California's flavor of the month will probably be next year's world trend.

TECHNOLOGY

California has led the world in computer technology. In the 1950s, Stanford University in Palo Alto needed to raise money to finance postwar growth, so it built Stanford Industrial Park, leasing space to high-tech companies that might benefit the university. Hewlett-Packard, Lockheed and General Electric moved in, forming what is now considered the germ cell of Silicon Valley. In 1971 Intel invented the microchip, and in 1976 Apple invented the first personal computer.

Digital technology reinvented our world view. But in the fat years of the 1990s, companies jumped on the dot-com bandwagon. Many reaped huge overnight profits, fueled by misplaced optimism, only to crash with equal velocity at the turn of the millennium.

The Oscar-winning documentary *The Times of Harvey Milk* (1983) tells the story of San Francisco's first openly gay city supervisor who, on a dark day in 1978, was shot dead in his City Hall office.

THE 21ST CENTURY

No place in America was more affected by the demise of the dot-coms than California. The same year brought rolling blackouts to California which were caused entirely by Enron's illegal manipulation of markets. But before the truth came out, Republican malcontents fingered then-Governor Gray Davis and called for a special recall election. (For an excellent account, watch *Enron: The Smartest Guys in the Room*.) Enter Arnold Schwarzenegger – Californians will always forgive an action hero more easily than a state bureaucrat. In 2006, Schwarzenegger won again, Democrats took back both houses of Congress in Washington, and San Francisco Congresswoman Nancy Pelosi became the new Speaker of the House, third in line for the presidency. Though the Republican Congress under George W Bush essentially ignored Democratically controlled California, the pendulum has swung. Thank goodness.

1976	2006
The first personal computer, the Apple I, is designed in Silicon Valley	Arnold Schwarzenegger (aka the Governor) is reelected governor of California

The Culture

The rest of America marvels at California, never quite sure how to categorize it. It's best not to try, since the state is forever reinventing itself. Remember, this is the place that gave the world both hippies *and* Ronald Reagan.

REGIONAL IDENTITY

Think of California as two states: Northern California and Southern California (SoCal). In fact there is a movement, however small, to divide the state. Culturally it makes sense, but economically it's not the best thing to do because the north has the natural resources (ie water) and the south has the money. The idea has never gone before voters, maybe because nobody can agree on where to draw the line.

Several neighboring counties in the extreme northern section of the state and next-door Oregon want to establish the 'State of Jefferson,' claiming they're ignored by their state capitals. Since 1941 they've lobbied for their cause, but ask average Californians if they've heard of the movement and nearly all will say no, effectively demonstrating the vast cultural differences – and lack of mutual awareness – between regions.

In any case, believe everything you've ever heard about Californians, so long as you realize the stereotypes are always exaggerated. Sure, valley girls snap chewing gum in the shopping malls east of Los Angeles, blond surfer boys shout 'Dude!' across San Diego beaches, and tree huggers toke on joints in the North Coast woods, but all in all, it's hard to peg the population. Bear in mind that the following exploration of identity addresses general trends, not hard-and-fast rules.

Woodsy types live in the north. Think buffalo-plaid flannel. There aren't a lot of people there – and there's not a lot of money floating around. Christian-fundamentalist radio stations screech on several strong frequencies. At the other end of the spectrum, you'll also find some of the state's most progressive liberals in the north (in Arcata, some of them border on fanatical). If you spot a beat-up old diesel Mercedes-Benz chugging along the highway, chances are it's running on biodiesel, possibly spent french-fry grease. There's a lot of ingenuity 'round here.

In the Bay Area, the politics are liberal and the people open-minded, with a strong live-and-let-live ethic. In Marin, there's a tremendous sense of civic pride that borders on narcissism. San Francisco is something of a melting pot, but there aren't a lot of lower-income citizens since rents are so high.

Los Angeles has greater racial tension – possibly because it's more diverse than San Francisco – but the unease likely reflects the disparity between the haves and have-nots. Whatever the case, it's hard to generalize about LA, but one thing is for sure: everybody drives. You're nothing – and nowhere – without a car.

Between LA and San Diego in Orange County – 'beyond the Orange Curtain' – George W Bush is welcomed with open arms at $2000-a-plate Republican fundraising dinners. Many people live in gated communities and have limited tolerance for (or exposure to) outsiders. The conservative politics extend to San Diego, perhaps because of the large number of navy people who live there.

LIFESTYLE & POPULATION

Just as it's impossible to generalize about what type of people live on the California coast, it's equally difficult to qualify *how* people live. The unifying theme, though, is a love of the outdoors. Perhaps that's why Frank

The California state flower is the orange California poppy, and it's illegal to pick them. Besides, they wilt almost instantly when plucked from the ground.

The Northern California coast has scores of nude beaches (people aren't so willing to drop their trousers in SoCal). For listings of where you can frolic au naturel, log on to the *San Francisco Bay Guardian*'s website, www.sfbg.com.

Lloyd Wright built so many homes in the LA area. In his designs he sought to bring the outdoors inside, with vast panes of glass opening up to patios that connected to other parts of the home. It's a recurring theme in modern California architecture, particularly in Southern California where many people have swimming pools (almost nobody on the coast north of Santa Barbara has a pool; it's too cold).

Nearly 30% of all Californians live in Los Angeles County.

People are pleasant – sometimes to a fault. In fact, everyone is so determined to get along that it can be hard to find out what somebody really thinks. This increases the further south you go. Political correctness thrives along the coast. Sometimes it's annoying. If you stick around one of the larger metropolitan areas for a while, you'll inevitably exchange telephone numbers with a person who expresses interest in seeing you again. In most parts of the world that means, 'Call me.' Not in California. It's just a nicety. Often the other person never calls, and if you make an attempt, you may never hear back.

Some might say that you're 'codependent' for having expectations of your new friend. Self-help-group jargon has thoroughly and completely infiltrated the daily language of Coastal Californians. For example, the word 'issue' is constantly bandied about; generally this is the polite way to refer to someone else's problems without implying that the person has…well, problems. It's all about getting along and being nice.

If you come across California slang that you don't understand, log onto www.urban dictionary.com for definitions. Word out.

This all flies out the window on an extended middle finger on the state's always-busy freeways. Road rage has become a serious problem. If you plan to do any driving whatsoever, take a deep breath before you put the key in the ignition, and meditate on remaining calm throughout your journey. Expect to encounter irrational people who won't hesitate to cut you off, then flip you the 'bird'. Such barbarism occurs mostly around major cities and heavily populated areas.

California ranks as the most populous state in the US. It's also one of the fastest growing, posting increases of more than five million residents between 1990 and 2000. The racial makeup continues to shift. Hispanic, Latino and Asian populations steadily increase, while Caucasians (non-Hispanic) post a decline. One in four residents is foreign-born, and approximately 30% of America's total immigrant population lives here, mostly in LA.

Southward from Oregon, population densities steadily increase, maxing out in the Bay Area and dropping off again south of San Francisco. Between Monterey and San Luis Obispo, few people live along the water. It's too remote, and the region is often isolated by closures of unstable Hwy 1. Greater LA sprawls along the coast toward San Diego in a continuous string of suburbs, small cities and incorporated towns, interrupted by long stretches of beach belonging to the US military, one of the region's major employers.

The flamboyant theatrical troupe the Cockettes performed whacked-out midnight shows (totally high on acid) in San Francisco from 1969–72. They skyrocketed to fame and even performed on Broadway – for one night. Check out David Weissman and Bill Weber's kick-ass feature-length documentary, *The Cockettes* (2002).

ARTS

Thanks to the movie industry, no other city can claim the pop-cultural influence that LA exerts worldwide. Southern California in particular has proved to be fertile ground for new architectural styles. Meanwhile, San Francisco's liberalism and humanistic tradition has established the Bay Area as a center for the arts – writers and musicians have been seeking inspiration there for decades.

Literature

The West Coast has always attracted artists and writers, and today the California resident literary community is stronger than ever including talent such as: Alice Walker, Pulitzer prize–winning author of *The Color Purple;* Chilean novelist Isabel Allende; Dorothy Allison, author of *Bastard Out of Carolina;* Amy Tan, who writes popular fiction like *The Joy Luck Club;* Maxine Hong

Kingston, coeditor of the landmark anthology *The Literature of California;* Dave Eggers, the hipster behind *McSweeney's* quarterly literary journal; Michael Chabon, author of the Pulitzer prize–winning *The Amazing Adventures of Kavalier and Clay;* and Adrienne Rich, progressive feminist poet.

Few writers nail California culture as well as Joan Didion. She's best known for her collection of essays, *Slouching Towards Bethlehem* (1968), which takes a caustic look at flower power and Haight-Ashbury. Tom Wolfe also put '60s San Francisco in perspective with *The Electric Kool-Aid Acid Test* (1968), which follows Ken Kesey's band of Merry Pranksters, who began their acid-laced 'magic bus' journey in Santa Cruz. Charles Bukowski's semiautobiographical novel *Post Office* (1971) captured down-and-out downtown LA. Richard Vasquez's *Chicano* (1970) took a dramatic look at LA's Latino barrio.

Back in the 1930s, San Francisco and LA became the capitals of the pulp detective novel, which were often made into noir films. Dashiell Hammett *(The Maltese Falcon)* made San Francisco's fog a sinister character. The king of hard-boiled crime writers was Raymond Chandler, who thinly disguised his hometown of Santa Monica as Bay City. A 1990s African-American renaissance of crime fiction was masterminded by James Ellroy *(LA Confidential),* Elmore Leonard *(Jackie Brown)* and Walter Mosley *(Devil in a Blue Dress).*

> San Diego's outwardly carefree appearance belies a dark underbelly. Get the dirt in *Under the Perfect Sun: The San Diego Tourists Never See,* by Mike Davis et al (2003).

Music

From smoky jazz clubs that once filled San Francisco's North Beach to hard-edged West Coast rap and hip-hop born in South Central LA, California has rocked the world.

In the 1930s and '40s, big swing bands toured LA. After WWII, the West Oakland blues sound developed up north, while the bebop of Charlie Parker and Charlie Mingus made LA swing. The cool West Coast Jazz of Chet Baker and Dave Brubeck evolved in the 1950s in San Francisco's North Beach, Hollywood, and Hermosa Beach near LA.

The first homegrown rock-and-roll talent to make it big in the '50s was Richie Valens, whose 'La Bamba' was a rockified version of a Mexican folk song. In the '60s, Jim Morrison & the Doors busted onto the Sunset Strip. Meanwhile, San Francisco had launched the psychedelic revolution with big-name acts such as the Grateful Dead and Janis Joplin.

The late '70s and early '80s saw the emergence of California's brand of punk. In LA, the rockabilly-edged band X stood out, while Black Flag led the hard-core way with singer Henry Rollins. San Francisco produced the Dead Kennedys and the Avengers. Jello Biafra, the lead singer of the DKs, became a social activist. The Red Hot Chili Peppers exploded out of LA in the late '80s with a highly charged, funk-punk sound, while the early '90s generated pop punksters blink-182 in San Diego and Green Day in East Bay, some of whose members started out playing at Berkeley's 924 Gilman Street club.

LA today is the hotbed for West Coast rap and hip-hop. Eazy E, Ice Cube and Dr Dre released the seminal NWA (Niggaz With Attitude) album, *Straight Outta Compton,* in 1989. Death Row Records, cofounded by Dr Dre, has since launched such artists as Long Beach bad-boy Snoop Dog and the late Tupac Shakur, who grew up in Marin.

> In *The White Album,* Joan Didion's essays capture the essence of contemporary California culture, from an architectural critique of the Governor's Mansion that Reagan built, to the psychology of driving Los Angeles' freeways.

Architecture

California's architecture, a fruitful jumble of styles, is as diverse as the state's population.

The first Spanish missions were built around courtyards with materials that were on hand: adobe, limestone and grass. Later, Californians adapted the original Spanish mission style to create the rancho-adobe style, as in San Diego's Old Town (p227).

Victorian architecture, including the Queen Anne style, is most prevalent in Northern California towns such as San Francisco, Ferndale (p115) and Eureka (p117), yet one of the finest examples of Victorian whimsy is San Diego's Hotel del Coronado (p229).

With its simpler, classical lines, Spanish colonial architecture – also called mission revival – was a rejection of frilly Victorian design. The train depots in LA and San Diego showcase this style, as do some buildings in San Diego's Balboa Park (p225), a legacy of the Panama–California Exposition in 1915.

By the early 1920s it had became fashionable to copy earlier periods. Various revival styles turn up in California's public buildings such as San Francisco's Palace of Fine Arts (p57). Hearst Castle (p164), a mixture of Moorish, Spanish and Mediterranean revival styles, is the grandest example.

Art deco took off during the 1920s and '30s, with vertical lines and symmetry creating a soaring effect. Heavy ornamentation featured floral motifs, sunbursts and zigzags. Downtown Oakland (p68) has a wealth of art deco buildings.

Also called the International Style, modernism was initiated in Europe by Bauhaus architects Walter Gropius, Ludwig Mies van der Rohe and Le Corbusier. Its characteristics include boxlike building shapes, open floor plans, plain facades and abundant glass.

Postmodernism was partly a response to the starkness of the International Style, and sought to reemphasize the structural form of the building and the space around it. Richard Meier transcended postmodernist vision with LA's Getty Center (p195). Canadian-born Frank Gehry is known for his deconstructivist buildings with almost sculptural forms and distinctive facade materials, such as at the high-profile Walt Disney Concert Hall (p198) in downtown LA.

Film

California's primary art form is its major export. Film is a powerful presence in the lives of not only Americans, but people around the world. Images of California are distributed far beyond its borders, ultimately reflecting back upon the state itself. Few tourists arrive without some cinematic reference to the place – nearly every street corner has been or will be a movie set. With increasing regularity, Hollywood films feature California as both a setting and a topic and, in some cases, almost as a character. LA especially loves to turn the camera on itself, often with a dark film-noir angle.

The Industry, as it's called, grew out of the humble orchards of Hollywoodland. The silent-movie era gave way to 'talkies' after 1927's *The Jazz Singer* premiered in downtown LA, ushering in Hollywood's glamorous Golden Age. Today Hollywood is no longer the focus. The high cost of filming in LA has sent location scouts beyond the San Fernando Valley (where most movie and TV studios are found) and north of the border to Canada, where they're welcomed with open arms in 'Hollywood North,' particularly in Vancouver, Toronto and Montréal. A few production companies are still based in the Bay Area, including Francis Ford Coppola's Zoetrope and George Lucas's Industrial Light & Magic, made up of high-tech gurus who produce computer-generated special effects for Hollywood blockbusters. Pixar Animation Studios is in Emeryville, near Berkeley.

MEDIA

A mere six corporations own nearly all major media outlets in the US. International coverage is weak, and there's little variation in what you read, hear or see on the news. Despite right-wing propaganda decrying the media's so-called liberal bias, close examination often shows just the opposite, particularly on Fox News. (For a slam-dunk read on the network, check out

'Few tourists arrive without some cinematic reference to the place – nearly every street corner has been or will be a movie set.'

the documentary *Outfoxed: Rupert Murdoch's War on Journalism*.) Other major TV-news networks – ABC, NBC, CBS and CNN – stick pretty much to the middle, but err on the side of conservatism. National Public Radio (NPR), with affiliate stations throughout the country, does a better job, particularly on its 'All Things Considered' news program, but the network receives substantial funding from Congress, so it too avoids anything too controversial. Public Radio International (PRI) takes bigger risks, with diverse programming that more accurately reflects the population at large. Listen out for PRI; it's a damn good network.

Several watchdog organizations keep tabs on media bias, with an eye toward protecting the endangered American democracy. The best among them is Fairness & Accuracy in Reporting (FAIR); log on to www.fair.org to learn what's really going on.

SPORTS

California boasts more professional sports teams than any other state. If you're in LA, San Francisco, Oakland or San Diego, depending on the season you'll have your pick of NFL football, NBA basketball or major-league baseball action. Pro games can be sold out – especially 49ers, Raiders and San Diego Chargers football, LA Lakers basketball and LA Kings hockey matches – so buy tickets early. You probably won't have to sell your firstborn child to score a ticket to pro hockey in Anaheim, or pro soccer and arena football action in San Jose or LA.

Intercity and intracity rivalries can be intense, so when football's San Francisco 49ers play the Oakland Raiders, basketball's LA Lakers play the LA Clippers or baseball's San Francisco Giants play the LA Dodgers or when the Oakland A's take on Anaheim's Angels, you best just stand back. Patrons of college sports rivalries, such as UC Berkeley's Cal Bears versus the Stanford Cardinals or the USC Trojans against the UCLA Bruins, are even more insane. In 2005, there was SoCal outrage over the Anaheim Angels renaming themselves the Los Angeles Angels of Anaheim, which is stretching the point geographically. Anaheim's civic leaders, who had custom-built the team's stadium back in the 1960s, sued the team but lost the suit in 2006: the new mouthful of a name stands.

Excepting championship play-offs, the regular season for major-league baseball runs from April to September, major-league soccer from April to mid-October, NFL football from September to early January, NHL ice hockey from October to March and NBA basketball from November to April. Professional beach volleyball holds major tournaments every summer at Hermosa and Manhattan Beaches near LA.

KCRW (www.kcrw.com), Santa Monica's National Public Radio affiliate, offers podcasts of its arts, culture and news programs. Listen online to its award-winning music shows for a slice of the California soundscape.

Environment

THE LAND

The third-largest state after Alaska and Texas, California covers about 156,000 sq miles, making it larger than Great Britain or Italy. The state's northern edge lies at about the same latitude as Boston and Rome, and the southern edge at the same latitude as Savannah in Georgia, and Tel Aviv, Israel.

Most of California is ringed by mountains, with the sea-level Central Valley in the middle. Think of it as a giant bathtub. The Coast Range runs along most of California's coastline, its western side plunging straight into the Pacific and its eastern side rolling gently toward the Central Valley. San Francisco Bay divides the range roughly in half. Three-quarters of the way down the state, the Coast Range is joined to the Sierra Nevada (along California's eastern border) by a series of mountains called the Transverse Ranges. These mountains, mostly around 5000ft high, divide the state into Southern and Northern California. To the south, the Los Angeles Basin directly fronts the ocean, bordered by a series of mountains that extend into Mexico. San Diego, on the edge of this plateau 120 miles south of LA, lies right on the border with Mexico.

California sits on one of the world's major earthquake fault zones, on the edge of two plates: the Pacific Plate, which consists of the Pacific ocean floor and much of the coastline, and the North American Plate, which covers all of North America and part of the Atlantic ocean floor. The primary boundary between the two is the infamous San Andreas Fault, which runs for 650 miles and has spawned numerous smaller faults. Walk the Earthquake Trail at Point Reyes (p82) for an up-close lesson in plate tectonics.

Earthquakes are common, although most are too small or too remote to be detected without sensors. In fact, small earthquakes are a good sign. The plates should move at a rate of about 1in per year. When they don't, the energy stores up, eventually resulting in large-scale quakes.

WILDLIFE
Animals

Spend even one day along the coast and you're likely to spot some sort of pinniped, perhaps an elephant or harbor seal, California sea lion or sea otter. See them frolic along the Central Coast, at either Point Lobos State Reserve (p158) near Carmel, Point Piedras Blancas (p164), just north of Hearst Castle, or on the Channel Islands (p182) off Santa Barbara. The Año Nuevo State Reserve (p71) on the San Francisco Peninsula is the largest elephant-seal breeding ground in the world. And right in San Francisco proper, you can watch sea lions up close at Pier 39 (p57).

Between December and March, people come from far and wide to see gray whales breach offshore on their annual southward migration. Get a good view at Point Reyes (p83). Pods of bottle-nosed dolphins and porpoises swim close to shore year-round from Morro Bay (p166) to Mexico.

Many bird species migrate along the Pacific Flyway, one of the four principal migration routes in North America, and there's a changing roster of birds overhead depending on the season. There are great places everywhere on the coast to hunker down with a pair of binoculars, but stellar standouts include Lake Earl (p137), Humboldt Bay National Wildlife Refuge (p117), Arcata Marsh (p122), and Audubon Canyon Ranch (p81). Year-round residents include gulls, grebes, terns, cormorants, sandpipers and little sanderlings that chase receding waves along the shore, looking for critters in the freshly turned sand.

The California Coastal Conservancy publishes books and pamphlets on accessing the California coast, including the quarterly *California Coast and Ocean*, which analyzes trends and events affecting the coast. Log on to www.scc.ca.gov/Publications/pubs.htm.

For more information about earthquake activity, see the US Geological Survey website (http://earthquake.usgs.gov). This government body collects and stores data on all earthquakes in the United States.

Monarch butterflies are beautiful orange creatures that follow remarkable migration patterns in search of milkweed, their only source of food. They spend winter in California by the tens of thousands, mostly on the Central Coast, notably in Pismo Beach (p173) and Pacific Grove (p155).

Plants

Coastal ecosystems range from drenched to parched. The northern end of the Coast Range supports stands of coast redwoods *(Sequoia sempervirens)*, towering giants with spongy red bark, flat needles and olive-size cones. These tree rely on fog as their primary water source. On the lush forest floor beneath them, look for sword ferns, redwood sorrel and deep green mosses. Because they're both so tall, redwoods are easily confused with Douglas fir trees; determine which is which by examining their bark. The redwood has fibrous, reddish-brown bark that spirals up the trunk in thick, sinewy lines. The bark of the Douglas fir isn't as red and looks like a jigsaw puzzle.

Along the Central Coast, the Monterey cypress and Monterey pine have thick, rough, grayish bark; long, reaching branches growing in clusters from the top of the trunk; and long needles. Depending where they stand, they're sometimes contorted by the coast's frequent and powerful wind. They too derive much water from the billowing fog.

Southern California, by comparison, is a much more arid region. Look for live oak, with hollylike evergreen leaves and fuzzy acorns; aromatic California laurel, with long slender leaves that turn purple; and manzanita, treelike shrubs with intensely red bark and small berries.

And throughout the state, both on the coast and inland, the hills turn green in winter, not summer. Because it almost never freezes, the dried-out brown grasses spring to life with new growth as soon as the autumn and winter rains arrive. Wildflowers pop up as early as February, and March is nicknamed the 'emerald month.' Along the coast look for little purple wild irises until June. And everywhere look for oak trees: California has 20 native species of them.

The Torrey pine, a species adapted to sparse rainfall and sandy, stony soils, is extremely rare. Look for it near San Diego and on Santa Rosa Island, which is part of Channel Islands National Park (p182).

Endangered Species

The coastline of California – indeed, much of the state – has been drastically altered by development. Imagine almost all of the land along the Pacific between the Oregon border and Santa Cruz covered with stands of giant redwoods. Today only 4.5% of them remain. They provide an important habitat: in recent years scientists have discovered that the complexity of these forests matches that of the tropical rainforests.

Near Ferndale (p115), the most famous casualty of logging in recent years, the spotted owl has been protected in the Headwaters Forest Reserve, but it's rarely open to the public.

California condors, giant birds weighing up to 20lb with a wingspan of 9ft, have all but disappeared, and conservationists are working hard to save them. Stop by Wild Animal Park (p227) near San Diego for a look at them.

All along the coast at state beaches, you're likely to hear about the threatened Western snowy plovers, tiny birds that nest in the sand. They scare easily. When threatened by dune buggies or joggers, they take off, leaving their eggs, which burn in the sun. The Monterey Bay Aquarium (p151) is working to restore their habitat by rescuing abandoned eggs and pairing the chicks with adult males, who raise the young.

The Audubon Society (www.audubon.org) prints a number of field guides on birds, plants, animals and weather. They're small enough to carry in a purse and useful for answering questions about California's natural environment.

The world's tallest tree was discovered in 2006, in Redwood National Park. It's named Hyperion and stands a whopping 378ft tall.

Introduced Species

Unfortunately California has been overrun by introduced species. Ice plant, the ropy green ground cover with purple-and-white flowers that creeps over beach dunes, originally came from South Africa. During construction of the railroads in the 19th century, fast-growing eucalyptus trees were imported from Australia to make railroad ties, but the wood proved poor and split when driven through with a stake. The trees now grow like weeds, fueling summertime wildfires with their flammable, explosive seed capsules. Even snails come from far away, brought to California in the 1850s from France to produce escargots. Now they're everywhere.

NATIONAL PARKS

The National Parks Service (NPS) protects spectacular stretches of coastline in California. Established in 1968, Redwood National Park (p130) covers 132,000 acres in a patchwork of public and private lands. Unlike the state's more famous inland parks, Sequoia and Yosemite, which were established in 1890, there simply wasn't enough land in the redwoods to delineate a big block. These forests were hotly contested, with loggers itching to get their hands on the valuable lumber. By making them national parks, the federal government sought to protect a disappearing habitat at a crucial time. Even so, logging on adjacent hillsides lasted until late 2005 and continuously threatened the park's health, since erosion fills stream beds and causes landslides; but now the entire ecologically sensitive Redwood Creek watershed is protected – even though much of it has been logged.

Further down the coast the NPS oversees the Golden Gate National Recreation Area (GGNRA; see p72), also an assemblage of lands abutting state parks. Among its sights are Muir Woods (p80), Alcatraz Island (p50) and San Francisco's Ocean Beach (p59).

Off the shore of Santa Barbara, Channel Islands National Park (p182) is largely undeveloped. The islands are prized for their rich marine life and aquatic environments. Unlike other national parks in California, they receive few visitors because of their remote locations: to reach them requires a long boat ride on choppy seas, though you can fly the 30 miles to Santa Rosa Island for day or overnight trips; and no bridge connects them to the mainland. The islands support several species of plant and animal, including the rare Torrey pine. From the shore on a day without fog or mist, look at the islands and see if you can spot splashes of yellow from the many coreopsis flowers.

ENVIRONMENTAL ISSUES

California's development has come at the expense of the environment. Pollution from mining washes into waterways that find their way to the ocean, polluting wetlands along the Pacific Flyway. Tons of particulate matter spews into the air from automobile and diesel emissions, contributing to asthma in children in urban areas. The ocean is overfished, land is disappearing beneath asphalt and landfills, and tankers leak oil off the coast.

But the news isn't all bad. Californians maintain a high awareness of environmental matters and often vote for preservation, especially in Northern California, land of the left. Take San Francisco for example. The city plans to recycle *all* of its trash by the year 2020. Indeed, it has already instituted citywide composting of perishable organic matter. The city's residents also overwhelmingly voted to fund construction of solar power plants that will produce 50 *megawatts* of electricity – and that's just to start. There's even talk of harnessing the tremendous tidal flows in and out of the Golden Gate to generate energy.

Environmentalists and egalitarians alike will want to know about Coastwalk (www.coastwalk.org), an organization dedicated to completing the California Coastal Trail, a continuous trail along the state's entire length, protecting the natural environment, and providing public access.

Amy Meyer's *New Guardian for the Golden Gate: How America Got a Great National Park* tells the remarkable story of how the lands surrounding the Golden Gate were saved from development and turned into a national recreation area.

The University of California at Berkeley's searchable digital-photo library has thousands of images of California landscapes, flora and fauna. Check it out at http://elib.cs.berkeley.edu/photos.

Along the coast air pollution isn't bad, due in large part to the prevailing westerly winds that blow in clean air off the ocean. But travel inland, particularly in the LA Basin, and you'll see that the air takes on a thick haze, obscuring vistas and creating health hazards. Fortunately California leads the nation in emissions control.

Of equal concern is water. There never seems to be enough to satisfy demand by coastal cities and inland farms. Most of it comes from the Sierra Nevada Mountains, in the eastern part of the state, but global warming and droughts both affect winter snowpack. If it rains in the Sierra – or doesn't snow at all – there's nothing to melt into the reservoirs that supply inland farms and coastal cities. Fortunately the citizenry has learned how to conserve. And you will too: expect a low-flow showerhead in your hotel room.

For more information about environmental issues in Coastal California, contact the Sierra Club (www.sierra club.org), America's oldest, largest and most effective environmental group.

Coastal California Outdoors

Though you'll feel plenty of wind through your hair and sun on your face while cruising Hwy 1 in your convertible, you'll need to get those muscles moving and adrenaline pumping to fully grasp the coast's spectacular riches. Californians know they're spoiled silly, so they express their gratitude by taking every chance to hit the trails, hop onto the saddle or grab a paddle. Now it's your turn: two-wheel it over the legendary 17-Mile Drive, launch your paraglider off a cliff and float over the glimmering ocean, spot a whale breaching off the bow of your boat, or live out your Beach Boys dream with a surf lesson or two. California may be where the car and mall culture gained a foothold, but the wise among us know that in reality, it's all about the Great Outdoors.

For the lowdown on surfing, pick up *Surfing California: A Complete Guide to the Best Breaks on the California Coast* by Raul Guisado and Jeff Klaas.

SURFING

Surf's up! Are you down? Even if you never set foot on a board – and we heartily recommend you do – there's no denying the influence of surfing on every aspect of California beach life. Invented by Pacific Islanders, surfing first washed ashore in 1907, when business tycoon Henry Huntington invited Hawaiian surfer George Freeth to LA to help promote Huntington's shoreside development. California hasn't been the same since Freeth's surfing demonstrations.

The state has plenty of easily accessible world-class surf spots, with the lion's share found in Southern California. You won't find many killer spots north of the Bay Area, but if your travels keep you up there check out resources at www.northerncaliforniasurfing.com.

Famous surf spots include Steamers Lane (p144) in Santa Cruz and Surfrider (p195) in Malibu. Both are point breaks (where swells peak into steep waves as they encounter a shelflike point), known for their consistently clean, glassy, big waves. The most powerful swells arrive in winter, while May and June are generally the flattest months, although they do bring warmer water. Speaking of which, don't be fooled by all those images you've seen of hot blonds surfing in just a bathing suit. You'll likely freeze your ass off in the water anywhere but Southern California in summer. Bring or rent a wet suit.

Crowds can be a problem in many places, as can overly territorial surfers, notably at Malibu, San Diego's Windansea (p233) and Orange County's Huntington Beach (p210). Try to befriend a local surfer for an introduction – and protection.

The best places to learn surfing are at beach breaks or long, shallow bays where waves are small and rolling. Mission Beach and Tourmaline (p233),

---

TWO GIRLS FOR EVERY BOY

Learning to surf can be intimidating, especially so for ladies; a growing number of outfits now specialize in female-only or female-centric lessons. The following are some of them:

Aloha Surfer Girls (☎ 858-427-0644; www.alohasurfergirls.com) On Mission Beach, San Diego.
HB Wahine (☎ 714-969-9399; www.hbwahine.com) On Huntington Beach, Orange County.
Linda Benson's SurfHer Surf School (☎ 858-345-1345; www.surfher.net) In Encinitas on the Central Coast. Men and boys welcome, too.
Surf Diva (☎ 858-454-8273; www.surfdiva.com; 2160 Av de la Playa) In La Jolla, San Diego.

KEITH GEAR: LA SURFER

Surfer and native Californian Keith Gear has been riding the waves up and down the coast for almost 30 years, and has these hot spots and tips to share.

Top Five Beginner Spots

- **Half Moon Bay** next to the harbor right off the highway
- **Cowell's Beach** or 38th Ave in Santa Cruz, and nearby Capitola
- **Gaviota to Carpentaria** (series of small beaches near Santa Barbara)
- **Malibu** (but beware of feisty locals) and a few miles south, where it says GLADSTONES-4-FISH on the cliff (no rentals here)
- **Doheny State Beach** in Orange County

Top Five Surf Spots

- **Steamers Lane (Santa Cruz)** – big, consistent, clean and long right break with left at middle peak on bigger days.
- **Rincon (Santa Barbara/Ventura)** – legendary right point break (peels forever).
- **Malibu** – long rides, and the clean right break gets better with bigger waves. You might even see a celebrity here.
- **Huntington Beach** – good summer spot and not too crowded. Always catches summer swells and has both right and left breaks.
- **Trestles (San Onofre/San Clemente)** – probably the premier summer spot, with big but forgiving waves, a fast ride and both right and left breaks.

Top Two Rules of Surfer Etiquette

- Don't get in the way of someone's ride. Plan your paddle out around the natural breaking wave direction. Better to duck under whitewater than try to beat a breaking wave with a rider on it.
- The surfer behind you riding in the same direction has right of way. Kick out when they start yelling at you.

both in San Diego, are good beginner spots, as is Seal Beach in Orange County and Cayucos (p166) on the Central Coast.

You'll find surfboard rental stands on just about every patch of sand where surfing is possible. Expect to pay about $15 per half-day, with wet suit rental another $10 or so. Group lessons start at around $50 per person, while the going rate for private, two-hour instruction starts at $100. If you're ready to jump in the deep end, many surf schools offer weekend-/week-long camps (around $150/from $350).

Safety issues to watch out for include riptides, which are powerful currents of water that pull you away from the shore (see p252). Sharks do inhabit California waters but attacks are extremely rare. Most take place in the so-called Red Triangle, or Shark Belt, between Monterey on the Central Coast, Tomales Bay just north of San Francisco and the offshore Farallon Islands.

Like cyclists, surfers can benefit from good sport-specific maps. Plan a coastal adventure using maps produced by the **Surf Report** (☎ 714-496-5922; www .surfmaps.net). The maps, which detail surf breaks and provide information on seasonal weather and water temperature, are sold county by county, or in a Southern California set ($40).

Enlightened surfers may also want to check out **Surfrider** (☎ 949-492-8170; http:// surfrider.org), a nonprofit organization that strives to protect the coastal environment. Water quality varies from beach to beach and day to day; for current conditions check the statewide 'Beach Report Card' at www.healthebay.org.

HIKING

With its unparalleled scenery, California is perfect for exploring on foot. This is true whether you've got your heart set on climbing sand dunes, rambling among the world's tallest trees or simply heading for a coastal walk accompanied by booming surf. Wherever you go, expect encounters with an entire cast of furry, feathered and flippered friends.

The Marin Headlands (p72), Mt Tamalpais (p79), the magical Muir Woods (p80) and Point Reyes National Seashore (p83) are all within an 90-minute drive of San Francisco and are crisscrossed by dozens of superb trails. Even in LA, you can ditch the car and head for the Santa Monica Mountains National Recreation Area's Malibu Creek State Park (p198), where the TV show *M*A*S*H* was filmed.

There's excellent hiking in Big Sur, like in redwood-heavy Pfeiffer Big Sur State Park (p160). On the North Coast, stroll through impossibly lush Fern Canyon (p132), which made its cinematic debut in *Jurassic Park 2*.

Parks and forests almost always have a visitors center or ranger station with clued-in staff happy to offer route suggestions and trail-specific tips. It also hands out or sells trail maps, which may be necessary depending on the length and difficulty of your hike. Look for contact information in the destination chapters throughout this book.

California state parks don't charge admission but most levy a parking fee ranging from $4 to $14. Once you pay the parking fee for one state park, it's good for all state parks that same day, which can be useful in places like Big Sur. There's also no charge if you walk or bike into a state park.

The entrance fee to national parks varies from $5 to $20 per vehicle and is good for unlimited entries over seven consecutive days. If you're going to visit many national parks, in California or elsewhere, consider getting the annual $50 National Parks Pass, which you can buy on-site at the entrance to any national park.

Coast Walks: 150 Adventures Along the California Coast (John McKinney, 1999) remains a quality source for hikes short and long, and includes helpful historical context.

DIVING & SNORKELING

Up and down the coast, rock reefs, shipwrecks and kelp forests teem with sea creatures ready for their close-up.

Thanks to the Monterey Bay National Marine Sanctuary, Monterey Bay (p152) offers year-round, world-renowned diving and snorkeling, though you'll need to don a wet suit. Nearby Point Lobos State Reserve is another diving gem. Further south, the fantastic San Diego–La Jolla Underwater Park Ecological Reserve (p234) is accessible via La Jolla Cove.

If you've already got your scuba certification you can rent dive outfits (including one tank of oxygen) for $70 to $100 – it's wise to reserve at least a day in advance. If you've got the time and the money to get certified, basic open-water classes cost around $300 and take from two to three weeks. Most programs require participants to be at least 16 years old. The website http://ladiver.com maintains exhaustive listings of dive sites and shops, certification programs, safety resources and weather conditions for the Los Angeles area, with links to its sister sites in Northern California, the Central Coast and the San Diego/Santa Barbara region.

Snorkeling kits can be rented from dive shops for around $40 a day, but if you're going to be taking the plunge more than twice or so, it's worth it to buy your own snorkel and set of fins. When you head out snorkeling, don't go alone, don't touch anything, and don't forget the sunblock!

WINDSURFING & KITESURFING   By Josh Krist

The idea of putting a sail on a surfboard was around for 20-odd years before two Southern Californians refined the idea and started selling sailboards in 1968 –

the first model was called 'Windsurfer.' A surf sport freed from the vagaries of waves and sometimes aggressive crowds was born. The popularity of this new sport also inspired the invention of kites that could launch a sailboard from the water – in the last few years the newest water sport has gone mainstream.

Experienced windsurfers tear up the waves up and down the coast, and new surfers (or those who want a mellower ride) skim along calm bays and protected beaches. There's almost always a breeze – with the best winds from March or April to the end of September – but the water is cold year-round and unless you're a polar bear a wet suit is a necessity. Any place that has good windsurfing has good kiteboarding. Look for the people doing aerial acrobatics as their parachutelike kites yank them from the water.

If you're on a kiteboard avoid places with obstacles like piers and power lines, and seek the wide-open spaces. Your sail-powered cohorts don't need to worry about unexpected flights that could slam them into concrete.

When in San Diego, beginners should check out Mission Bay (p229) near Santa Clara Point. The winds are steady and most of the time they blow toward the shore – perfect if you're a stranded first-timer. Santa Barbara's Leadbetter Beach (p179) is popular for all water sports and the area near Stearns Wharf in front of West Beach is a good starting spot.

The Bay Area has some of the most spectacular windsurfing backdrops in all of California, but the winds can be fierce and the water is always cold. Crissy Field (p58) is a favorite spot for experienced boarders and the wind literally howls here as it squeezes into the bay.

'Being in the shadow of the Golden Gate Bridge makes it one of the most dramatic places in the world to windsurf. That, and the freighters you need to dodge,' says Richard Bothwell, CFO (chief fun officer) of the Bay Area Outdoor Adventure Club. Currents can be very strong, and even experienced windsurfers should carry an emergency kit with a VHF radio and flares in case they get dragged out to sea.

The learning curve in windsurfing is steeper than other board sports – imagine balancing on a fast-moving plank through choppy waters while trying to read the wind and angle the sail just so. Lessons are available in most of the windsurfing hot spots for about $75 to $100 for a half-day beginner's lesson. Beginner kiteboarding lessons usually last a few days. The first day is spent learning kite control on the beach and the second day gets you into the water. Although it's harder to get started kiteboarding, experts say it's easier to advance quickly once the basics are down.

Most windsurfing businesses at least dabble in kiteboarding and many offer training in the $200 to $500 range for a full course (usually two or three lessons), including equipment hire. Shops usually won't rent kiteboarding gear to people who aren't taking lessons with them, but students often get a big discount on gear purchase.

Renting a windsurfing setup starts at around $20 per hour for a beginner's board and $15 to $25 for a wet suit and harness for the day. Wind reports are available at www.iwindsurf.com (membership is required for detailed reports) and a listing of schools and shops in California is available at www.worldwindsurf.com.

CYCLING

Top up those tires and strap on that helmet! California is outstanding cycling territory.

Just across the Golden Gate Bridge from San Francisco, the Marin Headlands (p72) offers a bonanza of biking trails for fat-tire fans. Classic, top-rated single-track rides include Prairie Creek Redwoods State Park (p132) on the North Coast and Montaña de Oro State Park (p167) on the Central Coast.

The California Coastal Records Project is an ongoing photographic endeavor to chart the coast inch-by-inch. At its highly addictive website, www.californiacoastline.org, you can browse the nearly 30,000 aerial photographs spanning from Oregon to Mexico. (Search 'Malibu' and see houses of celebs like Tom Hanks.)

Monterey Canyon, within the Monterey Bay National Marine Sanctuary, plummets to a depth of over 10,000ft, deeper even than the Grand Canyon.

California's cities are not terribly bike-friendly, although there are exceptions, most notably Santa Barbara (p179), San Luis Obispo (p168) and Santa Cruz (p144). And for the brave activists among you, don't forget all those Critical Mass (CM) events! See p168 for info on San Luis Obispo's ride with a twist, and check out www.critical-mass.org for a listing of cities that stage CMs. An excellent way to meet locals, too.

Even Los Angeles has some good cycling turf in the Santa Monica Mountains (p198) and along the beach on the South Bay Trail (p198). On the Central Coast, the Monterey Peninsula Recreational Trail (p157) travels for 18 car-free miles along the waterfront. Cyclists are thick on the ground on the 20-mile loop along the famously scenic 17-Mile Drive (p157).

Bikes are usually not allowed in designated wilderness areas at all and are limited to paved roads in national parks. Redwood National Park (p130), where you'll be cycling among the giant trees, is one bike-friendly national park. State parks are a little more relaxed but do check beforehand.

Most towns have at least one bike-rental shop and many are listed throughout this book. Prices range from about $5 to $8 per hour or $15 to $30 per day (more for high-tech mountain bikes), depending on the type of bike and the rental location. To get the inside scoop on the local scene, get information from the folks in rental shops. Before heading out, be sure to check tire inflation, and ask about renting a lock.

For more information on in-town biking or long-distance touring, check out these resources:

Adventure Cycling Association (☎ 800-775-2453; www.adventurecycling.org) Trip-planning resources such as the *Cyclist's Yellow Pages*.
Bicycle Rides in California (www.bikecal.com) Rides and resources in Northern California.
Los Angeles Bicycle Coalition (☎ 213-629-2142; http://labikecoalition.org)
Marin County Bicycle Coalition (☎ 415-456-3469; www.marinbike.org)
San Francisco Bicycle Coalition (☎ 415-431-2453; www.sfbike.org)
San Luis Obispo Bicycle Club (www.slobc.org) Local rides and a list of rental shops.
Santa Barbara Bicycle Coalition (www.sbbike.org) Includes downloadable tours of *Sideways* wine country.

KAYAKING

Few water-based sports are as accessible and fun for the whole gang as kayaking, and prior experience is rarely necessary. Gobs of rental outfitters can be found in Morro Bay (p166), whose waters are protected by a gorgeous 4-mile sand spit, and Monterey (p144), both on the Central Coast. Richardson Bay (p76) and in Marin County is a mere paddle's-length away from San Francisco's breathtaking skyline.

Most outfitters offer a choice between sit-upon (open or ocean) kayaks and sit-in (closed-hull) ones, the latter usually requiring a few minutes of training before you head out. Both start at around $30 per person for the day. With both open and closed, you'll usually have a choice between single and tandem. Whatever kind of kayak you get, a reputable outfitter will make sure you're aware of the tide schedule and wind conditions of your proposed route.

Many kayaking outfitters put forward a variety of half-day ($55 to $75) or day-long (from around $110) excursions, many with a theme like full-moon paddling or a kayak-hike combo. The best tours tend to have a small number of participants and are led by guides with some natural history training.

A few good choices:

Central Coast Outdoors (☎ 805-528-1080; www.centralcoastoutdoors.com) Based near San Luis Obispo.
Hum Boats Sail, Canoe & Kayak Center (☎ 707-443-5157; www.humboats.com) In Eureka on the Redwood Coast.

Information on freeway access for bicyclists, a guide to bicycle touring in California and links to free downloadable maps are available on www.cabobike.org, a site maintained by the California Association of Bicycling Organizations (CABO).

The outstanding *California Coastal Access Guide* (California Coastal Commission, 2003) gives comprehensive, map- and direction-heavy breakdowns to every public beach, reef, harbor, overlook and coastal campground in the state.

Monterey Bay Kayaks (☎ 800-649-5357; www.montereybaykayaks.com; 693 Del Monte Ave)
OE Express (☎ 858-454-6195; www.oeexpress.com; 2158 Av de la Playa) In La Jolla.

For general resources on kayaking in California, head to www.kayakonline.com/california.html

WHALE-WATCHING

Every summer 15,000 gray whales feed in the arctic waters between Alaska and Siberia, and every October, they start moving south down the Pacific coast of Canada and the USA to sheltered lagoons in the Gulf of California in Baja California. While there, the pregnant whales give birth to calves weighing up to 2500lb (who go on to live up to 50 years, grow to 50ft in length and weigh up to 45 tons). Around mid-March, these whales turn around and head back to the arctic. Luckily for us, during their 12,000-mile round-trip the whales pass just off the California coast.

The whales stay closer to shore on their southbound leg, so your best chances of catching a glimpse are in December and January. You can try your luck while staying shore-bound (free, but less probable and more removed from the action), or by taking a whale-watching trip. A few of the best dockside spots from which to point your binoculars include Point Reyes lighthouse (p83), Point Pinos lighthouse (p155) on the Monterey Peninsula and Cabrillo National Monument (p234) on San Diego's Point Loma.

Half-day trips (from $20 to $35 per adult and $15 to $20 per child) range from 2½ to four hours, and all-day trips range from $75 to $100, with some including meals and some not. Look for a tour that limits the number of people and has a trained naturalist on board. Ideally, the operator would also use biodiesel fuel in its boats like Sanctuary Cruises (p149), on the Monterey Peninsula, does. Many companies will let you go again for free if there are no spottings during your trip, and some have minimum age requirements, so check on this before the tears start. Binoculars are a must.

And it's not only gray whales that make appearances. Blue, humpback and sperm whales (not to mention tons of dolphins) can be seen off the California coast throughout the summer and fall, but these whale spottings tend not to be as predictable as the grays.

Spotting whales is a simple combination of patience and timing. Spouting, the exhalation of moist warm air, is usually the first sign that a whale is about. A series of spouts, about 15 seconds apart, may be followed by a sight of the creature's tail as the whale dives. If you're lucky, you may see whales spy hopping (sticking their heads out of the water to look around) or even breaching (leaping clear out of the water).

HANG GLIDING & PARAGLIDING

For a memorable fly-like-a-bird experience – and perhaps the most expensive 20 minutes of your life – you can't beat gliding. Very roughly speaking, paragliding is to hang gliding as a plane is to a hot-air balloon.

Some of the most unbelievable vistas and best gliding schools are found – surprise! – on the California coast. A tandem flight (the only kind you can do your first time) of either paragliding or hang gliding goes from $150 to $200 a pop, with the former on the cheaper side of the spectrum. Most companies won't allow kids under 12 to take the leap.

Two renowned gliding spots are Torrey Pines Gliderport (p234) north of La Jolla, and Santa Barbara's **Fly Above All** (☎ 805-965-3733; www.flyaboveall.com).

Even if you have no intention of going up yourself, swing by and watch the fun.

The age of a whale can be determined by counting the layers of wax in its ears, similar to counting the rings of a tree. Eeew!

For information and coupons for activities not discussed in this chapter – like horse riding and bungee-jumping – thrill-seekers should check out www.caladventures.com.

Food & Drink

California's food and drink compare with the world's finest and many great trends began here. North America's only indigenous beer-brewing style originates in California. San Francisco, not Seattle, gave rise to the current coffee culture. The organic-food industry is booming throughout the state, with seasonal-regional cooking growing in stature. Tying it all together, San Francisco and Los Angeles constantly play off each other, ever expanding the genre of California cuisine.

STAPLES & SPECIALTIES

The Golden State provides almost all of America's tomatoes and artichokes, and most of its lettuce and cabbage and a lot more besides. You name it, California grows it. Residents love produce. The single most common way to eat vegetables is in salad – served with a crusty loaf of freshly baked bread, it's a classic California meal.

California produces nearly all the nation's grapes, almonds and artichokes, 75% of its strawberries and lettuce and half its tomatoes. Dairy products are the cash cow, bringing in $4 billion annually.

Salad was once thought of as 'rabbit food' by many a Yankee. Men of Illinois saw men of California eating salads and labeled them gay (remember 'real men don't eat quiche'?). Thirty years and 300,000 coronary bypass surgeries later, the rest of America has followed suit – if only with iceberg lettuce (also grown locally). In California, where ripe avocados, fresh fruits and crunchy nuts originate, there's always something unusual thrown into the salad bowl.

With California's 1100 miles of coastline and innumerable rivers and streams, it's no wonder Californians love fish. Fishing is not only a huge industry, but a tremendously popular sport. As you travel the coast from spring through fall, you'll see salmon on every restaurant menu, much of it locally caught. (Try it cooked traditionally, on a cedar plank; it's delicious.) In the far north, pick up salmon jerky to nibble on in the car. Oysters, too, are very popular; though most indigenous species have been decimated or vanished altogether, look for oyster farms, such as Drakes Bay Oysters (p82) in Inverness.

Some people associate California with vegetarianism, but many locals ardently love meat. For years the paradigm for beef was corn-fed cattle from the Midwest. In California, however, a reverse trend is in progress. Better restaurants now serve grass-fed beef from cattle that range freely and are raised without the use of dietary or hormonal supplements. Not only does it improve the meat's texture and flavor, but it's environmentally friendly, since cattle aren't forced to consume a crop that requires vast amounts of water, fuel and electricity to grow and process into feed. On the flip side, corn is federally subsidized, which makes it cheap; it also causes the animals to grow faster, reducing costs for farmers and eventually consumers.

A stunning exposé about food in America, *Food Politics: How the Food Industry Influences Nutrition and Health*, by Marion Nestle (2003), tracks the influence of big businesses on the American diet.

Still, 'organic' meats and produce have taken off in California among savvy food-lovers and environmentalists alike. This is ironic since California's giant agribusiness companies produce huge amounts of genetically modified foods in the Central Valley. The cognoscenti won't buy it. Top chefs now insist on organics, claiming that they're not only environmentally safer, but taste better.

Corporate growers have lately been co-opting the term 'organic' and are working with large grocery chains. Note: just because produce is labeled organic doesn't mean it's fresh or from a small, independent producer. At large chains, produce sits for days – if not a week – in huge distribution centers before getting transported to stores, where it sits again until you buy it. When

CALIFORNIA CUISINE, THEN & NOW

What a difference a decade makes. Here's a comparison of what was hot in the mid-'90s, and what's hot in the mid-'00s

Then	Now
Cosmopolitans	Mojitos
Merlot	Pinot noir
Endive	Arugula
Foie gras	Rillettes
Seared-rare ahi tuna	Grass-fed beef
Crème brulée	Herb-infused ice cream

you shop at small, independent stores such as Bi-Rite in San Francisco (p65), which works exclusively with artisanal farmers, the food goes directly from the grower to the store. And that makes an enormous difference in flavor, not to mention nutritional content. As you drive through Half Moon Bay (p70) and other coastal agricultural regions, stop at little farm stands and buy whatever is in season; about half sell organically grown items. See if you can't taste the difference.

Californians adore culinary trends. Some crazes are stupid and doomed to failure (eg chocolate pasta), others are good but overused (eg foams), while still others get integrated from foreign countries, skyrocket in popularity and become a part of the California repertoire (eg duck confit). It's great that the 'molten chocolate cake' (read: undercooked) fad is on the outs. It was good in the right hands, but in the end, only B- and C-list restaurants continued doing it, and they did it badly, rendering the dish either cold and raw or hot and overcooked. And therein lies rub in Cal cuisine: copycats denigrate good ideas and dilute metaphors till they become bland and die. Thank heaven the metaphors keep evolving.

The outlandish 2004 film *Sideways* captures the folly and passion of California's wine-snob scene. Pinot noir, a highly sensitive grape that prospers only in rare climatic conditions, becomes a metaphor for the main character, Miles, brilliantly played by Paul Giamatti.

DRINKS

Californians love wine, and ever since Stag's Leap cabernet sauvignon and Chateau Montelena chardonnay (both from the Napa Valley) beat French rivals at the 1976 Paris Tasting – the 'World Cup of Wine' – California vintages have basked in the glow of international attention. From Mendocino to Santa Barbara, head inland just a few miles and you'll find yourself in some of the world's greatest wine-growing regions. Check out Sonoma County (p90) and Anderson Valley (p97) in the north, and the hills above Santa Barbara (p178) in the south.

Unlike in France, locally made wine is expensive – and many prefer to drink beer. During the Gold Rush, men wanted lager but couldn't brew it in the temperate San Francisco climate. Instead they devised a way to brew lager as one would brew ale, at higher temperatures. The result: steam beer, which has characteristics of both stout and lager. Some find it metallic, but you should definitely try it while you're in San Francisco.

For insider insight into wine, head to www.west coastwine.com, an interactive site with message boards, wine notes and chats.

Steam beer is the only indigenous American beer. All of it is made by hand in smallish breweries. Anchor Steam in San Francisco is the original steam brewer. Today, various ales have grown in popularity. Again, stop in the Anderson Valley (p97) or at any of the microbreweries listed in the destination chapters.

In cafés – which are everywhere – people love strong coffee. Don't be ashamed to wrinkle your nose at pale brown water. Most baristas respect those who like their coffee potent. Expect weak brews in roadside diners.

On the nonalcoholic front many vintners have started bottling their un-fermented wine-grape juice. Look for it on restaurant menus and at better nonchain food stores.

CULINARY CALENDAR & FOOD FESTIVALS

Masters of Food & Wine (☎ 800-401-1009; www.mfandw.com) California's most prestigious food-&-wine event features star chefs & vintners. Held in Carmel in February.

Rhône Rangers Wine Tasting (☎ 707-462-5943; www.rhonerangers.org) Around 120 American Rhône-style wine producers, with Bay Area artisanal food producers. Held in San Francisco in March.

Santa Barbara County Vintners' Festival (☎ 805-688-0881; www.sbcountywines.com) Quaff samples from storied wine country. Held in April.

California Strawberry Festival (☎ 888-288-9242; www.strawberry-fest.org; Oxnard) Family-fun festival celebrating the region's specialty: strawberries. Held in Oxnard, near Ventura, in May.

Cooking for Solutions (☎ 866-644-7561; www.montereybayaquarium.org) Celeb chefs show how to cook using sustainably farmed ingredients. Held in Monterey in May.

Chinese Food Festival Los Angeles (☎ 213-680-0243; www.chinesefoodfestivalla.com) Samples, demos and, of course, noodle-eating contests. Held in June.

Tofu Festival Los Angeles (☎ 213-473-3030; www.tofufest.org) Wacky tofu-eating contest and sake tastings in Little Tokyo. Held in August.

Russian River Food & Wine Festival (www.russianriverfoodandwinefest.com) Major-name Northern California chefs cook outdoors in Sonoma County. Held in September.

Pismo Beach Clam Festival (☎ 805-773-4382; www.pismochamber.com) Chowder cook-offs, a kids clam dig and plenty of the fried clams. Held in October.

San Diego Bay Wine & Food Festival (☎ 619-342-7337; www.worldofwineevents.com) Tastings, wine-maker dinners, classes and demos. Held in November.

The *San Francisco Chronicle* food and wine sections are treasure troves of contemporary recipes and reviews; check out the encyclopedic, user-friendly sections at www .sfgate.com/food.

For information and links to all things edible, see www.foodreference.com.

WHERE TO EAT & DRINK

Whenever possible pick a restaurant where the chef is also the owner. It makes all the difference in consistency and quality. There is no such thing as a typical California-cuisine restaurant. Many chefs draw influences from Europe, Asia or both. There are no rules, except that the food is extremely fresh, minimally processed and perfectly prepared. The point is to use few ingredients and let the foods' natural flavors sing. For sauces, chefs generally rely on flavor-packed reductions of stocks rather than fat-enriched gravies.

Coastal California has the requisite steak houses and seafood restaurants, but what makes the culinary scene special here are all the small, mom-and-pop spots that take advantage of the state's year-round growing season. Seasonal and regional are the new buzz words, and many restaurants now reveal the names of their purveyors on the menu. Perhaps the most extreme example of seasonal-regional cooking is the Seaweed Café in Bodega Bay (p89), where all the ingredients are sourced from small Sonoma County farmers, within a 30-mile radius of the restaurant. Now that's freshness!

The restaurant Chez Panisse in Berkeley is considered the birthplace of California cuisine.

VEGETARIANS & VEGANS

California may have more vegetarians and vegans per capita than any other state, but outside the Bay Area and greater LA, strictly vegetarian restaurants are few and far between. Take heart: vegetarians may go to virtually any proper sit-down restaurant in California and order a satisfying meal from the regular menu. Sometimes as much as 60% of the offerings will be vegetarian. This is especially true of Chinese and Indian restaurants, both of which are plentiful. Western-style restaurants have obligatory vegetarian-pasta dishes, salads, portobello mushrooms in season, baked squash and eggplant (aubergine), pilafs and pies. Dishes of steamed mixed vegetables dressed with olive oil or an emulsion sauce are popular, and people do astonishing things with tofu. Even many Mexican restaurants will offer vegetarian dishes, a thing

---

SLOW IS THE NEW FAST

The Slow Food movement is fast gaining ground across America, but nowhere like in California. Slow Food seeks to counteract fast food and reconnect people with traditional ways of cooking, raise awareness about all levels of the food chain, promote ecologically sound food production, and revive the table as a center of pleasure and community. Basically you eat what's in season where you live (which is difficult in Alaska, but easy in California). You can even start your own chapter (called a 'convivium') with a handful of friends, à la the 'gourmet clubs' of the mid-20th century. Learn more at www.slowfood.com.

---

unheard of in Mexico – just make sure lard wasn't used to cook the beans. You'll do very well along the North Coast and in Santa Cruz. Ravens in Mendocino, (p101) and Greens in San Francisco (p63) stand out for stellar, white-tablecloth dining; here you'll find no health food, no hippie food, just top-notch vegetarian cookery.

EATING WITH KIDS

If you're traveling with kids, you'll be pleased to know that most restaurants will be happy to see you. Always ask for a children's menu; it's sometimes printed on a take-home coloring book or placemat. There are also loads of midrange places where Mom and Dad can enjoy a good bottle of wine while the kids have an ice-cream sundae.

High-end restaurants, however, are not child-friendly. Meals in such places last two hours or more, too long to expect little ones to sit without squirming or screaming. Unless they're exceptionally well behaved, properly dressed and old enough to appreciate the meal, don't bring children to nice restaurants without first calling to inquire if it's appropriate (see also p249).

HABITS & CUSTOMS

In California, as throughout the US, the main meal of the day is dinner. Breakfasts are traditionally hearty, though busy lifestyles have cut into the eggs-and-bacon tradition. Lunch tends to be light – typically a sandwich, perhaps soup and salad. Americans are also big snackers.

If you're looking for huge, American-style portions, California may disappoint, at least at the higher-end places where the idea is to savor, not gorge. Considering they're gourmands, Californians eat relatively early. In fine restaurants, the peak hour is 7pm to 8pm. Always make reservations, even on weekdays.

California native and chef extraordinaire Julia Child said: 'America was just learning how to cook when nutrition reared its ugly head.'

COOKING COURSES

Balboa Park Food & Wine School (☎ 619-557-9441, ext 210; www.balboawinefood.com; Casa del Prado, Balboa Park, San Diego; per person $40 to $75) One-day demos by local chefs.
California Culinary Academy Weekend Gourmet (☎ 415-354-9198; www.baychef.com; 625 Polk St, San Francisco; per person $175) Professional cooking school with one-day programs for home cooks.
Chronicle Cooking School (☎ 415-777-7759; chroniclecooks@sfchronicle.com; Ferry Bldg, 1 Market St, San Francisco; classes $60) Cooking demonstrations at San Francisco's Ferry Building.
Laguna Culinary Arts (☎ 949-494-0745; www.lagunaculinaryarts.com; 550 South Coast Hwy, Laguna Beach; from $80) One-day introductory courses and multiday programs.
New School of Cooking (☎ 310-842-9702; www.newschoolofcooking.com; 8690 Washington Blvd, Culver City, Los Angeles; from $80) Lots of one-day classes, as well as degree programs.
Relish Culinary School (☎ 707-431-9999, 877-759-1004; www.relishculinary.com; from $70) Courses for home chefs; from cake-decorating to teen-pizza workshops. Various locations around Healdsburg (p90).

San Francisco & the Bay Area

You know you're someplace special when Bill O'Reilly suggests that Al Qaeda should blow it up. Ah, the Bay Area. Forever controversial. Endlessly fun. Maybe that's what gets everyone so upset. Locals always seem to be thumbing their noses at the status quo and goofing off – sailing the Bay's icy-blue waters, hiking Point Reyes, mountain-biking down Mt Tam, or lazing on the beaches from Marin to Santa Cruz. Even right beneath the Golden Gate Bridge, one of the world's most iconic monuments, there's a nude beach! Who has time to fight when there's so much beauty to explore?

And beauty does matter here – not the shiny-shiny Los Angeles kind, but the Mother Earth kind. Though the San Francisco Bay Area is America's fifth-largest metropolitan region, the coast looks much as it did a century ago, saved by prominent citizens working strategically to block development. Today hawks and eagles still soar over the Golden Gate.

Out-of-town finger-waggers may carp about the Bay Area's smugness, but they mistake gratitude for arrogance. People who live here know they've got something special, and they're grateful for it. Lucky for you, they love to show it off.

HIGHLIGHTS

- Staring down onto the Golden Gate Bridge from the **Marin Headlands** (p72)
- Biting into the Northern California food scene at the **Ferry Building Marketplace** (p49)
- Spotting whales offshore from windswept **Point Reyes National Seashore** (p83)
- Debating the architectural merit of the new **MH de Young Memorial Museum** (p56)
- Spotting the wild parrots of Telegraph Hill and wowing at the views on the perfect **San Francisco walking tour** (p58)

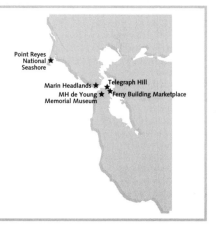

SAN FRANCISCO

pop 791,600

Welcome to the bubble, America's most liberal city, where you can say what you want, do what you want and act like a freak without anyone noticing. Even if you prefer khakis to chaps, and Bush to Gore (shhh!), you'll still have a blast in SF – don't call it Frisco, or San Fran; say Ess Eff. Locals love to party: nearly every weekend from spring to fall there's a street fair somewhere, with music and dancing and free-flowing margaritas. The city's culinary scene is spectacular. This is the birthplace of California cuisine and lately of the seasonal-regional, sustainable-foods movement. Surrounded by water on three sides and lorded over by 43 rolling hills dotted with Victorian homes and hidden stairway gardens, San Francisco is possibly the most beautiful city in the country, a photographer's dream. But the thing that makes the city so special is its people. If the idea of the American melting pot worked anywhere, it worked here. Once you've maxed your credit cards at downtown boutiques, ridden the cable cars and sailed to Alcatraz, explore the off-the-beaten-path neighborhoods to meet the locals and get a true sense of place. Don't underestimate the magic of the 'cool, gray city of love': a couple of weeks here and you may start shopping for apartments – or at least a pair of chaps.

ORIENTATION

Compact San Francisco sits at the tip of a 30-mile-long peninsula and measures seven-by-seven miles. To the west lies the Pacific, to the east San Francisco Bay.

The city can be roughly divided into three sections. Downtown resembles a slice of pie, its edges delimited by Van Ness Ave and Market St, with the rounded edge being the waterfront. Its major neighborhoods include the Financial District, North Beach, Chinatown, Union Sq, Nob Hill, Russian Hill and Fisherman's Wharf. To find numbered piers, note that from the Ferry Building even-numbered piers extend southward, and odd-numbered piers northward.

The area south of Market St is aptly called South of Market (SoMa). It's the upwardly mobile warehouse district, and bleeds into the hip, gritty Mission District.

The largest area lies west of Van Ness Ave and extends to the Pacific, encompassing many interesting neighborhoods, including posh Pacific Heights and the Marina, Japantown, the Castro (the city's gay center) and the Haight District (of 1960s fame). Also here are the city's best parks – the Presidio, Lincoln Park and Golden Gate Park.

INFORMATION

Bookstores

A Different Light Bookstore (Map p55; ☎ 415-431-0891; 489 Castro St; ⏲ 10am-11pm) Gay-specific titles.

Books Inc (Map p55; ☎ 415-864-6777; 2275 Market St; ⏲ 10am-11pm) General interest.

Café de la Presse (Map pp52-3; ☎ 415-398-2680; 352 Grant Ave at Bush St; ⏲ 7:30am-10pm) Carries some European papers and magazines; it's a chic café too.

City Lights (Map p54; ☎ 415-362-8193; 261 Columbus Ave; ⏲ 10am-midnight) Counterculture and literature; excellent readings.

Cody's (Map pp52-3; ☎ 415-773-0444; 2 Stockton St; ⏲ 10am-9pm) Branch of the famous, now-defunct Berkeley bookstore.

Fog City News (Map pp52-3; ☎ 415-543-7400; 455 Market St; ⏲ 8am-6pm Mon-Fri) Stellar selection of magazines, international periodicals and fabulous chocolate.

Get Lost (Map pp52-3; ☎ 415-437-0529; 1825 Market St) Tops for travel books and maps.

Modern Times (Map p55; ☎ 415-282-9246; 888 Valencia St; ⏲ 10am-9pm Mon-Sat, 11am-6pm Sun) Good in-store events; great for politicos.

Stacey's Books (Map pp52-3; ☎ 415-421-4687; 581 Market St) SF's oldest independent bookstore.

Emergency & Medical Services

California Pacific Medical Center (Map p51; ☎ 415-600-3333; 2333 Buchanan St) The city's most civilized ER; short waits, high fees without insurance. It's located near Sacramento St.

City Clinic (Map pp52-3; ☎ 415-487-5500; www.dph .sf.ca.us/sfcityclinic; 356 7th St; ⏲ 8am-4pm Mon, Wed & Fri, 1-6pm Tue, 1-4pm Thu) For treatment of sexually transmitted diseases.

Haight Ashbury Free Clinic (Map p51; ☎ 415-487-5632; 558 Clayton St; ⏲ 1-9pm Mon, 9am-9pm Tue-Thu, 1-5pm Fri) For nonemergencies, payable on sliding scale. Appointments required, except at drop-in hour of Monday and Tuesday 4:45pm, or Tuesday and Wednesday 8:45am; arrive at least 30 minutes early to secure a spot.

San Francisco General Hospital (Map p51; ☎ 415-206-8000; 1001 Potrero Ave) For severe trauma, go directly to one of the country's best trauma units; but

SAN FRANCISCO BAY AREA

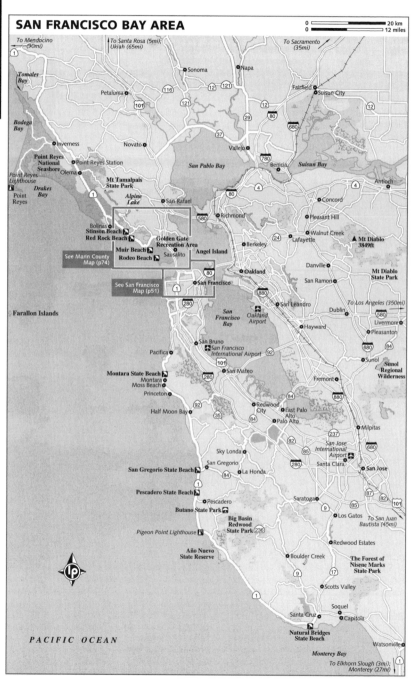

it's full of the destitute, and you might wait hours. Enter the ER from 23rd St.

Walgreen's The Castro (Map p55; ☎ 415-861-3136; 498 Castro St); The Marina (Map p54; ☎ 415-931-6417; 3201 Divisadero St) This is a 24-hour pharmacy.

Internet Access

Many cafés in SF have wi-fi. Most hotels provide internet access. Check the phone book for nearby Kinko's branches. The **Visitors Information Center** (right) provides more information on internet cafés around SF.

CompUSA (Map pp52-3; ☎ 415-743-3200; 750 Market St) Free access.

Main Library (Map pp52-3; ☎ 415-557-4400; cnr Larkin & Grove Sts) Six first-come, first-served 'express' terminals on the 1st floor, available for 15 minutes. Staff provide information on internet cafés. Located near the Civic Center BART/MUNI stations.

Internet Resources

Bay Guardian (www.sfbg.com) Features primers on politics and local events.

Craig's List (www.craigslist.org) SF's definitive community bulletin board.

National Weather Service (www.wrh.noaa.gov /Monterey)

SF Gate (www.sfgate.com) Mainstream news and listings; operated by the Chronicle.

SF Station (www.sfstation.com) Indie site for cultural events and goings-on.

SF Weekly (www.sfweekly.com) Cool site of up-to-the-minute goings-on.

Media

Northern California's largest daily, the *San Francisco Chronicle* (aka the *Comical*) is the best source for general news; the Sunday edition has the 'Datebook', one of the city's best entertainment resources.

SF has two intelligent weeklies, the *San Francisco Bay Guardian* and the *SF Weekly*, both published Wednesdays. They feature excellent events listings, in-depth articles and smart writing.

The *Bay Area Reporter* (the *BAR*) and the *Bay Times* are free gay papers distributed in the Castro and surrounding neighborhoods.

Money

Banks and ATMs are ubiquitous.

Travelex (Map pp52-3; ☎ 415-362-3453; 75 Geary St, Union Sq; ⏰ 9am-5pm Mon-Fri, 10am-4pm Sat) Currency exchange; there's another branch at San Francisco International Airport's International Terminal.

Post

Civic Center Post Office (Map pp52-3; ☎ 415-563-7284, 800-725-2161; 101 Hyde St) To receive poste restante mail, address it with: your name, c/o General Delivery, Civic Center Post Office, 101 Hyde St, San Francisco, CA 94142, USA.

Union Square Post Office (Map pp52-3; downstairs, Macy's department store, 170 O'Farrell St; Union Sq; ⏰ 10am-5:30pm Mon-Sat, 11am-5pm Sun)

Tourist Offices

California Welcome Center (Map p54; ☎ 415-981-1280; Ste 241-248; Bldg P; Pier 39; ⏰ 10am-5pm) Statewide information, brochures, maps and help with accommodations bookings (fees cost up to $5).

San Francisco Visitors Information Center (Map pp52-3; ☎ 415-391-2000; www.onlyinsanfrancisco .com; lower level, Hallidie Plaza, cnr Market & Powell Sts; ⏰ 8:30am-5pm Mon-Fri, 9am-3pm Sat & Sun) Carries maps, guidebooks, brochures, accommodations information and phonecards. Operates 24-hour automated phone line, with recorded information (☎ 415-391-2001).

DANGERS & ANNOYANCES

San Francisco is pretty safe, with several notable exceptions. Unless you know where you're going, avoid the Tenderloin, which is the downtown area bordered by Polk St (west), Powell St (east), Market St (south) and O'Farrell St (north). Avoid 6th St between Market and Folsom Sts. Market St between 5th St and Van Ness Ave is sketchy, but not terrible. In the Mission, junkies hang around Mission St between 15th and 17th.

The biggest nuisance comes from aggressive panhandlers loitering by the cable-car turnaround on Market St. Don't be cowed. Simply say 'Sorry,' and continue confidently on your way. Bicycle thieves linger at the east end of Haight St by the park.

SIGHTS & ACTIVITIES

If you're here a while, get Lonely Planet's *San Francisco* for comprehensive coverage.

The Embarcadero & Ferry Building

Stroll or bike the eastern waterfront, from South of Market to Fisherman's Wharf, along wide-open sidewalks, and take in picture-perfect views of Treasure Island and the Bay Bridge. At the foot of Market St, the elegant 1898 **Ferry Building** houses the not-to-be-missed **Ferry Building Marketplace** (Map pp52-3; ☎ 415-693-0996; www.ferrybuildingmarketplace.com; ⏰ 10am-6pm), which showcases gorgeous local, sustainable and regional foods by celebs such as Cowgirl Creamery, Hog Island Oyster Co and Acme Bread, and farmers whose names you see on überchic restaurant menus. Sample the goods, then stop for lunch at one of half-a-dozen stellar restaurants. Tuesday and Saturday mornings, there's an awesome organic **farmers market** (☎ 415-291-3276) out the front. Ferries to Sausalito with the **Golden Gate Ferry** (☎ 415-923-2000; www.goldengate.org) and to Tiburon with the **Blue & Gold Fleet** (☎ 415-773-1188; www.blueandgold fleet.com) dock out the back.

For drop-dead vistas, take your goodies south to **Pier 14** (Map pp52-3), a narrow pedestrian pier extending 600ft into the bay.

Vintage streetcars run along the Embarcadero from Fisherman's Wharf to the Ferry Building, then up Market St to the Castro district.

Golden Gate Bridge

The jewel in the crown of the Golden Gate National Recreation Area (GGNRA), the 1937 **Golden Gate Bridge** (Map p51; ☎ 415-921-5858; www .goldengatebridge.org; pedestrian walkway 5am-9pm Apr-Oct, to 6:30pm Nov-Mar, bicycles 24hr; ☺) remains San Francisco's most enduring symbol. A marvel of 20th-century engineering, it's nearly 2 miles long, with a main span of 4200ft. The name comes from the straits it crosses, not its color, which is actually 'international orange.'

Start your tour from the parking lot at the bridge's south end (via Lincoln Blvd through the Presidio; or via Hwy 101 northbound to the 10mph hairpin-exit marked 'Last SF Exit,' just before the toll plaza). There's a lookout here, along with a gift shop and a must-see cutaway of the 3ft-thick suspension cable. Follow the path to the bridge sidewalk. (If you're on a bicycle, follow signs to the appropriate sidewalk.) Bring a jacket, even if it's sunny inland. MUNI buses 28 (from Golden Gate Park) and 29 (from the Marina) run to the toll plaza.

SF'S COOLEST EPHEMERAL SIGHT

As summertime's afternoon fog blows in, look westward to Sutro Tower, the enormous Erector Set–like radio tower atop Twin Peaks. When the roiling clouds ascend its base and reach the cross pieces near the top, the tower magically transforms into a two-masted schooner sailing across a sea of fog. Fabulous.

If you drive across, stop at the first exit north of the bridge marked **Vista Point**. The views are superb, but you'll pay a $5 toll to return (there's no outbound toll). Before heading back, see Marin Headlands (p72).

Alcatraz Island

America's most notorious prison from 1933 to 1963, 12-acre Alcatraz Island sits isolated by chilly waters and strong currents. You can tour 'The Rock' by booking a ferry and self-guided audio tour through **Alcatraz Cruises** (Map p54; ☎ 415-981-7625; www.alcatrazcruises.com; ferry & audio tour $27; ☺). Check out the menu in the mess hall; it remains from the last day the prison was open. And listen for the howling of the wind in the walls. What a miserable place to be trapped in. Although prisoners found sunny days the worst (all those free, happy people on sailboats only reinforced the fact that the prisoners were locked up), the most atmospheric time to visit is during winter in the rain (when it's easier to get tickets, too). Reservations are essential: at peak summer periods, the parks service turns away 2000 people a day. Ask about the docent-led 'Alcatraz After Dark' tours.

Downtown, South of Market & Civic Center

The heart of the downtown area, **Union Square** (Map pp52-3) is where most visitors stay. Hotels, department stores, designer boutiques and theaters are clustered around the square. Anchoring its western edge, the grand 1904 **Westin St Francis Hotel** (335 Powell St) has glass elevators with primo downtown views; walk through the lobby to the concierge desk, and hang a right (don't tell 'em I told you!).

South of Market (SoMa), **Yerba Buena Gardens** (☎ 415-820-3550; www.yerbabuenagardens.com; ☺ 6am-10pm) is the neighborhood's centerpiece, with ice-skating, a bowling alley, children's museum, theaters and the handcarved 1906 **Loof carousel** (cnr 4th St & Howard St; $2; ☺ 10am-6pm; ☺).

Across the street is the excellent **San Francisco Museum of Modern Art** (☎ 415-357-4000; www.sfmoma .org; 151 3rd St; adult/child/student $12.50/free/$7; ☺ 11am-5:45pm Fri-Tue, to 8:45pm Thu), designed by Mario Botta. The permanent collection is strong in American abstract expressionism, but the galleries are boxy and small. Still, it's worth a visit, especially for the world-renowned

(Continued on page 56)

0 ——————— 2 km
0 ——————— 1 mile

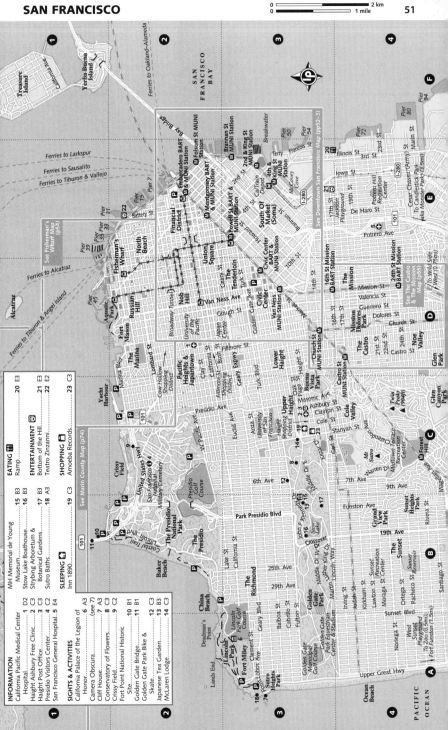

See Fisherman's Wharf Map (p54)

See Downtown San Francisco Map (pp52–3)

See Marin County Map (p74)

See The Castro & The Mission Map (p55)

Treasure Island

Yerba Buena Island

SAN FRANCISCO BAY

Alcatraz

Ferries to Oakland–Alameda
Ferries to Larkspur
Ferries to Sausalito
Ferries to Tiburon & Vallejo
Ferries to Alcatraz
Ferries to Tiburon & Angel Island

Bay Bridge

PACIFIC OCEAN

Ocean Beach

Golden Gate Park

The Presidio

The Richmond

The Sunset

The Marina

North Beach

Financial District

Union Square

Nob Hill

Russian Hill

Civic Center

Tenderloin

The Mission

The Castro

Noe Valley

Pacific Heights & Japantown

Lower Haight

Upper Haight

Cole Valley

Buena Vista Park

Glen Park

0 _____ 500 m
0 _____ 0.3 miles

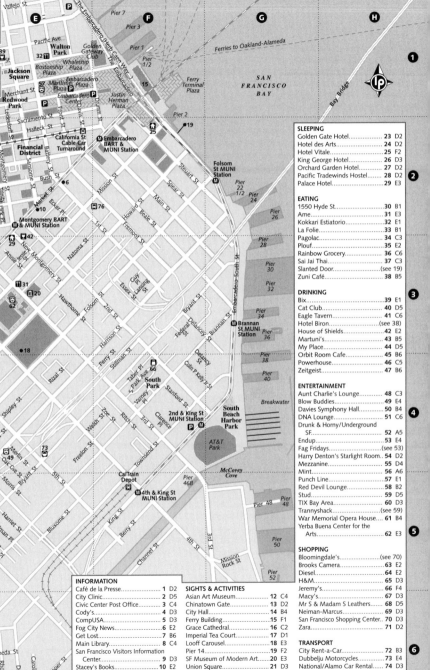

SAN FRANCISCO BAY

Ferries to Oakland-Alameda

Bay Bridge

SLEEPING
Golden Gate Hotel	23	D2
Hotel des Arts	24	D2
Hotel Vitale	25	F2
King George Hotel	26	D3
Orchard Garden Hotel	27	D2
Pacific Tradewinds Hostel	28	D2
Palace Hotel	29	E3

EATING
1550 Hyde St	30	B1
Ame	31	E3
Kokkari Estiatorio	32	E1
La Folie	33	B1
Pagolac	34	C3
Plouf	35	E2
Rainbow Grocery	36	C6
Sai Jai Thai	37	C3
Slanted Door	(see 19)	
Zuni Café	38	B5

DRINKING
Bix	39	E1
Cat Club	40	D5
Eagle Tavern	41	C6
Hotel Biron	(see 38)	
House of Shields	42	E2
Martuni's	43	B5
My Place	44	D5
Orbit Room Cafe	45	B6
Powerhouse	46	C5
Zeitgeist	47	B6

ENTERTAINMENT
Aunt Charlie's Lounge	48	C3
Blow Buddies	49	E4
Davies Symphony Hall	50	B4
DNA Lounge	51	C6
Drunk & Horny/Underground SF	52	A5
Endup	53	E4
Fag Fridays	(see 53)	
Harry Denton's Starlight Room	54	D2
Mezzanine	55	D4
Mint	56	A6
Punch Line	57	E1
Red Devil Lounge	58	B2
Stud	59	D5
TIX Bay Area	60	D3
Trannyshack	(see 59)	
War Memorial Opera House	61	B4
Yerba Buena Center for the Arts	62	E3

SHOPPING
Bloomingdale's	(see 70)	
Brooks Camera	63	E2
Diesel	64	E2
H&M	65	D3
Jeremy's	66	F4
Macy's	67	D3
Mr S & Madam S Leathers	68	D5
Neiman-Marcus	69	D3
San Francisco Shopping Center	70	D3
Zara	71	D2

INFORMATION
Café de la Presse	1	D2
City Clinic	2	D5
Civic Center Post Office	3	C4
Cody's	4	D3
CompUSA	5	D3
Fog City News	6	E2
Get Lost	7	B6
Main Library	8	C4
San Francisco Visitors Information Center	9	D3
Stacey's Books	10	E2
Travelex	11	D3
Union Square Post Office	(see 67)	

SIGHTS & ACTIVITIES
Asian Art Museum	12	C4
Chinatown Gate	13	D2
City Hall	14	B4
Ferry Building	15	F1
Grace Cathedral	16	C2
Imperial Tea Court	17	D1
Looff Carousel	18	E3
Pier 14	19	F2
SF Museum of Modern Art	20	E3
Union Square	21	D3
Westin St Francis Hotel	22	D3
Yerba Buena Gardens	(see 62)	

TRANSPORT
City Rent-a-Car	72	B3
Dubbelju Motorcycles	73	D4
National/Alamo Car Rental	74	D3
Speciality Rentals	75	B6
Transbay Terminal	76	F2

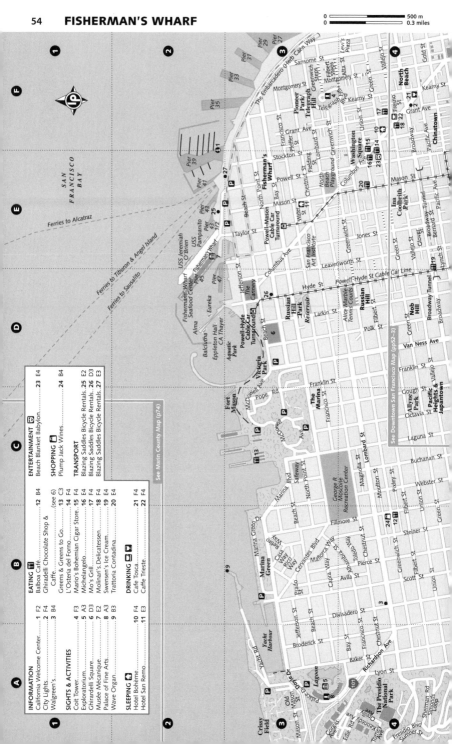

0 — 500 m
0 — 0.3 miles

INFORMATION
California Welcome Center................1 F2
City Lights.................................2 F4
Walgreen's................................3 B4

SIGHTS & ACTIVITIES
Coit Tower...............................4 F3
Exploratorium...........................5 A3
Ghirardelli Square......................6 D3
Musée Mécanique.......................7 E2
Palace of Fine Arts....................8 A3
Wave Organ............................9 B3

SLEEPING 🏨
Hotel Bohème...........................10 F4
Hotel San Remo.........................11 E3

EATING 🍴
Balboa Café.............................12 B4
Ghirardelli Chocolate Shop &
Caffe..................................(see 6)
Greens & Greens to Go................13 C3
L'Osteria del Forno....................14 F4
Mario's Bohemian Cigar Store.......15 F4
Michelangelo...........................16 F4
Mo's Grill..............................17 F2
Molinari's Delicatessen................18 F4
Swensen's Ice Cream..................19 E4
Trattoria Contadina....................20 E4

DRINKING 🍷 🍸
Caffe Tosca............................21 F4
Caffe Trieste..........................22 E3

ENTERTAINMENT 🎭
Beach Blanket Babylon................23 E4

SHOPPING 🛍
Plump Jack Wines......................24 B4

TRANSPORT
Blazing Saddles Bicycle Rentals......25 E2
Blazing Saddles Bicycle Rentals......26 D3
Blazing Saddles Bicycle Rentals......27 E3

See Marin County Map (p74)

See Downtown San Francisco Map (pp52-3)

(Continued from page 50)

photography collection. Thursday evenings are half-price; the first Tuesday of the month is free. NB: SoMa's blocks are long and not conducive to strolling; know where you're going or take a cab.

Up Market St in a transitional (read: sketchy) neighborhood, **Civic Center** is anchored by the magnificent Beaux Arts–style **City Hall** (☎ 415-554-4000; cnr Van Ness Ave & Grove St), its dome modeled after St Peter's Basilica in Vatican City. Wander in and see the grand rotunda. Opposite City Hall, at the other end of Civic Center Plaza, the **Asian Art Museum** (☎ 415-379-8800; www.asianart.org; cnr Larkin & McAllister Sts; adult/child/student $12/8/7; ☼ 10am-5pm Tue-Sun, 9pm Thu) used to be the library, until the new one was built next door (and they threw away 200,000 books to accommodate an atrium – what a crime. How do you say, 'Unclear on the concept of a library?'). The collection is the largest outside Asia; the Chinese works, especially the jade and bronze, are most impressive. If you don't go inside, marvel at the granite bas-relief on the building's face and be wowed by the entryway's travertine arches. Gorgeous.

Golden Gate Park

One of the world's finest urban parks, Golden Gate Park stretches nearly halfway across the peninsula. Pick up information at **McLaren Lodge** (Map p51; ☎ 415-831-2700; www.parks.sfgov.org; park's eastern entrance, cnr Fell & Stanyan Sts; ☼ 8am-5pm Mon-Fri).

The elegant **Conservatory of Flowers** (Map p51; ☎ 415-666-7001; www.conservatoryofflowers.org; admission $5; ☼ 9am-4:30pm Tue-Sun), the park's oldest building, houses rare plant species – some more than 120 years old – from 50 countries

around the world. The photogenic floral-topiary displays out the front make it a must-see for any gardener.

San Francisco's newest museum – and grandest architectural statement – the **MH de Young Memorial Museum** (Map p51; ☎ 415-863-3330; www.thinker.org/deyoung; 50 Hagiwara Tea Garden Dr; adult/student $10/6, 1st Tue of month free; ☼ 9:30am-5pm Tue-Sun, to 8:45pm Fri) isn't without its detractors. The entry hall resembles a 1950s-era secretarial pool: a vast room with bad lighting. But the galleries connect elegantly, one flowing seamlessly into another, showcasing the art beautifully. The works are engrossing and stimulating, especially the American and Oceanic collections. Don't skip the tower, which despite having disappointingly narrow windows, provides lovely views *downward* onto the city's western neighborhoods, if not upward to the glorious San Francisco sky. Some object to the tower's copper sheathing, but once it oxidizes in a few years, the boxy structure will blend in with the trees and aesthetes will stop squabbling. But for now, it's ugly and out of place.

The **Japanese Tea Garden** (Map p51; ☎ 415-831-2700; Hagiwara Tea Garden Dr; adult/child $2/1; ☼ 9am-6pm Mar-Oct, 8:30am-5pm Nov-Feb) is stunning in April when the wisteria blooms, but its always-lovely pagoda, gates, bridges and statues make it a picturesque destination year-round. For $2, revive with green tea and fortune cookies – the latter invented here (really!).

Strybing Arboretum & Botanical Gardens (Map p51; ☎ 415-661-1316; www.sfbotanicalgarden.org; Martin Luther King Dr; admission free; ☼ 8am-4:30pm Mon-Fri, 10am-5pm Sat & Sun) encompasses several gardens within 70 acres, including the Garden of Fragrance, the California Collection of Native Plants and the Japanese Moon-Viewing Garden. Stop by the bookstore – a fave of

---

DETOUR TO THE ISLANDS

There won't be cocktails with paper umbrellas waiting, but you'll find great photo ops at two nearby islands, both in San Francisco Bay.

Ride the ferry (adult/child $15/9) from Pier 41 to 750-acre **Angel Island State Park** (Map pp74-5; ☎ 415-435-1915, camping reservations ☎ 800-444-7275; www.parks.ca.gov), where you can bike and hike over 12 miles of trails, picnic and camp overnight (make reservations) on a wooded island opposite the city's northern waterfront. Call ☎ 415-897-0715 for bicycle rentals and tram tours.

For a lesser-known perspective on downtown's skyline, cross the western span of the eastbound Bay Bridge to **Treasure Island**. In the middle of the bridge, exit *left* at the 10mph hairpin ramp. Continue to the overlook for primo skyline vistas, day or night. (Not recommended during rush hour.)

> ### GET LOST & EXPLORE BY CLUE
>
> Ditch your guidebook for the day. On a piece of paper, transcribe the destinations and directional clues bulleted below. Get a detailed, to-scale city map with a street index – the official MUNI map ($2.50) is great and shows transit lines – then head to the city's geographical centerpoint, **Mt Olympus**, at the end of Upper Tce, near Buena Vista Park, and find your way via side streets to the following places. (A taxi from downtown costs $12 to $15, or take public transit to the Haight or Castro and walk up.) Each is a 30- to 60-minute adventure. Hint: Look for hidden staircases, and maintain your elevation on the hillsides as much as possible for the best views.
>
> **Noe Valley** Follow ridgelines south via Kite Hill, Corwin or Grand View; have a beer on 24th St.
>
> **Mission District** Follow the ridgelines south via Kite Hill, Seward St, 19th St and Mission Dolores Park; end at a Valencia St café.
>
> **Twin Peaks** Ascend via Tank Hill, then Twin Peaks Blvd; at the top, climb the two namesake peaks. Killer views!

gardeners – at the entrance for details on daily tours.

The park is packed with sporting facilities, including 7.5 miles of bicycle trails, countless miles of jogging trails, 12 miles of equestrian trails, an archery range, baseball and softball diamonds, fly-casting pools, a nine-hole golf course, lawn-bowling greens, four soccer fields and 21 tennis courts. Rent rowboats and pedal boats from the **Stow Lake boathouse** (Map p51; ☎ 415-752-0347; per hr $13-17; ⏰ 10am-4pm; ♿); bring bread to feed the ducks.

On Sunday, John F Kennedy Dr closes to traffic, and hordes of in-line skaters, cyclists and street-hockey players fill the roadway. The hot-hot scene is at 6th Ave and Kennedy Dr, where skaters bump and grind old-school style. Chill on the lawn and dig the show.

Rent skates from **Golden Gate Park Bike & Skate** (Map p51; ☎ 415-668-1117; 3038 Fulton St, cnr 6th Ave; per 24hr $6; ⏰ daily, weather permitting); rent bikes from **San Francisco Cyclery** (Map p51; ☎ 415-379-3870; 672 Stanyan St; per 2/8hrs $15/30; ⏰ Wed-Mon).

Fisherman's Wharf

North of the Embarcadero, **Pier 39** marks the beginning of **Fisherman's Wharf** (Map p54), the epicenter of (bland) tourism and home of the city's fishing fleet. Not much of a working wharf any more, it better resembles a waterfront shopping mall. Locals are baffled that tourists are drawn there. But two cable-car lines end here, there are attractions for kids, and you can eat to-go crab from fish stands. Snap photos of the **sea-lion colony** lazing off Pier 39's western end.

Blue & Gold Fleet (☎ 415-773-1188; www.blueandgoldfleet.com; Pier 41; adult/child $21/13; ♿) operates hour-long bay cruises; book online for discounts. Alternatively, stroll the wharf

and talk to fishermen; many give boat rides for less.

At Pier 45, next to the WWII warships, is the marvelous **Musée Mécanique** (☎ 415-346-2000; www.museemechanique.com; Shed A; Pier 45; admission free; ⏰ 10am-7pm; ♿) and its working collection of 19th-century antique carnival games; look for famous Laughing Sal and the opium den.

For a superfun half-day jaunt, rent a bicycle from **Blazing Saddles** (☎ 415-202-8888; www.blazingsaddles.com; per hr/day $7/28; ⏰ from 8am), ride over the Golden Gate Bridge and return via ferry from Sausalito. There are branches at Pier 41, Pier 43½ and 2715 Hyde Street.

Head to the Wharf's western end, past the Maritime Museum, and walk out along the fishing pier at **Aquatic Park**, which has rest rooms and a sandy beach safe for swimming – if you dare to brave the icy water!

The Marina

West of Aquatic Park, a footpath traverses a wooded hill toward the Marina, neighborhood of multimillion-dollar homes on seismically unstable ground. Stroll past the yacht harbor onto **Marina Green**, a six-block-long esplanade great for kite-flying, picnicking, skating and watching windsurfers and kiteboarders (who look like giant mosquitoes zipping up and down).

Bordering the Presidio, Bernard Maybeck's artificial classical ruin, the **Palace of Fine Arts** (Baker St at Bay St), was so popular when it was built for the 1915 Panama–Pacific Exposition that it was spared from its intended demolition. Behind the ruin is the **Exploratorium** (☎ 415-561-0360; www.exploratorium.edu; 3601 Lyon St; adult/child $12/8; ⏰ closed Mon; ♿), a museum of art, science and human perception – a must-visit for intellectually curious, hands-on sorts. Kids and adults

---

THE PERFECT SAN FRANCISCO DAY *John A Vlahides*

Whenever friends visit, I build a walking-tour itinerary for them around four elements: hills, neighborhoods, views and food: the four things that most define San Francisco. Wear comfy nonslip shoes and carry a day pack and water.

Meet in the Financial District at the **Ferry Building** (p49) for coffee overlooking the glittering blue bay; wander the food stalls and pick up Acme bread, Cowgirl Creamery cheese and farm-fresh local fruit to munch along the way. Ride the **California Street cable car** (p69), the line few tourists take because they don't know where it goes. Look back as you ascend **Nob Hill** (see boxed text, p62) for supercool Bay Bridge views. At the terminus, walk one block north up Van Ness Ave to Sacramento St and turn left (west). Amble past lovely **Lafayette Park**, where you can ascend the hill and see the cityscape. Turn right (north) on **Fillmore St**, the shopping street for Pacific Heights' skirt-and-sweater matrons. At Broadway, ooh and aah over the mesmerizing bay vistas and the mansions clinging to the hillsides, then descend the supersteep 18% grade through **Cow Hollow** into the **Marina** (p57). At the bay, turn right (east) and walk along the water, in view of **Alcatraz** (p50), the kite flyers at **Marina Green** (p57) and the bobbing sailboat masts of the small-craft harbor. Follow the footpath to **Fort Mason and Aquatic Park** (p57) and amble out along the pier. Bypass Fisherman's Wharf for **Columbus Ave and North Beach** (p62), the 'hood made famous by the Beats. Stop for meatball sandwiches at **Mario's Bohemian Cigar Store** (p54; ☎ 362-0536; 566 Columbus Ave), followed by espresso at **Caffe Trieste** (p65). If you've still got energy, climb **Telegraph Hill** to **Coit Tower** (see boxed text, p62), check out the Works Progress Administration (WPA) murals, then descend 28 stories down the rickety wooden **Filbert Street steps** to the Embarcadero waterfront and back to the Ferry Building. Look for the famous wild parrots of Telegraph Hill (yes, real parrots!) who live in the trees above the steps.

After a nap, meet for cocktails at **Cafe Flore** (p65), then watch a movie at the fabulous vintage-1920s **Castro Theatre** (see boxed text, p62), followed by dinner at **Chow** (p63) on Church St, the best cheap eat in the neighborhood. Then head off to the Mission to hear bands and shoot pool at the **Elbo Room** (p65), or swill cocktails on Valencia St.

---

love the museum's **Tactile Dome**, a pitch-black dome through which you crawl, climb and slide (reservations required).

The Presidio & Fort Point

For years the US Army occupied the northwest corner of the San Francisco Peninsula. The area remains largely undeveloped and much remains green, despite Hwys 1 and 101 merging here en route to the Golden Gate Bridge.

Established in 1776 and overseen by the Spanish, then Mexican, and finally the American military, the Presidio occupies 1480 acres currently under authority of the GGNRA and the National Parks Services (NPS). Debates continue over how best to use the valuable land and how to make the park financially self-sufficient by 2013, as mandated by Congress. One new tenant is George Lucas, whose world-famous digital studio, Letterman Digital Arts Center, is located here.

Get your bearings at the **Presidio Visitors Center** (Map p51; ☎ 415-561-4323; www.nps.gov/prsf; cnr Montgomery St & Lincoln Blvd; ☼ 9am-5pm).

Along the bay, former military airstrip **Crissy Field** has been restored to a tidal marsh, with hiking and biking trails, picnic areas with BBQs and a grassy former airstrip for pooches (San Franciscans *love* their dog play areas). The **Crissy Field Center** (Map p51; ☎ 415-561-7690; www.crissyfield.org; cnr Old Mason & Halleck Sts; ☼ 9am-5pm Wed-Sun) has a café and bookstore; download an MP3 Presidio walking tour from its website. For knock-your-socks-off bridge views, amble out the fishing pier opposite the Warming Hut, at the western end of Crissy Field. It's *way* cool at night.

Directly under the southern span of the Golden Gate Bridge, the **Fort Point National Historic Site** (☎ 415-556-1693; www.nps.gov/goga; ☼ 10am-5pm Fri-Sun) was built at the start of the 1861–65 Civil War, but it never saw battle and was abandoned in 1900. The triple-tiered brick fortress stands off Marine Dr.

Along the ocean side of the peninsula, **Baker Beach** is the city's most picturesque beach. Currents and cold water make swimming unappealing, but it's popular with sunbathers – the northern end is clothing-optional.

Lincoln Park, Point Lobos, Ocean Beach & Fort Funston

From the north-facing cliffs of **Lincoln Park**, west of the Golden Gate, the **California Palace of the Legion of Honor** (Map p51; ☎ 415-863-3330; www.thinker.org; adult/child $10/6, 1st Tue of month free; 9:30am-5pm Tue-Sun), one of San Francisco's finest art museums, displays medieval to 20th-century European art, including Rodin's *The Thinker*, located in the courtyard where Isadora Duncan once danced. Have lunch in the café. The museum is surrounded by an 18-hole **golf course** (☎ 415-750-4653, 415-221-9911).

At **Point Lobos**, the city's westernmost tip, the latest incarnation of the **Cliff House** (Map p51; ☎ 415-386-3330; www.cliffhouse.com) looks like a mausoleum. It's good for a drink, but eat at nearby **Louis'** (☎ 415-387-6330; 902 Pt Lobos Ave; dishes $5-10; 6:30am-4:30 Mon-Fri, to 6pm Sat & Sun) for the same view and burgers at half the price.

Behind the Cliff House, definitely see the mesmerizing 1946 **Camera Obscura** (Map p51; ☎ 415-750-0415; admission $2; 11am-sunset;), Leonardo da Vinci's invention that projects the view from outside the building onto a giant parabolic screen inside.

The ruins in the cove just north of the Cliff House are all that remain of the **Sutro Baths**, the magnificent six-pool, 3-acre indoor swimming-pool palace Adolph Sutro built in 1896. Hike the trail from the parking lot around to **Lands End** for brilliant Golden Gate views.

South of Point Lobos, wide-open **Ocean Beach** stretches 4 miles along the ocean. It's *not* safe for swimming, but you can have beach fires; call the NPS **park police** (☎ 415-561-5505) for regulations. Find wood at grocery stores.

The Great Hwy runs along Ocean Beach. Turn left on Sloat Blvd for the **San Francisco Zoo** (Map p51; ☎ 415-753-7080; www.sfzoo.org; Sloat Blvd & 45th Ave; adult/teen/child $11/8/5; 10am-5pm;), a

conservation-friendly menagerie, with jungle animals in the fog.

One mile south, watch hang gliders float above **Fort Funston**, and hike along windswept cliffs to the beach below. Bring your dog.

TOURS

The visitors information center (Map pp52–3) has a complete list of tour operators. **City Guides** (☎ 415-557-4266; www.sfcityguides.org), sponsored by the San Francisco Public Library, offers *free* walking tours led by savvy local historians.

The **Oceanic Society** (☎ 415-474-3385; www.oceanic-society.org; per person $78; Dec-May) sails to the Farallon Islands for whale-watching. Expect expert narration.

The **Victorian Home Walk** (☎ 415-252-9485; www.victorianwalk.com; per person $20) leads compelling architectural walking tours last 2½ hours.

Explore Chinatown and its culinary scene with **Wok Wiz Tours** (☎ 650-355-9657; www.wokwiz.com; with/without lunch $40/28).

Take an 80-minute amphibious tour of land and sea with **San Francisco Duck Tours** (☎ 415-431-3825; www.bayquackers.com; 2800 Leavenworth St; adult/child $35/12). Or see the bay from the sky on a 30-minute flight with **San Francisco Seaplane Tours** (☎ 415-332-4843; www.seaplane.com; Pier 39; adult/child $139/99).

FESTIVALS & EVENTS

The outrageous 14% hotel tax you pay funds our wacky street fairs (thanks!). The mother of 'em all is the **Folsom Street Fair**, in September, when 500,000 people wear their sex fetishes on the street. On the tamer side, June brings the Italian-American-flavored **North Beach Festival**; the hippie-inspired **Haight Street Fair**; and the *très civilisé* **Union Street Festival**. For a complete list, contact the visitors information center.

Critical Mass (www.critical-mass.org) Last Friday of every month; roving bicyclists take over the streets.

Chinese New Year (☎ 415-391-9680; www.chineseparade.com) Late January or early February; the Golden Dragon parade is the highlight.

San Francisco International Film Festival (☎ 415-929-5000; www.sfiff.org) Two weeks in March.

Bay to Breakers (☎ 415-359-2800; www.baytobreakers.com) On the third Sunday in May, more than 100,000 revelers turn out for this wacky footrace.

Carnaval (☎ 415-826-1401; www.carnavalsf.com) Samba till sunset at a huge Latino-flavored party and parade on Memorial Day weekend.

Gay Pride Parade (☎ 415-864-3733; www.sfpride.org) SF's largest event; held on the last Sunday in June.

GAY & LESBIAN SAN FRANCISCO

The mothership of gay culture, San Francisco is America's pinkest city, the easiest place in the US to be gay and where 'mos are accepted as part of mainstream society. (Remember, this is where gay marriage first became reality in the US.) New York Marys may label SF the retirement home of the young – indeed, the sidewalks roll up early – but when it comes to sexual outlaws and underground weirdness, SF kicks New York's ass.

The intersection of 18th and Castro Sts is the heart of the gay scene, and there are bars a go-go, but most are predictably middlebrow. Dancing queens and slutty boys head South of Market (SoMa), the location of most thump-thump clubs and sex venues. Cruise Castro by day, SoMa by night. On sunny days, Speedo-clad gay boys colonize the grassy hill at 20th and Church Sts, overlooking downtown. Be prepared for pot smoke: SF is stoner central.

Bars

The place on Sunday afternoons, the **Eagle Tavern** (Map pp52-3; ☎ 415-626-0880; www.sfeagle.com; 398 12th St), serves all-you-can-drink beer ($10) from 3pm to 6pm. Wear leather – or act like a whore – and blend right in. Thursday through Sunday are best at **Powerhouse** (Map pp52-3; ☎ 415-552-8689; www.powerhouse-sf.com; 1347 Folsom St), an almost-rough-trade SoMa bar; stoners smoke out and feel each other up on the back deck. **My Place** (Map pp52-3; ☎ 415-863-2329; 1225 Folsom St) – aka My Face – is a neighborhood stalwart for pervy men. Don't be fooled by the recently cleaned-up bathrooms: the place is still a dump – and you can smoke on the hidden back patio. At this writing, the notorious Hole in the Wall (aka Hole in the Head) had temporarily closed; ask locals. In the Castro, cologne-wearing 20-somethings (and gay-boy-loving straight girls) queue up nightly to dance in the light of flickering videos at **Badlands** (Map p55; ☎ 415-626-9320; 4121 18th St) – if you're over 30, you'll feel old. A better bet for cocktails is see-and-be-seen **Lime** (Map p55; ☎ 415-621-5256; 2247 Market St), which makes awesome mojitos. Shy types and A&F boys shoot pool in the glow of the fishtanks at neighborhood-esque **Moby Dick** (Map p55; ☎ 415-861-1191; 4049 18th St) or hang with pals at the **Pilsner** (Map p55; ☎ 415-621-7058; 225 Church St), where you can smoke on the patio.

For *grlz*, the Mission-hipster spot is the down-and-dirty **Lexington Club** (Map p55; ☎ 415-863-2052; www.lexingtonclub.com; 3464 19th St), which has SF's best bathroom graffiti. Cat fights aren't uncommon. Softball dykes go to off-the-beaten-path **Wild Side West** (Map p51; ☎ 415-647-3099; 424 Cortland St), but boys come to gab in the lush backyard's overgrown gardens. Power-to-the-pussy girls head to **Hot Pants**, held on the second and fourth Fridays at the **Cat Club** (Map pp52-3; ☎ 415-703-8964; www.catclubsf.com; 1190 Folsom St). Start the night at **Cafe Flore** (p65), a hip, gay coffeehouse and bar.

Clubs

For the latest, pick up the free rags *Odyssey* or *Gloss Magazine,* available at bars and A Different Light Bookstore (p47). **Juanita More** (www.juanitamore.com) throws the fiercest parties and they're *always* attended by sexy-hot boys; check her website. Ladies: log on to Craig's List (www.craigslist.org) and click on women-seeking-women; search for Mango, White Diamonds & Octopussy – or post a query.

Tuesdays at midnight, **Trannyshack** at the Stud (Map pp52-3; ☎ 415-863-6623; www.trannyshack.com; 399 9th St) packs in gorgeous 20-something boys, baby dykes and hagged-out trannies for the best drag show in SF. Think rocker bitch, not Barbra Streisand. On Thursdays the underground boy crowd crams into divey-chic Aunt Charlie's Lounge (p66) for **Tubesteak Connection** to cruise and grind to vintage bathhouse disco, spun by celeb DJ Bus Station John. (Check the rags for his fab-fab-fab monthly parties, the Rod and Double Dutch Disco.) At the notorious **EndUp** (Map pp52-3; ☎ 415-357-0827; www.theendup.com; 401 6th St), **Fag Fridays** is where to dance to house till 6am on Fridays. Saturdays, the hottest boys in town head to **Drunk & Horny** (Map pp52-3; ☎ 415-864-7386; www.drunkandhorny.net; 424 Haight St) at Underground SF. When it's time to get laid, head to the Disneyland of cock, **Blow Buddies** (Map pp52-3; ☎ 415-777-HEAD; www.blowbuddies.com; 933 Harrison St; admission $12, plus $8 membership fee; ☾ Thu-Sun nights, call for details) *No* cologne: sweat is the preferred scent.

Midnight Mass (☎ 415-267-4893; www.peacheschrist .com) Peaches Christ, the city's fiercest drag queen, screens classic camp films on Saturdays at midnight in July and August, each preceded by an even campier preshow, occasionally featuring cult celebs such as Mink Stole or Elvira.

SLEEPING

Staying downtown, by Union Square, puts you near all public transportation. It's a neighborhood of high-rises, not Victorians. Watch your back in the Tenderloin (see p49). North Beach is exciting, but use hotel garages, since street parking is impossible. Hostelling International (HI) has three locations in SF: log on to www.sfhostels.com.

Rates in this section are published high-season rates; you can often do better. The **visitors information center** (☎ 888-782-9673; www .sfvisitor.org) runs a reservation line.

Budget

Pacific Tradewinds Hostel (Map pp52-3; ☎ 415-433-7970, 800-486-7970; http://san-francisco-hostel.com; 680 Sacramento St; dm $24; 🖳) The city's spiffiest hostel sports a nautical theme, with ultraclean bathrooms with glass-brick showers. Run by a bunch of smiley, athletic 20-somethings, this is one happy hostel. Alas, it's a four-story walk-up.

Hotel San Remo (Map p54; ☎ 415-776-8688, 800-352-7366; www.sanremohotel.com; 2237 Mason St; r $60-90; 🅿) Long on Old West charm, the 100-year-old San Remo has rooms with shared bathroom. Its location between North Beach and the wharf makes it perfect for sightseers.

24 Henry Street (Map p55; ☎ 415-864-5686, 800-900-5686; www.24henry.com; r with bathroom $55-75, r without bathroom $90-110) A modest 19th-century house on a quiet, tree-lined lane, 24 Henry is like Grandma's house, assuming Grandma lives on a fixed income and doesn't often redecorate. It's a homey choice, good for unfussy, gay budget travelers.

Midrange

Inn 1890 (Map p51; ☎ 415-386-0486, 888-466-1890; www.inn1890.com; 1890 Page St; r incl breakfast $89-179; 🅿 🖳) A magical 16-bedroom Victorian mansion with little ornamentation, the Inn 1890 sits on a quiet residential street in the Upper Haight. Given the exceptional charm, personalized service and quality of accommodations, rates are a bargain. Book a fireplace room for romance. There's a big communal kitchen.

Hotel des Arts (Map pp52-3; ☎ 415-956-3232, 800-956-4322; www.sfhoteldesarts.com; 447 Bush St; r with bathroom $89-139, r without bathroom $89-109; 🅿 🖳) Art freaks: finally a budget hotel for you. Every wall in every room at Hotel des Arts has been painted with jaw-dropping murals by different underground, up-and-coming street artists. Part gallery, part hotel, it's like sleeping inside a painting. The budget-basic rooms are short on amenities, but oh! the art.

Golden Gate Hotel (Map pp52-3; ☎ 415-392-3702, 800-835-1118; www.goldengatehotel.com; 775 Bush St; r with bathroom $85-105, r without bathroom $150; 🅿 🖳) Like an old-fashioned boarding-house, the Golden Gate has kindly owners and simple rooms with mismatched furniture housed within a 1913 Edwardian, safely up the hill from the Tenderloin.

King George Hotel (Map pp52-3; ☎ 415-781-5050, 800-288-6005; www.kinggeorge.com; 334 Mason St; r $109-159; 🅿 🖳) One of downtown's bargains, the nine-story King George, opened 1912, has comfortable – if small – rooms. It serves breakfast, has a wine bar and offers English tea service on weekends.

our pick Hotel Bohème (Map p54; ☎ 415-433-9111; www.hotelboheme.com; 444 Columbus Ave; r $169-189; 🅿) Like a love letter to the jazz era, the Bohème is one smart hotel. Its moody color schemes – orange, black and sage-green – are a nod to the late 1950s. Inverted Chinese umbrellas hang from the ceiling, and photos from the Beat age decorate the walls. Rooms are smallish, and some front on noisy Columbus Ave, but the hotel is smack in the middle of North Beach's vibrant street scene. For quiet, book rooms at the back.

Top End

Orchard Garden Hotel (Map pp52-3; ☎ 415-399-9807, 888-717-2881; www.theorchardgardenhotel.com; 466 Bush St; r $149-299; 🅿 🖳) San Francisco's first all-green-practices hotel, opened in 2006, uses sustainably grown wood, recycled fabrics and chemical-free cleaning products. Rooms have deluxe touches like flat-screen TVs. Great location.

Hotel Vitale (Map pp52-3; ☎ 415-278-3700, 888-890-8688; www.hotelvitale.com; 8 Mission St; r $239-360; 🅿 🖳) Midcentury modern meets contemporary chic at the coolly minimalist Vitale, downtown's sexiest hotel. Rooms are done in a soothing spa theme, with a sprig of lavender outside every door and mud masks in the minibar. Splurge on a bay-view room. Top spot for a shag.

SAN FRANCISCO & THE BAY AREA

THE NEIGHBORHOOD CRAWL

San Francisco is a city of neighborhoods. To get a sense of the locals, see where they live.

North Beach

San Francisco's vibrant Italian district brims with locals and tourists alike. Stroll Columbus Ave and stop for cappuccino and cannoli, watch a game of boccie in Washington Square Park, poke your head into cool shops on Grant Ave, and gorge on pasta. This is the one San Francisco neighborhood that has successfully kept out *all* corporate chains. Looming above, 210ft-tall **Coit Tower** (Map p54; ☎ 415-362-0808; adult/child $4.50/2; ☙ 10am-6pm) stands atop Telegraph Hill, ride the elevator to the top. The neighborhood extends north from Broadway along Columbus and Grant Aves.

Chinatown

The largest Chinatown outside China stretches along Grant Ave and Stockton St, south of Broadway. Tourists flock to Grant Ave to see the pagoda-style **Chinatown Gate** (Map pp52-3; cnr Bush St) and nearby souvenir shops and restaurants, but the real action is on Stockton St, where local matrons elbow you out of the way to grab bok choy and still-swimming fish; come midday (Saturdays are busiest). Recharge with rare brews at moody **Imperial Tea Court** (Map pp52-3; ☎ 415-788-6080; 1411 Powell St)

The Castro

Ride vintage street cars up Market St to the Castro, the heart of the gay and lesbian communities. On weekends, the streets teem with people. Window-shop beneath towering palms on Market St, cruise the boys on Castro St, then catch a film at the gorgeous 1920s **Castro Theatre** (Map p55; ☎ 415-621-6120; 429 Castro St), where every show is preceded by a performance on the theatre's mighty Wurlitzer organ – classic San Francisco.

Palace Hotel (Map pp52-3; ☎ 415-512-1111, 888-627-7196; www.sfpalace.com; 2 New Montgomery; r from $279; P ☐ ☒) The landmark Palace stands, aglow with century-old Austrian crystal chandeliers, as a monument to 19th-century grandeur. The cushy (if staid) accommodations cater to expense-account travelers, but prices drop on weekends. Even if you're not staying here, see the opulent Garden Court, where you can sip tea in one of Northern California's most beautiful rooms.

EATING
Budget

Sai Jai Thai (Map pp52-3; ☎ 415-673-5774; 771 O'Farrell St; dishes $5-10; ☙ 11am-10:45pm) Mom and the cooks shout at each other in Thai, hardly anyone speaks English, and the room is grungey, but the cooking's spot-on. Just make sure when you're asked how hot, you reply, 'Spicy like for Thai people!'

Pagolac (Map pp52-3; ☎ 415-776-3234; 655 Larkin St; dishes $7-10; ☙ dinner Tue-Sun) Of the Vietnamese places in 'Little Saigon' along gritty Larkin St, Pagolac has the richest *pho* (noodle soups),

tastiest rice-noodle bowls and great char-grilled meats. Service is honest and kind, but the room gets loud. Tops for cheap eats.

Michelangelo (Map p54; ☎ 415-986-4058; 570 Columbus Ave; dishes $8-12; ☙ dinner; ♿) Finicky purists scoff at Michelangelo, but for a $10 plate of spaghetti Bolognese and a convivial crowd, it's hard to beat this hole-in-the-wall joint smack-dab in the middle of the Columbus St action. Wine comes in rooster-shaped pitchers, and big bowls of gummie bears get passed around for dessert. Fun, easy and fast – except when there's a line. Cash only.

Ramp (Map p51; ☎ 415-621-2378; 855 China Basin St; dishes $8-13; ☙ lunch/brunch only) Only locals lunch at the Ramp, in an industrial shipyard on the eastern waterfront. Sit on the docks at umbrella tables and purge your hangover with Bloodies. The food's OK, mostly sandwiches and salads, but the crowd is a cool cross section, and the not-yet gentrified area shows a side of SF few visitors see. Musicians play weekend afternoons, when the place become a bar. Head to the foot of Mariposa St, off 3rd St.

The Mission

The epicenter of cool, the unpredictable, gritty Mission District went from Mexican barrio to hipster central in the 1990s, when housing prices skyrocketed during the dot-com boom. Mexican grand-mothers still shop for *pollo* on Mission Street, but now blonde rivals brunette as the dominant hair color. **Mission Dolores**, the city's oldest building, is here at 300 Dolores St. Head to Valencia St for sec-ondhand boutiques and bookstores during the day, and übercool restaurants and bars at night.

Haight Street

The Haight rose to fame during the 1967 Summer of Love, when tripped-out hippy mystics danced in the streets. The psychedelic love fest ended, almost overnight, when speed hit the scene; yogis got strung out on China white, and the light went dark. Now there's a Gap store at the corner of Ashbury St, and the Haight seems a parody of its former self, but it's fun to shop at the many shoe stores and used-clothing boutiques. If street urchins annoy you, stay away. The 'hood begins at Masonic Ave and extends to Golden Gate Park.

Nob Hill

People who still wear fur in San Francisco convene on Nob Hill. Though luxury hotels stand at the crest of the hill, the neighborhood remains a residential area for the skirt-and-sweater elite. **Grace Cathedral** (Map pp52-3; ☎ 415-749-6300; 1100 California St) lords over very-civilized Huntington Park. All cable-car lines cross at California and Powell Sts. The only Nob Hill mansion that didn't burn after the 1906 earthquake stands on the corners of California and Mason Sts.

Russian Hill

Northwest of Nob Hill and east of Hyde St, crooked **Lombard St** twists and turns downhill for one block. Most take the Powell–Hyde cable-car line to the top, then walk down. But if you ascend the hill from Leavenworth St (a short walk from the wharf), you can reward yourself with homemade ice cream at **Swensen's** (Map p54; ☎ 415-775-6818; cnr Union & Hyde Sts). There are some wonderfully ro-mantic (and good) neighborhood restaurants along Hyde St between Washington and Union Sts.

Midrange

Chow (Map p55; ☎ 415-552-2469; 215 Church St; dishes $5-12; 11am-11pm;) The diverse menu here breaks the axiom that there's no good food in the Castro, and lists everything from pizza to pork chops, Thai-style noodles to spaghetti and meatballs. Most dishes come in two sizes, good for light eaters. The room is big, loud and busy; request a table on the back patio for quiet(er) conversations. Call ahead for the 'no-wait' list.

L'Osteria del Forno (Map p54; ☎ 415-982-1124; www.losteriadelforno.com; 519 Columbus Ave; dishes $8-15; closed Tue) Off-the-boat waiters serve trattoria-style Italian dishes at this tiny, eight-table spot that lines 'em up every night. Though little on the menu is truly authentic, the crispy-thin piz-zas and roasted meats have a soul-satisfying quality, the room is long on dressed-down romance, and prices are reasonable. For des-sert: *affogato* (espresso poured over ice cream). Cash only.

1550 Hyde St (Map pp52-3; ☎ 415-775-1550; www.1550hyde.com; 1550 Hyde St; dishes $16-19; din-ner Tue-Sun) One of several good neighborhood spots along the Hyde St cable-car line, 1550's Euro-Cal cooking uses sustainably grown, local ingredients in its earthy, honest, dishes. Locals pack the place every night; make res-ervations or wait in the tiny wine bar.

Trattoria Contadina (Map p54; ☎ 415-982-5728; www.trattoriacontadina.com; 1800 Mason St; dishes $10-20; dinner) Signed photos of baseball players line the walls at this old-school Italian-American joint that packs locals and tourists shoulder to shoulder for big, tasty plates of pasta. Make reservations.

Greens & Greens to Go (Map p54; ☎ 415-771-6222; www.greensrestaurant.com; Bldg A, Fort Mason; lunch $8-14, dinner $16-23; lunch Tue-Sun, dinner Mon-Sat;) Finally a place where herbivores can wear high heels. Long-running Greens bears the standard for vegetarianism, with inventive cooking so good that even hard-core meat eaters leave sated. The former industrial space juts out over the water, with stupen-dous Golden Gate Bridge views. Or picnic by the bay with salads, sandwiches and fantastic black-bean chili from Greens to Go, which is open daily.

Plouf (Map pp52-3; ☎ 415-986-6491; www.ploufsf .com; 40 Belden Place; dishes $15-25; ☻ closed Sat lunch & Sun) Plouf means 'splash' in French, and splashy it is. One of the city's best for seafood (especially mussels), it's bustling and loud, hip without being overbearing. Sexy waiters, a full bar and great wines. Sit outside in the alley, and imagine yourself in Paris.

Top End

Reserve well ahead for all restaurants in this section.

Slanted Door (Map pp52-3; ☎ 415-861-8032; slanteddoor .com; Ferry Bldg; lunch $9-18, dinner $15-28) Every foodie ought to visit the Slanted Door twice, the minimalist-chic Cal-Vietnamese inside the Ferry Building, lined with enormous plate-glass windows overlooking the bay. The menu blends Saigon street eats with the best of Nor-Cal ingredients, sourced locally and farmed sustainably. Dinners are jam-packed and loud; come at lunch, when prices drop, there's no push to finish your meal, and you can linger unfettered. Request a high-backed, bridge-view booth for maximum swank.

Kokkari Estiatorio (Map pp52-3; ☎ 415-981-0983; www.kokkari.com; 200 Jackson St; lunch $15-26, dinner $19-30; ☻ lunch Mon-Fri, dinner Mon-Sat) Retsina best accompanies the big Greek and eastern Mediterranean flavors at Kokkari, a haven for Dionysian revelry and table-hopping socialites. (When last there, we sat between Olympic skier Jonny Moseley and Mayor Gavin Newsom.) Open for a decade, it's still a standby for a splashy night out, and though the kitchen goes through ups and downs, the lamb chops are always excellent and the cushy booths and tables are some of the comfiest in town. It's a perfect place to drink too much and shout

Opah! Ladies wear a hot little black dress and blend right in. Request a table in the dining room by the bar, not the kitchen, and soak up the scene.

Ame (Map pp52-3; ☎ 415-284-4040; www.amerestaurant.com; 689 Mission St; lunch dishes $18-25, dinner $19-38; ☻ lunch and dinner daily) Japanese-born chef Hiro Sone trained in Italy and blends the delicacy of Eastern cookery with the robustness of European. Inside the coolly elegant St Regis Hotel, Ame (ah-*may*) – one of SF's hottest spots – has a spectacular (though pricey) sashimi bar, an impressive selection of sakes (filtered and unfiltered) and a rich menu of perfectly executed dishes such as sake-marinated black cod with shrimp dumplings, and risotto with eel and foie gras. Service could be better at this price, but the food is incredible.

La Folie (Map pp52-3; ☎ 415-776-5577; www.lafolie.com; 2316 Polk St; tasting menus $65-95; ☻ dinner Mon-Sat) Luxurious La Folie transforms food into art. French-born chef Roland Passot is one of SF's culinary stars, and though a serious chef, he's playful too – evident from the foie gras lollipops. Other standouts: butter-poached lobster and roasted squab with truffle-spiked jus. A top spot to hold hands and whisper by candlelight.

Groceries & Quick Eats

Rainbow Grocery (Map pp52-3; ☎ 415-863-0620; 1745 Folsom St; Ⓥ) A worker-owned cooperative, Rainbow is SF's hippest grocery. There's no meat, but a huge selection of natural foods, local organic veggies, fabulous cheeses, breads, wines and health items; this is the best spot to buy vitamins and supplements.

Molinari's Delicatessen (Map p54; ☎ 421-2337; 373 Columbus Ave) Stock up on Italian picnic supplies such as salami, olives, bread and Provolone

---

IN SEARCH OF THE PERFECT BURGER

SF is home to many burger joints and these are some of the best. Burgers cost $8 to $9 at all of these places. Eat away!

Balboa Café (Map p54; ☎ 415-921-3944; www.plumpjack.com; 3199 Fillmore St) When you're dressed up, but want burgers and a happening bar. Extraordinary wine selection. The Marina.

Burger Joint (Map p55; ☎ 415-824-3494; 807 Valencia St; 🚼) Uses Niman Ranch meat, but has few options other than burgers and fries. Cash only. The Mission.

Burgermeister (Map p55; ☎ 415-437-2874; www.burgermeistersf.com; 138 Church St; 🚼) All-natural Niman Ranch meat; killer milkshakes. Cash only. The Castro.

Mo's (Map p54; ☎ 415-788-3779; 1322 Grant Ave; 🚼) Grinds its own meat and hand cuts its fries. North Beach.

Zuni Café (Map pp52-3; ☎ 415-552-2522; 1658 Market St; ☻ closed Mon) Hobnob with the fancy-pants set. Hand-formed burgers on focaccia bread, served with matchstick fries. Civic Center.

18TH ST FOODIE PARADISE

Yeah, the Ferry Building is cool, but kind of theme parkish. To participate in the real day-to-day Nor-Cal food scene, head to 18th St, between Guerrero and Dolores Sts. Weekends are busy, busy.

Bi-Rite Market (Map p55; ☎ 415-241-9760; 3639 18th St) showcases local farmers, vintners, chocolatiers and cheese mongers – it's our favorite place to shop. Sample the season's best regional organic fruits, then take sandwiches to Dolores Park up the street. Next door, **Delfina** (Map p55; ☎ 415-552-4055; www.delfinasf.com; 3621 18th St; mains $17-21; ☒ closed lunch) turns out deliciously simple, ingredients-driven Cal-Italian cooking. Flavors are bright and clean and maximize what's in season right now. Make reservations, or try the neighboring **Pizzeria Delfina** (☎ 415-437-6800; 3611 18th St) for fresh-from-the-garden salads, vino and Italian-style pizzas. Sidewalk café and bakery **Tartine** (Map p55; ☎ 415-487-2600; www.tartinebakery.com; 600 Guerrero St; dishes $6; ☒ 8am-7pm, no dinner, closed Mon) makes fab French-style sandwiches, quiches and pastries as good as in Paris (really), and the best bread in SF (trust us), which comes out of the oven around 5pm, Thursday to Sunday. Expect a line.

---

at this famous delicatessen, then head to Washington Square Park.

DRINKING & ENTERTAINMENT

The *Sunday Chronicle*'s 'Datebook' lists almost everything happening around town. Also see the free *San Francisco Bay Guardian* and *SF Weekly*.

Cafes

While Seattle was still drinking Maxwell House, SF had already established itself as the epicenter of West Coast coffee culture.

Caffe Trieste (Map p54; ☎ 415-392-6739; 601 Vallejo St) The West Coast's first espresso bar and former Beat hangout still has poetry grafitti in the bathroom. There's Sinatra on the jukebox and live accordion shows on Saturday afternoons.

Café Flore (Map p55; ☎ 415-621-8579; 2298 Market St) Nicknamed the 'floor show' for its gorgeous parade of regulars, the Flore's outdoor patio is a cool scene on a sunny day. Inside feels like a window-lined gardening shed, surrounded by flowering trees.

Bars

Sorority girls and their pretty, blond boyfriends favor Union St, near Fillmore St, on a Saturday night. Cool cats hit the Mission: Valencia St, near 16th, is a good starting point.

Zeitgeist (Map pp52-3; ☎ 415-255-7505; 199 Valencia St) *The* hangout for urban bikers – pedal- and motor-powered – has an enormous back patio with pot smoke lingering in the air. Heavy pours and good beers.

House of Shields (Map pp52-3; ☎ 415-975-8651; 39 New Montgomery St) Has the look of a turn-of-

the-century fern bar taken over by hipsters. Sexy-tough bartenders, art heads and happening DJs lend to the gritty-chic atmosphere. Great after-shopping spot. Bummer that it closes at 10pm.

Hotel Biron (Map pp52-3; ☎ 415-703-0403; 45 Rose St) Aggressively intimate, but not overstyled, Biron looks like a cave; it's a happening spot for vino in wine-savvy SF.

Mint (Map pp52-3; ☎ 415-626-4726; 1942 Market St) Everyone's a star – in their own minds – at the Mint. The karaoke starts in the afternoon and runs till 2am. Bring a posse and get shitfaced.

Cafe Tosca (Map pp52-3; ☎ 415-986-9651; 242 Columbus Ave) A classic 1919 bar with old-world character, Tosca has a great jukebox with Rat Pack and Tin Pan Alley–American Songbook classics. If you want to stalk Sean Penn, start here.

Elbo Room (Map p55; ☎ 415-552-7788; www.elbo.com; 647 Valencia St) Shoot pool downstairs with Mission District scenesters, or hear DJs and live bands upstairs. Dig the photo booth!

Bix (Map pp52-3; ☎ 415-433-6300; 56 Gold St) Don high heels and tap your toes to jazz at the supper-club bar that started the West Coast's martini craze. Great food, perfect for a swanky date with your sweetheart.

Orbit Room Cafe (Map pp52-3; ☎ 415-252-9525; 1900 Market St) The Vespa crowd swills cocktails at this café-cum-bar near the Castro, where every drink is a fantasy in a glass. Fantastic mojitos and bloodies.

Clubs & live Music

The highest concentration of bars and clubs is around 11th and Folsom Sts.

Bottom of the Hill (Map p51; ☎ 415-621-4455; www.bottomofthehill.com; 1233 17th St) At the base of Potrero Hill, this indie-rock institution showcases local and national acts, and occasionally the odd folk band. It can be a bit self-consciously cool, but it's earned its laurels. Great back patio for smokers – or when the band gets too loud.

Red Devil Lounge (Map pp52-3; ☎ 415-921-1695; www.reddevillounge.com; 1695 Polk St) The up-and-coming and formerly famous (think Human League) play at this cozy club, an intimate spot to catch a show. The only disappointment may come in learning that your once-fave stars have lost their luster.

Aunt Charlie's Lounge (Map pp52-3; ☎ 415-441-2922; www.auntcharlieslounge.com; 133 Turk St) The city's best nitty-gritty old-school drag show happens on one of the worst blocks in town (take a taxi). Come on Friday or Saturdays after 10pm to see the Hot Boxxx Girls, hosted by Gina La Divina (aka the $65,000 silicon woman) and Vicki Marlane, the world's oldest-living, still-performing drag queen (really). Fierce! Note that this is a gay-boy bar and not an appropriate venue for a bachelorette party of giggling straight girls. If you're straight, be discreet. And remember to tip all the performers a dollar each.

Harry Denton's Starlight Room (Map pp52-3; ☎ 415-395-8595; www.harrydenton.com; 450 Powell St) The views are mesmerizing from the 21st floor of the Sir Francis Drake Hotel, where khaki-clad tourists let down their hair and dance to live bands or DJs. Safe space for tipsy dorks and conservative parents. The Sunday drag-show brunch is kooky.

LOCAL VOICES

SF Weekly clubs editor Brock Keeling likes to drink too much and occasionally gets asked to leave the clubs he's supposed to review. Here's what'll get you thrown out of a few San Francisco nightclubs:

- Martuni's (right) – Not knowing how to sing
- The Mint (p65) – Knowing how to sing
- Hotel Biron (p65) – Ordering white zinfandel
- Bottom of the Hill (p65) – Requesting show tunes
- Ruby Skye (downtown) – Snorting coke (openly) in the VIP area

---

El Rio (Map p55; ☎ 415-282-3325; www.elriosf.com; 3158 Mission St) This Mission stalwart hosts everything from DJ nights to rock bands to cabaret, but the big draw is Salsa Sundays (from 3pm, June through mid-November), when Latin bands perform outdoors and the whole joint shimmies and shakes. Come early for the free BBQ and dance lessons.

Martuni's (Map pp52-3; ☎ 415-241-0205; 4 Valencia St) Lounge lizards flock to mostly gay Martuni's, the city's last remaining seven-night-a-week piano bar with an open mic – but only for talented singers.

DNA Lounge (Map pp52-3; ☎ 415-626-1409; www.dnalounge.com; 375 11th St; ☺ usually Thu-Sat, call for details) One of the last arenalike nightclubs in SF, DNA occasionally hosts industrial bands and cabaret-burlesque shows, but its main focus is DJs, especially at 'Bootie' (second Saturday of the month), America's first mash-up club.

Mezzanine (Map pp52-3; ☎ 415-625-8880; www.mezzaninesf.com; 444 Jessie St; ☺ call for details) With possibly the best sound system in SF, behemoth Mezzanine hosts hip-hop artists, screaming divas, and a monthly gay tea dance (otherwise the crowd is 80/20 straight/gay). Dance all night.

Endup (Map pp52-3; ☎ 415-646-0999; www.theendup.com; 401 6th St; ☺ Thu night, then 24hr Fri-Sun) If you're grinding your teeth at 4am, desperately searching for a place to dance till noon on Saturday or Sunday, head to the Endup, where you can twirl, indoors and out, to electronica, house and club classics. The crowd is tweaky, but the place is an institution.

Live Theater

TIX Bay Area (Map pp52-3; ☎ 415-433-7827; www.theatrebayarea.org; Union Sq; ☺ closed Mon) This free-standing kiosk on Powell St sells half-price, day-of-performance tickets and full-price advance tickets. It also carries MUNI passes. Cash only for same-day seats.

Beach Blanket Babylon (Map p54; ☎ 415-421-4222; www.beachblanketbabylon.com; Club Fugazi, 678 Green St) If you see only one show, make it hilarious, zany Beach Blanket, where larger-than-life performers brilliantly spoof contemporary culture. And those hats! Wow.

Teatro Zinzanni (Map p51; ☎ 415-438-2668; http://zinzanni.org; Pier 27) A rotating cast of semi-celebs stars in Zinzanni's 19th-century, European-style circus – sort of a comedic Cirque du Soleil – with a damn good five-course meal.

The world-renowned San Francisco Symphony performs in **Davies Symphony Hall** (Map pp52-3; ☎ 415-864-6000; www.sfsymphony.org; cnr Grove St & Van Ness Ave). The beautiful **War Memorial Opera House** (Map pp52-3; ☎ 415-864-3330; 301 Van Ness Ave) hosts the San Francisco Opera and the **San Francisco Ballet** (☎ 415-865-2000; www.sfballet.org). **Yerba Buena Center for the Arts** (Map pp52-3; ☎ 415-978-2787; www.ybca.org; cnr Howard & 3rd Sts) hosts excellent contemporary performing arts.

For comedy, head to the **Punch Line** (Map pp52-3; ☎ 415-397-4337; www.punchlinecomedyclub .com; 444 Battery St).

Sports

San Francisco 49ers (☎ 415-656-4900; www.sf49ers.com) The 49ers play NFL football at Candlestick Park (aka Monster Park), south of the city.

San Francisco Giants (☎ 415-972-2000; www.sfgiants .com; ⚲) The Giants play Major League baseball at AT&T Park.

SHOPPING

If you've forgotten underwear or need a toaster or fur coat, head to Union Square, anchored by good-for-basics **Macy's** (Map pp52-3; ☎ 415-397-3333; 170 O'Farrell St) and chic **Neiman-Marcus** (Map pp52-3; ☎ 415-362-3900; 150 Stockton St). East along Post and Geary Sts lies the highest concentration of high-end boutiques; along Stockton St and Grant Ave are name-brand stores such as **Diesel** (Map pp52-3; ☎ 415-982-7077; 101 Post). A huge, fabulous **Bloomingdale's** (Map pp52-3; ☎ 415-856-5300; 845 Market St) is the hottest store at **San Francisco Shopping Centre** (Map pp52-3; cnr Market & 5th Sts). For disposable fashion, hit **H&M** (Map pp52-3; ☎ 415-986-4215; 150 Powell St). Dress like Euro-trash at **Zara** (Map pp52-3; ☎ 415-399-6930; 250 Post St).

Designers unload unsellable couture-grade suits and sportswear at **Jeremy's** (Map pp52-3; ☎ 415-882-4929; 2 South Park) – for as much as 90% off.

For souvenirs, go to Pier 39. For more civilized tourist shopping, hit **Ghirardelli Sq** (Map p54), at the wharf's west end; buy the namesake goodies at **Ghirardelli Chocolate Shop & Caffe** (☎ 415-474-1414).

Caveat emptor: don't get ripped off on electronics or cameras in Chinatown. Reputable **Brooks Camera** (Map pp52-3; ☎ 415-362-4708; 125 Kearny St) sells, rents and repairs them.

The cashmere-clad shop at Pacific Heights' indie boutiques, along **Fillmore St** (Map p51) between Bush and Sacramento Sts. Small de-

signers and high-end gift shops line Union St, between Franklin and Fillmore Sts, in **Cow Hollow** (Map p51); look in hidden courtyards. Nearby **Plumpjack Wines** (Map p54; ☎ 415-346-9870; www.plumpjack.com; 3129 Fillmore St) is famous for reasonable prices on stellar vintages.

For the hippest au courant underground shopping, head to **Hayes Valley** (Map pp52-3), on Hayes St between Franklin and Laguna Sts, near Civic Center.

Shop for vintage drag on **Haight St** (Map p51), from Masonic Ave to Stanyan St. **Amoeba Records** (Map p51; ☎ 415-831-1200; 1855 Haight St) carries SF's best selection of indie music.

In the Mission District, hit **Valencia St**, between 16th and 24th Sts, for vintage shops, locally designed clothing and Mexican folk art. Women-owned and -operated, **Good Vibrations** (Map p55; ☎ 415-522-5460; 603 Valencia St) is the street's most famous store, with sex-positive adult toys (read: vibrators).

A veritable emporium of fetish gear, **Mr S & Madam S Leathers** (Map pp52-3; ☎ 415-863-7764; 385 8th St) is a must-see for any serious sex freak.

GETTING THERE & AROUND
Air

The Bay Area has three airports: **San Francisco International Airport** (SFO; ☎ 650-876-7809; www.flysfo .com), 15 miles south of the city via Hwy 101 or I-280; **Oakland International Airport** (OAK; ☎ 510-577-4000; www.flyoakland.com), 12 miles north east, via the Bay Bridge and I-880; and **San Jose International Airport** (SJC; ☎ 408-277-4759; www .sjc.org), 45 miles south. Most international flights arrive at SFO. It's often cheapest to fly into OAK.

To/From the Airport

Take **Bay Area Rapid Transit** (BART; ☎ 415-989-2278; www.bart.gov) directly from SFO or OAK into downtown San Francisco ($5, 30 minutes).

Taxis charge about $35 for a trip into the city; follow signs from arrival areas at the airport. Add 15% gratuity to the metered fare.

Door-to-door shuttle vans cost less than taxis. Vans leave the departures level outside terminals. Try **Lorrie's** (☎ 415-334-9000; www.lorries -shuttles.com) and **Super Shuttle** (☎ 415-558-8500; www.supershuttle.com). Fares are about $15. Call ahead for city pick-ups.

Buses are cheapest. From SFO, take **SamTrans** (☎ 800-660-4287; www.samtrans.org) express-bus KX (adult/child $4/2, 30 minutes; carry-on luggage only, no suitcases) or bus

292 (adult/child $1.50/1, 60 minutes); buses depart from the lower level.

For services from OAK, reserve 48 hours ahead with **Bayporter Express** (☎ 415-467-1800; www.bayporter.com; 1st passenger $26, each additional $12).

To get from SJC to San Francisco, ride the **Santa Cruz Airporter** (☎ 800-497-4997, 831-475-0234; www.santacruzairporter.net) to San Francisco International Airport ($20), then take BART, a shuttle, or a taxi to downtown. Alternatively, take the **Valley Transit Authority** (VTA; ☎ 408-321-2300; www.vta.org) bus 10, the Airport Flyer ($1.75), to the Santa Clara Caltrain Station and ride the train to San Francisco ($6.75).

Bus

Intercity buses operate from the **Transbay Terminal** (Map pp52-3; 425 Mission St at 1st St). Take **AC Transit** (☎ 510-839-2882; www.actransit.org) to the East Bay, **Golden Gate Transit** (☎ 415-932-2000; www.goldengate.org) to Marin and Sonoma counties, and **SamTrans** (☎ 800-660-4287; www.samtrans .org) buses to points south.

THE OTHER SIDE OF THE BAY

Though San Franciscans avoid the East Bay, there are some damn cool sights to check out on the other side of the water.

In **Oakland**, start in the Rockridge neighborhood, on the skirts of the East Bay hills; park your car and wander **College Ave** and **Piedmont Ave** for indie shops, fun bars and bustling restaurants. Or take BART to Rockridge station.

Smack in the middle of downtown Oakland, **Lake Merritt** is ideal for an urban jog or nature walk. You'll spot hundreds of Canada geese (and their droppings) along a 3.5-mile perimeter path. Rent a boat and float beside Oakland's revitalized downtown. Kids love cute-as-a-button **Children's Fairyland** (☎ 510-452-2259; www.fairyland.org; 699 Bellevue Ave; admission $8; 👶), which apparently inspired Walt Disney when he was building Disneyland.

Also near the Lake Merritt BART station, the **Oakland Museum of California** (☎ 510-238-2200; www.museumca.org; admission adult/child $8/5; 🕙 10am-5pm Wed-Sun, noon-5pm Sun; 👶) has fantastic exhibits on California history, science and art and everything from sports to earthquakes.

It's a short walk to the bayside **Jack London Sq** (☎ 510-645-9292; www.jacklondonsquare.com), at the foot of Broadway, along the city's revitalized waterfront. (From I-880, exit at Broadway/Alameda; or take the ferry from SF.) Though some of it feels like a mall, there are worthwhile shops and waterside strolling. The Bay Area's premier jazz venue, cavernous **Yoshi's** (☎ 510-238-9200; www .yoshis.com; 510 Embarcadero West; 🕙 dinner daily, shows 8pm & 10pm Mon-Sat, 7pm & 9pm Sun) doubles as a fine Japanese restaurant. Alternatively take in a show – maybe Pink Floyd or the Oakland Symphony – at the oh-so-fabulous **Paramount Theatre** (☎ 510-893-2300; www.paramounttheatre .com), a National Historic Landmark dripping with art deco details.

And then there's **Berkeley** (aka Berserkeley), ground zero for radicalism in the 1960s and still a bastion of liberalism – even though it's no longer legal to walk around nude. Shoppers: check out the home decor and boho-chic boutiques inside converted warehouses along **4th St**, near University Ave.

Head inland and wander the wooded 178-acre **UC Berkeley Campus** (☎ 510-642-5215; www .berkeley.edu) and see its historic buildings and museums; pose for pictures by the oxidized-green Sather Gate. Take BART to the Berkeley station, or I-80 to University Ave.

Extending southward from UC, **Telegraph Ave** is chockablock with shops that cater to students, so you'll find good bargains on clothes and books.

And surprise, surprise: the roots of California cuisine lie *not* in San Francisco, but right here in Berkeley. Alice Water's **Chez Panisse** (☎ 510-548-5525; www.chezpanisse.com; 1517 Shattuck Ave; prix-fixe menu $50-85; 🕙 dinner Tue-Sat) continues to wow diners with seasonal, ingredients-driven cooking, available only as a set menu in the main dining room (reservations essential). It's easier to secure a table at the more-casual upstairs **Café at Chez Panisse** (☎ 510-548-5049; mains $17-26; 🕙 lunch & dinner Mon-Sat), which has a wood-fired oven and open kitchen.

The next time a San Franciscan tells you that East Bay is pig latin for beast, remember East Bay congresswoman Barbara Lee voted *against* the USA Patriot Act in 2001. San Francisco's Nancy Pelosi voted *for* it. Which side of the bay is the real beast? Get it, girl.

Greyhound (☎ 415-495-1575, 800-231-2222; www
.greyhound.com) operates nationwide buses.

Train
CalTrain (☎ 800-660-4287; www.caltrain.com; cnr 4th &
Townsend Sts) operates commuter lines down
the peninsula. MUNI's N-Judah streetcar line
serves the station.

Amtrak (☎ 800-872-7245; www.amtrak.com) stops
in Emeryville and Oakland, with connecting
bus services to San Francisco's Ferry Building.
Trains depart for Sacramento and the east.

Car & Motorcycle
Avoid driving, if only because parking sucks.
When parallel parking on hills, turn your
wheels to the curb or face fines.

Parking restrictions are strictly enforced, so
read the signs. For towed vehicles, call **City Tow**
(☎ 415-621-8605; Room 145, 850 Bryant St).

Rent a car for excursions out of town. For
good service, go to **National/Alamo** (Map pp52-3;
☎ 415-292-5300; www.nationalcar.com, www.alamo.com;
320 O'Farrell St) or **City Rent-a-Car** (Map pp52-3; www
.cityrentacar.com; 1433 Bush St).

For the best 4WDs and convertibles, call at
Specialty Rentals (Map pp52-3; ☎ 800-400-8412; www
.specialtyrentals.com; 150 Valencia St).

To rent a motorcycle, contact **Dubbelju** (Map
pp52-3; ☎ 415-495-2774; www.dubbelju.com; 689A Bryant St).

Public Transportation
MUNI (☎ 673-6864; www.sfmuni.com) runs buses,
streetcars and cable cars. Get the *Street &
Transit Map* ($2.50) at newsstands around
Union Square. Buses cost $1.50, cable cars $5.
Transfers are valid for two more trips within
90 minutes, except on cable cars. Buy multiday passes at the Visitors Information Center
or the TIX kiosk on Union Square.

BART (☎ 989-2278; www.bart.gov) runs trains
beneath Market and Mission Sts, linking San
Francisco and the East Bay via the Transbay
Tube. From downtown, it's a 10-minute ride
to the Mission district. Intracity fares cost
$1.40; intercity trips cost $2.50 to $6.

Taxi
Taxi fares start at $2.85 for the first mile and
cost 45¢ per fifth of a mile thereafter. Be
warned: taxis are almost impossible to hail
during Friday-evening rush. Call **Luxor Cab**
(☎ 415-282-4141), **Veteran's Cab** (☎ 415-552-1300) or
De Soto Cab (☎ 415-970-1300).

SOUTH OF THE BAY
Considering the Bay Area is America's fifth-
largest metropolitan area, it's amazing how
much of the land along the Pacific side of the
peninsula is undeveloped thanks in part to the
Peninsula Open Space Trust. The eastern side
is a tangle of suburbs, bisected by Hwy 101,
but along pastoral Hwy 1's 68-mile course to
Santa Cruz, all is quiet except for the roar of
the sea accompanying rolling hills carpeted in
crops, not subdivisions. Leave time to explore
hidden beaches and small towns, and stop at
farm stands in between.

PACIFICA TO HALF MOON BAY
Fifteen miles from downtown San Francisco,
Pacifica marks the end of coastside suburbs.
It's a nothing-special town, but has two sandy
beaches: **Rockaway Beach** to the north, popular
for fishing, and **Pacifica State Beach**, big with
surfers (beware riptides). The latter has outdoor showers and restrooms.

Just south of town, Hwy 1 emerges from
eucalyptus forests onto an unstable cliff called
Devil's Slide. The road often washes out during winter rains, but wow, it's breathtaking.

A half-mile south of Devil's Slide is **Gray Whale
Cove State Beach**, one of the coast's most popular
clothing-optional beaches. There are steep steps
down to the sand. Park on the inland side of
Hwy 1; but take care crossing the road!

Montara State Beach lies a mile south and
encompasses **McNee Ranch State Park**, a northern section of the Santa Cruz Mountains. To
ascend the pristine hills, hike the trails leading
from the Martini Creek parking lot on the
inland side of Hwy 1.

Point Montara Lighthouse HI Hostel (☎ 650-728-
7177; www.norcalhostels.org; cnr Hwy 1 & 16th St; dm $19-24,
r $53-63; 💻) stands next to a lighthouse built in
1900; make reservations.

The **Fitzgerald Marine Reserve** (☎ 650-728-3584;
www.fitzgeraldreserve.org), at Moss Beach, protects
way-cool tide pools. The rocks can be slippery.
Respect posted regulations. From Hwy 1 in
Moss Beach, turn west onto California Ave.

Stop for drinks at a former speakeasy, **Moss
Beach Distillery** (☎ 650-728-5595; cnr Beach Way & Ocean
Blvd; dishes from $15). The food's overpriced, but
the outdoor ocean-view bar is fun. Follow
signs from Hwy 1.

Just south, Princeton-by-the-Sea stretches
around Pillar Point Harbor. Eat fried fish and

DRIVING TOUR: PENINSULA RIDGELINE TOUR

What to See
The Coastal Range runs right down the San Francisco Peninsula (Map p48). Drive the spine along winding and wooded **Skyline Blvd** (Rte 35) to the crossroads in **Sky Londa**, near where Timothy Leary dropped acid with his Electric Kool-Aid gang. Motorcyclists *love* this road; let them pass. Stop for lunch – and check out all the bikes – at **Alice's Restaurant** (☎ 650-851-0303; 17288 Skyline Blvd; dishes from $5; 😊 8:30am-9pm). From here, drop west along **La Honda Rd** (Rte 84), down, down 1500ft elevation toward the sea, through rolling, oak-dotted hills to the sleepy hamlet of **San Gregorio**, before arriving back at the coast.

The Route
From San Francisco, take I-280 about 20 miles south to Hwy 92; go 0.2 miles west, and turn south on Skyline Blvd and continue 16 miles to Sky Londa; then it's 22 miles to Hwy 1.

Time & Mileage
Allow 90 minutes, without stops, from San Francisco; the one-way drive is about 60 miles.

---

coleslaw at **Barbara's Fishtrap** (☎ 650-728-7049; 281 Capistrano Rd; dishes $8-18). Or head just south to New England–style **Sam's Chowder House** (☎ 650-712-0245; www.samschowderhouse.com; 4210 N Cabrillo Hwy, aka Hwy 1; dishes $12-24)

At the west end of Pillar Point, **Maverick's** attracts the world's top surfers to its huge, steep and incredibly dangerous waves. The annual Quiksilver/Maverick's surf contest happens sometime between December and March, depending on conditions.

HALF MOON BAY
pop 11,300
Farms unfurl around Half Moon Bay, which feels worlds away from San Francisco, even though it's only 45 minutes south. Wander Main St and poke your head into home-furnishings and country-crafts shops – all pretty vanilla, but quaint nonetheless. Agriculture is the major industry, especially pumpkins, which dot the landscape orange in autumn. Then, otherwise-quiet farms transform into roadside attractions with corn mazes and jack-o-lanterns. Santa Cruz is 40 miles south.

Orientation & Information
Hwy 92 connects Half Moon Bay to inland freeways; avoid Hwy 92 during commute hours, unless traveling against traffic. Locally, Hwy 1 is called Cabrillo Hwy.

Shops, cafés and restaurants line five-block-long Main St, just east of Hwy 1. The **Half Moon Bay Coastside Chamber of Commerce** (☎ 650-726-8380; www.halfmoonbaychamber.org; 520 Kelly Ave;

😊 9am-4pm Mon-Fri) provides visitor information and details about ecofriendly businesses on its website (navigate to 'visiting,' then 'eco-tourism').

Sights & Activities
Frolic on 4 miles of open, sandy beach at **Half Moon Bay State Beach** (☎ 650-726-8819; day-use fee $4); access via Kelly Ave or further north at Venice Blvd.

Rent a horse at **Seahorse Ranch** (☎ 650-726-2362, 650-726-9903; www.horserentals.com/seahorse.html). Two-hour rides cost $60; arrive by 8am and it's only $35. Kids under five ride ponies.

Celebrate harvest at the annual **Art & Pumpkin Festival** (☎ 650-726-9652). The October event kicks off with the World Championship Pumpkin Weigh-Off; the winning pumpkins exceed 1000lb!

Sleeping & Eating
San Benito House (☎ 650-726-3425; www.sanbenito house.com; 356 Main St; r with bathroom $75-80, r without bathroom $95-149 all incl breakfast) Rent folksy, modest, Americana-style rooms above an old-fashioned bar. Downstairs is a deli with sandwiches on good bread (lunch under $10).

Mill Rose Inn (☎ 650-726-8750, 800-900-7673; www .millroseinn.com; 615 Mill St; r $150-310) The Mill Rose B&B provides cushy touches and the town's most eye-popping gardens – a riot of color.

Old Thyme Inn (☎ 650-726-1616, 800-720-4277; www .oldthymeinn.com; 779 Main St; r $140-325 incl breakfast) This 1898 inn has cheerful B&B rooms, some with Jacuzzis and fireplaces.

Flying Fish Grill (☎ 650-712-1125; cnr Hwy 92 & Main St; dishes from $3) This place has excellent fish tacos, along with other seafood plates that you can take out or eat in.

Cameron's Restaurant & Inn (☎ 650-726-5705; 1410 S Cabrillo Hwy; dishes from $8) Eat pub food, drink beer and play darts at Cameron's, a century-old, atmospheric English-style pub. If you don't mind bar noise, rent a room upstairs (from $99).

Cetrella (☎ 650-726-4090; www.cetrella.com; 845 Main St; mains $18-28; ☽ dinner, Sun brunch) Worth a drive from San Francisco, Cetrella's seasonally driven Mediterranean menu features flavors so clean and bright they dance on the palette. Try the (seasonal) zarzuella (crab-fish stew with smoked paprika, almonds and saffron). The room is huge, the look chic and there's live jazz Thursday to Saturday nights. Make reservations.

Getting There & Away

SamTrans (☎ 800-660-4287) bus 294 operates from the Hillsdale CalTrain station to Half Moon Bay, and up the coast to Moss Beach and Pacifica, daily until about 6pm ($1.50, 30 minutes).

HALF MOON BAY TO SANTA CRUZ

Santa Cruz is covered in the Central Coast chapter, p141.

San Gregorio State Beach (day-use fee $4) lies 10 miles south of Half Moon Bay. It has a clothing-optional stretch to the north, but it's usually too windy and cold. **Pomponio** and **Pescadero** state beaches extend further down the coast. **Butano State Park**, about 5 miles south of Pescadero, is good for day hikes.

An old farming village, **Pescadero** (www.pescaderovillage.com) lies 3 miles east of Hwy 1, between mountainous parks and forest preserves. The hamlet is well supplied with antiques and curiosity shops, but the best reason to visit is to eat at dressed-down **Duarte's Tavern** (☎ 879-0464; cnr Stage & Pescadero Rds; mains $16-23; ☽ 7am-9pm). It's most famous for artichoke soup and olallieberry pie, but there's homemade goat-cheese ravioli made with cheese from a nearby farm and great fish dishes: try the (seasonal) crab cioppino ($20). It's accessible from Hwy 1, south of San Gregorio State Beach on Pescadero Creek Rd.

Pigeon Point Lighthouse Hostel (☎ 650-879-0633; www.norcalhostels.org; 210 Pigeon Point Rd; dm $19-22, r $53-59) sits in the shadow of a 115ft-tall lighthouse.

Rooms are in the former lighthouse-keeper's quarters; reservations are highly recommended (but they'll always make room for bicyclists). Because of decaying ironwork, the lighthouse remains closed indefinitely, but the point is a dramatic spot to watch migrating gray whales from January to March.

Four miles south, **Costanoa** (☎ 650-879-1100, 877-262-7848; www.costanoa.com; 2001 Rossi Rd; lodge r with bathroom $210-270, cabin without bathroom $185-195, tent cabin without bathroom $115-155, tents & RVs $50-65; ⟨♿⟩) is part ecolodge, part campground and is tucked between three state parks. Great for outdoor enthusiasts, it feels like summer camp for former hippies turned moms and dads; enjoy hiking on gorgeous, wide-open hillsides and activities such as yoga and horseback riding. Accommodations range from smart-looking lodge rooms (with bathroom) to retreatlike modern duplex cabins (without bathroom) to tiny tent cabins with heated mattresses (turn off your light when you have sex, lest you put on a shadow-puppet show for your neighbors). Every room comes with extras like robes and slippers and aromatherapy soap; shared bathhouses have saunas, a nice touch. No TVs.

Año Nuevo State Reserve

Twenty-seven miles south of Half Moon Bay, elephant seals breed here in greater numbers than anywhere else in the world. It's wonderful to behold but to see them, plan well ahead.

Between 1800 and 1850, the elephant seal was driven to the edge of extinction by trappers. Only a handful survived around the Guadalupe Islands off the then-Mexican state of Baja California. With the development of substitutes for seal oil and the advent of ecological conservation, the elephant seal has made a comeback, reappearing on the Southern California coast around 1920. In 1955, seals returned to Año Nuevo beach.

The peak mating-and-birthing season falls between mid-December and the end of March; seal pups leave by April. During these months visitors are only allowed on the reserve for guided walks; book eight weeks ahead. The **park office** (☎ 650-879-0227; www.parks.ca.gov) can give advice, but to make reservations, call ☎ 800-444-4445 or 916-638-5883. Tours cost $5, plus $6 for parking. From the ranger station it's a 3- to 5-mile round-trip hike to the beach; the visit takes two to three hours. If you haven't booked, bad weather tends to bring last-minute cancellations. Advance reservations aren't necessary outside peak seasons, but you'll need a visitor permit from the entrance station; arrive before 3pm.

Big Basin Redwood State Park

Big Basin (☎ 650-338-8860; day-use fee $4) became California's first state park in 1902, following heated battles between conservationists and loggers. Many trees in this 25-sq-mile park in the Santa Cruz Mountains have stood more than 1500 years. Hike along running, fern-lined streams through old-growth redwood forests. The air is fragrant with stands of fir, cedar and bay.

You can access some trails from Hwy 1, but the main entrance lies off Hwy 236, which connects with Hwy 9 about 15 miles north of Santa Cruz. The park has 146 family **campsites** (☎ 800-444-7275 reservations; www.reserve america.com; sites $25). There are also 36 **tent cabins** (☎ 800-874-8368; www.bigbasintentcabins.com; cabins $50) with two double-bed platforms and wood-burning stoves.

MARIN COUNTY

Majestic redwoods cling to coastal hillside, while the surf endlessly carves new shapes into the cliffs below. Hundreds of miles of trails crisscross the Point Reyes National Seashore, Muir Woods and Mt Tamalpais National Park. But if there's one thing, other than their intense love of the outdoors, that binds the residents of Marin County, it's their equally passionate appreciation of the good life. And they can afford it. The region is populated by the überwealthy, though they pride themselves on their (seemingly) laid-back lifestyle. Towns may look like idyllic rural hamlets but shops cater to cosmopolitan tastes – pity the naïve restaurateur who tries to make a go of it using nonorganic ingredients.

Orientation

Hwy 101 heads north from the Golden Gate Bridge ($5 toll when heading back into San Francisco), spearing through Marin's middle; more bucolic Hwy 1 winds its way along the coast. In San Rafael, Sir Francis Drake Blvd cuts across west Marin from Hwy 101 to the ocean. Tank up before heading toward the coast – from Mill Valley onwards, the closest gas is in Point Reyes Station.

Hwy 580 comes in from the East Bay over the Richmond–San Rafael bridge ($3 toll for westbound traffic) to meet Hwy 101 at Larkspur.

Information

Marin County Convention & Visitors Bureau (☎ 866-925-2060, 415-925-2060; www.visitmarin.org; 1013 Larkspur Landing Circle, Larkspur; ☼ 9am-5pm Mon-Fri) handles tourist information for the entire county. Information is also available from the visitors center in Sausalito and the Mill Valley Chamber of Commerce. The **West Marin Chamber of Commerce** (☎ 415-663-9232; www.pointreyes.org) can give you more specifics on the Point Reyes region.

MARIN HEADLANDS

As you cross the Golden Gate Bridge, you could be forgiven for thinking you had been transported to the west coast of Ireland – especially in winter, when everything turns green. The hulking headlands are blanketed in emerald and fog, the waves crash on craggy cliffs below and there is little sound save whistling wind and cawing birds. The kamikaze cyclists sharing the narrow roads with you quickly bring you back to Northern California, as do the views of the city and the bridge. It's no wonder that this is one of the Bay Area's most popular hiking and biking destinations.

Orientation & Information

If you're coming from San Francisco, exit at Alexander Ave immediately after crossing the Golden Gate Bridge, then dip left under the highway and head out west. Conzelman Rd snakes up into the hills, where it eventually forks. Conzelman Rd continues west, becoming a steep, one-lane road as it descends to Point Bonita. From there it continues to Rodeo Beach and Fort Barry. McCullough Rd heads inland, joining Bunker Rd toward Rodeo Beach.

Information is available from the **Golden Gate National Recreation Area** (GGNRA; ☎ 415-561-4700; www.nps.gov/goga) and the **Marin Headlands Visitors Center** (☎ 415-331-1540; ☼ 9:30am-4:30pm), in an old church off Bunker Rd, three miles after turnoff from Hwy 101.

Sights & Activities

Every fall, 19 species of migrating birds – including hawks, falcons and eagles – congregate at **Hawk Hill**. Because open water doesn't support the thermals that the birds need to stay aloft, they use the headlands to gain altitude for the 2-mile crossing of the Golden Gate. Bring binoculars. Go 1.8 miles up Conzelman Rd, park along the road and walk up the west side of the hill past the gate and a few hundred feet from the top.

Near the end of Conzelman Rd is the still-operating **Point Bonita Lighthouse** (☉ 12:30-3:30pm Sat-Mon, free tours at 12:30pm), a breathtaking half-mile walk from the parking area. From the tip of Point Bonita, you can see the distant Golden Gate Bridge and beyond it the tips of the San Francisco skyline.

The **Marine Mammal Center** (☎ 415-289-7325; www.tmmc.org; admission free; ☉ 10am-4pm), on the hill above Rodeo Lagoon, is the largest marine-mammal hospital in the world. It's set to reopen in early 2008 after expansion. The solar-powered hospital will have observation decks for visitors to get close – but not too close – to the recovering patients, mostly seals. Spring is birthing season, and so the busiest and cutest time of year. The **Marine Mammal Visitors Center** (Bldg 1049; ☉ 10am-4pm; admission free), across from Rodeo Beach and open during the hospital's overhaul, has hands-on exhibits featuring cuddly creatures.

At the end of Bunker Rd sits black-sand **Rodeo Beach** (ro-*day*-oh), protected from wind by cliffs.

Sleeping

HI Marin Headlands Hostel (☎ 415-331-2777; www .norcalhostels.org/marin; Bldg 941, Fort Barry, Marin Headlands; dm/r $20/60; 💻) Set amidst towering eucalyptus trees, this friendly and ecosensitive hostel has lodging divided into two parts. The main building, formerly a military infirmary, houses the 76 dorm beds, while the annex, an old captain's house, has most of the private rooms and a more cozy, hardwood feel. The game room features a pool table, foosball and ping-pong. The hostel affords ready access to trails.

There are four small campgrounds in the headlands, and all involve hiking at least 1 mile from the nearest parking lot. **Kirby Cove Campground** (☎ 800-365-2267; sites $25; Apr-Oct) is in a spectacular shady nook near the entry to the bay. There's a small beach with the Golden Gate Bridge arching over the rocks nearby. Hawk, Bicentennial and Haypress campgrounds are inland; camping is free but

must be reserved through the Marin Headlands Visitors Center.

Getting There & Away

By car, take the second Alexander Ave exit just after the Golden Gate Bridge and dip left under the freeway. Get in the left lane and follow signs for 101S. Turn left at the stop sign and then right onto Conzelman Rd. Bicycles take roughly the same route. Conzelman Rd, to the right, takes you up along the bluffs; you can also take Bunker Rd.

Golden Gate Transit (☎ 415-923-2000; www.golden gatetransit.org) bus 2 leaves from the corners of Pine and Battery Sts and 7th and Folsom Sts in San Francisco to the Headlands ($3.40). On Sunday and holidays **MUNI** (☎ 415-673-6864; one way $1.50) bus 76 runs from the CalTrain depot in San Francisco to Fort Barry and Rodeo Beach. If you're taking either the **West Marin Stagecoach** (☎ 415-526-3239; www.marintransit.org) or **Golden Gate Transit** (☎ 415-455-2000; www.goldengate .org), have exact change ready.

SAUSALITO

pop 7184

Sausalito being the first town you hit after crossing the bridge from the City makes its appeal undeniable. Its main drag is a delicate curve hugging Richardson Bay and displaying postcard-worthy vistas of San Francisco and Angel Island. The fog rarely settles because of the ridgeline. But in summer, Sausalito becomes a victim of its own beauty – the 'tiny willows' that lent the town its name have been replaced by jostling daytrippers clogging the street, accompanied by the requisite glut of shops and eateries all too willing to help tourists part with their cash. Ferry over from San Francisco with a bike and escape the traffic.

When it became the terminus of the train line down the Pacific coast, Sausalito was transformed into a busy lumber port. After the war a new bohemian period began, with a resident artists colony living in 'arks' (houseboats moored along the bay). Creative genius Shel Silverstein lived on a nonmoored Sausalito houseboat on and off through the '60s and '70s.

Orientation & Information

Sausalito's commercial district is essentially one street, Bridgeway Blvd, on the waterfront. The town is actually on Richardson Bay, a

MARIN COUNTY

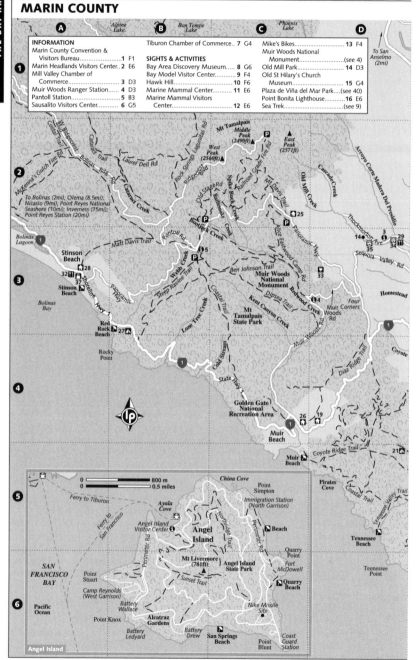

INFORMATION
Marin County Convention &
   Visitors Bureau.........................1 F1
Marin Headlands Visitors Center..2 E6
Mill Valley Chamber of
   Commerce.............................. 3 D3
Muir Woods Ranger Station...... 4 D3
Pantoll Station.............................5 B3
Sausalito Visitors Center............ 6 G5

Tiburon Chamber of Commerce.. 7 G4

SIGHTS & ACTIVITIES
Bay Area Discovery Museum..... 8 G6
Bay Model Visitor Center...........9 F4
Hawk Hill...................................10 F6
Marine Mammal Center.......... 11 E6
Marine Mammal Visitors
   Center................................... 12 E6

Mike's Bikes............................. 13 F4
Muir Woods National
   Monument.........................(see 4)
Old Mill Park...........................14 D3
Old St Hilary's Church
   Museum.................................15 G4
Plaza de Viña del Mar Park....(see 40)
Point Bonita Lighthouse...........16 E6
Sea Trek.................................(see 9)

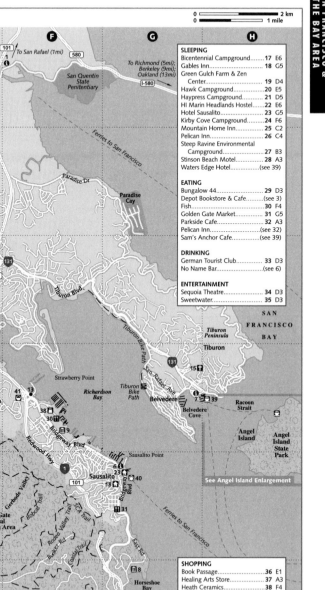

0 ———————— 2 km
0 ———————— 1 mile

SLEEPING
Bicentennial Campground........17 E6
Gables Inn...............................18 G5
Green Gulch Farm & Zen
  Center.................................19 D4
Hawk Campground...................20 E5
Haypress Campground.............21 D5
HI Marin Headlands Hostel.....22 E6
Hotel Sausalito........................23 G5
Kirby Cove Campground..........24 F6
Mountain Home Inn.................25 C2
Pelican Inn.............................26 C4
Steep Ravine Environmental
  Campground........................27 B3
Stinson Beach Motel................28 A3
Waters Edge Hotel................(see 39)

EATING
Bungalow 44...........................29 D3
Depot Bookstore & Cafe.........(see 3)
Fish..30 F4
Golden Gate Market...............31 G5
Parkside Cafe..........................32 A3
Pelican Inn...........................(see 32)
Sam's Anchor Cafe...............(see 39)

DRINKING
German Tourist Club...............33 D3
No Name Bar........................(see 6)

ENTERTAINMENT
Sequoia Theatre......................34 D3
Sweetwater.............................35 D3

SHOPPING
Book Passage..........................36 E1
Healing Arts Store...................37 A3
Heath Ceramics.......................38 F4

TRANSPORT
Ferries to Angel Island & San
  Francisco.............................39 H4
Ferries to San Francisco...........40 G5
Muir Woods Shuttle (Marin
  County)................................41 F4
Muir Woods Shuttle (Mill
  Valley)..................................42 E4

smaller bay within San Francisco Bay. The ferry terminal marks the town center. Housed in the old Ice House, the **Sausalito Visitors Center** (☎ 415-332-0505; 780 Bridgeway Blvd; ☻ 11:30am-4pm Tue-Sun) has local information and great historical exhibits.

Sights

Plaza de Viña Del Mar Park, near the ferry terminal, has a fountain flanked by 14ft-tall elephant statues from the 1915 Panama–Pacific Exposition in San Francisco.

Until computers demoted the system at the **Bay Model Visitor Center** (☎ 415-332-3871; 2100 Bridgeway Blvd; admission free, suggested donation $3; ☻ 9am-4pm Tue-Fri, 10am-5pm Sat & Sun) to a purely educational role, this 1.5-acre hydraulic model of the San Francisco Bay and the delta region helped scientists understand the effects of tides and currents on the land. A 24-hour period is represented in just 15 minutes. Look in the deepest water – under the Golden Gate Bridge – to see the most obvious tidal movement.

Aficionados of earthy, handcrafted tableware are likely already familiar with the pottery line **Heath Ceramics** (☎ 415-332-3732; www .heathceramics.com; 400 Gate Five Rd; ☻ 10am-5pm Sun-Wed, to 6pm Thu-Sat) founded by Edith Heath in the 1940s. The factory store sells the gorgeous stuff discounted at least 30% off retail and free tours of the factory are offered weekends at 11:30am. Reservations requested.

Spread out over half a dozen former bunkers and lying just under the north tower of the Golden Gate Bridge, the **Bay Area Discovery Museum** (☎ 415-487-4398; adult/child $8.50/7.50; ☻ 9am-4pm Tue-Fri, 10am-5pm Sat & Sun; ⓟ ⑤) caters to the curious kindergarten set. Kids can create art projects in the studios, climb around a shipwreck playground and try their hand at making waves.

Activities

Getting out on Richardson Bay is practically mandatory. Kayaks can be rented from **Sea Trek** (☎ 415-488-1000, 415-332-4465 Sat & Sun; www .seatrekkayak.com; kayaks per hr $15; ☻ 9am-5pm), in Schoonmaker Marina near the Bay Model Visitor Center. Lessons and group outings are also available.

Sausalito is also wonderful for **cycling**. If you venture across the Golden Gate Bridge, note that cyclists generally use the west side, except on weekdays between 5am and 3:30pm, when

they must share the east side with pedestrians (who have the right of way). After 9pm, cyclists can still cross the bridge on the east side through a security gate. For more information on rules and rides, contact the **San Francisco Bicycle Coalition** (☎ 415-431-2453; www .sfbike.org).

Mike's Bikes (☎ 415-332-3200; 1 Gate Six Rd; bikes for 24hr $30), at the north end of Bridgeway Blvd near Hwy 101, rents out road and mountain bikes. Reservations not accepted.

Sleeping & Eating

Gables Inn (☎ 415-289-1100, 800-966-1554; www.gables innsausalito.com; 62 Princess St; r $135-325; ⓟ) All nine rooms in this historic home share the same calming, beige-based color scheme, but the more expensive, upstairs rooms have Jacuzzi, fireplaces and balconies with spectacular views. Hot breakfast and evening wine and cheese are complimentary. For those towing kids, several rooms have sleeper sofas and there's a free video library.

Hotel Sausalito (☎ 415-332-4155; www.hotelsausalito .com; 16 El Portal; r $155-275; ⓟ ⑤) The guestrooms at this grand, smack-dab central 1915 hotel are on the small side, but are decorated in soft golden and green hues with some boasting stained-glass windows; they fairly glow from the inside out. The Scottish family that owns the place makes all feel welcome. Vouchers are given for continental breakfast at the restaurant next door. Parking costs $10.

Fish (☎ 415-331-3474; 350 Harbor Dr; dishes $12-30; ☻ Wed-Sun; ⑤) This joint at the end of Harbor Rd hooks the loyalty of locals with line-caught fish fresh off their own boats and down-home details such as picnic-table seating and Mason-jar glasses. Some complain it's overpriced – the Saigon salmon sandwich will set you back a whopping $18 – but the queue remains long. No credit cards.

Golden Gate Market (☎ 415-332-3040; 221 2nd St; ☻ 8am-9pm Mon-Sat, 9am-7pm Sun) For a bite that won't drain your wallet, grab a deli sandwich, some cheese and wine or some energy bars for the hike at this grocery-deli-liquor store on the south side of town.

No Name Bar (☎ 415-332-1392; 757 Bridgeway) Get a taste of what Sausalito must have been like before the yuppies invaded. The easy-going crowd at this bohemian dive gets down to live bands most nights. During daylight hours, throw some quarters in the jukebox and kick back with a game of Pictionary. Cash only.

Getting There & Away

Driving to Sausalito from San Francisco, take the Alexander Ave exit (the first exit after the Golden Gate Bridge) and follow the signs into Sausalito. There are five municipal parking lots in town, which are worth using as street-parking restrictions are strictly enforced.

Golden Gate Transit (☎ 415-923-2000; www.golden gatetransit.org) bus 10 runs daily to Sausalito from San Francisco (one way adult/child $3.40/1.70). Catch it at 7th and Market Sts.

The ferry is a popular way to get to Sausalito. **Golden Gate Ferries** (☎ 415-923-2000; one way adult/child 6-18 $6.75/3.35) operates to and from the San Francisco Ferry Building nine times daily. The trip takes half an hour and bicycles are welcome.

TIBURON

pop 8671

With a Lilliputian-sized Main St lined with clapboard buildings, Tiburon has retained more of the original wharf-rat vibe than its upper-crust neighbor to the west. Its name comes from the Spanish Punta de Tiburon (Shark Point). Until the 1930s, a drawbridge connected Tiburon to the town of Belvedere. Take the ferry from San Francisco, browse the shops on Main St, grab a bite to eat and you've done Tiburon. The town is also the jumping-off point for nearby Angel Island.

Orientation & Information

The central part of town is comprised of Tiburon Blvd, with Juanita Ln and Main St arcing off. Main St, also known as **Ark Row**, is where the old houseboats have found mooring on dry land and transformed into shops and boutiques.

The **Tiburon Peninsula Chamber of Commerce** (☎ 415-435-5633; www.tiburonchamber.org; 96B Main St; ☺ 8am-4pm Mon-Fri), on the lower level of the Ark Row shops, can provide information about the area. Their hours can be spotty, so if they're closed, pick up a historic walking guide at the Windsor Vineyards tasting room at 72 Main St.

Sights & Activities

Commanding splendid views from its perch, **Old St Hilary's Church Museum** (☎ 415-435-1853; 201 Esperanza St; admission free; ☺ 1-4pm Wed & Sun Apr-Oct) is one of the country's last examples of Carpenter Gothic architecture still in its original setting. The hillsides around the deconsecrated Catholic church comprise **St Hilary's Preserve**, which nurtures a treasure trove of rare wildflowers, including the black jewel flower and the Marin dwarf flax. Best in spring.

The Angel Island–Tiburon Ferry offers **sunset cruises** (☎ 415-435-2131; www.angelislandferry.com; adult/child $15/10) on Fridays and Saturdays from May to October. Pack your own picnic dinner to enjoy on board. Reservations recommended.

Friday nights from May through October, Tiburon throws its Main St **block party**, kicking off at 6pm.

Sleeping & Eating

Waters Edge Hotel (☎ 415-789-5999; www.marinhotels.com/waters.html; 25 Main St; r $189-439; P ⊠) This 23-unit hotel, its deck extending out over the bay, offers a variety of room sizes and amenities. Crisp white bedspreads, gas fireplaces and a view of the bay come with all rooms, though those with wood ceilings are the most atmospheric. There's also complimentary

---

WHY IS IT SO FOGGY?

When the summer sun's rays warm the air over the chilly Pacific, fog forms and hovers offshore; to grasp how it moves inland requires an understanding of California's geography. The vast agricultural region in the state's interior, the Central Valley, is ringed by mountains. Think of it as a giant bathtub. The only substantial sea-level break in these mountains occurs at the Golden Gate, to the west, which happens to be the direction from which prevailing winds blow. As the inland valley heats up and the warm air rises, it creates a deficit of air at surface level, generating wind that gets sucked through the only opening it can find: the Golden Gate. It happens fast; gusty wind is the only indication that the fog is about to roll in. But it's inconsistent: there can be fog at the beaches south of the Golden Gate and sun a mile to the north. Hills block fog – especially at times of high atmospheric pressure, as often happens in summer. Because of this, weather forecasters speak of the Bay Area's 'microclimates.' In July it's not uncommon for inland areas to reach 100°F, while the mercury at the coast barely reaches 70°F. But as the locals say, if you don't like the weather, just wait a minute.

continental breakfast in bed and a movie library in case you tire of the view.

Sam's Anchor Cafe (☎ 415-435-4527; 27 Main St; dishes $10-25) Everyone wants to sit on Sam's deck overlooking the marina, but you can't reserve outdoor seating at this popular, casual seafood and burger spot. Sam's is the oldest continuously operating restaurant in town – look for the trap door that was used to spirit the illicit liquids straight from the ships to the saloon. The cioppino is lip-smacking.

Getting There & Away

Golden Gate Transit (☎ 415-923-2000; www.golden gatetransit.org) bus 10 travels daily from San Francisco (one way $3.40) and Sausalito (one-way $2) to Tiburon, via Mill Valley. During the week, commuter bus 8 runs direct between San Francisco and Tiburon (one way $3.40).

On Hwy 101, look for the off-ramp for Tiburon Blvd, E Blithedale Ave and Hwy 131; driving east, it leads into town and intersects with Juanita Lane and Main St.

Blue & Gold Fleet (☎ 415-773-1188; Pier 41, Fisherman's Wharf; one way adult/child 5-11 $8.50/4.50) sails daily from San Francisco to Tiburon; ferries dock right in front of Guaymas restaurant at 5 Main St. You can transport bicycles for free. From Tiburon, ferries also connect regularly to nearby Angel Island.

MILL VALLEY

pop 13,286

BJ Honeycutt would often wax nostalgic about his picturesque hometown of Mill Valley on episodes of *M*A*S*H*, and nestled under the redwoods at the base of Mt Tam, it lives up to the accolades. To call Mill Valley home these days, however, you too will need to be pulling down a surgeon's salary. Though the 1892 Mill Valley Lumber Company still greets motorists on Miller Ave, the town is now packed with wildly expensive homes and pricey boutiques. It does manage to maintain its bohemian sensibility; in the central plaza, mothers breast-feed, goth kids sulk, alfresco painters dab, hippies hacky-sack and middle-aged men wearing berets play backgammon. The nearby trails of Mt Tam are the big draw.

Information is available from the **Mill Valley Chamber of Commerce** (☎ 415-388-9700; www.mill valley.org; 85 Throckmorton Ave; ◔ 10am-4pm Mon-Fri).

Sights & Activities

Several blocks west of downtown along Throckmorton Ave is **Old Mill Park**, perfect for a picnic.

Tennessee Valley (TV) Trail, in the Marin Headlands, is one of the most popular hikes in Marin (expect crowds on weekends), and offers beautiful views of the rugged coastline. It has easy, level access to the oft-windy 'black sand' beach and is a short 3.8 miles. From Hwy 101, take the Mill Valley–Stinson Beach–Hwy 1 exit and turn left onto Tennessee Valley Rd from the Shoreline Hwy; follow it 1.8 miles to the trailhead. Dogs aren't allowed on the TV Trail, but they are permitted on the Oakwood Valley Trail (1 mile up Tennessee Valley Rd from the Shoreline Hwy turn-off).

Sleeping & Eating

Mountain Home Inn (☎ 415-381-9000; www.mtnhome inn.com; 810 Panoramic Hwy; r $175-325; **P**) Set amid redwood, spruce and pine trees on a ridge of Mt Tam, this retreat is rustic yet sophisticated, though the presence of carpeting may turn off the most aesthetically minded. All 10 rooms face east and most have balconies. The smaller rooms – and they are small – are cozy dens. Rooms come equipped with fireplaces and wi-fi but no TVs. Its restaurant does prix fixe, and the morning view can't be beat. Dinner costs $38 and brunch costs $12 to $16. The restaurant is open Wednesday to Sunday.

Depot Bookstore & Cafe (87 Throckmorton Ave; meals under $10) Connected to the central plaza, the Depot is the community's de facto nerve center and occupies the space of the former railway station. It serves coffee, drinks and light meals and has free wi-fi. The bookstore sells lots of local publications, including trail guides.

Bungalow 44 (☎ 415-381-2500; 44 E Blithedale Ave; dishes $14-26; ◔ from 5pm) The Bungalow manages

---

LOCAL PICKS

■ For Robb Miller, design company executive, there's nothing more satisfying than fresh barbecued oysters, with garlic butter or traditional BBQ sauce, curbside at the Coast Cafe in Bolinas.

■ Marielle León, editor and new mom, loves to take son Max down to Tennessee Beach and watch the waves crash.

> ## IS IT BEER O'CLOCK YET?
>
> All those wholesome morning hikes in the mountains…it's enough to make you feel downright Teutonic. Which is why when your calves are aching and your lungs are searing, hop-step it to the **German Tourist Club** (30 Ridge Ave, Mill Valley; ⊙ 2-6pm), aka Die Naturfreunde. It's technically a private club that shuns overexposure, but the kind folks there seem to realize that their beer patio overlooking Muir Woods and Mt Tam is too good to keep to themselves. A stein of German draft will set you back around $7. If you're there at the right time, traditional alpine festivals are held in May, July and September on the third Sunday of the month (admission around $6).
>
> If you're car-bound, turn onto Ridge Ave from Panoramic Hwy, park in the gravel driveway at the end of the road, and start the 0.3-mile walk down the switchback driveway. Look to the right and you'll see the lodge through the trees. If you're hiking, the club is 1 mile into the Sun Trail from the Dipsea Trail.

to pull off a neighborhood feel despite upscale trappings such as straightback leather chairs. Portions are huge and the heritage is American, but the menu shines best through its appetizers – order a handful to share and call it a meal; the steak tartare is a local favorite. The front room can be awash in chatter and clatter, while the enclosed patio is prime for relaxing fireside.

Entertainment

Sweetwater (☎ 415-388-2820; www.sweetwatersaloon .com; 153 Throckmorton Ave) This intimate music club doesn't bother much with genres; if it makes the people move, be it funk, reggae, bluegrass or rollicking jam band, Sweetwater books it. Tuesdays bring happy-hour-priced drinks all night long.

Sequoia Theatre (☎ 415-388-4862; 25 Throckmorton Ave) This red velvet-seated historic theater screens indie films.

Getting There & Away

From San Francisco or Sausalito, take Hwy 101 north to the Mill Valley–Stinson Beach–Hwy 1 exit. Follow Hwy 1 (also called Shoreline Hwy) to Almonte Blvd (which becomes Miller Ave), then follow Miller Ave into downtown Mill Valley. From the north, take the E Blithedale Ave exit from Hwy 101, then head west into downtown Mill Valley.

Golden Gate Transit (☎ 415-923-2000; www.golden gatetransit.org) bus 4 runs from San Francisco to Mill Valley on weekdays; on weekends take bus 10, and transfer in Marin City to bus 15. All bus fares cost $3.40 for a one-way ticket. The **West Marin Stagecoach** (☎ 415-526-3239; www.marintransit.org) bus 61 connects Mill Valley with Marin City, Stinson Beach and Bolinas ($2).

MT TAMALPAIS STATE PARK

Visible from almost every spot in Marin, the 2571ft Mt Tamalpais (tam-il-*pie*-us) has wraparound views of ocean, bay and hills rolling into the distance. The coastal Miwok people, to whom Mt Tam was sacred, saw a figure of a sleeping maiden in its silhouette, and with enough squinting, you can see her too.

Mt Tamalpais State Park was formed in 1930 and its 6300 acres are home to deer, foxes, bobcats and mile after mile of hiking and biking trails. In 1896 the 'world's crookedest railroad' was completed from Mill Valley to the summit. The Old Railroad Grade is now one of Mt Tam's most popular hiking and biking trails.

Panoramic Hwy climbs from Mill Valley through the park to Stinson Beach. **Pantoll Station** (☎ 415-388-2070; 801 Panoramic Hwy) is the park headquarters. Get a detailed park map here for $1.

From Pantoll Station, it's 4.2 miles by car to **East Peak Summit**; take Pantoll Rd and then panoramic Ridgecrest Blvd to the top. Parking is $6 and a 10-minute hike leads to the top.

From Pantoll Station, the **Steep Ravine Trail** follows a wooded creek on to the coast (about 2.1 miles each way). For a longer hike, veer right (northwest) after 1.5 miles onto the **Dipsea Trail**, which meanders through trees for 1 mile before ending at Stinson Beach.

Just off Hwy 1 about 1 mile south of Stinson Beach is **Steep Ravine Environmental Campground** (☎ reservations 800-444-7275; campsites/cabins $15/60). This place has six beachfront campsites and several rustic five-person cabins overlooking the ocean. Reservations can – and should – be made seven months ahead.

To reach Pantoll Station by car, take Hwy 1 to the Panoramic Hwy and follow the signs.

The closest public transportation can get you (weekends only) is to the Mountain Home Inn. From Marin City, Mill Valley, Bolinas and Stinson Beach, take the **West Marin Stagecoach** (☎ 415-526-3239; www.marintransit.org; $2).

MUIR WOODS NATIONAL MONUMENT

Gazing up at the world's tallest trees is an experience to be had only in Northern California and a small part of Oregon. The old-growth redwoods at **Muir Woods** (☎ 415-388-2595; admission $3; ✆ 8am-sunset, to 5pm in winter), just 12 miles north of the Golden Gate Bridge, is the closest redwood stand to San Francisco. Try to come midweek, as soon as it opens, or late in the afternoon, when tour buses are less of a problem. But even at busy times, a short hike will get you out of the densest crowds.

Hiking

The brochure map you'll be given at the entrance shows only the most basic loops. If you are going to venture on a more substantial hike, buy the comprehensive park map ($1) when you pay the park fee.

The walk most people do is the **Main Trail Loop** (0.5 to 2 miles) alongside Redwood Creek to the 1000-year-old trees at **Cathedral Grove**; it returns via **Bohemian Grove**, where the tallest tree in the park stands 254ft high. The **Dipsea Trail** is a good 2-mile hike up to the top of aptly named **Cardiac Hill**.

Getting There & Away

By far the least stressful option – on you and the environment – is to take the **Rte 66 Muir Woods shuttle** (www.goldengate.org), which operates (at the time of writing) only on weekends and holidays, May to September. It costs $2 for the round-trip ($1 for kids and seniors) and runs every 30 minutes. There are two pickup spots in Mill Valley, from the Manzanita Park & Ride or across the street at Pohono St and Hwy 1. From Marin City, pickup is at Donohue St at the Gateway shopping center. Note that on the return trip to Mill Valley, the shuttle only stops at the Park & Ride, not at Pohono, so if you've parked at Pohono, just cross the street. Parking is free for shuttle users.

If you must drive, Muir Woods is 12 miles north of the Golden Gate Bridge. Driving north on Hwy 101, exit at Hwy 1 and continue north along Hwy 1/Shoreline Hwy to the Panoramic Hwy (a right-hand fork). Follow that for about 1 mile to Four Corners, where you turn left onto Muir Woods Rd.

THE COAST
Muir Beach

The longest row of mailboxes on the North Coast is found at the turnoff to Muir Beach from Hwy 1. There's not much town here, but the beach is pleasant and usually uncrowded.

There are superb views up and down the coast from the **Muir Beach Overlook**, located 2 miles north of Muir Beach. During WWII, watch was kept from the surrounding concrete lookouts for invading Japanese ships. Climb over the wooden gate and go down to the end of the overlook, where you may find yourself eye-to-beady-eye with some bird of prey or another. If it's a so-called Farallon day, you can make out the namesake islands.

When the fog rolls in, the jolly **Pelican Inn** (☎ 415-383-6000; www.pelicaninn.com; 10 Pacific Way; lunch dishes $10-15, dinner dishes $12-25) is where you'll want to end up. Downstairs, heavy timber beams support a liver-and-onions restaurant on one side and a wee pub on the other. Order a pint, throw some darts and bask in the fire's glow. Upstairs are seven impeccably English rooms, all with half-canopy beds (from $190).

About 2 miles north of the intersection with Panoramic Hwy and surrounded by magnificent redwoods, **Green Gulch Farm & Zen Center** (☎ 415-383-3134; www.sfzc.com; 1601 Shoreline Hwy) is a secluded Buddhist retreat above Muir Beach. Its Japanese-style **Lindisfarne Guest House** (☎ 415-383-3134; r $75-155) has 12 basic rooms surrounding a 30ft-tall atrium. Buffet-style vegetarian meals are offered, and bathrooms are shared.

On weekdays only, the **West Marin Stagecoach** (☎ 415-526-3239; www.marintransit.org) bus 61 connects Muir Beach with Marin City, Stinson Beach and Bolinas, and to Point Reyes Station on Wednesdays and Fridays ($2).

Stinson Beach

Stinson can't fail to please. It lacks sidewalks, so people amble to and fro without paying much mind to cars. Chockablock with restaurants, inns, gift shops and bookstores, Stinson feel downright cosmopolitan (until the sun sets, that is), relative to other Hwy 1 coast towns. Yet it preserves a barefoot bohemian sensibility; on a recent visit, across the street from each other, two jazz-accompanied spoken-word artists vied for café patrons' ears, while around the corner kids tried out the psychedelically colored hopscotch court, the trajectory of Frisbees forming graceful arcs over their heads.

Stinson's 3-mile beach has decent surfing, though frequent fog cover reminds you that you're not in Southern California. Swimming is only safe from May to mid-September. Call ☎ 415-868-1922 for weather and surf conditions. When the sun does make an appearance, escape the crowds by heading to the north end, where a lovely slender sand spit looks out over Bolinas.

Around 1 mile south of Stinson Beach is **Red Rock Beach**, a clothing-optional beach that attracts smaller crowds, probably because you have to scamper down a steep trail from Hwy 1 to reach it.

If you're traveling with kids, slip into the irresistibly named **Room of Self Discovery**, tucked behind the **Healing Arts Store** (3415 Hwy 1). It's a shed lined with miniature tchotchkes and a zen-garden sand tray in the center…the rest is up to you.

The **Stinson Beach Motel** (☎ 415-868-1712; www .stinsonbeachmotel.com; 3416 Hwy 1; r $125-200) is a collection of eight tidy beach cottages.

Patrons of the **Parkside Cafe** (☎ 415-868-1272; 43 Arenal Ave; dishes lunch $6-15, dinner $19-24) can glut themselves on small and large plates that trot the globe. Its breakfasts and lunches are supremely popular.

On weekdays, the **West Marin Stagecoach** (☎ 415-526-3239; www.marintransit.org) bus 61 connects Stinson Beach with Marin City, Bolinas and Muir Beach, and with Point Reyes Station

on Wednesdays and Fridays ($2). Take the 61w on weekends via Panoramic Hwy from Marin City.

Bolinas
pop 1246
Most well known for its tourist-allergic citizenry who kept removing the directional road signs until the highway department finally gave up posting them, Bolinas is a community that is close knit and highly self-aware. It supports a disproportionately large number of writers, artists and activists, a fact borne out all over town – the Lady of Bolinas Shrine on Wharf St, the fragments of art and poetry on the ramp down to the beach, and at least one barn sporting a giant peace sign. And almost in spite of itself, Bolinas can't help rewarding those who search it out.

From town you can go by foot to **Bolinas Beach**, which offers excellent strolling, especially if you're traveling with a four-legged friend. At high tide, however, you'll be hard-pressed to find much sand to walk on.

When you're ready for a fresh beach read, head to the **Bolinas Book Exchange** (22 Brighton Ave). For a quarter, you can surf the net for 15 minutes. Hours are at the proprietor's whim.

A crusty old place dating back to 1851, **Smiley's Schooner Saloon & Hotel** (☎ 415-868-1311; www .coastalpost.com/smileys; 41 Wharf Rd; r $79-89) has six simple but decent rooms (no phone or TV). The bar has live bands on weekends and is frequented by plenty of grizzled deadheads.

On a sunny day, the patio at **Coast Cafe** (☎ 415-868-2298; 48 Wharf Rd; dinner mains $14-25; Tue-Sun;) is where it's all at. Sample the freshest, organic food served by the freshest, organic staff. The menu is balanced between meat and meat-free options, and there's a kids menu.

On weekdays, the **West Marin Stagecoach** (☎ 415-526-3239; www.marintransit.org) bus 61 connects Bolinas with Marin City, Stinson Beach and Muir Beach, and with Point Reyes Station on Wednesdays and Fridays ($2). Take the 61w on weekends from Marin City, via Panoramic Hwy.

Olema
pop 245
About 2 miles south of Point Reyes Station, Olema was the main settlement in West Marin in the 1860s, during which the time the town supported six saloons – about the number

of buildings that make up the 'downtown' today. For years Olema held the distinction of being the epicenter of the 1906 Great Quake, but the most recent research finds that it was most likely a mile or so off the coast of San Francisco's Golden Gate Park. At the junction of Hwy 1 and Sir Francis Drake Blvd, Olema is a prime spot from which to explore Point Reyes.

The **Bear Valley Inn** (☎ 415-663-1777; www.bear vinn.com; Sir Francis Drake Blvd & Bear Valley Rd; r $115-180, cottage $150-200; ✗), built around 1910, epitomizes the West Marin B&B experience – organic breakfasts complete with fresh eggs, gracious proprietors and limitless nature at your doorstep. The three rooms are neat and snug. With sublime redwood floors, the light-flooded Hummingbird cottage sleeps six. The owners knock off 15% if you cycle here – call for details on the 20-mile ride from the Larkspur ferry. Free wi-fi.

The **West Marin Stagecoach** (☎ 415-526-3239; www.marintransit.org) bus 68 connects Olema with San Rafael, Point Reyes Station and Inverness Monday to Saturday ($2). On weekdays, the 61 takes the coastal route from Marin City up through Olema to Point Reyes Station.

Point Reyes Station

A patina of the Old West clings to this small town, which despite its diminutive size is the hub of West Marin. Dominated by dairies and ranches, the region was invaded by artists in the '60s, and is still beset by them, evidenced by the tie-dyed shops and Milquetoast galleries lining Main St. The all-organic **farmers market** is on Saturdays from 9am to 1pm.

With its nondescript brown carpet, **Station House Cafe** (☎ 415-663-1515; 11180 Shoreline Hwy; dinner dishes $9-19; ✆ 8am-9pm, to 10pm Fri & Sat, closed Wed) won't win any decorating awards, but the arrival of chef David Cook in 2006 has pumped some fresh blood into this Point Reyes institution. Organic bread? Niman Ranch meats? Produce grown behind the restaurant? Check, check, check. The Reuben sandwich and the oysters are exquisite.

At **Tomales Bay Foods & Cowgirl Creamery** (☎ 415-663-9335; 80 4th St; ✆ 10am-6pm Wed-Sun) you'll find picnic items and produce. Cowgirl Creamery's organic, artisan cheeses are made on the premises and are simply divine, though they average around $20 a pound. If you decide to splurge, try the Mt Tam triple-

cream cheese. Group tours ($3) can be arranged for 11:30am on Fridays. The attached **Cowgirl Cantina** delights epicures with gourmet soups, sandwiches and salads, from a menu that changes daily.

The only budget accommodations choice is the **Point Reyes Hostel** at the nearby Point Reyes National Seashore (see opposite).

The **West Marin Stagecoach** (☎ 415-526-3239; www.marintransit.org) bus 68 connects Point Reyes Station with San Rafael, Olema and Inverness Monday to Saturday ($2). On weekdays, the 61 takes the coastal route from Marin City up to Point Reyes Station.

Inverness
pop 995

The last outpost of civilization on your journey westward toward Point Reyes National Seashore, Inverness offers some outstanding lodging and dining choices among its hills and Tomales Bay shoreline.

West of town, stop for oysters at **Drakes Bay Oysters** (☎ 415-669-1149; www.drakesbayoyster.com; 17171 Sir Francis Drake Blvd; ✆ 8am-4:30pm); call ahead to make sure they've got some in stock.

At the Golden Hinde Inn, **Blue Waters Kayaking** (☎ 415-669-2600; www.bwkayak.com; 12938 Sir Francis Drake Blvd; kayak rental 2/4hrs $30/45) offers various Tomales Bay tours ($68 to $98), or you can rent a kayak and explore around secluded beaches by yourself.

The seven basic rooms (and one townhouse) at **Motel Inverness** (☎ 888-669-6909; 12718 Sir Francis Drake Blvd; r $109-275, room 8 & dacha $400-500) are comfy enough, with decor holding fast to the '70s, but the jewels of its crown are twofold: the Lodge, open to all guests and equipped with a champion pool table, fireplace and unbeatable views of the bay, and the pier-perched dacha, complete with splendiferous onion domes and room to sleep six.

Brimming with architectural curiosities, **Blackthorne Inn** (☎ 415-663-8621; www.blackthorne inn.com; 266 Vallejo Ave, Inverness Park; r $225-325) is a tree-house-reminiscent, adults-only inn built around a four-story wooden spiral staircase. The inn's three rooms are lovely, but a stay in the octagonal Eagles' Nest is honeymoon worthy, with private hot tub and a walkway connecting the Nest to the deck. Inverness Park is the tiny town 3.5-mile south of Inverness.

Three cottages make up **Rosemary B&B** (☎ 415-663-9338; www.rosemarybb.com) and all are sublime, built and maintained in harmony with nature, and equipped with wood stoves and vintage appliances. **Fir Tree** (from $295) is a two-bedroom house and sits on the land that **Rosemary Cottage** (from $255), which sleeps four in its cozy two rooms. Guests of both share access to a secluded hot tub. Nearby, the **Ark** (from $225), sleeps six and was built in the '70s by Cal architecture students using mostly recycled materials. All cottages have the option of an all-organic breakfast (for an additional $15).

The powers-that-be haven't fiddled much with the original leather-chair and stone-fireplace atmosphere at **Manka's Inverness Lodge** (☎ 415-669-1034; www.mankas.com; r $195-245), built as a hunting lodge in 1917. Local, wild game is still the order of the day for the $58 prix fixe dinners ($88 on Saturdays), though vegetarians can ask for alternatives. Mondays through Wednesdays see the chef loosening the geographic reins a bit. Upstairs are 14 rooms drenched in masculine elegance. To get to Manka's, turn left onto Argyle St, just north of town.

The **West Marin Stagecoach** (☎ 415-526-3239; www.marintransit.org) bus 68 connects Inverness with San Rafael, Olema and Point Reyes Monday to Saturday ($2). On weekdays, the 61 takes the coastal route (via Muir Beach, Stinson Beach and Bolinas) from Marin City up to Inverness via Point Reyes Station.

Point Reyes National Seashore

The windswept peninsula Point Reyes has a rough-hewn beauty that has always lured marine mammals and migratory birds as well as scores of shipwrecks, and more recently, cutthroat marijuana growers. In 2006 more than $50 million worth of pot was found all over West Marin, the growers having committed many dastardly environmental acts such as diverting streams filled with endangered species. When hiking, keep to the trails.

It was at Point Reyes that Sir Francis Drake landed to repair his ship the *Golden Hind* in 1579. During his five-week stay he mounted a brass plaque (which has never been found) claiming this land for England, and historians believe this happened at Drakes Beach. In 1595 the *San Augustine,* the first of scores of ships lost in these waters, went down.

Point Reyes National Seashore has 110 sq miles (72,000 acres) of pristine ocean beaches and the peninsula offers excellent hiking and camping opportunities. Be sure to bring warm

clothing, as even the sunniest days can quickly turn cold and foggy.

INFORMATION

The park headquarters, **Bear Valley Visitor Center** (☎ 415-464-5100; Bear Valley Rd; ☺ 9am-5pm Mon-Fri, 8am-5pm Sat & Sun), is near Olema and offers maps, information and worthwhile exhibits. You can also get information at the Point Reyes Lighthouse and the **Ken Patrick Center** (☎ 415-669-1250; ☺ 10am-5pm Sat, Sun & holidays) at Drakes Beach.

SIGHTS & ACTIVITIES

Limantour Rd, off Bear Valley Rd about 1 mile north of Bear Valley Visitor Center, leads to the Point Reyes Hostel and to **Limantour Beach**. The **Inverness Ridge Trail** heads from Limantour Rd up to 1282ft Mt Vision.

The **Point Reyes Lighthouse** (☎ 415-669-1534; ☺ 10am-4:30pm Thu-Mon) is at the very end of Sir Francis Drake Blvd. This spot, with its wild terrain and ferocious winds, offers the best **whale-watching** along the coast. The lighthouse sits below the headlands; to reach it requires descending (then ascending) more than 300 stairs. Nearby **Chimney Rock** is a fine short hike, especially in spring when the wildflowers are blossoming. A nearby viewing area allows you to spy on the park's **elephant-seal colony**.

On weekends during good weather, from late December through mid-April, the road to Chimney Rock and the lighthouse is closed to private vehicles. Instead you must take a shuttle ($5; children under 16 free) from **Drakes Beach**. Buy tickets at the Ken Patrick Center.

McClures Beach, near the north end, is a gem of a beach, with white sand, forceful surf, and excellent tide pools at low tide. Start the steep half-mile trail down to the beach at the end of Pierce Point Rd, where you can also access the stunning 3-mile blufftop walk to **Tomales Point** – through herds of Tule elk! (Keep your distance from the animals.)

SLEEPING

Just off Limantour Rd, the rustic and slightly threadbare **Point Reyes Hostel** (☎ 415-663-8811; dm from $16) lies in a secluded valley 2 miles from the ocean and is surrounded by hiking trails. The one private room (from $54) is reserved for families traveling with a child under the age of six.

SAN FRANCISCO &
THE BAY AREA

Point Reyes has four hike-in **campgrounds** (☎ 415-663-1092; sites $15) with pit toilets, untreated water and picnic tables (no fires). Permits are required; reserve at the Bear Valley Visitor Center or by calling ☎ 415-663-8054. Reaching the campgrounds requires a 2- to 6-mile hike.

GETTING THERE & AWAY

The slowest and curviest way to Point Reyes is along Hwy 1, through Stinson Beach and Olema. More direct is to exit Hwy 101 in San Rafael and follow Sir Francis Drake Blvd all the way to the tip of Point Reyes. For the latter route, if you're coming from the north, take the Central San Rafael exit and head west on 4th St, which turns into Sir Francis Drake Blvd. From the East Bay and San Francisco, follow signs for the Sir Francis exit. By either route, it's about 1½ hours to Olema from San Francisco.

Just north of Olema, where Hwy 1 and Sir Francis Drake Blvd come together, is Bear Valley Rd; turn left to reach the Bear Valley Visitor Center. If you're heading to the further reaches of Point Reyes, follow Sir Francis Drake Blvd through Point Reyes Station and out onto the peninsula, about an hour's drive.

On Saturdays, you can take the **West Marin Stagecoach** (☎ 415-526-3239; www.marintransit.org) bus 68, which cuts diagonally across the county from San Rafael to Inverness, and then on to Point Reyes National Seashore, dropping you at the Bear Valley Visitors Center ($2).

North Coast

Forget everything you've learned about California from the movies – unless you're a Hitchcock fan. The moody, isolated North Coast shatters the myth of sunny California: locals wear woolens, not bikinis. (Leave your Marc Jacobs home; pack Pendleton instead.) And unlike Southern California, there are no real freeways and barely any shopping malls. The trip here isn't about navigating the built environment, it's about finding your connection to the land. And wow, what stunning land it is.

Sun dapples through the canopy of towering redwoods, illuminating deep-green mosses and spiky ferns. Sea lions and elephant seals laze upon craggy rocks jutting out of the Pacific, barking and braying; beneath them sea cucumbers, orange starfish and white anemones cling to the rocks, despite the relentlessly pounding surf. In winter migrating whales breach offshore while eagles, falcons and vultures circle overhead.

Best of all, there's hardly anyone around. Looking for someplace to set down your yurt or escape the law? Look no further. There's a libertarian spirit on the North Coast that exists in few other places. Pot farmers live side by side with Republican loggers, and though they don't get along, they cut each other a wide swath. Take advantage of the solitude; this is where to bring your journal, watercolors or that novel you've been meaning to finish. Just don't forget your hiking boots.

HIGHLIGHTS

- Craning your neck at the world's tallest trees at **Redwood National Park** (p130)
- Spotting the San Andreas fault line from inside the 115ft-tall **Point Arena Lighthouse** (p95)
- Canoeing up California's longest undeveloped tidal estuary at **Big River** (p99), near Mendocino
- Howling at the moon from atop **King Peak** (p114) on the Lost Coast
- Feeling like you're driving a teeny-tiny Matchbox car along the **Avenue of the Giants** (p110)

Redwood ★
National Park

Avenue of the Giants ★

King Peak ★

Big River ★
Point Arena Lighthouse ★

Getting There & Away

Hwy 101 is the fast, inland route; Hwy 1 runs along the coast, then cuts inland and ends at Leggett, where it joins Hwy 101.

Amtrak (☎ 800-872-7245; www.amtrak.com) operates the *Coast Starlight* between Los Angeles and Seattle, with connecting bus services to several North Coast towns including Leggett and Garberville. Note that the train runs inland, not along the coast.

Greyhound (☎ 800-231-2222; www.greyhound.com) operates bus services up Hwy 101 from San Francisco to Santa Rosa, Ukiah, Willits, Rio Dell (near Scotia), Eureka and Arcata.

In Santa Rosa, the regional transit hub for bus services, **Golden Gate Transit** (☎ 707-541-2000, 415-923-2000; www.goldengate.org) bus 80 goes to SF, **Sonoma County Transit** (☎ 707-576-7433, 800-345-7433; www.sctransit.com) serves Sonoma County, and **Sonoma County Airport Express** (☎ 707-837-8700, 800-327-2024; www.airportexpressinc.com) operates buses to SFO and OAK airports.

The **Mendocino Transit Authority** (MTA; ☎ 707-462-1422, 800-696-4682; www.4mta.org) operates bus 65, which travels between Mendocino, Fort Bragg, Willits, Ukiah and Santa Rosa daily, with an afternoon return service. Bus 95 runs between Point Arena and Santa Rosa, via Jenner and Bodega Bay. Bus 75 heads north every weekday from Gualala to the Navarro River junction at Hwy 128, then runs inland through the Anderson Valley to Ukiah, returning in the afternoon. The North Coast route also heads out of Navarro River junction, passing through Albion, Little River, Mendocino and Fort Bragg, Monday to Friday. Please note: *Always flag down MTA buses!*

North of Mendocino County, the **Redwood Transit System** (☎ 707-443-0826; www.hta.org) operates buses Monday through Saturday between Scotia and Trinidad, stopping en route at Eureka and Arcata. **Redwood Coast Transit** (☎ 707-464-9314; www.redwoodcoasttransit.org) runs two buses a day, Monday to Saturday, between Crescent City, Klamath and Redwood National Park, with numerous stops along the way.

COASTAL HIGHWAY 1

Coastal Hwy 1 runs along vast stretches of rugged, largely undeveloped coastline that has been rigorously protected by local activists. In the 1960s, there were plans to turn the winding country road into a four-lane freeway, and subdivide the surrounding land into two-acre parcels. Can you imagine? It would have become another Southern California–style ecological nightmare. Instead the land looks as it always has, with fog-shrouded coves, rolling hills and dense forests. North of Jenner, grassy table bluffs yield to sheer cliffs as the road climbs hundreds of feet in twisty turns: apart from the Big Sur coast (p159), this is the premier coastal California drive (eat a fistful of crystallized ginger if you get car sick). The top destination is Mendocino (p97), but take time to investigate the many state parks en route, where you can spot lighthouses, whales and sea lions, and even walk along the San Andreas Fault.

BODEGA BAY
pop 950

When Alfred Hitchcock put Bodega Bay (and its tiny inland sister, Bodega) on the map in his 1963 film *The Birds*, it was a sleepy fishing village. Today it looks more like an East Coast seaside tourist town, with saltwater-taffy stands and giant dockside fish restaurants catering to tour buses. The gateway town to the Sonoma Coast, Bodega Bay makes a good base for exploring nearby beaches and dramatic coastal bluffs on a quick overnight trip from San Francisco, but if you have more than one night, there are prettier places to sleep further north (specifically Anchor Bay and Mendocino).

The town was saved from a terrible fate in 1962, when Pacific Gas & Electric (PG&E) attempted to build the world's largest nuclear power plant in the Bodega Bay Headlands – smack dab on the San Andreas Fault (duh!) – without permits from the Atomic Energy Commission (AEC). Thank heaven the AEC halted the project, but you can still see the enormous hole PG&E dug in the Headlands.

Orientation & Information

Hwy 1 runs along the east side of Bodega Harbor. On the west side, a peninsula resembling a crooked finger juts out to sea, forming the entrance to the harbor.

Business Services Unlimited (☎ 707-875-2183; 1400 Hwy 1, Pelican Plaza; per hr $12; ☻ 9am-5pm Mon-Fri, 10am-2pm Sat) Check email while doing wash at the launderette next door.

Sonoma Coast Visitors Center (☎ 707-875-3866; www.bodegabay.com; 850 Hwy 1; ☻ 9am-5pm Mon-Thu & Sat, to 6pm Fri, 10am-5pm Sun) Opposite the Tides

NORTH COAST

Wharf complex, the center provides information for the area north to Sea Ranch.

Sights & Activities

Outdoor activities are the major draw, but if you're an Asian-art lover, check out the fab collection of Japanese and California works at the **Ren Brown Collection Gallery** (☎ 707-875-2922; 1781 Hwy 1; ☺ 10am-5pm Wed-Sun).

Most views from the mainland are of the harbor. To see the ocean, head to Bodega Head, 265ft above sea level, where windswept grassy hills drop into the churning surf. Take the **Bodega Head trail** around the point, and look southward to spot Tomales Point, the northern tip of Pt Reyes – which is geologically related to Bodega Head – and eastward across the harbor. On a clear day, the views (and the whale-watching) are superb. Other fairly easy **hikes** here include a 3.75-mile trek to Bodega Dunes Campground and a 2.2-mile walk to Salmon Creek Ranch. To reach Bodega Head, go west from Hwy 1 onto Eastshore Rd, then turn right at the stop sign onto Bay Flat Rd. They don't call it 'Blow-dega Head' for nothing: bring a kite. **Candy & Kites** (☎ 707-875-3777; 1415 Hwy 1) sells single- and dual-line varieties.

For high romance, go horseback riding on the beach with **Chanslor Riding Stables** (☎ 707-875-3333; www.chanslor.com; 2660 Hwy 1). Conservationists: the ranch also offers excellent ecointerpretive horseback and electric-car tours of the surrounding watershed. Rides and tours range from $30 to $100.

On the oceanfront, **Bodega Harbour Golf Links** (☎ 707-875-3538; www.bodegaharbourgolf.com; green fees $45-90) is an 18-hole Scottish-style course designed by Robert Trent Jones Jr.

There's good seasonal surfing around Bodega Bay, depending on your level of expertise. **Bodega Bay Surf Shack** (☎ 707-875-3944; www.bodegabaysurf.com) rents boards ($15 per day), bicycles ($5 per hour), kayaks and wet suits, and offers surfing lessons and advice. **Bodega Bay Kayak** (☎ 707-875-8899; www.bodegabaykayak.com; 1580 Eastshore Rd) rents kayaks ($45 for four hours) and provides guided tours up quiet inland creeks. **Bodega Bay Pro Dive** (☎ 707-875-3054; www.bbprodive.com; 1275 Hwy 1) rents full gear for scuba diving ($60), but provides no instruction.

Make reservations for sport-fishing charters and, from December to April, popular whale-watching cruises. **Bodega Bay Sportfishing Center** (☎ 707-875-3344; www.usafishing.com; 1410 Bay Flat Rd), beside the Sandpiper Cafe, organizes harbor cruises ($15), full-day fishing trips ($75) and whale-watching excursions (adult/child $30/25); it also sells bait, tackle and fishing licenses. The **Boathouse** (☎ 707-875-3495; 1445 Hwy 1) also runs scheduled trips.

Festivals & Events

The **Bodega Bay Fishermen's Festival** in April is the big annual event and includes the blessing of the fleet, a flamboyant parade of vessels, an arts-and-crafts fair, kite-flying and feasting. The great **crab feed** takes place in February or March.

Sleeping

For a complete list of lodgings and rentals, contact the visitors center.

Bodega Harbor Inn (☎ 707-875-3594; www.bodegaharborinn.com; 1345 Bodega Ave; r $60-100, cottages $135-195) Half a block inland from Hwy 1, surrounded by grassy lawns, and furnished with both real and faux antiques, this modest blue-and-white shingled motel is the town's most economical option. Freestanding cottages have BBQ. Top choice for bargainistas.

Branscomb's Bodega Bay Inn (☎ 707-875-3388, 888-875-8733; www.bodegabayinn.com; 1588 Eastshore Rd; r incl breakfast $90-190) Local art fills this converted house, which feels like a cross between a B&B and a high-end hostel. There's no uniformity to the folksy decor (think Levitz furniture), but every room has a king-size bed. Outside there's a big garden courtyard. Wi-fi, too.

Chanslor Guest Ranch (☎ 875-2721; www.chanslorranch.com; 2660 Hwy 1; r $125-175) A mile north of town, this working horse ranch has six rooms, two with kitchenettes. This is one sweet place, with sweeping vistas across open grasslands to the sea.

Bodega Bay Lodge & Spa (☎ 707-875-3525, 800-368-2468; www.bodegabaylodge.com; 103 Hwy 1; r $170-295; ☺) This splurgeworthy lodge has rooms in satellite buildings overlooking marshlands and the sea. The more expensive the room, the more commanding the view. The look leans toward generic business-class fancy, but rooms are super-comfy, with high-thread-count sheets, feather pillows and all the usual amenities of a full-service hotel. Other features: fireplace rooms, ocean view pool, golf course, whirlpool, sauna, spa and fitness center.

Campgrounds fill up early. **Sonoma County Regional Park** (☎ information 707-875-3540, reservations 707-565-2267; campsites $18) operates **Doran Park** (201

Doran Beach Rd), which is best for tents, and **Westside Regional Park** (2400 Westshore Rd), best for RVs. It caters primarily to boaters and has windy exposures, beaches, hot showers, fishing and boat ramps.

Eating

Spud Point Crab Company (☎ 707-875-9472; 1860 Bay Flat Rd; dishes $7-10; 🕑 8:30am-5:30pm; 👶) In the classic tradition of dockside crab shacks, Spud Point makes sandwiches and salty-sweet crab cocktails served at picnic tables overlooking the marina. Take Bay Flat Rd to get here.

Dog House (☎ 707-875-2441; 573 Hwy 1; dishes $5-9; 🕑 11am-6pm; 👶) The Dog House has Vienna beef hot dogs, handcut fries and *real* shakes made with handscooped ice cream. There's even a view.

Gourmet Au Bay (☎ 707-875-9875; 913 Hwy 1; 🕑 11am-6pm Thu-Tue) Sit on the back deck of this wine bar with a glass of zinfandel and sniff the salt air.

Sandpiper Dockside Cafe & Restaurant (☎ 707-875-2278; 1410 Bay Flat Rd; mains $11-20; 🕑 8am-8pm; 👶) The classic tartare-sauce and fried-fish joint, Sandpiper overlooks the bay and serves straightforward, middle-of-the-road seafood with no surprises. There's breakfast too. Turn seaward from Hwy 1 onto Eastshore Rd and then go straight at the stop sign to the marina.

Seaweed Cafe (☎ 707-875-2700; www.seaweedcafe .com; 1580 Eastshore Dr; brunch mains $10-18, dinner $18-27; 🕑 brunch Sat & Sun, dinner Thu-Sun) Art heads and food-savvy *bon vivants* flock to this colorful little café, the culinary center point of the Sonoma County coast. Run by a French chef equally passionate about artistry and sustainability, Seaweed's dynamic menu uses farm-fresh greens, seafood, poultry and wine exclusively from indie purveyors within 30 miles of Bodega Bay. When there's red meat, it's an unusual cut like elk or beef cheeks. The menu's pricey, but you're paying for craftsmanship and supporting local farmers.

For seafood by the docks, **Tides Wharf & Restaurant** (☎ 875-3652; 835 Hwy 1; breakfast $6-12, lunch $12-22, dinner $15-25; 👶) and **Lucas Wharf Restaurant & Bar** (☎ 875-3522; 595 Hwy 1; dishes $14-25; 🕑 lunch & dinner; 👶) have views and similar menus of clam chowder, fried fish and coleslaw. Although Tides boasts a great fish market, Lucas Wharf feels less like a factory and has a take-out deli. Don't be surprised if a bus pulls up outside either of them.

SONOMA COAST STATE BEACH

The craggy shores and foggy coves of **Sonoma Coast State Beach** (☎ 707-875-3483) are actually a series of beaches, separated by crumbling, rocky headlands. The beaches stretch for 17 miles from Bodega Head to Vista Trail, north of Jenner. However inviting the water seems, these are *not* swimming beaches. The surf is treacherous, with rip currents and unpredictable sneaker waves, and it's often unsafe to wade. Never turn your back on the ocean, stay above the high-tide line and keep an eye on kids.

Heading north along the coast, notable beaches include **Bodega Dunes**; 2-mile-long **Salmon Creek Beach**; sandy **Portuguese** and **Schoolhouse Beaches**; **Duncan's Landing**, where small boats unload; **Shell Beach**, for tidepooling and beachcombing; and scenic **Goat Rock**, with its harbor-seal colony at the Russian River mouth. Most beaches are connected by coastal trails.

Bodega Dunes Campground (☎ 800-444-7275; www.reserveamerica.com; campsites $25) has high sand dunes and hot showers near a long, sandy beach – but a foghorn sounds all night, so bring earplugs. Another 5 miles further north, year-round **Wright's Beach Campground** (☎ 800-444-7275; www.reserveamerica.com; campsites $25) has popular beachside sites without much privacy; the surf is *treacherous*. People drown here: stay out of the water!

On Willow Creek Rd, inland from Hwy 1 on the southern side of the Russian River Bridge, are two first-come, first-served **environmental campgrounds** (campsites $15): Willow Creek and Pomo Canyon. Willow Creek has no water; Pomo Canyon has cold-water faucets. Both are usually open April to November.

JENNER
pop 170

There's not much here, but what a locale! Perched on high hills above the mouth of the Russian River, 15 minutes north of Bodega Bay, tiny Jenner is more of a crossroads than a town, where Hwy 116 (aka River Rd) originates and cuts inland along the Russian River into western Sonoma County's wine-growing regions (see p90). Look for the **harbor-seal colony** at the river's mouth; pups are born March to August.

North of here, the wide terraces of southern Sonoma yield to the rugged cliffs of the North Coast. Highway 1 climbs and twists, with drop-dead vistas out to sea. Stay focused,

DETOUR: HEALDSBURG & SONOMA WINE COUNTRY

Mention Wine Country and everyone thinks Napa, but you needn't fight inland traffic to sample some damn good California wines. Unless you're a cabernet sauvignon fetishist, stick to Sonoma County, which is far less fussy and closer to the coast – and unlike in fancy-pants Napa, nobody in Sonoma will care if you have bad hair.

From Jenner, head inland via Hwy 116, along the banks of the Russian River, 13 miles to Guerneville, where Main Street turns into River Rd. Continue eastward on River Rd for 5 miles and turn left onto Westside Rd. Wind your way 13 miles to Healdsburg, your ultimate destination. (If you miss the left turn, continue to Forestville and turn left on Wohler Rd, cross the Wohler Bridge, and turn right onto Westside Rd.)

Healdsburg lies between three dramatically different wine-producing valleys, where most wineries are free or charge only $2 to $5 for tastings; most allow picnicking too. Choose your destination based upon your favorite varietal – and avoid the big-name corporate wineries; stick to the little guys for real insight into local culture. Russian River (which you drive along en route from Jenner) gets blanketed with summertime fog, providing an ideal climate for pinot noir and chardonnay. Standouts along Westside Rd include **Roshambo** (☎ 707-431-2051, 888-525-9463; www.roshambowinery.com; 3000 Westside Rd; tastings free), with its way-cool pop-art gallery and pierced-and-tattooed wine-bar servers; head for the chardonnay and zinfandel. **De La Montoya** (☎ 707-433-3711; www.dlmwine.com; 2651 Westside Rd, at Foreman Lane; tastings free) makes a lip-smacking 'summer white' blend and gewürztraminer. Taste fab zins inside a geodesic dome at **Armida** (☎ 707-433-2222; www.armida.com; 2201 Westside Rd; tastings free, reserves $2).

North of Healdsburg, Dry Creek Valley is warmer and produces good zinfandel and sauvignon blanc; most people take busy Dry Creek Rd, but for a meandering country drive, take the narrow, slow and undulating West Dry Creek Rd instead, especially if you're on a bicycle. At the valley's north end, always-fun **Bella** (☎ 707-473-9171, 866-572-3552; www.bellawinery.com; 9711 W Dry Creek Rd; tasting free) has caves built into the hillside and makes big reds. Across the road, **Preston Vineyards** (☎ 707-433-3327, 800-305-9707; www.prestonvineyards.com; 9282 W Dry Creek Rd; tastings $3) is a vintage-19th-century organic farm with citrus-y sauvignon blanc and Rhône varietals; bring a picnic or buy snacks here – the tasting fee is refundable with a purchase. Though its tasting room is a windowless garage, **Unti** (☎ 707-433-5590; www.untivineyards.com; 4202 Dry Creek Rd; ☺ Sat & Sun, by appointment Mon-Fri) makes a big, fat, slutty syrah; if you love wine, don't miss it.

East of Hwy 101, gorgeous Alexander Valley is the last valley inland before Napa. Summers are hot. Consequently you'll find cabernet sauvignon, merlot and warm-weather chardonnay, but there's fine sauvignon blanc and zinfandel too. Wow, what a view from **Stryker Sonoma** (☎ 707-433-1944; www.strykersonoma.com; 5110 Hwy 128; tastings free), whose modern concrete-and-glass, hilltop tasting room overlooks the valley; head for the zin and sangiovese. For picnics and treats at the valley's south end, stop at the **Jimtown Store** (☎ 707-433-1212; www.jimtown.com; 6706 Hwy 128, Jimtown).

and use turnouts to allow nonsightseers to pass you.

It seems like half the town belongs to **Jenner Inn & Cottages** (☎ 707-865-2377, 800-732-2377; www.jennerinn.com; 10400 Hwy 1; creekside r $108-178, ocean view r $158-278, cottages $178-398; ☐), which offers everything from vacation houses to seaside cottages to river-view guest rooms. Rates include breakfast and afternoon tea. Most rooms have no TV; some are pet friendly.

There are simple ocean view cottages and comfortable knotty pine–paneled rooms, with no TVs or phones, at **River's End** (☎ 707-865-2484; www.rivers-end.com; 11048 Hwy 1; r & cabins $130-175, lunch

$14-26, dinner $20-34), a good spot for an overnight hideaway. It has a good, but overpriced, restaurant open Thursday to Monday. Come for drinks instead.

For good home-style cookin', head 10 minutes inland on Hwy 116 (River Rd) to Duncan's Mills and eat at **Cape Fear Café** (☎ 707-865-9246; 25191 Hwy 116; breakfast & lunch $8-14, dinner $16-24; ☺) and drink at the **Blue Heron** (☎ 707-865-9135; 25300 Steelhead Blvd; ☺ Tue-Sun). For a major splurge at a top Wine Country table, drive 40 minutes east to the romantic **Farmhouse Inn** (☎ 707-887-3300; www.farmhouseinn.com; 7871 River Rd; mains $25-32; ☺ dinner Thu-Sun).

Built around a leafy central square called the Plaza, Healdsburg is Sonoma County's new gastronomic capital. On the Plaza you can sample some of the region's best artisan products – nutty cheeses, small-batch chocolate, crusty breads, and fruit-dense gelato – without having to drive anywhere. Start at **Plaza Farms** (☎ 707-433-2345; 106 Matheson St; ☺ 10am-7pm), where 10 local purveyors share a single storefront. If you've never done a comparative taste test of olive oil, stop by Plaza Farms' DaVero, where you can sip three dramatically different vibrant and fruity varieties, including a delish Meyer lemon–infused oil. Bellwether Farms makes pungent sheep- and cows-milk cheeses that pair perfectly with Sonoma's spicy, jammy red wines, which you can sample from winemakers David Coffaro or Philip Staley at Plaza Farms. **Bovolo** (☎ 707-431-2962; 106 Matheson St; dishes $7-16; ☺ 11am-9pm Thu-Tue, 9am-9pm Sat & Sun, shorter in winter), the order-at-the-counter café in the back of the building, cures its own meats for succulent antipasti plates, crafts pizzas just like in Italy – thin-crusted and crackery, with combinations like prosciutto, arugula and fontina cheese – and turns its own gelato. Around the corner from Plaza Farms, pick up gooey sticky buns and dense brownies from **Downtown Bakery** (☎ 707-431-2719; www .downtownbakery.net; 308A Center St; ☺ 7am-5:30pm), followed by a cup of joe at **Flying Goat Coffee** (☎ 707-433-9081; www.flyinggoatcoffee.com; 324 Center St; ☺ 7am-6pm), where the locally roasted brew puts Starbucks to shame.

At dinner, there are two splurgeworthy spots. Sit on the veranda of a fabulous Victorian mansion at **Madrona Manor** (☎ 707-433-4231, 800-258-4003; www.madronamanor.com; 1001 Westside Rd; mains $17-29; r $195-445; ☺ dinner), a grand spot to pop the question, then spend the night. Or don your best Armani and sample the latest in grande-luxe Euro-Cal cuisine at **Cyrus** (☎ 707-433-3311; www.cyrusrestaurant.com; 29 North St; fixed-price menus $52-85; ☺ dinner Wed-Mon), one of the Wine Country's top tables. For something earthier, head north to **Santi** (☎ 707-857-1790; www .tavernasanti.com; 21047 Geyserville Ave, Geyserville; lunch $9-14, dinner $15-25; ☺ lunch Thu-Mon, dinner nightly) for rustic Italian cooking.

If you decide to spend the night, the best motel in Healdsburg is the **Best Western Dry Creek Inn** (☎ 707-433-0300, 800-222-5784; 198 Dry Creek Rd; r $129-139; ☒ ☒). Better yet, **Healdsburg Inn on the Plaza** (☎ 707-433-6991, 800-234-1425; www.healdsburginn.com; 110 Matheson St; r $200-250 Mon-Fri, $220-275 Sat & Sun; ☒) has airy, fresh-looking rooms with fine linens and gas fireplaces. For maximum chic, head directly to the **Hotel Healdsburg** (☎ 707-431-2800, 800-889-7188; www.hotelhealdsburg.com; 25 Matheson St; r incl breakfast $260-490; ☒ ☒ ☒). Or scope out some of the motels in Guerneville, back along the Russian River, where you can find cheaper rates.

If you just can't get enough of Sonoma County, pick up a map and drive to Sonoma Valley, then end up in the town of Sonoma, where you can sip wine – legally – under the giant trees on Sonoma Plaza, California's largest town square. If you must go to Napa, the north end of the valley is far prettier than the workaday city of Napa. Drive up the valley on Hwy 29, then back down via the parallel Silverado Trail; you'll spot about 200 wineries along the way, many of them architecturally stunning. Expect *extremely* heavy traffic on summer weekends.

FORT ROSS STATE HISTORIC PARK

In March 1812, a group of 25 Russians and 80 Alaskans (including members of the Kodiak and Aleutian tribes) built a wooden fort here, near a Kashaya Pomo village. The southernmost outpost of the 19th-century Russian fur trade on America's Pacific coast, Fort Ross was established as a base for sea-otter hunting operations and trade with Alta California, and for growing crops for Russian settlements in Alaska. The Russians dedicated the fort in August 1812 and occupied it until 1842, when it was abandoned because the sea-otter population had been decimated and agricultural production had never taken off.

Eleven miles north of Jenner, **Fort Ross State Historic Park** (☎ 707-847-3286; 19005 Hwy 1; admission per car $6; ☺ 10am-4:30pm) presents an accurate reconstruction of the fort. The original buildings were sold, dismantled and carried off to Sutter's Fort, in Sacramento, during the Gold Rush. The **visitors center** (☎ 707-847-3437; ☺ 10am-4:30pm) has historical displays and an excellent bookstore on Californian and Russian history and nature. Ask about hikes to the Russian cemetery.

On **Fort Ross Heritage Day**, the last Saturday in July, costumed volunteers bring the fort's

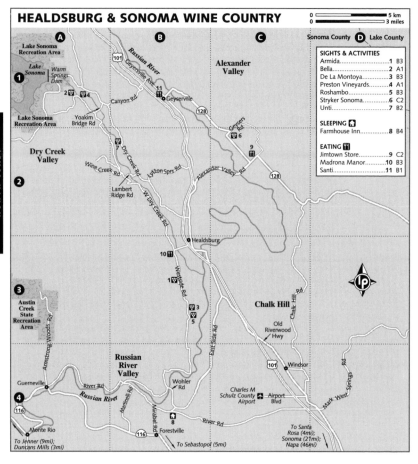

HEALDSBURG & SONOMA WINE COUNTRY

SIGHTS & ACTIVITIES	
Armida...............................1	B3
Bella.................................2	A1
De La Montoya................3	B3
Preston Vineyards...........4	A1
Roshambo......................5	B3
Stryker Sonoma...............6	C2
Unti................................7	B2

SLEEPING 🏠	
Farmhouse Inn.................8	B4

EATING 🍴	
Jimtown Store.................9	C2
Madrona Manor............10	B3
Santi.............................11	B1

history to life; check the website www.parks .ca.gov or call the visitors center for other special events.

Timber Cove Inn (☎ 707-847-3231, 800-987-8319; www.timbercoveinn.com; 21780 N Hwy 1; r Sat & Sun $110, ocean view from $222), a dramatic and quirky '60s-modern seaside inn, was once a top-of-the-line luxury lodge but today it needs work – lots of it. The grounds are overrun with raccoons, and the koi pond needs a good scrubbing, but the architectural shell is still stunning. You'll love it or hate it. If you're a nonrisk-taking, skirt-and-sweater traveler, keep heading north and choose Sea Ranch Lodge (opposite) instead.

Reef Campground (☎ 707-847-3286; campsites $15; ⌚ Apr-Oct), 2 miles south of the park, has first-come, first-served campsites (cold water, no showers) in a sheltered seaside gully, popular with abalone divers.

Stillwater Cove Regional Park (☎ information 707-847-3245, reservations 707-565-2267; www.sonoma-county .org/parks; 22455 N Hwy 1; campsites $18), 2 miles north of Timber Cove, has campsites (17 reservable, three first-come, first-served), hot coin-operated showers and hiking under Monterey pines. If Reef is full, you can usually get a site here.

SALT POINT STATE PARK

If you stop at only one park along the Sonoma Coast, make it 6000-acre **Salt Point State Park** (☎ 707-847-3221; admission per car $6), where sandstone cliffs drop dramatically into the sea and hiking trails crisscross windswept prairies and wooded hills, connecting pygmy forests and coastal coves rich with tide pools. The 6-mile-wide park is bisected by the San Andreas Fault – the rock on the east side is vastly different from that on the west. Check out the eerily beautiful *tafonis*, honeycombed-sandstone formations, near Gerstle Cove. For a good roadside photo op, there's a pullout at mileage marker 45, with views of decaying redwood shacks, grazing goats and headlands jutting to the sea.

For views of the pristine coastline, walk to the platform overlooking **Sentinel Rock**; it's just a short stroll from the Fisk Mill Cove parking lot, at the park's north end. Just south, **Stump Beach** has picnic areas with firepits and beach access. Further south, seals laze at **Gerstle Cove Marine Reserve**, one of California's first underwater parks (for shellfish biotoxins alerts, call ☎ 800-553-4133). Tread lightly around tide pools, and don't lift the rocks: even a glimpse of sunlight can kill some critters. Kids can check out an 'Adventure Pack' from the Gerstle Cove entrance station or the tiny **visitors center** (☎ 11am-3pm Sat & Sun), and use it to ID animals and plants in tide pools.

If it's springtime, you *must* see **Kruse Rhododendron State Reserve**. Growing abundantly in the forest's filtered light, magnificent, pink rhododendrons reach heights of over 30ft; turn east from Hwy 1 onto Kruse Ranch Rd, then follow the signs. A 2-mile mountain-biking trail connects the reserve and campgrounds.

The **Salt Point Lodge** (☎ 707-847-3234, 800-956-3437; www.saltpointlodgebarandgrill.com; 23255 Hwy 1, Jenner; r $90-140) has plain motel rooms and a restaurant; the kids playground is awesome (dig the slide!).

Two campgrounds, **Woodside** and **Gerstle Cove** (☎ 800-444-7275; www.reserveamerica.com; campsites $25), both signposted off Hwy 1, have campsites with cold water. Inland Woodside is well protected by Monterey pines. Gerstle Cove's trees burned over a decade ago and have only grown halfway back; it's actually kind of cool and ghostly looking, the dead snags towering above the thick new green growth, especially when the fog twirls between the branches. (Divers: Choose Gerstle Cove.) Walk-in **environmental campsites** (campsites $10) are half a mile from the parking area, on Woodside campground's east side.

SEA RANCH
pop 500

Approved for construction prior to the existence of the watchdog Coastal Commission, before anyone was talking about 'slow growth,' the upmarket subdivision of Sea Ranch sprawls 10 miles along the coast, and except for a lodge and small store, it's entirely residential. For supplies and gasoline, go to Gualala. Strict zoning laws require that houses be constructed of weathered wood only. According to *The Sea Ranch Design Manual*: 'This is not a place for the grand architectural statement; it's a place to explore the subtle nuances of fitting in…' Indeed. Though there are some lovely and recommended short-term rentals here, don't break any community rules – like throwing wild parties – or security will come knockin'.

After years of litigation, public throughways onto private beaches have been legally mandated. Hiking trails lead from roadside parking lots to the sea and along the bluffs (don't trespass on adjacent lands though). **Stengel Beach** (Hwy 1 mileage marker 53.96) has a beach-access staircase, **Walk-On Beach** (mileage marker 56.53) provides wheelchair access and **Shell Beach** (mileage marker 55.24) also has beach-access stairs; parking costs $4. For hiking details, including maps, contact the **Sea Ranch Association** (☎ 707-785-2444; www.tsra.org).

Sea Ranch Lodge (☎ 707-785-2371, 800-732-7262; www.searanchlodge.com; 60 Sea Walk Dr; r incl breakfast $230-395), a marvel of stark, '60s-modern California architecture, has spacious, cushy rooms, many with dramatic views; some have hot tubs and fireplaces. Recently acquired by Big Sur's famous Post Ranch Inn (p163), the lodge is undergoing upgrades; rates are sure to rise, so get in while you can. The fine contemporary restaurant serves throughout the day. Golf packages are available.

North of the lodge, stop for a meditation at Sea Ranch's iconic nondenominational **chapel** (Hwy 1 mileage marker 55.66), shaped like a wizard's hat; it's on the inland side of the highway.

Depending on the season, it can be surprisingly affordable to rent a house here; contact **Rams Head Realty** (☎ 707-785-2427, 800-785-3455; www.ramshead-realty.com), **Sea Ranch Rentals** (☎ 707-884-4235; www.searanchrentals.com), **Sea Ranch Vacation Rentals** (☎ 800-643-8899; www.searanchgetaway.com) or **Sea Ranch Escape** (☎ 888-732-7262; www.888searanch.com).

NORTH COAST

For crusty artisan breads and delicious pastries, visit **Two Fish Baking Co** (☎ 707-785-2443; 355090 Verdant View Dr, off Annapolis Rd; 7am-2pm Wed-Sun).

GUALALA
pop 585

Two-and-a-half hours north of San Francisco, Gualala was founded as a lumber-mill town in the 1860s; now it's the commercial center for the northern Sonoma–southern Mendocino coasts (the grocery store is excellent). Downtown is kinda cute, but bad zoning laws have permitted the construction of ugly buildings that hog the ocean view, and unlanterned high-wattage street lights adversely affect stargazing. It's much prettier just outside of town.

Redwood Coast Chamber of Commerce (☎ 707-884-1080, 800-778-5252; www.redwoodcoastchamber.com) has local business information. The **Dolphin Arts Gallery** (☎ 707-884-3896; 39225 Hwy 1; 10am-5pm), behind the post office, is the unofficial visitors center, with maps and information. Pick up books by regional authors at **Four-Eyed Frog Books** (☎ 707-884-1333; 39138 S Hwy 1).

The area's cultural hub, **Gualala Arts Center** (☎ 707-884-1138; www.gualalaarts.org; 9am-4pm Mon-Fri, noon-4pm Sat & Sun) has changing exhibitions, classes and musical performances in an outdoor grove, and organizes the worthwhile **Art in the Redwoods Festival** in August. Head inland along Old State Rd, at the south of town.

South of downtown, the 195-acre **Gualala Point Regional Park** (☎ 707-785-2377, reservations 707-565-2267; www.sonoma-county.org/parks; 42401 Hwy 1; day-use $5, campsites $18) has good camping and wooded hiking trails up the Gualala River.

In summer a sand spit forms at the mouth of the Gualala River, cutting it off from the ocean and turning it into a warm-water lake. **Adventure Rents** (☎ 707-884-4386, 888-881-4386; www.adventurerents.com) rents canoes and kayaks and provides instruction.

Ocean view motels line the main drag. The first choice is the straightforward, better-than-average **Surf Motel** (☎ 707-884-3571, 888-451-7873; www.gualala.com; r $95-120, ocean view r $135-179), which has cute touches like denim bedspreads.

There's no place like magical **St Orres Inn** (☎ 707-884-3303, dining room ☎ 707-884-3335; www.saintorres.com; 36601 Hwy 1; B&B $90-130, cottages $120-350, mains $40), famous for its trippy, redwood, Russian-inspired architecture. The main hotel has dramatic rough-hewn timbers and copper domes. On the property's 90 acres, handbuilt cottages range from rustic to luxurious. If you can swing it, eat once at the inn's dining room, open for dinner only, which serves oh-so-precious California cuisine in one of the coast's most romantic rooms. The menu never changes and the waiter's litany of nightly 'specials' is so long you'll need a notebook to keep up, but the food is very good.

Inland along Old State Rd camp (and hike) in redwoods at **Gualala River Redwood Park** (☎ 707-884-3533; www.gualalapark.com; day-use $10, campsites $36-42; Memorial Day–Labor Day).

For breakfast or lunch, stop for sandwiches, bagels, cakes and locally roasted coffee at **Trinks** (☎ 707-884-1713; 39410 S Hwy 1; 7am-5pm Mon-Sat, 8am-4pm Sun).

Smoked meats and Texas-style, wood-pit BBQ are the specialties at **Bones Roadhouse** (☎ 707-884-1188; 38920 S Hwy 1; 11:30am-9pm); if you're riding a Harley, you'll fit right in. On weekends there's live blues.

The hands-down best restaurant this side of Mendocino, bohemian **Pangaea** (☎ 707-884-9669; www.pangaeacafe.com; 39165 S Hwy 1; mains $22-35; dinner Wed-Sun) serves an eclectic, soulful menu of hearty dishes such as brined pork loin with polenta and bacon, and halibut with corn succotash. Reservations essential.

Of the two groceries, **Surf Supermarket** (☎ 707-884-4184; 39250 S Hwy 1) is best, with excellent wines and meat. If you're barbecuing, stock up here.

ANCHOR BAY
pop 500

Ten minutes north of Gualala, blink-and-miss-it Anchor Bay is the perfect place to disappear. There's not much other than two exceptional inns, a grocery, and heading north, a string of secluded, hard-to-find beaches. At night, fall asleep to the braying of sea lions.

Seven miles north of town, pull off at mileage marker 11.41 for **Schooner Gulch State Beach** (☎ 707-937-5804). A trail leads down cliffs to a sandy beach with tide pools. Bear right at the fork in the trail to reach **Bowling Ball Beach**, the next beach north, where at low tide rows of big, round rocks resemble bowling balls – but only at low tide. Consult tide tables for Arena Cove. The forecast low tide must be lower than +1.5ft on the tide chart; otherwise the rocks remain covered with water.

Perched on a hillside beneath towering trees and lovely gardens, **North Coast Country Inn** (☎ 707-884-4537, 800-959-4537; www.northcoast countryinn.com; 34591 S Hwy 1; r incl breakfast $185-225) has six extrabig, oh-so-cozy rooms with open-beam ceilings, fluffy down duvets, fireplaces, board games and private entrances. Some have kitchenettes. A hillside hot tub sweetens the deal. Pet-friendly.

ourpick **Mar Vista Cottages** (☎ 707-884-3522, 877-855-3522; www.marvistamendocino.com; 35101 S Hwy 1; 1-bedroom cottages $140-205, 2-bedroom cottages $200-230) is our favorite escape on the entire California coast. All 12 immaculate, vintage-1930s vacation cottages are outfitted with everything you need – delicious beds with feather-light duvets, comfy reading chairs, and full kitchens – and nothing you don't. On the 9-acre grounds are river-rock barbecues, hammocks, a redwood soaking tub, and organic grazing garden where you can snip herbs for omelettes you make using fresh eggs from the chickens outside. Across the road there's a hidden beach. Families and dogs are welcome. If you're looking for a retro-cozy hideaway cottage, this is it.

Shop and eat in Gualala. Pick up last-minute items at the good but pricey **Anchor Bay Store** (☎ 707-884-4245; Hwy 1). Next door are two so-so eateries.

POINT ARENA
pop 400

Thirty minutes north of Gualala, tiny downtown Point Arena looks like Main Street USA, but the centerpiece of the former fishing village is the namesake windswept point where a lighthouse has stood since 1908. **Point Arena Lighthouse** (☎ 707-882-2777; www.pointarenalighthouse.com; adult/child $5/1; 10am-4:30pm;) stands 10 stories high and is 2 miles north of town. It's the only lighthouse in California you can climb up. Check in at the museum, then ascend the 145 steps to the top and see the Fresnel lens and the jaw-dropping view. Dig the view of the San Andreas Fault to the east. Very cool.

One mile down Lighthouse Rd from Hwy 1, look for the Bureau of Land Management (BLM) signs on the left indicating the 1132-acre **Stornetta Public Lands** (☎ 707-468-4000; www.blm.gov), which has fabulous bird-watching, hiking on terraced rock past sea caves, and access to hidden coves. Scope your hike from atop the lighthouse.

Rent one of the three-bedroom former **Coast Guard homes** (homes $125-225) – think tract houses – next to the lighthouse. Contact the lighthouse keepers for more details.

A mile west of town at Arena Cove, there's a tourist restaurant, a small hotel, an ugly pier and the **Coast Guard House Inn** (☎ 707-882-2442; www.coastguardhouse.com; 695 Arena Cove; r $155-225), a 1901 Cape Cod–style house and cottage, with water-view rooms.

In downtown Point Arena, the **Sea Shell Inn** (☎ 707-882-2000; 135 Main St; r $55-70, str $90;) is the cheapest motel within 100 miles.

Downtown, **Carlini's Cafe** (☎ 707-882-2942; 206 Main St; dishes $5-8; breakfast & lunch Thu-Tue) serves the town's best food. Make it a point to stop at **Franny's Cup & Saucer** (☎ 707-882-2500; 213 Main St; 8am-5pm Wed-Sat) for big-city-quality pastries and kick-ass ginger snaps. Refuel on all-organic burritos at **El Burrito** (☎ 707-882-2910; 165 Main St; 11am-7pm) or pick up sandwiches, coffee and organic groceries at the **Record** (☎ 707-882-3663; 265 Main St; 7am-8pm Mon-Sat, 8am-6pm Sun), which has internet access.

Arena Cinema (☎ 707-882-3456; 214 Main St) shows mainstream and art films in a beautifully restored movie house. Sue, the ticket seller, has been in that booth for 40 years. Got a question about Point Arena? Ask Sue.

MANCHESTER STATE PARK & BEACH

The surf positively roars at this 5-mile-long, windswept **state beach** (☎ 707-882-2463), where long, rolling breakers pound the driftwood-littered coastline, smack dab on the San Andreas Fault. If you're looking to spend the day at a beach, this one's tremendous. Take the turnoff 9 miles north of Point Arena.

Ross Ranch (☎ 707-877-1834; www.elkcoast.com/ross ranch) at Irish Beach, 5 miles north, arranges two-hour horseback beach ($60) and mountain ($50) rides; make reservations.

Just before Manchester beach, an excellent **campground** (campsites $15) has grassy sites with cold water. Ten nonreservable **environmental campsites** (campsites $15) are hidden in the dunes, and are a 1.5-mile walk from the parking area; these have untreated creek water.

Closer to Hwy 1, **Mendocino Coast KOA** (☎ 707-882-2375, 800-562-4188; www.manchesterbeachkoa.com; tent/RV sites from $33/43, cabins $61-77;) has campsites beneath Monterey pines plus a cooking pavilion, hot showers, hot tub, pool, hiking and bicycles. It's a good backup if it's getting dark.

ELK

pop 250

Thirty minutes north of Point Arena, itty-bitty Elk is famous for its stunning clifftop views of 'sea stacks,' towering rock formations jutting out of the water. There's *nothing* to do after dinner, so bring a book – and sleeping pills if you're a night owl.

Orientation & Information

Elk's **visitors center** (5980 Hwy 1; 11am-1pm Sat & Sun mid-Mar–Oct) has exhibits on the town's logging past. At the southern end of town, **Greenwood State Beach** (☎ 707-877-3458) has a path to the beach where Greenwood Creek meets the sea – an excellent launch point for kayaking. **Force 10** (☎ 707-877-3505; www.force10tours.com) guides worthwhile ocean-kayaking tours ($115).

Sleeping

Elk's inns have mesmerizing views.

Griffin House (☎ 707-877-3422; www.griffinn.com; 5910 S Hwy 1; cottages $130-160, with ocean view $198-288; 🖳) Griffin House doesn't pretend to be more than it is – an unpretentious cluster of simple beachside cottages with low-pile carpeting, board games and wood-burning stoves.

Harbor House Inn (☎ 707-877-3203, 800-720-7474; www.theharborhouseinn.com; 5600 S Hwy 1; r & cottages incl breakfast $295-470) Elk's finest splurge-worthy inn is ideal for a honeymoon night. The 1915 Craftsman-style mansion has polished redwood interiors and stunning clifftop gardens; rates include an exceptional four-course dinner for two.

Elk has three other noteworthy inns:

Elk Cove Inn (☎ 707-877-3321, 800-275-2967; www.elkcoveinn.com; 6300 S Hwy 1; r $135-195, with ocean view $295-395) Lavender-scented B&B rooms with gazillion-thread-count linens, and the area's only full-service day spa.

Greenwood Pier Inn (☎ 707-877-9997; www.green woodpierinn.com; 5928 S Hwy 1; r $150-325) Feels a bit New-Agey and has sketchy service, but has well-placed ocean view cottages and lovely gardens.

Sandpiper House (☎ 707-877-3587, 800-894-9016; www.sandpiperhouse.com; 5520 S Hwy 1; r incl breakfast $155-260) Five rooms in a cheerful, grey-shingled 1916 house.

Eating

Queenie's Roadhouse Cafe (☎ 707-877-3285; 6061 S Hwy 1; dishes $6-10; 8am-3pm Thu-Mon) Always-good Queenie's is the top choice for breakfast or lunch, with terrific omelettes, scrambles, salads and sandwiches. Too bad it's closed for dinner.

Bridget Dolan's (☎ 707-877-1820; 5910 S Hwy 1; dishes $10-20; dinner Fri-Tue) This dressed-down pub serves straightforward cookin' like pot pies, and bangers and mash.

Zebo (☎ 707-877-3321; 6300 S Hwy 1; mains $21-25; dinner Wed-Sun) The tiny ocean view dining room at the Elk Cove Inn makes tasty Euro-Cal cooking like pan-roasted chicken, rack of lamb and crab ravioli. Make reservations.

VAN DAMME STATE PARK

Five minutes south of Mendocino, this gorgeous 1831-acre state **park** (☎ 707-937-5804, 707-937-5397; www.parks.ca.gov; admission per car $6) draws divers, beachcombers and kayakers to its easy-access beach, but it's also known for a **pygmy forest**, where the acidic soil and an impenetrable layer of hardpan just below the surface create a bonsai forest with decades-old trees half a foot high. There's a wheelchair-accessible boardwalk that provides access to the pine-scented forest; turn east off Hwy 1 onto Little River Airport Rd, a half-mile south of Van Damme State Park, and drive 3 miles. Alternatively, hike or bike up inland from the campground on the park's premiere trail, the lush 3.5-mile **Fern Canyon Scenic Trail**, which crosses back and forth over Little River beneath second-growth redwoods.

The **visitors center** (☎ 707-937-4016; 10am-4pm daily summer, Sat & Sun fall-spring) has a diorama of the park's marine conservation area, and videos and interpretive programs; a half-hour marsh loop trail starts nearby.

For sea-cave kayaking tours ($50), contact **Lost Coast Kayaking** (☎ 707-937-2434; www.lostcoastkayaking.com).

There are two gorgeous **campgrounds** (☎ 800-444-7275; www.reserveamerica.com; campsites $20-25) with hot showers, one off Hwy 1, the other in a highland meadow. *Make reservations!* Ten **environmental campsites** (campsites $15) lie just under a 2-mile hike up Fern Canyon; there's untreated creek water.

TOP EATS ALONG COASTAL HWY 1

- Rendezvous Inn (p104)
- Seaweed Cafe (p89)
- Pangea (p94)
- Cafe Beaujolais (p101)
- MacCallum House Restaurant (p101)

NORTH COAST

DETOUR: ANDERSON VALLEY & HWY 128

If you're in a hurry to get to San Francisco or weary of the coast's chilly weather, cut inland to the Anderson Valley via twisty Hwy 128, which originates 10 miles south of Mendocino; 60 miles ahead, you'll reach Hwy 101.

Wind past vineyards, apple orchards, pastureland and oak-dotted prairies. Most people come to winery-hop, but there's also good hiking and bicycling in the surrounding hills, and the chance to escape civilization. Tiny **Boonville** (population 700) and **Philo** (population 400) are the valley's principal towns. Get information from the **Anderson Valley Chamber of Commerce** (☎ 707-895-2379; www.andersonvalleychamber.com). Locals socially snub outsiders and even speak their own dialect, called Boontling.

Two miles east of Hwy 1, **Navarro Redwoods State Park** (☎ 707-895-3141) extends 11 miles under second-growth redwoods before emerging in the Anderson Valley. Don't tell locals you read this here, but you can swim in the warm-water Navarro River at a great beach near mileage-marker 3.66 on Hwy 128; walk through the woods to the river's sandy shore. Six miles after the junction, if you're stuck for a campsite, Paul M Demmick campground (bring your own water) makes a reasonable backup.

The valley's cool nights yield high-acid, fruit-forward, food-friendly wines like pinot noir, chardonnay and dry gewürztraminer. Most **wineries** (www.avwines.com) offer free tastings and are located outside Philo. **Navarro** (☎ 707-895-3686; 5601 Hwy 128; ☺ 10am-6pm) is the best option, and picnicking is encouraged. Romantic, tiny **Lazy Creek** (☎ 707-895-3623; 4741 Hwy 128) is up a half-mile dirt road; it's open when the gate is (call ahead). The tasting room at **Handley** (☎ 707-895-3876, 800-733-3151; www.handleycellars.com; 3151 Hwy 128; ☺ 10am-6pm) has cool tribal art. **Husch** (☎ 800-554-8724; 4400 Hwy 128; ☺ 10am-5pm) serves tastings inside a rose-covered cottage. For big reds, pack a picnic and head high up the rolling hills to **Esterlina** (☎ 707-895-2920; www.esterlinavineyards.com); call ahead.

Anderson Valley Brewing Co (☎ 707-895-2337; www.avbc.com; 17700 Hwy 153; tours $5), east of Hwy 128, crafts award-winning beers in a Bavarian-style brewhouse.

For the best fruit, head to the **Apple Farm** (☎ 707-895-2333; www.philoapplefarm.com; 18501 Greenwood Rd, Philo; cottages $175-200) for organic preserves, chutneys, heirloom apples and pears; open daylight hours. The farm also rents spiffy orchard cottages and hosts **cooking classes**.

Opposite the Boonville Hotel, **Boonville General Store** (☎ 707-895-9477; 17810 Farrer Lane; dishes $5-8; ☺ 9am-3pm Thu-Mon) is perfect for lunch – sandwiches on homemade bread, thin-crust pizzas and organic cheeses. Locals pack **Lauren's** (☎ 707-895-3869; 14211 Hwy 128, Boonville; mains $9-14; ☺ dinner Tue-Sat) for homemade Cal-American cookin'. **Boonville Hotel** (707-895-2210; www.boonvillehotel .com; 14040 Hwy 128; mains $13-25; ☺ dinner Thu-Mon) serves perfect New American roadhouse-style cooking, like roasted chicken and strawberry shortcake. Thursdays there's a three-course prix-fixe deal ($28) with no corkage.

Accommodations fill on weekends. **Anderson Valley Inn** (☎ 707-895-3325; www.avinn.com; 8480 Hwy 128, Philo; r $75-100, with kitchen $130-160) has fresh-looking motel rooms. Decked out in a contemporary American-country style that would make Martha Stewart proud, rooms at the **Boonville Hotel** (707-895-2210; www.boonvillehotel.com; 14040 Hwy 128; r $100-225, ste $180-275) are safe for urbanites who refuse to abandon style just because they've gone to the country. The dog-friendly **Other Place** (☎ 707-895-3979; www.sheepdung.com; cottages $175-250) rents secluded, private hilltop cottages surrounded by 500 acres of ranch lands. **Hendy Woods State Park** (☎ 707-937-5804, reservations 800-444-7275; www.reserveamerica.com; campsites $20-25; cabins $50) has wooded campsites by the Navarro River – with hot showers. **Wellspring Retreat Center** (☎ 707-895-3893; www .wellspringrenewal.org; Ray's Rd, Philo; campsites $20, cabins from $30) has rustic cottages without bathrooms; bring bedding and towels. Call ahead.

MENDOCINO
pop 1000

On a rocky headland jutting into the Pacific, picture-perfect feels more like Cape Cod than California, with tiny salt-box cottages surrounded by rose gardens, white picket fences and New England–style redwood water towers. In summer, fragrant bursts of lavender and jasmine permeate the foggy wind, tempered by salt air from the churning surf, which is never out of earshot.

Built by transplanted New Englanders in the 1850s, Mendocino thrived late into the 19th century, with ships transporting redwood timber to San Francisco. The mills shut in the 1930s, and the town fell into disrepair until it was rediscovered in the 1950s by bohemians. Today the whole of Mendo is listed on the National Register of Historic Places and has served as the backdrop for over 50 films, including *East of Eden* (1954) and *The Majestic* (2001). The culturally savvy, politically aware citizens welcome visitors, but eschew corporate interlopers, consistently blocking construction of cell-phone towers, straightening of winding approach roads, or anything that might alter the town's character.

Alas, Mendocino has become a victim of its own charms: many houses are now vacation homes, which has shot prices through the roof and driven out families. So many tourists come for the galleries, restaurants and B&Bs that, at times, Mendocino seems a parody of itself, earning it the nickname 'Spendocino.' But there's no arguing the stunning beauty of the place, and it's absolutely worth spending time here. Ideally come midweek or off-season, when the vibe is pure – and prices reasonable.

Information

Ford House Visitors Center & Museum (☎ 707-937-5397; www.gomendo.com; 735 Main St; suggested donation $2; 11am-4pm) Maps, books, information and exhibits including a scale model of 1890 Mendocino. There's also hot cider, picnic tables and rest rooms.

Gallery Books (☎ 707-937-2665; 319 Kasten St) History, nature, travel and children's books.

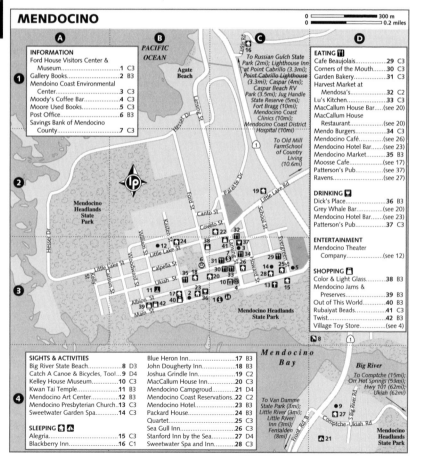

MENDOCINO

0 — 300 m
0 — 0.2 miles

INFORMATION
Ford House Visitors Center &
    Museum.................................1 C3
Gallery Books............................2 B3
Mendoino Coast Environmental
    Center..................................3 C3
Moody's Coffee Bar..................4 C3
Moore Used Books....................5 C3
Post Office...............................6 B3
Savings Bank of Mendocino
    County.................................7 C3

SIGHTS & ACTIVITIES
Big River State Beach................8 D3
Catch A Canoe & Bicycles, Too!..9 D4
Kelley House Museum..............10 C3
Kwan Tai Temple.....................11 B3
Mendocino Art Center.............12 C3
Mendocino Presbyterian Church.13 C3
Sweetwater Garden Spa..........14 C3

SLEEPING
Alegria...................................15 C3
Blackberry Inn........................16 C1

Blue Heron Inn.......................17 B3
John Dougherty Inn.................18 B3
Joshua Grindle Inn..................19 C2
MacCallum House Inn..............20 C3
Mendocino Campgroud...........21 D4
Mendocino Coast Reservations.22 C2
Mendocino Hotel.....................23 B3
Packard House........................24 B3
Quartet..................................25 C3
Sea Gull Inn...........................26 C3
Stanford Inn by the Sea...........27 D4
Sweetwater Spa and Inn.........28 C3

EATING
Cafe Beaujolais......................29 C3
Corners of the Mouth.............30 C3
Garden Bakery.......................31 C3
Harvest Market at
    Mendosa's.........................32 C2
Lu's Kitchen...........................33 C3
MacCallum House Bar......(see 20)
MacCallum House
    Restaurant...................(see 20)
Mendo Burgers......................34 C3
Mendocino Café...............(see 26)
Mendocino Hotel Bar.......(see 23)
Mendocino Market.................35 B3
Moosse Cafe...................(see 17)
Patterson's Pub................(see 37)
Ravens...........................(see 27)

DRINKING
Dick's Place...........................36 B3
Grey Whale Bar...............(see 20)
Mendocino Hotel Bar.......(see 23)
Patterson's Pub......................37 C3

ENTERTAINMENT
Mendocino Theater
    Company........................(see 12)

SHOPPING
Color & Light Glass..............38 B3
Mendocino Jams &
    Preserves.........................39 B3
Out of This World..................40 B3
Rubaiyat Beads.....................41 C3
Twist....................................42 B3
Village Toy Store...............(see 4)

Mendocino Coast Clinics (☎ 707-964-1251; 205 South St; ☺ 9am-6pm Mon-Fri, to 1pm Sat) For nonemergencies.
Mendocino Coast District Hospital (☎ 707-961-1234; 700 River Dr, Fort Bragg) With a 24-hour emergency room.
Moody's Coffee Bar (☎ 707-933-4843; www.moodys coffeebar.com; 10450 Lansing St; per min $0.10; ☺ 5:30am-9pm) Internet access, good coffee and the *New York Times*.
Moore Used Books (☎ 707-937-1537; 990 Main St)
Post office (☎ 707-937-1650; 10500 Ford St)
Savings Bank of Mendocino County (☎ 707-937-0545; 10500 Lansing St) 24hr ATM.

Sights

The **Mendocino Art Center** (☎ 707-937-5818, 800-653-3328; www.mendocinoartcenter.org; 45200 Little Lake St; ☺ 10am-5pm daily Apr-Oct, to 4pm Tue-Sat Nov-Mar) hosts exhibitions, arts-and-crafts fairs, theatrical performances and a nationally recognized program of over 200 art classes. Art galleries around town hold events on the second Saturday of each month from 5pm to 8pm.

The 1861 **Kelley House Museum** (☎ 707-937-5791; www.mendocinohistory.org; 45007 Albion St; admission $2; ☺ 11am-3pm Thu-Tue Jun-Sep, Fri-Mon Oct-May) has a research library and changing exhibits on early California and Mendocino. In summer the museum hosts walking tours for $10 from Friday to Monday; call for times.

At the 1852 **Kwan Tai Temple** (45160 Albion St), peer in the window to see the old Chinese altar. Back on Main St, near the visitors center, you can spot one of town's famous **water towers**.

The restored 1909 **Point Cabrillo Lighthouse** (☎ 707-937-0816; www.pointcabrillo.org; Point Cabrillo Dr; admission free; ☺ 11am-4pm Sat & Sun Jan & Feb, daily Mar-Oct, Fri-Mon Nov & Dec; ♿) stands on a 300-acre wildlife preserve north of town, between Russian Gulch and Caspar Beach. The lightkeeper's home is now a B&B (see p100). Guided walks of the preserve leave at 11am on Sundays from May to September.

Activities

Mendocino Headlands State Park (☎ 707-937-5804) surrounds the village, where trails crisscross bluffs and rocky coves. Ask at the visitors center about guided weekend walks, including spring wildflower walks and whale-watching walks.

Catch A Canoe & Bicycles, Too! (☎ 707-937-0273, 800-331-8884; www.stanfordinn.com; cnr Comptche-Ukiah

Rd & Hwy 1; ☺ 9am-5pm; ♿) rents bikes, kayaks and outrigger canoes for self-guided trips up the 8-mile **Big River tidal estuary**, the longest undeveloped estuary in Northern California. There are no highways or buildings, only beaches, forests, marshes, streams, abundant wildlife and historic logging sites, including century-old train trestles and log dams.

Tiny Albion, hugging the north side of the Albion River mouth, 5 miles south of Mendocino, has a navigable river and ocean bay for **kayaking**.

Sweetwater Garden Spa (☎ 707-937-4140, 800-300-4140; 955 Ukiah St; ☺ noon-10pm) offers massage and bodywork. A one-hour private tub-and-sauna session costs $18; the public tub costs $10 ($7.50 Wednesdays).

Build beach fires and make driftwood forts at **Big River State Beach** (☎ 707-937-5804). Park behind the Presbyterian church on Main St and take the stairs down.

Play golf 3 miles south of town at the **Little River Inn** (☎ 707-937-5942, 888-466-5683; Hwy 1, Little River; www.littleriverinn.com; greens fees $25-40).

Festivals & Events

For the complete list of festivals, check with the visitors center or www.gomendo.com.
Mendocino Whale Festival Early March, with wine and chowder tastings, whale-watching and music.
Mendocino Music Festival Mid-July, with orchestral and chamber music concerts on the headlands, children's matinees and open rehearsals.
Mendocino Wine & Mushroom Festival Early November, guided mushroom tours and symposia.
Mendocino Coast Candlelight Inn Tour Christmas-time inn tours and caroling.
Mendocino Crab & Wine Days Late December to early February, with wine tasting, cooking classes, whale-watching and crab cruises.

Sleeping

Most Mendocino B&Bs embrace the cabbage-rose-wallpaper, lace-curtain aesthetic. Rates plummet in winter. Fort Bragg (p103) is cheaper, if less charming.
Mendocino Coast Reservations (☎ 707-937-5033, 800-262-7801; www.mendocinovacations.com; 45084 Little Lake St; ☺ 9am-5pm) books vacation homes and B&Bs.
Sweetwater Spa & Inn (☎ 937-4076, 800-300-4140; 44840 Main St; www.sweetwaterspa.com; r & cottages $125-200) owns a variety of accommodations, in town and nearby. Rates include spa privileges.

NORTH COAST

NORTH COAST

CAMPING

Russian Gulch State Park (☎ reservations 800-444-7275; www.reserveamerica.com; campsites $20-25) After Van Damme State Park (p96), make this your first choice. In a wooded canyon 2 miles north of town, Russian Gulch has secluded drive-in sights and hot showers, a sandy beach, a small waterfall and Devil's Punch Bowl, a collapsed sea arch.

Mendocino Campground (☎ 707-937-3130; www .mendocino-campground.com; Comptche-Ukiah Rd; campsites $25-35; ☽ Apr-Oct) High above Hwy 1, this woodsy option has 60 sites (some with views) hot showers and forested trails. Dogs welcome.

Caspar Beach RV Park (☎ 707-964-3306; www .casparbeachrvpark.com; 14441 Cabrillo Dr; campsites $25, RV sites $30-35) In a sheltered gully beside Caspar Beach, 3.5 miles north of Mendocino.

B&BS

All prices include breakfast; most have no TVs.

Fensalden (☎ 707-937-4042, 800-959-3850; www .fensalden.com; 33810 Navarro Ridge Rd, Albion; r $129-198, bungalow $239) An 1880s stagecoach stop, 8 miles south of town, Fensalden's B&B rooms are OK, but the supercool weathered-redwood bungalow, which sleeps four, is fantastic!

John Dougherty House (☎ 707-937-5266; 800-486-2104; www.jdhouse.com; 571 Ukiah St; r $150-275) Decked out in a spiffy-looking, blue-and-white nautical theme that would do any gay sailor boy proud, rooms at this fashionable little B&B have more urban style than others in town (think flat-panel TVs); some have fireplaces and ocean views. Wonderful garden. Top choice for gay travelers (but all welcome). Ask about the Packard House, by the same owners.

Joshua Grindle Inn (☎ 707-937-4143, 800-474-6353; www.joshgrin.com; 44800 Little Lake Rd; r $179-259) We love the Grindle. The ideal choice for aficionados of historic accommodations, it's also Mendo's first B&B, with bright, airy, uncluttered rooms in an 1869 house, a weathered saltbox cottage and water tower. There are afternoon goodies, warm hospitality and gorgeous gardens.

Lighthouse Inn at Point Cabrillo (☎ 707-937-6124; 866-937-6124; http://mendocinolighthouse.pointcabrillo .org; Point Cabrillo Dr; r $177-272) On 300 acres, in the shadow of Point Cabrillo Lighthouse, the lighthouse keeper's house and several cottages have been turned into B&B rooms, with atmospheric details like redwood paneling. At

night the light from the brilliant Fresnel lens sweeps overhead, making it a fabulous spot for a nighttime stroll. Rates include a private night tour of the lighthouse and a five-course breakfast.

Alegria (☎ 707-937-5150, 800-780-7905; www.ocean frontmagic.com; 44781 Main St; r $139-159, with ocean view $209-279, cottage with kitchen $210) The perfect romantic hideaway, Alegria's rooms have ocean view decks and wood-burning fireplaces; outside there's private beach access, a rarity in Mendo. The ever-so-friendly innkeepers also rent housekeeping cottages, and rooms across the street at Quartet, formerly McElroy's Cottage Inn, a 1900s Craftsman-style house with simple accommodations.

Stanford Inn by the Sea (☎ 707-937-5615, 800-331-8884; www.stanfordinn.com; Comptche-Ukiah Rd; r $240-295; 🖳 🖳) There's not a stitch of Victoriana at Mendo's first-choice lodge, where every rough-hewn-pine-paneled room has a wood-burning fireplace, top-quality mattress with fine linens, and extras like stereos and fine art. On the 10 rolling acres, gorgeous organic gardens, with the Pacific as backdrop, provide produce for the dining room. The solarium-enclosed pool and hot tub are open 24 hours. On-site spa. Free bicycles. Pets welcome.

MacCallum House Inn (☎ 707-937-0289, 800-609-0492; www.maccallumhouse.com; 45020 Albion St; r $195-375; 🖳) Stay in an 1882 refurbished barn, a cozy cottage or a fab water tower with a glass panel over the original well (but skip the suburban-looking MacCallum Suites). All have cushy details like robes, DVD players, stereos, plush linens and spa services. Pets welcome.

Other options:

Sea Gull Inn (☎ 707-937-5204, 888-937-5204; www .seagullbb.com; 44960 Albion St; r $65-145, barn $165) Cozy rooms, meandering gardens – and a bargain!

Old Mill Farm School of Country Living (☎ 707-937-0244, 707-937-3047; www.oldmillfarm .org; rustic cabin $95) Self-sustaining organic farm with rustic cabin. Call ahead. Check the website for info on farm events and workshops.

Blue Heron Inn (☎ 707-937-4323; 390 Kasten St; www.theblueheron.com; r $95-115) Spartan rooms above a restaurant; crisp linens; some shared bathrooms.

HOTELS & MOTELS

Mendocino Hotel (☎ 707-937-0511, 800-548-0513; www .mendocinohotel.com; 45080 Main St; r $95-115, with bathroom $135-165, ste $225-395) Built in 1878 as the town's first hotel. Many of the Victorian guestrooms share bathrooms. For thicker walls, book a modern garden suite. Look for the ghost. (Fear not: she's mellow and lingers in the dining room.)

Blackberry Inn (☎ 707-937-5281, 800-950-7806; www.mendocinomotel.com; 44951 Larkin Rd; r $140-200) On a hill above town, the Blackberry looks like a row of Old West storefronts. Inside, the Americana-style rooms are comfy and have distant ocean views and fireplaces. Rates are best online.

Eating

For cheap(ish) evening meals, try the **MacCallum House Bar** (☎ 707-937-0289; www.maccallumhouse.com; 45020 Albion St) or **Patterson's Pub** (☎ 707-937-4782; 10485 Lansing St), or drive to Fort Bragg (p104). Organic produce and locally raised meats are the rule – Mendo is nothing if not PC. Make reservations.

RESTAURANTS

Mendocino Cafe (☎ 707-937-6141; 10451 Lansing St; lunch mains $9-14, dinner $11-20; ♿) A good-value choice for a sit-down garden lunch or mid-priced dinner, Mendocino Cafe's diverse menu weaves together Mexican, Asian and American cooking, like fish tacos, Thai burritos, steaks, pasta and seafood.

Cafe Beaujolais (☎ 707-937-5614; www.cafebeaujolais.com; 961 Ukiah St; mains $24-29; ☯ dinner) Mendocino's iconic, much-beloved country-Cal-French restaurant occupies an 1896 house restyled into a monochromatic urban-chic dining room, perfect for holding hands by candlelight. The refined, inspired cooking draws diners from San Francisco, who make this the centerpiece of their trip. Bring your credit card; you'll need it.

MacCallum House Restaurant (☎ 707-937-0289; www.maccallumhouse.com; 45020 Albion St; café dishes $6-12, mains $21-32; ☯ dinner) The sure-handed owner-chef's earthy Euro-Cal menu features duck, lamb, gnocchi and seafood, served in a redwood-paneled Victorian dining room. The food is consistently good, but the otherwise romantic dining room suffers from too many tables, too close together. Sit on the veranda or request a table on the wall. Good breakfasts.

Moosse Cafe (☎ 707-937-4323; www.theblueheron.com; 390 Kasten St; dishes lunch $10-14, dinner $20-25) The ideal spot for a lingering lunch, bright and airy Moosse Cafe serves creamy-delicious mac-'n'-cheese, housemade paté and Niçoise salads. At dinner, roast chicken and cioppino are the standouts. Save room for chocolate pudding. Monday nights, three-course dinners cost $20, and there's no corkage fee.

Ravens (☎ 707-937-5615; www.stanfordinn.com; Stanford Inn, Comptche-Ukiah Rd; breakfast $8-13, dishes $14-28; ☯ breakfast & dinner; Ⓥ) Who knew vegetarian could be so good? Omnivores may foreswear meat after dining at the Ravens, where the haute-contemporary menu features everything from pizza to sea-palm strudel. Produce comes from the inn's own organic gardens, where you can stroll after dinner. The breakfasts are Mendocino's best, when you can look over rolling hills to the sea beyond.

GROCERIES & QUICK EATS

Harvest Market at Mendosa's (☎ 707-937-5879; 10501 Lansing St; ☯ 7:30am-10pm) Finally Mendocino has a decent grocery store, with good meats and produce.

Corners of the Mouth (☎ 707-937-5345; 45016 Ukiah St; ☯ 9am-7pm) Carries natural foods.

Mendocino Market (☎ 707-937-3474; 45051 Ukiah St; sandwiches $6-9; ☯ 10am-6:30pm) Locals get sandwiches here. There's wild seafood, meat and local wine too.

Mendo Burgers (☎ 707-937-1111; 10483 Lansing St; meals $6-9; ☯ 11am-4:30pm Thu-Tue; ♿) Behind Mendocino Bakery, this old-fashioned lunch counter makes great burgers and handcut fries; veggie burgers too.

Lu's Kitchen (☎ 707-937-4939; 45013 Ukiah St; dishes $7-10; ☯ 11:30am-5:30pm; ♿) Lu makes fab organic-veggie burritos in a tiny shack; outdoor-only tables.

Garden Bakery (☎ 707-937-3140; 10450 Lansing St; ☯ 8:30am-4pm Wed-Sat) The town's best bakery makes sweeties and good bread. Enter off Albion St.

Mendocino Hotel Bar (☎ 707-937-0511; 45080 Main St; bar food $6-15; ☯ 11am-10pm) On a gloomy day, warm up with chowder at this moody, dark wood–paneled bar.

Drinking

Sip cocktails at the **Mendocino Hotel Bar** (☎ 707-937-0511; 45080 Main St) or the **Grey Whale Bar** (☎ 707-937-0289, 800-609-0492; www.maccallumhouse.com; MacCallum House Inn, 45020 Albion St).

Patterson's Pub (☎ 707-937-4782; 10485 Lansing St) This cozy Irish-style pub serves a menu of good pub grub ($9 to $14) till 11pm Friday and Saturday, 10pm weeknights.

Dick's Place (☎ 707-937-5643; 45080 Main St) Do shots with rowdy locals.

Entertainment

Mendocino Theater Company (☎ 707-937-4477; www.1mtc.org; 45200 Little Lake St) Performs good contemporary theater in an 88-seat house.

Shopping

Village Toy Store (☎ 707-937-4633; 10450 Lansing St) Great selection of wooden toys and games you won't find in the chains – and hardly anything requires batteries!

Mendocino Coast Environmental Center (☎ 707-937-1035; www.mcecenter.org; 10483 Lansing St) Learn the latest local environmental issues and to get involved with community actions on everything from reforestation to offshore drilling. It also doubles as a retail shop selling earth-friendly products.

Out of this World (☎ 707-937-3335; 451000 Main St) Bird-watchers, astronomy buffs and science geeks: head directly to this telescope, binocular and science-toy shop.

Rubaiyat Beads (☎ 707-937-1217; 10550 Lansing St) Fantastic selection of beaded jewelry and silver.

Twist (☎ 707-937-1717; 45140 Main St) Twist stocks ecofriendly, natural-fiber clothing and trippy handblown 'tobacco-smoking accessories' (dude: that means bongs).

Mendocino Jams & Preserves (☎ 707-937-1037; 440 Main St) Mendo Jams offers tastes of its goodies. Try the ketchup.

Color & Light Glass (☎ 707-937-1003; 10525 Ford St; ⊙ Fri-Tue) Inside an artist's studio, see original fuse- and stained-glass works.

Getting There & Away

See the Fort Bragg section (p105) for details on regional buses.

JUG HANDLE STATE RESERVE

Even if you're not a rock geek, Jug Handle's **ecological staircase** is conceptually fascinating. Five wave-cut terraces ascend in steps from the seashore, each 100ft and 100,000 years removed from the previous, each with its own distinct geology and vegetation. See it on a 5-mile (round-trip) self-guided nature trail. One of the terraces has a pygmy forest, similar to the better-known example at Van Damme State Park (p96). Pick up a printed guide from the parking lot. If you're not the heady sort, you might shrug your shoulders and say, So what? – in which case you should head directly for the headlands and whale-watch or lounge on the beach. Look for the turnoff, just

north of Caspar, halfway between Fort Bragg and Mendocino.

Jug Handle Creek Farm & Nature Center (☎ 707-964-4630; http://jughandle.creek.org; campsites $12, r & cabins adult $30-38, child $13, student $23-30) is a non-profit 39-acre farm with rustic cabins and hostel rooms in a 19th-century farmhouse. Call ahead about work-stay discounts and environmental-education opportunities.

Opposite the state reserve, **Annie's Jughandle Beach B&B** (☎ 707-964-1415, 800-964-9957; www.jughandle.com; Hwy 1, mileage marker 55; r incl breakfast $120-220) is an 1880s farmhouse with cheery rooms, some with Jacuzzis and gas fireplaces.

FORT BRAGG

pop 7025

Mendocino's stepsister was for years defined by its lumber mill. Then the mill closed in 2002, leaving the blue-collar town struggling for an identity. Tourists and retirees are filling the gap: shops that once sold work clothes are being replaced with specialty boutiques selling fancy socks, and at the local hospital, geriatrics are replacing prenatal programs. Though downtown is sweet in a Mayberry kind of way, the southern end of town is hideous: unlike the *entire* franchise-free 180-mile stretch of Coastal Hwy 1 between here and the Golden Gate, southern Fort Bragg sprawls, with Mc-Donald's and Starbucks polluting the coastal aesthetic. Put on blinders, and don't stop till you're downtown, where you'll find way better hamburgers, locally roasted coffee, old-school architecture and residents eager to show off their cute little town. Alas, would that they would shield their too-bright streetlights to restore the stargazing, but they're making other efforts to overcome their dowdy image, and they're on the right track.

Orientation & Information

Twisting, nausea-inducing Hwy 20 connects with Hwy 101. Most facilities are near Main St, a 2-mile stretch of Hwy 1. Shops, a movie theater and post office are on Franklin St, which runs parallel, one block east. Fort Bragg's wharf, with its fishing-boat docks and seafood restaurants, lies at grungey Noyo Harbor – the mouth of the Noyo River – south of downtown.

Fort Bragg-Mendocino Coast Chamber of Commerce (☎ 707-961-6300, 800-726-2780; www.fortbragg.com, www.mendocinocoast.com; 332 N Main St; ⊙ 9am-5pm Mon-Fri, to 3pm Sat) Information about Fort Bragg, Mendocino and surrounding areas.

Sage's Computer (☎ 707-964-9955; 325a Redwood Ave; per 10min $1.25) Internet access using Macs.

Seal of Approval (☎ 707-964-7099; 260 N Main St; per 10min $1.50; ☺ 8am-8pm Mon-Fri, 10am-6pm Sat) Internet access.

Sights & Activities

Everybody loves the **Skunk Train** (☎ 707-964-6371, 866-457-5865; www.skunktrain.com; Laurel St; adult $28-45, child 3-11 $18-20; ☝), the historic logging train that chugs from Fort Bragg and Willits (p107), passing through redwood-forested mountains, along rivers, and through deep mountain tunnels en route to Northspur, the midway point, where it turns around – a plenty-long 3½-hour trip. There's also a 90-minute jaunt if you're tight on time. The depot is downtown at Laurel St, west of Main St.

The jaw-droppingly stunning **Mendocino Coast Botanical Gardens** (☎ 707-964-4352; www.garden bythesea.org; 18220 N Hwy 1; adult/child/teen/senior $7.50/ 1/3/6; ☺ 9am-5pm Mar-Oct, to 4pm Nov-Feb) displays native flora year-round along serpentine paths on 47 seafront acres south of town. Primary trails are wheelchair-accessible.

Famous **Glass Beach** is named for (what's left of) the sea-polished glass in the sand. This was once the city dump; now it's part of MacKerricher State Park (p105), so you can't take the glass anymore. Take the headlands trail from Elm St, off Main St.

The 1892 **Guest House Museum** (☎ 707-964-4251; 343 N Main St; admission $2; ☺ 11am-2pm Mon-Fri, 10am-4pm Sat & Sun Jun-Oct; 11am-2pm Thu-Sun Nov-May), a majestic Victorian, displays relics of Fort Bragg's history. Literally and figuratively on the other side of the street, the **Triangle Tattoo & Museum** (☎ 707-964-8814; www.triangletattoo.com; 356B N Main St; ☺ noon-7pm) is flanked by galleries that unveil new shows and stay open till 8pm on the second Saturday of each month. **Northcoast Artists** (☎ 707-964-8266; http://northcoastartists.org; 362 N Main St) is a co-op gallery. Antique and book shops line Franklin St, one block east. Holy cow: check out the crazy-cool storefront full of physics experiments at **Larry Spring, Experimental Analysis of Electromagnetic Energy** (☎ 707-964-2116; 225 Redwood Ave).

Nearby **North Coast Brewing Co** (☎ 707-964-2739; 455 N Main St) offers brewery tours Monday to Saturday; call ahead.

Small boats at Noyo Harbor offer coastal and whale-watching cruises and deep-sea fishing and crabbing trips. Try **Noyo Fishing Center** (☎ 707-964-3000; www.fortbraggfishing.com; 32440 N Har-

bor Dr) or **All-Aboard Adventures** (☎ 707-964-1881; www.allaboardadventures.com; 32400 N Harbor Dr).

Festivals & Events

Fort Bragg Whale Festival Third weekend in March, with microbrew tastings, crafts fairs and whale-watching.

Rhododendron Show Late April or early May.

World's Largest Salmon BBQ Held at Noyo Harbor on the Saturday nearest 4th of July.

Caspar World Folk Festival Folk music, early August.

Paul Bunyan Days Celebrates California's logging history with a logging show, square dancing, parade and fair, Labor Day weekend.

Sleeping

Fort Bragg's lodging is cheaper than Mendocino's, but many motels along noisy Hwy 1 don't have air-conditioning so you'll hear traffic through your open windows. The following do not have noise problems. Summer weekends sell out; book ahead.

CAMPING

California Department of Forestry (☎ 707-964-5674; www.fire.ca.gov/php/rsrc-mgt_jackson.php; 802 N Main St; ☺ Mon-Fri) has maps, permits and camping information for the Jackson State Forest, east of Fort Bragg, where camping is *free*!

Pomo RV Park & Campground (☎ 707-964-3373; www.infortbragg.com/pomorvpark; 17999 Tregoning Lane; tent/RV sites $24/35) A mile south of town, this wooded campground is back from Hwy 1. Gates close at 11pm.

B&BS & INNS

Most B&Bs have no TVs; all prices include breakfast.

Caspar Inn (☎ 707-964-5565; www.casparinn.com; 14957 Caspar Rd; r $65-75) If you can tolerate sleeping above a bar with bands playing till 1:30am, head 5 miles south to this rockin' roadhouse. Rooms share bathrooms; those in front are quieter.

Lodge at Noyo River (☎ 707-964-8045, 800-628-1126; www.noyolodge.com; 500 Casa del Norte Dr; r $95-175) The modern suites have oversized tubs and bling appeal, but the best rooms are in the 19th-century lumber-baron's house, rich with character and lovely woodwork, but no space-occupying froufrou. Full breakfast is included.

Rendezvous Inn (☎ 707-964-8142, 800-491-8142; www.rendezvousinn.com; 647 N Main Dr; r $110, cottage $170) The North Coast's best chef cooks your breakfast at this simple B&B, good for low-maintenance travelers. A cottage out back sleeps four.

Weller House Inn (☎ 707-964-4415, 877-893-5537; www.wellerhouse.com; 524 Stewart St; r $115-180) Fort Bragg's top-choice B&B is a beautifully restored 1886 Victorian with a fabulous redwood ballroom on the top floor, where guests take breakfast and play cards. Rooms have fluffy down comforters and period details. The water tower is the tallest structure in town – and has a hot tub inside!

MOTELS

Colombi Motel (☎ 707-964-5773; www.colombimotel .com; 647 Oak St; 1- & 2-bedroom units $45-70) The Mendocino Coast's best bargain has sparkling-clean, two-room units with either a bedroom and kitchen or two bedrooms. Check in at the Market at Oak and Harold Sts. Launderette next door.

Anchor Lodge (☎ 707-964-4283; www.anchor-lodge .com; 32260 N Harbor Dr; r $55, with ocean view $90, with kitchen $135) Fishermen and salty dogs favor this motel under the Wharf Restaurant at Noyo Harbor. Some rooms have water views, some have kitchens.

Super 8 (☎ 707-964-4003, 800-206-9833; www.super8 .com; 888 S Main St; r $77-95; 🐾) Of the nothing-special motels lining Hwy 1, this one's appropriately priced, clean and has air-conditioning, microwaves and refrigerators.

Hi-Sea Inn (☎ 707-964-5929, 800-990-7327; www .hiseainn.com; 1201 N Main St; r $79-109) North of downtown are three oceanfront motels. This one's the least pretentious – just a plain motel with killer views, within earshot of the pounding surf.

Holiday Inn Express (☎ 707-964-1100, 800-465-4329; www.holidayinnexpress.com; 250 Hwy 20; r $119-139; 🖳) Yes, it's a chain, but it's got extras like a hot tub and fitness center. And the indoor pool – a rarity – is a godsend for parents.

Beachcomber Motel (☎ 707-964-2402, 800-400-7873; www.thebeachcombermotel.com; 1111 N Main St; r $89-129, with ocean view $109-149, with kitchen $159) Fussier travelers who want an ocean view motel with upgraded furniture should choose this over the Hi-Sea, next door. Book upstairs for maximum privacy.

Eating

Headlands Coffeehouse (☎ 707-964-1987; 120 E Laurel St; dishes $4-8; 🕑 7am-10pm) Fort Bragg's most happening café serves Belgian waffles at breakfast; at lunch and dinner try homemade soups, veggie-friendly salads, paninis and lasagna. First choice for budgeteers.

Laurel Deli (☎ 707-964-7812; Depot Shopping Center, 401 N Main St; mains $6-8; 🕑 breakfast & lunch; 👶) Locals pick the Laurel for cheap breakfasts and good sandwiches; kids *love* the giant, real locomotive parked in the middle of the cavernous room.

Piaci Pub & Pizzeria (☎ 707-961-1133; 120 W Redwood Ave; pizza $8-12; 🕑 lunch Mon-Fri, dinner nightly) Pair local wines and microbrews with Piaci's always-good thin-crust pizzas for a tasty but easy meal. Expect waits at peak times.

North Coast Brewing Co (☎ 707-964-3400; 444 N Main St; mains $8-17; 🕑 11:30am-9pm) For burgers, great garlic fries and handcrafted beers, this is the place. There's a mellow dining room, but the raucous bar is more fun if you wanna catch a buzz.

Chapter & Moon (☎ 707-962-1643; 32150 N Harbor Dr; mains $10-15; 🕑 8am-8pm) The top spot at Noyo Harbor serves down-home American-style cooking (think meatloaf and chicken with dumplings) overlooking the water in a whitewashed room with pinewood tables and ladder-back chairs. Mains are cheap; starters aren't. Good breakfasts.

Nit's (☎ 707-964-7187; 322 N Main; lunch $8-15, dinner $18-22; 🕑 Tue-Sat) Mains are pricey, but plates are huge, beautifully presented and dynamically spiced at this tiny French-Thai storefront café run by a Thai-born chef-owner. After the Rendezvous Inn (below), Nit's serves the town's best food. Cash only.

Mendo Bistro (☎ 707-964-4974; www.mendobistro .com; 301 N Main St; dishes $14-22; 🕑 dinner; 👶) Choose a meat, a preparation, and an accompanying sauce from Mendo Bistro's crowd-pleasing, mix-and-match menu. The loud, bustling room is big enough that kids can run around and nobody will notice. Good crab cakes.

** our pick Rendezvous Inn** (☎ 707-964-8142; www .rendezvousinn.com; 647 N Main St; mains $24-29; 🕑 dinner Wed-Sun) The North Coast's top restaurant (really) blends rustic charm with big-city cooking in a converted redwood-paneled Craftsman-style house. Protégé of Michelin-three-star-rated, celebrity French chef Georges Blanc, chef-owner Kim Badenhop showcases seasonal, regional ingredients like lavender, wild boar, blackberries and venison in his down-to-earth, French-provincial menu; the wintertime crab-tasting menu is worth the three-hour drive from San Francisco. If you want chowder and baked potatoes, look elsewhere, but if you're a serious foodie, don't miss the Rendezvous. Make reservations, and bring a sweater: the old house gets drafty.

Of Noyo Harbor's seafood joints, Chapter & Moon (opposite) is best, then **Sharon's by the Sea** (☎ 707-962-0680; 32096 N Harbor Dr; lunch $6-17, dinner $11-24), a pretty little dockside fish grotto with picnic tables outside. For fried fish, coleslaw and fries, skip the pricey Wharf restaurant and head next door to **Cap'n Flint's** (☎ 707-964-9447; 32250 N Harbor Dr; ☿ 11am-9pm; ♨) and get (nearly) the same food for half the price.

For self-caterers and those in search of a quick meal:

Cowlick's Ice Cream (☎ 962-9271; 250B Main St)
Farmers market (☎ 707-937-4330; cnr Laurel & Franklin Sts; ☿ 3:30-6pm Wed May-Oct) Downtown.
Harvest Market (☎ 707-964-7000; cnr Hwys 1 & 20; ☿ 5am-11pm) The best groceries.
Mendocino Cookie Company (☎ 964-0282; 303 N Main St)

Drinking & Entertainment
Headlands Coffeehouse (☎ 707-964-1987; www.headlandscoffeehouse.com; 120 E Laurel St) The town's informal cultural center point features live music nightly – jazz, folk and classical – and kick-ass jazz jams Sunday afternoons. Free wi-fi.

North Coast Brewing Company (☎ 707-964-3400; 444 N Main St) If it's microbrews you're after, North Coast makes some of the best. Head for the stouts.

Caspar Inn (☎ 707-964-5565; www.casparinn.com; 14957 Caspar Rd) Five miles south of Fort Bragg, off Hwy 1, Caspar Inn has live music every night but Monday – reggae, hip-hop, rockabilly, R&B, world beat and open-mic Sundays. There's a cover charge ($3 to $25) Tuesday to Saturday and big names occasionally show up unannounced.

Opera Fresca (☎ 707-937-3646, 888-826-7372; www.operafresca.com) This ambitious company performs fully staged operas year-round and hosts a Christmas sing-along *Messiah*.

Gloriana Opera Company (☎ 707-964-7469; www.gloriana.org; 721 N Franklin St) Gloriana stages operettas and popular musicals like *Funny Girl*.

Getting Around
Mendocino Transit Authority (MTA; ☎ 707-462-1422, 800-696-4682; www.4mta.org) operates Route 5, 'BraggAbout' buses, weekdays between Noyo Harbor and downtown. Bus 60 operates weekdays to Mendocino ($1, 30 minutes). Bus 65 operates daily to Willits ($3.25, one hour), then heads south along Hwy 101 via Ukiah to Santa Rosa ($20, three hours), where you can connect with Golden Gate Transit to San Francisco (see the San Francisco chapter, p67).

Fort Bragg Cyclery (☎ 707-964-3509; www.fortbraggcyclery.com; 221-A N Main St) rents bicycles.

MACKERRICHER STATE PARK
Lose yourself in the roaring surf and wide-open sightlines of **MacKerricher State Park** (☎ 707-964-9112; www.parks.ca.gov), 4 miles north of Fort Bragg, where rocky headlands, tide pools, sandy beaches and pristine dunes unfurl for nine gorgeous miles up the coast

The **visitors center** (☿ 10am-6pm Sat & Sun Jul-Sep, 11am-3pm Sat & Sun Oct-Jun) sits next to the whale skeleton at the park entrance. Hike the **Coastal Trail** along dark-sand beaches and spot wildlife and rare and endangered plant species (tread lightly; no dogs allowed north of the parking lot). Take the easy boardwalk around **Lake Cleone**, a 30-acre freshwater lake stocked with trout and a great spot for birding. At nearby **Laguna Point** an interpretive boardwalk overlooks seals and, December to April, migrating whales. Most people linger around the lake and Laguna Point; to ditch the crowds, walk north. Or ride bikes south along a dedicated **bicycle path** that includes passage over a way-cool train trestle leading to Fort Bragg.

Ricochet Ridge Ranch (☎ 707-964-7669; www.horse-vacation.com; 24201 N Hwy 1) offers horseback-riding trips through redwoods or along the beach ($45, 90 minutes). Guides are terrific, the horses top quality.

Popular **campgrounds** (☎ 800-444-2725; www.reserveamerica.com; campsites $20-25), nestled in pine forest, have hot showers and water; the first-choice reservable campsites are numbers 21 to 59. Ten superb, secluded walk-in campsites (numbers 1-10; campsites $25) are first-come, first-served.

Cleone Gardens (☎ 964-2788, 800-400-2189; www.cleonegardensinn.com; 24600 N Hwy 1; r $98-112, with kitchen $170), a vintage-1970s cedar-sided motel, is slowly being upgraded by new owners. Its good-sized rooms, some with fireplaces and garden-view decks, have vaulted redwood ceilings and are worth checking out if you're not the fussy sort. Hot tub.

WESTPORT
pop 200
The last hamlet before the Lost Coast (p112), sleepy Westport feels like a frontier settlement, with romantic beaches and abundant peace. It's a twisting 15-mile drive from Fort

Bragg, and another 22 miles to Hwy 1's terminus at Hwy 101 in Leggett. (For details on accessing the Lost Coast's southernmost reaches from Westport, see entry on Usal Beach Campground, p115.)

Bring a picnic to **Pacific Star Winery** (☎ 707-964-1155; www.pacificstarwinery.com; 33000 N Hwy 1; tastings free; ☻ 11am-5pm) and sample Italian-style wines from atop stunning ocean view bluffs.

Head north of town for 1.5 miles for the **Westport-Union Landing State Beach** (☎ 707-937-5804; campsites $15), which extends along 3 miles of rugged coastline. It's mostly a primitive campground (with water), but a rough hiking trail passes by tide pools and streams, accessible at low tide. A mile south, **Westport Beach RV & Camping** (☎ 707-964-2964; www.westportbeachrv .com; 37700 N Hwy 1; campsites $22, RV sites $32-36) has showers and beachside tent camping (gates close at 10pm).

For in-town accommodations, the **Westport Inn** (☎ 707-964-5135; 37040 N Hwy 1; r $60) has cheap motel rooms.

North of town, wonderful **Howard Creek Ranch** (☎ 707-964-6725; www.howardcreekranch.com; 40501 N Hwy 1; r $75-125, ste $155-185 all incl breakfast) occupies 60 stunning acres of forest and farmland abutting the wilderness, and has accommodations in an 1880s farmhouse or a carriage barn, whose way-cool redwood rooms have been expertly handcrafted by the owner. Bring hiking boots, not high heels. If you're looking for a rural retreat, look no further.

Want to rent a house? Consider the two-bedroom 1832 **Westport House** (☎ 707-937-4007; www.vrbo.com/61409; per night $200), overlooking pounding surf (there's a two-night minimum stay), or the four-bedroom **Seagate Vacation Rental** (☎ 530-873-6793; www.vrbo.com/30340; 36875 N Hwy 1; per night $250).

INLAND HIGHWAY 101

The fastest route from the Bay Area to the North Coast is Hwy 101, which runs north from San Francisco as a freeway, then as a two- or four-lane highway north of Sonoma County, occasionally passing through small towns with traffic lights. If you're on a budget, consider staying along 101 – but understand that you're trading atmosphere for price.

Timing is everything. Between 4pm and 7pm, northbound traffic snarls. Expect bumper-to-bumper delays any time of day through Santa Rosa – locals use the freeway like it's Main St – and at Willits, where trucks bound for the coast turn onto Hwy 20.

HOPLAND
pop 818

One hundred miles north of San Francisco, cute little Hopland is the gateway to Mendocino County's wine country and has good wine-tasting rooms. Spend an hour getting lost in (and eating your way through) the **Fetzer Vineyards Organic Gardens** (☎ 800-846-8637; www.fetzer.com; 13601 Eastside Rd; ☻ 9am-5pm), possibly the most gorgeous meandering gardens in Northern California; from Hwy 101, turn east onto Hwy 175 and drive one mile. Drop by way-cool **Real Goods Solar Living Center** (☎ 707-744-2100; www.solarliving.org; 13771 S Hwy 101; suggested donation $1-5; ☻ 10am-7pm; ☻) to learn about alternative energy.

Fill up on Americana cooking at the **Bluebird Cafe** (☎ 707-744-1633; 13340 S Hwy 101; breakfast & lunch $5-10, dinner $10-15; ☻ 7am-2pm Mon-Thu, 8am-8pm Fri-Sun; ☻). Spend the night at the 1890 **Hopland Inn** (☎ 707-744-1890, 800-266-1890; www.hoplandinn .com; 13401 S Hwy 101; r $100-130; ☻); book a room in back for maximum quiet.

UKIAH
pop 15,500

Fourteen miles north, downtown Ukiah is pretty dull, but there are some cool nearby sights. **Vichy Hot Springs Resort** (☎ 707-462-9515; www.vichysprings.com; 2605 Vichy Springs Rd; RV campsites $20, lodge s/d $120/165, creekside r $170/215, cottages $295; ☻ ☻) has the only warm-water, naturally carbonated mineral baths in North America; two-hour day-use costs $25, all day runs to $38. Three miles east of Ukiah, via Talmage Rd, the **City of Ten Thousand Buddhas** (☎ 707-462-0939; www.advite.com/sf; 2001 Talmage Rd; ☻ 8am-6pm) is a former state mental hospital that's now a 488-acre Chinese-Buddhist community. Don't miss the temple hall, which really does have 10,000 Buddhas! Be discreet. Stay for lunch in the vegetarian-Chinese **restaurant** (4951 Bodhi Way; dishes $6-9; ☻ 11am-3pm Mon, Wed & Thu, to 6pm Fri-Sun; ☻).

The hands-down best eats are at **Patrona** (☎ 707-462-9181; www.patronarestaurant.com; 130 W Standley St; dishes lunch $9-15, dinner $15-25; ☻ lunch Thu & Fri, dinner Tue-Sat), which specializes in organic, seasonal Euro-Cal cooking. This place alone is worth the detour to Ukiah. **Schat's Courthouse**

Bakery & Cafe (☎ 707-462-1670; 113 W Perkins St; lunch $3-7, dinner $8-14; ☺ 6am-8:30pm Mon-Sat) makes tasty hot dishes and good sandwiches on home-made bread. **Oco Time** (☎ 707-462-2422; 111 W Church St; lunch mains $7-10, dinner $8-16; ☺ lunch Tue-Fri, dinner Mon-Sat) serves surprisingly good Japanese.

Request a remodeled room at the budget-friendly **Sunrise Inn** (☎ 707-462-6601; www.sunriseinn .net; 650 S State St; r $48-68; ☒). **Holiday Inn Express** (☎ 707-462-5745, 800-465-4329; www.hiexpress.com/ukiahca; 1720 N State St; r $89-99; ☒ ☒ ☒) is the best (and newest) of the cookie-cutter chains. **Discovery Inn Motel** (☎ 707-462-8873; www.5motels.com; 1340 N State St; r $85-90; ☒ ☒) has a big pool and clean (if tired-looking) rooms.

Far-out, clothing-optional **Orr Hot Springs** (☎ 707-462-6277; hotwater@pacific.net; campsites $45-50, dm $55-65, s $100-125, d $135-155, cottages $185-215; ☺ 10am-10pm) is *the* place for back-to-the-land hipsters and backpackers who like to get naked. Shy types wear sarongs. Rates include access to the communal redwood hot tub, private porcelain tubs, outdoor tile-and-rock heated pools, sauna, spring-fed rock-bottom swimming pool, steam, massage and magical gardens. There's also a communal kitchen. Day-use costs $25; reservations are required. From Hwy 101 in Ukiah, take N State St exit, go north a quarter of a mile to Orr Springs Rd, then 9 miles west. The steep, winding mountain road takes 30 minutes to drive. (Continue westward, via Comptche–Ukiah Rd, and you'll wind up in Mendocino, p97.)

WILLITS
pop 5000
Twenty miles north of Ukiah, Willits has a NorCal boho vibe; tie-dye is de rigueur. It's the last town before the redwoods, but is most famous as the eastern terminus of the **Skunk Train** (☎ 707-459-5248, 866-457-5865; www.skunktrain .com), which runs between Willits and Fort Bragg (for details, see p103).

Some of the in-town motels are dumps; choose carefully. Cheaper options include the way-dated but clean **Edgewood Motel** (☎ 707-459-5914; fax 707-459-4875; 1521 S Main St; r $50-60; ☒); **Best Value Inn Holiday Lodge** (☎ 707-459-5361, 800-835-3972; www.bestvalueinn.com; 1540 S Main St; r $69-99; ☒ ☒); or the quiet, Old West-themed **Old West Inn** (☎ 707-459-4201, 800-700-7659; fax 707-459-3009; 1221 S Main St; r $69-89; ☒ ☒).

Up-market motels include the top-choice **Baechtel Creek Inn & Spa** (☎ 707-459-9063, 800-459-9911; www.baechtelcreekinn.com; 101 Gregory Lane; r $90-

120; ☒ ☒ ☒) and second-choice **Super 8 Motel** (☎ 707-459-3388, 800-800-8000; www.super8.com; 1119 S Main St; r $69-89; ☒ ☒).

Tiny **Ardella's Kitchen** (☎ 707-459-6577; 35 E Commercial St; meals $5-8; ☺ 6am-noon Tue-Sat) is tops for breakfast. **Anna's Asian House** (☎ 707-459-6086; 47 Mendocino Ave; mains $6-10; ☺ 11am-9pm Mon-Sat) serves respectable, MSG-free Szechuan cooking.

REDWOOD COAST

Welcome to the land of tall trees, timber wars and marijuana farms. People 'beyond the red-wood curtain' pride themselves on their life-styles, and if you haven't yet seen a Mercedes chugging down the highway on vegetable oil, you will now. Hardly any travelers venture north of Mendocino, so you'll pretty much have the road to yourself. North of Leggett, the redwoods appear, trees so big that you'll lose perspective on size. It takes a while to adjust to nature's scale here: avoid jumping out of the car only to snap pictures, or you won't really grasp what you're seeing. Instead, leave time to lollygag and bask in the haunting grandeur of it all.

LEGGETT
pop 200
Hwy 1 ends and redwood country begins at Leggett, a good stopping point between the far north and the Bay Area. There ain't much but an expensive gas station, lunch counter, good pizza joint with beer, and two markets. The town center is just off Hwy 1. (Bicyclists: If you're riding south on Hwy 1, you may want to hitchhike over the mountains toward West-port. The road twists and turns for 20 miles before hitting the coast, and there's hardly a shoulder. If you do ride, don't wear your iPod so you can hear approaching trucks.)

The 1000-acre **Standish-Hickey State Recrea-tion Area** (☎ 707-925-6482; 69350 Hwy 101; per car $6), 1.5 miles to the north, has picnicking, river swimming and fishing, and 9 miles of hiking trails among virgin and second-growth red-woods (check out the 225ft tall Miles Standish Tree). Salmon and steelhead fishing is best in the fall and winter. There are year-round **campgrounds** (☎ 800-444-7275; www.reserveamerica .com; campsites $15-20) with hot showers here; book in summer and avoid the highway-side sites.

Chandelier Drive-Thru Tree Park (☎ 707-925-6363; Drive-Thru Tree Rd; per car $5; ☺ 8am-dusk; ☒) has 200 private acres of virgin redwoods with pretty picnicking and nature walks. And yes, there's a 315ft-tall, 2000-year-old redwood with a square hole carved out, large enough to accommodate a Chevy Suburban. Only in America.

Love it or hate it, **Confusion Hill** (☎ 707-925-6456; www.confusionhill.com; 75001 N Hwy 101; adult/child gravity house $5/4, train rides $7/5; ❧ 9am-6pm summer, 10am-5pm winter; ⚓) is pure cheese, a classic, old-fashioned tourist trap from 1949. In the (overpriced) 'gravity house,' gravity plays tricks on you, and some claim to feel dizzy (we did), which makes sense because you're standing at a 40-degree angle trying to keep your balance. Water reportedly flows uphill: we stared and stared, eager to be impressed, but it just didn't happen. Still, kids go nuts for the playhouse quality of the space, and the narrow-gauge train rides are exciting for toddlers. Cynics: Stay away.

Across from Confusion Hill, **Redwoods River Resort** (☎ 707-925-6249; www.redwoodriverresort.com; 75000 Hwy 101; campsites $22-29, RV sites $33-35, cabins $95-110, lodge r $83-130) has a range of lodgings, good for families.

For basic supplies, groceries, sandwiches and cookies and brownies worth stopping for, visit the **Peg House** (☎ 707-925-6444; 69501 Hwy 101; ❧ 8am-9pm). There's BBQ food in the garden most afternoons. For diner food and pizza, head to the center of town.

RICHARDSON GROVE STATE PARK

Fifteen miles north, bisected by the Eel River, **Richardson Grove** (☎ 707-247-3318; Hwy 101; per car $6) occupies 1400 acres of virgin forest. Many trees are over 1000 years old and 300ft tall, but there aren't many hiking trails. In winter, there's good fishing for silver and king salmon. The **visitors center** (☎ 707-247-3318; ❧ 9am-2pm) sells books and gifts inside a 1930s lodge, which often has a fire going during cool weather. The park is primarily a **campground** (☎ reservations 800-444-7275; www.reserveamerica.com; campsites $15-20) with three separate areas with

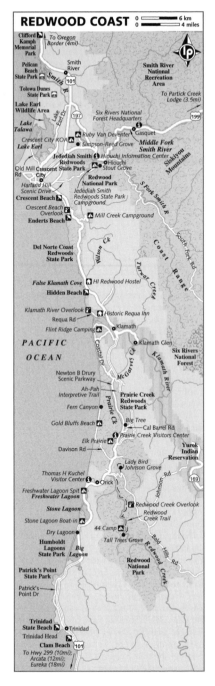

REDWOOD COAST

0 ——— 6 km
0 ——— 4 miles

TOP 5 ROMANTIC HIDEAWAYS ON THE REDWOOD COAST

- **Shelter Cove Bed & Breakfast** (p113)
- **Historic Requa Inn** (p133)
- **Benbow Inn** (opposite)
- **Carter House** (p118)
- **Casa Rubio** (p138)

hot showers; some remain open year-round. Summer-only Oak Flat on the east side of the river is shady and has a sandy beach.

BENBOW LAKE

On the Eel River, 2 miles south of Garberville, the 1200-acre **Benbow Lake State Recreation Area** (☎ summer 707-923-3238, winter 707-923-3318; per car $6) exists when a seasonal dam forms 26-acre Benbow Lake, mid-June to mid-September. In mid-August, avoid swimming in the lake or river until two weeks after the Reggae on the River festival (right), when 25,000 people use the river as a bathtub. The water is cleanest in early summer.

A monument to 1920s rustic elegance, **Benbow Inn** (☎ 707-923-2124, 800-355-3301; www.benbowinn.com; 445 Lake Benbow Dr; r $130-305, cottage $375; ☒ ☒) is a national historic landmark and the Redwood Empire's first luxury resort. Hollywood's elite once frolicked in the Tudor-style resort's lobby, where you can play chess by the crackling fire, and enjoy complimentary afternoon tea and evening hors d'oeuvres. Moss-covered oaks shade the lawns fronting on the river, a perfect place for reading. Rooms have top-quality beds, antique furniture, a decanter of sherry and paperbacks in a basket. The window-lined dining room (breakfast and lunch $10 to $15, dinner mains $22 to $32) serves good Euro-Cal cuisine and Sunday brunch. There's an adjoining golf course and smart-looking RV resort.

Across Hwy 101, the year-round riverside **campground** (☎ reservations 800-444-7275; www.reserveamerica.com; campsites $23-28) is subject to wintertime bridge closures due to flooding, but this is when the fishing is best. There's one shower; sites endure highway noise. Expect crowds in summer because of the easy proximity to recreation – golf (at Benbow Inn), swimming, biking and hiking.

GARBERVILLE
pop 1800
The main supply center for southern Humboldt County and the primary jumping-off point to the Lost Coast and the Avenue of the Giants, Garberville looks like Main Street USA – until you notice all the hooligans on the sidewalks. There's an uneasy relationship between the old-guard fisher-logger types and the hippies, many of whom came in the 1970s to grow sinsemilla (potent, seedless marijuana) after the feds chased them out of

Santa Cruz. At last count, the hippies were winning the culture wars, with tie-dye shirts edging out fishing vests. But the war rages: a sign on the door of a local bar lays plain who is, and is not, welcome. It reads simply: 'Absolutely NO patchouli oil!!!'. Two miles west, Garberville's ragtag sister Redway has fewer services, but a noteworthy restaurant. Garberville is four hours north of San Francisco, one hour south of Eureka.

Information
Garberville-Redway Area Chamber of Commerce (☎ 707-923-2613, 800-923-2613; www.garberville.org; 784 Redwood Dr; ☷ 8am-4pm Mon-Fri, 10am-4pm Sat & Sun Jul-Sep) Inside the Redwood Dr Center; has tourist information.
KMUD FM91 Find out what's really happening by tuning in to community radio.
Treats (☎ 707-923-3554; 764 Redwood Dr; per min $0.15; ☷ 10am-6pm) Internet access and wi-fi.

Activities
The area's sights and activities are in surrounding parks and on the Lost Coast (p112). If you want to kayak down the Eel River, visit **Tsunami Surf & Sport** (☎ 707-923-1965; 445 Conger; ☷ Mon-Sat).

Festivals & Events
Reggae on the River (☎ 707-923-4583; www.reggaeontheriver.com) in early August draws huge crowds for reggae, world music, arts-and-craft fairs, camping and swimming in the river. Headliners include luminaries like the always-barefoot Michael Franti and Spearhead. Three-day passes ($175) go on sale March 1 and sell out fast; no single tickets. This is by far the North Coast's biggest event.

Other annual events:
Avenue of the Giants Marathon (www.theave.org) May foot race.
Harley-Davidson Redwood Run (www.redwoodrun.com) Held in June.
Garberville Rodeo June rodeo.
Summer Arts & Music Festival September event at Benbow Lake.
Humboldt Hempfest Celebrate all things hemp in November.
Winter Arts Fair A mid-December fair.

Sleeping
Prices drop significantly in winter.
Best Western Humboldt House Inn (☎ 707-923-2771, 800-528-1234; 701 Redwood Dr; r $119-129; ☒ ☒)

Though generic, it's by far the best place in town, with good beds, upgraded furnishings and refrigerators. Call ahead; it fills nearly every night in summer.

Redwoods Getaway (☎ 707-923-2061; www.redwoods getaway.com; Redway; house $200) A three-bedroom house right on the Eel River; call ahead.

For cheaper lodging, there are two satisfactory motels. First try **Sherwood Forest** (☎ 707-923-2721; www.sherwoodforestmotel.com; 814 Redwood Dr; r $66-84; 🔲 🐾), then **Humboldt Redwoods Inn** (☎ 707-923-2451; www.humboldtredwoodsinn.com; 987 Redwood Dr; r $59-95; 🔲 🐾), but the desk clerks are hardly ever there, so call ahead.

There's also camping and lodging at Benbow Lake (p109) and the Avenue of the Giants (right).

Eating
Nacho Mama (☎ 707-923-4060; 375 Sprowel Creek Rd; meals under $6; 🕑 11am-7pm Mon-Sat) This tiny shack on the corner of Redwood Dr has organic fast-food Mexican. Tops for budget eats.

Woodrose Cafe (☎ 707-923-3191; 911 Redwood Dr; meals $7-11; 🕑 breakfast & lunch; 🚼) Garberville's much-beloved cafe serves organic-egg omelettes, veggie scrambles, and buckwheat pancakes with *real* maple syrup. Lunch brings crunchy salads, sandwiches with all-natural meats, and good burritos. There's lots for vegetarians too. This is the one place everyone in town can agree is great. Too bad it's closed at dinner. No credit cards.

Eel River Cafe (☎ 707-923-3783; 801 Redwood Dr; dishes under $10; 🕑 6am-2pm Thu-Mon; 🚼) Breakfast is the thing at this old-school diner, where locals line up every morning to score booths. Order the blueberry pancakes. Alas, they're served with Log Cabin–like syrup; BYO maple.

Calico's Deli & Pasta (☎ 707-923-2253; 808 Redwood Dr; dishes $6-13; 🕑 11am-9pm; 🚼) Calico's has house-made pasta and sandwiches, good if you're with kids or want a hot dinner for 10 bucks, but don't be surprised if there's water on the plate under your noodles.

Mateel Cafe (☎ 707-923-2030; 3342-44 Redwood Dr, Redway; lunch $8-12, dinner $20-26; 🕑 11:30am-9pm Mon-Sat) After the Woodrose, Mateel Cafe (in Redway) makes the best eats in the area. The wildly diverse menu lists everything from steaks and chops to stone-baked pizzas to rice and veggies. The salads are terrific. If there's lemon tart on special, order it without hesitation.

Chautauqua Natural Foods (☎ 707-923-2452; 436 Church St; 🕑 Mon-Sat) Sells natural groceries. Has a small dining area and a great bulletin board.

Drinking & Entertainment
You can also sip cocktails in an elegant 1920s Tudor-style inn at the Benbow Inn (p109).

Sicilito's (☎ 707-923-2814; 445 Conger St; meals $6-14; 🕑 11:30am-10pm) Behind the Best Western, Sicilito's serves microbrews and frat-boy food worth skipping.

Garberville Theatre (☎ 707-923-3580; 766 Redwood Dr) First-run movies.

HUMBOLDT REDWOODS STATE PARK & AVENUE OF THE GIANTS
Of all of California's redwood parks, **Humboldt Redwoods State Park** (☎ 707-946-2409) packs the biggest punch, if only because it's easily accessible by car. The park covers 53,000 acres – 17,000 old-growth – and protects some of the world's most magnificent trees, including 74 of the 100 tallest.

Exit Hwy 101 when you see the **Avenue of the Giants** road sign, and travel parallel to Hwy 101 along this incredible 32-mile, two-lane stretch, which winds beneath the canopy of the biggest trees you may ever see. The ribbon of asphalt below them looks ridiculously small by comparison, like a child's toy-car racetrack. Pick up free driving guides at roadside signboards at the avenue's southern entrance, 6 miles north of Garberville (Hwy 101 Exit 645), and at the northern entrance, south of Scotia (Hwy 101 Exit 674); there are access points off Hwy 101. Driving the Avenue instead of Hwy 101 adds only 15 minutes to your northbound travel time.

South of Weott, a volunteer-staffed **visitors center** (☎ 707-946-2263; 🕑 9am-5pm summer, 10am-4pm winter; 🚼) has shady picnic areas. If you're into history and ecology, plan to spend an hour here. The small **museum** has cool taxidermy, photo albums of locals floods and fires, hands-on exhibits, summertime kids' programs and informative displays on logging and salmon. The *pièce de résistance* is the historic 1917 'Travel Log,' a life-sized RV made from the trunk of a carved-out redwood. Wow.

Primeval **Rockefeller Forest**, 4.5 miles west of the avenue via Mattole Rd, appears as it did a century ago. It's the world's largest contiguous old-growth redwood forest, and contains about 20% of all such remaining trees. In **Founders Grove**, north of the visitors center, the **Dyerville Giant** was knocked over in 1991 by another falling tree. A walk along its gargantuan 370ft length, with its humongous trunk towering above, helps you appreciate how huge these ancient trees are.

Walking Trails

The park has over 100 miles of trails for hiking, mountain biking and horseback riding. Trails don't dry or get cleaned up until mid-June, and fallen trees lie across the paths – don't wear new white tennies in spring! Seasonal river bridges go up in mid-June. Easy walks include short nature trails in Founders Grove and Rockefeller Forest and the **Drury-Chaney Loop Trail**. The **Bull Creek Flats trail** is the only trail that loops through the heart of the contiguous old-growth forest – and it's moderately easy. Schedule half a day and plan to swim in the creek (summer only). The most challenging is the **Grasshopper Peak Trail**, south of the visitors center, which climbs to the 3379ft fire lookout.

For a break from hiking, taste wine at **Riverbend Cellars** (☎ 707-943-9907; www.riverbendcellars.com; 12990 Ave of the Giants, Myers Flat; ◷ 11am-6pm).

Other sights

If you love JRR Tolkien's story *The Hobbit*, stop at fabulously wacky **Hobbiton USA** (☎ 707-923-2265; 1111 Ave of the Giants, Phillipsville; ◷ 11am-7pm May-Sep; ⚑), and follow Bilbo's story as you wander through the woods pressing buttons to hear sounds of creatures, castles and hobbits. It's pure cheese, like a bedtime story in the woods.

Steer your Buick through the **Shrine Drive-thru Tree** (☎ 707-943-1658; 13078 Ave of the Giants, Myers Flat; per person $1.50; ◷ 10am-5pm; ⚑), a living tree hollowed out by lightning. This is the original drive-thru tree, open since the 1920s. There's a kid's walk-thru tree like Old Mother Hubbard's shoe – a great photo op!

Sleeping & Eating

Several towns along the avenue have simple lodgings – but choose wisely: some are creepy, some deceptively cheerful, some run by bigots. (One innkeeper told me, 'I run a safe place. I don't allow any gays, freaks or troublemakers.' Uh, dude, doesn't that describe about half of Lonely Planet's readership?)

Campgrounds (☎ reservations 800-444-7275; www .reserveamerica.com; campsites $15-20) The park runs three campgrounds with hot showers, two environmental camps, five trail camps, a hike-bike camp and an equestrian camp. One of the three, Burlington, is beside the visitors center and is open year-round. It's near trailheads and the road, but it's in the redwoods and kids like it. The other two are open mid-May to early autumn: Hidden Springs, 5 miles south, is on oak mountainsides with sites surrounded by brush; it has more privacy and the best swimming. Albee Creek, on Mattole Rd past Rockefeller Forest, is the prettiest, with meadows and apple orchards where wildlife comes to feed; it's nearest the backcountry trailheads.

Giant Redwoods RV & Campground (☎ 707-943-3198; www.giantredwoodsrvcamp.com; 455 Boy Scout Camp Rd, Myers Flat; tent/RV sites $25/37) If the campgrounds are full, come here. This place has showers, hookups, riverside sites, beaches and activities.

BERRIES, BERRIES EVERYWHERE

August to October, blackberry bushes bear fruit as big as your thumb – and they're *everywhere*. Here's how to pick 'em. If you're reading this before your trip, pack gardening gloves; the stalks of the bushes are covered in sharp thorns. Wear long sleeves to protect your skin. Stomp your feet to shake the ground and scare off snakes, and carry a stick to whack at the bushes and warn animals you're coming. The sweetest berries come right off the branch without any tugging. If they resist picking, they're still sour.

If you can't bear to venture into a thicket of prickers, stop at **Flood Plain Produce** (3117 Ave of the Giants, Pepperwood), a self-serve roadside farm stand that sells homemade blackberry popsicles. Take your popsicle across the street and head 100 yards north to the break in the bushes. A short way ahead you'll find an *enormous* 100-year-old walnut tree, perfect for climbing. (If you're unsure, ask at the fruit stand.) On your way back to the road, stain your fingers purple picking more berries!

Miranda Gardens Resort (☎ 707-943-3011; www .mirandagardens.com; 6766 Ave of the Giants, Miranda; cottages $105-165, cottages with kitchen $155-265; ☒) One of the best in the area and family friendly. The cozy, slightly rustic cottages have redwood paneling; some have fireplaces. They're a tad musty – as is everything under the redwoods – but the bathrooms are clean and there's a pool. Across the street there's a family restaurant.

our pick **Vacation House in the Redwoods** (☎ 707-722-4330; www.redwoodvisitor.org; 31117 Ave of the Giants, Phillipsville; house $135) This is a lovely one-bedroom cottage surrounded by a sunny flower farm. It sleeps up to five. A hammock, deck and hot tub sweeten the deal.

Riverwood Inn (☎ 707-943-3333; www.riverwoodinn .info; 2828 Ave of the Giants, Phillipsville; ☺ lunch Sat & Sun, dinner Wed-Mon). Packed with Harley riders, this inn is a raucous haunted roadhouse near Garberville, which hosts blues, folk and rock bands, mixes strong drinks and serves OK Mexican cooking. It also rents rooms ($55 to $80).

Chimney Tree (☎ 707-923-2265; 1111 Ave of the Giants, Phillipsville; ☺ 10am-7pm May-Sep; ☐) The burgers here are worth a detour. The restaurant raises its own grass-fed beef. Alas, the fries are frozen, but those burgers…mmm-mmm! Wander into the namesake burned-out redwood tree while waiting for your burger.

At the time of writing, worthwhile Knights restaurant in Myers Flat had closed, but may reopen.

SCOTIA
pop 1000

Scotia is a rarity in modern times: it's one of the last 'company towns' in California, entirely owned and operated by the Pacific Lumber Company (Palco), which runs the world's largest redwood lumber mill. Times are changing, though. The mill sawed its last big tree in 1997 and no longer has a blade big enough to cut giant redwoods. There's talk of the mill selling the town to its inhabitants. Find out more at the **Scotia Museum & Visitors Center** (☎ 707-764-2222; www.palco.com; cnr Main & Bridge Sts; ☺ 8am-4:30pm Mon-Fri summer), at the town's south end. Free self-guided mill tours are available Monday to Friday. The museum's **fisheries exhibit** is remarkably good and informative – ironic, considering that logging destroys fish habitats. In summer, go to the museum for information; otherwise head to the guardhouse at the mill's entrance.

As you drive along Hwy 101 and see what appears to be a never-ending redwood forest, understand that this 'forest' sometimes consists of trees only a few rows deep – called a 'beauty strip' – a carefully crafted illusion for tourists. Most old-growth trees have been cut. Once you've grasped Palco's party line about 'forestry stewardship,' log on to the website of the **Bay Area Coalition for Headwaters Forest** (www .headwaterspreserve.org) to learn about clear-cutting and the politics of the timber wars. Also tune in to community-radio station KMUD FM 90.3 and 91.1.

But keep your mouth shut. For Scotia's official 'Code of Conduct,' consult placards posted around town. There's one at Hoby's Market, directly opposite the Scotia Inn's front door. You may neither yell, scream nor sing loud enough for anyone else to hear; in other words, no protesting or you'll get arrested.

Scotia is downright creepy, like a set from the *Twilight Zone*. If you're under 50, need a haircut, and forgot to carry your American flag, you'll get suspicious looks. Watch your back: if you feel like you're being followed, you *are*.

There's no compelling reason to linger. At the time of writing, the **Scotia Inn** (☎ 707-764-5683, 707-764-2222; 100 Main St) had closed, it reopened for weekend business, but again appears closed.

Hoby's Market (☎ 707-764-5331; 105 Main St) sells sandwiches and groceries and has great prices on meat – stock up here if you're barbecuing for a crowd.

There are nothing-special motels and diners in **Rio Dell** (aka 'Real Dull'), across the river. Back in the day, this is where the debauchery happened: because it wasn't a company town, Rio Dell had bars and hookers. In 1969, the freeway bypassed the town, and it died.

LOST COAST

The North Coast's premier backpacking destination, California's 'Lost Coast' extends from where Hwy 1 cuts inland, north of Westport, to just south of Ferndale. It became 'lost' when the state's highway system bypassed the region early in the 20th century. It's not feasible to run a road through here. The rugged King Range rises 4000ft, within 3 miles of the coast, with cliffs plunging to the sea. The range is extremely unstable and in a recent earthquake rose nearly 4ft at once!

The Lost Coast is one of California's most pristine coastal areas. The central and southern stretches fall respectively within the King Range National Conservation Area and the Sinkyone Wilderness State Park. The area north of the King Range is more accessible, but the scenery less dramatic.

In autumn the weather is clear, if cool. Wildflowers bloom from April through May, and gray whales migrate from December through April. The warmest, driest months are June to August, but days are foggy. The weather can quickly change.

Information

Although there are several one-horse rural settlements (Petrolia and Honeydew, for example), the significant community is Shelter Cove, an isolated unincorporated town 25 long miles west of Garberville. Get supplies in Garberville, Ferndale, Eureka or Arcata. The area is a patchwork of government-owned land and private property. Take it easy while driving, especially in fog, and pull over to let people pass. Check for ticks: Lyme disease is common. Don't jump fences or trespass, especially in October at harvest time; this is pot-growing country, and some locals won't hesitate to fire a shotgun in your direction. Locals claim that nearby Cape Mendocino is the westernmost point in the contiguous US. It's not. That honor belongs to Cape Alava, Washington.

Shelter Cove

pop 500

The only sizable community on the Lost Coast, remote Shelter Coves is surrounded by King Range National Conservation Area and abuts a large south-facing cove. It's a tiny seaside subdivision with an airstrip in the middle – indeed, many visitors are private pilots. Fifty years ago, southern California swindlers subdivided the land, built the airstrip, and flew in potential investors, fast-talking them into buying seaside land for retirement. But they didn't tell buyers that a steep, winding, one-lane dirt road provided the *only* access, and that the seaside plots were eroding into the sea.

Today, there's still only one route, but now it's paved. Cell phones don't work here: if you want to disappear this is a good place. The town is a mild disappointment, with not much to do, but stunning **Black Sands Beach** stretches for miles northward, a perfect place for long, romantic walks.

SLEEPING

For a complete list of lodgings, log on to www .sojourner2000.com. **Northern California Properties** (☎ 707-986-7346; 101 Lower Pacific Dr) rents vacation properties.

Shelter Cove RV Park, Campground & Deli (☎ 707-986-7474; 492 Machi Rd; tent/RV sites $25/35) This park has hot showers and outdoor tables.

Shelter Cove Beachcomber Inn (☎ 707-986-7551, 800-718-4789; www.sojourner2000.com; 412 Machi Rd; r $65-105) Slightly inland, the Beachcomber Inn has some rooms with kitchens and woodburning stoves; all have BBQ and picnic tables; they could use upgrades, but they're a bargain.

Marina Motel (☎ 707-986-7595; 533 Machi Rd; r $100) There are plain-jane rooms at this bland, last-choice motel.

Oceanfront Inn & Lighthouse (☎ 707-986-7002; http://sheltercoveoceanfrontinn.com; 10 Seal Court; r $125-145, ste $175) The tidy, modern rooms here have microwaves, refrigerators, and balconies overlooking the sea. The decor is spartan so as not to detract from the view. Splurge on a kitchen suite; the best is upstairs, with its peaked ceiling and giant windows.

Inn of the Lost Coast (☎ 707-986-7521, 888-570-9676; www.innofthelostcoast.com; 205 Wave Dr; r $145-250) This inn has clean, albeit charmless, motel rooms, with full ocean views; downstairs there's the Lost Coast Coffee Company.

Cliff House at Shelter Cove (☎ 707-986-7344; www .cliffhousesheltercove.com; 141 Wave Dr; ste $149-169) The rooms feel prefab and sterile at this oceanfront place, but they have kitchens.

Shelter Cove Bed & Breakfast (☎ 707-986-7161; www.sheltercovebandb.com; 148 Dolphin Dr; r $175-195) This is the best place to stay (by far). This sparkling oceanfront retreat is managed by supercool, design-savvy owners. It sits high on a bluff overlooking the crashing surf and is so clean that even the windows get washed once a week. Decked out with natural linen furniture and white beadboard wainscotting, the place is gorgeous, a real love nest; leave the kids at home. Oh, if you don't like B&Bs, note that the owners live off-site.

EATING

Cove Restaurant (☎ 707-986-1197; 10 Seal Court; dishes $6-19; ✆ dinner Thu-Sun) This first-choice restaurant has everything from veggie stir-fries to New York steaks.

Mario's (☎ 707-986-1401; 533 Machi Rd; breakfast & lunch $6-11, dinner $10-20; ✆ Fri-Wed) For straight-

NORTH COAST

forward American, there's this eatery, which has a bar.

Shelter Cove RV Park, Campground & Deli (☎ 707-986-7474; 492 Machi Rd; ☺ 8am-6pm daily Jul-Sep, Tue-Sun Oct-Mar) Serves up good fish and chips.

Get groceries and gasoline at **Shelter Cove General Store** (☎ 707-986-7733; 7272 Shelter Cove Rd), 2 miles beyond town.

King Range National Conservation Area

Stretching over 35 miles of virgin coastline, with ridge after ridge of mountainous terrain plunging to the surf, the 60,000-acre area tops out at namesake King's Peak (4087ft). The wettest spot in California, the range receives over 120in – and as much as 240in – of annual rainfall, causing frequent landslides; in winter snow falls on the ridges. (By contrast, nearby sea-level Shelter Cove gets only 69in of rain and no snow.) Two-thirds of the area is awaiting wilderness designation.

Nine miles east of Shelter Cove, the **Bureau of Land Management** (BLM; ☎ 707-986-5400, 707-825-2300; 768 Shelter Cove Rd; ☺ 8am-4:30pm Mon-Sat Memorial Day–Labor Day, 8am-4:30pm Mon-Fri May-Sep) has maps and directions for trails and campsites; they're posted outside after hours. For overnight hikes, you'll need a backcountry-use permit. Note that many travelers mistakenly turn left onto Briceland-Thorn Rd in an attempt to find the 'town' of Whitethorn. But there is no town, just boarded up buildings. Whitethorn is the BLM's name for the *general* area. To reach the BLM office from Garberville/Redway, follow signs to Shelter Cove; look for the roadside information panel, 0.25 miles past the post office. Information and permits are also available from the BLM in Arcata (p124).

Fire restrictions begin July 1 and last until the first soaking rain, usually in November. During this time, there are no campfires allowed outside developed campgrounds.

HIKING

The best way to see the Lost Coast is to hike. (Call the BLM for current trail conditions.) Some of the best trails start from Mattole Campground, near Petrolia. It's at the ocean end of Lighthouse Rd, 4 miles from Mattole Rd, southeast of Petrolia.

The **Lost Coast Trail** follows 24.7 miles of coastline from Mattole Campground in the north to Black Sands Beach at Shelter Cove in the south. The prevailing northerly winds make it best to hike from north to south; plan three or four days. In October and November, and April and May, the weather is iffy and winds can blow south to north, depending on whether there's a low-pressure system overhead. The best times to come are summer weekdays at the end of August, early June, and September and October. The busiest times are Memorial Day, Labor Day and summer weekends. For information on backpacker shuttles, call the BLM or contact **Lost Coast Trail Transport Services** (☎ 707-986-9909; www.lostcoasttrail.com) or **Lost Coast Shuttle** (☎ 707-223-1547).

Highlights include an abandoned lighthouse at Punta Gorda, remnants of early shipwrecks, tide pools and abundant wildlife including sea lions, seals and more than 300 bird species. The trail is mostly level, passing beaches and crossing over rocky outcrops. Along the Lost Coast Trail, **Big Flat** is the most popular backcountry destination. Carry a tide table, lest you get trapped: from Buck Creek to Miller Creek, you can only hike during an outgoing tide.

A good **day hike** starts at the Mattole Campground trailhead and travels 3 miles south along the coast to the Punta Gorda lighthouse (return against the wind).

People have discovered the Lost Coast Trail. To ditch the crowds, take any of the (strenuous) upland trails off the beach toward the ridgeline. For a satisfying, hard 21-mile-long hike originating at the Lost Coast Trail, take Buck Creek Trail to King Crest Trail to Rattlesnake Ridge Trail. The 360 degree views from **King Peak** are stupendous, particularly on the full moon or during a meteor shower. Note that if you hike up, it can be hellish hot on the ridges, though the coast remains cool and foggy; wear removable layers. Carry a topographical map and a compass: signage is limited along these trails.

Both Wailaki and Nadelos have developed **campgrounds** (campsites $8) with toilets and water. There are another four developed campgrounds around the range, with toilets but no water (except Honeydew, which has purifiable creek water). There are multiple primitive walk-in sites. Outside developed campgrounds, you'll need a bear canister and backcountry permit, both available from BLM offices.

Sinkyone Wilderness State Park

Named for the Sinkyone people who once lived here, this 7367-acre wilderness extends south of Shelter Cove along pristine coastline.

The **Lost Coast Trail** continues here for another 22 miles, from Whale Gulch south to Usal Beach Campground, taking at least three days as it meanders along high ridges, providing bird's-eye views down to deserted beaches and the crashing surf; side trails descend to water level. Near the park's northern end, the (haunted!) **Needle Rock Ranch** (☎ 707-986-7711; campsites $10) serves as a remote visitors center; register here for the adjacent campsites. This is the only source of potable water. For information when the ranch is closed (most of the time), call **Richardson Grove State Park** (☎ 707-247-3318).

To get to Sinkyone, drive west from Garberville and Redway on Briceland-Thorn Rd, 21 miles through Whitethorn to Four Corners. Turn left (south) and continue for 3.5 miles down a very rugged road to the ranch house; it takes 1½ hours.

There's access to the **Usal Beach Campground** (campsites $15) at the south end of the park from Hwy 1 (you can't make reservations): north of Westport, unpaved County Rd 431 begins from Hwy 1's milepost 90.88 and travels 6 miles up the coast to the campground. The road is graded yearly in late spring, and is passable in summer via two-wheel-drive vehicle. Most sites are past the message board by the beach. Use bear canisters or keep food in your trunk. Look for giant elk feeding on the tall grass – they live behind sites No 1 and 2 – and osprey by the creek's mouth.

North of the campground, Usal Rd (County Rd 431) is much rougher and recommended only if you have a high-clearance 4WD and a chainsaw. Seriously.

North of the King Range

You can reach the Lost Coast's northern section year-round via paved, narrow Mattole Rd. Plan three hours to navigate the winding 68 miles from Ferndale in the north to the coast at Cape Mendocino, then inland to Humboldt Redwoods State Park and Hwy 101. Don't expect redwoods: the vegetation is grassland and pasture. It's beautiful in spots – lined with wildflowers, with sweeping vistas out to sea – but there are few places to stop. It's prettiest in spring, while the hills are still green. (Note that if you're a nervous driver, you'll hate this route.)

You'll pass two tiny settlements. **Petrolia** is the site of California's first oil well, capped-off on private property. Locals dislike outsiders.

Visit the cemetery instead. Or better yet, pick blueberries at **Lost Coast Blueberries** (☎ 707-629-3563; 41774 Matole Rd), but call ahead. There's also a post office and **store** (☎ 707-629-3455; ☻ 9am-5pm) with bear-canister rentals (cash only), gasoline, propane and kerosene. At **Honeydew** there's a semireliable gas station, post office and **store** (☎ 707-629-3310; ☻ 9am-5pm). Locals are friendly, but there's nothing to do but hang out on the front porch. The drive is enjoyable, but the Lost Coast's wild, spectacular scenery lies further south in the more remote regions.

There's creekside camping with flush toilets and cold showers at the developed **AW Way County Park** (☎ 707-445-7651; Mattole Rd; per vehicle $15), 6 miles southeast of Petrolia, on the road toward Honeydew.

FERNDALE
pop 1400

The North Coast's most charming town has so many impeccable Victorians that the entire place is listed as a state and federal historical landmark. It's the kind of town where people say hello on the street and stop to pet each other's dogs. When Hollywood location scouts came to Ferndale, hoping to use the local fairgrounds to film *Seabiscuit*, locals said no way would they allow anything to stop the Humboldt County Fair, which has been held in the same spot every year, rain or shine, since 1896. Dairy farmers built the town in the 19th century, and it's still run by the 'milk mafia': you're not a local till you've lived here 40 years. Stroll Main St and poke your head into galleries, old-fashioned emporiums and soda fountains. Although Ferndale relies on tourism, it has refreshingly avoided becoming a tourist trap – and has no chain stores. It's a lovely place to spend the night, but it's dead as a doornail in winter.

Information

Look for free copies around town of the souvenir edition of the *Ferndale Enterprise* for walking and driving tours.

Computer Assistance (☎ 707-786-1016; 524b Main St) Check email.

Ferndale Chamber of Commerce (☎ 707-786-4477; www.victorianferndale.org/chamber) The website has current information, or use the phone service.

Ferndale Library (☎ 707-786-9559; 807 Main St; ☻ noon-5pm & 7-9pm Tue-Thu, noon-4pm Fri, to 5pm Sat) Internet access, one-hour limit.

NORTH COAST

Sights & Activities

As Ferndale's settlers grew wealthy from dairy farming, some built ornate mansions called 'butterfat palaces.' The **Gingerbread Mansion** (400 Berding St), an 1898 Queen Anne-Eastlake, is the town's most photographed building. **Shaw House** (703 Main St) was the first permanent structure in Ferndale. The town's founder, Seth Shaw, started constructing the gabled Carpenter Gothic in 1854; it wasn't completed until 1866. Called 'Fern Dale' for the 6ft-tall ferns that grew here, it housed the first post office, of which Shaw was the postmaster – hence the town's name. The 1866, 32-room **Fern Cottage** (☎ 707-786-4835; www.ferncottage.org; Centerville Rd; adult/senior/student/under 7 $5/4/2.50/free; ☺ 10am-4pm Wed-Sun Jul-Sep), west of town, was originally a Carpenter Gothic that grew as the family did. Only one family ever lived here, so nothing got thrown away, and it's all been preserved. Call ahead for winter hours.

The **Ferndale Museum** (☎ 707-786-4466; www.ferndale-museum.org; cnr Shaw & 3rd Sts; admission by donation; ☺ 11am-4pm Wed-Sat, 1pm-4pm Sun) is jam-packed with artifacts. Some of the installations are cheesy, but there are cool light-up diorama-style dollhouses and a working seismograph; after a tremor, the whole town comes here to find out its magnitude.

Don't miss a gander at some of the crazy contraptions at the **Kinetic Sculpture Museum** (www.kineticsculpturerace.org; 580 Main St; admission free; ☺ 10am-5pm Mon-Sat, noon-4pm Sun; ♿), which houses fanciful, astounding kinetic sculptures used in the town's annual Kinetic Sculpture Race (see the boxed text, p125).

Half a mile from downtown via Bluff St, enjoy short tramps through fields of wildflowers, beside ponds, redwood groves and eucalyptus trees at 110-acre **Russ Park**. The **cemetery**, also on Bluff St, is way cool. Five miles down Centerville Rd, **Centerville Beach** is one of the few off-leash dog beaches in Humboldt County.

Head to **Parasol Arts** (☎ 707-786-4444; 405 Main St; ☺ 10am-9pm Wed-Sun, noon-5pm Sun; ♿) to paint unfinished pottery, then leave it to be fired and mailed home to you. It's a great foggy-day activity and remarkably inexpensive.

Festivals & Events

Contact the Chamber of Commerce for details of the town's festivals.
Kinetic Sculpture Race The famous race is held during the Memorial Day weekend (see p125).

Tour of the Unknown Coast This bicycle race takes place the Saturday before Mother's Day.
Humboldt County Fair In mid-August; horse racing is the big event. This is an unexceptionally good county fair.
Bargain Lovers' Weekend Shops and houses have sidewalk sales the weekend after Labor Day.
Christmas celebrations Ferndale is famous for its elaborate Christmas festivities.

Sleeping
CAMPING
Humboldt County Fairgrounds (☎ 707-786-9511; www.humboldtcountyfair.org; 1250 5th St; tent/RV sites $10/25) The fairgrounds provide lawn camping, hookups and showers; turn west onto Van Ness St.

B&BS
Ferndale's B&Bs are heavy on the Victorian frill and space-occupying froufrou. All have wi-fi.

Collingwood Inn B&B (☎ 707-786-9219, 800-469-1632; www.collingwoodinn.com; 831 Main St; r $110-215, cottage $190) The cute-as-a-button 1885 Hart House has four rooms with extras like featherbeds, bathrobes, coffee delivered to your door and breakfast at your convenience. Gay friendly. Pets welcome.

Shaw House (☎ 707-786-9958, 800-557-7429; www.shawhouse.com; 703 Main St; r $115-175, ste $245-275) California's oldest B&B is also Ferndale's first grand home. Original details remain, including painted wooden ceilings and three gracious parlors. If you like B&Bs, this one's a charmer.

Gingerbread Mansion Inn (☎ 707-786-4000, 800-952-4136; www.gingerbread-mansion.com; 400 Berding St; r $160-400) Ferndale's iconic B&B drips with gingerbread trim. The 11 exquisitely detailed rooms are decked out with high-end 1890s Victorian furnishings. Rates include high-tea service, evening wine and three-course breakfast. No kids under 12.

HOTELS & MOTELS
Francis Creek Inn (☎ 707-786-9611; 577 Main St; r $73-83) This motel has four well-kept, pretty rooms, but no outdoor areas.

Fern Motel (☎ 707-786-5000; www.fern-motel.com; 332 Ocean St; r $75-95) The rooms are standard issue, but there's a big grassy lawn and miniature Victorian playhouse for kids.

Hotel Ivanhoe (☎ 707-786-9000; www.ivanhoe-hotel.com; 315 Main St; r $95-145) Ferndale's oldest hostelry opened in 1875. It has four antique-laden rooms and an Old West–style 2nd-floor porch, perfect for morning coffee.

Victorian Inn (☎ 707-786-4949, 888-589-1808; www .a-victorian-inn.com; 400 Ocean Ave; r $95-245 incl full breakfast) The bright, sunny rooms inside this 1890 two-story, former bank building are comfortably furnished with thick carpeting, good linens and antiques.

Eating

Bakeries, cafés, a pizzeria and old-fashioned lunch counters line Main St.

Buttercream (☎ 707-786-4880; 385 Main St; dishes $5-7; ☽ lunch Tue-Sun) A country-style tea salon in the back of an antiques store, Buttercream has a daily changing menu of soup, salad, one main and chicken salad. Good muffins and French-press coffee too.

Poppa Joe's (☎ 707-786-4180; 409 Main St; dishes $5-7; ☽ 6am-2pm Mon-Fri, to noon Sat & Sun; ♿) You can't beat the atmosphere at this wacky diner, where trophy heads hang from the wall and old men play poker all day. The American-style breakfasts are good too – especially the pancakes.

Curley's Grill (☎ 707-786-9696; 400 Ocean Ave; dishes $8-21) Curley's bar and grill serves everything from steak sandwiches and meatloaf to lamb shank and Niçoise salads, served on brightly colored Fiestaware at exposed oak tables. Great bar. Alas, the food is inconsistent, but when you hit it right, it's spot-on.

Hotel Ivanhoe (☎ 707-786-9000; 315 Main St; mains $14-23; ☽ dinner Wed-Sun) Chicken marsala is the specialty at this Victorian dinner-house and pub, but when it's available, lamb is the standout. There's prime rib on Friday and Saturday (and sometimes Sunday), and on Tuesday great beef stroganoff made with the weekend's leftover prime rib. There's a small-portions menu ($10 to $14), also available at the bar. Top choice for dinner.

Entertainment

Ferndale Repertory Theatre (☎ 707-786-5483; www .ferndale-rep.org; 447 Main St) This theatre produces worthwhile shows and musicals year-round.

Shopping

Blacksmith Shop & Gallery (☎ 707-786-4216; www .ferndaleblacksmith.com; 455 & 491 Main St) From wrought-iron art to hand-forged furniture, this is the largest collection of contemporary blacksmithing in America. Of all Ferndale's shops, this one's not to be missed.

Abraxas (☎ 707-786-4288; 505 Main St) Chockablock full of fun jewelry, from silver to turquoise. Tons of earrings and hats too.

Golden Gait Mercantile (☎ 707-786-4891; 421 Main St) The shelves of this old-fashioned store are filled with yesteryear's goods, as well as fun bric-a-brac and tasty jams.

Hobart Gallery (☎ 707-786-9259; 393 Main St) Check out the mixed-media art here; some is for sale.

Silva's (☎ 707-786-4425; Victorian Inn, 400 Ocean Ave) Silva's has fancy high-end jewelry, the kind you buy when you propose.

HUMBOLDT BAY NATIONAL WILDLIFE REFUGE

Even if you're not into birding, you'll be wowed by this **wildlife refuge** (☎ 707-733-5406; ☽ sunrise-sunset), at the southern end of Humboldt Bay, that protects wetlands habitats for more than 200 species of birds migrating annually along the Pacific Flyway. In one single day in 2004, there were a whopping 26,000 Aleutian cackling geese counted outside the visitors center!

Gulls, terns, cormorants, pelicans, egrets and herons come year-round. Peak season for waterbirds and raptors runs September to March, for black brant geese and migratory shorebirds mid-March to late April. Look for harbor seals offshore; bring binoculars.

Pick up a map from the **visitors center** (1020 Ranch Rd; ☽ 8am-5pm). It highlights two 30-minute interpretive walks. Exit Hwy 101 at Hookton Rd (exit 696), 11 miles south of Eureka, and turn north along the frontage road on the freeway's west side. In April, look for the **Godwit Days festival** (www.godwitdays.com).

EUREKA

pop 25,600

The Humboldt County seat, Eureka fronts on giant Humboldt Bay, the largest bay north of San Francisco. Despite a diverse and interesting community of artists, writers, pagans and other free-thinkers, Eureka is ultimately an old-guard Catholic town that goes to bed at nine o'clock. The city lacks the dynamism of its trippy-dippy neighbor Arcata. The town fathers don't allow much to change, and until they die off, nothing will. The suburban strip along Hwy 101 south of town is unimpressive, but it's worth seeing Old Town with its colorful Victorians, good shops, impressive museums, and refurbished waterfront.

And keep your eyes peeled for art: there's lots around town, some quite good. Eureka is an hour north of Garberville.

Orientation & Information

Streets lie on a grid; numbered streets cross lettered streets. For the best window-shopping, head to 2nd St between D and G Sts. There's a California Welcome Center in Arcata (p124).

Eureka Chamber of Commerce (☎ 707-442-3738, 800-356-6381; 2112 Broadway; ☯ Mon-Sat) This is the main visitors information center and is located on Hwy 101.

Eureka-Humboldt County Convention & Visitors Bureau (☎ 707-443-5097, 800-346-3482; www.redwoods.info; 1034 2nd St; ☯ Mon-Fri) Has maps and brochures.

Going Places (☎ 707-443-4145; 328 2nd St) Travel-oriented bookstore. One of three excellent bookshops in Old Town.

Has Beans (☎ 707-442-1535; 738 2nd St, at I St; per min $0.15) Internet access, homemade pastries.

Pride Enterprises Tours (☎ 707-445-2117, 800-400-1849) Local historian leads outstanding personalized tours. Licensed to guide in the national parks.

Six Rivers National Forest Headquarters (☎ 707-442-1721; 1330 Bayshore Way; ☯ Mon-Fri) Has maps and information.

Sights

The most famous of Eureka's impressive Victorians is the ornate **Carson Mansion** (143 M St), 1880s home of lumber baron William Carson, designed by Samuel and Joseph Newsom, the famous 19th-century architects. It took 100 men a full year to build. Today it's a private club. The pink house opposite, the **Wedding Mansion** (202 M St), is an 1884 Queen Anne Victorian by the same architects, built as a wedding gift for Carson's son.

Who says they don't build houses like that any more? The **Carter House** (cnr 3rd & L St), was built in the 1980s by bon vivant Mark Carter, using 19th-century blueprints he'd found in an antique store. He's a local celeb; you can meet him at the Hotel Carter, across the street.

Don't miss **Blue Ox Millworks & Historic Park** (☯ 707-444-3437, 800-248-4259; www.blueoxmill.com; 1 X St; adult/child $7.50/3.50; ☯ 9am-4pm Mon-Sat; ☯). One of only seven of its kind left in America, the millworks uses antique tools and mills to produce authentic gingerbread trim and decoration for Victorian buildings. One-hour self-guided tours take you through the mill and surrounding historical buildings, including a blacksmith shop and recreated 19th-century skid camp. Kids love the oxen. Master craftsman Eric Hollenbeck does everything by hand, and even manufactures his own stains. (When colleagues laughed, saying, 'Why waste time making stain when you can buy it for $10?,' Eric replied, 'The hidden cost of convenience is knowledge.' Indeed.) If you spend Saturdays watching *This Old House* on PBS, you'll go nuts at Blue Ox. At the time of publication, there were tentative plans to move; call ahead.

The **Morris Graves Museum of Art** (☎ 707-442-0278, events 442-9054; www.humboldtarts.org; 636 F St; admission by donation; ☯ noon-5pm Wed-Sun) is Eureka's cultural hub and has rotating exhibitions by California artists inside a 1904 Carnegie library, the state's first public library. It hosts weekend jazz, dance and spoken-word performances (September to May).

The free *Eureka Visitors Map*, available at tourist offices, details architectural and historical walking tours and drives. **Old Town**, along 2nd and 3rd Sts, from C St to M St, was once Eureka's down-and-out area, but has been refurbished into an inviting pedestrian district of galleries, shops, cafés and restaurants. The F Street Plaza and Boardwalk run along the waterfront at the foot of F St.

The **Romano Gabriel Wooden Sculpture Garden** (315 2nd St) is enclosed by glass, between D and E Sts. For 30 years the brightly painted folk art in Gabriel's front yard delighted locals. After he died in 1977, the city moved the collection here.

For little kids, there's the **Discovery Museum** (☎ 707-443-9694; 517 3rd St; admission $4; ☯ 10am-4pm Tue-Sat, noon-4pm Sun; ☯), a hands-on interactive museum.

South of downtown via Hwy 101 to Highland Ave, the 1853 **Fort Humboldt State Historic Park** (☎ 707-445-6567; 3431 Fort Ave; admission free; ☯ 8am-5pm; ☯) overlooks Humboldt Bay. Only one structure remains, the tiny hospital, now a museum, but cool outdoor exhibits show the old equipment used to fell redwoods. The park fires up the machinery on the 3rd Saturday of the month, May through September.

Sequoia Park (☎ 707-442-6552; 3414 W St; admission by donation; ☯ 10am-7pm Tue-Sun May-Sep, to 5pm Oct-Apr; ☯), a 77-acre old-growth redwood grove, has biking and hiking trails, a children's playground and picnic areas, and a small zoo.

Activities

Hum-Boats Sail, Canoe & Kayak Center (☎ 707-443-5157; www.humboats.com; Startare Dr), at Woodley Island Marina, rents kayaks and sailboats. It has lessons and tours (some dog-friendly), ecotours, a water taxi, sailboat charters, sunset sails and full-moon paddles.

Board the 1910 *Madaket*, America's oldest continuously operating passenger vessel, for a **harbor cruise** (☎ 707-445-1910; www.humboldtbaymaritimemuseum.com; F St; adult/child/senior $15/7.50/13; ☼ May-Oct; ♿). The *Madaket* originally ferried mill passengers until the Samoa Bridge was built in 1972.

Northern Mountain Supply (☎ 707-445-1711; 125 W 5th St) rents camping and backpacking gear.

Pro Sport Center (☎ 707-443-6328; 508 Myrtle Ave) has a full-service bike-repair shop (no rentals) and sells camping gear; it rents and sells kayaks, and scuba diving and skiing gear.

Festivals & Events

On the first Saturday every month, 'Arts Alive!' is a progressive gallery tour. Summer concerts are held at the F Street Pier. Contact the visitors bureau for details on festivals.

Redwood Coast Dixieland Jazz Festival (www.redwoodjazz.org) April jazz.

Rhododendron Festival April flower festival.

Blues by the Bay (www.redwoodcoastmusicfestivals.org) July waterfront concerts.

Kinetic Sculpture Race (www.kineticsculpturerace.org) The race happens on the Memorial Day weekend in September, when folks on self-propelled contraptions travel 38 miles from Arcata to Ferndale. (See the boxed text, p125.)

Sleeping

Rate are high midsummer; you might find cheaper in Arcata.

CAMPING

Eureka KOA (☎ 707-822-4243, 800-562-3136; www.koakampgrounds.com; 4050 N Hwy 101; campsites $25-29, RV sites $30-37, cabins $50-60; ♿) About halfway to Arcata, Eureka KOA has a heated pool, store, laundry, playground and bicycle rentals, but it's next to a mill and noisy at 8am.

There's also camping on Samoa Peninsula (p121).

B&BS

Abigail's Elegant Victorian Mansion (☎ 707-444-3144; www.eureka-california.com; 1406 C St; r $115-155, incl breakfast $155-195) This National Historic Landmark is practically a Victorian living-history museum, dripping with period details. The sweet-as-could-be innkeepers lavish guests with warm hospitality, including a ride around Eureka in 1920s automobiles. Save money by forgoing breakfast.

Cornelius Daly Inn (☎ 707-445-3638, 800-321-9656; www.dalyinn.com; 1125 H St; r $125, with bathroom $165-180) This impeccably maintained 1905 Colonial Revival mansion has individually decorated rooms with turn-of-the-20th-century European and American antiques. Guest parlors are trimmed with rare woods; outside are century-old flowering trees.

Upstairs at the Waterfront (☎ 707-444-1301, 888-817-5840; www.upstairsatthewaterfront.com; 102 F St; r $175, ste $225) This grand Victorian apartment above the Café Waterfront has superb details and a

---

THE INDIAN ISLAND MASSACRE

In 1860, Eureka had been settled only 10 years. Like all frontier settlements, there'd been the usual back-and-forth hostilities between the Native Americans and White settlers, but nothing like what happened on February 25, 1860. The tribe had just finished a celebration on Indian Island, across Humboldt Bay, and the men set out on a hunting expedition, leaving the women and children alone. Under cover of night, a militia of settlers bearing hatchets stormed the island and viciously murdered 100 women, children and elders. The militia continued up the coast, and by the time the killing spree was over, the tribe had been decimated. The immediate outcry came not from the community, which did nothing, but from young journalist Bret Harte, who lived in Union (now Arcata). In a front-page editorial, he accused the settlers of 'barbarity' – and within two weeks, he was run out of town.

It took Eureka more than 120 years to acknowledge the massacre, though some still deny it ever happened. The Wiyots – what's left of them – are now at Table Bluff, next to Humboldt Bay National Wildlife Refuge, and relations between the tribe and city have improved, but they're not great. You can see an abstract mural memorializing the event on the wall of the **Eureka Theater** (612 F St), next to the Morris Graves Museum, called *The Sun Set Twice on the People That Day.*

fabulous shared kitchen dividing the space into two. Pictures on the website don't do it justice. You can rent just a bedroom, but the suite's the thing, with a *huge* living room overlooking the harbor. If you're two couples, book the whole place.

Carter House Victorians (☎ 707-444-8062, 800-404-1390; www.carterhouse.com; r $190-275, ste $350-450, cottage $595) Stay in one of three sumptuously decorated houses: a single-level 1900 house, a honeymoon-hideaway cottage or a replica of an 1880s San Francisco mansion (see p118). Unlike elsewhere, you won't see the innkeeper unless you want to. Guests can have an in-room breakfast or eat at the adjacent hotel's understatedly elegant restaurant.

HOTELS & MOTELS

Motels line Hwy 101. Most cost $60 to $100 and have no air-conditioning: choose places back from the road for less noise. The cheapest are south of downtown on the suburban strip.

Bayview Motel (☎ 707-442-1673, 866-725-6813; www.bayviewmotel.com; 2844 Fairfield St; r $90, ste $150) The upscale Bayview has spotless rooms with extras including refrigerators and patios overlooking Humboldt Bay. Jacuzzi suites have fireplaces.

Best Western Humboldt Bay Inn (☎ 707-443-2234, 800-521-6996; www.humboldtbayinn.com; 232 W 5th St; r $125-145; ⌨) This upper-end motel has firm mattresses and thick carpeting; upgraded rooms have DVDs, 27in TVs, robes, microwaves and refrigerators. Request a quiet room.

Eagle House Inn (☎ 707-444-3344; www.eaglehouseinn.com; 139 2nd St; r $105-185, ste $195-225) A hulking Victorian hotel in Old town, the Eagle House has 24 rooms above a turn-of-the-century ballroom perfect for hide-and-seek. Rooms have opulent, but not overly precious period furniture – carved headboards, floral-print carpeting, antique armoires. Kid friendly.

Hotel Carter (☎ 707-444-8067, 800-404-1390; www.carterhouse.com; 301 L St; r with breakfast $155-205, ste $275-350) Hotel Carter bears the standard for North Coast luxury. Recently constructed in period style, it's a Victorian lookalike without drafty windows. Stylish without being fussy, rooms have top-quality linens, unfinished pine antiques, and modern amenities; suites have in-room whirlpools and marble fireplaces. Rates include made-to-order breakfast, plus evening wine and hors d'oeuvres.

Eating

La Chapala (☎ 707-443-9514; 201 2nd St; dishes $6-14; ⏰ 11am-9pm; ♿) For Mexican, family-owned La Chapala is consistently good. The margaritas are cheap – $12.50 a liter! Don't get so hammered you forget to order the homemade flan.

Ramone's (☎ 707-445-2923; 209 E St; dishes under $10; ⏰ 7am-6pm Mon-Sat, 8am-4pm Sun) It's little more than a deli counter, but Ramone's makes good soups and wraps.

Waterfront Cafe Oyster Bar & Grill (☎ 707-443-9190; 102 F St; lunch $8-13, dinner $13-20; ⏰ 9am-9pm) The Waterfront overlooks the bay from its casual vintage-Victorian dining room and serves steamed clams, fish-and-chips, oysters and chowder. Top spot for Sunday brunch, with jazz and Ramos fizzes.

Hurricane Kate's (☎ 707-444-1405; www.hurricanekates.com; 511 2nd St; mains lunch $9-14, dinner $16-26; ⏰ Tue-Sat) The favorite spot of local *bon vivants*, Kate's open kitchen pumps out pretty-good, eclectic, tapas-style dishes ($10 to $14), and roast meats, but the wood-fired pizzas are the standout. Full bar.

Cafe Marina & Woodley's Bar (☎ 707-443-2233; 601 Startare Dr; dishes $10-16; ⏰ 11am-10pm) For an atmospheric sunny-day lunch, watch the bobbing sailboat masts in the small-craft harbor from the deck of Cafe Marina, which makes great bloodies and pretty good American food.

Kyoto (☎ 707-443-7777; 320 F St; dishes $15-25; ⏰ dinner Wed-Sat) The chef-owner lovingly crafts every plate at this tiny Japanese joint, where the waiter tells bad jokes while serving good sushi and sake-marinated deep-sea cod. Make reservations.

O.H.'s Townhouse (☎ 707-443-4652; 206 W 6th St; mains $15-21; ⏰ dinner Tue-Sun; ♿) Pick your own meat from the display case at Eureka's best steakhouse, which hasn't changed a whit since 1978 (think wood-veneer paneling). The mushy veggies are awful, but the steaks are delish.

Roy's (☎ 707-442-4574; 218 D St; dishes $14-20; ⏰ dinner Tue-Sat; ♿) If Eureka had a Mafia, they'd eat pasta at Roy's. The five-cheese ravioli and balsamic vinaigrette are delicious, but avoid complicated dishes.

Restaurant 301 (☎ 707-444-8062; www.carterhouse.com; 301 L St; breakfast $11, dinner $20-34, 4-course menu $45; ⏰ breakfast & dinner) Eureka's top table, romantic, sophisticated 301 serves a contemporary California menu, using produce from its organic gardens (tours available). Mains are pricey, but the five-course prix-fixe menu ($45) is a good deal. This is the place on date night. The encyclopedic wine list is stunning.

Pick up groceries at **Eureka Natural Foods** (☎ 707-442-6325; 1626 Broadway) or **Eureka Co-op** (☎ 443-6027; cnr 4th & A Sts). There's also a **farmers market** (☎ 707-441-9999; Old Town Gazebo, cnr 2nd & F Sts; ♥ 10am-1pm Tue Jun-Oct) and cafés and sandwich shops in Old Town.

Drinking

Shanty (☎ 707-444-2053; 213 2nd St; ♥ noon-2am) Kick it on the patio with hipsters at this way-cool grunge bar, where you can play Donkey Kong, pool or Ping Pong between shots. Shanty is gay friendly, but not gay per se. Sunday there's a Bloody Mary bar, 10am to 2pm.

Pearl (☎ 707-444-2017; 507 2nd St) Eureka's swankiest, most fashion-forward bar caters to the over-30 set, with live jazz weekends.

Lost Coast Brewery (☎ 707-445-4480; 617 4th St) The suds are good at Lost Coast – try the Downtown Brown – and there's pub grub 11am until midnight. Try the spicy-hot buffalo wings.

Casa Blanca (☎ 707-443-6190; 1436 2nd St, at P St; ♥ 4-9pm) Sip margaritas at this bay-view Mexican restaurant; come before sunset.

321 Coffee (☎ 707-444-9371; 321 3rd St; ♥ 8am-9pm) Play chess and sip with local students at this living-room-like coffeehouse. Good soup.

Entertainment

For gay events, log onto **Queer Humboldt** (www.queerhumboldt.com).

Morris Graves Museum of Art (☎ 707-442-0278, events 442-9054; www.humboldtarts.org; 636 F St) The museum hosts performing-arts events, September to May, Saturday evenings and Sunday afternoons.

Broadway Cinema (☎ 707-444-3456; Broadway) Screens first-run movies near 14th St.

Club Triangle at Indigo Nightclub (☎ 707-268-8888; 535 5th St) Sunday nights, this becomes the North Coast's big gay dance club.

Getting There & Around

Horizon Air (☎ 800-547-9308; horizonair.alaskaair.com) and **United Express** (☎ 800-241-6522; www.united.com) serve Arcata-Eureka Airport, 20 miles north.

Greyhound (☎ 800-231-2222; 1603 4th St) has a limited-service stop on 4th St (Hwy 101); there's one bus daily to San Francisco ($40, seven hours).

Redwood Transit Service (☎ 707-443-0826; www.hta.org) operates buses between Trinidad, Arcata, Eureka, Fernbridge (near Ferndale), and Scotia, Monday to Saturday. Buses to Arcata cost $1.95 and stop along 5th St at D, H, K, O and U Sts.

Eureka Transit Service (☎ 707-443-0826; www.hta.org/ets) operates local buses around town, Monday to Saturday.

SAMOA PENINSULA

Grassy dunes and windswept beaches extend along half-mile-wide, 7-mile long Samoa Peninsula, demarking Humboldt Bay's western boundary. Stretches of it are downright spectacular, particularly the dunes – part of a 34-mile-long dune system, the largest in Northern California – and the wildlife viewing is excellent. The shoreline road (Hwy 255) is the backdoor route between Arcata and Eureka.

At the peninsula's south end, **Samoa Dunes Recreation Area** (☎ 707-825-2300; ♥ sunrise-sunset) is good for picnicking and fishing. For wildlife, head to **Mad River Slough & Dunes**; from Arcata, take Samoa Blvd west 3 miles, then turn right at Young St, the Manila turn-off. Park at the community center lot, from where a trail passes mudflats, salt marsh and tidal channels. There are over 200 species of birds: migrating waterfowl in spring and fall, songbirds in spring and summer, shorebirds in fall and winter, and waders year-round.

At the peninsula's north end, 475-acre **Lanphere Dunes Preserve** protects one of the finest examples of dune succession on the entire Pacific coast. These undisturbed dunes reach heights exceeding 80ft. Because of the environment's fragility, access is by guided tour only. **Friends of the Dunes** (☎ 707-444-1397; www.friendsofthedunes.org) leads 2½-hour rain-or-shine Saturday guided walks at 10am through Lanphere Dunes and Manila Dunes. The first and third Saturdays of the month, walks depart from the **Pacific Union School parking lot** (3001 Janes Rd, Arcata). On the second and fourth Saturdays, meet at **Manila Community Center** (1655 Peninsula Dr, Manila). Volunteer restoration workdays are scheduled on alternate Saturdays. Call or check the website.

A couple of miles south from Lanphere Dunes, the 100-acre **Manila Dunes Recreation Area** (☎ 707-445-3309) is open to the public, with access from Peninsula Dr, with trails through beach pines. On-leash dogs are permitted. In

NORTH COAST

DRIVING TOUR: SOUTH SPIT & THE MOUTH OF HUMBOLDT BAY

What to See

Though giant Humboldt Bay (Map p284) is the second-largest bay in California, you'd never know it from the mainland. To get a stunning perspective on the size of this vast body of water, take a short drive from Eureka out South Spit, the narrow, 800-acre peninsula that separates the mighty Pacific's churning waves from the bay's placid waters. Along the way, you'll pass through **Table Bluff Reservation**, the ancestral home of the local Wiyot Tribe, and **Humboldt Bay National Wildlife Refuge** (p117), where you can spot an amazing array of birdlife.

But the money shot comes at the end of the peninsula, where you can walk out **South Jetty**, the pier that extends into the ocean and delineates the entrance to the bay, a narrow channel where huge amounts of water roar in and out with the tides. Be careful! If it's storming or seas are high, do not walk out on the jetty, lest a rogue wave knock you into the ocean. If seas are calm, walk out on the pier and be dazzled by the view. Part of the thrill lies in the calculated risk of meandering out along a low pier surrounded by roaring water; use your best judgment. If you're nervous, walk along the beach and dunes instead, and lose yourself in the wide-open vistas of the sky and the whoosh of the wind and waves. Keep your eyes peeled for itty-bitty Snowy Plovers, which nest near the end of the spit. And watch out for all-terrain vehicles; they're allowed on the beach in places. Dogs are allowed on a leash only. On your way back, before you turn back onto Table Bluff Rd, stop at the high cliffs at **Table Bluff County Park**; December through April it's a great spot for whale-watching. If you plan to picnic, bring drinking water. Three miles south of the park is the 2100-acre **Eel River Wildlife Area**; the wildlife-rich river delta is home to one of the North Coast's largest remaining riparian forests.

The Route

Head 11 miles south of Eureka, via Hwy 101, to Hookton Rd (exit 696). Cross Eel River Dr and continue westward on Hookton Rd for 5 miles. Veer right onto South Jetty Rd, the beginning of South Spit. If you have time on your way back, continue south along the water toward the mouth of the Eel River, an additional 3 miles.

Time & Mileage

From Eureka, budget 20 minutes to reach the beginning of South Spit. The peninsula is 4.5 miles long; it takes about 10 minutes to reach the end. For a quick peek, plan 60 to 90 minutes, longer if you plan to picnic and bird- or whale-watch. If you continue to Eel River Wildlife area, add 3 miles one way, plus the time you'll spend ogling flora and fauna.

2005 the BLM acquired **Ma-Le'l Dunes** (☎ 707-825-2300), immediately south of Lanphere Dunes. There are several walking trails through dunes and beach forest; dogs are allowed off leash at the southern end. Access is from Young Lane, at the northern end of the peninsula, off Hwy 255.

The West's last surviving lumber-camp cookhouse, the ever-so-fun **Samoa Cookhouse** (☎ 707-442-1659; www.humboldtdining.com/cookhouse; off Samoa Blvd; breakfast/lunch/dinner $9/10/14; ♿) serves all-you-can-eat family meals at long tables with checkered tablecloths. Kids eat for half-price. Stop by the little museum. The cookhouse is five minutes northwest of Eureka, across the Samoa Bridge; follow the signs. From Arcata, take Samoa Blvd (Hwy 255).

There's shadeless, windy camping at **Samoa Boat Ramp County Park** (☎ 707-445-7651; campsites $14), on the peninsula's bay side, 4 miles south of Samoa Bridge, with limited tent camping (it's mostly RVs) and few facilities but good views.

ARCATA

pop 16,500

The North Coast's most progressive town, patchouli-dipped Arcata initially looks like a quaint little town built around a pretty central square, but scratch the surface and find a bastion of alternative lifestyles and liberal politics that lean so far left, the Green Party is considered moderate. In April 2003, the City Council not only voted to condemn the USA

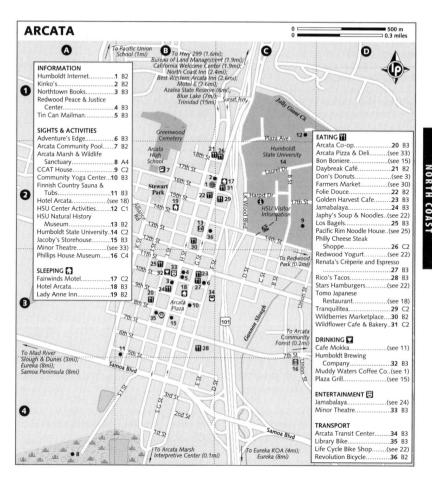

ARCATA

INFORMATION
Humboldt Internet.............1 B2
Kinko's.............................2 B2
Northtown Books.............3 B3
Redwood Peace & Justice
  Center...........................4 B3
Tin Can Mailman.............5 B3

SIGHTS & ACTIVITIES
Adventure's Edge..............6 B3
Arcata Community Pool....7 B2
Arcata Marsh & Wildlife
  Sanctuary.......................8 A4
CCAT House.....................9 C2
Community Yoga Center...10 B3
Finnish Country Sauna &
  Tubs.............................11 B3
Hotel Arcata.................(see 18)
HSU Center Activities.....12 C1
HSU Natural History
  Museum.........................13 B2
Humboldt State University..14 C2
Jacoby's Storehouse.........15 B3
Minor Theatre.............(see 33)
Phillips House Museum....16 C4

SLEEPING
Fairwinds Motel..............17 C2
Hotel Arcata..................18 B3
Lady Anne Inn................19 B2

EATING
Arcata Co-op..................20 B3
Arcata Pizza & Deli.......(see 33)
Bon Boniere..................(see 15)
Daybreak Café.................21 B2
Don's Donuts...............(see 3)
Farmers Market............(see 30)
Folie Douce....................22 B2
Golden Harvest Cafe........23 B3
Jamabalaya.....................24 B3
Japhy's Soup & Noodles..(see 22)
Los Bagels......................25 B3
Pacific Rim Noodle House..(see 25)
Philly Cheese Steak
  Shoppe.........................26 C2
Redwood Yogurt...........(see 22)
Renata's Crêperie and Espresso
  ....27 B3
Rico's Tacos....................28 B3
Stars Hamburgers.........(see 22)
Tomo Japanese
  Restaurant.................(see 18)
Tranquilitea....................29 C2
Wildberries Marketplace....30 B2
Wildflower Cafe & Bakery..31 C2

DRINKING
Cafe Mokka..................(see 11)
Humboldt Brewing
  Company.......................32 B3
Muddy Waters Coffee Co..(see 1)
Plaza Grill....................(see 15)

ENTERTAINMENT
Jamabalaya..................(see 24)
Minor Theatre................33 B3

TRANSPORT
Arcata Transit Center.......34 B3
Library Bike....................35 B3
Life Cycle Bike Shop......(see 22)
Revolution Bicycle...........36 B2

Patriot Act, but *outlawed* voluntary compliance with it. If you like to argue politics, you're gonna love it here. Liberal or conservative, you'll appreciate the town's forward-thinking ecological practices. While the rest of America is only just starting to consider the idea of sustainability, Arcata has been living it for years: garbage trucks run on biodiesel, recycling gets picked up by tandem bicycle, wastewater gets filtered clean in marshlands, and almost every street has a bike lane.

Founded in 1850 as a base for nearby lumber camps, Arcata is now a college town – everyone looks 22, versus Eureka, where everyone looks 50. The Humboldt State University (HSU) aesthetic is decidedly scruffy, and posses of earnest, fun-loving, Birkenstock-shod students roam downtown on weekend evenings. Yes, there's a tenacious smugness about Arcata – blame it on youth – but there's also an interesting discourse happening here, and it's worth listening to. But for God's sake, if you want to keep the peace, don't mention George W!

Orientation

Streets run on a grid, with numbered streets traveling east–west and lettered streets north–south. G and H Sts run north and south (respectively) to HSU and Hwy 101. The plaza is bordered by G and H and 8th and 9th Sts. Eureka is 5 miles, or 10 minutes, south on Hwy 101. Or, take Samoa Blvd to Hwy 255 for a scenic route around Arcata Bay.

Information

Arcata Eye (www.arcataeye.com) Free newspaper listing local events; the 'Police Log' column is hysterical! (On the website, it's under 'Public Safety.')

Bureau of Land Management (BLM; ☎ 707-825-2300; 1695 Heindon Rd) Has information on the Lost Coast.

California Welcome Center (☎ 707-822-3619; www.arcatachamber.com; 1635 Heindon Rd; ☺ 9am-5pm) Two miles north of town, off Giuntoli Lane, Hwy 101's west side. Operated by the Arcata Chamber of Commerce. Provides local and statewide information. Get the free *Official Map Guide to Arcata*.

Humboldt Internet (☎ 707-825-4638; 750 16th St; per hr $3; ☺ 10am-5pm Mon-Fri) PC internet access.

Kinko's (☎ 707-822-8712; 1618 G St; per min $0.20; ☺ 8am-11pm Mon-Thu, 7am-9pm Fri, 9am-6pm Sat) Has Macs and PCs.

Northtown Books (☎ 707-822-2384; 957 H St) New books, periodicals, travel maps and guides.

Redwood Peace & Justice Center (☎ 707-826-2511; http://rpjc.net; 1040 H St) Ground zero for grassroots political actions and resources.

Tin Can Mailman (☎ 707-822-1307; 1000 H St) Used volumes on two floors; excellent for hard-to-find books.

Sights

Around Arcata Plaza are two National Historic Landmarks: the 1857 **Jacoby's Storehouse** (cnr H & 8th Sts) and the 1915 **Hotel Arcata** (cnr G & 9th Sts). Other standouts include the vintage 1914 **Minor Theatre** (1013 10th St) and the 1854 **Phillips House Museum** (☎ 707-822-4722; www.arcatahistory.org; cnr 7th & Union Sts; admission by donation; ☺ 2-4pm Sun & by appointment), which has historical exhibits and tours.

On the northeastern side of town, **Humboldt State University** (HSU; ☎ 707-826-3011; www.humboldt .edu) is Arcata's *raison d'être*. The Campus Center for Appropriate Technology (CCAT) is a world leader in sustainable technologies; take a self-guided tour at 2pm on Friday of the **CCAT House** (☎ 707-826-3551; Buck House, HSU; ☺ 9am-5pm Mon-Fri; ♿), a converted residence that uses only 4% of the energy of a comparably sized dwelling. Dig the pedal-powered TV! The **HSU Natural History Museum** (☎ 707-866-4479; www .humboldt.edu/~natmus; 1315 G St; adult/child $3/2; ☺ 10am-5pm Tue-Sat; ♿) has kid-friendly interactive exhibits of fossils, live animals, a beehive, tide pool tank, and cool tsunami and seismic displays.

On the shores of Humboldt Bay, **Arcata Marsh & Wildlife Sanctuary** has 5 miles of walking trails and outstanding birding – and it doubles as the city's (nearly) odor-free wastewater treatment facility (ya gotta love this town's ingenuity).

Friends of Arcata Marsh guide tours Saturdays at 2pm from the **Arcata Marsh Interpretive Center** (☎ 707-826-2359; 600 South G St; admission free; ☺ 9am-5pm Tue-Sun, 1pm-5pm Mon; ♿). The **Redwood Region Audubon Society** (☎ 707-826-7031; www.rras.org; donation welcome) offers guided walks of the marsh on Saturdays at 8:30am, rain or shine, from the parking lot at I Street's south end.

At the east end of 11th and 14th Sts, **Redwood Park** has beautiful redwoods and picnic areas. Adjoining the park is the **Arcata Community Forest**, a 575-acre old-growth forest crisscrossed by 10 miles of trails, with dirt paths and paved roads good for hikers and mountain bikers.

Northeast of Arcata, 2 miles east of Hwy 101, **Azalea State Reserve** (☎ 707-488-2041; Hwy 200) bursts into bloom late April to late May; otherwise it's just a pretty wood.

Activities

Especially if sore from hiking, you mustn't leave Arcata without visiting the **Finnish Country Sauna & Tubs** (☎ 707-822-2228; cnr 5th & J Sts; ☺ noon-10pm Sun-Thu, to 12:30am Fri & Sat), where you can sip chai by the fireside or in meditative gardens, then rent a private open-air redwood hot tub ($8 per half hour) or sweat in a sauna. Reserve ahead, especially on weekends.

From Tai Chi and African dance to backpacking and kayaking, **HSU Center Activities** (☎ 707-826-3357; www.humboldt.edu/~cntract) sponsors myriad activities, workshops, outings, sporting-gear rentals and consignment sales; nonstudents welcome. It's in the University Center, beside the campus clock tower.

Community Yoga Center (☎ 707-440-2111; www .innerfreedomyoga.com; 890 G St; classes $10) offers drop-in classes. **Arcata Community Pool** (☎ 707-822-6801; 1150 16th St; adult/child/senior $6/5/4) has lap swimming, a coed hot tub, sauna and exercise room.

Adventure's Edge (☎ 707-822-4673; www.adventures edge.com; 650 10th St; ☺ 9am-6pm Mon-Sat, 11am-5pm Sun) rents, sells and services outdoor equipment. The **Outdoor Store** (☎ 707-822-0321; 876 G St; ☺ 10am-6pm Mon-Sat, noon-5pm Sun) sells outdoor gear, and rents snowboards and kayaks.

Festivals & Events

Arcata's most famous event is the **Kinetic Sculpture Race** (www.kineticsculputurerace.org) held on the Memorial Day weekend, when people on self-propelled contraptions travel 38 miles from Arcata to Ferndale (see the boxed text, opposite).

CRAZY CONTRAPTIONS

The Kinetic Sculpture Race was born in 1969 when Ferndale artist Hobart Brown decided to spruce up his son's tricycle to make it more interesting, creating a wobbly, five-wheeled red 'pentacycle.' Initially, five odd contraptions raced down Main St on Mother's Day, and a 10ft turtle sculpture won. The race was expanded in the early '70s and has now blossomed into a three-day, amphibious event with contraptions competing over 38 miles from Arcata to Ferndale. Held over Memorial Day weekend (late May), the race attracts thousands of spectators and usually at least a few dozen entrants (one year there were 99). Cities around the world have followed in Ferndale's footsteps, with far-flung places like Perth, Australia, now holding their own kinetic races.

A few of the race rules are as bizarre as the entrants, including 'It is legal to get assistance from the natural power of water, wind, sun, gravity and friendly extraterrestrials (if introduced to the judges prior to the race)' and the Mom Rule, which states the following:

'If a Pilot is pregnant and in labor, that Pilot may be excused for a reasonable length of time (an hour or so) without penalty. However, the Pilot must return with a gloss 8 x 10 color photo for publicity purposes. The baby may then be carried as a passenger in the Barnacle Category for one leg of the course.'

The **Arcata Bay Oyster Festival** (www.oysterfestival .net) happens in June. In July and August, there's **Shakespeare in the Park** (www.arcataparksand rec.com). Sundays in August and September, attend **Summer Music & Art on the Plaza** (www .arcatamainstreet.com). September brings the **North Country Fair**.

Sleeping

Arcata has limited lodgings; it's a good base for exploring the parks further north. The nearest camping is Eureka KOA (p119). Also see Trinidad (p128) and Patrick's Point (p129).

A brand-spanking-new bayside ecohostel was scheduled to open in 2007; log on to www.humboldtbayhostel.org for the latest on construction.

Fairwinds Motel (☎ 707-822-4824; www.fairwinds motelarcata.com; 1674 G St; s $67-73, d $73-84) This standard-issue motel has OK rooms, but there's a constant whoosh of freeway noise from nearby Hwy 101.

Hotel Arcata (☎ 707-826-0217, 800-344-1221; www .hotelarcata.com; 708 9th St; r $84-105, ste $135-155) The renovated 1915 brick Hotel Arcata anchors the plaza and has high ceilings and comfortable, if small, rooms. Plaza-side rooms are loud; book one facing the air shaft for maximum quiet.

Lady Anne Inn (☎ 707-822-2797; www.humboldt1 .com/ladyanne; 902 14th St; r $100-130) Roses line the walkway to this 1888 mansion full of Victorian bric-a-brac. The frilly rooms are pretty, but there's no breakfast.

Arcata Stay (☎ 707-822-0935, 877-822-0935; www .arcatastay.com; apt $130-175) Live like a local in a beautifully furnished apartment or cozy cottage hideaway; all apartments in this lodging network are within walking distance of the plaza and have kitchens, and lots of privacy.

Other motels lie 2 miles north off Hwy 101's Giuntoli Lane exit.

Motel 6 (☎ 707-822-7061, 800-466-8356; www.motel6 .com; 4755 Valley West Blvd; s $50-56, d $56-62; ❄ ⬛)

North Coast Inn (☎ 707-822-4861, 800-406-0046; www.northcoastinn.com; 4975 Valley West Blvd; r $80-85; ❄ ⬛) Satisfactory option, with on-site restaurant and airport transfers.

Best Western Arcata Inn (☎ 707-826-0313, 800-528-1234; www.bestwestern.com; 4827 Valley West Blvd; r $99; ❄ ⬛) First choice motel.

Eating

Renata's Crèperie & Espresso (☎ 707-825-8783; 1030 G St; dishes $5-8; ☽ 8am-3pm & 5pm-9pm Fri-Sat, 8am-3pm Wed, Thu & Sun) We love Renata. She formerly served crepes out of a truck, but finally has permanent digs, and her café is the new hot spot, with organic sweet and savory crepes, salads and coffee. All the cool cats hang here.

Japhy's Soup & Noodles (☎ 707-826-2594; 1563 G St; dishes $3-6; ☽ 11:30am-8pm Mon-Fri) The budgeteers first choice serves big salads, tasty coconut curry, cold noodle salads and great homemade soups. Best of all, you can fill up for about $6. Score!

Wildflower Cafe & Bakery (☎ 707-822-0360; 1604 G St; dishes $5-8; ☽ 8am-8pm Mon-Sat, 9am-1pm Sun; Ⓥ)

The place for vegetarians, Wildflower serves fab frittatas and pancakes, and big crunchy salads. At dinner there's mushroom stroganoff, veggie lasagna and other substantial dishes.

Pacific Rim Noodle House (☎ 707-826-7604; 1021 I St; dishes $4-7; ☼ 11am-7pm Mon-Sat) Super-duper noodles, rice bowls, potstickers and sushi rolls are mainstays at this take-out favorite, with tables outside.

Golden Harvest Cafe (☎ 707-822-8962; 1062 G St; breakfast $4-8; ☼ breakfast & lunch) Tops for breakfast with a hangover (it's windowless), Golden Harvest serves classic Benedicts, four-egg omelettes, and pancakes with *real* maple syrup. Alas, the coffee sucks.

Tranquilitea (☎ 707-822-0153; 1540 G St; mains $8-12; ☼ 11am-7pm Mon-Sat; V) Sunny and mellow Tranquilitea is part teahouse-cafe, and part wellness center – it's so Arcata! On the menu, organic-vegetarian salads, smoothies, grilled-panini sandwiches and excellent teas are served with panache. The atmosphere is mellow and girly, good for a tarot reading. Nice garden patio. In back there's massage and bodywork; call ahead.

Daybreak Cafe (☎ 707-826-7543; 768 18th St; mains $5-9; ☼ 7am-4pm) The veggie-heavy breakfasts are tasty, with omelettes and burritos, but the blueberry cornmeal pancakes take the prize. At lunch there's turkey in some dishes, but the place is mostly vegetarian.

Tomo Japanese Restaurant (☎ 707-822-1414; 708 9th St; lunch $8-11, dinner $14-17; ☼ lunch Mon-Sat, dinner nightly) Everybody loves Tomo. Sushi is the thing and the cuts are good, but the tempura is weak, with flavorless batter and uninteresting veggies. Stick to fish.

Jambalaya (☎ 707-822-4766; 915 H St; lunch mains $7-9, dinner $15-20; ☼ lunch Mon-Fri, dinner nightly) In a cavernous space, Jambalaya serves a mishmash of Caribbean-influenced dishes – at lunch Cuban sandwiches, at dinner wild salmon and (of course) jambalaya. Good midrange option with lots of local wines and beers.

Folie Douce (☎ 707-822-1042; 1551 G St; brunch mains $8-14, dinner $23-32; ☼ dinner Tue-Sat, brunch Sun) Arcata's best, Folie Douce presents a short but inventive menu of seasonally inspired bistro cooking, from Asian to Mediterranean, with an emphasis on local organics. Wood-fired pizzas ($12 to $18) are a specialty. Sunday brunch too. Reservations essential.

There are fantastic **farmers markets** (☎ 707-441-9999; Arcata Plaza ☼ 9am-2pm Sat Apr-Nov; Wildberries

☼ 3:30-6:30pm Tue Jun-Oct) on Arcata Plaza and outside **Wildberries Marketplace** (☎ 707-822-0095; 747 13th St; ☼ 7am-11pm), which is Arcata's best grocery, with natural foods, a good deli, bakery and juice bar. **Arcata Co-op** (☎ 707-822-5947; cnr 8th & I Sts; ☼ 6am-10pm) carries natural foods and has a good butcher with grass-fed beef.

Arcata has good cheap eats:

Arcata Pizza & Deli (☎ 707-822-4650; 1057 H St; ☼ 11am-1am Sun-Thur, to 3am Fri & Sat) Fill up after bar-hopping.

Bon Boniere (☎ 707-822-6388; 791 8th St; ☼ 11am-10pm; ♿) Inside Jacoby's Storehouse, get ice-cream sundaes here.

Don's Donuts (☎ 707-822-6465; 933 H St; ☼ 24hr) Get a Southeast Asian sandwich.

Los Bagels (☎ 707-822-3150; 1061 I St; dishes $2.50-6; ☼ Wed-Mon) Everyone stops in here sooner or later.

Philly Cheese Steak Shoppe (☎ 707-825-7400; cnr 18th & G Sts; ☼ 11am-9pm) Ever-popular with hungry, cash-strapped students.

Redwood Yogurt (☎ 707-826-7677; 1573 G St; ☼ noon-8pm Mon-Sat; ♿) Makes its own frozen yogurt.

Rico's Tacos (☎ 707-826-2572; 686 F St; mains $5-7; ☼ 9am-9pm) Next to Safeway, Rico's is arguably town's best taqueria.

Stars Hamburgers (☎ 707-826-1379; 1535 G St; burgers $3-5; ☼ 11am-8pm Mon-Thu, to 9pm Fri, to 7pm Sat, noon-6pm Sun; ♿) Uses grass-fed beef to make fantastic burgers.

Drinking

Dive bars and cocktail lounges line the plaza's northern side. Arcata is awash in coffeehouses.

Humboldt Brewing Company (☎ 707-826-2739; 856 10th St; pub grub $5-10) Humboldt has 15 brews on tap, fab fish tacos and bitchin' buffalo wings. There's live music Wednesday to Saturday nights.

Plaza Grill (☎ 707-826-0860; 791 8th St; ☼ 5-11pm) Professors and the literati head upstairs in Jacoby's Storehouse to the handsomest bar in town. Great pork chops too.

Muddy Waters Coffee Co (☎ 707-826-2233; 1603 G St) The coolest happenin' joint in town has occasional live music, coffee, beer and wine.

Cafe Mokka (☎ 707-822-2228; cnr 5th & J Sts) Bohos head to this cafe at Finnish Country Sauna & Tubs (p124) on weekends for mellow hearthside acoustic music – usually European folk. Other nights, read international newspapers and join multilingual conversations.

DETOUR TO BLUE LAKE

Six miles inland from Arcata, via Hwy 299, in **Blue Lake** (pop 1300) the **Dell'Arte International School of Physical Theatre** (☎ 707-668-5663; www.dellarte.com) is America's only school of trad-itional *Commedia Dell'Arte,* the wacky Italian physical-comedy theatrical genre dating back to the Renaissance. The school mounts productions year-round, both traditional and contemporary, but the **Mad River Festival** (June and July) is the big draw, when international high-energy perform-ers present music, plays and general buffoonery, culminating in the Blue Lake Pageant, a parade with dancers, musicians and huge *papier mâché* puppets.

At the **Mad River Fish Hatchery** (☎ 707-822-0592; 1660 Hatchery Rd; www.dfg.ca.gov/lands/fh; admission by donation; ☼ sunrise-sunset), see over 170,000 steelhead trout growing in giant concrete 'raceways.' Spawning begins in December, and yearlings are released March 1. There's good river access too, with wheelchair-accessible fishing, picnic tables, summertime swimming and berry picking.

Entertainment

Center Arts (☎ 707-826-4411, tickets 707-826-3928; www.humboldt.edu/~carts) You'd be amazed who shows up at HSU, from Diana Krall and Dave Bru-beck to Lou Reed and Ani Difranco.

Minor Theatre (☎ 707-822-3456; 1013 H St) Screens first-run and classic films.

Jambalaya (☎ 707-822-4766; 915 H St) Hosts live music after 10pm Fridays and Saturdays.

Getting There & Around

Eureka is 10 minutes south. See p121 for airport information. **Redwood Transit System** (☎ 707-443-0826; www.hta.org), **Greyhound** (☎ 800-231-2222; www.greyhound.com) and **Arcata city buses** (☎ 707-822-3775; ☼ Mon-Sat) stop at the **Arcata Transit Center** (☎ 707-825-8934; 925 E St at 9th St). For shared rides, read the bulletin board at the Arcata Co-op (opposite).

Bicyclists: Hwy 101 entering town from the north is scary because you have to cross freeway on-ramps. Here's an alternate route: from McKinleyville in the north, take Mur-ray Rd west from Hwy 101, to the Hammond Trail south (a dedicated bike route), to Mad River Rd south into Arcata.

Revolution Bicycle (☎ 707-822-2562; 1360 G St) and **Life Cycle Bike Shop** (☎ 707-822-7755; 1593 G St; ☼ Mon-Sat) rent, service and sell bicycles.

Only in Arcata: borrow a bike from **Library Bike** (☎ 707-822-1122; www.arcata.com/greenbikes; 865 8th St) for a $20 deposit, which gets refunded when you return the bike – up to six months later! They're beaters, but they ride. And hello – they're basically free.

TRINIDAD

pop 400

Fifteen miles north of Eureka, picture-perfect Trinidad sits on a bluff overlooking a glitter-ing blue-water harbor, with gorgeous hiking and lovely sand beaches. Several water-view B&Bs make terrific romantic getaways. The town gained it name when Spanish sea cap-tains arrived on Trinity Sunday in 1775 and named the area La Santisima Trinidad (the Holy Trinity). Trinidad didn't boom, though, until the 1850s, when it became an important port for miners. Schooners from San Fran-cisco brought supplies for inland gold fields, and carried back lumber from the North Coast. Today, tourism and fishing keep the economy going.

Orientation & Information

Trinidad is tiny. Approach via Hwy 101 (exit at Trinidad) or from the north via Patrick's Point Dr (which becomes Scenic Dr further south).

Beachcomber Café (☎ 707-677-0106; 363 Trinity St; per hr $5; ☼ 7am-4pm Mon-Thu, to 9pm Fri, 9am-4pm Sat & Sun) Internet access and wi-fi.

Information kiosk (cnr Patrick's Point Dr & Main St) Just west of the freeway, pick up the pamphlet *Discover Trinidad,* which has an excellent map.

Trinidad Chamber of Commerce (www.trinidadcalif.com) Provides information via the internet.

Sights & Activities

Overlooking the bay on a bluff at the foot of Main St, the iconic **Trinidad Memorial Lighthouse** (cnr Trinity & Edwards Sts) is a replica of an 1871 lighthouse. It's normally closed to visitors, except during the annual **Trinidad Fish Festival**, held in mid-June.

Take the kids to **HSU Telonicher Marine Labora-tory** (☎ 707-826-3671; www.humboldt.edu/~marinelb; Ewing St; admission free; ☼ 9am-4:30pm Mon-Fri mid-Mat–Sep, noon-4pm Sat Sep–mid-May; ⏫), near Edwards St; there's a touch tank, several aquariums (look for the giant octopus!), an enormous whale jaw and a cool 3-D map of the ocean floor.

The free map available from the information kiosk shows several good hiking trails, especially the definitive **Trinidad Head Trail**, which affords superb coastal views and great whale-watching (April to June and December to February). Stroll along an exceptionally beautiful cove at **Trinidad State Beach**; take Main St and bear right at Stagecoach, then take the second turn left (the first is a picnic area) into the small lot.

Eroding Scenic Dr twists south along coastal bluffs. About two miles south of town, **Baker Beach** is nude; take the marked trail through the grass, opposite No 1237 Scenic Dr. A third of a mile past Baker, Scenic Dr leads to broad **Luffenholtz Beach** (accessible via the staircase). The road washed out south of here, so to reach fabulous **Moonstone Beach**, one of the few white-sand beaches along the North Coast not littered with giant driftwood, ask locals to direct you. Further south Moonstone becomes **Clam Beach County Park**, a gorgeous stretch of sand, but Scenic Dr ends sooner, forcing you onto Hwy 101 to reach the county park.

Trinidad is famous for fishing. Arrange a trip through **Salty's Surf 'n' Tackle Tours** (☎ 707-677-0300; 332 Main St) or **Trinidad Bay Charters** (☎ 707-839-4743, 800-839-4744; www.trinidadbaycharters.net). The harbor is at the bottom of Edwards St, at the foot of Trinidad Head. Five-hour trips cost $80.

Surfing is best fall through spring, but potentially dangerous, particularly in winter. Unless you know how to judge conditions and get yourself out of trouble – there are no lifeguards here – you can also surf in better-protected Crescent City (see p135). To find the best surf breaks, talk to Salty's Surf 'n' Tackle (above).

North Coast Adventures (☎ 707-677-3124; www .northcoastadventures.com; lessons per 2hr/day $50/90) gives sea- and river-kayaking lessons and guided ecotrips (including tide pool tours) around the North Coast.

Sleeping

Clam Beach (☎ 707-445-7491; campsites per vehicle $10) South of town off Hwy 101, Clam Beach has excellent beach camping. Pitch your tent in the dunes (look for natural windbreaks). Facilities include pit toilets, cold water, picnic tables and fire rings.

View Crest Lodge & Campground (☎ 707-677-3393; www.viewcrestlodge.com; 3415 Patrick's Point Dr; tent/RV sites $16/26, 1-bedroom cottages $95-135) On a hill above the ocean on the inland side, some of these modern, well-maintained cottages have views and Jacuzzis; most have kitchens. There's also a good campground. Good bargain.

Trinidad Inn (☎ 707-677-3349; www.trinidadinn.com; 1170 Patrick's Point Dr; r $65-100) The rooms are sparklingly clean and attractively decorated at this gray-shingled, single-story motel, Trinidad's best. Most rooms have kitchens.

Bishop Pine Lodge (☎ 707-677-3314; www.bishop pinelodge.com; 1481 Patrick's Point Dr; cottages $90-100, with kitchen $100-165) It feels like summer camp at Bishop Pine, where you can rent freestanding redwood cottages in a grassy meadow on a sunny hillside. All but two have kitchens, woodsy charm, and unintentionally retro-funky furniture.

Trinidad Retreats (☎ 707-677-1606; www.trinidad retreats.com; per day from $150) Rents local houses.

Trinidad Bay B&B (☎ 707-677-0840; www.trinidad baybnb.com; 560 Edwards St; r $200) On bluffs overlooking the harbor and Trinidad Head, this cute little Cape Cod–style saltbox is the only lodging downtown, with four individually decorated rooms done in a cozy, inviting beach-house style with classy white furniture (parents beware). One room has a kitchen; two others have fireplaces. There's homemade honey at breakfast.

Lost Whale Inn (☎ 707-677-3425; www.lostwhaleinn .com; 3452 Patrick's Point Dr; r incl breakfast $225-250, ste $300) Fall asleep to the sound of braying sea lions at this spacious, modern clifftop B&B surrounded by flowering gardens. The ocean views are mesmerizing, and there's a 24-hour hot tub. Rooms have knotty-pine trimmings, redwood floors and homey touches like country quilts. Kids welcome.

Eating

Catch Café (☎ 707-677-0390; 355 Main St; mains $6-9; ⏲ 11am-7pm Tue-Sun; ♿) Across from the Chevron station, this fun little hippie-dippie joint makes good food fast, using mostly organic ingredients – from pizzettas and grass-fed burgers to brown rice and veggies. Order at the counter, sit outside.

Seascape Restaurant (☎ 707-677-3762; Trinidad Harbor; breakfast & lunch $8-10, dinner $11-22; ⏲ 7am-10pm; ♿) Sit in a vinyl booth and watch the fishermen from this harborside greasy spoon that serves good breakfasts and standard-American seafood dishes. It's open shorter hours in winter.

TOP ROADSIDE PULLOUTS FOR PER-SPECTIVE ON THE REDWOOD COAST

- Klamath River Overlook (p133)
- Crescent Beach Overlook (p134)
- Clam Beach County Park (opposite)
- Thomas H Kuchel Visitor Center, Redwood National Park (p130)
- False Klamath Cove (p134)

Trinidad Bay Eatery (☎ 707-677-3777; cnr Parker & Trinity Sts; breakfast & lunch $7-12, dinner $17-23; ☯ 7am-3pm Mon & Tue, to 8pm Wed-Sun; ♿) Chowder and blackberry cobbler are the standouts at this diner that otherwise serves standard American fare.

Katy's Smokehouse & Fishmarket (☎ 707-677-0151; www.katyssmokehouse.com; 740 Edwards St; ☯ 9am-6pm) Katy's uses line-caught seafood to make its own chemical-free smoked and canned fish, some vacuum-packed for convenient transport.

Larrupin Cafe (☎ 707-677-0230; 1658 Patrick's Point Dr; mains $20-30; ☯ dinner Thu-Tue) Everybody loves Larrupin, where Moroccan rugs, chocolate-brown walls, gravity-defying floral arrangements and deep-burgundy Oriental carpets create a moody atmosphere perfect for a lovers' tryst. On the menu, expect consistently good mesquite-grilled seafood and meats. In summer book a table on the garden patio. No credit cards.

Drinking

Beachcomber Café (☎ 707-677-0106; 363 Trinity St) If you really wanna know what's happening in Trinidad, talk to Jackie and Melissa, the hella-fun owners of this sweet little café that makes good organic coffee, sandwiches, bagels and homemade cookies.

Moonstone Grill (☎ 707-677-1616; Moonstone Beach; ☯ Wed-Sun) For drop-dead sunset views over a picture-perfect beach, have cocktails at fancypants Moonstone. Call for directions.

PATRICK'S POINT STATE PARK

Dense pine forests yield to grassy meadows, and sandy beaches abut rocky headlands at 1-sq-mile-big **Patrick's Point** (☎ 707-677-3570; 4150 Patrick's Point Dr; day-use $6; ♿). Five miles north of Trinidad, with supereasy access to dramatic coastal bluffs, it's a best bet for families. Stroll scenic overlooks, climb giant rock formations, watch whales breach, gaze into tide pools or listen to barking sea lions and singing birds.

Sumêg is an authentic reproduction of a Yurok village, with hand-hewn redwood buildings where Native Americans gather for traditional ceremonies. (Local Native Americans built solid structures, instead of temporary ones, because the land here is so productive that tribes didn't need to migrate with the seasons.) In the native plant garden you'll find species for making traditional baskets and medicines.

On **Agate Beach** look for bits of jade and shiny sea-polished agate. Follow the signs to **tide pools**; tread lightly and obey regulations. The 2-mile **Rim Trail**, a former Yurok trail around the bluffs, circles the point with access to huge rocky outcroppings. Don't miss **Wedding Rock**, one of the park's most romantic spots. Other trails lead around unusual formations like **Ceremonial Rock** and **Lookout Rock**.

The park's three well-tended drive-in **campgrounds** (☎ reservations 800-444-7275; www.reserveamerica.com; campsites $15-20) have coin-operated hot showers. Penn Creek and Abalone campgrounds are more sheltered than Agate Beach.

HUMBOLDT LAGOONS STATE PARK

Hwy 101 drops out of the forest at **Humboldt Lagoons** (☎ 707-488-2041), where long, sandy beaches stretch for miles. Two large coastal lagoons – **Big Lagoon** and **Stone Lagoon** – have stellar bird-watching and kayaking (rent boats in Arcata, p124). Of all the places to kayak on the Redwood Coast, this is my favorite. Sunsets are spectacular, with no man-made structures in sight. The Stone Lagoon Visitors Center, on Hwy 101, has closed due to staffing shortages, but there's a toilet and a bulletin board displaying information. About a mile north, **Freshwater Lagoon** is also great for birdwatching; picnic at its north end near the Thomas H Kuchel Visitor Center of Redwood National Park (p130). South of Stone Lagoon, itty-bitty **Dry Lagoon** (actually a freshwater marsh) has a fantastic day hike. Park at Dry Lagoon's picnic area and hike north on the unmarked trail to Stone Lagoon, which skirts the southwestern shore and ends up at the ocean, passing through woods and marshland rich with birds and wildlife. It's about 2.5 miles one way, and mostly flat – and nobody takes it because it's unmarked.

All campsites are first-come, first-served. The state park runs two **environmental campgrounds** (campsites $12; Apr-Oct), bring water. Stone Lagoon has six canoe-in environmental campsites; Dry Lagoon, off Hwy 101, has six walk-in campsites. Check in at Patrick's Point State Park (p129), at least 30 minutes before sunset. **Humboldt County Parks** (707-445-7651; campsites $14) operates a lovely cypress-grove picnic area and campground beside Big Lagoon, a mile off Hwy 101, with flush toilets and water, but no showers.

Redwood Trails RV & Campground (707-488-2061; rv4fun.com/redwood.html; Hwy 101; tent/RV sites $15/26), opposite the turn-off to Dry Lagoon, has a general store, bakery, arcade, horseback rides and, if you're lucky, elk lazing in the meadow outside.

REDWOOD NATIONAL PARK

The world's tallest living trees have been standing here for time immemorial, predating the Roman Empire by over 500 years. Prepare to be impressed – or at least dwarfed.

Jointly administered by the state and federal governments, Redwood National and State Parks are actually a string of parks, starting in the north at Jedediah Smith Redwoods (p137) and continuing southward to Del Norte Coast Redwoods (p133), Prairie Creek Redwoods (opposite) and Redwood National Park. Together, these parks have been declared an International Biosphere Reserve and World Heritage Site.

The small town of **Orick** (population 650), at the southern tip of the park, *should* be a bustling gateway town, since it's the only settlement on the 40-mile stretch between Trinidad and Klamath. Instead, pick-up trucks rust in people's front yards. (Locals blame the park for their demise. A one-sided telling of the tale is spelled out in *Orick 911,* which you can rent free from the local video store.) There's a good Mexican restaurant (La Hacienda), a diner serving tasty pie (Palm Café), and a great running joke: the marquis of the (closed) Orick Theater, which might read anything from 'Dean Martin and Jerry Lewis Live!' to 'Naked Cowgirl Mud Wrestling, Tonight Only!' Stop for lunch and gasoline, but sleep elsewhere.

Orientation & Information

There are no fees and no entrance stations, so it's imperative to pick up the free official map either at the park headquarters (p135) in Cres-

cent City or at the **Thomas H Kuchel Visitor Center** (Redwood Information Center; 707-465-7765; www.nps .gov/redw; Hwy 101; 9am-5pm;) in Orick, where there's a 12-minute introductory video. Rangers issue permits here for Tall Trees Grove (below). For in-depth redwood ecology, buy the official parks handbook ($7.50). Outside are ocean view picnic areas and boardwalks over the dunes – a great spot to let kids run.

Reserve campgrounds in advance, lest you be relegated to the less-attractive nearby RV parks.

Sights & Activities

Just north of the visitors center, turn east on Bald Hills Rd 2 miles to **Lady Bird Johnson Grove**, one of the park's most beautiful groves, accessible via a gentle 1-mile loop trail. Follow signs. Continue another 5 miles up Bald Hills to **Redwood Creek Overlook**. On the top of the ridgeline at 2100ft elevation, you'll see over the trees and the entire watershed – provided it's not foggy. Past the overlook lies the gated turn-off for the **Tall Trees Grove**, location of some of the world's tallest trees. Rangers issue only 50 vehicle permits per day, but they rarely run out. Pick one up, along with the gate-lock combination, from the Thomas H Kuchel Visitor Center (above) or park headquarters in Crescent City (p135). Allow four hours for the round-trip, which includes a 6-mile drive down a rough dirt road (speed limit 15mph) and a steep 1.3-mile one-way hike, which descends 800ft to the grove.

The 4.5-mile **Dolason Prairie Trail** drops 2400ft in elevation, passing through various ecological zones, from open grasslands high above the trees, into the lush forest below. The trailhead is 11 miles up Bald Hills Rd from Hwy 101; preposition a shuttle car at Tall Trees Grove and spare yourself the uphill return.

LOCAL VOICE

Al Muelhoeffer leads tours for the Sierra Club and is the only known person to have trekked *all* 200+ miles of trails in Redwood National and State Parks on behalf of the parks service. His favorites are:

- Dolason Prairie Trail (above)
- The Hidden Beach section of the Coastal Trail (p133)
- Emerald Ridge Trail (opposite)

COAST REDWOODS: THE TALLEST TREES ON EARTH

Though they covered much of the northern hemisphere millions of years ago, redwood trees now grow only in China and two areas of California (and a small grove in Oregon). Coast redwoods *(Sequoia sempervirens)* are found in a narrow, 450-mile-long strip along California's Pacific coast between Big Sur and southern Oregon. They can live for 2200 years, grow to 370ft tall (the tallest tree ever recorded) and achieve a diameter of 22ft at the base, with bark up to 12in thick.

In summer 2006, researchers found three new record-breaking trees in Redwood National Park. The tallest, Hyperion, measures a whopping 378ft – that's nearly 40 stories tall! Coming in a close second and third are Helios at 376ft and Icarus at 371ft. These just-discovered trees displace the old record-holder, the 370ft-high Stratosphere Giant in Rockefeller Forest (p110). But the trees bear no signs, so you won't be able to find them – too many boot-clad visitors would compact the delicate root systems, so the park's not telling where they are. No matter, though, because you wouldn't be able to distinguish them from others around them anyway.

The tallest trees reach their maximum height some time between 300 and 700 years of age. Because they're narrow at their bases, they generally aren't the ones you notice as you walk through the forest. The dramatic, fat-trunked giants, which make such a visually stunning impact from the ground, are ancient, as much as 2000 years old. But they're not as tall as the younger ones because their tops have been blown off in intense storms that have occurred over the centuries.

The structure of coast redwoods has been compared to a nail standing on its head. Unlike most trees, coast redwoods have no deep taproot and their root system is shallow in relation to their height – only 10ft to 13ft deep and spreading out 60ft to 80ft around the tree. The trees sometimes fall due to wind, but they are very flexible and usually sway in the wind as if they're dancing.

What gives these majestic giants their namesake color? It's the redwoods' high tannin content. It also makes their wood and bark resistant to insects and disease. The thick, spongy bark also has a high moisture content, enabling the ancient trees to survive many naturally occurring forest fires.

Coast redwoods are the only conifers in the world that can reproduce not only by seed cones, which grow to about the size of an olive at the ends of branches, but also by sprouting from their parents' roots and stumps, using the established root systems. Often you'll see a circle of redwoods standing in a forest, sometimes around a wide crater; this 'fairy ring' is made up of offspring that sprouted from one parent tree, which may have deteriorated into humus long ago. Burls, the large bumpy tissue growths on trunks and fallen logs, are a third method of reproduction.

There's a whole ecosystem in the canopy of the trees. Critters and birds such as the wandering salamander, marbled murrelet, and the famous northern spotted owl spend their entire existence high above the forest floor, where they need not fight for food, nor get caught by predators.

Today only 4% of the North Coast's original two million acres of ancient redwood forests remain standing. Almost half of these old-growth forests are protected in Redwood National and State Parks.

The 2.7-mile **Emerald Ridge Trail** originates 600ft from the Tall Trees trailhead and drops to Redwood Creek, crisscrossing the stream and gravel bars (bring appropriate footwear and attempt this trail in summer only, when the water is low). Note that instead of following trail markers downstream, make an *upstream* detour for swimming holes, stunning scenery and total solitude.

There are several longer trails, including awe-inspiring **Redwood Creek Trail**, which also reaches Tall Trees Grove. You'll need a free backcountry permit to camp along the route, which is accessible only from Memorial Day to Labor Day, when footbridges are up. Otherwise, there's no way across the creek. (Note that there are more automobile break-ins at Redwood Creek trailhead than anywhere else in the park. Hide valuables.)

There's primitive camping in the park; inquire at visitors centers.

PRAIRIE CREEK REDWOODS STATE PARK

Famous for virgin redwood forests and unspoiled coastline, this 14,000-acre section of Redwood National and State Parks has 70 miles of hiking trails and spectacular scenic drives. Pick up information and sit by the fire at **Prairie Creek Visitors Center** (☎ 707-465-7354; 🕙 9am-5pm Mar-Oct, 10am-4pm Nov-Feb; 🚭), which has the best bookstore of all the redwood parks' visitor centers – including park headquarters. Kids love the taxidermy dioramas and their push-button, light-up displays. Outside, Roosevelt elk roam grassy flats.

Sights & Activities

Don't skip the 8-mile **Newton B Drury Scenic Parkway**, which parallels Hwy 101, passing through untouched ancient redwood forests. It's worth the short detour off the freeway to view the magnificence of these trees from your car. Numerous trails branch off from roadside pullouts. Intersecting scenic drives include the 3-mile-long **Cal Barrel Rd**, which intersects the parkway just north of the visitors center (this is the *only* road in any of the parks where you can walk dogs).

There are 28 mountain-biking and hiking trails through the park, from simple to strenuous. If you're tight on time or have mobility impairments, stop at **Big Tree**, an easy 100yd walk from the car park. Several other short nature trails start near the visitors center, including the Revelation Trail, Five-Minute Trail, Elk Prairie Trail and Nature Trail. If you're depressed by the overall destruction of redwood forests, stop in at the **Ah-Pah Interpretive Trail** at the park's north end and stroll the recently reforested logging road: you'll be surprised at how quickly the forest recovers and be inspired by humanity's ingenuity. Other fine treks include the 11.5-mile **Coastal Trail** and the 3.5-mile **South Fork-Rhododendron-Brown Creek Loop**, particularly beautiful in spring when rhododendrons and wildflowers bloom. Approach from the Brown Creek to South Fork direction – unless you like tramping uphill. Kids like splashing in the creek alongside the easy-access **Prairie Creek Trail**, which roughly parallels Drury Scenic Pkwy.

The **Coastal Drive** follows Davison Rd to Gold Bluffs. Go west 3 miles north of Orick and doubleback north along a sometimes-rough gravel road for 3.5 miles over the coastal hills to the **fee station** (per vehicle $6), then head up the coast to **Gold Bluffs Beach**, where you can picnic or camp. One mile ahead, take an easy half-mile trail to prehistoric-looking **Fern Canyon**, whose 60ft fern-covered sheer-rock walls can be seen in Steven Spielberg's *Jurassic Park 2:*

The Lost World. This is one of the most photographed spots on the North Coast – damp and lush, all emerald green – and *totally* worth getting your toes wet to see.

Sleeping & Eating

There are no motels or cabins. Pitch a tent in the campgrounds at the southern end of the park.

Elk Prairie Campground (☎ reservations 800-444-7275; www.reserveamerica.com; campsites $15-20) Elk roam this popular campground, where you can sleep under redwoods or at the prairie's edge. The camp has hot showers and some hike-in sites. There's also a shallow creek to splash in. Sites 1 to 7 and 69 to 76 are on grassy prairies and get full sun; sites 8 to 68 are wooded. To camp in a mixed redwood forest, book sites 20 to 27.

Gold Bluffs Beach (campsites $15) This campground sits between 100ft cliffs and wide-open ocean, but there are some windbreaks and solar-heated showers. Look for sites up the cliff under the trees. You can't make reservations.

The park also has three backcountry **campsites** (per person $3), as well as one **environmental campsite** (per person $12).

KLAMATH

pop 1420

Giant cast-metal golden bears stand sentry at the southern end of town, as Hwy 101 crosses the Klamath River Bridge. But for them, you could drive right past Klamath and not even know it. Pull off the highway onto Klamath Rd to reach downtown. Klamath is an hour north of Eureka.

There's not much here except water and trees, making it an excellent base for outdoor adventurers. For information or to learn about August's **Salmon Festival**, contact the **Klamath Chamber of Commerce** (☎ 800-200-2335; www.klamathcc.org). For hiking maps, stop by the Redwood National and State Parks Headquarters in Crescent City (p135) or the Thomas H Kuchel Visitor Center in Orick (p130). **Fun Bus Tours** (☎ 707-482-1030, 888-386-2872; www.fun bustours.com; adult/child $30/2.50) leads tours of the nearby parks.

All the land for 40 miles upriver, and 1 mile on either side of the Klamath River's centerline, falls under the jurisdiction of the Yurok tribal police, *not* Del Norte County's sheriff. For more on the tribe, see www .yuroktribe.org.

Sights & Activities

The mouth of the **Klamath River** is a dramatic sight. Marine, riparian, forest and meadow ecological zones all converge: the birding is exceptional! For the best views, head north of town to Requa Rd and the **Klamath River Overlook**, and picnic on high bluffs above driftwood-strewn beaches. On a clear day, this is one of the most spectacular viewpoints on the North Coast (no exaggeration), and one of the best whale-watching spots in California. For a good hike, head north along the Coastal Trail. You'll have the sand to yourself at **Hidden Beach**; access the trail at the northern end of Motel Trees (right).

Just south of the river, on Hwy 101, follow signs for the scenic **Coastal Drive**, a narrow, winding country road (unsuitable for RVs and trailers) atop extremely high cliffs over the ocean. Come when it's not foggy, and mind your driving. Though technically in Redwood National Park, it's much closer to Klamath.

Dude, is that Abe Lincoln with an axe? No! That's Paul Bunyon and his pal Babe the Blue Ox towering over the parking lot at Cheese of... er, **Trees of Mystery** (☎ 707-482-2251, 800-638-3389; www.treesofmystery.net; 15500 Hwy 101; adult/child/senior $13.50/6.50/10; ☼ 8am-7pm Jun-Aug, 9am-5pm Sep-May; ☝), a shameless tourist trap with a gondola running through the redwood canopy. The **End of the Trail Museum**, hidden behind the gift shop, has an amazing collection of Native American arts and artifacts – and it's *free*.

Sleeping & Eating

Woodsy Klamath is cheaper than nearby Crescent City, but there aren't as many places to eat or buy groceries, and there's nothing to do at night but play cards. There's a market and diner in town.

Flint Ridge Campground (☎ 707-464-6101 campsites free) Four miles from the Klamath River Bridge via Coastal Drive, this tent-only, hike-in campground has sites in a meadow, a five-minute walk east from the dirt parking area. No water; pack out trash. And it's free!

Kamp Klamath (☎ 707-482-0227, 866-552-6284; www.kampklamath.com; tent/RV sites $19/24; ☐) If park campgrounds are full, pitch a tent on the river's south shore at this spacious, well-shaded campground, with bicycle rentals and family-friendly events like Saturday BBQs and campfire songs. There's an onsite store with beer and camping equipment. RV sites have hookups.

Ravenwood Motel (☎ 707-482-5911, 866-520-9875; www.ravenwoodmotel.com; 131 Klamath Blvd; r/ste with kitchen $58/105) The spotlessly clean rooms are better than anything in Crescent City and individually decorated with furnishings you'd expect in a city hotel, not a small-town motel. Mattresses are good, with fairly high-thread-count sheets. Outside there are BBQs.

Motel Trees (☎ 707-482-3152, 800-848-2982; www.treesofmystery.com; 15495 Hwy 101 S; d/q $60/103) Opposite Trees of Mystery, Motel Trees has standard-issue rooms and theme rooms. The family-style restaurant (open 8am to 8pm in summer, closed Tuesday and Wednesday in winter) serves plain-old American cooking.

Steelhead Lodge (☎ 707-482-8145; Hwy 169; r $65, mains $16-25; ☼ dinner nightly summer, Fri-Sun Feb-Jun, closed Nov-Jan) Three miles upriver in Klamath Glen, this Western-style lodge is known for its knock-down 'fishbowl' margaritas. The steak dinners are OK, but folks really come to get hammered. (What else is there to do here after dark?) The lodge also rents clean, basic motel rooms with kitchens ($65).

Woodland Villa Cabins (☎ 707-482-2081, 888-866-2466; www.klamathusa.com; 15870 Hwy 101; d cottage $69-75, cottage with kitchen $84-93; ☐) Rent modest, cozy cottages here. There's a picnic area and small market on-site.

our pick **Historic Requa Inn** (☎ 707-482-1425, 866-800-8777; www.requainn.com; 451 Requa Rd; r incl breakfast $85-155) A woodsy country lodge on high bluffs overlooking the mouth of the Klamath, the 1914 Requa Inn is one of our North Coast favorites. Many of the charming country-style rooms have mesmerizing views over the misty river, as does the dining room, where guests have breakfast and dinner. After a day hiking, play Scrabble by the fire in the common area and compare tales with other travelers. The restaurant is sometimes open to the public; call 24 hours ahead. No TVs.

DEL NORTE COAST REDWOODS STATE PARK

Marked by steep canyons and dense woods, 3200 acres of this **park** (per vehicle per day $6) are virgin redwood forest, crisscrossed by 15 miles of hiking trails. In December 2005, the park grew by 25,000 acres, logged-out land purchased from a lumber company. Now the entire ecologically important Redwood Creek watershed is fully protected – good news for salmon, since the watershed is one of the biggest spawning

WHAT'S ALL THE SQUAWK ABOUT SALMON?

In 2006 salmon-fishing season was drastically shortened and almost got canceled altogether, seriously threatening the livelihood of local tribes and fishermen. There simply weren't enough fish. The problem lay not so much with overfishing – salmon fishing is heavily regulated – but habitat destruction by dams, logging, and lately the Bush Administration.

Rivers in Northern California once teemed with salmon, especially the Klamath, California's second-largest waterway, where 100 years ago, the annual upriver migration exceeded a million fish. But in 2005, that number had dropped to under 30,000. What happened?

The crisis began 100 years ago with major dam construction and large-scale logging. Dams not only block spawning adults and chew up weak, immature fish in giant rotating hydroelectric turbines, but they cause diminished flows downriver, which cause water temperatures to rise, sparking the growth of toxic, oxygen-depriving blue-green algae blooms, a persistent and serious problem. Logging causes silt runoff from deforested hillsides, filling in the clear, cold-water pools and gravel beds that salmon require for spawning.

But the latest news is about the Bush Administration, which instead of finding new solutions to old problems, has created huge new ones. Get this: In 2002, Gale Norton, a Bush appointee, directed the Bureau of Reclamation to divert huge amounts of Klamath River water to inland farmers, some of whom grow crops *in the desert.* When the salmon returned to spawn that autumn, there wasn't enough water in the river, and that which did flow got so warm that it killed the fish. Over 30,000 spawning salmon died on the muddy banks. (You have to see it to grasp the scope; search Google Images for 'Klamath River fish kill.') Because newborn fish don't spawn for approximately four years, the effects of the kill weren't fully felt until 2006. The local tribes, fishermen, sport anglers and tourism agencies are up in arms.

Before you start bumming out too much, know that there's real hope. In March 2006, the US District Court in Oakland set caps on how much water could be diverted from the Klamath to farms, in order to protect migrating salmon. And there's growing momentum to decommission some or all of the four dams along the lower Klamath. In 2006, Bill Fehrman, the President of Pacificorp, the owner of the dams, said, 'We are not opposed to dam removal.' But the Federal Energy Regulatory Commission (FERC), under Bush, has refused even to consider the dam-removal proposal. Politics aside, there are other issues at play, such as a century's worth of silt behind the dams, but according to the California Coastal Conservancy, a state agency, the silt is clean, and decommissioning the dams would be safe and inexpensive – around $100 million – and pay big returns down the line with the restoration of salmon runs. Other than the farmers, those who object to the idea are primarily inland landowners on the shores of upstream reservoirs; they don't want to see their land values diminish.

The debate rages. Nearly every other day in 2006 the Eureka newspaper, the *Times Standard,* ran articles on the Klamath and will likely do so well into the future. To learn the latest, search back issues online at the **Times-Standard** (www.times-standard.com). Better yet, talk to a local member of the Yurok tribe, which has water rights to the lower Klamath. Stop by the easy-to-find tribal office in the town of Klamath and chat up Tammy Prouty, the tribe's secretary. But for the opposing view, you'll have to drive to the desert.

areas in all of Northern California, but it's currently closed to the public.

Pick up maps and inquire about guided walks at the Redwood National and State Parks Headquarters in Crescent City (opposite) or the Thomas H Kuchel Visitor Center in Orick (p130).

At the park's north end, watch the surf pound at **Crescent Beach**, just south of Crescent City via Enderts Beach Rd. Continue uphill to **Crescent Beach Overlook** for picnicking and win-

tertime whale-watching. Hike via the Crescent Beach Trail (or along the Coastal Trail from the south) to **Enderts Beach** for magnificent tide pools at low tide (tread lightly).

Tall trees cling precipitously to canyon walls that drop to the rocky, timber-strewn coastline, and it's almost impossible to get to the water, except via the gorgeous but steep **Damnation Trail**. If you don't want to hike, head south to **False Klamath Cove**, where you can picnic and stretch your legs on the sand.

The **HI Redwood Hostel** (☎ 707-482-8265, 800-909-4776; www.norcalhostels.org/redwoods; 14480 Hwy 101; dm/r $20/49; ☽ 8am-10am & 5-10pm Mar-Nov) is a rambling 1908 farmhouse on a bluff overlooking False Klamath Cove. The window-lined kitchen is glorious at breakfast, when the sun lights up the churning surf outside. Linen and towels are included. Doors lock at 10pm but once you've checked in, there's no curfew. Reserve ahead, especially for family rooms. There's a small on-site store selling rice, pasta and yummy homemade chocolates.

The **Mill Creek Campground** (☎ 800-444-7275; www.reserveamerica.com; campsites $20) has 145 sites in a redwood grove, 2 miles east of Hwy 101, 7 miles south of Crescent City. It's quieter than Jedediah Smith Redwoods (p137), but it's in a second-growth, not old-growth forest. Sites 1 to 74 are woodsier; sites 75 to 145 sunnier. Hike-in sites are prettiest.

CRESCENT CITY
pop 8800

Twenty minutes north of Klamath, on a crescent-shaped bay, Crescent City is California's last big town north of Arcata. Though founded in 1853 as a seaport and supply center for inland gold mines, Crescent City retains few old buildings: half the town was destroyed by a tsunami in 1964, a defining event that has oddly become a point of civic pride, as evidenced by the tsunami-logo flags decorating downtown lampposts (see boxed text, p136). Completely rebuilt, it lacks charm, but has a certain '60s-kitsch appeal, with ticky-tacky-box architecture – evidence the local Denny's. Considering the entire town is on the water, city planners have done a terrible job of maximizing the views – except at Beachfront Park and along Pebble Beach Dr, the town's only pretty residential neighborhood. The economy depends heavily on shrimp and crab fishing, hotel tax, and on Pelican Bay maximum-security prison, just north of town, which adds tension to the air (watch for cops). Despite all this ho-humness, there is a teeny-tiny arts community trying to establish itself. Time will tell if a tsunami of blandness drowns it out.

Orientation & Information

Hwy 101 splits into two parallel one-way streets, with the southbound traffic on L St, northbound on M St. Front St runs west toward the lighthouse. The tiny downtown is centered along 3rd St.

Crescent City-Del Norte Chamber of Commerce (☎ 707-464-3174, 800-343-8300; www.delnorte.org; 1001 Front St; ☽ 9am-5pm daily Jul-Sep, Mon-Fri Oct-Jun) Pick up local information.
Redwood National & State Parks Headquarters (☎ 707-465-7306; 1111 2nd St; ☽ 9am-5pm) On-staff rangers and information about all four parks under its jurisdiction. On the corner of K St.

Sights & Activities

One of the last-remaining light stations with a live-in lighthouse keeper, the 1856 **Battery Point Lighthouse** (☎ 707-464-3089; www.delnortehistory.org/lighthouse), at the south end of A St, operates on a tiny, rocky island you can reach at low tide. April to October, tour the **museum** (☎ adult/child $3/1; ☽ 10am-4pm Wed-Sun May-Sep; Sat & Sun Dec-Feb); hours vary with tides and weather. Phone ahead, or check the bulletin board in the parking lot.

Six miles offshore, the **St George Reef Lighthouse** (☎ 707-464-8299; www.stgeorgereeflighthouse.us; ☽ Oct-May) is visible on clear days. The only way in is via helicopter ($170; book ahead).

Skip the downer Ocean World aquarium; instead visit the feel-good **North Coast Marine Mammal Center** (☎ 707-465-6265; www.northcoastmmc.org; 424 Howe Dr; admission by donation; ☽ 10am-5pm; ♿), just east of Battery Point, where injured seals, sea lions and dolphins recuperate after being rescued.

Beachfront Park (Howe Dr), between B & H Sts, has a great harborside beach for little ones – with no waves – and picnic tables and a bicycle trail. Further east on near J St, you'll come to **Kidtown** (Howe Dr), with slides and swings and a make-believe castle. For a scenic drive, head north on Pebble Beach Dr, which ends at **Point St George**, where you can walk through grassy dunes.

Crescent City is a mellow place to learn to surf (head to South Beach); rent a board and wet suit from **Rhyn Noll Surf & Skate** (☎ 707-465-4400; 275 L St). The fishing is great, too: book a deep-sea expedition or whale-watching trip aboard the **Tally Ho II** (☎ 707-464-1236; Crescent City Harbor). There's weekend glow-in-the-dark bowling at **Tsunami Lanes** (☎ 707-464-4323; 760 L St).

Festivals & Events

The best reason to visit may be the **Aleutian Goose Festival** (www.aleutiangoosefestival.org), at the end of March, to see the dawn sky fill with thousands of migrating geese. Less impressive, the **Del Norte County Fair** takes place in August.

Sleeping

Most people stop for only one night, en route between San Francisco and Portland, so motels are overpriced. Town's south side is quietest. Also see Pelican State Beach (p138).

Curly Redwood Lodge (☎ 707-464-2137; www.curly redwoodlodge.com; 701 Hwy 101 S; r $62-67) Aficionados of '50s-modern love this motel, whose rooms are paneled with the lumber of one single giant curly redwood, but the place needs upgrades such as thicker carpeting and door seals.

Bayview Motel (☎ 707-465-2050, 800-446-0583; 310 Hwy 101 S; r $65-80, tr $90; 🐾) Nonsmoking rooms at this nondescript motel are nicer than the smoking rooms; they also have air-conditioning (nonsmoking rooms don't) and are further from the road, providing maximum quiet. Good housekeeping. On-site diner.

Crescent Beach Motel (☎ 707-464-5436; www.cres centbeachmotel.com; 1455 Hwy 101 S; ocean view s/d $92/98; nonview r $70) Just south of town, this basic, old-fashioned motel has no phones (though it has TVs) and ugly bedspreads, but wow! the views: ocean view rooms are within spitting distance of the crashing surf. Try here first, but skip the nonview rooms.

Light House Inn (☎ 707-464-3993, 877-464-3993; www .lighthouse101.com; 681 Hwy 101 S; s/d/tr $89/99/115; 🐾 🖳) Rooms are big and spotless at this three-story motel. The lobby has too many frilly details (think dollhouses), but rooms have fridges and microwaves. Good choice for families.

Castle Island Getaway (☎ 707-465-5102; www.castle islandgetaway.com; 1830 Murphy Ave; r $100-150) Two blocks from the ocean, this B&B has three rooms (reservations required) in a home owned by a charming, sophisticated innkeeper; the upstairs suite has the most space. Top choice for a B&B.

Cottage by the Sea (☎ 707-464-9068, 877-642-2254; www.waterfrontvacationrental.com; 205 South A St; cottage with kitchen $150) Near the lighthouse, this sparkling-clean cottage is decorated with too many pillows on the bed. It's by the sea but has no view. There are B&B rooms in the type-A owner's house, but stick to the cottage for maximum privacy.

Hampton Inn (☎ 707-465-5400; www.hamptoninn .com; 100 A St; r $159-199; 🐾 🖳 🕿) Crescent City's only chain-style hotel is in a gorgeous spot on oceanfront bluffs. Too bad the prefab building is so ugly. In terms of amenities, it's the town's best.

The county operates two reservable **campgrounds** (☎ 707-464-7230; campsites $10) just outside town. **Florence Keller Park** (3400 Cunningham Ln) has 50 sites in a beautiful redwood grove (take Hwy 101 north to Elk Valley Cross Rd and follow the signs). **Ruby Van Deventer Park** (4705 N Bank Rd) has 18 sites along the Smith River, off Hwy 197.

Eating & Drinking

Restaurants close early, before 9pm. Of the Mexican joints in town, **Perlita's** (☎ 707-465-6770; 297 Hwy 101 S; 🕑 11:30am-8:30pm) is arguably best.

Good Harvest Cafe (☎ 707-465-6028; 700 Northcrest Dr; dishes $7-10; 🕑 breakfast & lunch; 🕿) The hands-down-best place to eat in Crescent City serves

---

CRESCENT CITY'S GREAT TSUNAMI

On March 28, 1964, most of downtown Crescent City was destroyed by a tsunami. At 3:36am, a giant earthquake occurred on the north shore of Prince William Sound in Alaska. Measuring a whopping 9.2 on the Richter scale, the quake was the most severe ever recorded in North America. The first of the ensuing giant ocean swells reached Crescent City only a few hours later.

Officials warned the sheriff's office, and at 7:08am evacuation of the waterfront began. The waves arrived an hour later. The first two were small, only about 13ft above the tide line, and many rejoiced, thinking the worst had passed. Then the water receded until the bay was emptied, leaving boats that had been anchored offshore sitting in the mud. Frigid water surged in, rising all the way up to 5th St, knocking buildings off their foundations, carrying away cars, trucks and anything else in its path. By the time the fourth and final wave receded, 29 blocks of town were destroyed, with more than 300 buildings displaced. Five gasoline storage tanks exploded. Eleven people died, three of whom were never found.

Many old-timers are still remembered for their heroic acts during and after the waves, helping to save their neighbors and later rebuild the town. Today the modern little downtown shopping center that replaced many of the destroyed buildings bears an unusual but appropriate name – Tsunami Landing.

big salads, homemade soups, smoothies, sandwiches, omelettes, beer and lots for vegetarians. Too bad it's closed at dinner. It's on the corner of Hwy 101.

Thai House (☎ 707-464-2427; 105 N St; dishes $8-11; ⏱ lunch & dinner; ♿) Behind Safeway, the Thai House serves pretty good Thai and Vietnamese cooking, with a few Chinese dishes too.

Beachcomber Restaurant (☎ 707-464-2205; 1400 Hwy 101 S; meals $13-19; ⏱ dinner Fri-Tue; ♿) It's basically a diner with vinyl booths and a salad bar, but it has full ocean views. Expect fried fish with tartare sauce and iceberg lettuce. 'Small dinners' cost $8 to $12.

Bistro Garden (☎ 707-464-5627; 110 Anchor Way; lunch mains $8-11, dinner $17-27; ⏱ lunch Mon-Fri, dinner Mon-Sat) The food here is better than you typically find in Crescent City. It actually uses sauces! The fish-heavy menu features seafood stew, grilled oysters and filet mignon. The ocean views are stellar. Come before sunset.

Java Hut (☎ 707-465-4439; 437 Hwy 101 N; ⏱ 5am-10pm) It's almost impossible to get strong coffee on the North Coast, but you'll do OK here.

Getting There & Around

United Express (☎ 800-241-6522; www.united.com) flies into tiny **Jack McNamara Field Airport** (CEC; ☎ 707-464-7229), north of town. Rent a vehicle, by reservation only, at **Hertz** (☎ 707-464-5750, 800-654-3131; www.hertz.com), or the local **Two Guys Car Rental** (☎ 707-464-6818, 800-308-7813). **Redwood Coast Transit** (☎ 707-464-9314, 707-464-6400; www.redwoodcoasttransit.org) operates two daily buses (except Sunday) between Crescent City and Arcata for $20 one way, or $30 for a five-day pass. It also serves Klamath and Smith River. Service between Klamath and Crescent City costs $1. (NB: The transit company's website is woefully inadequate; call for up-to-date information.)

TOLOWA DUNES STATE PARK & LAKE EARL WILDLIFE AREA

A naturalist's wonderland, five minutes north of Crescent City via Northcrest Dr, the **park and wildlife area** (☎ 707-465-2145; ⏱ sunrise-sunset) encompass about 10,000 acres of terrain, including wetlands, dunes, meadows, wooded hillsides and two lakes, **Lake Earl** and **Lake Tolowa**, which are connected by a narrow waterway. Everywhere there are birds, over 250 species of them – low warbles and high-pitched whistles fill the air. This is a major stopping point along the Pacific flyway for Aleutian geese. Keep an

eye out for peregrine falcons too. Offshore spot whales, harbor seals and sea lions. Fish for cutthroat trout in the lakes.

There are 20 miles of hiking and horseback trails, most level and sandy. Tread lightly. In summer inquire about guided walks. The best wetland trails lie in the northern portion of the park, where a delicate balance exists between freshwater and marine habitats. Pick up information from the Crescent City-Del Norte County Chamber of Commerce or the Redwood National and State Parks office in Crescent City (p135). Come in spring and early summer, while everything is green and lush. In winter it's sopping wet, in fall crackling dry.

The park and wildlife area is split into a patchwork of lands administered by California State Parks and the Department of Fish & Game (DFG); it's hard to tell where one area begins and another ends. The DFG focuses on single-species management, hunting and fishing, while the State Parks' focus is on ecodiversity and recreation. Thus you might be hiking a vast expanse of gorgeous and pristine dunes, with peerless views of mountains and sea, when out of nowhere you'll hear a shotgun in the woods. Fear not: there are strict regulations limiting where and when you can hunt, and such places are clearly marked.

There are two primitive **campgrounds** (campsites $7): a walk-in environmental campground (no water) and an equestrian campsite (nonpotable well water). Both are first-come, first-served. Register at Jedediah Smith (below) or Del Norte Coast Redwoods State Park (p133) campgrounds. Bring firewood, and be prepared for mosquitoes in late spring and early summer.

JEDEDIAH SMITH REDWOODS STATE PARK

The sparkling-clear Smith River, California's only undammed major river, runs through the state's northernmost redwood park, **Jedediah Smith** (per day $6), which lies 10 miles northeast of Crescent City (via Hwy 101 east to Hwy 197). The redwood stands are so dense that there are few trails through the park, but the outstanding 11-mile **Howland Hill Scenic Drive** cuts through otherwise inaccessible areas (take Hwy 199 to South Fork Rd; turn right after crossing two bridges). It's a rough, unpaved road, impassable for RVs over 22ft, and it gets graded only once a year in spring, but if you can't hike it's the best way to see the forest.

NORTH COAST

NORTH COAST

DETOUR: SMITH RIVER NATIONAL RECREATION AREA

West of Jedediah Smith Redwoods, the Smith River, the state's last remaining undammed water-way, runs right beside Hwy 199. Originating high in the Siskiyou Mountains, its serpentine course cuts through deep rock canyons beneath thick forests. Chinook salmon and steelhead trout annually migrate up its clear waters. Camp, hike, raft and kayak; check regulations if you want to fish. **Lunker Fish Trips** (☎ 707-458-4704, 800-248-4704; 2590 Hwy 199) leads excursions and rents inflatable kayaks. (Note that when it rains, the water rises fast because the riverbed is mostly rock; but it recedes fast too.) Stop by the **Six Rivers National Forest Headquarters** (☎ 707-457-3131; www .fs.fed.us/r5/sixrivers; 10600 Hwy 199, Gasquet; ☒ 8am-4:30 daily summer, Mon-Fri fall-spring) to get your bearings; opening hours can vary. Pick up pamphlets for the **Darlingtonia Trail** and **Myrtle Creek Botanical Area**, both easy jaunts into the woods where you can see rare plants and learn about the area's geology. The **South Fork & Middle Fork confluence** is one of the most photographed spots around, and it's easy to reach: take Hwy 199 to South Fork Rd, and turn right. Several hundred feet ahead, turn right again; pull off at the next right, just ahead. Bring a picnic.

Stroll the interpretive trail through the **Simpson-Reed Grove**. The longer **Mill Creek** Trail, off Howland Hill Scenic Drive, passes through redwoods and along a creek, and ends at the park's campground, on the Smith River. **Boy Scout Tree Trail** leads through the lush woods to a 20ft waterfall (December to May), the only waterfall in any of the redwood parks. There's a terrific **river beach** and picnic area near the park entrance, off Hwy 199, 5 miles east of Hwy 101. An easy half-mile path, departing from the far side of the campground, crosses the Smith River via a summer-only footbridge, leading to **Stout Grove**, the park's most famous grove. The **visitors center** (☎ 707-465-2144; ☒ 10am-4pm daily summer, Sat & Sun fall & spring) sells hiking maps and nature guides. If you wade in the river, be careful in spring when currents are swift and the water cold.

The popular **campground** (☎ reservations 800-444-7275; www.reserveamerica.com; campsites $20) has hot showers and sits beneath giant redwoods beside the river. Fabulous. Make reservations.

Just east, **Hiouchi Information Center** (☎ 707-464-6101, ext 5064; ☒ 9am-5pm mid-Jun–mid-Sep) stocks maps and books. Families can borrow free activity backpacks with projects for kids. When the visitors centers are closed, go to Redwood National & State Parks Headquarters in Crescent City (p135).

A mile east of the park in **Hiouchi**, rent inner tubes, inflatable kayaks and mountain bikes at **Lunker Fish Trips** (☎ 707-458-4704, 800-248-4704; 2590 Hwy 199), one of the North Coast's finest steelhead-fishing guides (fishing is best September to April).

Hiouchi Motel (☎ 707-458-3041, 866-446-8244; www .hiouchimotel.com; 2097 Hwy 199; s $45, d $60-65; ☐) has

straightforward motel rooms. Across the street, **Hiouchi Hamlet RV Resort** (☎ 707-458-3321, 800-722-9468; campsites $15, RV sites $22-27) also has a small market for supplies and fishing licenses.

Patrick Creek Lodge (☎ 707-457-3323; www.patrick creeklodge.net; r $100-130), a 1926 log cabin–style roadhouse, has simple accommodations and serves three surprisingly good meals a day (lunch $6 to $11, dinner $15 to $22).

PELICAN STATE BEACH

Smack dab on the Oregon border, five-acre **Pelican State Beach** (☎ 707-464-6101, ext 5151) is easy to miss. From the south, pull off Hwy 101 just before the state agricultural inspection station. There are no facilities. It's a great beach for kite flying; pick one up just over the border.

The best reason to visit is to stay at secluded, charming **Casa Rubio** (☎ 707-487-4313; 17285 Crissey Rd; www.casarubio.com; r $98-158), where three of the four ocean view inn rooms have kitchens. Think summer cottage, with mismatched furniture and meandering gardens. Lovely.

Next door, the **Nautical** (☎ 707-487-5006; 16850 Hwy 101 N; mains $19-29; ☒ dinner Wed-Sun) has spectacular sunset views and good, but pricey, dinners.

White Rock Resort (☎ 707-487-1021, 888-487-4659; www.whiterockresort.com; 16800 Hwy 101 N; r $175-195) has expensive 'cottages' (converted mobile homes); pay the extra $20 for oceanfront views.

Sea Escape (☎ 707-487-7333; www.seaescape.us; 15370 Hwy 101 N; r $95-135) has clean, but frumpy, motel-style suites, some with ocean views and kitchens.

Pitch a tent by the ocean (no windbreaks) at **Clifford Kamph Memorial Park** (☎ 707-464-7230; 15100 Hwy 101; campsites $5); no RVs.

Central Coast

Yes, San Francisco and LA are givens, but no trip to California is worth its salt without a jaunt down the Central Coast. Much of the state's mystique and lore can be traced to here, but obvious right off the bat is the area's intense loveliness – the Monterey Peninsula's rocky outcroppings, the shimmering waterfalls and forested mountains of Big Sur, Guadalupe's towering sand dunes, the Santa Barbara wine country's cultivated perfection, the primordial rawness of the Channel Islands.

In the north, flower-power Santa Cruz stands as the ideological and physical counterpoint to aggressively charming Carmel, the gateway to Big Sur country, where Hwy 1 pulls out all the stops scenery-wise.

The warmth of Southern California can be felt starting in the historic college town of San Luis Obispo. SoCal's distinctive Mission-style architecture is laid on extrathick in gracious, moneyed Santa Barbara, where even the homeless shelter sports whitewash adobe and an elegant red-tile roof. North of the city is the fabled wine country that has the starring role in the film *Sideways*.

To do the Central Coast justice, plan on at least a week, more if you take advantage of the myriad opportunities for hiking, biking, cycling or kayaking.

CENTRAL COAST

HIGHLIGHTS

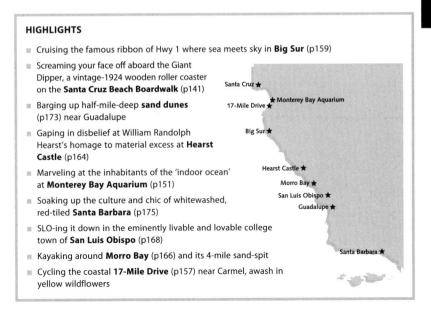

- Cruising the famous ribbon of Hwy 1 where sea meets sky in **Big Sur** (p159)
- Screaming your face off aboard the Giant Dipper, a vintage-1924 wooden roller coaster on the **Santa Cruz Beach Boardwalk** (p141)
- Barging up half-mile-deep **sand dunes** (p173) near Guadalupe
- Gaping in disbelief at William Randolph Hearst's homage to material excess at **Hearst Castle** (p164)
- Marveling at the inhabitants of the 'indoor ocean' at **Monterey Bay Aquarium** (p151)
- Soaking up the culture and chic of whitewashed, red-tiled **Santa Barbara** (p175)
- SLO-ing it down in the eminently livable and lovable college town of **San Luis Obispo** (p168)
- Kayaking around **Morro Bay** (p166) and its 4-mile sand-spit
- Cycling the coastal **17-Mile Drive** (p157) near Carmel, awash in yellow wildflowers

Santa Cruz ★
17-Mile Drive ★ ★ Monterey Bay Aquarium
Big Sur ★
Hearst Castle ★
Morro Bay ★
San Luis Obispo ★
Guadalupe ★
Santa Barbara ★

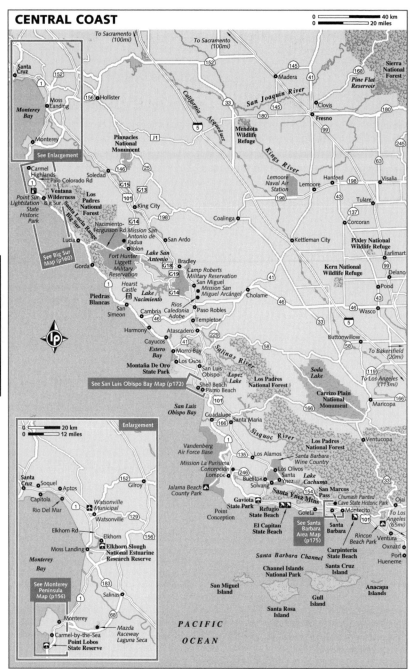

CENTRAL COAST

MONTEREY BAY

The Monterey Bay is the constant backdrop to life on the peninsula. Along its half-moon coastline, you'll find miles of often-deserted beaches and a span of towns bubbling with idiosyncratic charm. Yet even more diverse is the bay itself, protected as the Monterey Bay National Marine Sanctuary, and one of the richest and most varied marine environments anywhere on the planet.

SANTA CRUZ
pop 57,200
On the north end of Monterey Bay, Santa Cruz is counterculture central, a touchy-feely city famous for its leftie-liberal politics and live-and-let-live ideology – except when it comes to dogs (not allowed off leash or downtown), parking (meters run seven days a week), and Republicans (shot on sight). According to local banker John Rossell, 'North Korea, Cuba and Santa Cruz are the last-remaining bastions of communism on the planet.' A slight exaggeration perhaps, but the City Council has actually twice voted to impeach Bush and spends much of its time writing letters of outrage on behalf of the Burmese people's plight instead of focusing on the terrible parking problems downtown.

Local politics aside, Santa Cruz is a fun city, with a vibrant downtown that staged a remarkable comeback from the devastation caused by the 1989 Loma Prieta earthquake. On the waterfront is the famous beach boardwalk, and in the hills, the University of California at Santa Cruz (UCSC). Plan to spend at least a day, but to begin appreciating the aesthetic of jangly skirts and waist-length dreadlocks you'll need to stay longer. Santa Cruz is 90 minutes south of San Francisco and 50 minutes north of Monterey.

Orientation
Santa Cruz stretches along the coast, blending into Capitola, a low-key beach town, and Aptos beyond. The San Lorenzo River divides the town in an un-neat fashion into a sort of yin and yang. Pacific Ave is downtown's main street. Hwy 1 from the north leads into Mission St; Hwy 17, the main route from the Bay Area, turns into Ocean St. The UCSC campus is uphill 2.5 miles northwest of the center.

Carry plenty of quarters for parking meters, which operate seven days a week until 8pm.

Those with blue poles have 12-hour limits; others have two-hour limits. Watch out: meter maids are merciless!

Information
Bookshop Santa Cruz (☎ 831-423-0900; 1520 Pacific Ave; ☺ 10am-10pm) Excellent bookstore with a vast selection of new books, a few used ones, popular and unusual magazines and a café. Also the city's unofficial cultural center point.
Dominican Hospital (☎ 831-462-7700; 1555 Soquel Dr; ☺ 24 hr) 24-hour emergency services.
Kinko's (☎ 831-425-1177; 105 Laurel St; ☺ 7am-11pm) Internet access, $0.20 per minute.
KPIG FM107.5 Plays the classic Santa Cruz soundtrack (think Bob Marley, Joni Mitchell, and jam bands like the Dead).
Post office (☎ 831-426-0144; 850 Front St)
Santa Cruz County Conference & Visitors Council (☎ 831-425-1234; www.santacruz.org; 1211 Ocean St; ☺ 9am-5pm Mon-Sat, 10am-4pm Sun) Has brochures, maps and free internet access.

Sights
Stroll, shop and people-watch downtown along Pacific Ave, a 10-minute walk from the beach. The 200 block of Walnut St (downtown) is the prettiest street in town, with gracefully arcing trees and 100-year-old homes.

SANTA CRUZ BEACH BOARDWALK
The 1907 **boardwalk** (☎ 831-423-5590; www.beachboardwalk.com; admission free; ☺ 11am-11pm daily summer, to 5pm Sat & Sun winter; ♿) is the oldest beach-front amusement park on the West Coast. The boardwalk has a glorious old-school Americana vibe, with the smell of cotton candy mixing with the salt air, punctuated by the distant squeals of kids hanging upside down on carnival rides. Its most famous include the half-mile-long Giant Dipper, a vintage-1924 wooden roller coaster, and the 1911 Looff carousel – both National Historic Landmarks. For kids, the Cave Train is unexpectedly fun for its portrayal of cavemen in modern times. But the thing that makes it so great is the proximity to the beach. When you're feeling dopey from too much sun, don your flip-flops, leave your towel on the beach, and hit the rides. When you're good and dizzy, head back to the sand. Individual rides cost between $2 and $4, or you can buy an all-day pass for $27. On Friday nights in summer there are free concerts by rock veterans you may have thought were dead.

CENTRAL COAST

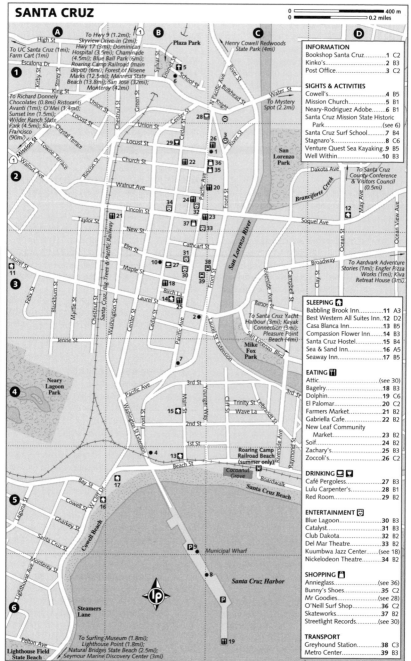

SANTA CRUZ

WOODIES ON THE WHARF *Heather Dickson*

No need to cover your eyes; this is all about cars. Woodies are hulking, practical, wooden-bodied beasts developed as commercial station wagons in the 1920s. They became popular with the West Coast surf community in the 1950s and '60s, when they started to lose their luster and could be purchased for as little as $125. As Jim Ferdinand, President of Santa Cruz Woodies, said, 'They were popular with surfers because of their price and the amount of room they had in them – you could fit your board and your buddies and go to the beach.'

Today, you can still see woodies on the third Saturday in June at **Woodies on the Wharf** (www .santacruzwoodies.com), the premier show on the West Coast for these classic cars. It's a free, one-day, annual event that showcases over 200 vehicles and brings the Beach Boys image back to town. Jim says, 'Lots of the California owners are surfers or past surfers who've tried to recapture their youth, the car they had when they were in high school, or it's just something they've always loved.' As for the cars, many of them are in pristine condition and look more like works of art but, as Jim says, 'If your car has wood that's rotting and rust holes in it you can still come and have a great time.' The club's roots are in laid-back surf culture after all.

So what coastal California route would a woodie owner take? Jim says he loves following Hwy 1 down the coast from Santa Cruz to San Diego. He adds, 'If there's surf, we'll stop and surf.' Indeed, however well Jim keeps his car, 'It's still got sand in the carpet and goes to the beach.'

MUNICIPAL WHARF
You can drive the length of the wharf, where restaurants, gift shops and barking sea lions compete for attention. A few shops rent poles and fishing tackle, if you're keen to join the fisherfolk along the wharf waiting patiently for a bite. The views here are first rate.

MISSION SANTA CRUZ
Though the 1791 Mission Santa Cruz (Mission of the Holy Cross) gave the town its name, today it's one of California's most unremarkable missions. The **Santa Cruz Mission State Historic Park** (425-5849; 144 School St; 10am-4pm Thu-Sun), one block off Mission Plaza, includes only one original structure, the 1791 **Neary-Rodríguez Adobe**. If you want to see a real mission, drive an hour to San Juan Bautista instead, where Hitchcock filmed parts of *Vertigo*. Or worship at the altar of the redwoods, up at Big Basin Redwoods State Park (p80).

WEST CLIFF DRIVE
This road follows the cliffs southwest of the wharf. It's an excellent drive or, better, walk. The tip, **Lighthouse Point**, overlooks **Steamers Lane**, one of the top – and most accessible – surfing spots on the West Coast. Fittingly, the lighthouse is home to the tiny **Surfing Museum** (831-420-6289; www.santacruzsurfingmuseum.org; admission free; noon-4pm Thu-Mon;). Across the street, the wild expanse of **Lighthouse Field** was saved from development into a convention hotel by community action in the 1970s and '80s.

Tops for sunsets, **Natural Bridges State Beach** (831-423-4609;) is at the end of W Cliff Dr, 3 miles from the wharf. There are tide pools for exploring and the state's only monarch-butterfly preserve, where monarchs roost in big bunches November to March. Unfortunately, the iconic main natural bridge has collapsed.

UNIVERSITY OF CALIFORNIA, SANTA CRUZ
Established in 1965 in the hills above town, the **University of California Santa Cruz** (UCSC; 831-459-4008; www.ucsc.edu) has over 13,000 students known for their creative and liberal bent, and a rural campus with redwood stands and architecturally interesting buildings – many of recycled materials – designed to blend in with the rolling grassland. There are two top-notch galleries, a beautiful **arboretum** (831-427-2998) and a number of decaying 19th-century structures from the Cowell Ranch, on which the campus was built. Ag is big here, and there's a **farm cart** (cnr High & Bay Sts; noon-6pm Tue-Fri Jun-Oct) selling produce grown on campus. Check it out: a banana slug is the school mascot!

Seymour Marine Discovery Center (831-459-3800; near cnr Delaware Ave & Swift St; adult/student $5/3; 10am-5pm Tue-Sat, noon-5pm Sun;), west of town near Natural Bridges, is part of UCSC's famous Long Marine Laboratory. The interactive exhibits include aquariums and the world's largest blue whale skeleton that is lit up at Christmas.

CENTRAL COAST

THE MYSTERY SPOT

A classic old-fashioned tourist trap, the **Mystery Spot** (☎ 831-423-8897; off Branciforte Dr; admission $5; ⌚ 9am-7pm; ♿) has scarcely changed since the day it opened in the 1940s. On this steeply sloping hillside, compasses point crazily, mysterious forces push you around and buildings lean at weird angles. Yes, it's silly, but it's classic kitsch. Make reservations, or be stuck waiting. It's 3 miles north of town: take Water St to Market St, turn left and continue into the hills.

Activities

CYCLING & HIKING

Santa Cruz is a beach-cruiser and road-bike, not mountain-bike, town. An easy walk or ride with million-dollar views follows winding W Cliff Dr along the coastline. From the boardwalk it's 1 mile to Lighthouse Point and 3 miles to Natural Bridges State Beach. It's especially nice toward sunset. (If you have dogs, ask locals en route to point you to 'It's Beach,' one of the only pooch-friendly beaches in Santa Cruz.) Or head east on a bike along East Cliff Dr, stopping at beaches along the way. Nearby state parks offer many good walks and hikes, including **Henry Cowell Redwoods** (off Hwy 9), as well as Wilder Ranch (good for kids) and Forest of Nisene Marks.

SPAS

Santa Cruz has a surprising number of spas with private soaking tubs. Locals call them 'soak and pokes.' At **Kiva Retreat House** (☎ 831-429-1142; kivaretreat.com; 702 Water St; ⌚ noon-11pm), a private tub for two people is $20 per hour; massages start at $65 per hour. The **Well Within** (☎ 831-458-9355; www.wellwithinspa.com; 417 Cedar St; ⌚ 11am-midnight) has indoor and outdoor spas at comparable prices. For a traditional skirt-and-sweater spa, head to **Chaminade** (☎ 831-475-6500; www.chaminade.com; 1 Chaminade Ln; ⌚ 10am-8pm).

SWIMMING, SURFING & KAYAKING

The north side of Monterey Bay is warmer than the south. Consequently beach activities are more feasible in Santa Cruz than Monterey. Still, the water averages a shivery 55°F.

Surfing is huge in Santa Cruz, especially at **Steamers Lane** (p143). Other favorite surf spots are **Pleasure Point Beach** (E Cliff Dr), toward Capitola, and **Manresa State Beach**. Rent surfboards and related gear at **Cowell's** (☎ 831-427-2355; 30 Front St; surfboards per day $30; ⌚ 8am-6pm). The veterans at this shop have heaps of local knowledge.

Want to learn to surf? Both **Santa Cruz Surf School** (☎ 831-426-7072; www.santacruzsurfschool.com; 322 Pacific Ave) and **Richard Schmidt Surf School** (☎ 831-423-0928; www.richardschmidt.com) will have you standing and surfing the first day out. Both charge $70 to $80 for beginners lessons, including equipment.

Kayaking is a popular way to discover the kelp beds and craggy coastline up close. **Venture Quest Sea Kayaking** (☎ 831-427-2267; www.kayaksantacruz.com; Municipal Wharf) rents kayaks, provides instruction and leads nature tours. **Kayak Connection** (☎ 831-479-1121; 413 Lake Ave), at the Yacht Harbor, also offers rentals and tours. Rentals cost $25 to $35 for three hours and $50 to $60 per day. Tours cost $50 to $70.

WHALE-WATCHING & HARBOR CRUISES

Whale-watching trips, harbor cruises and fishing expeditions depart year-round from the municipal wharf. **Stagnaro's** (☎ 813-427-2334;

KIDSTUFF

If it's too cold for the beach or you don't feel like riding a roller coaster, take the **Roaring Camp Railroad** (☎ 831-335-4400; www.roaringcamp.com; Mt Hermon Rd; adult/child from $18/12), which operates standard-gauge trains from the boardwalk that connect in Felton, 6 miles north of town, with narrow-gauge trains into the redwoods. Opening hours vary according to the seasons. The trains only operate May through September.

Local moms and dads call **Blue Ball Park** (Old San Jose Rd, Soquel), north of Soquel Dr, the area's best playground, so named *not* for the husbands of breast-feeding mothers, but for several giant blue balls that appear to be rolling uphill; it's a 10-minute drive east of town in Soquel.

At **Aardvark Adventure Stories** (☎ 831-423-9900; www.aardvarkadventurestories.com; 519 Seabright Ave), kids can star in their own adventure books. First you do a photo shoot, then use computers to design the story line; call ahead.

LOCAL LUMINARIES KEEPING SANTA CRUZ WEIRD

LA can keep its celebrities; Santa Cruz has its own and they're easier to spot. Look for **Robert (aka the Umbrella Man)**, who's on Pacific Ave every day, walking in ultraslow motion, usually wearing nothing but pink. He's kinda the ambassador of SC: he never asks for anything, just makes eye contact and smiles, and continues his inch-worm's pace down the street.

The **Great Morgani** dresses in a full-body stocking, like something from Burning Man, and plays the accordion with great enthusiasm – but a little off key. He used to be a broker, then gave it all up to become a street performer. What he lacks in talent, he makes up for with sheer enthusiasm and costuming.

Neil Coonerty owns Bookshop Santa Cruz (p141). A child of the '60s with the twinkle of Santa Claus in his eye, he knows just about everyone in town and is responsible for the 'Keep Santa Cruz Weird' bumper stickers, a backlash against the influx of dot-com money in the '90s. In the 1989 earthquake, when everything downtown fell, he opened – the *next day* – under a tent, which became the gathering point for shell-shocked locals. This man's got heart! Say hello, and he'll probably remember you the next time you see him.

Jack O'Neill, the granddaddy of local surf culture, is rarely spotted. He's the guy who invented the wet suit and made a gazillion dollars, but never moved out of the same small house by Pleasure Point. Jack is by far the town's biggest celebrity, all because he wanted to be warmer while surfing. Look for the man with the eye patch.

---

www.stagnaros.com; Municipal Wharf; cruises from $12) is a longstanding operator. Whale-watching trips run from December to April, though there's plenty of marine life to see on a summer bay cruise. There's also a range of fishing trips available. Fishing trips cost $45 to $70.

Festivals & Events

Shakespeare Santa Cruz (☎ 831-459-2121; www.shakespearesantacruz.org) Presents damn good productions by the Bard, outdoors in a redwood grove, July and August.

Open Studio Art Tour (☎ 831-475-9600; www.ccscc.org) Local artists open their studios for tours one weekend in October.

Sleeping

Santa Cruz does not have not enough beds to satisfy demand: expect outrageous prices at peak times for nothing-special rooms. Choose places between downtown and the beach for easy foot access to both. If looking for a straightforward motel, also check Ocean St. Places near the boardwalk run the gamut from friendly to frightening.

HOSTELS

Santa Cruz Hostel (☎ 831-423-8304; www.hi-santacruz.org; 321 Main St; dm/d $21/45; registration 8-11am & 5-10pm) The best deal in town – by far – this lovely hostel occupies several century-old cottages surrounded by flowering gardens. It's just two blocks from the beach and five

blocks from downtown. Note: there's a three-night maximum and an 11pm curfew. Make reservations.

B&BS

Compassion Flower Inn (☎ 831-466-0420; www.compassionflowerinn.com; 216 Laurel St; r $115-125, with bathroom $135-175;) Owned by staunch supporters of the medical-marijuana movement, Compassion Flower integrates pot into seemingly every detail – even the phone number spells 'Inn o'420.' But this is no stoner flophouse. Indeed, it's an elegant old four-bedroom 1865 Gothic Revival that's been lovingly restored, particularly its gorgeous woodwork (the inlaid pot leaves are a new addition). Rooms are small with a touch of fussiness, but nothing overbearing. And they're *spotless*. Outside there's a clothing-optional hot tub next to a little garden with demonstration pot plants. The organic, country-style breakfasts are all-vegetarian. No TVs.

Babbling Brook Inn (☎ 831-427-2437; www.babblingbrookinn.com; 1025 Laurel St; r $180-250) Built around a running stream, with meandering gardens and towering trees, the inn has cozy rooms in small satellite buildings, decorated with a nod to French-provincial style. Most have gas fireplaces, some have Jacuzzi tubs, and all have featherbeds and downy-soft pillows. Rates include afternoon wine, fantastic fresh-from-the-oven cookies, and full breakfast. Fear not: there's lots of privacy too.

MOTELS

Sunset Inn (☎ 831-423-7500; www.sunsetinnsantacruz .com; 2424 Mission St; r $95-165; ✷) On the outskirts of town, this single-story motel has big rooms with fridges and microwaves. It's a plain-Jane place, but it's clean, well kept, and one of the best deals in town.

Seaway Inn (☎ 831-471-9004; www.seawayinn.com; 176 W Cliff Dr; r $100-140; ✷) Across the road from the ocean, rooms at this two-story motel have partial ocean views across the top of the parking lot; book upstairs for maximum privacy and better views. There's a dated tropical theme, with blond wood and faux rattan headboards, but there are fridges, microwaves and DVDs to compensate. There's also a two-bedroom family suite ($200).

Sea & Sand Inn (☎ 831-427-3400; www.santacruz motels.com; 201 W Cliff Dr; r $169-279; 🖳) The spiffiest motel in town overlooks Main Beach and the Wharf and has a grassy lawn at the cliff's edge. Fall asleep to braying sea lions! Rooms are smallish, but have solid pine, not veneer, furniture. Bathrooms could use updating and have showers only, not tubs, but they're clean, disregarding the occasional mildew spot. It's pricey for a motel, but the views are stellar. For more space book a double-queen room.

Casa Blanca Inn (☎ 831-423-1570, 800-644-1570; www.casablanca-santacruz.com; 101 Main St at Beach St; r $185-225; ✷) Built around a former mansion right near the Wharf, Casa Blanca's quaint rooms look like they were decorated 20 years ago by Laura Ashley and Martha Washington, with an odd mix of white-wicker chairs and dark, colonial-style tables. But they're clean, comfy and well kept, and some overlook the ocean. Betty White stayed here – not at the ugly Coast Hotel – when filming a movie in town. And if it's good enough for Miss Betty, I'd feel OK putting my mom here.

Best Western All Suites Inn (☎ 831-458-9898; www.bestwestern.com; 500 Ocean St at Soquel Ave; r $139-300; ✷ 🖳 ✷) Every room is a large-ish suite with a kitchenette, and sleeps up to four. The furniture is upper-end generic, but the place was redone in 2006 so it looks fresh. This is a good choice for families or business travelers needing space and amenities. There are other chain motels nearby.

Eating

Alas, Santa Cruz's food scene lacks luster, but there are some stellar standouts. If you're grazing, Pacific Ave is lined with eateries.

RESTAURANTS & CAFÉS

Zachary's (☎ 831-427-0646; 819 Pacific Ave; dishes $5-9; ✷ breakfast; ✷) This is the breakfast spot that covetous locals don't want you to know about (hide your guidebook). Brave the line for huge portions that'll keep you going all day. 'Mike's Mess' is the kitchen-sink standout.

Bagelry (☎ 831-429-8049; 320A Cedar St; ✷ 7:30am-5:30pm; ✷) The bagels here are real (boiled, then baked), and come with fantastic spreads, especially the hummus and egg salad. Check out the bulletin board for local goings-on.

Zoccoli's (☎ 831-423-1711; 1534 Pacific Ave; ✷ 9am-6pm; ✷) An old-style Italian deli with outdoor seating, Zocolli's makes great sandwiches and picnic fixin'. Note: If you've a kitchen, get the homemade meatballs and make spaghetti for dinner. Delicious.

Attic (☎ 831-460-1800; www.theatticsantacruz.com; 931 Pacific Ave; mains $6-10) For big, crunchy organic salads, homemade soups, vegan dishes, and a huge menu of teas, head to this order-at-the-counter café-cum-gallery and performance space. There are meat dishes too, but the emphasis is on veggies. Save room for the vegan shortbread cookies, which defy the law that says vegan equals tasteless.

El Palomar (☎ 831-425-7575; 1336 Pacific Ave; meals $10-20; ✷) Always packed and consistently good (if not great), El Palomar serves tasty Mexican staples – try the seviches – and good margaritas. The tortillas are made fresh by charming women in the covered courtyard.

Engfer Pizza Works (☎ 831-429-1856; www.engfer pizzaworks.com; 537 Seabright Ave; pizzas $8-$17; ✷ 4-9:30pm Tue-Sun; ✷) Inside an old factory, Engfer makes Santa Cruz's best pizza from a wood-fired oven, using homemade dough and sauces. Expect all the usuals, plus a 'no-name' pizza that's like a giant salad on roasted bread. There's even a vegan pie. Play ping-pong and sip beer on tap or local wine while you wait.

Dolphin (☎ 831-426-5830; Municipal Wharf; mains $9-16; ✷ breakfast, lunch & dinner; ✷) For fish on the wharf, you'll get the most bang for your buck at this totally unpretentious family-owned diner way out the end of the pier. There's also a takeout window and picnic tables outside, great for parents with fidgety kids.

O'Mei (☎ 831-425-8458; 2316 Mission St; mains $13-19) It's pricey for Chinese, but everything is fresh and preparations are spot on. The crisp-fried sweet potatoes and red-oil dumplings both merit a special trip – some drive all the way from San Francisco for them. Make reservations.

Soif (☎ 831-423-2020; www.soifwine.com; 105 Walnut Ave; small plates $4-6, mains $17-22; ☺ dinner) *Finally* Santa Cruz has a restaurant that could compete in San Francisco. Part wine shop, part wine bar and restaurant, Soif is where the city's food-savvy *bon vivants* flock for a heady selection of 50 unusual wines by the glass – all available in 2oz pours – designed to pair with a sophisticated, seasonally driven, Euro-Cal small-plates menu. Expect dishes like watermelon with fresh goat cheese; octopus salad with arugula, olives and mint; lamb meatballs with almond sauce; and duck confit with blackberry gastrique. Don't miss the stuffed candied tomato for desert, which once and for all proves that tomatoes are indeed a fruit.

Ristoranti Avanti (☎ 831-427-0135; 1711 Mission St; mains $12-25; ☺ lunch Mon-Fri, dinner nightly; ☖) Don't be fooled by its shopping-center location: mom-and-pop Avanti makes some of Santa Cruz's best food. The accessible Cal-Italian menu features earthy pasta dishes like homemade ravioli and lasagna made with lamb, chicken and fontina. Chicken cacciatore is the house specialty, but look for seasonal knockouts too, like roast chicken breast with corn fritters and heirloom tomatoes, lamb loin with tapenade, or pork chops with figs and pancetta-wrapped radicchio. The produce is organic and local. The room has a warm, casual vibe, with the owner's collection of pottery adorning the walls. Good Italian and California wines by the glass. Families always welcome. Make reservations.

Gabriella Cafe (☎ 831-457-1677; 910 Cedar St; mains $15-25) Intimate and romantic, with tiny tables and twinkling lights, Gabriella's is the perfect date spot, with a charming outdoor garden great for a long, lingering lunch. The food at dinner could be better, but if you're in love, who cares?

GROCERIES & QUICK EATS

Farmers market (☎ 831-454-0566; cnr Lincoln & Center Sts; ☺ 2:30-6:30pm Wed) For organic fruits and vegetables and a taste of the local vibe, cruise by the farmers market. You may think I'm kidding, but take care to protect yourself from unwieldy dreadlocks tossed over the shoulder of an unsuspecting hippie dude leaning in to squeeze a peach.

Richard Donnelly Chocolate (☎ 831-458-2414; www.donnellychocolates.com; 1509 Mission St) The Willy Wonka of Santa Cruz makes chocolates on par with those in the big city. This guy is an alchemist! Try the cardamom truffles.

New Leaf Community Market (☎ 831-426-1306; 1134 Pacific Ave; ☺ 8am-9pm) Good meats, organic produce and a full selection of groceries, right downtown.

Drinking

Pacific Ave has a number of bars.

Cafe Pergolesi (☎ 831-426-1775; 418 Cedar St; ☺ 9am-9pm; ▣) Discuss conspiracy theories over superstrong coffee with local under-30s at this way-popular landmark café in an old house with a big veranda overlooking the street. Free wi-fi.

Lulu Carpenter's (☎ 831-429-9804; 1545 Pacific Ave; ☺ 6am-midnight; ▣) If you wear your collar up and like to spread out with the *Sunday Times*, you'll dig this clean-hands café with brick walls and casement windows. There's outdoor seating on Pacific Ave or in the garden. Free wi-fi.

Red Room (☎ 831-426-2994; 1003 Cedar St) If you're a beautiful scenester, you hang out at Red – but this is Santa Cruz, so don't panic if you didn't pack Prada. Upstairs is more style-y with moody lighting, big sofas, old-school architectural details, and a fireplace. Downstairs is grungier and looks like a vintage-'50s mafia hangout, with lots of red tufted leather – and you can smoke (signs say you can't, but everyone does anyway).

Entertainment

Metro Santa Cruz (www.metrosantacruz.com) and **Good Times** (www.gtweekly.com) are free weeklies with comprehensive entertainment coverage.

Catalyst (☎ 831-423-1338; www.catalystclub.com; 1011 Pacific Ave) With an 800-seat capacity, Catalyst is a major Santa Cruz music venue; over the years it's hosted national acts from Gillian Welch to Black Uhuru to Nirvana. When there's no music, the upstairs pool room remains open.

Kuumbwa Jazz Center (☎ 831-427-2227; www.kuumbwajazz.org; 320 Cedar St) Sponsoring jazz luminaries since 1975, Kuumbwa is for serious jazz heads who come for the big-name performers and intimate room.

Club Dakota (☎ 831-454-9030; 1209 Pacific Ave) The sign at the entrance reads: 'all lifestyles respected,' which in the all-inclusive, gender-neutral, big-rainbow-tent language of Santa

CENTRAL COAST

Cruz means, 'this is a gay bar.' It's a fun, fun place to dance, and has a sexy, happening bar scene – when it's busy; otherwise it's dead. But if you're a 'mo, this is the place.

Blue Lagoon (☏ 831-423-7117; 923 Pacific Ave) Blue Lagoon used to be a gay dance club till girls started coming to escape the aggro stares of straight dudes, but the dudes soon followed, and now there's hardly a gay boy in sight. The crowd varies with the night's theme, ranging from hip-hop to goth industrial. It's a fun spot for billiards too.

Skyview Drive-In (☏ 831-475-3405; 2260 Soquel Dr; Soquel; &) See first-run movies at an old-fashioned drive-in. Kids under 12 free. On Thursday it's $4 per person. Friday through Sunday in the daytime, it's a flea market.

Nickelodeon Theatre (☏ 831-426-7500; 210 Lincoln St) shows indie and foreign films, while the landmark **Del Mar Theatre** (☏ 831-469-3220; 1124 Pacific Ave) shows midnight and first-run art-house movies.

Shopping
Downtown Santa Cruz boasts numerous locally owned stores. Plan several hours wandering Pacific Ave and the side streets.

O'Neill Surf Shop (☏ 831-469-4377; 110 Cooper St) This is the mother ship for the locally based, internationally popular brand of surf wear and gear.

Streetlight Records (☏ 831-421-9200; 939 Pacific Ave) Streetlight sells unusual new and used CDs and records; it buys too.

Skateworks (☏ 831-427-4292; www.skateworks.com; 1125 Pacific Ave) Skaters come here for kick-ass accessories and to trip out on skate movies on the big-screen TV.

Annieglass (☏ 831-427-4620; www.annieglass.com; 110 Cooper St) If you're into home entertaining and fancy dinnerware, don't miss Annieglass, which is sold in ultrachic New York stores like Bergdorf's, but made right here in Santa Cruz. Go figure.

Mr Goodies (☏ 831-427-9997; 1541 Pacific Ave) Like a collector's giant curio cabinet, Goodies carries wacky cultural detritus, from cast-off jewelry to Pez dispensers.

Bunny's Shoes (☏ 831-423-3824; 1350 Pacific Ave) Cheap shoes for fun, frilly girls. Great purses and handbags too.

Getting There & Around
Santa Cruz is 75 miles south of San Francisco, via I-280 to Hwy 85 to Hwy 17, the latter a fast-moving and sometimes peril-ous route. Monterey is 43 miles (50 minutes) south via beautiful Hwy 1. Without your own wheels, the easiest way to reach Santa Cruz is by bus.

Greyhound (☏ 831-423-1800; www.greyhound.com; 425 Front St), next to the Metro Center, has daily buses to San Francisco ($13, three hours), Salinas ($15, 70 minutes) and Los Angeles ($49, eight to 10 hours). To reach Monterey, change buses in Salinas (p154).

Santa Cruz Airporter (☏ 831-423-1214, 800-497-4997) runs shuttles to/from the airports at San Jose ($40) and San Francisco ($50).

Santa Cruz Metro (☏ 831-425-8600; www.scmtd.com) is the local public transit operation. It operates Hwy 17 Express buses from Santa Cruz to the San Jose CalTrain/Amtrak station ($4) and connects with trains to San Francisco. Metro also operates extensive bus services (tickets $1.50, day pass $4.50) throughout the county and is an excellent way to get around. Most routes converge on the Metro Center between Pacific and Front Sts downtown. Useful routes follow:

Bus No	Destination
3	Natural Bridges State Beach
35	Felton, then on to Boulder Creek and near Big Basin State Park (limited service)
40 & 42	Davenport and the north coast beaches
69	Capitola Transit Center

SANTA CRUZ TO MONTEREY
Capitola
pop 57,200
Five miles east of Santa Cruz, the cute little seaside town of Capitola is quieter than Santa Cruz, with affluent crowds less inclined to hold drum circles on the beach. Downtown is good for strolling, with shops, restaurants and pretty houses built to human scale. Streets can get crowded, and parking is a nightmare on weekends; try the lot behind City Hall, off Capitola Ave at Riverview Dr.

The **Capitola Chamber of Commerce** (☏ 831-475-6522; www.capitolachamber.com) has local tips and information about mid-September's **Capitola Art & Wine Festival** and the famous **Begonia Festival** (☏ 831-476-3566), on Labor Day weekend, with a flotilla of flowered floats on Soquel Creek.

Catch a caffeine buzz while overlooking Soquel Creek at **Mr Toots Coffeehouse** (☏ 831-475-3679; 231 Esplanade; ⏱ 7am-10pm). For the best picnics, head inland to **Gayle's** (☎ 831-462-1200; 504 Bay Ave; ☼ 6:30am-8:30pm), an amazing bakery with a big deli area where you can assemble beach picnics. If relatives are visiting (and picking up the tab), ride the tram to romantic **Shadowbrook** (☎ 475-1511; 1750 Wharf Rd; brunch $12-22, dinner $17-28; ☼ dinner nightly, Sunday brunch), a huge, old wooden house-turned-restaurant; open since 1947, it's surrounded by vast gardens overlooking Soquel Creek. Alas, the food could be better, but the atmosphere is fantastic.

South Santa Cruz County

Aptos is a cute little town with a very fun **July 4 Parade** (America's shortest). It's reached from the Aptos/Seacliff exit on Hwy 1. Nearby is **Seacliff Sate Beach** (☎ 831-685-6440; 201 State Park Dr; per vehicle $6) where the beach is fine but the real attraction is the 'cement boat,' a quixotic freighter built from concrete that floated fine but had a star-crossed life that ended here on the coast as a fishing pier. South of the park are miles of free beaches.

Ten miles south of Santa Cruz, the La Selva Beach exit on Hwy 1 leads to **Manresa State Beach** (☎ 831-724-3750; per vehicle $6) and **Sunset State Beach** (☎ 831-763-7063; per vehicle $6) further south. At both, you'll have miles of sand and surf to yourself just a few yards from the parking lots.

Moss Landing & Elkhorn Slough

Hwy 1 returns to the coast at Moss Landing, just south of the Monterey County line, 25 miles south of Santa Cruz and 18 miles north of Monterey. There are several interesting shops, some good cafés and a working fishing harbor – all (unfortunately) in the shadow of a giant power plant. Maybe the best reason to visit, **Sanctuary Cruises** (☎ 831-917-1046; www .sanctuarycruises.com; adult/preteens $42/32) operates year-round whale-watching and dolphin-spotting cruises, led by marine biologists. Tours last four to five hours (compared with the average three-hour tours), so you've got much better chances of spotting whales. Boats are spotless and even run on biodiesel.

Just north of Moss Landing, you can hike 5 miles of trails, spot eagles and pelicans and see how Monterey Bay naturally meets the land at 1400-acre **Elkhorn Slough National Estuarine Research Reserve** (☎ 728-2822; www.elkhornslough .org; 1700 Elkhorn Rd, off Hwy 1, Watsonville; ☼ 9am-5pm Wed-Sun). It's free to see the visitors center, but adults pay $2.50 to hike. Call for docent-led tour times. Fret not if you forgot your binoculars; borrow a pair, along with a bird book, from the visitors center. Kayaking may be the best way to see the slough (but not on a windy day); contact **Kayak Connection** (☎ 831-479-1121; 413 Lake Ave) about tours. Or book a seat on a 27ft pontoon boat with **Elkhorn Slough Safari** (☎ 831-633-5555; www.elkhornslough .com; adult/senior/child $28/26/20) for a naturalist-guided ecology tour. Bring a camera; you'll be glad you did!

MONTEREY

pop 29,210

What draws many tourists to Monterey is its world-class aquarium, overlooking the Monterey Bay National Marine Sanctuary. Until 2006 the largest such sanctuary in the country, it protects dense kelp forests and a stunning variety of marine life, including seals and sea lions, elephant seals, dolphins and whales. But the city also possesses the most well-preserved evidence of the state's Spanish and Mexican periods, with many restored adobe buildings open for exploring. An afternoon's wander through the town's historic quarter promises to be more edifying than time spent in the tourist ghettos of Fisherman's Wharf and Cannery Row. A snorkeling excursion on the bay? Even better.

History

The Ohlone tribe, who had been on the peninsula since around 500 BC, may have spotted Spanish explorer Juan Rodríguez Cabrillo, the first European visitor, who sailed by in 1542. He was followed in 1602 by Sebastián Vizcaíno, who landed near the site of today's downtown Monterey and named it after his patron, the Duke of Monte Rey. A long hiatus followed before the Spanish – including mission founder Padre Junípero Serra – returned in 1770 to establish Monterey as their first presidio in Alta (Upper) California. A year later, Serra decided to separate church and state by shifting the mission to Carmel, a safer distance from the military presence.

After a brief spell as the capital of Alta California after Mexico broke from Spain, the town spent 30 years as a backwater. But when a luxurious hotel was built, San Franciscans discovered Monterey as a convenient getaway. Around the same time, fishermen began capitalizing on the teeming marine

CENTRAL COAST

life in Monterey Bay. By the 1930s, Cannery Row had made the port the 'Sardine Capital of the World,' but overfishing and climatic changes caused the industry's sudden collapse in the 1950s.

In more recent decades, the city has been successful in netting schools of tourists, with no collapse in sight.

Orientation & Information

Monterey's historic downtown is a compact area surrounding Alvarado St, which ends with Portola and Custom House plazas, near Fisherman's Wharf. This area is known as Old Monterey, as distinct from Cannery Row, about a mile northwest. Cannery Row segues into Pacific Grove.

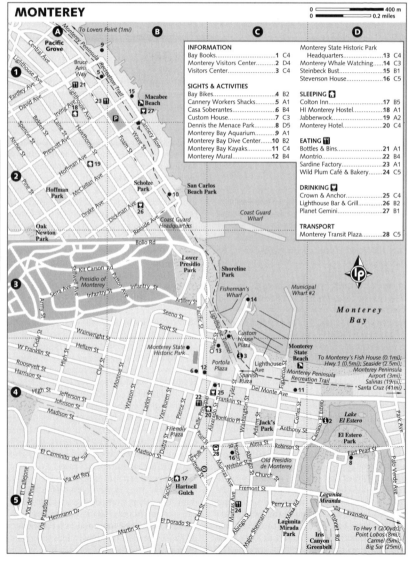

MONTEREY

INFORMATION	
Bay Books	1 C4
Monterey Visitors Center	2 D4
Visitors Center	3 C4

SIGHTS & ACTIVITIES	
Bay Bikes	4 B2
Cannery Workers Shacks	5 A1
Casa Soberantes	6 B4
Custom House	7 C3
Dennis the Menace Park	8 D5
Monterey Bay Aquarium	9 A1
Monterey Bay Dive Center	10 B2
Monterey Bay Kayaks	11 C4
Monterey Mural	12 B4

Monterey State Historic Park	
Headquarters	13 C4
Monterey Whale Watching	14 C3
Steinbeck Bust	15 B1
Stevenson House	16 C5

SLEEPING	
Colton Inn	17 B5
HI Monterey Hostel	18 A1
Jabberwock	19 A2
Monterey Hotel	20 C4

EATING	
Bottles & Bins	21 A1
Montrio	22 B4
Sardine Factory	23 A1
Wild Plum Café & Bakery	24 C5

DRINKING	
Crown & Anchor	25 C4
Lighthouse Bar & Grill	26 B2
Planet Gemini	27 B1

TRANSPORT	
Monterey Transit Plaza	28 C5

Bay Books (☎ 831-375-1855; 316 Alvarado St; ☺ 7am-10pm; ⬜) The best bookstore on the Monterey Peninsula with a wide range of books, a coffee bar and community bulletin board.

Monterey visitors center (☎ 831-649-1770, 888-221-1010; www.montereyinfo.org; cnr Camino El Estero & Franklin St; ☺ 9am-5pm) Free phone system for checking lodging availability.

Visitors center (☎ 831-657-6400; 150 Olivier St; ☺ 8am-5pm Mon-Fri) Near the State Historic Park.

Sights

The entire Monterey Bay is part of the **Monterey Bay National Marine Sanctuary** (☎ 831-647-4201; www.mbnms.nos.noaa.gov), which extends from Marin County south past San Simeon. The Bush administration has hinted that oil drilling may be necessary in this treasure to fuel the nation's unquenchable thirst for fuel, but so far it's safe, and there's even a push by environmentalists to extend its southern boundary by 40 coastline miles.

MONTEREY BAY AQUARIUM

Monterey's most mesmerizing experience is a visit to the **aquarium** (☎ 831-648-4888; www .montereybayaquarium.org; 886 Cannery Row; adult/child 3-12 $22/13; ☺ 10am-6pm Aug-Apr, from 9:30am May-Sep; ♿), built on the site of what was once the city's largest sardine cannery. All forms of aquatic creatures are on proud display, from kid-tolerant sea stars and slimy sea slugs to animated sea otters and surprisingly nimble 800lb tuna. But the aquarium is more than an impressive collection of glass tanks – thoughtful placards underscore the bay's cultural and historical contexts.

Every minute, upwards of 2000 gallons of seawater are pumped into the three-story **kelp forest**, re-creating as closely as possible the natural conditions you see out the windows to the east. (At night, the water flows in unfiltered, balancing the system even more.) The large fish of prey are at their charismatic best during mealtimes; divers handfeed at 11:30am and 4pm.

More giggle-inducing are the sea-otter feeding sessions (at 10:30am, 1:30pm and 3:30pm). At other times, the critters can often be seen basking in the **Great Tide Pool** outside the aquarium, where they lounge around while they are readied for reintroduction to the wild.

Even New Age-y music and the occasional infinity-mirror illusion don't detract from the appeal of the hall of jellies, where jelly-fish show off their mysterious, diaphanous beauty.

Throughout the aquarium there are **touch pools**, where you can get close to sea cucumbers, bat rays and various tide-pool creatures.

A visit can easily become a full-day affair, so consider getting your hand stamped so you can break up the visit with lunch. (Anyone feel like seafood?) To avoid long lines in summer, on weekends and holidays, get **tickets** (☎ 831-648-4937, 800-756-3737; transaction fee $3) in advance from hotels or via the web or phone. Before you leave, make sure to pick up the wallet-sized Seafood Watch, an essential seafood-dining guide to keeping fish and shellfish populations sustainable.

MONTEREY STATE HISTORIC PARK

Old Monterey is an assemblage of 19th-century brick and adobe buildings covered on a 2-mile self-guided walking tour called the **Path of History**. Admission to the buildings is free, though expect some buildings to be open while others aren't.

Grab a brochure for the self-guided tour and find out what's open from the **park headquarters** (☎ 831-649-7118; Custom House Plaza; ☺ 10am-5pm) in the Pacific House. You can join a docent-led 90-minute tour (adult/child $5/2; phone to confirm times), during which you'll pick up tidbits like how the roads of early Monterey were covered in crushed whalebones as protection from mud. Below are details on a few of the park's highlights.

Custom House

In 1822, newly independent Mexico ended the Spanish trade monopoly but stipulated that any traders bringing goods to Alta California must first unload their cargoes at the **Monterey Custom House** (Custom House Plaza) for duty assessment. The restored 1827 building displays an exotic selection of the goods traders brought in to exchange for Californian cowhides. In 1846, the American flag was raised over the Custom House, and California was formally annexed from Mexico.

Casa Soberanes

A beautiful garden fronts **Casa Soberanes** (336 Pacific St), built in 1842 during the late Mexican period. Across Pacific St, the large and colorful **Monterey Mural** mosaic, on the modern Monterey Conference Center, tells the history of Monterey.

Stevenson House

Scottish writer Robert Louis Stevenson came to Monterey in 1879 to meet with his wife-to-be, Fanny Osbourne, and this building, then the French Hotel, was reputedly where he stayed while writing *Treasure Island*. The rooms were pretty primitive, but he was still a penniless unknown at that time. The 1840 **building** (530 Houston St) houses a superb collection of Stevenson memorabilia.

CANNERY ROW

Back in Steinbeck's day, Cannery Row was a stinky, hardscrabble melting pot, the epicenter of the sardine-canning industry that was Monterey's lifeblood in the first half of the 20th century. The area's grit and energy were immortalized in Steinbeck's novel *Cannery Row*. Sadly, there's precious little evidence of that era now. A bronze **bust** of the writer sits at the bottom of Prescott Ave, wearing an expression easily read as resigned disappointment at the sterile and unabashedly commercial experience his row has devolved into. Chockablock with chain restaurants and souvenir shops hawking saltwater taffy, there are still a few spots worth making time for, such as the aquarium, but once you've done with that and the obligatory stroll, best move on. Do check out the **Cannery Workers Shacks** at the base of flowery Bruce Ariss Way. A row of small rooms maintained with historical accuracy depicts the stark and strenuous lives led by Filipino, Japanese and Spanish laborers during the cannery's heyday.

THE WHARVES

Like its larger namesake in San Francisco, **Fisherman's Wharf** is a tacky tourist trap at heart and is the jumping-off point for many whale-watching expeditions and deep-sea fishing trips. On the flip side, the refreshingly authentic **Municipal Wharf #2** is a short walk to the east. Fishing boats bob and sway, painters work on their canvases, and seafood purveyors hawk their fresh catches.

DENNIS THE MENACE PARK

A must for fans of kick-ass playgrounds, this **park** (☎ 831-646-3860; 777 Pearl St; ♿) was the brainchild of Hank Ketcham, the creator of the classic comic strip, who lived in Pebble Beach until his death in 2004. This ain't your standard dumbed-down playground,

suffocated by Big Brother safety regulations. With lightning-fast slides and towering climbing structures, even adults can't resist its charms.

Activities

CYCLING

Thanks to stunning scenery and paved bike paths, cycling is a terribly popular peninsula activity. The **Monterey Peninsula Recreational Trail**, a former train line, travels for 18 car-free miles along the waterfront from Lovers Point in Pacific Grove to Seaside, passing by downtown and Cannery Row in Monterey.

Many people like to make the 20-mile round trip to Carmel by bike along 17-Mile Drive (p157).

Maps and rentals are available from **Bay Bikes** (☎ 831-655-2453; 585 Cannery Row; ☼ 9am-7pm; bike rentals per hr/half-day from $6/18).

DIVING & SNORKELING

The Monterey Bay offers world-renowned diving and snorkeling, though the water is chilly. Excellent spots for both are off Lovers Point in Pacific Grove and in the Point Lobos State Reserve (see p158).

One of the best places to organize a dive or snorkel trip is at **Monterey Bay Dive Center** (☎ 831-656-0454; www.montereyscubadiving.com; 225 Cannery Row), which offers instruction and equipment rental. Full standard dive outfits go for $75; snorkeling kits cost $39. The shop can also advise on snorkeling in the inlets of the bay.

KAYAKING

Monterey Bay Kayaks (☎ 800-649-5357; www.montereybaykayaks.com; 693 Del Monte Ave) rents open and closed kayaks from $30 per day, offers instruction courses every weekend and operates a range of natural-history tours.

WHALE-WATCHING

You can spot whales off the coast of Monterey pretty much year-round. The season for blue and humpback whales runs from May to November, while gray whales pass by from mid-December to April. **Monterey Whale Watching** (☎ 831-372-2203; www.montereywhalewatching.com; 96 Old Fisherman's Wharf; adult/child $35/25) boats leave daily on three-hour tours. **Sanctuary Cruises** (p149), operating out of Moss Landing, runs five-hour cruises of Monterey Bay from biodiesel vessels.

Festivals & Events

Reserve lodging well in advance if you're going to be in the vicinity during these events.

AT&T Pebble Beach National Pro-Am (☎ 831-649-1533; www.attpbgolf.com) Famous golf tournament mixing pros and celebrities in late January or early February.

Red Bull US Grand Prix (www.laguna-seca.com /events) The largest motorcycle race on the continent, usually at the end of July.

Monterey Wine Festival (☎ 800-656-4282; www .montereywine.com) Usually early June.

Monterey Jazz Festival (☎ 831-373-3366; www .montereyjazzfestival.org) The world's longest running jazz festival, which began in 1954, takes place in September.

Sleeping

Book well ahead for summer visits – the events listed above can sell out the town crazy early. Generally there are a lot of inexpensive chain motels east toward Seaside and downtown. The cheapest accommodations – other than the first two listed below – are along Monterey's motel row, about 2.5 miles east of downtown on N Fremont St, east of Hwy 1 (take the Fremont St exit).

HI Monterey Hostel (☎ 831-649-0375; www.monterey hostel.org; 778 Hawthorne St; dm/r $25/54; ☒ reception 8-10am & 5-10pm; Ⓟ 🖳) This well-run hostel with the spiff exterior paint job is blocks from Cannery Row and has recently added a BBQ patio. There's room for 45 heads, but reservations are strongly recommended.

Colton Inn (☎ 831-649-6500, 800.848.7007; www.colton inn.com; 707 Pacific St; r $139-249; Ⓟ) This champ of a motel prides itself on cleanliness and friendliness, and as its reward has earned a solid base of repeat guests. There's no pool and zero view, but it loans out DVDs and videos, continental breakfast is included and there's free wi-fi throughout the property. It even has a sauna.

Monterey Hotel (☎ 831-375-3184, 800-727-0960; www.montereyhotel.com; 406 Alvarado St; r $150-300; Ⓟ) Fresh off a centennial renovation, this 1904 hotel in the heart of downtown is grand in the traditional Victorian manner, though as a historic building, it has no elevator. Its 64 rooms feature old-world features like plantation shutters and handcarved furniture, though with modern perks such as free wi-fi. Rates include a good-sized continental breakfast. Booking online can save you up to 50%. Parking costs $5.

our pick **Jabberwock** (☎ 831-372-4777; www.jabber wockinn.com; 598 Laine St; r $155-275; Ⓟ) High atop a hill and barely visible through a shroud of foliage, this emerald-carpeted 1911 Craftsman house hums a playful Alice in Wonderland tune through its seven immaculate rooms with names like The Brillig (flaunting gorgeous handpainted wallpaper) and Tulgey Wood (one of several rooms with a killer view). Over the full gourmet breakfast, ask about the house's many salvaged architectural elements. And be sure to notice the book clock near the door. All in all, a sublime place to celebrate your un-birthday.

Eating

Bottles & Bins (☎ 831-375-5488; 898 Lighthouse Ave; ☒ 10:30am-midnight) Vince Poma's liquor store is the peninsula's top spot to pick up wine and nonstandard beers – lots of Belgians and Pacific Northwest microbrews – and in the corner his spirited wife Karlen serves up her love-infused deli sandwiches ($6) from 10:30am to 3pm weekdays.

Wild Plum Cafe & Bakery (☎ 831-646-3109; 731 Munras Ave B; mains $5.50-9; ☒ 7am-6:30pm Tue-Fri, to 5pm Sat & Mon) Locals crowd in to this slender nook at lunch time for soups from scratch, sandwiches on homemade bread and heftier fare like BBQ pork tacos. The Mediterranean on focaccia is sublime, too. A small deli caters to picnickers.

Monterey's Fish House (☎ 831-373-4647; 2114 Del Monte Ave; mains $14-17; ☒ lunch Mon-Fri, dinner daily)

CENTRAL COAST

Ten bucks says you're the only nonlocal in the joint. Italian-Japanese chef David DiGirolamo prepares spanking-fresh seafood with the occasional Asian twist, watched over by photos of his Sicilian fishermen ancestors. Though reservations are next to required, Hawaiian shirts seem to be *de rigueur* for gentlemen. Try the barbecued oysters or, for those stout of heart, the large Mexican squid steak.

Montrio (☎ 831-648-8880; 414 Calle Principal; tapas around $5, mains $15-25; ❤ dinner) It's fitting that Montrio occupies the old firehouse, because this place is hot. Gracious and well-trained servers will set before you internationally accented dishes concocted from mostly organic and market-driven ingredients. Despite its hip interior – think leather walls and iron trellises – the tables have butcher paper and fat crayons. There's also a kids menu, but it's hard to imagine children sitting still long enough for their parents to scrape the plates of their white chocolate bread pudding, though sitting near the action of the open kitchen may do the trick. Ask about the 'backroom bargain' wines.

Sardine Factory (☎ 831-373-3775; 701 Wave St; mains $27-40; ❤ dinner) For a formal sit-down dinner with pampering service, the Sardine Factory is it. It's a 40-year-old institution that still prepares fine steaks and seafood, but its real strength lies in its atmosphere and wine list. It can be pricey, so consider its three-course prix-fixe dinners (5pm to 7pm) or simply something off the tapas menu and a glass of wine. Each of its dining rooms is ornately and uniquely decorated, but my favorite is the glass conservatory.

Drinking & Entertainment

Crown & Anchor (☎ 831-649-6496; 150 W Franklin St) Descend into the basement of this British pub and the first thing you'll notice is the red plaid carpeting. Perhaps not the most authentic decor imaginable, but these blokes do know their way around a bar, with 20 draft beers and the peninsula's best selection of single malts, not to mention the damn fine fish-and-chips.

Lighthouse Bar & Grill (☎ 831-373-4488; 281 Lighthouse Ave; ❤ from 11am Wed-Sun, from 5pm Mon & Tue) Draped in Christmas lights and featuring the requisite pool table, Monterey's only queer bar attracts the boys, the girls and everyone in between to its cozy, friendly quarters. Sunday beer bashes at 2pm.

Planet Gemini (☎ 831-373-1449; www.planetgemini.com; 3rd fl, 625 Cannery Row) All done up in red walls and purple velvet curtains, Planet Gemini draws a youthful crowd with its comedy shows (Friday and Saturday) and Latin dance nights (Wednesday and Sunday).

Getting There & Away

Monterey Peninsula Airport (MRY; ☎ 831-648-7000; Olmsted Rd) handles flights operated by American Eagle (Los Angeles), America West (Las

---

DETOUR: SALINAS

Known for being the birthplace of John Steinbeck and as 'The World's Salad Bowl', alluding to the six million heads of iceberg lettuce harvested each summer day, Salinas makes a vivid contrast with the conspicuous affluence of Monterey. Its historic center stretches along Main St, whose northern end is punctuated by the town's main attraction, the National Steinbeck Center. Pick up information and maps at the **Salinas Valley Chamber of Commerce** (☎ 831-424-7611; www.salinaschamber.com; 119 E Alisal St; ❤ 9:30am-5pm Mon-Fri), a few blocks southeast of Main St.

The **National Steinbeck Center** (☎ 831-796-3833; www.steinbeck.org; 1 Main St; adult/students & seniors/child 13-17/child 6-12 $11/9/8/6; ❤ 10am-5pm; 🚻) will enthrall even those who don't know a lick about Salinas' Nobel Prize–winning native son. John Steinbeck (1902–68) called Salinas Valley 'the valley of the world,' a reference to the workers from all over creation who came to scrape out a living from the earth, and his literary explorations were influenced and inspired by the people who settled here. The interactive, kid-accessible exhibits chronicle the writer's life and works in an engaging way. The other side of the center is taken up with the Rabobank Agricultural Museum, which takes you on a journey through the modern-day agriculture industry, from water to pesticides to transportation. More interesting than it sounds.

Steinbeck is buried in the Hamilton family plot at **Garden of Memories Cemetery** (Abbott St & Romie Ln), 1 mile south of the center.

See opposite for details on getting here via Monterey–Salinas Transit (MST).

Vegas and Phoenix) and United Express (Los Angeles, San Francisco and Denver). It's 4 miles southeast of downtown off Hwy 68. **Monterey/Salinas Airbus** (☎ 831-373-7777; www .montereyairbus.com) links those cities with the San Jose and San Francisco airports several times daily ($30 to $40).

If you aren't flying or don't have wheels, getting to the Monterey Peninsula can be tricky. The best you can do is take Greyhound or Amtrak to Salinas (opposite) 17 miles east of Monterey and then catch a local Monterey–Salinas Transit (MST) bus.

Getting Around
Monterey–Salinas Transit (MST; ☎ 831-899-2555; www .mst.org) runs local buses in the region. Fares are $2 to $4 for one ride or $4.50 to $9 for a day pass depending on distance covered. Routes converge at the **Monterey Transit Plaza** (Jules Simoneau Plaza, Alvarado St). Bus 20 makes the 50-minute run to/from Salinas every 30 to 60 minutes.

Between late May and early September, you can take a free trolley-style bus that loops around downtown, Fisherman's Wharf and Cannery Row between 10am and 7pm.

PACIFIC GROVE
pop 16,117
Pacific Grove, or PG, is a tranquil community that began as a Methodist retreat in 1875, and maintained a quaint, holier-than-thou attitude until well into the 20th century – the selling of liquor was illegal up until 1969. For many, PG is the perfect respite from the Monterey-Carmel hubbub. In winter PG hosts swarms of monarch butterflies, which make the local pine groves their temporary home. The **chamber of commerce** (☎ 831-373-3304, 800-656-6650; www .pacificgrove.org; cnr Central & Forest Aves; 9:30am-5pm Mon-Fri, 10am-3pm Sat) dispenses information and has an outdoor courtesy phone.

Sights & Activities
Appropriately named **Ocean View Blvd** affords fine views from Lover's Point east to Point Pinos. Here the road becomes the again appropriately named **Sunset Drive** with numerous turn-outs where you can enjoy the pounding surf, rocky outcrops and teaming tidal pools. The entire route is great for walking or cycling and some think it surpasses the 17-Mile Drive (p157) for beauty, and it's free.

If you're in town during monarch season (roughly October to March), the best place

to see them cluster by the millions – if the temperature is behaving – is at the **Monarch Grove** (Ridge Rd), a thicket of trees off Lighthouse Ave.

At the northwestern end of Lighthouse Ave, on the tip of the Monterey Peninsula, you'll find the humble-looking **Point Pinos Lighthouse** (☎ 831-648-5716; suggested donation adult/ child $2/1; 11:30am-5pm summer, shorter hr winter), the oldest continuously operating lighthouse on the West Coast, having been warning ships off this hazardous point since 1855. Don't miss the basement museum, with displays on shipwrecks and lighthouse technology such as lens structure and signal systems. The lighthouse grounds overlook the stunning **Pacific Groves Municipal Golf Links**, where black-tailed deer wander freely among the golfers. The lighthouse makes an excellent spot for gray whale–watching in late fall to early spring.

Sleeping & Eating
Martine Inn (☎ 831-373-3388, 800-852-5588; www .martineinn.com; 255 Ocean View Blvd; r $139-360;) This Pepto-Bismol-hued B&B, favored primarily by couples of a certain age, is one of several mansions lining the water. Its 24 rooms are filled with antiques and other luxuries like four-poster beds (some units have wood-burning fireplaces and stunning views), though the inn's not so spit-and-polish as to detract from its (unintentional) kitschiness. The 1890s billiard table is the star of the game room. Wake to a hearty breakfast that employs much silver and crystal ware in its presentation.

Holly's Lighthouse Cafe (☎ 831-372-7006; 602 Lighthouse Ave; mains $5-8; breakfast & lunch) This diminutive diner has achieved local institution status with its checkered blue tablecloths and waitresses that ask regulars how their moms are doing. The oatmeal, of all things, gets rave reviews. Breakfast served until 3pm.

Passionfish (☎ 831-655-3311; www.passionfish.net; 701 Lighthouse Ave; meals $16-26; dinner) Fresh, sustainable seafood is served in any number of inventive ways here – to wit, Alaskan halibut with cilantro-citrus sauce and garlic noodles – though the menu also carries slow-cooked meats and locally grown vegetables. The earth-tone decor is spare, complementing and not distracting from the food. The pages-long wine list is priced at retail, and for tea-lovers, there are twice as many Chinese teas on offer as wines by the glass.

CENTRAL COAST

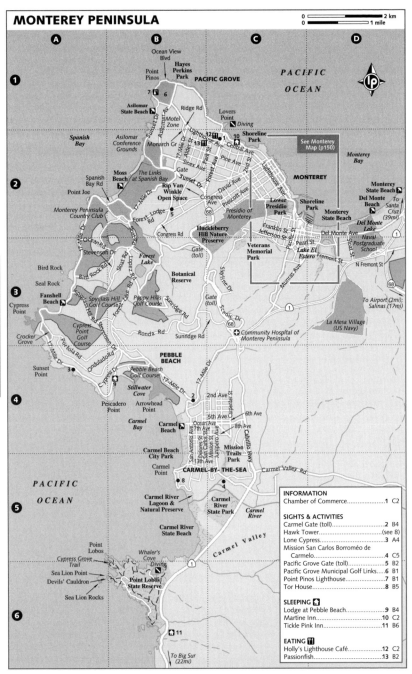

MONTEREY PENINSULA

0 _____ 2 km
0 _____ 1 mile

INFORMATION
Chamber of Commerce...................1 C2

SIGHTS & ACTIVITIES
Carmel Gate (toll)............................2 B4
Hawk Tower.................................(see 8)
Lone Cypress.................................3 A4
Mission San Carlos Borroméo de
  Carmelo.....................................4 C5
Pacific Grove Gate (toll)..................5 B2
Pacific Grove Municipal Golf Links...6 B1
Point Pinos Lighthouse.....................7 B1
Tor House.....................................8 B5

SLEEPING
Lodge at Pebble Beach.....................9 B4
Martine Inn..................................10 C2
Tickle Pink Inn.............................11 B6

EATING
Holly's Lighthouse Café...................12 C2
Passionfish.................................13 B2

17-MILE DRIVE

The only private toll road west of the Mississippi, the spectacularly scenic 17-Mile Dr (which is actually a hair shorter these days), connects Pacific Grove and Carmel, meandering through Pebble Beach, a private resort and residential area that epitomizes the jaw-dropping wealth of the area. It's no chore staying within the 25mph limit – every curve in the road reveals another postcard vista, especially in summer when the landscape shows off its throw rugs of yellow wildflowers. If you're driving, you'll be sharing the road with cyclists, some undeniably wobbly on their wheels.

Open sunrise to sunset, entry is controlled by the **Pebble Beach Company** (☎ 831-647-7500; www.pebblebeach.com; per vehicle $8.75, bicycles free). If it makes you feel better, your entry fee can be put towards any shopping you do in Pebble Beach. There are five gates; for the most scenic portion, enter the Pacific Grove Gate off Sunset Dr and exit at the Carmel Gate.

Using the map provided when you enter, you can easily pick out landmarks such as **Spanish Bay**, where explorer Gaspar de Portolá dropped anchor in 1769; treacherously rocky **Point Joe**, which in the past was often mistaken for the entrance to Monterey Bay and thus became the site of several shipwrecks; and **Bird Rock**, which is a bird and seal haven. The ostensible pièce de résistance of the drive is the **Lone Cypress**, the trademarked symbol of the Pebble Beach Company that perches on a seaward rock. The tree's already more than 250 years old, and is now reinforced with wire supports, which fortunately aren't that visible in photographs (of which you will take many, not matter how hard you try to resist).

Besides the coast, the real attractions here are the world-famous **golf courses** such as Spyglass Hill, Cypress Point and, of course, Pebble Beach. The renowned **Lodge at Pebble Beach** (☎ 831-624-3811; www.pebblebeach.com; r from $580; 🖳 🖳) boasts world-class spas, restaurants and extravagant shops. If your folks forgot to leave you that seven-figure inheritance, you can still soak up the atmosphere in the art-filled public spaces and café.

Cycling the Drive is enormously popular, but if you can, do the ride during the week, when vehicular traffic isn't as heavy. There's no shoulder on the road, so keep your wits about you. On weekends the flow of bikes goes primarily north to south. While not strictly illegal, doing the ride from Carmel to Pacific Grove on weekends is discouraged, and is harder on the cyclists and drivers alike. For rental shops in Monterey, see p152.

CARMEL-BY-THE-SEA
pop 3995

The town's hyphenation distinguishes it from Carmel Valley just inland and Carmel Highlands to the south, but as everyone knows, there's really only one Carmel – which is not to say that it's the Carmel that it once was. Founded as a seaside resort in the 1880s – in itself surprising since the beach is nearly always clouded over with fog – Carmel quickly attracted famous artists and writers (including Sinclair Lewis and Jack London) and their hangers-on. This indulgence in the arts survives in the town's 100-plus galleries, but sky-high property values and the steady incursion of tour buses hungry to sample Carmel's much-vaunted quaintness and quirkiness have obliterated its salt-of-the-earth bohemia.

With impressive coastal frontage, upscale shipping venues and borderline fanatical devotion to its canine residents, Carmel simply glows with smugness. Local bylaws forbid neon signs and billboards. Fairytale Comstock cottages, with their characteristic stone chimneys and pitched gable roofs, dot the town. Buildings have no street numbers, so addresses always specify the block and side of street, and residents pick up their mail from the post office. For all its village charm, it's also the kind of place where Beemers slam on their brakes if you glance sideways at a crosswalk, but the same folks studiously avoid eye contact when walking past you on an empty street. Don't take it personally.

Orientation & Information

Ocean Ave is the wide east–west road with trees-and-flower-filled medians. It's the main strip in town, and much of the action is found near the intersection with San Carlos St.

The **Carmel Business Association** (☎ 831-624-2522; www.carmelcalifornia.com; San Carlos St btwn 5th & 6th Aves; ⏰ 10am-5pm) distributes town maps.

Sights

One of the pleasantest things to do in Carmel is escape the shopping streets and stroll through the tree-lined neighborhoods on the lookout for domiciles charming and peculiar. The Hansel and Gretel houses at Torres St and Ocean Ave are just how you'd imagine them, and a home at 13th Ave and Monte Verde St is covered in bark. A wicked, cool house in the shape of a ship, made from stone and salvaged ship parts, is near 6th Ave and Guadalupe (the road west of Carpenter St). There's more. Go and find them.

For a more formal introduction to the town, consider a **Carmel Heritage Society** (☎ 831-624-4447; tours $10) walking tour, which is 90 minutes long and leaves at 9:30am most Saturdays from **First Murphy House** (cnr 6th Ave & Lincoln St). No reservations required.

Despite being perennially overcast, the **Carmel Beach** is a nice crescent of white sand.

MISSION SAN CARLOS DE BORROMÉO DE CARMELO

The original Monterey mission was established by Padre Serra in 1769, but poor soil forced the move to Carmel in 1771. Although the missionaries founded 20 other California missions, this **mission** (☎ 831-624-1271; 3080 Rio Rd; adult/child $5/1; 9:30am-5pm) remained Serra's base.

Today it's one of the most attractive and complete of the California missions. The **mission church** was originally built of wood, then replaced by an adobe structure and, in 1793, by the present stone church.

Don't overlook the gravestone of 'Old Gabriel', a Native American convert whom Father Serra baptized personally, and whose dates put him at 151 years old when he died. Supposedly the oldest man to have ever lived in the modern era, he smoked like a chimney and outlived seven wives. There's a lesson in there somewhere.

TOR HOUSE

Even if you've never heard of the 20th-century poet Robinson Jeffers, a pilgrimage to the structures he built with his own hands – **Tor House** (☎ 831-624-1813; 26304 Ocean View Ave; tours adult/student $7/2; 10am-3pm Fri & Sat) and the Celtic-inspired Hawk Tower – offers fascinating insight into both the man and the ethos of Carmel he embodied, not to mention a host of intriguing architectural aspects; one of the portholes in the tower came from the wrecked ship that carried Napoleon from Elba. The only way to visit the property is to reserve space on a tour.

POINT LOBOS

About 4 miles south of Carmel, **Point Lobos** (☎ 831-624-4909; pt-lobos.parks.state.ca.us; per vehicle $8) has a dramatically rocky coastline. It takes its name from the Punta de los Lobos Marinos, or the 'Point of the Sea Wolves,' named by the Spanish for the howls of the resident sea lions. The full perimeter hike is 6 miles, but several short walks take in the wild scenery. Favorite destinations include **Sea Lion Point** and **Devil's Cauldron**, the latter a whirlpool that gets splashy at high tide.

Sleeping & Eating

You're more likely to see a gray whale breaching in September than find cheap accommodations in Carmel. You *will* find a slew of small boutique hotels and cozy B&Bs, but these fill up quickly, particularly in summer.

Carmel Village Inn (☎ 831-624-3864; www.carmel villageinn.com; cnr Ocean & Junipero Aves; r with fireplace $175-245, without fireplace $145-195) With cheerful flowers decorating its exterior, this central motel diagonally across from Devendorf Park has 34 pleasant rooms each with a fridge, TV and coffeemaker. Free wi-fi and continental breakfast, to boot.

Pine Inn (☎ 831-624-3851, 800-228-3851; www.pine inn.com; cnr Ocean Ave & Lincoln St; r $149-300;) Antiques and cozy lighting create an ambience of 19th-century comfort in the Pine's 49 rooms, and the lobby is a stunner in bordello red and brass trim. Right in the heart of town, it's surprisingly affordable, relatively speaking, though the less expensive rooms are short on cat-swinging space. Continental breakfast at the adjoining Italian restaurant is included in the rate. Try not to arrive after 9pm.

Tickle Pink Inn (☎ 831-624-1244; www.ticklepinkinn .com; 155 Highland Dr; r $239-500;) Perched on a hill a few miles south of downtown, the Tickle Pink is almost sinfully romantic, with a bottle of sparkling wine awaiting your arrival and a staff that specializes in making guests feel warm and fuzzy. Every room has a decadent ocean view and a balcony from which to admire it, and if you've forgotten your binoculars they'll lend you a pair. Lots of upscale inns do evening wine-and-cheese and extended continental breakfast, but here it's done with real style.

Bruno's Market & Deli (☎ 831-624-3821; cnr 6th Ave & Junipero St; meals $5-9; 7am-8pm) The best local grocery store, Bruno's has a superb deli for creating picnics. Daily lunch specials are popular. It also stocks Sparky's fresh draft root beer, based in Pacific Grove.

Bouchée (☎ 831-626-7880; Mission St btwn Ocean & 7th Aves; mains $17-32; from 4:30pm) One of Carmel's culinary highlights, Bouchée delivers refined French dining with a tapas twist. Its menu of 'small bites' is divided into light, medium and full-bodied – playing off its adjoining wine-bar and wine-merchant venture – though many of the dishes are available in main-course portions as well. The black capellini pasta highlights red abalone caught in the Monterey Bay. The 14 tables are packed in fairly tight, so watch those elbows.

Jack London's (☎ 831-624-2336; Dolores St btwn 5th & 6th Aves; dishes $6-20) Secreted away down a walkway off Dolores, it serves hot food until...wait for it...midnight! A Carmel mainstay since 1973, Jack's pairs upscale pub grub with a selection of microbrews and potent mixed drinks. With a cozy fireplace, the bar is also a fine place for just a drink.

Getting There & Around

Carmel is only 5 miles south of Monterey by Hwy 1. MST buses 4 and 5 run north to Monterey (p155) and south to the mission. Bus 22 passes through en route to Big Sur. Free unlimited parking can be found at **Vista Lobos Park** (cnr 3rd Ave & Torres St).

BIG SUR TO SAN LUIS OBISPO

On this 130-mile stretch of Hwy 1, you'll snake along the unbelievably picturesque coast south until it joins with Hwy 101 at San Luis Obispo. Even if your driving skills are up for the myriad of hills and switchbacks, others aren't: expect to average under 40mph for the route. Parts of the road are battle-scarred, evidence of the eternal struggle to keep it open after landslides.

BIG SUR

You know you've arrived somewhere special when the bathroom graffiti doesn't relate who hearts whom or when so-and-so was there, but instead counsels that 'the untouched world lies only beyond the limitations of man'. Yet Big Sur is more an experience than one tangible place. With a population hovering around 2000 scattered amid 250 sq miles, Big Sur has no traffic lights, banks or strip malls, and when the sun goes down, the moon and stars are the only streetlights, if summer's dense fog hasn't extinguished those as well. Much

ink has been spilled extolling the raw beauty and energy of this stretch of land shoehorned between the Santa Lucia Range and the Pacific Ocean, but nothing quite prepares you for your first glimpse of the craggy, unspoiled coastline, painted with nature's most intense color palette.

In the 1950s and '60s, Big Sur – so named by Spanish settlers living in Carmel who referred to the wilderness as *el pais grande del sur* (the big country to the south) – became a favorite retreat for writers and artists, including Henry Miller and Lawrence Ferlinghetti. And still it attracts mystics, artists and eccentric types looking to contemplate their navels along with harried city slickers ready to disengage from their cell phones and reflect deeply in and on this emerald edge of continent.

Although it's only 90 miles from Carmel to San Simeon, driving along this narrow two-lane highway is slow going. Allow at least four hours to cover the distance. Traveling after dark is perilous and futile, since you won't be able to see any of the countryside. Watch for cyclists, and remember, downhill traffic yields to uphill traffic on single-lane roads.

Orientation & Information

Visitors often wander into businesses along Hwy 1 and ask, 'How much further to Big Sur?' In fact, there is no town of Big Sur as such, though you may see the name on maps. The little commercial activity here is concentrated along the stretch between Andrew Molera State Park to the north and Pfeiffer Big Sur State Park to the south. Sometimes called 'The Village,' this is where you'll find many of the restaurants and lodging options, and the post office.

Just south of Pfeiffer Big Sur State Park is the **Big Sur Ranger Station** (☎ 831-667-2315; ☒ 8am-4:30pm), your source for information and maps for Los Padres National Forest, the Ventana Wilderness and the state parks. In southern Big Sur, south of the turn-off to the Nacimiento–Fergusson Rd is the **Pacific Valley Ranger Station** (☎ 805-927-4211; ☒ 9am-5pm).

Look for the free annual **Big Sur Guide** (www .bigsurcalifornia.org) published by the Big Sur Chamber of Commerce.

Note that road and emergency services here are distant – in Monterey in the north or Cambria in the south. Fill up the tank beforehand, and be careful.

Sights & Activities

These are listed north to south. Note: if you pay the entrance fee for one state park, you get in free to any others that day.

BIXBY BRIDGE

About 13 miles south of Carmel, the much photographed landmark Bixby Bridge, spanning Rainbow Canyon, is one of the world's highest single-span bridges at 714ft long and 260ft high. Completed in 1932, it was built by prisoners eager to lop time off their sentences. There's a photo-op pull-off just north of the bridge. Don't be tricked into thinking that the similar-looking Rocky Creek Bridge, just north of Bixby, is the real deal.

POINT SUR LIGHT STATION STATE HISTORIC PARK

A little more than 6 miles further south of Bixby Bridge, Point Sur looks like a velvet green fortress rising out of the plain. It's actually an imposing volcanic rock that looks like an island but is connected to land by a sandbar. Atop the rock is the 1899 **Point Sur Light Station** (☎ 831-625-4419; www.pointsur.org; tours adult/child $8/4), which remained in operation until 1974. Views and details of life here are engrossing, to partake you need to join a three-hour tour. Meet at the farm gate on Hwy 1 at 10am or 2pm Saturday or 10am Sunday year-round. There are also some weekday tours from spring through to fall – call for details.

ANDREW MOLERA STATE PARK

This oft-overlooked **park** (☎ 831-667-2315; per vehicle $8; ⏰ 8am-5pm) enjoys a remote and wild setting, lots of wildlife and great beachcombing – at last visit condors were making quick work of a whale carcass about a half-mile south down the beach. The first-come, first-served, 24-hour, **walk-in campground** (campsites $9), a little under half a mile from the parking lot, has fire pits, vault toilets and drinking water, but no water views. A quarter-mile trail leads from the campground to a beautiful beach where the Big Sur River runs into the ocean. **Molera Horseback Tours** (☎ 831-625-5486, 800-942-5486; www .molerahorsebacktours.com; ⏰ Mar-Nov) offers a variety of guided trail rides from $25.

PFEIFFER BIG SUR STATE PARK

Named after Big Sur's first European settlers who arrived in 1869, **Pfeiffer Big Sur State Park** (☎ 831-667-2315; day-use $8) is the largest state

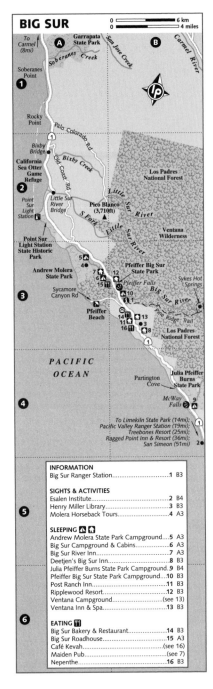

BIG SUR

0 ——— 6 km
0 ——— 4 miles

INFORMATION	
Big Sur Ranger Station............................1	B3

SIGHTS & ACTIVITIES	
Esalen Institute.......................................2	B4
Henry Miller Library...............................3	B3
Molera Horseback Tours..........................4	A3

SLEEPING	
Andrew Molera State Park Campground....5	A3
Big Sur Campground & Cabins.................6	A3
Big Sur River Inn....................................7	A3
Deetjen's Big Sur Inn..............................8	B3
Julia Pfeiffer Burns State Park Campground..9	B4
Pfeiffer Big Sur State Park Campground...10	B3
Post Ranch Inn.....................................11	B3
Ripplewood Resort................................12	B3
Ventana Campground.....................(see 13)	
Ventana Inn & Spa................................13	B3

EATING	
Big Sur Bakery & Restaurant...................14	B3
Big Sur Roadhouse................................15	A3
Café Kevah....................................(see 16)	
Maiden Pub......................................(see 7)	
Nepenthe..16	B3

BIG SUR IN A DAY

Pity the harried traveler who can't carve out a few days to absorb the enchantment of Big Sur, but sometimes you have to make do with what you've got. Assuming you're driving north to south, get thee first to **Big Sur Bakery & Restaurant** (p163) for coffee that will put hair on your chest, then calm yourself with a stroll on fantastic **Pfeiffer Beach** (below). Do lunch at the classic **Nepenthe** (p164) restaurant or its downstairs sister **Kivah** before getting in touch with your literary boho side at the **Henry Miller Library** (below). Gawp at the kelp forests in **Partington Cove** (below) before snapping your very own postcard-perfect photo of **McWay Falls** (below). If you find time to stay overnight, go yurt-style at **Treebones Resort** (p163). If you're up late and down with nudity, reserve hot-tub space at the **Esalen Institute** (p162), open to the public from 1am to 2am.

---

park in Big Sur. There are miles of pristine hiking through redwoods in its 964 acres, though the popular trail to reach long and lean **Pfeiffer Falls** is only a 1.4-mile round-trip walk.

A 218-site **campground** (☎ reservations 800-444-7275; www.parks.ca.gov; campsites $25-35) is beside the Big Sur River in a valley shaded by redwood groves; facilities include showers. Summer crowds are the drawback to this otherwise idyllic scene.

PFEIFFER BEACH
Just west of Pfeiffer Big Sur State Park, this phenomenal, crescent-shaped **beach** (day-use $5) is notable for its huge double rock formation through which waves crash with life-affirming power. It's often windy, and the surf is too dangerous for swimming. Dig down into the wet sand – it's purple!

To get there from Hwy 1 south, pass the turn-off for Andrew Molera State Park, about a quarter-mile south of the Big Sur Ranger Station, then make a sharp right onto the unmarked road with the small brown sign that says 'narrow road' at the top. Follow this for 2.3 miles to the parking lot, and the beach is a two-minute walk away.

HENRY MILLER LIBRARY
A denizen for 17 years, Henry Miller wrote, 'it was here in Big Sur I first learned to say "amen"'. The **Henry Miller Library** (☎ 831-667-2574; www.henrymiller.org; suggested donation $1; ☺ usually 11am-6pm Thu-Sun; ☐) is Big Sur's most cultured venue, but was never Miller's home. (He lived about 4 miles to the south.) The house belonged to Miller's friend, the painter Emil White, until his death and is now run by a nonprofit group. The library has all of Miller's

written works, many of his paintings and a great collection of Big Sur and Beat Generation material, including copies of the top 100 books Miller claimed were most influential on him. Stop by for a browse, some free coffee and a game of ping-pong. Check the website for details on the library's numerous cultural events.

The library is a quarter-mile south of Nepenthe restaurant.

PARTINGTON COVE
From the western side of Hwy 1, a poorly marked steep dirt trail descends half a mile along Partington Creek to Partington Cove, a little-visited but very beautiful section of Big Sur. On the 1-mile loop you cross a cool bridge and then walk through an even cooler tunnel. During Prohibition it was a landing spot for rum-runners. The water in the cove is unbelievably aqua and within it grow incredible kelp forests. There's no real beach access, but you can scamper on the rocks and look for tide pools as waves cuff ominously.

The turn-off is inside a large hairpin turn 8 miles south of Nepenthe restaurant and 1.8 miles north of Julia Pfeiffer Burns State Park.

JULIA PFEIFFER BURNS STATE PARK
This **park** (☎ 831-667-2315; day-use $8) hugs both sides of Hwy 1 and features redwood, tan oak, madrona and chaparral. At the park entrance (on the east side of Hwy 1) are picnic grounds along McWay Creek. The 4.5-mile **Ewoldsen Trail** offers views of the ocean and the Santa Lucia Range.

The park's highlight is California's only coastal waterfall, the 80ft **McWay Falls**, which drops straight into the sea – or onto the beach, depending on the tide. We dare you to take fewer than a dozen photos. To reach the waterfall viewpoint, take the short Overlook Trail heading west and cross beneath Hwy 1. Nearby, two small walk-in **campgrounds** (☎ reservations 800-444-7275; www.parks.ca.gov; campsites $15-20) sit on a semiprotected bluff. Camper registration is at Pfeiffer Big Sur State Park campground, 12 miles north.

ESALEN INSTITUTE

Eleven miles south of Nepenthe, world-renowned workshop and hot springs mecca the **Esalen Institute** (☎ 831-667-3000; www.esalen.org) is like hippie camp for adults. Week- or weekend-long workshops run the gamut from your standard Deepening your Yoga Practice to Ericksonian Hypnosis & Gestalt and Women's Leadership. Fun fact: Hunter S Thompson was the gun-toting caretaker here in 1960.

When space is available, you can stay at Esalen without participating in a workshop, but you'll have to check at the guardhouse. Accommodations are in rooms sleeping up to three people (per person $150 to $180) or in four- to six-bed dorms (per person $105 to $110). The bathrooms can be leaky and the bunk beds lumpy, so don't go in expecting Post Ranch luxury. The rates include three organic buffet-style meals...which even offer meat!

The Esalen baths are fed by a natural hot spring and sit on a ledge above the ocean. Dollars to doughnuts you'll never take another shower that compares view-wise with the one here. The clothing-optional 'nightly bathing' is open to the public from 1am to 3am by **reservation** (☎ 831-667-3047; bathing $20) only. The fee is payable by credit card only.

Sleeping

Lodging in Big Sur ranges from basic four walls and a mattress to glossy mag-worthy resorts. Campers will find many options as well, though reserving is also advised. Worse comes to worse, you can pull over and crash out in your car. If the police come a-knockin', just tell them you were grabbing a catnap – you had gotten drowsy and didn't want to fall asleep at the wheel. They're pretty understanding – just don't sleep in your vehicle in the same spot two nights in a row.

BUDGET

There's camping in three of Big Sur's state parks: Andrew Molera State Park (p160), Pfeiffer Big Sur State Park (p160) and Julia Pfeiffer Burns State Park (p161).

Ventana Campground (☎ 831-667-2712; www .ventanawildernesscampground.com; campsites $27-40; ☾ Mar-Oct) Just south of Pfeiffer Big Sur State Park and set in a 40-acre redwood grove, this 80-site campground has beautiful secluded campsites with a lot of privacy.

Big Sur Campground & Cabins (☎ 831-667-2322; campsites $25-29, tent cabins $54-59, cabins with bathroom & kitchen $100-225) In the Village, this option, popular with RVs, has 79 sites and some small cabins shaded by redwoods right on the Big Sur River. The camping store stocks the basics, and there are laundry facilities, hot showers and a playground.

Limekiln State Park Campground (☎ 831-667-2403, reservations 800-444-7275; www.parks.ca.gov; camp-sites $25) This park gets its name from the four remaining lime kilns originally built here in the 1880s. A short hike leads to a 100ft waterfall. The campground sits right by the park entrance, tucked under a bridge next to the ocean; it has flush toilets and hot showers. Sites 1 and 2 are tops – secluded and with ocean views.

MIDRANGE

Deetjen's Big Sur Inn (☎ 831-667-2377; www.deetjens .com; r $75-195) Nestled among redwoods and wisteria along Castro Creek, this enchanting conglomeration of rustic rooms and cottages was built by Norwegian immigrant Helmuth Deetjen in the 1930s. He salvaged the red-wood to add on more rooms and cottages – now totaling 20 thin-walled units – for the myriad transients who were showing up at his doorstep. Some rooms are warmed by wood-burning fireplaces, and the cheaper ones share a bathroom, but all book up far in advance. The cozy dining room serves hearty breakfasts and dinners. Deetjen's is a quarter of a mile south of the Henry Miller Library, and operates on a nonprofit basis.

Ripplewood Resort (☎ 831-667-2242; www.ripple woodresort.com; cabins $90-150) Ripplewood has struck a blow for fiscal equality by having the same rates year-round. Cabins vary in details: all have kitchens and private bathrooms, some have fireplaces. The riverside cabins – like Nos 1 and 2 – are quiet and surrounded by red-woods, but the hillside ones can be noisy.

Big Sur River Inn (☎ 831-667-2700, 800-548-3610; www.bigsurriverinn.com; r $85-150, ste $180-225; ☒) In business since 1888, this inn – the most northern of the bunch – offers 20 comfy, country-style rooms, some with balconies overlooking the river (which many would call a creek). The grassy lawn between the water and the inn is a magnet for kids. There are several good eating and drinking options here, like the Big Sur River restaurant and the Maiden Pub. The enlightening community bulletin board carries notices about kundalini classes, acreage for sale, and entreaties to improve your karma by returning a stolen chainsaw.

Ragged Point Inn & Resort (☎ 805-927-4502; www .raggedpointinn.com; r $129-279) Fifteen miles north of San Simeon stands Ragged Point, an appropriately named cliff outcropping with views of the coastline in both directions. This sprawling and expanding resort, inexplicably popular with middle-aged motorcyclists and Japanese tour groups, has 30 rooms, some with ocean views – No 5 is especially nice – and you score a fireplace, Jacuzzi and kitchenette if you spring for a deluxe.

our pick **Treebones Resort** (☎ 877-424-4787; www .treebonesresort.com; 71895 Hwy 1; yurts/campsites $129-189/55; ☒) Don't let the word 'resort' throw you. Yes, it's got an ocean view hot tub, a heated pool and massage treatments, but this delightful charmer is actually a ridiculous bargain, especially for families. And when was the last time you slept in a yurt? The exteriors of the 16 circular tentlike constructions belie their polished pine floors, sumptuous quilt-covered beds, sink vanities (dispensing fresh well water) and redwood decks. One of the four family-sized yurts even has a ping-pong table inside. The bathrooms and showers are a quick stroll away in the main lodge, but fresh air's why you're in Big Sur, right? Five ocean view campsites are set aside for tent-bearing guests. The complimentary make-your-own waffle breakfast will stand you in good stead for your morning's adventures. Treebones is 3 miles south of Plaskett Campground in southern Big Sur, and its sign is pretty tiny.

TOP END

Post Ranch Inn (☎ 831-667-2200, 800-527-2200; www .postranchinn.com; r $550-1385) The last word in luxurious coastal getaways, the legendary Post Ranch pampers guests with lodgings that feature slate spa tubs, private decks, fireplaces, and even walking sticks for those coastal hikes. There are 30 individual units, but you'd be forgiven for thinking you were the only guests here. Ocean-facing rooms have the best view on the Central Coast, while the nonview tree houses have a bit of sway supplied by your

own motion. One sour note: the staff can be stiff and standoffish. Nonmillionaires can take a free half-hour tour on weekdays at 2pm. The inn is just under a mile south of the Big Sur Bakery & Restaurant.

Ventana Inn & Spa (☎ 831-667-2331, 800-628-6500; www.ventanainn.com; r from $460; ☐ ☒) Other than the introduction of flat-screen plasma TVs in the suites, serene, romantic Ventana hasn't changed all that much since it opened in 1975. Madame Ventana wears Post Ranch clothes but has an Esalen soul, and caters to honeymooning couples and paparazzi-fleeing celebs. Guests can pad from yoga class to the Japanese bathhouse to the indigenous plant gardens to the clothing-optional pool, or chose instead to hole up all day next to the wood-burning fireplace in their rustic-style room or cabin.

Eating

For more options, see the Sleeping section.

Big Sur Bakery & Restaurant (☎ 831-667-0520; pizza $14-19, dinner mains $27-36; ☒ bakery daily, restaurant Tue-Sun) This funkily decorated, warmly lit house behind the Shell station in the Village has offerings that change through the day and season. Wood-fired pizzas and stellar burgers share the lineup with more refined – but just as satisfying – dishes like wild salmon with succotash. The bakery pours the best coffee in Big Sur and sells its own house granola. In the words of one local, 'their ham and cheese croissant is...mwa! Tasty shit.' Poke around the spirit garden next door. Just south of the post office.

Big Sur Roadhouse (☎ 831-667-2264; mains $13-24; ☒ dinner Wed-Mon) Marcus and Heather Foster opened the Latin-flavored Roadhouse after working together at Sierra Mar, the Post Ranch Inn's hoity-toity eatery. Thankfully, they've chosen to share with us fresh, impeccable cuisine (like plantain *tostones* with tiger prawns) minus the haute attitude. Inside, the restaurant fairly glows from the corner fireplace and copper-top bar, not to mention the smiles from diners' faces. The front patio is more often than not covered in exuberant chalk drawings. Just south of the River Inn.

Big Sur River Inn (☎ 831-667-2700; mains $11-23; ☒ breakfast, lunch & dinner) This inn in the Village has a woodsy old supper-club feel, a fireplace that could eat you alive and a deck that overlooks the river teeming with throaty frogs. The food is classic American, sourced from organic local produce and hormone-free meat.

CENTRAL COAST

Tucked next door to the south is Maiden Pub, with an incredible beer bible and a motley group of local musicians jamming their hearts out on the weekends.

Nepenthe (☎ 831-667-2345; mains $13-32) Nepenthe (nuh-*penth*-ee) comes from a Greek word meaning 'isle of no sorrow', and indeed, it'd be hard to feel blue while sitting on its clifftop terrace, the vast ocean vista spread out before you. The food, while tasty (try the renowned Ambrosia burger), is secondary to the view and Nepenthe's place in history. Orson Welles and Rita Hayworth bought the land in 1944, and in 1947 Bill and Lolla Fassett opened the restaurant. Nepenthe is 3 miles south of Pfeiffer Big Sur State Park.

Cafe Kevah (dishes $8-12; ☺ breakfast, lunch; 🏃) For cheaper eats and almost the same views as Nepenthe, go downstairs to this outdoor café.

Getting There & Away

Although there are seasonal buses from Monterey to the northern sections of Big Sur, the area is best explored by car, since you'll be itching to stop frequently to take in the rugged beauty and stunning vistas that reveal themselves at every turn.

If you opt for public transit, MST bus 22 ($4, 75 minutes, twice daily) goes from Monterey (p155) via Carmel as far south as Nepenthe restaurant between late May and early September. The buses are equipped to take two bicycles.

PIEDRAS BLANCAS

Nearly extinct 100 years ago, elephant seals have made a remarkable comeback along California's coast. There are seals hanging around much of the year (though mid-August to mid-October they're thin on the ground) just 4.4 miles north of Hearst Castle, but from December through February the males return and the year's births begin. On sunny days, the seals usually 'lie around like banana slugs,' in the words of one **Friends of the Elephant Seal** (☎ 805-924-1628; www .elephantseal.org) docent, 'but when the temperature drops, they get aggro.' The behemoth bulls, who can weigh between 3000lb and 5000lb, engage in mock and sometimes real combat, all the while emitting toilet-plunger grunts.

HEARST CASTLE

Though newspaper magnate William Randolph Hearst (1863–1951) didn't call his 165-room monstrosity a castle – preferring its official name Cuesta Encantada (the Enchanted Hill) or more often simply 'the ranch' – it beats the pants off most castles in the world in the ostentatious contest. It's a wondrous, historic (Winston Churchill penned anti-Nazi essays here in the 1930s), over-the-top homage to material excess perched high on a hill, and a visit is a must.

Architect Julia Morgan based the main building, or Casa Grande, on the design of a Spanish cathedral, and over the next 28 years catered to Hearst's every design whim, deftly integrating the spoils of his fabled European shopping sprees (ancient artifacts, entire monasteries etc) into the whole. The estate sprawls out over 127 acres of lushly landscaped gardens (and at the time, the largest private zoo in the world), accentuated by shimmering pools and fountains and statues from ancient Greece and Moorish Spain.

Hearst and his longtime mistress Marion Davies (his first wife refused to grant him a divorce) adored entertaining at the ranch, and it saw a steady stream of the biggest movers and shakers of the era. Invitations were highly coveted and much fun was had, but Hearst had his quirks – he despised drunkenness, and restricted his guests' alcohol consumption to two drinks. Guests were also forbidden to speak of death.

To see anything of **Hearst Castle** (☎ general information 805-927-2020, reservations 800-444-4445; www .hearstcastle.com; tours adult/child May-Sep $24/12, Oct-Apr $20/10), you will need to take a tour. For most of the year, you will absolutely need reservations for these tours. In the peak summer months you'll need these a week or more in advance. Before you leave, or if someone fell down on reservation duty, visit the museum area in the back of the visitors center.

Tours start daily at 8:20am, with the last leaving at 3:20pm (sometimes later during summer). There are four main tours; for each you depart from the visitors center and make the 10-minute bus ride up the hill. No matter how many tours you go on you have to make the journey up and down each time. Each of the tours lasts about 1¾ hours, and every tour includes the highlight Neptune and Roman pools.

It's best to start with **Tour 1**, aka the 'Experience Tour,' as you get an overview of the estate and a chance to see a film about Hearst's life. This answers all the basic questions and prepares you to delve deeper. Unless you have just a passing interest in the castle, you'll likely be sucked into wanting to take more tours. The docents are almost preternaturally knowledgeable – just try and stump 'em.

Tours 2, 3 and **4** change their itineraries occasionally, but generally focus on the upstairs, pools or gardens, and are much less crowded than the Experience Tour.

The new **Evening Tours** (adult/child $30/15; ☉ tours Fri & Sat Mar-May & Sep-Dec) offer an overview as well, but the special twist is that visitors – make that guests – get to spy on what the house felt like while Hearst was entertaining (which was always), thanks to the costumed performers-cum-docents around every corner, lounging and preening. Reserve far in advance for this 2¼-hour tour.

Getting to Hearst Castle without your own wheels can be a challenge. However San Luis Obispo's RTA (p171) makes two daily round-trips ($2.50, 90 minutes) between San Luis Obispo (SLO) and the visitors center via Morro Bay and Cambria.

CAMBRIA
pop 6100

One of Cambria's early nicknames was Slabtown, after the rough pieces of wood its early buildings were constructed from. Though the name was changed to the more melodious-sounding Cambria in 1870, the modest, self-effacing temperament of Slabtown seems to have stuck. Cambria has three distinct parts: the historic center a half-mile off Hwy 1 with cafés, shops and restaurants along Main St; the tourist-choked newer center often called 'Cambria West,' also on Main St but right off Hwy 1; and the motel-lined Moonstone Beach, which, though its eponymous moonstones – aka jasper – are long gone, still tempts meanderers to its boardwalk and stretches of sand.

All places following are on the east side, except the **chamber of commerce** (☎ 805-927-3624; www.cambriachamber.org; 767 Main St; ☉ 9am-5pm Mon-Fri, noon-4pm Sat & Sun).

Bridge Street Inn (☎ 805-927-7653; www.bridge streetinncambria.com; 4314 Bridge St; dm $25, r $40-70 all incl breakfast) Framed by an exuberant jasmine bush, this 1895 B&B-cum-hostel has character and charm at a great price, though the beds could be comfier. There is a communal kitchen – and let's not forget the wi-fi and

the volleyball court. It's small, so reserve ahead.

Olallieberry B&B (☎ 805-927-3222; www.olallieberry .com; 2476 Main St; r $135-220) A stay at one of the Olallieberry's nine cozy, cheerful guest rooms, replete with pastels, quilts and not a few ruffles, is like a visit to the fun grandma's house. All rooms have their own private bathroom and all but one has a fireplace. If the expansive gardens and deck don't relax you enough, get an on-site massage from innkeeper and massage therapist Marilyn Draper. FYI, an olallieberry is similar to a blackberry.

Robin's (☎ 805-927-5007; 4095 Burton Dr; lunch $7-10, dinner $13-24; ☉ 11am-9pm) The best place to eat in town, Robin's has been whipping up fresh quasi-international cuisine using local ingredients for more than two decades. The curry chicken salad gets high marks, and there's plenty for nonmeat-eaters, like the portobello and spinach lasagna. Dine inside, out in on the wisteria-draped patio or get something to go from the deli counter.

Lily's Coffeehouse (☎ 805-927-7259; 2028 Main St; ☉ 8:30am-5pm Wed-Mon) Something of a community gathering spot, Lily's has a peaceful front garden patio where you can tap into free wi-fi while sipping your $1 espresso. Drop in on Saturday from 11am to 4pm and order a crepe made to your exact specifications.

Camozzi's Saloon (☎ 805-927-8941; 2262 Main St E) Grab one of the eight beers on tap and take a long look at the walls covered in photographs of old-time Cambria. Pool tables, shuffleboard and a jukebox will be waiting when you're done with your history lesson.

ESTERO BAY

Estero Bay is a long, shallow, west-facing bay with Cayucos at its northern end and Montaña de Oro State Park at its southern end. Morro Bay, a deep inlet guarded by Morro Rock and separated from the ocean by a 12-mile-long sand spit, sits about halfway between the two and has most of Estero Bay's services and tourist activity. Morro Rock is the bay's unmistakable landmark.

San Luis Obispo's RTA (p171) bus 12 ($1 to $2.50, hourly 7am to 7pm, Monday to Saturday) travels up Hwy 1 from San Luis Obispo, stopping in Morro Bay. Two runs every day continue on to Cayucos, Cambria and San Simeon.

CENTRAL COAST

Cayucos

pop 3100

The main drag of amiable, slow-paced Cayucos (ki-*you*-kiss) calls to mind an old frontier town, while a block to the west, surf's up. Cayucos developed around a wharf and warehouse built by Captain James Cass in 1867, and Ocean Ave, which parallels Hwy 1, maintains its historic storefronts and most of the town's hotels, eateries and its abundance of antique shops. At the town's northern end is the blissfully uncommercialized, knock-kneed pier, built in 1875.

Cayucos is a good spot for beginner surfers. **Cayucos Surf Company** (☎ 805-995-1000; 95 Cayucos Dr; ☑ 10am-6pm) sells and rents surfboards (full day $18) as well as wet suits and boogie boards. Lessons are available for $70 for two hours.

SLEEPING & EATING

Shoreline Inn (☎ 805-995-3681; www.cayucosshorelineinn .com; 1 N Ocean Ave; r $130-170) Fresh off a renovation, this friendly, clean 28-room motel right on the water is terribly good value, and it welcomes pets. Wi-fi, fridges, microwaves and continental breakfast round out the package.

ourpick Ruddell's Smokehouse (☎ 805-995-5028; 101 D St; mains $4-10; ☑ 11am-6pm; ♿) 'Smoker Jim' transforms fresh-off-the-boat seafood into succulently smoked slabs that delight locals and visitors alike. His fish tacos (in smoked albacore, salmon or ahi) come slathered in a unique relish of mayo, apples and celery. Fish and pork sandwiches ($8) and salads are also available, as is a small selection of grab-and-go items from the deli case (ahi jerky, anyone?). Squeeze yourself in the door to place your order and then scarf it down at an outside table. Try to land on a Sunday afternoon, when local musicians – think a guitar or two, drums and an upright bass – convene for a rollicking acoustic jam session. The music kicks off around 3pm.

Bill & Carol's Sea Shanty (☎ 805-995-3272; 296 S Ocean Ave; mains $7-23; ☑ breakfast, lunch & dinner; ♿) The burgers, omelettes and seafood here hold their own for sure, but the lineup of desserts is what makes this place awesome – try the strawberry shortcake or the olallieberry cobbler. A bazillion baseball caps hang from the ceiling – they happily accept donations in kind.

Morro Bay

pop 10,208

Morro Bay...that's the one with the big rock and those huge smokestacks, right? Er, yes. Morro Rock, a 578ft volcanic peak jutting dramatically from the ocean floor, is part of a 21-million-year-old chain of nine such rocks stretching between here and San Luis Obispo, nicknamed the Nine Sisters. Morro Bay's less boast-worthy landmark comes courtesy of the power plant, which threw up three cigarette-shaped smokestacks on the north side of town, to the dismay of residents. But in ironic contrast to its vertical scars, the town harbors extraordinary natural riches, well worth a day's exploration, and ideally via kayak. The bay is a giant estuary inhabited by two dozen threatened and endangered species, including the brown pelican, sea otter and steelhead trout. In winter, about 120 migratory bird species make the bay their home.

Leading south from Morro Rock is the Embarcadero, a small waterfront boulevard lined with touristy shops and restaurant. It's also the launching area for boat tours. The **chamber of commerce** (☎ 805-772-4467; www.morrobay.com; 845 Embarcadero; ☑ 10am-4pm Mon- Sat, 11am-3pm Sun) is in the thick of things. Three blocks up the hill from the water, Main St is the more interesting, less tourist-driven part of town.

SIGHTS & ACTIVITIES

On the way to get a close-up look at the Rock, you'll pass the **power plant** (1290 Embarcadero) – the 'How it Works' display at the entrance is actually quite interesting. Community action saved **Morro Rock** from being pulverized into asphalt, and it's now the nesting ground of peregrine falcons. You can fish off its south side or laze at the small beach on the north side, but you can't drive all the way around.

Across the street from the chamber of commerce, on Saturdays you can watch noon-time demonstration tournaments on a **giant chessboard**. Up the hill, the **fishermen & farmers market** (☎ 805-772-4467; Main St near Morro Bay Blvd; ☑ 3-6pm Sat) also draws a Saturday crowd.

The **Museum of Natural History** (☎ 805-772-2694; adult/child under 17 $2/free; ☑ 10am-5pm; ♿) features interactive exhibits showing how the forces of nature affect us, geared toward kids but intriguing to all. It's within the 2700-acre **Morro Bay State Park**, which incorporates an 18-hole golf course, a marina with kayak rentals and a campground.

Opportunities to get out on the water abound. One of the best is a kayaking tour with **Central Coast Outdoors** (☎ 805-528-1080; www .centralcoastoutdoors.com), and it offers exhilarating biking and hiking tours of the area as well.

CENTRAL COAST

Rock Kayak Co (☎ 805-772-2906; www.rockkayak.com; 845 Embarcadero) rents kayaks and offers tours.

Especially if venturing out on your own, be aware of the tide schedules; you'll ideally want to ride the tide out and then back in. Wind is calmest in the mornings.

For views of kelp forests and schools of fish, take a spin on **Sub-Sea** (☎ 805-772-9463; 699 Embarcadero #9; www.subseatours.com; adult/child 3-12 $14/7; ☺ May-Oct), a semisubmersible that plies the waters.

SLEEPING
Motels cluster along Main and Harbor Sts. It's crucial to make reservations in summer and for October's family-friendly Harbor Festival.

Pleasant Inn Motel (☎ 805-772-8521; www.pleasant innmotel.com; 235 Harbor St; r $70-115) The posy-patterned rooms aren't anything to write home about, but this family-run motel keeps them clean, and the price is right. Some units have kitchens, and pets are welcome.

Embarcadero Inn (☎ 805-772-2700; www.embarcadero inn.com; 456 Embarcadero; r incl continental breakfast $110-175; ▯) Every room at this classy, if slightly bland, inn on the south side of town faces the bay, and most have balconies with views of the rock. Room 255 has a particularly splendid view. The breakfast room is a wi-fi access point.

Inn at Morro Bay (☎ 805-772-5651; www.innatmorro bay.com; 60 State Park Rd; r $149-279; ▨ ▨) On the south side of town on 4000 acres within the state park – and the only lodging in town that's right on the water – this resort delivers calm surroundings and attentive service. The 97 rooms run the gamut of views and amenities, but all are airy and comfortable. Being adjacent to the golf course, the inn attracts lots of golfers, hence the bucket of range balls in each room. Beach cruisers are available at no cost.

EATING
Giovanni's Fish Market (☎ 805-772-2255; 1001 Front St; mains $6-14; ☺ 11am-7pm) This family-run place is a classic California seafood shack in every good sense of the word. The fish and chips drive folks mad. Inside there's a market with an amazing selection of smoked fish and other treats.

Taco Temple (☎ 805-772-4965; 2680 Main St; mains $8-13; ☝) Locals rave, and for good reason. Overlook the frontage road location and

come for megaportions of scrumptious creative Mexican grub in a shorts-and-T-shirt setting. Try one of the specials – they deserve the name. Cash only.

Sunshine Health Foods (☎ 805-772-7873; 415 Morro Bay Blvd; ☺ Mon-Sat; ▼) Stock up on your natural, organic snacks here. In the back is Shine Cafe (mains $6 to $10), a mostly organic eatery with karma-cleansing grub like tempeh tacos and a vegan club sandwich.

GETTING THERE & AWAY
If you're driving, exit 297A from Hwy 1 will take you right to Main St.

San Luis Obispo's **Regional Transit Authority** (RTA; ☎ 805-541-2228; www.slorta.org; fares $1-2.50) Route 12 bus operates daily except Sundays, and connects Morro Bay with San Simeon, Cambria, Cayucos and San Luis Obispo.

Montaña de Oro State Park
About 6 miles southwest of Morro Bay, Montaña de Oro State Park covers nearly 8000 acres of undeveloped mountain and seaside terrain. In spring the hills are blanketed by bright poppies, wild mustard and other wildflowers that give the park its name, meaning 'mountain of gold' in Spanish. Its coastal bluffs are a favorite spot for hiking, mountain biking and horseback riding. The northern half of the park includes a row of sand dunes (some 85ft high) and the 4-mile-long sand spit that separates Morro Bay from the Pacific. The park's southern section consists of fingerlike bluffs and an ancient marine terrace, which after seismic uplifting is now a series of 1000ft peaks.

The park's **visitors center** (☎ 805-528-0513; ☺ 11am-3pm), 3 miles south of the park boundary, has an interpretive garden and serves as the ranger station and natural history museum. It sits right above **Spooners Cove**, once used by smugglers and now a beautiful sandy beach and picnic area. Several **hiking trails**, including the outstanding 4-mile Bluff Trail, which skirts the cliffs and has beach access points, start from here. To get to the sand dunes, turn off onto Sand Spit Rd from the main park road until it dead-ends into the Sand Spit day-use area, about 1.8 miles north of the visitors center. There's no fee.

Near the visitors center is the lovely and primitive **Montaña de Oro State Park Campground** (☎ 805-528-0513, reservations 800-444-7275; www.parks .ca.gov; campsites $11-15) with 50 sites, each near the creek or against the hillside. Fees include use of fire rings, pit toilets and drinking water. There are more remote, walk-in sites further into the park.

The park is about 7 miles from Hwy 1. Exit at South Bay Blvd and follow the signs, which will lead you through the towns of Los Osos and Baywood Park.

Montaña de Oro is located at the end of Pecho Rd near Los Osos. From Hwy 101, take the Los Osos Valley Rd exit just south of San Luis Obispo. Drive approximately 12 miles on this road until you reach the Ranger Headquarters & Visitor Center, adjacent to Spooner's Cove.

SAN LUIS OBISPO
pop 43,500

Almost equidistant between LA and San Francisco, San Luis Obispo (sun *loo*-is o-*bis*-po) has long been the classic stopover point for those making the journey. With no must-see attractions, SLO might not seem to warrant high ranking on the itinerary. But not only does it make the ideal base for Central Coast exploration, it's one of those small cities that doles out urban pleasures and rural charm in equal measure. Nestled at the base of the Santa Lucia foothills and a grape's throw from a thriving wine industry, SLO gets high marks for livability; the gorgeous ridgeline are protected from development and drive-thrus are illegal downtown. The 18,000 students at Cal Poly (the co-eds of which have been dubbed 'Poly Dollies') keep the streets hopping during the school year.

Orientation

SLO's downtown is walkable and compact. The main roads are Higuera St, which travels one way going southwest, and Marsh St, parallel to Higuera St, running northeast. San Luis Obispo Creek, once used to irrigate mission orchards, flows through downtown. By the way, the 'P' you see on the peak from town is for Cal Poly, and the 'M' peak is for Mission College Prep (and not for the Cal Poly Mustangs, as even some locals believe.)

Information

Banks are along Higuera and Marsh Sts, near the main post office. The hostel has a computer guests can use, and most cafés, including Uptown Espresso and Linnaea's, have free wi-fi.

Chamber of commerce (☎ 805-781-2777; www .visitslo.com; 1039 Chorro St; ◷ 10am-5pm Sun-Wed, to 7pm Thu-Sat) You can use the free phone to check for lodging availability.
Main post office (☎ 805-541-3062; cnr Marsh & Morro Sts)

Sights & Activities

SLO's attractions cluster around **Mission Plaza**, a shady oasis with restored adobes and fountains overlooking San Luis Obispo Creek, right in the heart of downtown. Look for the Moon Tree, a coast redwood grown from a seed that was on board Apollo 14's lunar mission.

The satisfyingly reverberatory bells you'll hear at noon emanate from the **Mission San Luis Obispo de Tolosa** (☎ 805-543-6850; Monterey St; suggested donation $2; ◷ 9am-5pm Apr-Oct, to 4pm Nov-Mar) between Chorro and Broad Sts. The fifth of the California missions, it was established in 1772 and named for a French saint. Often called the 'Prince of the Missions,' its still-active church has an unusual L-shape and whitewashed walls decorated with the Stations of the Cross. Hour-long tours start at 1:15pm daily except Saturdays.

For an overview of local history, check out the **San Luis Obispo County Historical Museum** (☎ 805-543-0638; 696 Monterey St; admission free; ◷ 10am-4pm Wed-Sun), just southwest of the mission. It's housed in the 1905 Carnegie Library, an elegant sandstone building.

The San Luis Obispo Creek is lined with shady trails and public art, and leads to the **San Luis Obispo Art Center** (☎ 805-543-8562; 1010 Broad St;

BIKE SUMO

Yeah, tons of cities have some version of Critical Mass, but how many culminate in bike sumo? If you're in town on the first Thursday of the month, join cycle-happy Slobispans at Mission Plaza at 9:30pm for The Happening: costume-accentuated, free-spirited loops around downtown on bikes. The riders then convene at **Wally's Bike Works** (306 Higuera St), where two contestants (armed with fear-striking aliases) enter the circle, and the one left sitting is the winner. What conspires in the middle is a cross between acrobatics on bikes and Fight Club. The bouts are tournament format, so participants can't simply drop in, but spectating is riotous fun.

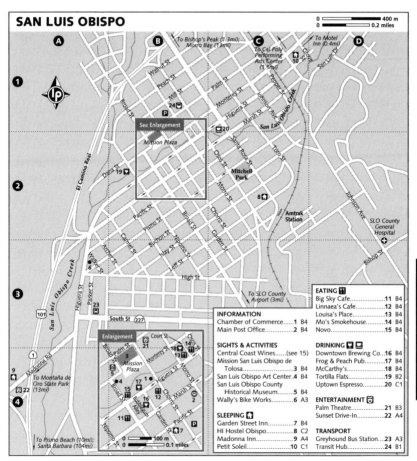

SAN LUIS OBISPO

INFORMATION	
Chamber of Commerce......1	B4
Main Post Office..............2	B4

SIGHTS & ACTIVITIES	
Central Coast Wines......(see 15)	
Mission San Luis Obispo de Tolosa..........................3	B4
San Luis Obispo Art Center..4	B4
San Luis Obispo County Historical Museum..........5	B4
Wally's Bike Works...........6	A3

SLEEPING	
Garden Street Inn..............7	B4
HI Hostel Obispo..............8	C2
Madonna Inn...................9	A4
Petit Soleil.....................10	C1

EATING	
Big Sky Cafe..................11	B4
Linnaea's Cafe...............12	B4
Louisa's Place................13	B4
Mo's Smokehouse..........14	B4
Novo............................15	B4

DRINKING	
Downtown Brewing Co...16	B4
Frog & Peach Pub..........17	B4
McCarthy's...................18	B4
Tortilla Flats..................19	B2
Uptown Espresso..........20	C1

ENTERTAINMENT	
Palm Theatre.................21	B3
Sunset Drive-In.............22	A4

TRANSPORT	
Greyhound Bus Station....23	A3
Transit Hub...................24	B1

admission free; 11am-5pm Wed-Mon), which has no permanent collection but rather showcases local artists and visiting exhibits from around the state.

Germophobes beware: SLO's quirkiest attraction is **Bubblegum Alley**, a narrow walkway on the 700 block of Higuera St (between the shops Atmospheres and Girl2Girl) on which folks have been leaving their masticatory mark since 1960. Every inch is plastered with ABC gum, and creative types have attempted to impose some aesthetic design on their contributions. Watch where you step.

If you can only stay for a night, make it a Thursday, when the well-known **farmers market** (5-9pm Thu) turns Higuera St between Nipomo and Osos St and adjacent lanes into a giant street party. In the midst of the requisite fruit and veggie stands, witness garage bands, salvation peddlers, signature-collectors, balloon-animal twisters, face painters and copious amounts of food-on-a-stick.

There are plenty of good hikes around SLO, many of which start from Poly Canyon Rd on the Cal Poly campus. Hiking maps and parking information are available at the booth on the right as you enter the campus. The most popular hike is to the top of the **Bishop's Peak** (1559ft), the tallest of the **Nine Sisters**, a chain of volcanic peaks. The trail (about 2.5 miles) starts in a grove of live oaks and heads along rocky, exposed switchbacks. To get to the hike, go northwest from downtown on Santa Rosa St (Hwy 1) for 1.5 miles, turn west onto

Highland Dr and after a little less than 1 mile the road ends at the trailhead.

Central Coast Wines (☎ 805-784-9463; www.ccwines .com; 712 Higuera St) For those needing some guidance before – or instead of – venturing into the wine country. Geographically, the small shop carries wines from Santa Barbara to Paso Robles, and every bottle stocked is hand-picked by the staff. On Thursday from 6pm to 9pm, winemakers hold pourings: for $5 you get a tasting of two whites and four reds.

Sleeping

Motels cluster along the northeastern end of Monterey St near Hwy 101 and at the Hwy 101 exit for Hwy 1 at Santa Rosa St. Midcentury history buffs should check out the shell of the Motel Inn, the world's very first motel, at 2223 Monterey St just south of Hwy 1.

HI Hostel Obispo (☎ 805-544-4678; www.hostelobispo .com; 1617 Santa Rosa St; dm $23, r $55-70; ☺ check-in 7:30-10am & 4:30-10pm; ☐) A gem among hostels, Hostel Obispo, in a converted Victorian on a tree-lined street a minute's walk from the train station, is fresh off a renovation that brought a games room, a rooftop garden and solar power to an already special place. The staff is unfailingly helpful, kitchen scraps go to the owner's chickens, linens are line-dried, bikes can be rented and the morning coffee is organic. Simply put, you can feel the love. There are 22 beds, and credit cards aren't accepted.

Petit Soleil (☎ 805-549-0321; www.psslo.com; 1473 Monterey St; r $139-199, ste $209-269; ⊠) This golden-hued, 16-unit 'bed *et* breakfast' charms you at every turn. Each room is beautifully, tastefully decorated according to its name and several – including Chocolat – feature painted murals. Breakfast is a gourmet feast and guests enjoy wine tastings every evening. The two front rooms catch some street noise.

Garden Street Inn (☎ 805-545-9802; www.garden streetinn.com; 1212 Garden St; r $165-225; ⊠ ☐) This restored 1887 Victorian B&B, ideally located downtown, has 13 comfy and spacious rooms and suites, but decor-wise, suffers from a touch of grandma's-house-itis. A big breakfast is served in a stylish room with original stained-glass windows.

Madonna Inn (☎ 805-543-3000, 800-543-9666; www .madonnainn.com; 100 Madonna Rd; r $168-300; ⊠) You'd expect a place like this in Vegas, not SLO, but here it is, in all its campy, over-the-top extravagance. Japanese tourists, vacationing Midwesterners and ironic city folk come for the 109

themed rooms – including Yosemite Rock, Floral Fantasy and the hot-pink Sugar & Spice. Check out photos of all the rooms online, or you can wander the halls and spy into the ones being cleaned. The urinal in the men's room is a waterfall – ladies, go ahead and take a peek.

Eating

Big Sky Cafe (☎ 805-545-5401; 1121 Broad St; dinner mains $8-18; ☺ breakfast, lunch & dinner) A perennial, casual favorite, Big Sky is a big room, and still the wait can be long; food this good takes a few extra minutes – its tagline is 'analog food for a digital world.' The decor is influenced by the Southwest but the menu is all over the place (in a good way), though much of the ingredients are sourced locally. Try the 'BLT that Time Forgot.' Vegetarians will, for once, have more options than meat-eaters.

Louisa's Place (☎ 805-541-0227; 964 Higuera St; mains $6-10; ☺ 6am-3pm) The eggs served up at this busy-bee, no-frills greasy spoon come straight from Cal Poly. Snag a table on the sidewalk and automatically earn cool-kid status. Be prepared to wait.

Linnaea's Cafe (☎ 805-541-5888; 1110 Garden St; meals $5-9; ☺ breakfast, lunch & dinner; ☐) SLO's first coffeehouse, and perhaps the one with the most fervent following, Linnaea's carries an ever-expanding menu that changes daily. Weeknights carry a theme (soup night, waffle night etc) until 10pm. There's a lovely garden out back and wi-fi to boot.

Mo's Smokehouse BBQ (☎ 805-544-6193; 970 Higuera St; mains $7-15; ♿) Sink your tush into an antique chair before sinking your teeth into some authentic BBQ, hickory-smoked on the premises. You order at the counter, so it's a good option for those short on time. The ribs are lip-smacking.

Novo (☎ 805-543-3986; 726 Higuera; dishes $8-26; ☺ lunch & dinner) Sharing an owner with the esteemed Robin's in Cambria and open again after a renovation and menu-expansion, Novo spins out Mediterranean, Brazilian and Asian-inspired tapas, with an eye towards freshness and presentation. Doll yourself up, choose one of the dozens of international wines or beers and savor the view from the creekside decks.

Drinking

Uptown Espresso (☎ 805-783-1300; 1065 Higuera St; ☺ 5:30am-11pm) Dose up at the 'home of the velvet foam.' There's free wi-fi and a double-sided fireplace.

Mccarthy's (805-544-0268; 1019 Court St) This post-age stamp of an Irish pub just off Higuera earns fierce loyalty – both from its gruffly friendly bartenders, some of whom sport tattoos in honor of the joint, and its patrons; don't be surprised if the guy next to you is perched on the same stool his grandfather fell off of two generations ago. Incredibly, Mccarthy's was Jameson Whiskey's largest US account in 2005. Cash only, and no dancing allowed.

Frog & Peach Pub (☎ 805-595-3764; 728 Higuera St) Dark and musty, this near-dive is the place for a game of darts among an eclectic crowd. Tuesdays showcase beer specials. The pub books the occasional band; if it's crap, chill on the back patio.

Downtown Brewing Co (☎ 805-543-1843; 1119 Garden St) More often called just SLO Brew, this study in rafters and exposed brick has plenty of homemade beers to go with its upscale pub grub (Tuesday to Sunday). Downstairs, you'll find live music along the lines of Camper Van Beethoven or Refugee All-Stars most nights. Catch dollar pints on Tuesdays after 9pm.

Tortilla Flats (☎ 805-544-7575; 1051 Nipomo St) By day, the Flats is a passable Mexican restaurant. Night brings the booty-shaking. Its schedule's always in flux, but there's usually salsa on Sundays, and queer nights several times a week.

Entertainment

Palm Theatre (☎ 805-541-5161; 817 Palm St) The country's first solar-powered movie theater (cool!), this old-style movie house showcases foreign and indie films. Tickets are a few bucks off on Mondays.

Cal Poly Performing Arts Center (PAC; ☎ 805-756-2787; www.pacslo.org; 1 Grand Ave) This state-of-the-art facility is the town's main cultural venue and presents an eclectic schedule of concerts, theater and dance.

Sunset Drive-In (☎ 805-544-4475; 255 Elks Ln; adult/child 6-11 $6/2; ☼ summer only) Never made out at a drive in? Here's your chance. The movies are mindless summer blockbusters. Right across the highway from the Madonna Inn.

Getting There & Around

Greyhound (☎ 805-543-2121; 150 South St) runs daily buses to Los Angeles ($32, five hours) via Santa Barbara ($19.50, two hours), and to San Francisco ($40.50, seven hours).

San Luis Obispo's **Regional Transit Authority** (RTA; ☎ 805-541-2228; www.slorta.org; fares $1-2.50) operates buses daily except Sunday across the region, including Paso Robles, San Simeon, Cambria, Morro Bay and the bay cities including Pismo Beach. Lines converge on the **transit hub** (cnr Palm & Osos Sts).

Amtrak (1011 Railroad Ave) has good train service at SLO. The *Pacific Surfliner* train serves Santa Barbara ($25), Los Angeles ($30) and San Diego ($45). The Seattle–LA *Coast Starlight* stops at SLO daily. There are several daily buses that link to regional trains in Santa Barbara and San Jose.

SAN LUIS OBISPO BAY

This broad bay is home to a string of laid-back, little beach towns including Avila Beach and Pismo Beach. If you're looking for a sandy respite from your trip, this is a good spot to break the journey.

Getting There & Away

San Luis Obispo's RTA (see left) operates buses from SLO to the bay cities including Pismo Beach. Hwy 1 ends its brief relationship with Hwy 101 that began in SLO just south of Pismo Beach as it veers off to stay near the coast.

Avila Beach

pop 836

Quiet, sunny Avila (*ah*-vi-la) Beach has had a rough decade. In the late 1980s it was discovered that for decades pipes from the nearby Unocal refinery and port had been leaking into the soil, massively contaminating it with a toxic soup of petroleum products. In 1999 Unocal began a legal settlement that involved tearing down the town and carting off the beach. The crowds were lured back by the freshly built seafront commercial district and new sand on the beaches. Then a fatal shark attack in 2003 scared them off again, but only temporarily. Barring any new catastrophe – or shark sightings – Avila's upswing is underway. The **Avila Beach Trolley** loops around town on weekends. The **Fish & Farmer's Market** (☼ 4-8pm Fri) is on the southernmost pier.

About 1 mile north of the center is **Port San Luis**, a working fishing harbor. The barking of sea lions will serenade you as you stroll **Harford Pier**, one of the most authentic fishing piers on the coast. At the tip of the pier is the seafood restaurant **Olde Port Inn** (☎ 805-595-2515; mains $12-26), with glass-top tables so diners can see down into the water. Next door, the unpretentious **Pete's Pierside Cafe** (mains $4-16) has some of everything,

CENTRAL COAST

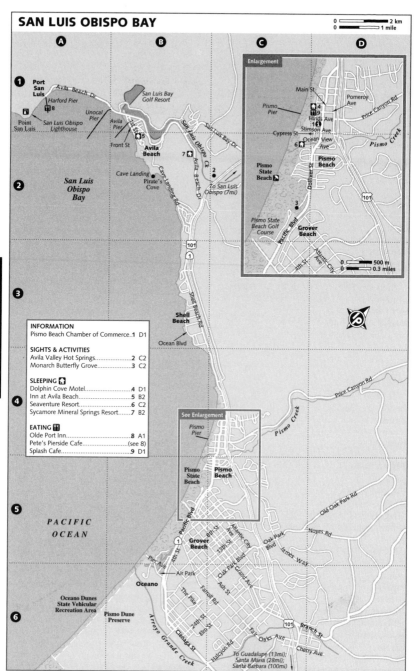

SAN LUIS OBISPO BAY

0 —————— 2 km
0 —————— 1 mile

Port San Luis
Avila Beach Dr
San Luis Bay Golf Resort
Harford Pier
Point San Luis
San Luis Obispo Lighthouse
Unocal Pier
Avila Pier
Front St
Avila Beach
San Luis Bay Dr
San Luis Obispo Cr.
To San Luis Obispo (7mi)
Cave Landing
Pirate's Cove
Cave Landing Rd
Avila Beach Dr

San Luis Obispo Bay

Shell Beach
Shell Beach Rd
Ocean Blvd

PACIFIC
OCEAN

101
1

Price Canyon Rd
Pismo Creek

See Enlargement
Pismo Pier
Pismo State Beach
Pismo Beach

Old Oak Park Rd
Price Canyon Rd

Pacific Blvd
Grover Beach
1
Pier Ave
Air Park
Oceano
The Pike
Fairoff Rd
Ash St
Oak Park Blvd
Grand Ave
Oak Park Blvd
Oak Park Blvd
Noyes Rd
Atlantic City
13th St
8th St
4th St
James Way

Oceano Dunes State Vehicular Recreation Area
Pismo Dune Preserve
Arroyo Grande Creek
Cienaga St
Elm St
24th St
Halcyon Rd
Fair Oaks Ave
101
Branch St
Cherry Ave
To Guadalupe (13mi);
Santa Maria (28mi);
Santa Barbara (100mi)

Enlargement

Main St
Pismo Pier
Pomeroy Ave
Price Canyon Rd
Cypress St
Hinds Ave
Stimson Ave
Ocean View Ave
Pismo Creek
Pismo State Beach
Pismo Beach
Dolliver St
101
Pismo State Beach Golf Course
Pacific Blvd
Grover Beach
4th St
Atlantic City Ave

0 —————— 500 m
0 —————— 0.3 miles

INFORMATION
Pismo Beach Chamber of Commerce...1 D1

SIGHTS & ACTIVITIES
Avila Valley Hot Springs.................2 C2
Monarch Butterfly Grove.................3 C2

SLEEPING 🏠
Dolphin Cove Motel.........................4 D1
Inn at Avila Beach...........................5 B2
Seaventure Resort...........................6 C2
Sycamore Mineral Springs Resort...7 B2

EATING 🍴
Olde Port Inn.................................8 A1
Pete's Pierside Cafe.......................(see 8)
Splash Cafe...................................9 D1

including fresh oysters sliced open in front of you and an excellent salsa bar to doctor up your fish taco with.

The pier is also home to **fish markets** that sell rockfish, sole, salmon or anything else right off the boats.

Just south of Avila Beach, **Cave Landing** is a 150ft promontory used as a dock for large ships in the early 1900s. A rocky trail from the parking lot's southern end leads down to the cave and to **Pirate's Cove**, a beautiful sandy beach where clothing is optional and personal caution is urged. From Avila Beach Dr going east, take a right on Cave Landing Rd.

In town, the **Inn at Avila Beach** (☎ 805-595-2300; www.avilabeachca.com; 256 Front St; r $90-210; 🖳) has a cheerful mix of Mediterranean and Mexican styles, with vibrant colors, handpainted tiles and wrought iron. Its roof deck is kitted out with TVs, grills, hammocks and other toys. Rooms span the gamut, so shop and compare.

Melt away your tensions in a private hot mineral spa at the **Sycamore Mineral Springs Resort** (☎ 805-595-7302; www.sycamoresprings.com; 1215 Avila Beach Dr; r $169-449; 🔀 🖳 🎇). Even if you're not staying at the resort, you can treat yourself in one of 20 private redwood hot tubs ($20 per hour), scattered over a woodsy hillside. They're open 24 hours.

For those less flush with cash, the nearby **Avila Valley Hot Springs** (☎ 805-595-2359; 250 Avila Beach Dr; adult/child $9/7; 🕑 8am-8pm; 🚼), in operation since 1907, features a slightly sulphuric, lukewarm swimming pool, with a pretty cool tube slide.

Pismo Beach
pop 8419
Pismo Beach, the largest of the bay towns, fronts a more commercial, more party-hearty visage than neighboring Avila, but its beach is still wide and sandy. The town still likes to call itself the 'Clam Capital of the World,' but these days, the beach is pretty much clammed out.

Now, butterflies are Pismo's most prevalent animal attraction. Tens of thousands of migrating monarch butterflies descend upon the town between late November and March, making their winter home in the secluded **Monarch Butterfly Grove**. Forming dense clusters in the tops of eucalyptus and pine trees, these creatures are easily mistaken for leaves. Free access to the grove is via the Pismo State Beach North Beach Campground, south of town off Hwy 1.

For information visit the **Pismo Beach Chamber of Commerce** (☎ 805-773-4382; www.pismochamber.com; 581 Dolliver St; 🕑 9am-5pm Mon-Sat, 10am-4pm Sun).

SLEEPING & EATING
Dolphin Cove Motel (☎ 805-773-4706; www.dolphincovemotel.com; 170 Main St; r $80-180) This friendly property has 21 basic rooms with fridges. Room 8 is the only one with a deck, which is why it was the one James Dean always chose for his congo-drum sessions and trysts with Pier Angeli. You must be at least 21 years old to rent a room.

Seaventure Resort (☎ 805-773-4994; www.seaventure.com; 100 Ocean View Ave; r $129-449; 🔀 🖳 🎇) The motel-ish decor leaves some guests kvetching about the price, but if you score an oceanside room you'll be too distracted by the view from your balcony to care. The staff is ever so accommodating and the use of beach cruisers and beach chairs is complimentary, as is the continental breakfast.

Splash Cafe (☎ 805-773-4653; 197 Pomeroy Ave; mains $4-8; 🕑 10am-9pm) Lines go out and wrap around this boisterous veteran hole-in-the-wall that makes award-winning clam chowder – in a sourdough bread bowl, naturally – and a long lineup of grilled and fried briny delights. It's open shorter hours in winter.

Guadalupe
Though a mere 16 miles south of Pismo Beach, you almost expect to have to dodge tumbleweed as you drive into the one-road agricultural town of Guadalupe. It's a quirky place, best known as the jumping-off point for sand dune exploration, but worth an hour or two outside dune duty. One of the town's main landmarks is the huge **Gold Medal Flour mural** taking up an entire building side. Passers-through assume it's a relic of the 19th century, but in fact it was painted to intentionally look old for the shooting of *Odd Couple 2* in 1997. If you're up for a shot of local lore, go chat with John, the proprietor of the **Napa Auto & Antiques**, whose store is under the mural and doubles as a local museum. Hours are at John's whim. There's also the official **Guadalupe Historical Museum** (☎ 805-343-5901; 1005 Guadalupe St; 🕑 1-3pm Sat & Sun). Ask there about the Guadalupe raid.

The excellent **Dunes Center** (☎ 805-343-2455; www.dunescenter.org; 1055 Guadalupe St; 🕑 10am-4pm Tue-Sun) gives out information on visiting the largest coastal dunes on the continent, which take up 18 miles and are up to a half-mile deep in places. The center has exhibits about their ecology as well as a half-dozen films – including one on the Dunites, the mysterious folks who called the dunes home during the 1930s. The Dunes Center will open its hugely expanded visitors center in 2008.

One of the several areas to 'barge' up the dunes (the technical verb for the activity) is the **Rancho Guadalupe Dunes Preserve** (admission free). From Hwy 1 south, turn right onto Hwy 166 at the cemetery. Go 3 miles, pass the kiosk and the sand factory, and you'll soon dead-end into the parking lot. Mussel Rock, the highest coastal dune in the country at 500ft, is a 25-minute walk south from the parking lot.

The dunes are also famous for being the site of the **Lost City of DeMille** (www.lostcitydemille.com). In 1923 a huge Hollywood crew came to the sands for the filming of Cecil B DeMille's remake of *The Ten Commandments*. Enormous sets were constructed complete with huge sphinxes and more. After filming, DeMille saved money by leaving the sets in place and burying them in the sand. Over the following decades legends about the lost wonders of Egypt – albeit ones constructed from plaster, hay and paint – swirled like sand in a dune wind.

Starting in 1983 a team began looking for what has become known as the Lost City of DeMille. Numerous artifacts have been found and the location of the main structures pinpointed. Now all that needs to happen is for funds to be found to excavate the enormous sets. Depending on the direction of the wind, you can sometimes see small pieces of the set on your way to the Rancho Guadalupe Dunes Preserve. On your left as you crest the hill

after the sand factory, they'll look like broken pieces of wood and foam, though better examples can be seen up close at the Dunes Center. Check out the website for current information on the excavations.

Back in town, slide into a cowhide booth and order up a steak at the **Far Western Tavern**, just past the Napa Supply Store. It covers its bases by pairing a jukebox and sports-blaring TV with velvet wallpaper and candlelit tables.

There's no lodging in Guadalupe. (The building with 'hotel' painted on it houses farm workers.)

Amtrak (barely) maintains a station at 330 Guadalupe St, but there's no ticket office, so be sure to buy a round-trip ticket, which from San Luis Obispo is $20.

SANTA BARBARA AREA

Frankly put, this area is damn pleasant to putter around. Chic, Mediterranean-style Santa Barbara anchors the region, with a superb and appropriately photogenic wine country to the north, the unspoilt Channel Islands National Park to the south, and quirky enclaves like New Agey Ojai to the east and Danish-esque Solvang to the west. Or, don't even leave the beaches of Santa Barbara – plenty of people don't.

SOLVANG
pop 5141

Oh, Solvang. In 1911 bona fide Danes did indeed found the town – and start a folk school for the preservation of Danish heritage – but

---

A WINE COUNTRY PRIMER

Though large-scale winemaking has only been happening here since the 1980s, Santa Barbara's climate has always been perfect for growing grapes. Two parallel, east–west-trending mountain ranges (the Santa Ynez and the San Rafael) cradle the region and funnel coastal fog eastward off the Pacific into the valleys between. The further inland you go, the warmer it gets. At the shore, fog and low clouds can hover all day, keeping the weather downright chilly, even in July, while only a few miles inland, temperatures can soar a full 30°F hotter, sometimes approaching 100°F in mid-July. These delicately balanced microclimates support two major varieties of grape.

Near the coast in the Santa Maria Valley, pinot noir – a particularly fragile grape – and other Burgundian varieties thrive in the fog. Inland in the warmer Santa Ynez Valley, where there can be as much as a 50°F variance in temperatures from day to night, Rhône-style grapes do best; these include syrah, morvedre, and viognier. Bordeaux-styles wines, such as cabernet franc and cabernet sauvignon, get a bad rap in Santa Barbara County, and are usually associated only with Napa, Sonoma and Alexander Counties in Northern California. Nonetheless, there are a few pockets in the Santa Ynez Valley where you'll find some fine cabernet franc, often at good prices, too.

the intervening decades have seen Solvang (loosely meaning Sunny Field) cash in hard on its euro-charm. Grumpy families and charmed blue-hairs plod down the main drag of Copenhagen Dr, which is lined with over-priced trinket shops and fronted with faux-Scandinavian facades featuring Danish flags and nonoperational windmills. It's a Danish Disneyland without the rides, but nonetheless strangely irresistible to chasers of kitsch and those in need of some exercise in the eye-rolling department. You'll be most susceptible to Solvang's appeal at dusk, with the day-trippers gone and the strings of white lights illuminated, outlining the town's silhouette.

The **Elverhøj Museum** (☎ 805-686-1211; cnr 2nd St & Elverhoy Way; admission by donation; ☺ 12:30-4pm Wed-Sun) is one of the only spots in town where you can learn about what real Danish life in the area was like. Check out its 'farmer's door.' One of the better of Solvang's many bakeries is **Solvang Restaurant** (☎ 805-688-4645; 1672 Copenhagen Dr; mains $3-13; ☺ breakfast & lunch) which does brisk business in *aebleskivers* (though it means 'apple slice,' it's like a round glazed doughnut) as well as typical diner fare. It's also where Jack

proclaims his prenuptial intentions to Miles in the movie *Sideways*.

For a more modern bite, **Panino** (☎ 805-688-0608; 475 1st St, sandwiches $7.50) does excellent gourmet sandwiches, with plenty for vegetarians.

Solvang is 3 miles east of Buellton along Hwy 246.

SANTA BARBARA
pop 86,000

Just an hour's drive north of Los Angeles, Santa Barbara basks smugly in its near-perfection. It's blessed with almost freakishly good weather, a stunning masterpiece of a courthouse, and a backdrop of mountains to complement its foreground of ocean. And that's not to mention what's apparent as soon as you drive into town: the remarkable architectural matching. After a 1925 earthquake leveled the downtown, planners chose to go with a Mediterranean-style rebuild, thus the city's trademark red-tile roofs, whitewashed adobe walls and strings of palm trees. Some view this consistency as aesthetically calming, others as stifling and uncreative. Regardless, no one can deny the real appeal of the public beaches that line the

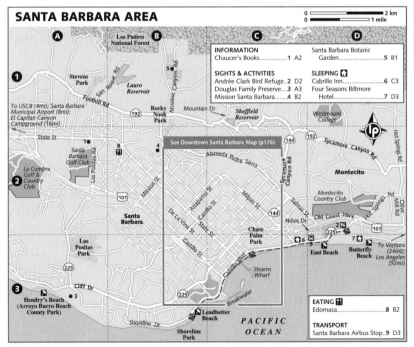

SANTA BARBARA AREA

INFORMATION		SLEEPING
Chaucer's Books...........1 A2	Santa Barbara Botanic Garden..........5 B1	Cabrillo Inn..........6 C3
SIGHTS & ACTIVITIES		Four Seasons Biltmore
Andrée Clark Bird Refuge..2 D2		Hotel..........7 D3
Douglas Family Preserve....3 A3		
Mission Santa Barbara......4 B2		EATING
		Edomasa..........8 B2
		TRANSPORT
		Santa Barbara Airbus Stop..9 D3

CENTRAL COAST

city tip to toe. Just ignore those pesky oil derricks out to sea.

Orientation

Downtown Santa Barbara is laid out in a square grid, its main drag being State St, which runs roughly northwest–southeast. Unless you're keen for a slow tour, don't use State St as your uptown–downtown connector – you'll hit a light every 30ft or so. Lower State St (south of Ortega St) has a large concentration of cafés and bars, while upper State St (north of Ortega St) has most of the shops. Palm-lined Cabrillo Blvd hugs the coastline and turns into Coast Village Rd as it enters the suburb of Montecito.

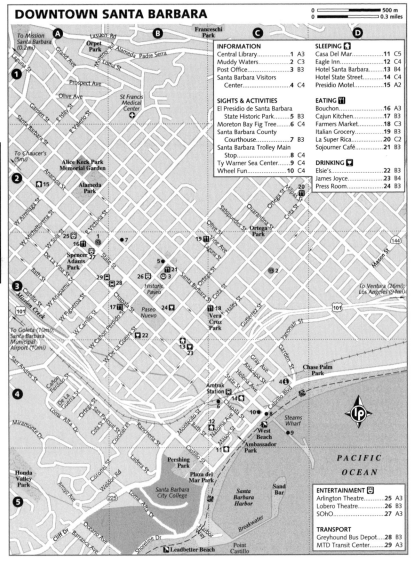

DOWNTOWN SANTA BARBARA

0   500 m
0   0.3 miles

INFORMATION
Central Library.......................1 A3
Muddy Waters......................2 C3
Post Office...........................3 B3
Santa Barbara Visitors
    Center..............................4 C4

SIGHTS & ACTIVITIES
El Presidio de Santa Barbara
    State Historic Park.........5 B3
Moreton Bay Fig Tree........6 C4
Santa Barbara County
    Courthouse...................7 B3
Santa Barbara Trolley Main
    Stop..............................8 C4
Ty Warner Sea Center.......9 C4
Wheel Fun.........................10 C4

SLEEPING
Casa Del Mar....................11 C5
Eagle Inn..........................12 C4
Hotel Santa Barbara.........13 B4
Hotel State Street.............14 C4
Presidio Motel...................15 A2

EATING
Bouchon...........................16 A3
Cajun Kitchen...................17 B3
Farmers Market................18 C3
Italian Grocery..................19 B3
La Super Rica....................20 C2
Sojourner Café..................21 B3

DRINKING
Elsie's...............................22 B3
James Joyce......................23 B4
Press Room.......................24 B3

ENTERTAINMENT
Arlington Theatre.............25 A3
Lobero Theatre.................26 B3
SOhO................................27 A3

TRANSPORT
Greyhound Bus Depot.....28 B3
MTD Transit Center.........29 A3

Santa Barbara is surrounded by small, affluent communities: Hope Ranch to the west, Montecito the east. UCSB is just west of Hope Ranch in Isla Vista, and most of Santa Barbara's college crowd lives around the campus or in neighboring Goleta (go-*lee*-ta).

Information

BOOKSTORES

Chaucer's Books (Map p175; ☎ 805-682-6782; 3321 State St) Knowledgeable staff, and floor to ceiling with new books.

INTERNET ACCESS

There are scads of access spots in town. Here are two:

Central Library (Map p176; ☎ 805-962-7653; 40 E Anapamu St) Free use of computers for nonresidents, plus wi-fi.

Muddy Waters (Map p176; ☎ 831-966-9328; 58 E Haley St; per 30min $3; ⊙ 6am-6pm Mon-Sat, also 8pm-midnight Fri & Sat) Wi-fi, plus a computer where you can surf the Net. A good place to find out what the young artsy crowd is up to. Cash only.

MEDICAL SERVICES

Santa Barbara Cottage Hospital (Map p175; ☎ 805-682-7111; cnr Pueblo & Bath Sts; ⊙ 24hr)

POST

Post office (Map p176; ☎ 805-564-2226; 836 Anacapa St; ⊙ 8am-6pm Mon-Fri, 9am-5pm Sat)

TOURIST INFORMATION

Santa Barbara Visitors Center (Map p176; ☎ 805-965-3021; www.santabarbaraca.com; 1 Garden St; ⊙ 9am-5pm Mon-Sat, 10am-5pm Sun) Excellent service with maps and brochures.

Sights

SANTA BARBARA COUNTY COURTHOUSE

If you've only time – or patience – for one 'attraction', make it the **courthouse** (Map p176; ☎ 805-962-6464; 1100 Anacapa St; admission free; ⊙ info desk 8:30am-4:30pm), often called the most beautiful government building in the country. The L-shaped structure, built in 1929 in the Spanish-Moorish castle style, features hand-painted ceilings, tiles from Tunisia and Spain, gorgeously kept grounds and the best view of the city from El Mirador, the 85ft clock tower. You must peek your head into the law library, with its vaulted blue ceiling covered in golden stars. Breathtaking. You're free to explore the courthouse on your own, but the best way to

see it is on a free docent-led tour regularly at 2pm Monday to Saturday, and a few days at 10am as well.

MISSION SANTA BARBARA

Called the 'Queen of the Missions,' **Mission Santa Barbara** (Map p175; ☎ 805-682-4713; www.sbmission.org; 2201 Laguna St; adult/child $4/free; ⊙ 9am-5pm) sits on a hilltop perch half a mile north of downtown. It was established on December 4 (the feast day of St Barbara) in 1786, as the 10th California mission, though the current pink sandstone version dates only from 1820. It's the only California mission to have twin bell towers as well as the sole one to have been occupied without interruption by the Franciscans since its founding. To the side is an extensive cemetery where an estimated 4000 Chumash (*shoe*-mash) are buried in unmarked graves. The **Madonnari Italian Street Painting Festival** over Memorial Day weekend (late May or early June) blankets the mission's parking lot with astonishing chalk drawings, which last for as long as the weather and the trampling feet allow.

EL PRESIDIO DE SANTA BARBARA STATE HISTORIC PARK

The former Spanish **fort** (Map p176; ☎ 805-966-9719; E Cañon Perdido St btwn Anacapa & Santa Barbara Sts; adult/child $3/free; ⊙ 10:30am-4:30pm) was founded in 1782 to protect the missions between Monterey and San Diego, and work is underway to restore it to its 18th-century condition, when it was Spain's last military stronghold in California as well as the town's social and political hub. Be sure to visit the chapel, with an interior that

---

THE MORETON BAY FIG TREE

Near the corner of Montecito and Chapala Sts stands the imposing Moreton Bay fig tree (Map p176). The story goes, in 1876 an Australian sailor gave a local girl a seed as a token of his affection, and a year later another girl replanted it in its present location. (Did the first girl die of a broken heart?) The tree is believed to be the largest of its kind in North America; not only is it a whopping 78ft tall, but it has a 171ft canopy, reputedly enough to provide shade to 1000 people at a time. The tree used to provide shelter to Santa Barbara's homeless population, who were dubbed 'tree people'; some even tried to use the tree as a mailing address.

explodes in kaleidoscopic color and features some interesting trompe l'oeil effects.

SANTA BARBARA BOTANIC GARDEN
This stunner of a **botanic garden** (Map p175; ☎ 805-682-4726; www.sbbg.org; 1212 Mission Canyon Rd; adult/child 13-17/child 2-12 $8/6/4; ☺ 9am-sunset) is devoted to the native plants of California. About 5.5 miles of trails meander through cacti, redwoods and wildflowers. Around 23 of the garden's 78 acres have recently been granted County Historic Landmark recognition, including the old mission dam and aqueduct, built by the Chumash to irrigate the mission's fields.

LOTUSLAND
The eccentric Madame Ganna Walka bought the 37 acres that make up **Lotusland** (☎ 805-969-9990; www.lotusland.org; adult/child under 10 $20/10; ☺ tours 10am & 1:30pm Wed-Sat Feb-Nov) in 1941, with

money from the fortunes she inherited after marrying – and then divorcing – a string of wealthy men. She spent the next four decades tending and expanding her incredible collection of plants. On the grounds are 170 varieties of aloe alone, and the cycad garden is packed with rare species. Reservations are required for the intimate tours. The phone is attended from 9am to noon on weekdays only; call ahead to reserve tours and receive directions on how to find the garden.

THE WATERFRONT
At the southern end of State St, the entrance to **Stearns Wharf** (Map p176) is marked by a sculpture of three dolphins – an identical one is in Puerta Vallarta, Mexico, SB's sister city. Built in 1872, the wharf is the oldest one continuously operating on the West Coast. On the wharf is the **Ty Warner Sea Center** (Map p176; ☎ 805-962-2526;

DRIVING TOUR: HWY 154 & THE SANTA BARBARA WINE COUNTRY

What to See
Santa Barbara's Wine Country (Map p287), made up of the Santa Maria and Santa Ynez Valleys, unfurls along winding country lanes amid oak-dotted rolling hills that stretch for miles. If you're pressed for time (haha), plan to visit only the Santa Ynez Valley, which is closer to Santa Barbara and has the highest concentration of wineries. The charming town of **Los Olivos** is the center of the area's wine country, and there you'll find the **Los Olivos Tasting Room** (☎ 805-668-7406; 2905 Grand Ave), the state's first independent tasting room, which specializes in pinot noir you can't find anywhere else. Family-run **Sunstone Winery & Vineyards** (☎ 805-688-9463; 125 Refugio Rd; tastings $5; ☺ 10am-4pm) does bang-up merlot, and all its grapes are grown organically and bio-sustainably. Back on Hwy 154, you'll skirt **Lake Cachuma**, its handful of trails beckoning you to walk off your wine buzz. Hungry yet? The legendary **Cold Spring Tavern** (☎ 805-967-0066; 5595 Stagecoach Rd; ☺ 11am) was a stagecoach stop on a woodsy curve of the road that still functions as a relay station of sorts. Leather-clad bikers, young families and smart-looking couples form crowds in the bar, at the restaurant and BBQ-side. There's music on Sunday afternoons. Back on Hwy 154, make a quick detour to gaze at the 400-plus-year-old pictographs at the **Chumash Painted Cave State Historic Park** (☎ 805-733-3713; www.parks.ca.gov; ☺ dawn-dusk). The cave is protected by a metal screen, so bring a flashlight for a decent view.

The Route
Hwy 154 (San Marcos Pass Rd) heads south from Hwy 101, 6 miles north of Buellton and 35 winding miles later deposits you back onto 101 just a few miles northwest of downtown Santa Barbara. Hwy 154 will take you directly into Los Olivos, and Refugio Rd goes due south – via Robler Rd – to hit the Sunstone Winery. To get back on Hwy 154, backtrack north a mile or so, take 246 east, which will hit 154. From there it's a straight shoot to Santa Barbara, not counting the minor turn-offs if you want to visit Cold Spring Tavern (turn right onto Stagecoach Rd just past the San Marcos Bridge, and follow it 1.5 miles into the canyon) or the Chumash Painted Cave (look for the turn-off to Painted Cave Rd, about 8 miles north of Santa Barbara.)

Time & Mileage
This route covers around 40 miles, but with all the stops (and the engine-straining mountain inclines) you could – and should – make a day of it.

adult/child 13-17/child under 13 $7/6/4; ⊙ 10am-5pm; ♿), which takes you up close and personal with the ocean. The coolest exhibit is the crawl tunnel through a 1500-gallon surge tank.

Activities
BEACHES
Long and sandy and equipped with a playground, **East Beach** (Map p175) is the stretch between Stearns Wharf and Montecito, and is Santa Barbara's most popular beach. Chic **Butterfly Beach** (Map p175), at its eastern end, is across from the Four Seasons Biltmore Hotel.

Between Stearns Wharf and the harbor, **West Beach** (Map p176) has calm water and is popular with families. On the other side of the harbor, **Leadbetter Beach** is a good spot for beginning surfers and windsurfers. Climbing the stairs on the west end takes you to **Shoreline Park** (Map p175), with picnic tables, stunning views and awesome kite-flying conditions.

West of Santa Barbara near the junction of Cliff Dr and Las Positas Rd, **Hendry's Beach** (Map p175), whose official name is Arroyo Burro Beach County Park, has free parking and a good restaurant. Above the beach is the **Douglas Family Preserve** (Map p175), with cliffside strolls for humans and dogs. The land was slated for development (you can still find some street curbs and drains) and residents despaired of raising the funds to save it – until an 11th-hour donation by actor Michael Douglas.

CYCLING & SKATING
The Cabrillo Blvd **beachfront bike path** runs for 3 miles along the water, between Andrée Clark Bird Refuge and Leadbetter Beach. The **Goleta Bikeway** continues west to UCSB. Ask local bikers for more details of local routes.

Wheel Fun (Map p176; ☎ 805-966-2282; www.wheel funrentals.com; 23 E Cabrillo Blvd) rents bikes, surreys and in-line skates.

Tours
The **Red Tile Tour** is a self-guided 12-block walking tour that's an excellent way to take in all major downtown sights and historic landmarks, including the Santa Barbara County Courthouse, Museum of Art, Historical Museum and El Presidio. Pick up a free map from the visitors center.

Santa Barbara Trolley (Map p176; ☎ 805-965-0353; www.sbtrolley.com; adult/child 13-17 $18/9) makes a narrated 105-minute loop past Stearns Wharf, the

courthouse, the botanical garden, the mission and sights in between. Tickets are valid all day between 10am and 4pm, allowing you to get off and on as you please. Order online and get a few bucks off.

Sleeping
Don't show up in Santa Barbara and expect to find a cheap room at the last minute, especially on weekends.

BUDGET
A number of fairly affordable motels, especially in the off season, cluster along upper State St near Las Positas Rd.

Presidio Motel (Map p176; ☎ 805-963-1355; www .thepresidiomotel.com; 1620 State St; r incl continental breakfast $70-150; ℗ ⊠ 💻) Just north of downtown, this great little motel has hotel aspirations, with charming staff and crisp, modern rooms that break the Super 8 mold – wonderful beds, unique art on the walls and high plank ceilings. The sundeck is perfect for mountain gazing (never mind busy State St below). Free wi-fi.

Hotel State Street (Map p176; ☎ 805-966-6586; 121 State St; r $79-105; ℗ 💻) Despite the whimsical origami cranes hanging from the lobby ceiling, this 52-room hotel has a slight institutional feel. The price and location are hard to beat, though you'll be sharing a bathroom. Rooms are clean (the bathrooms can be less so) and many have big windows, a sink and TV, but no phone. Only two blocks to the beach, and even closer to the railroad tracks – complimentary wake-up call courtesy the 7am train.

MIDRANGE
There's a host of midrange places in the blocks behind West Beach. Castillo St can be busy, streets such as Bath St further in are not.

Cabrillo Inn (Map p175; ☎ 805-966-1641; www.cabrillo -inn.com; 931 Cabrillo Blvd; r $129-199; ℗ 💻) Great value for families – the two pools don't hurt either – this large motel right on the beach on the east side has rooms heavy on florals and carpet, but most have at least a partial ocean view.

Hotel Santa Barbara (Map p176; ☎ 805-957-9300, 888-259-7700; www.hotelsantabarbara.com; 533 State St; r $160-270; ℗ ⊠ 💻) Right in the heart of downtown, this classic, restored 1926 hotel has 75 yellow-and-blue Cal-Med rooms, and a staff that goes the extra mile. Guests get their own newspaper to peruse during breakfast. The less expensive rooms can be on the small side.

Eagle Inn (Map p176; ☎ 805-965-3586; www.theeagle inn.com; 232 Natoma Ave; r incl continental breakfast $137-220; P) The flowery decor of the rooms doesn't quite match up with the exterior's elegant tile-and-whitewash Mission style, but a mere two blocks from the beach on a residential street, this cozy 23-room inn is a fine choice for those looking for some quietude. Some rooms come with a balcony, gas fireplace and a Jacuzzi.

Casa Del Mar (Map p176; ☎ 805-963-4418; www.casa delmar.com; 18 Bath St; r $169-279) Half a block from the sand – though not sporting any ocean views – this 1920s Spanish-style inn is a small gem. The 21 rooms vary greatly – some have kitchenettes or fireplaces, and there are suites ideal for families – but all soothe the soul with pure white bedspreads, clean lines and flat-screen TVs. Soothe the stomach at the buffet breakfast and evening wine and cheese. Check the website for special online rates.

El Capitan Canyon Campground (☎ 805-685-3887; 11560 Calle Real; safari tents $135, cabins $185-345; P ▣) Situated 17 miles west of downtown on 3500 dazzling acres between the mountains and the beach, El Capitan is for those who love to camp but hate to wake up with dirt under their nails. The amenities in the tents and cabins vary – some have fireplaces, decks and Jacuzzis – but all feature high-thread-count sheets on beds to die for, and private BBQ pits. Cars are stashed away from the lodgings, so kids can dart to and fro, and adults can mingle. The Upper Meadow sites are the most secluded. Follow a horseback-riding tour with an on-site massage.

TOP END

Four Seasons Biltmore Hotel (Map p175; ☎ 805-969-2261, 800-332-3442; www.fourseasons.com; 1260 Channel Dr; r $500-800; P ▨ ▣ ▣) When a place throws down $250 million on a renovation (bank-rolled by Beanie Baby billionaire Ty Warner, no less), one expects perfection down to the de-tail, and that's just what the Biltmore delivers. With more proprietary and lavish elements than you can shake a swizzle stick at – note the wine-bottle stained glass in the lobby, the ceiling dusted with 23-karat gold to catch the light just so, the tiled Islamic foot bath, picture-window views at every turn – the Biltmore is worth a visit. Even if you don't stay here, stroll its 22 acres (which happen to be home to an impressive collection of rare botanica), sip a cocktail on the terrace or indulge in a spa treatment while overlooking the ocean. Guests are often of the honeymoon and anniversary variety (Room 703 boasts one of the few ocean view balconies) while the fantastically expensive detached cottages and suites attract celebs looking to hide out.

Eating

Santa Barbara doesn't (yet) push the envelope when it comes to daring, creative cuisine, but they've got the standards down pat, and have excellent offerings for every budget.

our pick La Super Rica (Map p176; ☎ 805-963-4940; 622 N Milpas St; dishes under $6; ⏰ 11am-9pm, to 9:30pm Fri & Sat) You'll see the line roping around this half-shack, half-tent institution before you see any sign. But the queue goes fast, and you'd better be snappy with your order when the time comes, though it's easy to be distracted watching the hands flying and the tortillas smoking in the cubicle-sized kitchen. This was Julia Child's all-time-favorite Mexican restaurant, and I like to imagine her with the copious amounts of peanut oil they use dripping off her chin. Try one of the creative daily specials, or on Friday or Saturday get the famous tamales. One downer: vegetarians won't starve, but options are slim.

Italian Grocery (Map p176; ☎ 805-966-6041; 415 E de la Guerre St; torpedoes $4-5.50; ⏰ 9am-6pm Mon-Sat, 10am-2pm Sun) Tino's, as it's often known to locals (who will kill me for letting outsiders know about this place) does the best damn subs – or torpedoes – in town, and has a deli counter that makes grown Italian men weep with pleasure.

Cajun Kitchen (Map p176; ☎ 805-965-1004; 901 Chapala St; mains $5-8; ⏰ breakfast & lunch) One of the best – and easiest on the wallet – breakfast spots in town, it's got the requisite gigantic menu (veg-etarians have at least eight omelettes to choose from), as well as authentic Cajun creations like crawfish *etoufée*. Watch the short-order cooks do their stuff through big windows.

Sojourner Cafe (Map p176; ☎ 805-965-7922; 134 E Cañon Perdido; mains $7-17; ⏰ 11am-11pm, to 10pm Sun; V) With origami boxes hanging from the ceiling, crunchy, funky Soj has been kicking since 1978 and shows no signs of slowing down. However, it has morphed from strict vegetarianism to including fish and poultry on its Mediterranean- and Asian-heavy menu. The dessert list is infamous, and most are vegan (though you'd never guess it). Fun fact: chef Edie Robertson was in an all-girl rock band before donning her chef's hat.

Edomasa (Map p175; ☎ 805-687-0210; 2710 De La Vina St; mains $10-12; ⏰ 6pm-midnight Mon-Thu, to 1am

Fri & Sat) Edomasa manages a neighborhood feel and solid Japanese food with way less price-gouging than some other sushi places I could name. The staff is attentive, rolls are generously sized if not terribly creative, and the nonsushi dishes – like the ramen – are fabulous. And did you notice how late they stay open? Popular with the young people.

Bouchon (Map p176; ☎ 805-730-1160; 9 W Victoria St; mains $24-35; ☼ dinner) Meaning 'wine stopper' in French, convivial yet intimate Bouchon epitomizes upscale California cuisine, with mains like pear-glazed Pacific salmon. (Though some find the portion sizes un-American). Produce and meats are sourced locally from small-scale farms and the 50-plus local wines are available by the glass. Reserve a table on the patio if you and your sweetie feel like making sheep's eyes at each other.

Farmers market (Map p176; ☎ 805-962-5354; cnr Cota & Santa Barbara Sts; ☼ 8:30am-12:30pm Sat) This splendid farmers market also hosts a Tuesday version from 3pm to 7pm along the 500 and 600 blocks of State St.

Drinking

Santa Barbara's after-dark scene revolves around lower State St, though on Saturday night the street can look like a scene out of *Attack of the Preppy Clones*. Be prepared to flash your ID if you're even vaguely young looking. The Four Seasons Biltmore Hotel (opposite) is a magical spot to clutch a cocktail while overlooking the ocean.

Press Room (Map p176; ☎ 805-936-8121; 15 E Ortega St) Blessedly unpretentious, the Press Room attracts locals, Brooks photography students and a slew of European travelers. There's no better place to catch the game, stuff the jukebox and be lovingly abused by the bartender. The owner is from Manchester and is a stitch and a half, so We'll forgive the heterocentric rest-room signs.

Elsie's (Map p176; ☎ 805-963-4503; 117 De la Guerra St) Occupying an ivy-covered building, Elsie's thumbs its nose at its neighbors, the upscale chain stores of Paseo Nuevo. Her walls are covered in local art, her pool table is purple, her crowd is hip yet friendly scenesters, and her calendar is packed with open mics, open turntables, open what-have-yous. Best of all, she's got Ms Pac-Man.

James Joyce (Map p176; ☎ 805-962-2688; 513 State St) In the thick of the State St drag, this institution's most endearing quality is the inch-thick carpet of peanut shells. Live music plays every night but Monday, and the pool and dart playing is fast and furious.

Entertainment

The free weekly **Independent** (www.independent.com) has complete events listings and reviews. The **Santa Barbara News-Press** (www.newspress.com) has a daily events calendar and a Friday supplement called 'Scene' that has good dining reviews.

SOhO (Map p176; ☎ 805-962-7776; www.sohosb.com; 1221 State St) One unpretentious brick room plus scores of live music-lovers plus performances every night of the week equals SOhO, situated above a McDonald's. Lineups run from David Wilcox to Ozomatli.

Arlington Theatre (Map p176; ☎ 805-963-4408; 1317 State St) Harking back to 1931, the mission-style Arlington is a must-see for fans of classic theaters. There's a Spanish courtyard, and the gorgeous ceiling is spangled with stars. A splendid place to see a film or concert. Before Sunday matinees, the pipe organ struts its stuff.

Lobero Theatre (Map p176; ☎ 805-963-0761; 33 E Cañon Perdido St) This is one of California's oldest theaters (1873), and presents modern dance, ballet, chamber music and special events, often featuring internationally renowned talent.

Getting There & Around

If you don't use a private vehicle to get to Santa Barbara, you're eligible for a substantial discount at select hotels, plus a nice swag bag of coupons for restaurants and activities, courtesy of **Santa Barbara Car Free** (www.santabarbaracarfree.org).

Santa Barbara Municipal Airport (SBA; ☎ 805-967-7111; 500 Fowler Rd), in Goleta, is 8 miles west of downtown off Hwy 101. All major car-rental firms are here.

Santa Barbara Airbus (Map p175; ☎ 805-964-7759, 800-423-1618; www.santabarbaraairbus.com) shuttles between Los Angeles International Airport (LAX) and Santa Barbara (one way from $42, 2½ to three hours).

Greyhound (Map p176; ☎ 805-965-7551; 34 W Carrillo St) has up to nine daily buses to Los Angeles ($12.50, 2¼ to three hours) and up to five to San Francisco ($40.50, 7½ to nine hours).

Santa Barbara is a stop on the daily Seattle–LA *Coast Starlight*, run by **Amtrak** (Map p176; 209 State St). It is also the terminus for most of the frequent *Pacific Surfliner* regional trains to LA ($21, 2½ to three hours) and San Luis Obispo ($22). If you take the *Surfliner* to Santa

CENTRAL COAST

DETOUR: OJAI

Ojai (pronounced *oh*-hi, meaning 'moon' to the Chumash) is a town that has long drawn artists and New Agers. It's a local point of pride that Frank Capra chose the Ojai Valley to represent the mythical Shangri-La in his 1937 movie *Lost Horizon*, but the truth is that the valley had only four seconds of screen time. Ojai is known for the rose-colored glow that emanates from the Topa Topa mountains at sunset, the so-called Pink Moment. For information on the town, head to the **Ojai Chamber of Commerce** (☎ 805-646-8126; www.ojaichamber.org; 150 W Ojai Ave; ☻ 9:30am-4:30pm Mon-Fri, 10am-4pm Sat & Sun).

The Arcade Plaza, a maze of mission revival–style buildings on Ojai Ave contains interesting shops, cafés and art galleries. The giant tree that **Bart's Books** (☎ 805-646-3755; 302 W Matilija St; ☻ 9:30am-sunset) was built around had to be chopped down in 2006, but by the time you read this the salvaged wood may have been reconstructed into a tree-house in the same spot. Bart's is just north of Ojai Ave, and used-book-lovers will not want to miss it.

The best times to catch a Pink Moment are slightly cloudy evenings in spring and fall, and the ideal vantage point in town is the lookout at **Meditation Mount**. To get there, take a left at Boccali's (see above), then head 2.7 miles up Reeves Rd.

Ojai is also known for its number of indulgent wellness spas. The **Ojai Valley Inn & Spa** (☎ 805-646-5511, 800-422-6524; www.ojairesort.com; Country Club Rd) is a gorgeous place to pamper yourself or let others do it for you. Monday through Thursday, nonguests can pay $20 for access to its pools and other facilities, with the purchase of a treatment.

Blue Iguana Inn (☎ 805-646-5277; www.blueiguanainn.com; cnr Hwy. 33 & Loma Dr; r $99-149, ste $139-239; ☒ ☒) is a cheerful study in tile work, terracotta and southwest-style furnishings. On the west end of town, it also offers free wi-fi and memory foam pillow-top mattresses to go along with its charm.

Boccali's (☎ 805-646-6116; 3277 Ojai Ave; mains $7-15; ☻ 11:45am-9pm Wed-Sun, 4-9pm Mon & Tue), replete with red-and-white-checkered plastic tablecloths, does simple Italian and does it well. Much of the produce is grown right behind the restaurant, and excess is sold off the front porch. The tomatoes in the fresh tomato salad are often still warm. No credit cards accepted. To get here, head east from downtown two miles.

Ojai (Map p287) is about 35 miles east of Santa Barbara and 14 miles inland from Ventura off Hwy 33. The only direct bus service is from the city of Ventura. Take the **SCAT** (☎ 805-487-4222; www.scat.org) bus 16 from Main and Figueroa Sts ($1.25; 45 minutes, hourly).

Barbara, ask the conductor for your two free tickets on any MTD bus.

The **Downtown-Waterfront Shuttle** bus route ($0.25, every 10 minutes, 10am to 6pm) runs along State St to Stearns Wharf. A second route ($0.25, every 30 minutes, 10am to 6pm) travels along the waterfront between the zoo and Harbor Way.

Santa Barbara Metropolitan Transit District (MTD; ☎ 805-683-3702; www.sbmtd.gov; fares $1.25) runs buses throughout the city and surrounding county. The **MTD Transit Center** (Map p176; 1020 Chapala St) has details on routes and schedules.

CHANNEL ISLANDS NATIONAL PARK

An eight-island chain lying off the coast from Newport Beach to Santa Barbara, the Channel Islands are named for the troughs that separate them from the mainland. These four islands, along with tiny Santa Barbara island 38 miles west of San Pedro, comprise the fascinating Channel Islands National Park. Here you'll find almost 150 (mostly plant and a few animal) species not found anywhere else on the globe.

Information

National Parks Service (NPS) runs the excellent **Channel Islands National Park Visitors Center** (☎ 805-658-5730; www.nps.gov/chis; 1901 Spinnaker Dr, Ventura; ☻ 8:30am-5pm), your one-stop shop for all things Channel-related, including information on trips and a lookout from where you can see the islands on a clear day. The center is at the far tip of Ventura Harbor, off Harbor Blvd southwest of Hwy 101, via E Harbor Blvd.

Sight and Activities

Anacapa, which is actually three separate islets, is the closest to the mainland and offers a nice, easy introduction to the islands' ecology. Snorkeling, diving, swimming and kayaking are all possible in the rich kelp beds surrounding the island, and boats make the trip year-round.

Santa Cruz, the largest island, is laced with hiking trails and is probably the best island for exploring on your own. Popular activities include swimming, snorkeling, scuba diving and kayaking. Keep your eyes peeled for bald eagles, participants in a DDT-recovery release project.

Beautiful sandy beaches, nearly 200 bird species and the Painted Cave (the largest and deepest sea cave on the planet) are highlights on **Santa Rosa**, which is the best destination for longer trips.

San Miguel offers solitude and a wilderness experience, but it's often shrouded in fog and is very windy. There are interesting natural formations (eg Caliche Forest, made of calcium-carbonate castings of trees) and an elephant seal colony at Point Bennett at various times during the year.

Santa Barbara is home to the humongous northern elephant seal and is a remote playground for birds and marine wildlife. Facilities include a visitors center and a primitive campground. Hikers, bird-watchers, divers, snorkelers and anglers will all find their fill here.

Sleeping

All islands have primitive **campgrounds** (☎ reservations 800-365-2267; reservations.nps.gov; campsites $10), which are open year-round. Each one has pit toilets and picnic tables, but you must take everything in (and out). Water is only available on Santa Rosa and Santa Cruz Islands. Due to fire danger, campfires are not allowed, but enclosed camp stoves are OK. Be prepared to carry your stuff a half-mile to 1.5 miles to the campground from the landing areas.

Getting There & Away

Two boat companies offer camper transportation and excursions to the islands.

Island Packers (☎ 805-642-1393, recorded information 805-642-7688; www.islandpackers.com; 1691 Spinnaker Dr, Ventura), near the visitors center, offers numerous day trips and packages to all the islands. Rates begin at $42/25 per adult/child for the East Anacapa day trip. Going to the other islands costs more and campers pay extra for their gear. Nonlanding whale-watching tours start at $26/17 for a 3½-hour gray whale trip (January to March).

Truth Aquatics (☎ 805-962-1127; www.truthaquatics .com), the park's Santa Barbara–based operator, offers similar excursions as Island Packers.

Most trips require a minimum number of participants and may be canceled at any time due to surf and weather conditions. In any case, landing is never guaranteed, again because of changeable weather and surf conditions. Reservations are recommended for weekend, holiday and summer trips.

VENTURA
pop 104,000

Ventura, or San Buenaventura by its official name, started life as an agricultural and manufacturing center, but these days is largely a pushing-off point for adventurers to the Channel Islands (opposite). Its historic downtown along Main St supports a delightful assortment of used bookstores and ungentrified cause-supporting thrift shops – the winner of the most un-PC name: the Retarded Children's Thrift Store (it's also the best one). If you've had enough of Santa Barbarian perfection, sit back and drink in this marginally scruffy, some say supremely haunted, town. Main St is north of Hwy 101 via Seaward Ave.

The gorgeously rickety Carpenter Gothic church is now the **Victorian Rose B&B** (☎ 805-641-1888; www.victorian-rose.com; 896 E. Main St; r $99-175), but retains its original 96ft steeple. Each of the five rooms is unique, though all come with stained-glass windows, gothic furnishings... and the possibility of making the acquaintance of the resident ghosts, who have been known to offer guests foot massages.

Across the street from the mission and occupying a historic building that used to be a grocer's, upscale yet convivial **Jonathan's at Peirano's** (☎ 805-648-4853; 204 E Main St; dinner mains $17-35; ☽ lunch Tue-Sat, dinner Tue-Sun) fires off Mediterranean tapas and mains with panache. Its long and varied menu – three versions of paella, for starters – offers wine pairings for each plate, and the martini list is equally comprehensive. Make reservations for the dining room for a more intimate setting.

Greyhound (☎ 805-653-0164; 291 E Thompson Blvd) runs buses daily from LA ($12.50, 2½ hours) en route to Santa Barbara ($9.50, 40 minutes). **Amtrak** (cnr Harbor Blvd & Figueroa St) operates daily trains to Santa Barbara ($14, 40 minutes) and LA ($22, two hours).

Los Angeles & Orange County

Driving north from San Diego or south from Santa Barbara, you start to feel a vortex sucking you in. And you thought it was just the cruise control! You've just entered the throbbing jugular of Southern California, the land of countless starstruck dreams, a place never so easily defined as when it's contained in a screen. It's the nucleus of all the stereotypes borne of nearly a century of Tinseltown magic bludgeoned into our collective subconscious. Even – nay, especially – if you're one of those out-of-hand LA-haters (some of you close-minded San Franciscans out there, I'm talking to you), you've got to see la-la land for yourself.

You won't need much to act out your own LA story. Credit card, wheels, beach towel, and you're golden. What you can forget are your preconceptions. Though you'll find your share of surgically enhanced blondes and industry types weaving lanes at 80mph, Los Angeles is intensely diverse – 70% of LA county residents are not white – and the town bristles with fascinating neighborhoods and characters that have nothing to do with the 'biz'.

LA likes to think that if it's focaccia, tortillas and rice bowls, then Orange County is Wonder Bread. Well, that's part arrogance and part truth. Though the county could be generalized as a hodgepodge of suburbs, the beach towns maintain unique personalities, like surf-serious Huntington Beach and gracious Laguna Beach. And let's not forget that the OC also contains that high temple of kitsch…Disneyland.

It's a siblinglike relationship between LA and the OC. But at the end of the day, boundaries don't exist much around here. Especially in the imagination.

HIGHLIGHTS

- Watching the death-wish bodyboarders face the towering waves at the **Wedge** (p211) in Newport Beach
- Browsing the junk, treasure and everything in between on display on Long Beach's **Retro Row** (p197)
- Spending the day gazing at priceless works of art high above LA at the **Getty Center** (p195), in itself a spectacular piece of work
- Screaming through the galaxy on Space Mountain at **Disneyland** (p209), then sticking around for the fireworks display
- Joining in on the human freak parade at Ocean Front Walk in **Venice** (p196)
- Watching the sun dip below the horizon in artsy **Laguna Beach** (p213)
- Eating your way through the **Third Street Farmers Market** (p187)
- Playing 'Name that Celeb' while cruising down the star-studded streets of **Beverly Hills** (p194)

LOS ANGELES

pop 384,500

Of the beach towns, Santa Monica is the most equipped for tourists and the most accessible from Downtown, though Malibu is tops for star-spotting. Everything about Venice is colorful: the hippies, murals and boardwalk, making it an especially appealing stop. Bustling Long Beach has some big showcases in the aquarium and the Queen Mary, but what's most interesting is a stroll through its burgeoning arts district.

About 12 miles inland, Downtown LA combines outstanding architecture and museums with global-village pizzazz. Hollywood has its happening 'hoods of Los Feliz and Silver Lake, and *très* gay West Hollywood (WeHo) is all about urban chic. South of Hollywood, Mid-City's main draw is Museum Row, while further west is swank Beverly Hills.

HISTORY

Following the common pattern, the hunter-gatherer existence of the Gabrieleño and Chumash peoples ended with the arrival of Spanish missionaries and pioneers in the late 18th century. Known as El Pueblo de la Reina de Los Angeles, the first civilian settlement became a farming community but remained an isolated outpost for decades. LA was incorporated as a Californian city in 1850, but a series of events caused LA's population to swell by 1930: the collapse of the Northern California Gold Rush, the arrival of the transcontinental railroad, the birth of the citrus industry, the discovery of oil, the launch of the port of LA and the birth of the movie industry in 1908. The deluge of new residents after WWII shaped LA into the megalopolis of today, with its attendant problems including suburban sprawl, air pollution and racial strife. Add soaring real estate to the list of problems that continue to cloud LA's sunny skies. But with a strong economy, low unemployment and a now-decreasing crime rate, overall morale remains high.

ORIENTATION

Getting around is easiest by car. The Fwy system isn't as convoluted as you may fear, despite the fact that most interstates go by several names in addition to their route number and direction. (For example, US-101 northbound is called the Santa Monica Fwy, but southbound it's the Hollywood Fwy. Pay attention!) Hwy 1 still hugs the coast, with the 405 running roughly parallel a few miles to the east. The I-10 lies east–west, deadending at the ocean in Santa Monica. US-101 cuts diagonally through Downtown until merging with I-5 on its way down to San Diego.

For navigating within neighborhoods the maps in this book should be sufficient. Otherwise, pick up a street map at a gas station or bookstore.

INFORMATION

Bookstores

Listed here are some favorite indie bookstores.

Acres of Books (☎ 562-437-6980; 240 Long Beach Blvd, Long Beach; 🕑 10am-9pm Mon-Sat, to 5pm Sun) The largest used bookstore in the state – around a million titles – and a favorite hang of Ray Bradbury. The shelving system is gleefully random: a category label may read 'insects, circus, guns, fraternal groups'.

California Map & Travel Center (Map pp192-3; ☎ 310-396-6277; 3312 Pico Blvd, Santa Monica) Travel bookstore with frequent readings.

Equal Writes (☎ 562-491-5600; 344 E 4th St, Long Beach; 🕑 11am-7pm Tue-Fri, 10am-5pm Sat, 1-5pm Sun) This part bookstore, part queer community center carries hilarious bumper stickers.

Internet Access

Cybercafés are notoriously short-lived, so call ahead to confirm that the following are still in business.

Cyber Java (Map p191; ☎ 323-466-5600; 7080 Hollywood Blvd, Hollywood; per 10min $1.75, wi-fi free; 🕑 7am-11:30pm)

Interactive Café (Map pp192-3; ☎ 310-395-5009; 215 Broadway, Santa Monica; per 10 min $1; 🕑 6am-1am Sun-Thu, to 2am Fri & Sat) Doubles as an art space.

Media

For entertainment-listings magazines, see p203.

KPFK 90.7 fm (www.kpfk.org) Part of the Pacific radio network; news and talk.

LA Weekly (www.laweekly.com) Free alternative news and listings magazine.

Los Angeles Times (www.latimes.com) Nation's fourth-largest daily and winner of 37 Pulitzer Prizes.

Medical Services

Cedars-Sinai Medical Center (Map pp188-9; ☎ 310-855-5000; 8700 Beverly Blvd, West Hollywood; 🕑 24hr emergency room)

Post
Call ☎ 800-275-8777 for the nearest branch, or see the maps to Downtown LA (p190) or Hollywood & Los Feliz (p191) for locations.

Telephone
Thanks to the growth of electronic communication devices, LA County is now divided into six (and counting) area codes; all telephone numbers in this chapter are accompanied by the appropriate area code. When making local calls from a land line between numbers with 310 area codes, you must dial a '1' and the area code first.

Tourist Offices
California Welcome Visitors Center (Map p207; ☎ 714-667-0400; www.visitcwc.com; Westfield Shoppingtown Mainplace, Suite 112, 2800 N. Main St, Santa Ana; ◷ 9am-5pm Mon-Fri)
Downtown Los Angeles Visitor Information Center (Map p190; ☎ 213-689-8822; www.visitlosangeles.info; 685 S Figueroa St, Downtown; ◷ 9am-5pm Mon-Fri)
Hollywood Visitors Center (Map p191; ☎ 323-467-6412; Hollywood & Highland complex, Hollywood; ◷ 10am-10pm Mon-Sat, 11am-7pm Sun) Sells discounted theater tickets.
Santa Monica Visitors Center (Map pp192-3; ☎ 310-393-7593; www.santamonica.com; 1920 Main St, Santa Monica; ◷ 10am-6pm)

DANGERS & ANNOYANCES
Extra caution should be exercised in East LA, Compton and Watts, sections which are still plagued by gangs and drugs. Hollywood and Venice also yield dangers, especially in poorly lit side streets. Downtown LA is safe in the daytime, but only empties out after sundown. Downtown is also home to numerous homeless folks, especially on Skid Row, an area roughly bounded by 3rd, Alameda, 7th and Main Sts.

SIGHTS
Hollywood, Los Feliz & Silver Lake
Hollywood Blvd (Map p191), where Richard Gere cruised Julia Roberts in *Pretty Woman*, has been spruced up in recent years, though it's still far from recapturing its Golden Age glamour. Historic movie palaces bask in restored glory, Metro Rail's Red Line makes public transport easy and some of LA's hottest bars and nightclubs have found their footing here. The most interesting mile runs between La Brea (la *bray*) Ave and Vine St along the

---

> **ALL ABOUT THE HOLLYWOOD SIGN**
> LA's most recognizable landmark first appeared atop its perch in 1923 as Hollywoodland, an advertising gimmick for a real-estate development. Over the years pranksters have altered the sign's 50ft-tall letters to variously read 'Hollyweed' and 'Holywood', among other monikers. A letter mailed to Peg Entwistle – the 24-year-old starlet who jumped from the 'H' in 1932 – the day before she killed herself was an offer to star in a play…about a woman driven to suicide.

Hollywood Walk of Fame, which honors more than 2000 celebrities (a good half of whom you've likely never heard of) with stars embedded in the sidewalk.

The Hollywood & Highland Mall dwarfs the 1927 **Grauman's Chinese Theatre** (Map p191; ☎ 323-464-6266; 6925 Hollywood Blvd), famous for its forecourt where screen legends have left their imprint in cement: feet, hands and – in the case of Jimmy 'Schnozzle' Durante – his noseprint.

Following Hollywood Blvd east beyond Hwy 101 (Hollywood Fwy) takes you to the neighborhoods of **Los Feliz** (loss *fee*-les) and **Silver Lake**, both boho-chic enclaves with offbeat shopping, funky bars and a hopping restaurant scene and resident cool kids like Beck and Flea.

The Metro Red Line (p205) serves central Hollywood (Hollywood/Highland station) and Los Feliz (Vermont/Sunset station) from Downtown LA.

Griffith Park
Five times the size of New York City's Central Park, **Griffith Park** (Map p187; 4370 Crystal Springs Dr; admission free; ◷ 6am-10pm; 🏃) is an escape from urbanity, embracing an outdoor theater, the city zoo, an historic merry-go-round, an observatory, two museums, playgrounds, hiking trails and even the Hollywood Sign.

For information and maps stop by the **Griffith Park Ranger Station** (Map p187; ☎ 323-913-4632; 4730 Crystal Springs Dr; ◷ 5:30am-10:30pm). Trails include the 3-mile **Mt Hollywood Hiking Trail** with spectacular view of the sign.

On the southern slopes of Mt Hollywood, the landmark 1935 art-deco **Griffith Observatory** (Map p187; ☎ 323-664-1181; www.griffithobs.org; 2800 E

GRIFFITH PARK

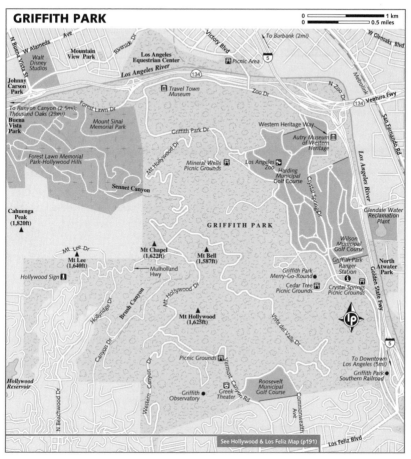

See Hollywood & Los Feliz Map (p191)

Observatory Rd; P &) has flung open its doors once again after a face-lift, showing off new exhibition halls and a snazzy underground 'event horizon theater'. The planetarium's technology has also been upgraded to cutting-edge (even as one of its planets has been downgraded).

Access to the park is easiest via the Griffith Park Dr or Zoo Dr exits off I-5.

West Hollywood

Brash, brassy West Hollywood is an independent city that packs more personality into its 2 sq miles than you can shake a boa at. And how fabulous is it that the city, the epicenter of LA's gay scene, is abbreviated WeHo? It's also the heart of SoCal's design community

and the adopted home of about 6000 immigrants from the former Soviet Union. LA's fabled nightlife mecca, the Sunset Strip, is its main artery.

Mid-City

Fresh produce is an afterthought at the landmark **Third Street Farmers Market** (off Map p191; ☎ 323-933-9211; www.farmersmarketla.com; 6333 W 3rd St; ☒ 9am-9pm Mon-Fri, to 8pm Sat, 10am-7pm Sun; P), in business since 1934. The scene is more about the specialty grocers (don't miss the hot-sauce shop with its lineup of bottles sporting R-rated labels), the vendors proffering edibles from every corner of the globe and the intense

(Continued on page 194)

Map labels

Agoura Hills
101
Santa Monica Mountains
Topanga
Topanga State Park
Malibu Creek State Park
Santa Monica Mountains National Recreation Area
27
Pacific Palisades
N1
Malibu Canyon Rd
Malibu
See Enlargement
Pacific Coast Hwy
Topanga Beach
Will Rogers State Beach
To Ventura (37 mi)
1
Zuma Beach
Pretty Point Dume State Beach
Encino Reservoir
Mulholland Dr
Runyon Canyon
405
Studio City
Universal City
101
Glendale
134
West Hollywood
Hollywood Fwy
See Griffith Park Map (p187)
See Hollywood & Los Feliz Map (p191)
UCLA Medical Center
3
UCLA
Beverly Hills
Wilshire Blvd
Santa Monica Blvd
Santa Monica Fwy
See Downtown Los Angeles Map (p190)
110
Los Angeles
Brentwood
2
10
Santa Monica
Culver City
USC Exposition Park
5
Venice
Vernon
Marina del Rey
405
90
Slauson Ave
South Central
Santa Monica Bay
See Santa Monica & Venice Beach Map (pp192–3)
Inglewood
110
Dockweiler State Beach
Los Angeles International Airport (LAX)
Watts
El Segundo
Century Fwy
105
Manhattan Beach
Pacific Coast Hwy
San Diego Fwy
Compton
91
CSU Dominguez Hills
Hermosa Beach
107
Redondo Beach
Hawthorne Blvd
Western Ave
Torrance
405
710
Malaga Cove
1
110
103
1
Palos Verdes Point
Palos Verdes Peninsula
213
47
Long Beach
47
5
7
Rancho Palos Verdes
San Pedro
Point Vicente
Abalone Cove
Royal Palms State Beach
Outer Los Angeles Harbor
Outer Lon
Middle Breakwater
White Point
Point Fermin
San Pedro Breakwater

Enlargement

Santa Monica Mountains National Recreation Area
N1
0   1 km
0   0.5 miles
Pepperdine University
Malibu
Malibu Canyon Rd
9
1
Pacific Coast Hwy
Malibu Rd
1
8
Malibu Pier
Malibu Beach
Malibu Lagoon State Beach / Surfrider Beach
Carbon Beach
Enlargement

Legend

INFORMATION
Cedars-Sinai-Medical Center.....1 C1

SIGHTS & ACTIVITIES
Aquarium of the Pacific.............2 D3
Getty Center............................3 C1
Getty Villa..............................4 B1
Queen Mary............................5 D3
Rodeo Drive............................6 C1
Wayfarers Chapel.....................7 C3

SLEEPING
Casa Malibu Inn.......................8 B3

EATING
Nobu Malibu............................9 B3

PACIFIC OCEAN

Santa Catalina Island
Two Harbors
Avalon

A B C D
1 2 3 4 5 6

0 — 10 km
0 — 6 miles

Pasadena 210 Foothill Fwy · Monrovia · San Antonio Heights
Caltech **E** Arcadia **F** · Azusa **G** Glendora **H**
· San Marino Temple City Santa Fe Dam Recreation Area
Pasadena Fwy Rosemead Blvd 210 Rancho Cucamonga
Alhambra · San Gabriel 605 Baldwin Park 30 Bonelli Regional County Park · Upland **1**
10 Monterey Park El Monte San Bernardino Fwy Montclair Ontario
Whittier Narrows Recreation Area West Covina Covina 10 57 71 Pomona Ontario International Airport 15
60 East Los Angeles Industry · La Puente Pomona Fwy 60 Diamond Bar Chino 60 Mira Loma

Pico Rivera Schabarum Regional Park Rowland Heights 142 83 **2**
Downey Whittier La Habra Heights Carbon Canyon Rd Chino Hills State Park Norco
605 Los Angeles County Orange County Prado Flood Control Basin
aramount La Mirada La Habra Imperial Hwy Brea 71
tesia Fwy Norwalk Santa Ana Fwy CSU Fullerton Yorba Linda Blvd Yorba Linda Corona Home Gardens
akewood Cerritos Buena Park Fullerton Placentia 90 91 El Cerrito
ng Beach Municipal Airport Carson St Lincoln Ave 39 Knott's Berry Farm Riverside Fwy 5 91 Anaheim 55 Villa Park Irvine Regional Park 231 **3**
Willow St Cypress Disneyland & Disney's California Adventure 57 Orange Cleveland National Forest Santa Ana Mountains
CSU Long Beach 605 Los Alamitos Reserve Center Stanton Garden Grove Fwy Garden Grove 22 22
lmont Shore United States Naval Weapons Station Westminster Beach Blvd Santa Ana Tustin Eastern Transportation Corridor (toll) Portola Hills **4**
aples Seal Beach National Wildlife Refuge 405 Irvine Center Dr
ach Harbor Seal Beach Pier Pacific Coast Hwy Costa Mesa Fwy John Wayne Airport (Orange County) 5 231 Lake Forest
ng Beach eakwater Bolsa Chica State Beach Santa Ana River 55 Irvine Mission Viejo
an Pedro Bay Huntington Beach 1 73 UC Irvine
Huntington Pier Huntington City Beach Huntington State Beach Costa Mesa 74 **5**
Newport Beach
San Pedro Channel Corona del Mar State Beach, Newport Bay Corona del Mar Crystal Cove State Park
Crystal Cove Beach Cottages 133 73
Laguna Beach San Juan Capistrano
Aliso Beach 5
Laguna Niguel
Dana Point Capistrano Beach San Diego County
Doheny State Beach San Clemente
San Clemente State Beach San Onofre Camp Pendleton (US Marine Corps) **6**
San Onofre State Beach

See Orange County Map (p206)

To Oceanside (12mi)

0 ————— 600 m
0 ————— 0.4 miles

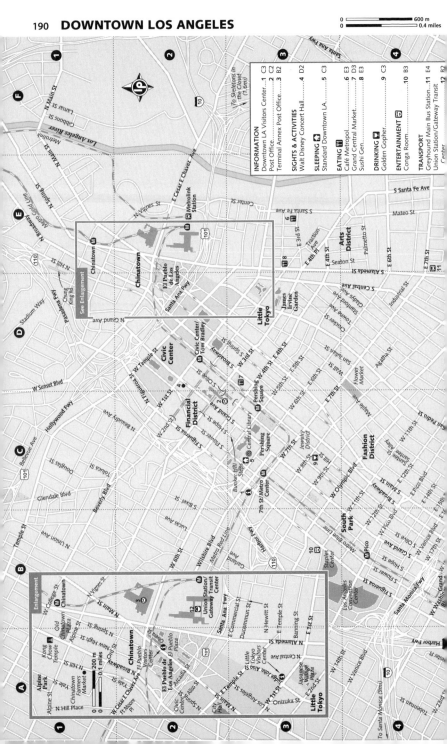

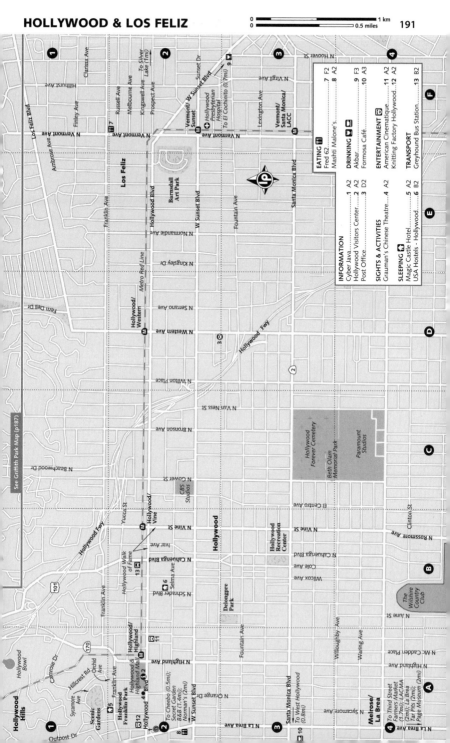

HOLLYWOOD & LOS FELIZ

191

INFORMATION
Cyber Java	1 A2
Hollywood Visitors Center	2 A2
Post Office	3 D2

SIGHTS & ACTIVITIES
Grauman's Chinese Theatre	4 A2

SLEEPING 🏨
Magic Castle Hotel	5 A2
USA Hostels - Hollywood	6 B2

EATING 🍴
Fred 62	7 F2
Mashti Malone's	8 A2

DRINKING 🍷 🍸
Akbar	9 F3
Formosa Café	10 A3

ENTERTAINMENT 🎭
American Cinematique	11 A2
Knitting Factory Hollywood	12 A2

TRANSPORT
Greyhound Bus Station	13 B2

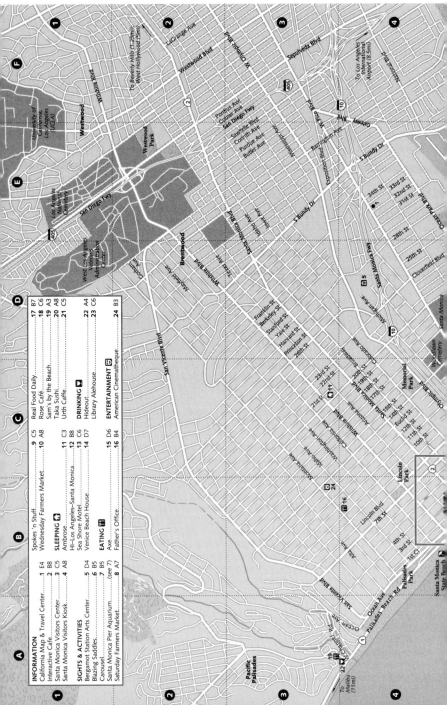

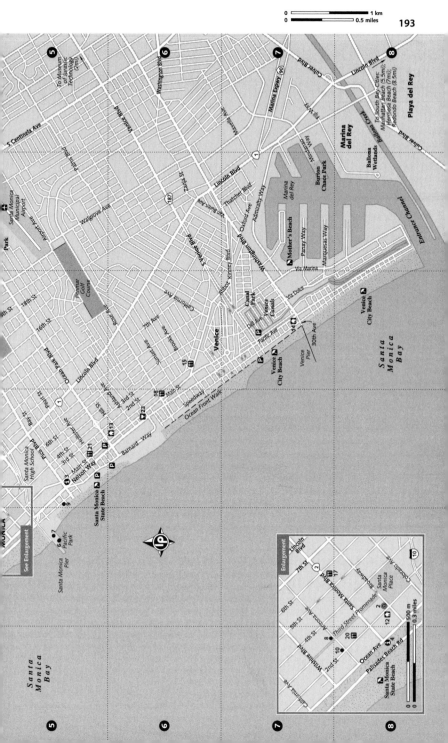

0 _____ 1 km
0 _____ 0.5 miles

To South Bay Cities:
Manhattan Beach (5.5mi);
Hermosa Beach (7mi);
Redondo Beach (8.5mi)

Playa del Rey

Lincoln Blvd

Culver Blvd

Ballona Creek

Culver Blvd

Marina del Rey

Ballona Wetlands

Burton Chace Park

Admiralty Way

Via Marina

Panay Way

Marquesas Way

Mother's Beach

Marina del Rey

Via Dolce

Via Marina

Entrance Channel

Venice City Beach

Santa Monica Bay

Marina Expwy

Culver Blvd

Washington Blvd

Lincoln Blvd

Thatcher Blvd

Oxford Ave

Washington Blvd

Abbot Kinney Blvd

Lincoln Blvd

S Venice Blvd

California Ave

Palms Blvd

Zanja St

7th Ave

Brooks Ave

Sunset Ave

Venice

Canal Park

Dell Ave

Pacific Ave

30th Ave

Venice Canals

Venice City Beach

Venice Pier

Ocean Front Walk

Speedway

Main St

2nd St

3rd St

4th St

5th St

Electric Ave

Abbot Kinney Blvd

Grand Blvd

Peacock Golf Course

Walgrove Ave

18th St

16th St

Ocean Park Blvd

Lincoln Blvd

Pearl St

Bay St

Pico Blvd

Highland Ave

Barnard Way

Nelson Way

Santa Monica High School

Santa Monica State Beach

Santa Monica Municipal Airport

S Centinela Ave

Airport Ave

Park

To Museum of Jurassic Technology (2mi)

MONICA

See Enlargement

Santa Monica Pier

Pacific Park

Santa Monica Bay

Enlargement

Lincoln Blvd

7th St

Santa Monica Blvd

6th St

5th St

4th St

2nd St

Arizona Ave

Wilshire Blvd

Broadway

Third Street Promenade

Santa Monica Place

Colorado Ave

Ocean Ave

California Ave

Palisades Beach Rd

Santa Monica State Beach

0 _____ 500 m
0 _____ 0.3 miles

(Continued from page 187)

people-watching. Parking's free for two hours with validation.

LACMA (off Map p191; ☎ 323-857-6000; www.lacma .org; 5905 Wilshire Blvd; adult/child/student/senior $9/free/5/5, admission after 5pm free; ☯ noon-8pm Mon, Tue & Thu, to 9pm Fri, 11am-8pm Sat & Sun) is one of the country's top art museums and is about to get even better. Right now it brims with several millennia's worth of paintings, sculpture and decorative arts from around the world, and it's currently undergoing an immense expansion that will bring, among other things, the reimagining of the cube-shaped atrium and the creation of the 70,000-sq-ft Broad Contemporary Art Museum, to be complete by the end of 2007.

Between 40,000 and 10,000 years ago, critters like mastodons and saber-toothed cats prowled the land, and many of them got stuck in the gooey gunk that bubbles up from deep beneath the earth's surface along Wilshire Blvd. Despite the misleading name (the black stuff is actually asphalt, the lowest grade of crude oil), the **La Brea Tar Pits** is one of the world's most fecund Ice Age fossil sites. The most spectacular excavations are on display at the **Page Museum** (off Map p191; ☎ 323-934-7243; www.tarpits.org; 5801 Wilshire Blvd; adult/child/student/senior $7/2/4.50/4.50; ☯ 9:30am-5pm Mon-Fri, 10am-5pm Sat & Sun; Ⓟ ♿). From mid-June to mid-September you can observe scientists digging up treasure at the adjacent **Pit 91** (admission free; ☯ 10am-noon & 1-4pm Wed-Sun).

Beverly Hills & Brentwood

No trip to LA is complete without a drive through Beverly Hills, the manicured, palm-tree-lined bastion of the richest and famousest. (Even better if you're driving a clunker from last century with out-of-state plates. The haughty disdain to which you'll be subjected is too amusing.) For ease of access, **Sunset Blvd** is a good bet for mansion-gawking. Hyper-

---

WHAT TO DO IF YOU SEE A STAR *Amy C Balfour*

The odds of seeing a star in the 30-mile zone surrounding Hollywood are actually pretty good. Whether shopping at The Grove, walking in Runyon Canyon or catching a movie at the ArcLight, stars have to live their lives somewhere. So what should you do if you happen upon Brad, Halle or Reese? Follow these pointers to maximize your celebrity-spotting experience:

- Keep sunglasses handy – It may be hard to place a famous face, especially out of context. Or maybe you can't believe Orlando Bloom actually walks his dog in the park. Either way, slipping on shades allows a few extra seconds of surreptitious staring.

- Respect their personal space – Take stock of your surroundings and remember you're looking at a person, not a product. George Clooney is a living, breathing human being. Yes, he sells movies, but he's not a can of soda (although he may be a bag of chips). Piercing shrieks and convulsive hyperventilating can be off-putting.

- Don't mimic their most famous catchphrase – Jake Gyllenhaal doesn't want to hear 'I wish I knew how to quit you!' yelled across the Hollywood Farmer's Market in a faux cowboy accent. Although imitation is the sincerest form of flattery, it's not always polite. And he's probably heard it before.

- Compliment their work – Everyone loves a compliment, and stars are no different.

- Don't comment on their height or lack thereof – Most stars are short. Some of them are very short. See Orlando Bloom, above. Understanding this before entering Hollywood will work in your favor. Blurting, 'Wow, you're a lot shorter in real life!' will endear you to no one.

- Don't be creepy – This should go without saying, but I know a grown man who still believes he has an outstanding date with Milla Jovovich based on a brief conversation at Bookstar. She probably remembers it differently. Or not at all. Along these lines, don't mention your collection of Queen Amidala figurines to Natalie Portman while waiting for your caramel ice blended at the Sunset Coffee Bean. Just don't.

- Keep conversation light – If the setting seems right for an extended conversation, then friendliness with a touch of nonthreatening familiarity is the way to go. If you're met with silence, don't take it personally and keep an eye out for the next one.

posh **Rodeo Drive** is a three-block artery of style for the Prada and Gucci brigade. During daylight hours, Beverly Hills is thick on the ground with A-listers. If spotting some is a goal, we recommend keeping an eye out for paparazzi, with their telltale earpieces and telephoto lenses. It's like finding the kill by watching for the circling vultures.

High above the 405 in neighboring Brentwood, the **Getty Center** (Map pp188-9; ☎ 310-440-7300; www.getty.edu; 1200 Getty Center Dr, Brentwood; admission free; ☷ 10am-6pm Sun & Tue-Thu, to 9pm Fri & Sat; ☷ ☷) attends a world-class art collection, from the Renaissance to David Hockney. Each of the four main pavilions' top floors is illuminated by natural light so that the paintings can be viewed under the conditions the artist intended. The largest piece of art is the Getty's architecture itself. Richard Meier's billion-dollar expression in travertine marble seems to glow with an inner warmth, and is full of human-scale details like the leaf fossils still visible in the stone – examples of these can be seen on the wall next to the steps going down to the cactus roof garden. On clear days, you can take in breathtaking views of the city. Even getting up to the 110-acre 'campus' aboard a driverless tram is fun, though you can walk it in 20 minutes if you're craving the workout.

The best time to visit is in the late afternoon after the crowds have thinned and you can watch the sunset.

To avoid the parking fee, park in the lot on Sepulveda Blvd at Constitution Ave (just north of Wilshire Blvd) and take the free shuttle. Both Metro bus 761 and the Big Blue Bus 14 stop here.

Malibu

Malibu…it's fragrance, soda, sunscreen, plane and car. But here it's a narrow, 27-mile stretch of Hwy 1/PCH with no discernible center, inhabited by people richer than God – many are movie stars, who think they're God – and a place far less scenic than you likely imagine it. Cruising past mile after mile of multimillion-dollar beachside houses – which don't look like much from the road – will leave you with precious few panoramas of the ocean.

Though it doesn't look particularly posh, Malibu has been celebrity central since the 1930s, when money troubles forced landowner May Rindge to lease out property to her famous Hollywood friends. Celebs including Tom Hanks, Richard Gere and Whoopi Goldberg maintain homes in this well-policed neighborhood.

There are some fine beaches, including **Point Dume**, **Zuma** (this one especially is packed on weekends) and **Surfrider**, a world-famous surf spot. Most have a $7 parking fee, if you don't strike gold and find a spot on the highway.

There *are* a few ways to cut through the houses and hit the beach, thanks to the nonprofit group Access for All. One **public accessway** is at Carbon Beach, a mile east of the pier at 22132 Hwy 1.

Rising behind Malibu is **Malibu Creek State Park**, part of the Santa Monica Mountains National Recreation Area and laced with hiking trails (p198).

Malibu's starring cultural attraction is the **Getty Villa** (Map pp188-9; ☎ 310-440-7300; www.getty.edu; 17985 Pacific Coast Hwy; admission free; ☷). This display of J Paul Getty's precious Greek, Roman and Etruscan antiquities reopened to great fanfare in 2006, but the institution quickly found egg on its face when allegations of 'illegally obtained' antiquities within the collection grew to a fevered pitch. At the time of writing, the Getty had returned several pieces to Greece and was in delicate negotiations with Italy. At least the exquisite architecture of the villa, modeled after a 1st-century Herculaneum country house, is here to stay.

LOS ANGELES & ORANGE COUNTY

Santa Monica

Self-assuredly holding court as the quintessential LA beach town, Santa Monica, with her requisite early-20th-century pier anchored by a delightful amusement park (rather than yet another Ruby's Diner outpost), pedestrian-friendly Downtown and miles of sandy beaches. It's also politically progressive and environmentally aware; the city recently put the kibosh on both smoking on the Third Street Promenade and the use of Styrofoam in restaurants.

The demographic is as melting-pot as it gets on the southern coast; bronzed women toting yoga mats share the sidewalk with hacky-sacking scruffians in overalls, and thanks to rent control, the people who keep the buses and vacuum cleaners running can actually afford to live in the town they work in. Bob Dylan, Adam Sandler and Courteney Cox Arquette are some bigwigs that call Santa Monica home.

Stop by the visitors center for information. The city's most recognizable landmark is the **Santa Monica Pier** (Map pp192-3; ☎ 310-458-8900; www.santamonicapier.org; admission free; ♿), the oldest amusement pier in California (1908), it contains a vintage **carousel** and small **amusement park** (☼ daily in summer, Fri-Sun rest of year) complete with solar-powered Ferris wheel, a roller coaster and other rides. And setting aside the tragedy in 2003 that left 10 people dead (an 86-year-old supposedly mistook his car's accelerator for the brake), the city's **farmers market** is hugely popular; many chefs think it's one of the best in the country. The market rotates locations throughout the week, but the best days are Wednesday (Arizona Ave and 2nd St) and Saturday (Arizona Ave and 3rd St), from 8:30am to around 1:30pm.

Meandering right by the pier is the **South Bay Bicycle Trail**, a paved bicycle and walking path. Bike or in-line skate rentals are available on the pier and at beachside kiosks (see p198).

The car-free **Third Street Promenade** –between Wilshire Blvd and Broadway – is a great place for a stroll and a spot of people-watching. Jugglers, skateboarders and Bible-thumpers share space with – incongruously enough – dinosaur topiaries. There are plenty of opportunities to whip out the ol' credit card, but for the most part the stores are chains like Anthropologie and Abercrombie & Fitch.

Art-lovers should continue inland for 3 miles to the **Bergamot Station Arts Center** (Map pp192-3; 2525 Michigan Ave; ☼ 10am-6pm Tue-Sat; Ⓟ), home to more than 30 avant-garde galleries and a great café. Clever gifts can be had at its **Gallery of Functional Art**, in space E3. To get there, go northeast on Olympic Blvd, take a right on Cloverfield Blvd, and then a left on Michigan Ave.

Main St, on the border with Venice, is connected to Downtown by the electric Tide Shuttle ($0.25 per ride).

Venice

If Santa Monica is San Francisco in miniature – sophisticated, gracious and liberal – then Venice is Berkeley; artsy, bombastic and so left-leaning it's close to toppling over. Originally swampland, Venice started out as the dream of one eccentric tobacco heir by the name of Abbot Kinney. He envisioned an amusement park and seaside resort called 'Venice of America' complete with Ferris wheel and Italian *gondolieri* who poled tourists around canals. Most of his harebrained schemes enjoyed success, but after Abbot Kinney's death Venice faded from the radar until the 1950s and '60s, when its European vibe and funky canals drew beatniks and hippies like Jim Morrison. Venice is still a cauldron of creativity, peopled by karmically correct New Agers and a few celebs, including Dennis Hopper and Julia Roberts.

Pick up a free, comprehensive Maphawk map from shops all over town. One good place to snag the map, alternative weeklies and other local publications is the **Beyond Baroque Literary Arts Center** (☎ 310-822-3006; www.beyondbaroque.org; 681 Venice Ave), housed in the former city hall.

Ocean Front Walk (Map pp192-3; Venice Pier to Rose Ave; admission free; ☼ 24hr) is what most people have in mind when they think of Venice: the human zoo of wannabe Schwarzeneggers, a Speedo-clad 'snake man' and a roller-skating Sikh minstrel. Known locally as Venice Boardwalk, its vibe is at its most surreal on summer weekends.

An excellent place for a stroll is the mile-long stretch of **Abbot Kinney Blvd** between Venice Blvd and Main St, chockablock with boutiques, galleries, bars and restaurants.

Feel like a head trip? About 5 miles east of downtown Venice, the **Museum of Jurassic Technology** (off Map pp192-3; ☎ 310-836-6131; www.mjt.org; 9341 Venice Blvd, Culver City; adult/youth 12-21/child under 12 $5/3/free; ☼ 2-8pm Thu, noon-6pm Fri-Sun) has

---

DETOUR: THE GREAT WALL OF LOS ANGELES

Here's a side of LA a world away from the Pacific playground, billion-dollar museums and celebrity sightings. The longest mural in the world at half a mile, the Great Wall of Los Angeles depicts Californian and Angelino history in broad, colorful strokes, warts and all: the treatment of Native Americans, the Zoot Suit Riots, McCarthyism, Japanese internment and so on, all from the standpoint of the folks who didn't get to write the textbooks – they painted theirs instead. Even more inspiring is that the mural was created, in the late '70s and early '80s, by a ragtag group of 400 youths organized by the **Social & Public Art Resource Center** (SPARC; ☎ 310-822-9560; www .sparcmurals.org; 685 Venice Blvd, Venice). The center is still a vibrant part of LA's 'socially responsible art-making' scene and is ramping up for a massive Great Wall restoration project, which will restore the fading sections and eventually expand the mural to cover LA's history from the '60s through to the present.

The Wall is along the Tujunga flood wash, near North Hollywood. It's not an especially salubrious location: you view it from the far side of a sometimes algae-coated culvert and through a chain-link fence. But its challenging setting only serves to underscore the mural's beauty and power – not to mention the strength of will its very creation required.

To get there from Hwy 101/Ventura Fwy, exit Coldwater Canyon and head north. The mural runs from Burbank Blvd to Oxnard St.

---

little to do with technology and absolutely nothing to do with dinosaurs. Rather, the MJT messes with your sense of reality as fantastical phenomena are laid out for your quizzical examination. Camaroonian stink ants, decaying dice, fruit stone carvings, nothing is too obscure or arcane. The Tula Tea Room doles out free tea and cookies (from an hour after the museum opens to an hour before closing), and the Borzoi Kabinet Theater screens Slavic films with MJT-appropriate titles like *Levsha: The Tale of a Cross-Eyed Lefty from Tula and the Steel Flea.*

Long Beach
Long Beach, on the border with Orange County, has come a long way from its working-class oil and navy days, but the inevitable gentrification process hasn't yet stripped the city of all of its grit. The action is divided between southern **Pine Ave**, lined with restaurants, nightclubs and bars, and the fledgling East Village Arts District, roughly bordered by 7th St and Ocean Ave to the north and south and Alamitos Ave and Long Beach Blvd to the east and west. Looking south into the harbor you'll notice several islands studded with palm trees and waterfalls – these are actually well-disguised oil-drilling platforms.

Downtown Long Beach is the southern terminus of the Metro Blue Line. A shuttle service, called **Passport**, serves all major places of interest on four routes (free within Downtown; $0.90 otherwise, exact change

only). A **Long Beach Visitor Information Kiosk** (☎ 562-436-3645, 800-452-7829; ☉ 10am-5pm Jun-Sep, to 4pm Fri-Sun Oct-May) is outside the Aquarium of the Pacific.

You won't be able to miss the 1929 grand dame apartment building **Villa Riviera** (800 E Ocean Blvd at Alamitos Ave). Sadly, it's not open to the public, but if you've got binocs, check out its gargoyles.

A bibliophile's dream is dusty, musty **Acres of Books** p185). Heading east on 4th St brings you to 'Retro Row', lousy with vintage stores, antiques and coffeehouses. Hit **Equal Writes** (p185) to stock up on left-wing bumper stickers before hitting the OC.

The **Aquarium of the Pacific** (Map pp188-9; ☎ 562-590-3100; www.aquariumofpacific.org; 100 Aquarium Way; adult/child $20/12; ☉ 9am-6pm; (P) (占)) is a high-tech romp through an underwater world. Its 12,500 creatures hail from tepid Baja California, the frigid northern Pacific, coral reefs of the tropics and local kelp forests. It's also the only facility in the world that has successfully bred the Seussian-looking weedy sea dragon.

The **Museum of Latin American Art** (☎ 562-437-1689; www.molaa.org; 628 Alamitos Ave; adult/child/student $5/free/3, Fri free; ☉ 11:30am-7pm Tue-Fri, 11am-7pm Sat, to 6pm Sun) is one of only two museums in the country to exclusively showcase contemporary Latin American art. The museum is open during its ambitious expansion, due for completion by early 2007.

Long Beach's flagship (ha ha) attraction is the supposedly haunted British ocean liner

Queen Mary (Map pp188-9; ☎ 562-435-3511; www.queen
mary.com; 1126 Queens Hwy; adult/child/senior $23/12/20;
☺ 10am-5pm Mon-Thu, to 6pm Fri-Sun, hours vary by season;
Ⓟ). Larger than the *Titanic*, the *Queen Mary*
transported royals, dignitaries, immigrants
and troops during its 1001 Atlantic crossings
between 1936 and 1964. It's now an overpriced hotel and tourist attraction.

Downtown

Though heretofore attempts to create a living,
breathing center of Los Angeles have been
largely futile, that hasn't stopped forward-
thinking people like architect Frank Gehry
from trying. It may be presumptuous to believe that anything as organic as a city center
can be architected into existence, but the so-
called Grand Avenue Cultural Corridor, with
the Walt Disney Concert Hall (see below) as
its pièce de résistance, comes close. And it's
getting closer by the day.

Gehry has just embarked on construction
of his next ambitious Downtown revitaliza-
tion project. By 2009, when the first phase
is slated for completion, LA's skyline will
see the addition of two L-shaped towers (the
taller of which will be translucent and 47
stories high), both with terraced green space.
A 16-acre park is intending to help create
'the scale of a community', and plazas and
walkways will connect the existing cultural
sights with each other and with those who are
strolling to and fro. (Pedestrians in LA…how
revolutionary!)

For the moment, however, Grand Ave's
centerpiece is still Gehry's **Walt Disney Concert Hall**
(Map p190; ☎ 213-972-4399 ext 5; http://wdch.laphil.com;
111 S Grand Ave; self-guided audio tours adult/student/senior
$10/8/8, guided tour $10; ☺ audio tours 9am-3pm nonmatinee

days, guided tours 10am-11:30am matinee days). It's a grav-
ity-defying sculpture of curving and billowing
stainless-steel walls. Soon after it opened in
2003, people living in the neighboring con-
dominiums started complaining of atrocious
glare and skyrocketing air-conditioning bills
caused by the reflection off the structure. In
2005 the metal surfaces were sandblasted down
to a more manageable sheen.

Union Station (Map p190; 800 N Alameda St), built
in 1939, is often called the 'last of the grand
railroad stations' in the nation. Indeed, it's a
glamorous exercise in Spanish mission and
art deco.

Little Tokyo was established by immigrants in
the 1880s. It has a mix of traditional gardens,
Buddhist temples and sushi bars to support
tourists as well as its 250,000-strong community of Japanese-Americans.

In the industrial section southeast of Little
Tokyo, an increasingly lively **Arts District** (www.la
dad.org) is emerging, with some 1200 (and
counting) scrappy artists living and working
in studios above abandoned warehouses and
small factories, enough to support a number
of cafés, restaurants and shops.

ACTIVITIES
Cycling & In-Line Skating

The best place for skating or riding is along
the paved **South Bay Bicycle Trail** that parallels
the beach for 22 miles, from north of Santa
Monica to Torrance. You'll also find lots of
information at www.labikepaths.com. There
are numerous bike-rental places along the
beaches. Here are two:

Blazing Saddles (Map pp192-3; ☎ 310-393-9778;
Santa Monica Pier, Santa Monica)

Spokes 'n' Stuff (Map pp192-3; ☎ 310-395-4748; 1750
Ocean Front Walk, Santa Monica) On the paved boardwalk
behind Loews Hotel.

Hiking

For a quick ramble, head to **Griffith Park** (p187)
or to **Runyon Canyon** (Map p187; www.runyon-canyon
.com). The latter is a favorite playground of
fitness-obsessed locals and their dogs. You'll
have fine views of the Hollywood Sign and
the city. The southern trailhead is at the end
of Fuller St, off Franklin Ave.

Malibu Creek State Park (Map pp188–9) has a
great trail leading to the set of the TV series
M*A*S*H, where an old Jeep and other relics
rust in the sunshine. The trailhead is in the
park's main parking lot on Malibu Canyon Rd,

SKELETONS IN THE CLOSET

The fun, macabre gift shop **Skeletons in
the Closet** (off map p190; ☎ 323-343-0760;
1104 N Mission Rd; ☺ 8:30am-4:30pm Mon-Fri) is
operated by the LA County Coroner's Office
and located two floors above the morgue.
Items include personalized toe-tags, body
outline beach towels, hearse-shaped coin
banks, and travel garment 'body bags',
along with classic 'LA County Coroner' T-
shirts. Proceeds benefit the Youthful Drunk
Driving Visitation program, an alternative
sentencing program.

which is called Las Virgenes Rd if coming from Hwy 101 (Hollywood Fwy). Parking is $8.

The **ParkLink Shuttle** (☎ 888-734-2323; tickets $1) loops around the western half of the recreation area, stopping at many of the places mentioned above. Buses run only on weekends between 8am and 5pm from October through March and until 8pm from April through September.

Swimming & Surfing

Water temperatures peak at about 70°F in August and September. Water quality varies; for updated conditions check the 'Beach Report Card' at www.healthebay.org. Good surfing spots for nonbeginners include Malibu Lagoon State Beach, aka Surfrider Beach, and the Manhattan Beach pier.

Surfing novices can expect to pay about $100 to $125 for a two-hour private lesson or $50 to $75 for a group lesson, including board and wet suit. Contact these schools for details:

Learn to Surf LA (☎ 310-920-1265; www.learntosurf la.com)

Malibu Ocean Sports (☎ 877-952-9257; www.malibu oceansports.com)

Surf Academy (☎ 310-372-1036, 877-599-7873; www .surfacademy.org)

TOURS

Los Angeles Conservancy (☎ 213-623-2489; www.la conservancy.org; tours $10) Thematic walking tours, mostly of Downtown LA, with an architectural focus. Reservations required.

Starline Tours (☎ 323-463-333, 800-959-3131; www .starlinetours.com; tours from $35) Your basic narrated bus tours of the city, stars' homes and theme parks.

FESTIVALS & EVENTS

LA has a packed calendar of annual festivals and special events. We've only got space for the blockbusters, but for more ideas download the **LA Festival Calendar** (www.culturela.org) and click on 'Events'.

Rose Parade (☎ 626-449-4100; www.tournamentof roses.com) Cavalcade of flower-festooned floats along Pasadena's Colorado Blvd, followed by the Rose Bowl football game. Held on January 1.

Chinese New Year (☎ 213-680-0243, 213-617-0396) Colorful Dragon Parade, plus free entertainment, fireworks, food, games, carnival rides and other traditional revels in the heart of Chinatown during late January or early February.

Sunset Junction Street Fair (☎ 323-661-7771; www .sunsetjunction.org) A mid-August street party celebrating Silver Lake's wackiness.

GAY & LESBIAN LOS ANGELES

LA is one of the country's gayest cities, with the rainbow flag flying especially proudly along Santa Monica Blvd in West Hollywood. Freebie magazines containing up-to-date listings and news are strewn about in bars, restaurants and gay-friendly establishments around town.

A Different Light (☎ 310-854-6601; 8853 Santa Monica Blvd, West Hollywood) is LA's bastion of queer literature, nonfiction and magazines. Another resource is the bookstore and community center **Equal Writes** (p185) in Long Beach.

LA Pride (www.lapride.org) is a three-day festival in mid-June with nonstop partying and a parade down Santa Monica Blvd.

SLEEPING

As a general rule, lodging Downtown is soulless, overpriced and underloved. Hollywood, West Hollywood and Santa Monica have more memorable digs. Always check online for special rates.

Budget

USA Hostels-Hollywood (Map p191; ☎ 323-462-3777, 800-524-6783; www.usahostels.com; 1624 Schrader Blvd, Hollywood; dm $24-27, r $58-64; 🖳) Well run and central, this hostel is a convivial spot with plenty of activities, a big kitchen and lots of freebies, including pancake breakfasts.

HI-Los Angeles-Santa Monica (Map pp192-3; ☎ 310-393-9913, 800-909-4776 ext 137; www.lahostels.org; 1436 2nd St, Santa Monica; dm $28, r from $69; 🖳) This enormous, generic but newly renovated hostel may be low on charm, but the location – between the beach and Third Street Promenade – is the envy of much fancier places.

Midrange

Secret Garden B&B (off map p191; ☎ 323-656-3888, 877-732-4736; www.secretgardenbnb.com; 8039 Selma Ave, Hollywood; r incl breakfast $95-165; 🅿 🖳) Under new ownership as of 2006, this Pepto-Bismol Spanish Moorish jewel with its Rapunzel tower and lush garden sits a mere block away from Sunset Strip. The common areas give off more exoticness than its five guest rooms, some of which fall into motel territory. Free wi-fi.

Turret House (☎ 562-624-1991, 888-488-7738; www .turrethouse.com; 556 Chestnut Ave, Long Beach; r incl breakfast $109-135) This butter yellow corner Victorian with wraparound porch has five cozy rooms, each with fireplace, TV and bathroom with clawfoot tub, and a fuzzy robe to slip into. Rates include passes to a nearby gym, and there's a hot tub on the premises. Dog-lovers only, as the owners Brian and Jeff have four of the adorable guys.

Sea Shore Motel (Map pp192–3; ☎ 310-392-2787; www.seashoremotel.com; 2637 Main St, Santa Monica; r $110-120, ste $130-250; P ✖) This 20-room family-owned motel is one of a dying breed: a clean, budget-priced place mere steps from the beach and restaurants. The tiled rooms are attractive enough – though beds are on the firm side – but the new suites with full kitchens and balconies are killer. Free wi-fi. Bring earplugs, and book far in advance for a summer stay.

Farmer's Daughter (☎ 323-937-3930, 800-334-1658; www.farmersdaughterhotel.com; 115 S Fairfax Ave, Mid-City; r $139-200; P ✖ 🖳 🐾) Tongue firmly in cheek, the Daughter delivers a carefully architected blend of down-home folksiness and slick hipster touches. Its 63 rooms come kitted with wide-plank wood floors, denim bedspreads and gingham curtains, but the bold use of primary colors and clever shower curtains goes beyond what grandma would have dared. There's an iMac in the lobby and poolside bean bags, the latter equally likely to be supporting a rocker nursing a hangover as a gaggle of giggly kids.

Elan Hotel Modern (☎ 323-658-6663, 888-611-0398; www.elanhotel.com; 8435 Beverly Blvd, West Hollywood; r incl breakfast $140-220; P ✖ 🖳) Well, the secret's out. This place is rock solid in every important way, and a steal for LA. Let's hope it doesn't go to their heads. Look past the motel facade into the rooms, decked out in natural tones, and sporting plenty of beyond-standard-issue amenities, including Egyptian cotton sheets, goose-down comforters and fancy bath stuff. It's got a little B&B thing going too, with evening wine and cheese, ample breakfast, and a staff that treats you like family…in a good way.

Venice Beach House (Map pp192–3; ☎ 310-823-1966; www.venicebeachhouse.com; 15 30th Ave, Venice; r $130, with bathroom $145-235; P) The most pleasing place to stay in Venice, this ivy-shellacked 1911 house with its emerald lawn moat is close enough to the ocean for you to be lulled to sleep by the sound of waves. Its nine rooms are unique and vary in size and amenities – some have a balcony, some have a fireplace. The very plaid, though masculine colored, Abbott Kinney room is a delight.

ourpick Magic Castle Hotel (Map p191; ☎ 800-741-4915; www.magiccastlehotel.com; 7025 Franklin Ave, Hollywood; r $159-179, ste $219-259; P ✖ 🖳 🐾) This gem simply sparkles with pale blond furniture, white goose-down duvets, free wi-fi and fancy bathroom accessories, but the best amenity of all is the genuinely delightful staff. Most of the 40 units are one- or two-bedroom suites with kitchenettes, a stellar option for families. Start your day with freshly baked goods and gourmet coffee on your balcony (some rooms) or by the pool. A stay here earns guests 21 and over access to the nightly dinner-and-a-show ($20 plus the price of dinner) at the adjacent and appropriately castley-looking Magic Castle Club, otherwise open only to professional magicians.

Top End

Standard Downtown LA (Map p190; ☎ 213-892-8080; www.standardhotel.com; 550 S Flower St, Downtown; r from $150; P ✖ 🖳 🐾) With its trademark upside-down sign, this painfully hip hotel seems to bring out the fabulousness of self-assured guests, while making those cut from more introverted cloth want to hide in the peek-through shower. There's a huge variety of rooms, but all are mod affairs with platform beds, and all the cheap rooms (they really call them that) are smoker-friendly. The rooftop pool bar has an intense pick-up scene.

Casa Malibu Inn (Map pp188–9; ☎ 310-456-2219, 800-831-0858; 22752 Pacific Coast Hwy, Malibu; ocean view r from $159, garden view r $219-350; P) Ignore the motel-ish facade; this small family-run establishment overlooks a small private beach and has 21 clean, attractive rooms surrounding a vine- and flower-festooned courtyard. It's worth splurging on an ocean-view room, most of which have private decks and fireplaces or kitchenettes, though all the beds tend to sag more than is ideal. There's also free wi-fi, and each room has a fridge. Fun fact: glamour queen Lana Turner once spent 18 months living in the Catalina Suite.

Ambrose (Map pp192–3; ☎ 310-315-1555, 877-262-7673; www.ambrosehotel.com; 1255 20th St, Santa Monica; r incl breakfast $175-250; P ✖ 🖳) As soon as you step into this chocolate and cream hotel, you start wondering how you can redecorate your house to capture some of Ambrose's Asian cool and craftsman warmth. It's got 76 rooms (and one studio apartment), but the attentive service makes you feel like you're staying at a B&B. Beds support organic mattresses and are dressed in Matteo linens, the limestone bathrooms stock Aveda products, and the organic continental breakfast (including Starbucks coffee) is worthy of a way better name. Since the hotel isn't within walking distance to the beach, a London cab can shuttle you around free of charge. Tiny spoiler – the plumbing can be loud. Free parking and wi-fi.

EATING

The original **Third Street Farmers Market** (off Map p191; 6333 W 3rd St; 9am-9pm Mon-Fri, 9am-8pm Sat, 10am-7pm Sun; P) is a great spot for a casual meal any time of day, as is the **Grand Central Market** (Map p190; ☎ 213-624-2378; 317 S Broadway, Downtown; 9am-6pm; P).

Budget

Zephyr (☎ 562-435-7113; 340 E 4th St, Long Beach; dishes $5-8; Tue-Sun; V) All vegan, with several raw options, and mostly organic, relative newcomer Zephyr has become ground zero for Long Beach's food-conscious hipsters.

Fred 62 (Map p191; ☎ 323-667-0062; 1850 N Vermont Ave, Los Feliz; dishes $6-14; 24hr) The flickering blue neon sign pulls you in with its tractor beam – don't fight it. Craving large-portioned, easy-on-the-wallet, punny-titled grub in a setting with meticulously stylish and rumpus-room cozy? Whatever you're craving – bagel 'n' lox, vegetarian chicken pot pie, spicy Asian salad, perhaps a 5am bottle of Champagne – a perky waitress in a racing-stripe apron will happily oblige. Drew Barrymore is reported to make regular appearances.

Rose Café (Map pp192-3; ☎ 310-399-0711; 220 Rose St at Main St, Venice; dishes $7-10; dining room 8am-3pm, counter service until 5:30pm most days) Around since 1979, this Venice mainstay has it all: café,

---

MOST EXOTIC ICE CREAM IN LA

Though **Mashti Malone's** (Map p191; ☎ 323-874-6168; 1525 N La Brea Ave, Hollywood; 11am-11pm) ice-cream shop handles the standards just fine, it's the delicate Iranian concoctions like lavender, *falludeh* and rosewater saffron that keep the hordes coming and the celebs bulk-ordering. The story goes that the storefront used to be Mugsy Malone's Ice Cream, and when Mashti bought it, he could only afford to change out half of the sign. Sample the 'herbal snow', but we don't recommend getting it.

---

dining room, bakery, art space – and each is a class act. Brunch is atrociously popular. Order up some rave-worthy frittatas from the varied menu once you snag a seat on the lovely semi-enclosed patio. (Frank Gehry popped in soon after its overhang was constructed, and commented that that he'd have done it 'differently'.) There are plans to open for dinner sometime in 2007. No reservations taken on weekends.

Real Food Daily (Santa Monica Map pp192-3; ☎ 310-451-7544; 514 Santa Monica Blvd; dishes $7-13; West Hollywood ☎ 310-289-9910; 414 N La Cienega Blvd; V) Vegan cooking guru Ann Gentry gives meat and daily substitutes the gourmet treatment. Classics like the Salisbury *seitan* feed the body and soul, though no items are real envelope-pushers and you're advised to keep the salt and Tabasco within reach.

New Paradise (☎ 562-218-0066; 1350 E Anaheim St, Long Beach; dishes $8-12) Long Beach has a strong community of Cambodians, and one of the best culinary manifestations is New Paradise. It's also wedding reception central for LB's Cambodian-Americans, so if you come on a weekend, expect a party. Wedding or no, there's live music every Friday night and during the day Saturday and Sunday. There's not a dud on the menu, but the 'beef sticks' are tremendous.

El Cochinito (☎ 323-668-0737; 3508 W Sunset Blvd, Los Feliz; dishes $8-13; lunch & dinner) Arguably the best Cuban food in the city, 12-table hole-in-the wall El Cochinito (the little pig) is family run and neighborhood adored. This is traditional 'pre-Castro' Cuban at its finest. The *tostones* are thin and crispy and the roasted pork melt-in-your-mouth tender, but really, you can't order wrong.

Midrange

Malo (☎ 323-664-1011; 4326 Sunset Blvd, Silver Lake; dishes $6-15; from 6pm) Trendy, lowlit quasi-Mexican Malo is usually packed with young stylish things checking each other out over flights of salsa and homemade chips. That is, until their tapas and entrées arrive, and then it's all eyes on the plates. The beef and pickle tacos? Way better than they sound. Waitstaff can be laughably inattentive, especially on the weekends, so order those margaritas in bulk.

Urth Caffe (dishes $7-15; 6am-midnight) Beverly Hills (☎ 310-205-9311; 267 S Beverly Dr); Santa Monica (Map pp192-3; ☎ 310-314-7040; 2327 Main St); West Hollywood

LOS ANGELES & ORANGE COUNTY

(☎ 310-659-0628; 8565 Melrose Ave) The West Hollywood branch has been packed with hotties, producers and gawkers for more than a decade. The organic teas and coffees are all primo quality but it's the see-and-be-seen patio that gives this place its edge. For sustenance, try the pastries, salads or panini. The desserts (around $6) are fantastic and can easily feed two normal people, or nine aspiring actresses.

Café Metropol (Map p190; ☎ 213-613-1537; 923 E 3rd St; dishes $7-15; ⏱ 8am-10pm Mon-Sat; **P**) This exposed-brick, high-ceilinged, art-studded bistro embodies the ways in which the Arts District is transforming Downtown. Metropol's a bit tricky to find, but the gourmet sandwiches and panini, organic salads and pizzas make it worthwhile. Live jazz, bebop and DJ-spun tunes emanate Thursday through Saturday night (cover usually $5 to $8).

Sushi Gen (Map p190; ☎ 213-617-0552; 422 E 2nd St, Little Tokyo; dishes $7-15; ⏱ lunch & dinner Mon-Sat; **P**) You won't find any truffle-oil-infused wasabi nonsense at this shoot-from-the-hip sushi joint. Fish doesn't get any fresher, so best focus on sashimi and rolls. Coming midday means competing with businessfolk who seem ready to kung-fu-fight you for the chance to order the sashimi lunch special. Lots of Japanese expats in attendance. 'Nuff said.

Taka Sushi (Map pp192-3; ☎ 310-394-6540; 1345 2nd St, Santa Monica; dishes $7-15; ⏱ lunch Mon-Fri, dinner daily) Popular and centrally located near the Promenade, this magenta-seated sushi joint is an excellent spot for a casual, if not a quick, bite. (It gets supercrowded, especially during lunch.) As an appetizer, go for the grilled green mussels. Sake-lovers will be in heaven – Taka carries an enormous selection of premium brands.

Canter's Deli (☎ 323-651-2030; 419 N Fairfax Ave, Mid-City; dishes $7-16; ⏱ 24hr) Across from the Farmers Market and still wheezing along after more than 80 years, Canter's isn't really about the food, though it covers the Jewish deli basics decently, gets high marks for its waffles (of all things) and even serves full Thanksgiving dinners ($11.50) nightly and pea soup on Wednesdays. It ain't about the service, either, which is indifferent on a good day. And it's not about sophistication – it serves Coor's on tap, for Pete's sake. But it's an LA institution, there's only a $2 minimum, and it's open All. The. Time. Check out the stained-glass ceiling.

Nate 'n Al's (☎ 310-274-0101; 414 N Beverly Dr, Beverly Hills; dishes $8-15; ⏱ 7:30am-8:45pm Sun-Fri, to 9:30pm Sat) This 1943 institution will have you scarfing down what may be the best deli nosh this side of the Mississippi. (Ever try brie matzo?) Doris Day used to walk over in her bathrobe every day for breakfast. With luck, you'll get a free helping of star sightings yourself, especially in the mornings.

Cheebo (☎ 323-850-7070; 7533 W Sunset Blvd, Hollywood; breakfast & lunch $6-14, dinner $10-27; ⏱ 8am-11:30pm) This cheerful hipster joint is the spot for creative organic, hormone-free fare, especially pizzas – try the sausage and fennel. The porkwich is a winning combo of slow-roasted pork doused with Manchego cheese. Tables are covered in butcher paper and crayons are supplied, for the kids and those Silver Lake arty types.

Father's Office (Map pp192-3; ☎ 310-393-2337; 1018 Montana Ave at 10th St, Santa Monica; burgers $12; ⏱ 5pm-10pm) Okay, it's technically a bar – and one with a stellar lineup of beers – but the best damn fancy-pants burger in LA is here, gunned out with caramelized onion, applewood bacon compote, blue and gruyere cheeses and arugula. If you know what's good for you, you won't ask for substitutions or for ketchup. Claustrophobes will want to get there as soon as it opens.

Top End

Axe (Map pp192-3; ☎ 310-664-9787; 1009 Abbot Kinney Blvd, Venice; dishes lunch $7-12, dinner $10-26; ⏱ lunch & dinner Tue-Sun) At the end of Abbot Kinney, this exercise in minimalist refinement writes the book on 'California soul food'. Its name derives from a Yoruba word meaning 'go with the power of the gods and goddesses', and presumably this power comes from the all-organic, farm-fresh ingredients. You can create your own salad, or if you don't feel like thinking, order the rice bowl, which is orgasmic. Flesh-lovers don't fret – there's plenty of meat on the menu, especially at dinner. Whatever you do, don't repeat our mistake and pronounce it phonetically: it's 'ah-shay', sweetie.

Nobu Malibu (Map pp188-9; ☎ 310-317-9140; Ste 18a, 3835 Cross Creek Rd; dishes $14-32; ⏱ dinner daily, lunch Sat & Sun; **P**) Tucked in the Malibu Country Mart shopping center, Nobu dishes up creative Japanese fare (seviche, anyone?) if slightly inconsistent, portion-challenged and at sticker-shock prices. However, it's tops for weeknight celeb sightings. Reserve a table on the dimly lit patio, and to blend in, do not dress up. On a recent visit, Meg Ryan was behind us and Fran Drescher was to our right. Don't expect ingratiating service unless you're similarly befamed.

Sam's by the Beach (Map pp192-3; ☎ 310-230-9100; 108 W Channel Rd, Santa Monica; dishes $19-24; ☯ dinner Tue-Sun) If Sam hasn't come over to your table and introduced himself by dessert, I'll eat my hat. He and his merry band of locals – those who crave high quality Cal-Med and gracious attention in equal parts – seem to be conducting a passionate yet respectful love affair. Seafood (procured daily from LA's fish market), wild game and pastas all shine. The daredevils among you should try the sea-urchin risotto.

Our pick Norman's (off map p191; ☎ 310-657-2400; 8570 W Sunset Blvd, Sunset Millennium, Hollywood; dishes $18-40; ☯ dinner Tue-Sat) Norman's proves that an outstanding dinner experience can be had on the Strip; let's just hope that LA's foodies find out quick enough for it to stay open. The menu is French based with creative Asian influences, and changes monthly. Diners in the know rave about the roast pig ($19), served Fridays only. Decor is spare, updated steakhouse, with glass panels allowing guests to spy on the kitchen. Service is exceptional as well; you'll want to take master sommelier Peter Birmingham home in your pocket. For an especially romantic date, reserve a curtained-off booth.

DRINKING
For the following places that have a parking icon, this means valet, unless otherwise noted.

Downtown, Hollywood & Los Feliz
Golden Gopher (Map p190; ☎ 213-614-8001; 417 W 8th St, Downtown; ☯ from 8pm Sat-Mon, from 5pm Tue-Fri) This campy lounge manages to draw drinkers from all stripes to its somewhat sketchy neighborhood. The furnishings cover the bases too, with chandeliers *and* Ms Pac-Man. Those who haven't had enough at closing time can stock up for later at the in-house liquor store.

Akbar (Map p191; ☎ 323-665-6810; 4356 W Sunset Blvd, Los Feliz; ☯ from 7pm) The Akbar refuses to be pigeonholed. The facts: it's a divey, lightly Moroccan-themed watering hole with a killer jukebox and a drink wheel. But try to pin down if it's gay or straight, smoking or non,

neighborhood-friendly or hipster-tetchy, and you're outta luck.

Formosa Cafe (Map p191; ☎ 323-850-9050; 7156 Santa Monica Blvd, Hollywood; ☯ from 4pm Mon-Thu, from 6pm Fri & Sat; Ⓟ) Bogie and Bacall used to knock 'em back here, making it a great spot for sopping up some Old Hollywood nostalgia. Mai tais and martinis are the cocktails of choice. Smoking patio.

Santa Monica & Venice
Library Alehouse (Map pp192-3; ☎ 310-314-4855; 2911 Main St, Santa Monica) This not-exactly-quiet-as-a-library pub is regularly voted as having LA's best beer selection. With 29 beers on draft, including four Belgians, and a continuously updated bottle list, who am I to argue? If you just can't make up your mind, get a five-beer sampler. Head to the back patio for more intimate surroundings. Often closes at midnight.

Hideout (Map pp192-3; ☎ 310-429-9920; 112 W Channel Rd, Santa Monica; ☯ from 7pm Mon-Fri, from noon Sat & Sun) Back in the day, this beachfront building on the north side of town housed Will Rogers' favorite speakeasy, Doc Law's Drugstore, which Rogers dubbed the hideout. These days it's a hideout for folks who can't be bothered spending two hours primping before hitting the bar. DJs mix it up on weekend nights (no cover on Friday), and there are free (decent) tacos from 8pm to 11pm on Thursdays.

ENTERTAINMENT
The freebie *LA Weekly* and the *Los Angeles Times* Calendar section (especially Thursday's tabloid-sized pullout) are your best sources for plugging into the local scene. Buy your tickets at the box office or through **Ticketmaster** (☎ 213-480-3232; www.ticketmaster.com). Half-price tickets to many shows are sold online by **LAStageTIX** (www.theatrela.org).

Cinemas
Tickets for most theaters can be prebooked through **Moviefone** (☎ from any LA area code 777-3456).

American Cinematheque (☎ 323-466-3456; www.americancinematheque.com) Hollywood (Map p191; 6712 Hollywood Blvd); Santa Monica (Map pp192-3; 1328 Montana Ave) Eclectic film fare from around the world for serious cinephiles.

Silent Movie Theatre (☎ 323-655-2520; www.silentmovietheatre.com; 611 N Fairfax Ave, Mid-City; adult/student $15/10) 'Silents are golden' at this unique theater where screenings are accompanied by live music.

Live Music & Dance Clubs

Some live-music spots are free, but most average between $5 and $10. If you're determined to do the nightclub thing – at least in Hollywood or WeHo – come armed with a hot bod or a fat wallet in order to impress the goons presiding over the velvet rope. Clubs elsewhere are more laid-back. Covers range from $5 to $20.

Knitting Factory Hollywood (Map p191; ☎ 323-463-0204; 7021 Hollywood Blvd, Hollywood; ⏱ from 9pm) This bastion of indie bands welcomes patrons of all ages and offers up top-notch world music, progressive jazz and other alterna-sounds. Headliners take the main stage, the rest make do with the intimate AlterKnit Lounge.

Conga Room (Map p190; www.congaroom.com; Figueroa & Olympic Blvds in the LA Live complex, Downtown) LA's premier venue for Latin music – partly owned by J-Lo – is moving digs, to the Nokia-sponsored 'entertainment destination' LA Live. When the Conga Room opens its doors in summer 2008, you can look forward to more sizzling nights courtesy of groups like Ozomatli and Aterciopelados.

Babe & Ricky's (☎ 323-295-9112; 4339 Leimert Blvd, Leimert Park; ⏱ from 6pm Mon, Thu-Sat) LA's oldest blues club has nourished bodies and souls for nearly four decades. The Monday night jam session, with free food, brings the house down.

SHOPPING

No matter whether you're a penny-pincher or a power shopper, you'll find lots of opportunities to drop some cash around town.

Fashionistas flock to **Robertson Blvd** (btwn N Beverly & W 3rd St) and **Melrose Ave** (btwn San Vicente & La Brea) in West Hollywood, while bargain hunters haunt Downtown's Fashion District.

DETOUR: LAS VEGAS

Sin City isn't even remotely near the coast, but if you've had it up to here with all that natural beauty, head 270 miles east of LA (four to five hours) to Las Vegas. We don't need to tell you what's there. The quickest route is I-10 east to I-15 north all the way to the Strip. A slower, more scenic option is to detour off from I-15 at Baker and head north through Death Valley National Park or trace a smaller loop south through the Mojave National Preserve.

If money is no object, Beverly Hills beckons with international couture, jewelry and antiques, especially along Rodeo Dr. East of there Silver Lake has cool kitsch and collectibles, especially around **Sunset Junction** (Hollywood & Sunset Blvds). Santa Monica has good boutique shopping on Montana Ave and Main St. In nearby Venice, you'll find bizarre knickknacks along the Venice Boardwalk, although locals prefer Abbot Kinney Blvd with its spirited mix of art, fashion and New Age emporiums.

GETTING THERE & AWAY
Air

The main gateway to LA is **Los Angeles International Airport** (LAX; Map pp188-9; ☎ 310-646- 5252; www.lawa.org). A free minibus for the mobility-impaired can be ordered by calling ☎ 310-646-6402.

Bus

The main bus terminal for **Greyhound** (Map p190; ☎ 213-629-8421; 1716 E 7th St) is in an unsavory part of Downtown, so avoid arriving after dark. Bus 58 makes the 10-minute trip to the transit plaza at Union Station with onward service across town, including Metro Rail's Red Line to Hollywood.

Greyhound buses serve Santa Barbara ($12.50) and San Francisco ($45.50).

Car & Motorcycle

All the major international car-rental agencies have branches at LAX and throughout Los Angeles (see p263 for central reservation numbers). If you haven't prebooked, use the courtesy phones in the arrival areas at LAX.

Train

Amtrak trains roll into Downtown's historic **Union Station** (Map p190; ☎ 800-872-7245; 800 N Alameda St). The *Pacific Surfliner* travels daily to San Diego ($28, 2¾ hours), Santa Barbara ($21, 2½ to three hours) and San Luis Obispo ($29, 5½ hours). See p265 for full details.

GETTING AROUND
To/From the Airport

Door-to-door shuttles, such as those operated by **Prime Time** (☎ 800-473-3743) and **Super Shuttle** (☎ 310-782-6600), leave from the lower level of all terminals. Typical fares to Santa Monica, Hollywood or Downtown are $20, $25 and $15, respectively. Practically all airport-area

DRIVING TOUR: PALOS VERDES PENINSULA & THE SOUTH BAY

What to See

This jaunt on the Palos Verdes Peninsula gets you out of the smog and back to the ocean. San Pedro (san *pee*-dro) is on the edge of the third-busiest container port on the planet, and you don't have to be a transportation geek to be awestruck by – and grudgingly appreciative of – the choreography and sheer volumes of steel at play between ship, crane, train and truck as witnessed from the Vincent Thomas Bridge/Hwy 47. North of downtown is **Green Hills Memorial Park** (27501 S Western Ave, Ocean View plot 875), where writer Charles Bukowski is buried. His epitaph reads 'Don't Try,' which he meant not in the nihilist but in the Yoda sense. In town, you'll find the **Los Angeles Maritime Museum** (☎ 310-548-7618; www.lamaritimemuseum.org; Berth 84, Harbor Blvd & 6th St; adult/child $3/1; ☟ 10am-5pm Tue-Sat, noon-5pm Sun), with intricate ship models, navigational equipment and views of docked container ships from the top floor. From San Pedro, the houses thin out and the ocean and sky open up as you head west on Palos Verdes Rd. You'll notice the road rippling and tilting around Portuguese Bend from the earthquake faults below. The **Wayfarers Chapel** (Map pp188-9; ☎ 310-377-7919; www.wayfarerschapel.org; 5755 Palos Verdes Dr S; admission free; ☟ 8am-5pm) is an enchanting hillside structure surrounded by redwood trees. The work of Lloyd Wright (Frank's son), it's built almost entirely of glass. As the road swoops north, speed by the McMansions but pull off along the water for a stroll along one of the many clifftop trails. Then take your pick of eateries or bars in **Manhattan Beach**, **Redondo Beach** or **Hermosa Beach**. One fine spot is Italian family-style **Mama D's** (☎ 310-546-1492; 1125 Manhattan Ave, Manhattan Beach; dishes $8-12; ⛾), with mix-and-match noodles and sauces.

The Route

You can get here any number of ways. From Long Beach, head over the Vincent Thomas Bridge/Hwy 47 and then head south to reach downtown San Pedro. Then Palos Verdes Rd will start you westward. Stay on this as it swings northward, and connects with your old pal Hwy 1 south of Redondo Beach. Or go counterclockwise if coming from Downtown LA (I-10W to I-405S to Hwy 1).

Time & Mileage

It's around 50 miles to do the loop from Long Beach, or about 80 miles if you start from Downtown LA. The trip could take anywhere from two hours (outside of rush hour) to all day, if you make time for things like the Maritime Museum, a beach hike and a bite in one of the beach towns.

hotels and some hostels have arrangements with shuttle companies for free or discounted pick-ups. The **airport bus** (☎ 714-978-8855; www.airportbus.com) travels hourly or half-hourly from LAX to the main Disneyland resorts for $19 one way or $28 round-trip for adults.

Using public transportation is slower and less convenient but cheaper. From outside any terminal catch a free Shuttle C bus to the LAX Transit Center, the hub for buses serving all of LA. Trip planning help is available at ☎ 800-266-6883 or www.metro.net.

Bicycle

Most buses are equipped with bike racks, although you must securely load and unload it yourself. Bikes are also allowed on Metro Rail trains except during rush hours. For rental places, see p198.

Car & Motorcycle

Parking at motels and cheaper hotels is usually free, while fancier ones charge anywhere from $8 to $25. Valet parking at nicer restaurants and hotels is commonplace. Keep *plenty* of change in your car for meters. It goes without saying that you should try to avoid rush hours.

Public Transportation

LOCAL BUSES

Some neighborhoods are served by local **DASH minibuses** (☎ your area code + 808-2273; www.ladottransit.com), which only run on weekdays, and only until 7pm. Fare per boarding is $0.25.

METRO

LA's main public transportation agency is **Metro** (☎ 800-266-6883; www.metro.net), which operates about 200 bus lines as well as four rail lines. The rail line most used by visitors, the **Red Line**, connects Downtown's Union Station to North Hollywood, via central Hollywood and Universal Studios. The **Blue Line** links Downtown with Long Beach. The **Gold Line** connects Union Station to Pasadena, via Chinatown Station. (Its East LA arm is still under construction.)

Tickets cost $1.25 per boarding or $3 for a day pass with unlimited rides. Bus drivers sell single tickets and day passes (exact fare required), while train tickets are available from vending machines at each station.

Taxi

Except for those taxis lined up outside airports, train stations, bus stations and major hotels, cabbies only respond to phone calls. Some recommended companies:
Independent (☎ 800-521-8294)
Yellow Cab (☎ 800-200-1085)

ORANGE COUNTY

Although it's a mosaic of 34 independent cities, Orange County identifies itself as a county more than any other in SoCal. And thanks to the indulgent TV show of the same name, 'the OC' has become its standard shorthand, cementing its identity as a place seething with spoiled rich kids (and adults, for that matter). Angelinos like to poke fun at their neighbors with the nickname 'the Orange

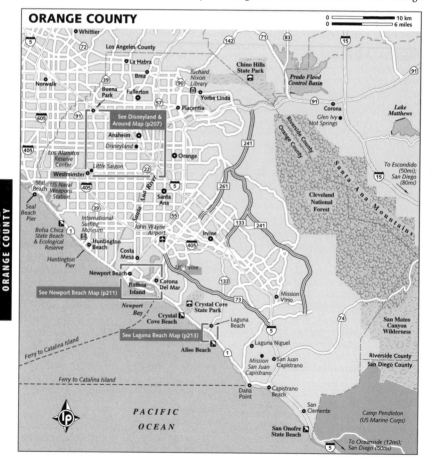

ORANGE COUNTY

0 ————— 10 km
0 ————— 6 miles

Whittier
Los Angeles County
La Habra
Brea
Norwalk
Buena Park
Fullerton
Placentia
Yorba Linda
Richard Nixon Library
Chino Hills State Park
Prado Flood Control Basin
Corona
Glen Ivy Hot Springs
Lake Matthews
See Disneyland & Around Map (p207)
Anaheim
Disneyland
Orange
Los Alamitos Reserve Center
Little Saigon
Westminster
Seal Beach
US Naval Weapons Station
Santa Ana
Seal Beach Pier
Santa Ana River
International Surfing Museum
John Wayne Airport
Irvine
Bolsa Chica State Beach & Ecological Reserve
Huntington Beach
Costa Mesa
Huntington Pier
UC Irvine
Newport Beach
See Newport Beach Map (p211)
Balboa Island
Corona Del Mar
Newport Bay
Crystal Cove Beach
Crystal Cove State Park
Laguna Beach
See Laguna Beach Map (p213)
Mission Viejo
Cleveland National Forest
Orange County
Riverside County
Santa Ana Mountains
To Escondido (50mi); San Diego (80mi)
San Mateo Canyon Wilderness
Ferry to Catalina Island
Aliso Beach
Laguna Niguel
Mission San Juan Capistrano
San Juan Capistrano
Riverside County
San Diego County
Ferry to Catalina Island
Dana Point
Capistrano Beach
San Clemente
Camp Pendleton (US Marine Corps)
PACIFIC OCEAN
San Onofre State Beach
To Oceanside (12mi); San Diego (50mi)

Curtain', referring to the county's brand of conservatism – an amalgam of Christian fundamentalism, libertarianism and immigrant bashing, though Laguna Beach does support a thriving arts scene as well as a strong queer community to go with its wide beaches and aquamarine ocean.

But materialism, rather than conservatism, does seem to be the OC's one unifying sentiment. Preteens flaunt baby-Ts reading 'Me, my Cell and I' and Mercedes SUVs sport decals that brag 'Powered by Daddy's Money'. At least they've got a sense of humor about it.

Information

The knowledgeable folks at the **Anaheim/ Orange County Visitors & Conference Bureau** (Map p207; ☎ 714-765-8888; www.anaheimoc.org; 800 W Katella Ave, Anaheim; ☺ 8am-5pm Mon-Fri) can help with all aspects of OC planning.

DISNEYLAND RESORT

Whether you're as rigid with excitement as the kids or are entertaining the notion of reading in the car for 12 hours, there's no denying the saccharine, singsong pull of Disneyland.

Looking out over the throng of humanity, you're likely to not see a single cell phone – folks are too busy being happy. This is, after all, the happiest day of their lives, or so the loudspeakers inform them as they approach the gates. Er…freaky. Still, you simply can't help but be amazed by this alternate universe, where each detail has been carefully 'imagineered,' from the pastel sidewalks to the personal hygiene of the park's 21,000 employees (called 'cast members' in Disney-speak). Disney's California Adventure (DCA) right next door pays unholy 'tribute' to the state's history and natural wonders.

Tickets & Opening Hours

Both parks are open 365 days a year, but hours can vary. During peak season (mid-June to early September) Disneyland's hours are usually 8am to midnight. The rest of the year it's open from 10am to 8pm or until 10pm. DCA closes at 10pm in summer, earlier in the off-season. Check on the current schedule at ☎ 714-781-4565 or ☎ 714-781-7290 (live assistance) or on http://disneyland.disney.go.com.

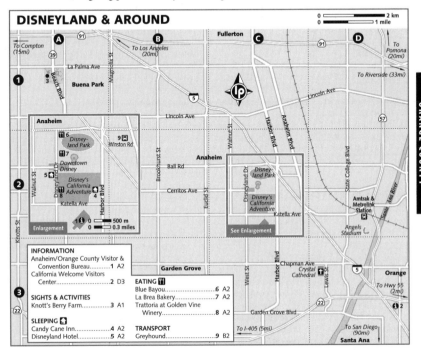

DISNEYLAND & AROUND

INFORMATION
Anaheim/Orange County Visitor &
  Convention Bureau.....................1 A2
California Welcome Visitors
  Center..2 D3

SIGHTS & ACTIVITIES
Knott's Berry Farm................3 A1

SLEEPING
Candy Cane Inn.....................4 A2
Disneyland Hotel...................5 A2

EATING
Blue Bayou............................6 A2
La Brea Bakery......................7 A2
Trattoria at Golden Vine
  Winery................................8 A2

TRANSPORT
Greyhound............................9 B2

DOING DISNEY RIGHT

Here are some tips to help you make the most of your visit:

■ Plan on at least one day for each park, more if you want to go on all the rides. Lines are longest during summer and around major holidays. In December and the first week of January crowds pack the resort to see the holiday decorations. In general, visiting midweek is better than Friday, Saturday or Sunday, and arriving early in the day is best.

■ Bring a hat, sun block and bottled water.

■ If you're not going back to your hotel to eat, make lunch reservations as soon as you arrive.

■ Consider returning to your hotel in the heat of the day. The kids can frolic in the pool while you doze with a book on your face. Come 9pm, while you're standing around waiting for the fireworks display, you'll be *really* glad you did.

At the time of writing, one-day admission to *either* Disneyland *or* DCA costs $63 for adults, $53 for children aged three to nine. To visit *both* parks in one day costs $83/73 per adult/child.

Take advantage of the free Fastpass system, which preassigns specific boarding times for selected attractions, slashing wait times. Fastpass machines are near the entrances to the rides. Simply show up at the time printed on the ticket and go straight to the Fastpass line. There's still a wait, but it'll be much shorter. You can't get a second Fastpass for two hours or until you've used the first.

Disneyland

Upon entering the gates of **Disneyland** (☎ recorded info 714-781-4565, live assistance 714-781-7290; www .disneyland.com; 🚼), you're immediately funneled onto Main Street USA, fashioned after Walt's hometown of Marceline, Missouri. Main St ends in the Central Plaza, the center of the park and the point from which all the 'lands' extend (Frontierland, Tomorrowland etc). Lording it over the plaza is **Sleeping Beauty Castle**.

Disney's California Adventure

DCA covers more acres than Disneyland, feels less crowded than Disneyland, and has a mix of attractions and straightforward amusement park-style rides.

The **Hollywood Pictures Backlot** includes a mishmash of building styles. Especially if the weather is cooperating, you'll do a serious double-take at the end of the **Hollywood Pictures Backlot** street, where a forced-perspective sky-and-land mural makes it look like the street keeps going. One of DCA's big attractions is the 183ft-tall **Twilight Zone Tower of Terror**, which is essentially a drop down an elevator chute in a haunted hotel. It opened just three years after 9/11, causing some controversy over the choice of name. Another is the **California Screamin'** roller coaster, which covers 10 acres and resembles an old wooden coaster, but it's got a smooth-as-silk steel track.

Sleeping & Eating

Candy Cane Inn (☎ 714-774-5284, 800-345-7057; www .candycaneinn.net; 1747 S Harbor Blvd; r $139-179; 🆇 🆂) *This* might be the happiest place around, actually. Guests rave about its sparkling pool and spotless rooms (though the standards are on the cramped side), and pluses like free wi-fi, continental breakfast and gorgeous gardens. The staff members take obvious pride in their work. To top it off, the inn's adjacent to the main gate to Disneyland.

Disneyland Hotel (☎ 714-778-6600; 1150 Magic Way; r $235-270; 🆇 🖳 🆂) The park's original hotel, with a whooping 990 rooms, hasn't lost its appeal, though its three towers feel a bit retro-mod these days. Turn off the lights in your room and Tinker Bell's pixie dust glows in the dark on the walls. The hotel has good-sized rooms, some of which sleep four or more. The Neverland-themed pool has a 110ft waterslide. *Sweet.*

Besides the following sit-down options, each 'land' has several cafeteria-style options.

La Brea Bakery (☎ 714-490-0233; 1556 S Disneyland Dr; breakfast $7-9, lunch & dinner $8-20; 🕑 breakfast, lunch & dinner) Downtown Disney's bakery serves up sandwiches and salads.

Trattoria at Golden Vine Winery (☎ 714-781-3463; dishes $6-17; 🕑 11am-6pm) This is DCA's best place for a relaxing sit-down lunch and serves surprisingly inexpensive pasta, salads and gourmet sandwiches.

TOP DISNEYLAND ATTRACTIONS

■ Space Mountain (Tomorrowland) – Don't be fooled by the Atari-esque molded plastic rocketship. This sucker hurls you through space and leaves you crying for mommy by the end.

■ Indiana Jones Adventure (Adventureland) – You're strapped into a Humvee and forced to contend with all the breaking rope bridges and poisonous snakes the movie Indie faces. The huge rolling ball thing? Wicked cool.

■ Pirates of the Caribbean (New Orleans Sq) – The longest ride and usually the longest wait (no Fastpass). You'll float through the subterranean haunts of pirates, where buccaneers' skeletons perch atop their mounds of booty. If this is a must-see for you, get in line as soon as you arrive.

■ Peter Pan's Flight (Fantasyland) – One of the park's original attractions. You get to fly over London in your own galleon.

■ Splash Mountain (Critter Country) – A pleasant flume ride accompanied by singing and dancing stuffed animals. A camera snaps your picture during the final descent. Enough women were lifting their shirts to earn the ride the nickname 'Flash Mountain'. If you try that now, you'll find a digital Mickey Mouse T-shirt cover-up in your pic.

■ Buzz Lightyear Astro Blasters (Tomorrowland) – A hit with single-digit-aged boys in particular, this is more game than ride. Earn points by blasting the enemy with hand-held laser cannons.

■ Fireworks Display (Central Plaza) – Nightly fireworks over the Magic Castle, complete with flying Tinker Bell.

■ It's a Small World (Fantasyland) – Incessant singing by animatronic dolls from around the world. At first charming, then unnerving, then downright irritating. But hey, it's a classic.

Blue Bayou (☎ 714-781-3463; New Orleans Sq, Disneyland; dishes lunch $11-18, dinner $25-40) Surrounded by the 'bayou' inside Pirates of the Caribbean, this place is famous for its Monte Cristo sandwiches at lunch, and Creole and Cajun specialties at dinner. Reserve early.

Getting There & Away
The Anaheim Resort is just off I-5 on Harbor Blvd, about 30 miles south of Downtown LA. The park is bordered by Ball Rd, Disneyland Dr, Harbor Blvd and Katella Ave. Parking costs $10, cash only. Enter the 'Mickey & Friends' parking structure from southbound Disneyland Dr at Ball Rd (the largest parking structure in the world, with room for 10,300 vehicles).

The **airport bus** (☎ info 714-938-8937; www.airportbus.com) runs between Disneyland-area hotels and Los Angeles International Airport (LAX) at least hourly (one way/round-trip $19/28).

Frequent departures are available with **Greyhound** (☎ 714-999-1256; 100 W Winston Rd) to/from Downtown LA ($9.50, one hour).

The depot next to Angels Stadium is where **Amtrak** (☎ 714-385-1448; 2150 E Katella Ave) trains stop. Tickets to/from LA's Union Station are $9.50 (45 minutes).

Getting Around
Many hotels and motels have free shuttles to Disneyland and other area attractions.

The bus company **Anaheim Resort Transit** (ART; ☎ 888-364-2787; www.rideart.org) provides frequent service to/from Disneyland from hotels in the immediate area. An all-day pass costs $3 per day. You must buy the pass before boarding; pick one up at one of a dozen kiosks or online. Otherwise it's $3 per one-way trip.

HUNTINGTON BEACH
pop 195,000
Welcome to 'Surf City, USA,' according to the old Jan and Dean song, and now according to the law. In 2006, Huntington Beach (HB) won its nasty trademark battle with Santa Cruz over the use of the name 'Surf City, USA', a story that neatly symbolizes the distinctly Californian balance between beach-bum blasé and cutthroat competitiveness. But such contradictions aren't new to HB; in 1907, simply to attract home buyers, megadeveloper Henry Huntington brought over Hawaiian-Irish surfing star George Freeth to give demonstrations, an event considered to be the birth of the mainland

KNOTT'S BERRY FARM

If financial, moral or agoraphobic reasons are putting you off a visit to that Other theme park, consider smaller, quainter, less commercially frenzied **Knott's Berry Farm** (Map p207; ☎ 714-220-5200; www.knotts.com; 8039 Beach Blvd, Buena Park; adult/child 3-11 $40/15; 🚻). It's popular with preteens, especially those raised with limited exposure to the cult of Disney. Just 4 miles northwest of Anaheim off the I-5, the park opened in 1932, when Mr Knott's boysenberries (a loganberry-blackberry-raspberry hybrid) and Mrs Knott's fried-chicken dinners attracted crowds of local farmhands. Mr Knott built an imitation ghost town to keep their guests entertained, and eventually hired local carnival rides and started charging admission.

These days, it's the thrill rides that are the draw, like the **Xcelerator**, a '50s-themed roller coaster that blasts you from 0mph to 82mph in only 2.3 seconds and the teeth-chattering **GhostRider** is one of the best wooden roller coasters in California. It hurtles along a neck-breaking 4530ft track, at one point plunging 108ft with a G-force of 3.14.

Halloween is taken very seriously at 'Knott's Scary Park'. The entire month of October is devoted to scaring the bejesus out of visitors, with a dozen walk-through mazes, four 'scare zones' and countless varieties of the undead on the prowl for fresh blood.

surfing scene. HB's 8½ miles of wide sandy beaches attract as many sun-worshippers as surf-worshippers, so long as they're not put off by the helicopters roaring overhead or the view of the oil pumps and construction work stretching north parallel the beach. You won't be disturbed by any of that once you snag a beachside fire pit (most south of the pier), watch the sunset and then s'more away…until 10pm.

Huntington Beach Convention & Visitors Bureau (☎ 714-969-3492; www.surfcityusa.com; Ste 208, 301 Main St; ☺ 9am-5pm Mon-Fri) provides information.

Sights & Activities

Surfing in HB is competitive. Control your longboard or draw ire from locals. For lessons, check out **M&M Surfing School** (☎ 714-846-7873; www.mmsurfingschool.com) in neighboring Seal Beach, which offers single-day instruction for $40 to $60. **HB Wahine** (☎ 714-969-9399; www.hb wahine.com) is a great female-only surf school. Private lessons cost $100 for two hours.

The **International Surfing Museum** (☎ 714-960-3483; www.surfingmuseum.org; 411 Olive St; admission $2; ☺ noon-5pm daily in summer, Wed-Sun rest of year), on Main St, has exhibits chronicling the sport's history through photos, film, music and memorabilia. Hours can be inconsistent – out surfing, perhaps? – so call ahead.

Car buffs should get up early for a meander through the **Donut Derelicts Car Show** (www.donut derelicts.com; ☺ 6-8:30am Sat), a weekly gathering of woodies, beach cruisers and pimped-out street rods at the corner of Magnolia St and Adams Ave.

Sleeping & Eating

HB suffers from a dearth of interesting lodging options. For more charm factor, head to Laguna Beach.

Hotel Huntington Beach (☎ 714-891-0123, 877-891-0123; www.hotelhb.com; 7667 Center Ave; r $119-149; Ⓟ 🚻 🖥 🐾) This office building clone lacks personality, but its 224 rooms come standard with king-size beds and free perks include parking, wi-fi and a fitness pass.

Bodhi Tree (☎ 714-969-9500; 501 Main St; dishes $4.50-9; ☺ 11am-9pm; Ⓥ) On the north side of town, this 100% vegan, white-tableclothed, mostly Vietnamese joint carries a huge and varied menu. The orange 'chicken' is delish, as is the Vietnamese sandwich.

Sugar Shack (☎ 714-536-0355; 213 Main St; dishes $5-8; ☺ breakfast & lunch) Huge-portion breakfasts are served up here, and if you get here at 6am you can watch surfer dudes don their wet suits. Expect a wait, especially if you want to sit outside. The photos plastering the walls raise it almost to museum status.

Getting There & Away

OCTA (☎ 714-560-6282; www.octa.net) bus 1 connects HB with the rest of OC's beach towns.

NEWPORT BEACH

pop 83,000

By virtue of its long peninsula and maze of manmade islands and inlets, Newport Beach is one of the largest pleasure harbors on the globe – for the miniscule percentage of humans who can afford to drop anchor here. Indeed, Newport Beach oozes wealth. For the rest of us though, the town beckons with family-friendly beaches and several stroll-worthy historical areas.

Newport Beach Conference & Visitors Bureau (☎ 800-942-6278; www.newportbeach-cvb.com; 110 Newport Center Dr, Ste 120, Gateway Plaza Bldg 110; ⊗ 8am-5pm Mon-Fri) provides maps, brochures and other tourist information at its main office near Fashion Island.

Sights

Six miles long, **Balboa Peninsula** has a white-sand beach on its ocean side and a number of stylish homes. Hotels, restaurants and bars cluster around the peninsula's two piers: **Newport Pier**, near its western end, and **Balboa Pier** at the eastern end.

Massive changes are afoot for the historic Balboa Fun Zone, opposite Balboa Pier on the harbor side. The **Newport Harbor Nautical Museum** has bought the property and will be opening up its expanded facility by 2009. The arcades and carousel will be shipping out as their leases expire, but happily, the Ferris wheel is staying put, as is the landmark 1905 **Balboa Pavilion**, which is illuminated at night.

At the very tip of the peninsula adjacent to West Jetty View Park, the **Wedge** is a famous bodysurfing spot. When the timing's right – always in summer – a wave bouncing off the jetty meets another barreling in from sea, and the resulting hollow tunnel can reach 30 bone-crushing feet tall. Watching people get 'thumped' is a popular spectator sport.

In the middle of the harbor sits the island that time forgot, its streets still largely lined with tightly clustered cottages built in the 1920s and '30s – and precious little parking. The promenade that circles Balboa Island makes a terrific walk. The island is connected to the peninsula via a tiny car and passenger **ferry** (per person $0.60, car & driver $1.50; ⊗ 5:30am-2:30am). It lands at Agate Ave, about 11 blocks west of Marine Ave, the main drag.

Sleeping & Eating

Newport Channel Inn (☎ 949-642-3030, 800-255-8614; www.newportchannelinn.com; 6030 W Coast Hwy; r $119-149; P ☷) Right on the highway but just one block from the beach, this kid-friendly motel is one of the better deals in town.

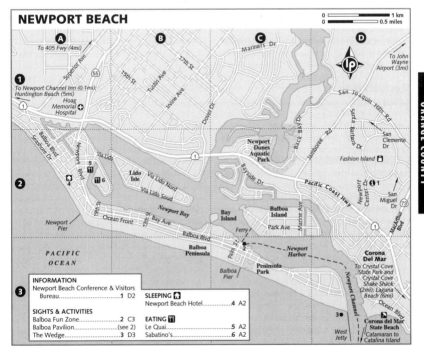

CRYSTAL COVE BEACH COTTAGES

So, the bad news is that you're more likely to win the lottery than score reservations. The good news is, well, that they exist at all. Built throughout the 1920s and '30s, the beach cottages bunched along the 3.5-mile Crystal Cove State Park shoreline between Newport Beach and Laguna Beach slowly evolved into a year-round community, with children romping in the surf while their parents saluted the daily raising of the martini flag.

In 1979 the state park system bought the land from the Irvine Co and extended 20-year leases to the cottages' residents, but when the lease was up, the park system made quick plans for an upscale resort. Enter the Crystal Cove Alliance (www.crystalcovealliance.org), a group of residents who banded together under the leadership of president Laura Davick (who grew up in one of the cottages) to protect the 12-acre property's unique physical and historical fabric.

After five years of fundraising and painstaking work, 22 of the 46 original cottages have been restored to mid-century era condition, with 14 of these now for rent. (The phase two cottages – including the lovely brown-shingled one where Beaches was filmed – are awaiting restoration money.) Each cottage is distinctively decorated, and appliances like the stove and ice box actually work, even though they're period pieces. Three of the cottages are dorm-style, but only the kitchen and bathroom are shared and it's likely you'll barely see your cottage-mates. Two-person, ocean-panoramic 39C is a favorite.

Guests and day-trippers park their cars at on the east side of Hwy 1 at the Los Trancos parking lot and take a 1940s-era school bus ($1) down to the cottages. Without cars, the sandy paths are filled with folks meandering between their cottage, the beach and the Beachcomber's restaurant. And yes, the martini flag-raising ritual has been reinstated.

So, how much are you willing to spend for a night in a lovingly restored oceanfront cabin? $250? $300? Try this on for size: dorm-style cottages go from $30 a night and the most expensive cottages top out at $175 for four people (some can sleep up to nine, at $20 extra per person).

For your spot in paradise you have to plan a half-year out. First browse www.crystalcove beachcottages.com to scope the cottages. Then set up an online account with **Reserve America** (☎ 800-444-7275; www.reserveamerica.com). Finally you're ready to call or log on to Reserve America exactly six months before your intended visit. For example, if you want to book a stay for any night in August, start dialing at 8am sharp on February 1. Better yet, divvy up the family, one half working the phones and the other half the computers.

If unsuccessful, you can always do a day trip to the sparkling beach (parking $10). And keep checking back for cancellations.

The spacious rooms suffer from ugly-bedspreaditis, but do have fridges and microwave ovens.

Newport Beach Hotel (☎ 949-673-7030; www.the newportbeachhotel.com; 2306 W Oceanfront Blvd at 23rd St; r $225-375; P ⊠) As of 2006, this hotel is armed with a new name, new staff and, well, new everything. Its superlative feature has remained, and that is that you can wake up and basically roll into the sand. The 15 rooms sport a clean, modern look, with ivory bedspreads, 400-thread-count sheets, hardwood floors, LCD TVs, wi-fi and marble showers.

Crystal Cove Shake Shack (7703 E Coast Hwy; shakes $5, sandwiches $6-9)This historic spot between Newport Beach and Laguna Beach just got a face-lift and menu expansion, but lost some of its character lines. But the (in)famous – and

enormous – date shake is still delicious, even if you don't like dates.

Sabatino's (☎ 949-723-0621; Ste D, 251 Shipyard Way; lunch $10-17, dinner $12-25; ⊠ lunch & dinner daily, breakfast Sat & Sun) It's so nice to go to an Italian joint and actually hear Italian. Sabatino's claim to fame is its handmade sausage, blended with goats cheese for that cholesterol double-whammy; try the sausage platter, if you dare. The family-sized deli sandwiches, spanking-fresh seafood and Sicilian-style pastas keep the locals coming back. Bring mints – the amounts of garlic used could kill a horse. A place this authentic is appropriately hard to find: it's on the Lido Peninsula, so take Newport Blvd south, then left onto Via Lido. Veer right as the road turns into Lafayette, turn left at the cannery, and follow the road into the Lido shipyard. When you get lost, just call.

Le Quai (☎ 949-673-9463; 2816 Lafayette Rd; dishes $16-35; 🕑 dinner Wed-Sat) If money is no object, Le Quai is an excellent choice for an elegant dinner. Pronounced lu-*kay*, this oh-so-romantic outdoor bistro affords diners the opportunity to gaze out over the boats slipping past while tucking into the well-prepared French fare. Overall, service is gracious, but watch out for wine-pushing pressure tactics.

Getting There & Around

OCTA (☎ 714-560-6282; www.octa.net) bus 1 connects Newport Beach with the rest of OC's beach towns. Bus 71 stops at the corner of Pacific Coast Hwy and Hwy 55, and goes south to the end of the Balboa Peninsula.

LAGUNA BEACH

pop 24,200

There's a good reason why MTV chose this beach town as the setting for its quasireality-based teen melodrama of the same name –Laguna is drop-dead gorgeous, and full of people who share the same attribute. With wooded hillsides, seaside cliffs, pristine beaches and azure waves, this is hands-down the prettiest stretch of coast south of LA. To its unending credit, much of Laguna's 7-mile coastline has been set aside as public space. Artist Norman St Clair 'discovered' Laguna around 1910, and soon other artists influenced by French impressionism, who came to be known as the 'plein air' ('open air') school, were setting up camp. By the late '20s, more than half of the

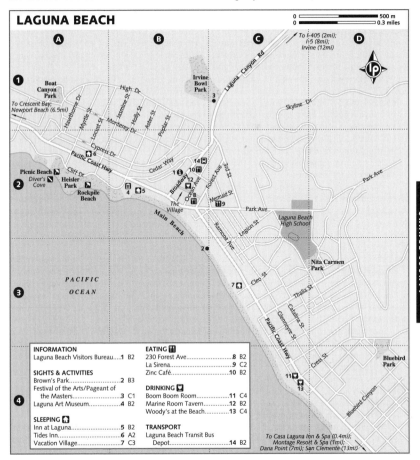

LAGUNA BEACH

INFORMATION		
Laguna Beach Visitors Bureau.....**1** B2		
SIGHTS & ACTIVITIES		
Brown's Park............................**2** B3		
Festival of the Arts/Pageant of		
the Masters.........................**3** C1		
Laguna Art Museum.................**4** B2		
SLEEPING		
Inn at Laguna.........................**5** B2		
Tides Inn...................................**6** A2		
Vacation Village.....................**7** C3		

EATING		
230 Forest Ave.........................**8** B2		
La Sirena...................................**9** C2		
Zinc Café.................................**10** B2		
DRINKING		
Boom Boom Room..................**11** C4		
Marine Room Tavern.............**12** B2		
Woody's at the Beach............**13** C4		
TRANSPORT		
Laguna Beach Transit Bus		
Depot..................................**14** B2		

LOS ANGELES & ORANGE COUNTY

town's 300 residents were artists. Real-estate prices make such ratios impossible these days, but the town's artistic heart still beats vigorously. Public sculpture graces the streets and parks, dozens of galleries feature local artists and the city hosts several renowned festivals. It's also the center of the OC's gay scene.

Orientation & Information

Beguiling shops, restaurants and bars, many hidden in courtyards and housed in funky shacks, are concentrated along a quarter-mile stretch in the Village along three parallel streets: Broadway, Ocean Ave and Forest Ave.

Laguna Beach Visitors Bureau (☎ 800-877-1115; www.lagunabeachinfo.org; 252 Broadway; ☯ 9am-5pm Mon-Fri) provides information, including the interesting public art guide.

Sights & Activities

Laguna Beach has 30 public beaches and coves. Though many are hidden from view by multimillion-dollar homes, most beaches are accessible by stairs off Pacific Coast Hwy; just look for the 'beach access' signs.

Main Beach has volleyball and basketball courts and a playground, and is the best beach for swimming. Northwest of Main Beach, the area is too rocky to surf; tide pooling is best. Delightful **Brown's Park** (551 S Coast Hwy), more of an art-filled garden alley, deadends in a deck overlooking Main Beach.

Just northwest of Main Beach, the grassy, bluff-top **Heisler Park** has sweeping views of the craggy coves and deep blue sea. Drop down below the park to **Diver's Cove**, a deep,

protected inlet popular with snorkelers and, of course, divers.

The **Laguna Art Museum** (☎ 949-494-8971; www.lagunaartmuseum.org; 307 Cliff Dr; adult/child under 12/student $10/free/8; ☯ 11am-5pm) has changing exhibits usually featuring California artists, plus a permanent collection heavy on California landscapes and vintage photographs.

Even if you have no intention of staying there, head to the **Montage Resort & Spa** (☎ 949-715-6000; www.montagelagunabeach.com; 30801 S Coast Hwy; r $500-750; P 🖳 🖭). Swing by for a decadent spa treatment, a cocktail in the lounge (with its view down to the dazzling inlaid sunburst in the pool) or just a stroll on the public walkway through the grounds and down to the beach. There's underground public parking ($0.25 for 10 minutes) on the south end of the resort.

Sleeping & Eating

Tides Inn (☎ 949-494-2494, 888-777-2107; www.tides laguna.com; 460 N Coast Hwy; r $115-225; 🖳 🖭) For Laguna, this place is a bargain, especially considering its location three blocks north of the Village, bend-over-backwards service and comfortable rooms – though some bathrooms are miniscule. Certain rooms have kitchenettes and ocean views. Rooms on the road can be noisy.

Vacation Village (☎ 949-494-8566; 647 S Coast Hwy; r $159-339; P 🖭) Just two blocks from town center, this family-centric, nonhoity-toity resort has 130 clean rooms. About half have ocean views, and many are suites with kitchenettes. Management provides beach towels,

---

FULL MOON PARTY

If you're going to be in SoCal during the second Saturday in July – and you're into lowbrow, drop-trough humor – get your ass over to the annual Amtrak Mooning (www.moonamtrak.org). This loosely organized, all-day and much-of-the-evening event attracts folks looking to expose the passengers of the Amtrak and Metrolink trains to some free entertainment by exposing themselves.

Supposedly in 1979, a man at the **Mugs Away Saloon** (☎ 949-582-9716; 27324 Camino Capistrano, #102) in Laguna Niguel, 4.5 miles north of San Juan Capistrano, announced that he'd buy a round for anyone who ran outside and mooned the next train. Many did, and a beautiful tradition was born.

If you too want to partake, gather on the east side of the tracks. (There's Night Mooning too, for those of shy persuasion.) Cheek decorating is encouraged. If you'd rather be a train-bound lookie-loo, board at any stop from Irvine in the north to San Juan Capistrano in the south (for Amtrak) or Laguna Niguel (for Metrolink).

The easiest way to get to the Laguna Niguel tracks by car is from I-5. Take the Avery Parkway exit, head west at the end of the off-ramp, and then right at the T.

PAGEANT OF THE MASTERS

Laguna Beach's landmark event, the **Festival of the Arts** (☎ 800-487-3378; www.foapom.com; 650 Laguna Canyon Rd; adult/student $7/4; ☺ from 10am Jul & Aug), a seven-week juried exhibit of 160 artists whose work varies from paintings to handcrafted furniture to scrimshaw. Begun in 1932, the festival now attracts patrons and tourists from around the world.

The most thrilling part of the fair by far is the **Pageant of the Masters** (☎ 800-487-3378; tickets $20-80), in which human models (resident Lagunans) blend seamlessly into re-creations of famous works of art – mostly paintings – but sometimes sculptures, coins, even hood ornaments. The lineup of works changes every year, but *The Last Supper* is always included. The viewings are accompanied by live orchestral music and engaging narration.

The pageant began in 1933 as a sideshow to the main festival. Tickets generally go on sale around the beginning of December of the previous year, but even through April your chances are still good at snagging seats. Nightly performances begin at 8:30pm. Beg, borrow or steal a pair of binoculars – no matter where you're sitting – they will enhance the experience a thousand-fold. Bring a jacket; the venue is an outdoor amphitheater.

---

lounge chairs and umbrellas for doing time on its stretch of private beach.

Casa Laguna Inn & Spa (☎ 949-494-2996, 800-233-0449; www.casalaguna.com; 2510 S Coast Hwy; r $200-590; P ⊗ ⚏ ⚏) Cascading down a terraced hillside on the south side of town, this gorgeous mission-style B&B has 22 rooms and suites interspersed within an acre of gardens. Each of the rooms is uniquely furnished, but all feature seven layers of bedding – heaven! The fastidious attention to detail shines through from the gourmet breakfast straight on to the evening cordial. Watch the sun set from the ocean view hot tub and know utter satisfaction.

La Sirena (☎ 949-499-2301; 347 Mermaid St; dishes $4-10; ☺ 11am-9pm Mon-Sat) La Sirena, which means mermaid in Spanish, takes the best elements of Mexican cuisine and whips them up into a Cali-style frenzy – fresh, zesty and healthy. There's no lard in those handmade tortillas, and the salsa bar rocks. Try the salmon-fish tacos or the chicken tortilla soup. Other than a picnic table outside, there's no place to sit – and no alcohol is served – so get your order to go and head to the beach.

Zinc Café (☎ 949-494-6302; 350 Ocean Ave; dishes $5-8; ☺ breakfast & lunch; Ⓥ) Come on a weekend especially and you'll be waiting a while, but in the meantime there will be dogs to pet, bulletin boards to peruse and locals' conversations to eavesdrop on. Once you're seated on the shady patio, you're ready to order from the relatively limited, all-vegetarian menu. It's also got prepared sandwiches for those on the run.

230 Forest Avenue (☎ 949-494-2545; 230 Forest Ave; dishes $16-32; ☺ dinner) This chic, bustling bistro is a perennial local favorite as much for the people-watching through the floor-to-ceiling windows as for its finely crafted menu. It specializes in seafood – the hazelnut-crusted Alaskan halibut is a joy – but the pastas and meats hold their own as well, both in taste and presentation. Martini-lovers will be spoilt for choice.

Drinking

Marine Room Tavern (☎ 949-494-3027; 214 Ocean Ave; admission $5-10) This place packs in a crowd of Harley riders and PYTs, but not a Marine in sight. Full bar, no food, and rockin' live music every night but Monday.

Woody's at the Beach (☎ 949-376-8809; 1305 S Coast Hwy) Woody's offers elegant dishes like herb-grilled chicken to go with its lively bar scene. Its outdoor deck overlooks, you guessed it, the beach.

Boom Boom Room (☎ 949-494-7588; 1401 S Coast Hwy; ☺ Tue-Sun) To the dismay of OC's queer community, efforts to 'Save the Boom!' may have failed, and this venerable club dating back to the 1920s will likely lose its lease as of September 2007. Until then, gays and straights alike whoop it up on Friday, Saturday and Wednesday (drag show night). The Boom is inside the Coast Inn.

Getting There & Around

To reach Laguna Beach from the I-405, take Hwy 133 (Laguna Canyon Rd) southwest. Laguna is served by OCTA bus 1, which

SAN JUAN CAPISTRANO

Famous the world over for the swallows that return from their winter migration on the same day every year, the town of San Juan Capistrano is also home to the 'jewel of the California missions.'

Located about 10 miles southeast and inland of Laguna Beach, the **Mission San Juan Capistrano** (Map p206; ☎ 949-234-1300; www.missionsjc.com; 31882 Camino Capistrano; adult/child/senior $6/4/5; ⏰ 8:30am-5pm) was built around a series of 18th-century arcades, each of which enclose charming fountains and lush gardens that range from rose to cactus to water lilies, and often awash in Monarch butterflies. The whitewashed Serra Chapel is considered the oldest building in California and is the only chapel still standing in which Father Junípero Serra gave Mass.

To celebrate the swallows' return from their Argentine sojourn, the city puts on the **Festival of the Swallows** every year on March 19. Calling the ceilingless Great Stone Church 'the American Acropolis' is a bit of a stretch, but in its walls is where the beloved swallows make their summer home until around October 23.

From Laguna Beach, take OCTA bus 1 south to K-Mart Plaza, then connect to bus 191/A in the direction of Mission Viejo, which drops you near the mission ($2, about one hour). Drivers should exit I-5 at Ortega Hwy and head west for about a quarter of a mile.

runs along the coast from Long Beach to San Clemente.

Parking is a perpetual problem. Hoard your quarters. If you're spending the night, leave your car at the hotel and ride the local bus. Pacific Coast Hwy through town moves slowly in summer, especially on weekend afternoons.

Laguna Beach Transit (☎ 949-497-0746; 300 block of Broadway) has its central bus depot on Broadway, just north of the visitors bureau in the heart of the Village. It operates three routes at hourly intervals (approximately 7am to 6pm Monday to Friday, 9am to 6pm Saturday). Rides cost $0.75.

San Diego Area

California's second-largest city doesn't seduce like San Francisco or thrill like Los Angeles, but life in San Diego is so persistently pleasant that you won't care much, what with its 70 miles of coastline and the country's most enviable climate. It seems appropriate that a map of the metropolitan area resembles the profile of an elephant's head (or is it just me?); conservative and slow-moving yet gracious, good-looking and highly likable.

Actually, the first part of the metaphor is loosening its grip with each passing year; San Diego's biotech-fueled economy continues to attract new blood to a region long overloaded by retirees and military types. You can feel a fresh snap in the air (only figuratively, of course) and spring in the step.

The city's offerings can easily keep you entertained for the good part of a week, as you hopscotch between the outstanding museums and gardens in Balboa Park (one of the country's largest urban parks), the sizzling nightlife of the Gaslamp Quarter and the requisite vegging out wave-side.

Spreading north from the city, a necklace of beach communities runs the gamut from bohemian to bourgeois, with as many chances for adventure as you're willing to take, be it hiking and snorkeling or, for adrenaline junkies, paragliding and hang gliding.

If San Diego's orderly perfection starts getting to you, overload your senses in Tijuana, Mexico, just a short trolley ride away.

HIGHLIGHTS

- Checking out the lions and tigers and bears at the world-renowned **San Diego Zoo** (p227) and the **Wild Animal Park** (p227)
- Gorging yourself on knowledge and art at the museums in **Balboa Park** (p225)
- Poking around the neighborhood of **Hillcrest** (p228) – used bookstores, vintage clothes, funky bars and the center of San Diego's queer community
- Sipping a cocktail at the **Hotel del Coronado** (p236) overlooking the blinding-white beach.
- Making a run for the border and living *la vida loca* in tacky, trippy **Tijuana** (p244)
- Beach-hopping along the string of easygoing coast towns in North County, like hippie-dippy **Encinitas** (p242)
- Watching the sunset – and hearing the crowd break out in applause – at **Crystal Pier** (p230) on Pacific Beach

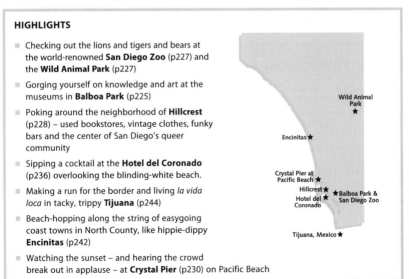

SAN DIEGO AREA

SAN DIEGO

pop 1.3 million

Though it's undergoing rapid growth, San Diego has so far managed to retain a laid-back resort feel amid the skyscrapers, with the Old Town and Gaslamp Quarter pulling their historical weight. Neighborhoods like Hillcrest, Bankers Hill and South Park are luring the young and the hip to a city long mired in its military and blue-hair image. And few cities can compare on the kid-friendly meter, what with two world-famous zoos and other kid-positive attractions like SeaWorld. In San Diego, you can't escape the presence of the water, whether you're whale-watching from the tip of Point Loma, frolicking on Ocean Beach, building a championship-worthy sandcastle on Imperial Beach or getting snorkel-happy in La Jolla Cove.

HISTORY

By the time Spanish explorer Juan Rodríguez Cabrillo became the first European to sail into San Diego Bay in 1542, the region was divided peaceably between the native Kumeyaay and Luiseño/Juaneño peoples. Their way of life continued undisturbed until Junípero Serra and Gaspar de Portolá arrived in 1769, founding a mission and a military fort on the hill now known as the Presidio, making it the first permanent European settlement in California.

The discovery of gold in the hills east of San Diego in 1869 soon brought the railroad to San Diego, but when the gold played out, the economy took a nosedive and the city's population plummeted. So when San Francisco hosted the Panama-Pacific International Exposition in 1914, the next year San Diego responded with its own Panama-California Exposition, hoping to attract investment. To give San Diego a unique image, boosters built exhibition halls (see p225) in the Spanish colonial style that still defines much of the city today.

However, it was the bombing of Pearl Harbor in 1941 that really made San Diego. The US Pacific Fleet needed a mainland home for its headquarters and it settled on San Diego, whose excellent deepwater port affords protection in almost all weather. The military literally reshaped the city, dredging the harbor

and building landfill islands. The opening of the University of California campus in the 1960s heralded a new era as students slowly drove a liberal wedge into the city's homogenous, flag-and-family culture.

ORIENTATION

San Diego is user-friendly, geographically speaking. The airport, train station and bus terminal are within, or very close to, the city center. (You'll get used to the planes' alarmingly low take-off and landing patterns.) Downtown consists of a compact grid of streets east of San Diego Bay and encompasses the Gaslamp Quarter, the Embarcadero and Little Italy. Balboa Park and the zoo sit north of town, and at the northwest edge of the park lie the Uptown and Hillcrest districts. Keep heading northwest from Hillcrest and you arrive in Old Town.

Coronado, the peninsula that guards San Diego Bay, is accessible from downtown by bridge or a short ferry. Across the mouth of the bay lies another, rockier peninsula, which comes to a dramatic end at Point Loma and offers great views over city and sea. Moving

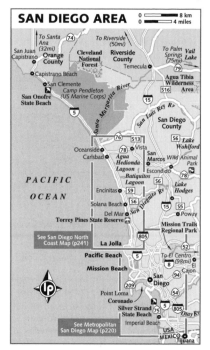

north up the coast, you arrive at Ocean Beach followed by Mission Bay, with its tranquil parks and lagoons. Beyond Mission Bay and Beach lies Pacific Beach. Finally, you hit upscale La Jolla.

INFORMATION
Bookstores

Book hounds should peruse the old, new and rare offerings of bookstores on 5th Ave between University and Robinson Aves in Hillcrest.

Bluestocking Books (Map pp222-3; ☎ 619-296-1424; 3817 5th Ave; ⏱ 11am-7pm Tue-Thu, to 9:30pm Fri-Mon) Despite the name, this isn't a 'womens' bookstore, but a funky, all-encompassing spot with new and used tomes.

DG Wills Books (☎ 858-456-1800; 7461 Girard Ave, La Jolla; ⏱ 10am-7pm Mon-Sat, 11am-6pm Sun) Dennis Wills himself will likely be holding down the fort of his bookstore, a fixture in the area. A must for those of bookish bent.

Le Travel Store (Map p221; ☎ 619-544-0005; 745 4th Ave; ⏱ 10am-7pm Mon-Sat, noon-6pm Sun) Next to STA Travel, it's got maps, travel guides and accessories.

Emergency & Medical Services

Scripps Mercy Hospital (Map pp222-3; ☎ 619-294-8111; 4077 5th Ave; ⏱ 24hr) An urgent-care clinic operates in addition to an emergency room.

Internet Access

All public libraries provide free internet access. Or try the following:

David's Coffee House (Map pp222-3; ☎ 619-296-4173; 3766 5th Ave, Hillcrest; ⏱ 7am-11pm Sun-Thu, to midnight Fri & Sat) Wi-fi, plus three computers if you're laptopless. And…wait for it…both Pac-Man and Centipede video games.

Living Room Coffeehouse (Map pp222-3; ☎ 619-295-7911; 1417 University Ave, Hillcrest; ⏱ 6am-midnight) Another coffeehouse with connections.

Media

KPBS 89.5FM Public radio, high-quality news and information.

San Diego Reader What's happening in town, particularly on the active music, art and theater scenes; pick up a free copy all over town.

Post

For local post office locations, call ☎ 800-275-8777 or log on to www.usps.com.

Downtown post office (Map p221; ☎ 619-232-8612; 815 E St; ⏱ 8:30am-5pm Mon-Fri)

Tourist Information

International Visitors Information Center (Map p221; ☎ 619-236-1212; www.sandiego.org; 1040-1/3 W Broadway at Harbor Dr; ⏱ 9am-5pm daily Jun-Aug & Thu-Tue Sep-May) The on-site official visitors center for the city sits across from Broadway Pier, along the Embarcadero.

DANGERS & ANNOYANCES

Areas of interest to visitors are well defined and mostly within easy reach of downtown by foot or by public transportation. San Diego is a fairly safe city, though you should be cautious venturing east of about 6th Ave in downtown, especially after dark. Hostile panhandling is the most common problem. Steer clear of Balboa Park after nightfall.

SIGHTS
Downtown

Just south of the city's stretch of skyscrapers lies the historic Gaslamp Quarter, and closer to the bay and near the city's mammoth convention center looms Petco, San Diego's baseball stadium, which has helped seal the renewal of the entire downtown. To the west lies the Embarcadero district, a fine place for a bayfront jog. A short walk north lands you in Little Italy, where mom-and-pop eateries alternate with high-end design stores.

GASLAMP QUARTER

Founded in 1867, the Gaslamp Quarter has, almost since its inception, catered to the vices of travelers. During San Diego's Gold Rush of the 1870s, the neighborhood quickly degenerated into a string of saloons, bordellos, gambling halls and opium dens. In San Diego's postwar boom, the Victorian and beaux arts buildings were left to molder while the rest of downtown was razed and rebuilt. When developers started to eye the area in the early 1980s, preservationists organized to save the old brick and stone facades from the wrecking ball.

These days, the Gaslamp Quarter is again the focus of the city's nightlife, though of a significantly tamer variety. Come after nightfall on a Friday or Saturday and watch as men flash their plastic money and women their plastic cleavages, to the entertainment of all.

(Continued on page 225)

SAN DIEGO AREA

0 —————— 6 km
0 —————— 4 miles

Torrey Pines
State Reserve
Torrey Pines
City Park
Gliderport
Salk Institute
Black's
Beach
UCSD
Scripps
Pier
Scripps Research
Institute
La Jolla
Shores
La Jolla
Soledad
Mtn
(822ft)
Windansea
Beach
Pacific
Beach
Tourmaline
Surfing Park
Crystal Pier
Garnet Ave
Grand Ave
See Mission
Bay & the
Beaches
Map (p224)
Mission Beach
Ocean Beach
Park
Ocean
Beach Pier
Point Loma
Ave
Ocean Beach
Sunset Cliffs
Park
Point Loma
Point
Loma Sport
Fishing
Shelter
Island
Harbor Island
Cabrillo National
Monument
Point Loma
Old Point
Loma Lighthouse
North Island
US Naval
Air Station
Holland's
Bicycles
Orange Ave
Hotel del
Coronado
Coronado
Coronado
Bay Bridge
Silver Strand
State Beach
US Naval
Communication
Station
Imperial
Beach Pier
Palm Ave
Imperial
Beach
Border
Field
State
Park
South
San Diego
PACIFIC
OCEAN
Ferry to Catalina
See La Jolla
Map (p231)

To Del Mar (6mi);
Solana Beach (8.5mi);
Encinitas (12mi);
Carlsbad (23mi)
To Escondido (15mi)
Miramar Rd
US Marine Corps
Air Station - Miramar
University
Towne Centre
La Jolla Village Dr
Genesee Ave
See San Diego
North Coast
Map (p241)
Mission Trails
Regional Park
San Diego River
Clairemont Mesa Blvd
Tierrasanta Blvd
Balboa Ave
Tecolote
Canyon
National
Park
Mission Gorge Rd
Navajo Rd
Jackson Dr
Lake Murray
To El Cajon (10mi)
Mission
San Diego
de Alcalá
Qualcomm
Stadium
San Diego
State University
Montezuma Rd
El Cajon Blvd
El Cajon Blvd
University Ave
La Mesa
East
San Diego
Lemon
Grove
Akins Ave
San Diego
Trolly
Paradise Valley Rd
Sweetwater River
KOA
National
City
Bonita Rd
Chula
Vista
Telegraph Canyon Rd
Main St
Otay Valley Rd
Otay River
Otay Mesa Border
Crossing (8mi)
San
Ysidro
Border
Crossing
Tijuana River
California (U S A)
Baja California (M E X I C O)
Tijuana
University
of San Diego
Fashion
Valley
Hazard Centre
Mission Valley
Friars Rd
Old Town
San Diego
International
Airport
Harbor Dr
Broadway
Market St
Imperial Ave
National Ave
San Diego
Bay
Silver Strand Blvd
Hillcrest
University
Heights
Normal
Heights
Washington St
University Ave
San Diego
See Balboa Park, Hillcrest
and Old Town Map (pp222–3)
Balboa
Park
Fairmount Ave
See Downtown San
Diego Map (p221)
SeaWorld
San Diego
Sports Arena
Mission
Bay

DOWNTOWN SAN DIEGO

0 — 500 m
0 — 0.3 miles

To Midway Postal Station (2mi); Old Town (1mi); Mission Bay (4mi)

San Diego International Airport

To Point Loma (4mi)

To Hillcrest (2.5mi)

To San Diego Zoo (0.3mi)

El Prado

Cabrillo Bridge

Pan American Plaza

Balboa Park

Kalmia St
Juniper St
Ivy St

Middletown

Hawthorn St

Grape St

Fir St

Elm St

Kalmia St
Juniper St
Ivy St

Curlew St
Brant St
Albatross St
Front St

6th Ave

Balboa Blvd

163

Cabrillo Fwy

San Diego Fwy
To El Cajon & Tijuana

5

To San Diego Zoo (0.5mi)

Piers

San Diego Bay

Hawthorn St

Grape St

California St
Kettner Blvd
Columbia St
India St
Juniper St
Ivy St

San Diego Trolley

13
11
20
10

Little Italy

Date St

Cedar St

Beech St

Ash St

A St

B St

C St

Broadway

E St

F St

County Administration Center

County Center/ Little Italy

Pacific Hwy

N Harbor Dr

Santa Fe Train Depot (Amtrak)

San Diego Trolley American Plaza Terminal

8
5

18
19

San Diego City College

San Diego City College

San Diego Trolley

San Diego Fwy

Civic Center

Fifth Avenue

San Diego Trolley

Horton Plaza Park
15

Weston Horton Plaza

Broadway Circle

San Diego-Coronado Ferry

3
1
17
6

Broadway Pier

Navy Pier

Navy Broadway Complex

Pantoja Park

Seaport Village

Market St

Park

Tuna Ln
G St Ln

Tuna Harbor

Pier

Seaport Village

Embarcadero Marina Park

San Diego Convention Center

Harbor Dr

San Diego Trolley

Gaslamp Quarter

Island Ave

Convention Center
12

14
9

Petco Park

Gaslamp Quarter

2

G St

F St

Market St
13th Ave
14th Ave
12th & Market
11th Ave
12th Ave
10th Ave
9th Ave
8th Ave
7th Ave

J St

K St

L St

National Ave

12th & Imperial Transfer Station

Convention Way

See Balboa Park & Hillcrest Map (pp222–3)

5th Ave

1st Ave
2nd Ave
3rd Ave
4th Ave
5th Ave
6th Ave

Kettner Blvd
Columbia St
State St
Union St
Front St
India St

16

1
3

INFORMATION		SLEEPING		DRINKING	
International Visitors Information Center............1 A3		500 West Hotel..............8 B3		Café Bassam..........14 C4	
Le Travel Store.................2 C4		HI San Diego Downtown Hostel............9 C4			
		La Pensione Hotel.........10 B2		ENTERTAINMENT	
SIGHTS & ACTIVITIES		Little Italy Inn.............11 B2		Times Art Tix............15 C3	
Hornblower Cruises.........3 A3					
Maritime Museum...........4 A3		EATING		TRANSPORT	
Museum of Contemporary Art San Diego - Downtown..5 B3		Gaslamp Strip Club.......12 C4		Cruise Ship Terminal.........16 A3	
		Mona Lisa...............13 B1		Ferry Landing............17 A3	
San Diego Aircraft Carrier Museum..............6 A4				Greyhound Station...........18 B3	
San Diego Harbor Excursion..7 A3				Transit Store............19 C3	
				West Coast Rent a Car.....20 B2	

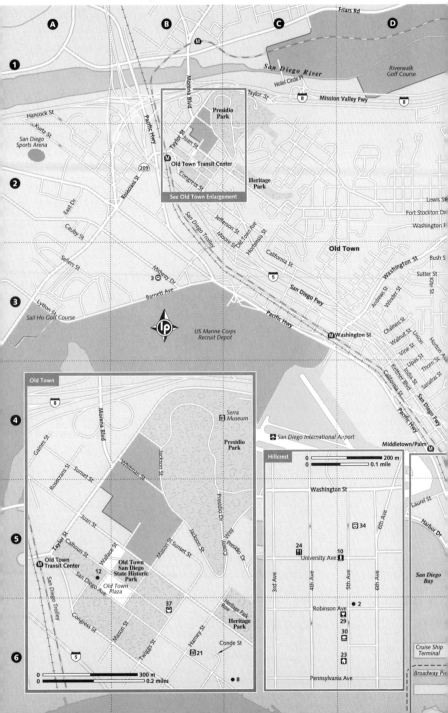

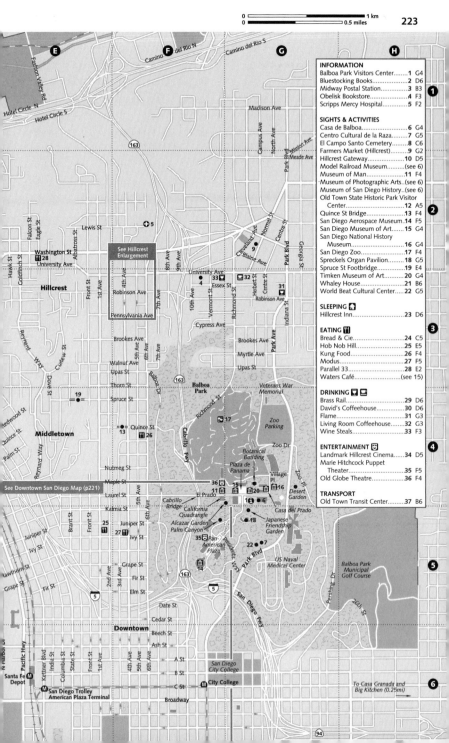

INFORMATION
Balboa Park Visitors Center.........1 G4
Bluestocking Books....................2 D6
Midway Postal Station...............3 B3
Obelisk Bookstore.....................4 F3
Scripps Mercy Hospital..............5 F2

SIGHTS & ACTIVITIES
Casa de Balboa.........................6 G4
Centro Cultural de la Raza.........7 G5
El Campo Santo Cemetery........8 C6
Farmers Market (Hillcrest).........9 G2
Hillcrest Gateway.....................10 D5
Model Railroad Museum...........(see 6)
Museum of Man.......................11 F4
Museum of Photographic Arts..(see 6)
Museum of San Diego History..(see 6)
Old Town State Historic Park Visitor
  Center................................12 A5
Quince St Bridge.....................13 F4
San Diego Aerospace Museum.14 F5
San Diego Museum of Art.......15 G4
San Diego National History
  Museum..............................16 G4
San Diego Zoo........................17 F4
Spreckels Organ Pavilion.........18 G5
Spruce St Footbridge...............19 E4
Timken Museum of Art............20 G4
Whaley House........................21 B6
World Beat Cultural Center......22 G5

SLEEPING
Hillcrest Inn............................23 D6

EATING
Bread & Cie.............................24 C5
Hob Nob Hill..........................25 E5
Kung Food..............................26 F4
Modus.....................................27 F5
Parallel 33...............................28 E2
Waters Café...........................(see 15)

DRINKING
Brass Rail................................29 D6
David's Coffeehouse................30 D6
Flame......................................31 G3
Living Room Coffeehouse........32 G3
Wine Steals.............................33 F3

ENTERTAINMENT
Landmark Hillcrest Cinema....34 D5
Marie Hitchcock Puppet
  Theater...............................35 F5
Old Globe Theatre..................36 F4

TRANSPORT
Old Town Transit Center.........37 B6

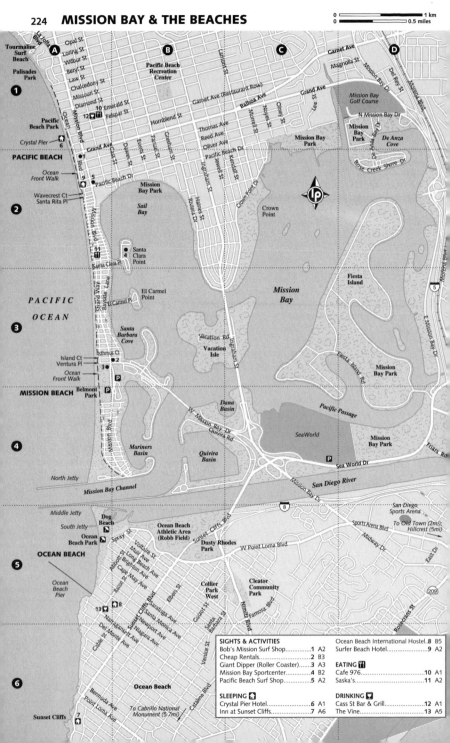

0 | 1 km
0 | 0.5 miles

A **B** **C** **D**

1
Tourmaline
Surf Beach
Palisades
Park
Opal St
Loring St
Wilbur St
Beryl St
Law St
Chalcedony St
Missouri St
Diamond St
Emerald St 10
Felspar St 12
Pacific Beach
Recreation Center
Garnet Ave (Restaurant Row)
Balboa Ave
Grand Ave
Garnet Ave
Magnolia St
Mission Bay Golf Course
N Mission Bay Dr
Mission Bay Park
Lee St
Olney St
Morrell St
Noyes St
Lamont St
Mission Bay Park
De Anza Cove
Del Rey St
Modena Blvd

2
Pacific Beach Park
Crystal Pier
PACIFIC BEACH
Ocean Front Walk
Wavecrest Ct
Santa Rita Pl
Hornblend St
Thomas Ave
Reed Ave
Oliver Ave
Pacific Beach Dr
Grand Ave
Ingraham St
Jewell St
Kendall St
Mission Bay Park
Crown Point
Sail Bay
Haines St
Riviera Dr
Crown Point Dr
5
Rose Creek Shore Dr

3
PACIFIC
OCEAN
Santa Clara Point
El Carmel Point
Mission Bay
Fiesta Island
11
Santa Clara Pl
El Carmel Pl
Vacation Rd
Ingraham St
Mission Bay Park
Fiesta Island Rd
Friars Rd

4
Island Ct
Ventura Pl
Ocean Front Walk
MISSION BEACH
Belmont Park
Isthmus Ct
Santa Barbara Cove
Mariners Basin
North Jetty
Mission Bay Channel
Dana Basin
Vacation Isle
W Mission Bay Dr
Quivira Rd
Quivira Basin
SeaWorld
Pacific Passage
Mission Bay Park
Sea World Dr
San Diego River
Mission Bay Dr

5
Middle Jetty
South Jetty
Ocean Beach Park
OCEAN BEACH
Ocean Beach Pier
Dog Beach
Ocean Beach Athletic Area (Robb Field)
Spray St
Voltaire St
Muir Ave
Abbott St
St Louis Mall Ave
W Point Loma Blvd
Sunset Cliffs Blvd
Dusty Rhodes Park
Collier Park West
Cleator Community Park
Nimitz Blvd
Famosa Blvd
Sports Arena Blvd
Midway Dr
San Diego Sports Arena
To Old Town (2mi); Hillcrest (5mi)
East St
Rosecrans St

6
Sunset Cliffs
7
Ocean Beach
13
8
Bacon St
Cape May Ave
Brighton Ave
Narragansett Ave
Del Monte Ave
Cable St
Bermuda Ave
Point Loma Ave
Santa Monica Ave
Newport Ave
Niagara Ave
Saratoga Ave
Ebers St
Guizot St
Venice St
Catalina Blvd
Santa Barbara St
To Cabrillo National Monument (5.7mi)
209

SIGHTS & ACTIVITIES	
Bob's Mission Surf Shop	1 A2
Cheap Rentals	2 B3
Giant Dipper (Roller Coaster)	3 A3
Mission Bay Sportcenter	4 B2
Pacific Beach Surf Shop	5 A2
SLEEPING	
Crystal Pier Hotel	6 A1
Inn at Sunset Cliffs	7 A6
Ocean Beach International Hostel	8 B5
Surfer Beach Hotel	9 A2
EATING	
Cafe 976	10 A1
Saska's	11 A2
DRINKING	
Cass St Bar & Grill	12 A1
The Vine	13 A5

(Continued from page 219)

MUSEUM OF CONTEMPORARY ART SAN DIEGO – DOWNTOWN

As of January 2007, **MCASD** (Map p221; ☎ 619-234-1001; 1001 Kettner Blvd; admission free; ☣ 11am-5pm Thu-Tue) completed work on its ambitious expansion, with renovation of the existing building – which used to be the train station's baggage building – plus a three-story contemporary art space, which adds a modern counterpoint to the museum's mission-style architecture. MCASD is the downtown branch of the La Jolla–based institution (p230) that has brought groundbreaking art to San Diegans since the 1960s.

LITTLE ITALY

Italian immigrants, mostly fishermen, began settling this rise of land just up from San Diego Bay in the 19th century. The community had its heyday in the 1920s, when Prohibition opened up new 'business opportunities' (read 'bootlegging'). Unfortunately, the construction of I-5 tore apart its cultural fabric. Nevertheless, the hardiest of the old family businesses have survived and, thanks to the city's recent urban renaissance, they've gained new clientele. Now old-world grocery stores alternate with slick cafés and high-end boutiques.

Embarcadero

This whole area, west of downtown, is undergoing a dramatic transformation in the form of a 1.2-mile tree-lined esplanade, and construction of a pier and a wharf, among other ambitious projects. The final results won't be seen until around 2009.

The 100ft masts of the square-rigger *Star of India* will help you spot the **Maritime Museum** (Map p221; ☎ 619-234-9153; 1492 N Harbor Dr; all 3 vessels adult/child 6-17 $12/8; ☣ 9am-8pm). Launched in 1863, the tall ship plied the England-India trade route and carried immigrants to New Zealand. The museum takes you on a journey through the history of water voyage, plus a fair amount of navy stuff.

The main attraction, though, is the **San Diego Aircraft Carrier Museum** (Map p221; ☎ 619-544-9600; www.midway.org; Navy Pier; adult/child 6-17/senior & student $15/8/10; ☣ 10am-5pm; Ⓟ) aboard the USS *Midway*, the navy's longest-serving aircraft carrier (1945–91). A self-guided audio tour takes in the berthing spaces, the galley, the sick bay and, of course, the flight deck with its restored aircraft.

Balboa Park

After receiving her botany degree in 1881, Kate O Sessions came to San Diego as a teacher but soon began working as a horticulturist, establishing gardens for the fashionable homes of the city's emerging elite. In 1892, in need of space for a nursery, she suggested to city officials that they allow her the use of 30 acres of city-owned Balboa Park for her nursery in return for planting 100 trees a year and donating 300 others for placement throughout San Diego. The city agreed, and within a decade Balboa Park had shade trees, lawns, paths and flowerbeds. San Diegans soon began referring to her as 'The Mother of Balboa Park.' Today, it's one of the country's finest urban parks, with flower gardens and shaded walks, tennis courts and swimming pools, museums and theaters, a velodrome, golf courses, an outdoor organ and one of the world's great zoos. The park is also the city's premier cultural center, with a cluster of theaters and museums arrayed along the El Prado promenade.

To visit everything would take a full two days, so plan your visit carefully. Note that many museums are closed Monday, and several per week (on a rotating basis) are free Tuesday. The best spot within the park to assuage hunger pangs is Waters Cafe (p237).

The **Balboa Park Visitors Center** (Map pp222-3; ☎ 619-239-0512; 1549 El Prado; ☣ 9am-4pm) in the House of Hospitality sells the Balboa Passport (adult single entry to 13 of the park's museums for one week) for $30.

Balboa Park is easily reached from downtown on bus 7, 7A or 7B along Park Blvd. By car, Park Blvd provides easy access to free parking areas. From the west, El Prado is an extension of Laurel St, which crosses Cabrillo Bridge.

The free Balboa Park Tram stops at various points on a continuous loop through the main areas of the park. (It's actually a bus rather than a tram and is not to be confused with the Old Town Trolley tour bus.)

EL PRADO

Originally built for the 1915–16 Panama-California Exposition, these Spanish colonial buildings are particularly beautiful in the morning and evening. The original exposition

SAN DIEGO AREA

halls, which were mostly constructed out of stucco, chicken wire, plaster, hemp and horsehair, were only meant to be temporary. However, they proved so popular that, over the years, they have been gradually replaced with durable concrete replicas.

California Building & Museum of Man

As you enter Balboa Park via Laurel St, you cross the picturesque Cabrillo Bridge and then pass under an archway and into an area called the California Quadrangle, with the **Museum of Man** (Map pp222-3; ☎ 619-239-2001; www.museumofman.org; adult/child under 6/child 6-17/senior $6/free/3/5; ☺ 10am-4:30pm). Its richly decorated **Tower of California** has become a symbol of San Diego itself. The museum specializes in Native American artifacts, in particular from the American Southwest.

Old Globe Theatre

Built in the style of Shakespeare's Old Globe in London, this **theater** (Map pp222-3; ☎ 619-239-2255; www.oldglobe.org) won a Tony award in 1984 for its ongoing contribution to theater arts. You can catch performances year-round.

San Diego Museum of Art

This small but elegant **museum** (Map pp222-3; ☎ 619-232-7931; www.sdmart.org; adult/child 6-17/student $10/4/7; ☺ 10am-6pm Tue-Sun, to 9pm Thu) has no truly famous works in its permanent collection, but includes a decent survey of European art, from Giotto to Josef Albers, as well as some noteworthy American landscape paintings and Asian art.

Timken Museum of Art

Distinctive for *not* being in imitation Spanish style, this tiny **building** (Map pp222-3; ☎ 619-239-5548; www.timkenmuseum.org; 1500 El Prado; admission free; ☺ 10am-4:30pm Tue-Sat, 1:30-4:30pm Sun Oct-Aug) houses works by Rembrandt, Rubens and El Greco. There's also a remarkable selection of Russian icons. The museum is named after the Timken family, who rode to fame and fortune on the invention of the roller bearer used in horse-drawn carriages.

Casa de Balboa

The permanent collection at the stellar **Museum of Photographic Arts** (Map pp222-3; ☎ 619-238-7559; www.mopa.org; adult/child under 12/student/senior $6/free/4/4, 2nd Tue of month free; ☺ 10am-5pm Fri-Wed, to 9pm Thu) traces the history of photography in terms of both technology and aesthetics, with particular strength in social documentary and photojournalism.

The previously blah-ish **Museum of San Diego History** (Map pp222-3; ☎ 619-232-6203; www.sandiegohistory.org; adult/youth 6-17/student & senior $5/2/4; ☺ 10am-5pm) has sexed itself up a bit, most notably with a cool interactive walk-on map of San Diego. The city's history is also displayed through thousands of historical costumes.

Downstairs, the **Model Railroad Museum** (☎ 619-696-0199; www.sdmodelrailroadm.com; adult/child under 15/student $6/free/3, 1st Tue of month free; ☺ 11am-4pm Tue-Fri, to 5pm Sat & Sun; 🚻), the largest indoor model-railroad display in the world, has working models of real railroads in Southern California, past and present. Awesome.

San Diego Natural History Museum

Kids dig this temple to the natural world, which has a particular focus on the ecosystems of southern California and the Baja California peninsula. Giant-screen films are included in the admission to the **museum** (Map pp222-3; ☎ 619-232-3821; www.sdnhm.org; adult/child 3-12/youth 13-17 $11/7/6, 1st Tue of month free; ☺ 10am-5pm; 🚻).

SPRECKELS ORGAN PAVILION

Heading south from Plaza de Panama, you can't miss the extravagantly curved colonnade that provides shelter for one of the world's largest **outdoor organs** (Map pp222-3). Donated by the Spreckels family of sugar fame, the organ has some 4400 pipes, the smallest the size of a pencil and the largest nearly 10m long. Free concerts are held at 2pm every Sunday, and at 7:30pm Monday from mid-June to August.

SAN DIEGO AEROSPACE MUSEUM

In a distinctive round structure at the end of Pan American Plaza, this **museum** (Map pp222-3; ☎ 619-234-8291; www.aerospacemuseum.org; adult/under 18 $10/5; ☺ 10am-4:30pm, to 5pm Jun-Aug) houses a small but interesting collection that ranges from the balloon age to the space age.

MARIE HITCHCOCK PUPPET THEATER

This **theater** (Map pp222-3; ☎ 619-685-5990; www.balboaparkpuppets.com; adult/child $5/3; 🚻) puts on shows at 11am, 1pm and 2:30pm Wednesday to Sunday (reduced show times in winter), and has puppet-making workshops for kids.

CENTRO CULTURAL DE LA RAZA
Devoted primarily to Mexican and Native American art, this **cultural center** (Map pp222-3; ☎ 619-235-6135; www.centroraza.com; 2125 Park Blvd; admission $2; ☺ noon-5pm Thu-Sun), sits on the fringe of the main museum area (easiest access is via Park Blvd). The round, steel building is actually a converted water tank decked out by Chicano muralists. Inside, exhibits can run the gamut from contemporary Chicano and indigenous artwork to photographs documenting San Francisco's first gay marriage ceremonies in 2004.

WORLD BEAT CULTURAL CENTER
Also housed in a converted water tank, this nonprofit multicultural arts **center** (☎ 619-230-1190; www.worldbeatcenter.org; 2100 Park Blvd; admission free; ☺ hr vary) presents performances and exhibits on the African and indigenous cultures of the world, but perhaps the most fun for visitors is dropping in on one of their classes (free to $15), from West African drumming for children to capoeira and qi gong.

SAN DIEGO ZOO
Packed into 100 acres of clever design in the northwestern corner of Balboa Park, the **zoo** (Map pp222-3; ☎ 619-231-1515; www.sandiegozoo.org; adult/child $22/14.50, deluxe package $32/20; ☺ 9am-9pm summer, to 4pm rest of year; ♿) is a compendium of some of nature's largest, smallest, noblest, oddest and most endangered creatures. (Check the website for news of the most recent zoo baby arrivals.)

One of the ways the San Diego Zoo shines is through its pioneering methods of housing and displaying animals to mimic their natural habitat, leading to a revolution in zoo design and, so the argument goes, to happier animals. The zoo also plays a major role in the protection of endangered species.

In its efforts to re-create those habitats, the zoo has also become one of the country's great botanical gardens, tricking San Diego's near-desert climate to yield everything from bamboo and eucalyptus to mini-African rain forests.

A big, free, parking lot is off Park Blvd. Bus 7 will get you there from downtown. The zoo is open daily at 9am, but closing times vary with the season; call for current hours.

The 'deluxe admission package' includes a 40-minute guided bus tour and a round-trip aerial tram ride on the Skyfari cable car. The extras probably aren't worth it, unless you have sore feet or are in a hurry. A combined ticket to visit both the San Diego Zoo and the Wild Animal Park within a five-day period costs $54.50/33.50 for an adult/child. It's wise to arrive early, as many of the animals are most active in the morning, and many are fed between 9am and 11am. Animal shows are held in the two amphitheaters (no extra charge).

Old Town
Until the 1860s, the city of San Diego was little more than a cluster of wood and adobe buildings just below Presidio Hill. Today this

DETOUR: SAN DIEGO WILD ANIMAL PARK
Since the early 1960s, the San Diego Zoological Society has been developing the **Wild Animal Park** (Map p218; ☎ 760-747-8702; www.sandiegozoo.org; 15500 San Pasqual Valley Rd, Escondido; adult/child 3-11 $28.50/17.50; ☺ 9am-8pm summer, to 4pm rest of year; ♿), an 1800-acre, open-range zoo where herds of giraffes, zebras, rhinos and other animals roam the open valley floor. A spiffed-up new route of the Wgasa Bush Line Railway (included in admission price) is currently under development, the first leg of which will be complete by early 2008, but through 2007 you can take a shortened, 45-minute ride, which gives spectacular views of the animals and is accompanied by commentary. Sit on the right side (inside the loop) for the best viewing.

Admission includes the monorail and all shows. A combined ticket to visit the San Diego Zoo and Wild Animal Park within a five-day period costs $54.50/33.50 per adult/child. Parking is $6 extra. The park offers many extra animal-encounter experiences – like photo caravan tours that drive right up alongside the animals, and the chance to stand ringside as a cheetah whizzes by you chasing a mechanical rabbit – but they're pricey, and reservations are required.

The park's just north of Hwy 78, 5 miles east of I-15 from the Via Rancho Parkway exit. Plan 45 minutes transit by car from San Diego, except in rush hour when that figure can double. For bus information contact **North San Diego County Transit District** (☎ 619-233-3004, from North County 800-266-6883; www.gonctd.com).

SAN DIEGO AREA

area is called Old Town, although it is neither very old (most of the buildings are reconstructions), nor exactly a town (more like a leafy suburb). But it's good for those who need to quell their beach-guilt with a spot of history.

The **Old Town State Historic Park Visitors center** (Map pp222-3; ☎ 619-220-5422; Wallace St; ☼ 10am-5pm) houses a California history slide show and a neat model of Old Town. Several guided tours leave daily in summer.

Two blocks from the Old Town perimeter sits **Whaley House** (Map pp222-3; ☎ 619-297-7511; 2482 San Diego Ave; admission $5; ☼ 10am-10pm in summer, to 4:30pm rest of year), the city's oldest brick building, having served as courthouse, theater and private residence. In the '60s it was officially certified as haunted by the US Department of Commerce. Inside, the period furniture is watched over by knowledgeable costumed docents. Ask one of them about the theater's slanted stage.

In 1769 Padre Junípero Serra and Gaspar de Portolá established the first Spanish settlement in California on **Presidio Hill**, overlooking the valley of the San Diego River. The walk from Old Town along Mason St rewards you with views of the bay.

El Campo Santo, between Arista and Conde Sts on San Diego Ave is a tiny, touching cemetery dating back to the earliest Spanish settlers. One grave near the gate was so placed because the man, 'Jesus the Indian', died while

'completely drunk'. The construction of San Diego Ave accidentally covered many resting spots, so you may notice some medallions marking grave sites embedded in the street.

The Old Town Transit Center, on the trolley line at Taylor St, is a stop for the *Coaster* commuter train, the San Diego Trolley (orange and blue lines) and buses 4 and 5 from downtown.

Uptown & Hillcrest

Uptown consists roughly of the triangle north of downtown, east of Old Town and south of Mission Valley. As you head north from downtown along the west side of Balboa Park, you arrive at a series of bluffs that, in the late 19th century, became San Diego's most fashionable neighborhood – only those who owned a horse-drawn carriage could afford to live here. Known as Bankers Hill after some of the wealthy residents, these upscale heights had unobstructed views of the bay and Point Loma before I-5 went up.

As you head northward toward Hillcrest, detour across the 375ft **Spruce Street Footbridge** (Map pp222–3), a 1912 suspension bridge built over a deep canyon between Front and Brant Sts. The nearby **Quince Street Bridge**, between 4th and 3rd Aves, is a wood-trestle structure built in 1905 and refurbished in 1988.

Just up from the northwestern corner of Balboa Park, you hit **Hillcrest** (Map pp222–3),

---

GAY & LESBIAN SAN DIEGO

Ironically, the roots of San Diego's thriving gay community can be traced to the city's strong military presence. During WWII, gay men from around the country left the relative isolation of their hometowns and, amid the enforced intimacy of military life, were suddenly able to create strong if clandestine social networks. When the war was over, these new friends often settled in the cities where they were decommissioned, including San Diego.

In Hillcrest you'll find queer-friendly bars, restaurants, cafés and bookstores thick on the ground. **San Diego Gay Pride** (☎ 619-297-7683; www.sdpride.org) takes place in Hillcrest and Balboa Park at the end of July. For more complete listings and events, get a copy of *Buzz* and the *Gay and Lesbian Times,* both widely available in the neighborhood. You can also check out the following:

Brass Rail (Map pp222-3; ☎ 619-298-2233; 3796 5th Ave) The city's oldest gay bar has a different music style nightly, from African to Top 40.

David's Coffeehouse (Map pp222-3; ☎ 619-296-4173; 3766 5th Ave, Hillcrest; ☼ 7am-11pm Sun-Thu, to midnight Fri & Sat) Homey Hillcrest classic, plus Ms Pac-Man.

Flame (Map pp222-3; ☎ 619-295-4163; 3780 Park Blvd) The Flame was the city's oldest lesbian bar until it started divvying up its nights by theme. Ever since Six Degrees shuttered its doors in 2006, Saturday night at the Flame (alternately 'The lame' or 'The F me', depending on what part of its neon sign is burnt out) is the only show in town for the ladies. And it goes *off.*

Obelisk Bookstore (Map pp222-3; ☎ 619-297-4171; 1029 University Ave; ☼ 10am-10pm Mon-Fri, to 11pm Fri & Sat, 11am-10pm Sun) All the usual queeraphernalia, and the place to pick up your '92103' T-shirt.

the heart of Uptown (buses 1, 3 and 25 go to/from downtown along 4th and 5th Aves). The neighborhood began its life in the early 20th century as a modest middle-class suburb. Today, it's San Diego's most bohemian district. University and 5th Aves are lined with coffeehouses, thrift shops and excellent restaurants in all price ranges. The **Hillcrest Gateway** (Map pp222–3), a neon sign that arches over University Ave at 5th Ave, marks the center of the action.

Hillcrest's **farmers market** (Map pp222-3; 5th Ave, cnr Normal & Lincoln Sts; ☺ 9am-1pm Sun) is tops for people-watching.

Coronado

Across the bay from downtown, **Coronado** (Map p220) provides natural protection to San Diego's port – and just as carefully guards its own conservative ambience. Locals call it an island, but although it's administratively separated from San Diego, it's connected to the mainland by the spectacular, 2.12-mile Coronado Bay Bridge (opened in 1969), as well as by a long, narrow spit of sand known as the Silver Strand.

There are two reasons to come to Coronado Island: the remarkable Hotel del Coronado (known as 'the Del') and the stunning strand it sits on.

When the **Hotel del Coronado** was built in 1888, it was designed to 'be the talk of the western world'. While that's surely an exaggeration these days, the Del does harbor plenty of lore to go along with its 26 acres of grounds overlooking an impossibly white beach. The hotel's main building is a sprawling timber palace with billowing turrets, dramatic ballrooms and nearly 700 rooms, all connected by a maze of dark corridors, bright courtyards, and elegantly carved stairways. Though it has hosted every US president since Johnson, the Del achieved its widest exposure in the 1959 movie *Some Like It Hot*, which earned its lasting association with Marilyn Monroe.

Cars with driver only pay a $1 toll when coming over the bridge to Coronado, but it's free for vehicles with passengers. Buses 901, 902 and 903 from downtown run the length of Orange Ave to the Hotel del Coronado.

A regular ferry ($2.25) operates hourly between Broadway Pier and Coronado. A **water taxi** (☎ 619-235-8294) makes a regular connection between Seaport Village and Coronado. Rent a bike at Coronado's Ferry Landing

Marketplace or bring one on the ferry for 50¢. Alternatively, use the electric Coronado Shuttle to get around (free). The Old Town Trolley tour stops in front of Mc P's Irish Pub, on Orange Ave at 11th St.

Point Loma

On the southern tip of Point Loma, you'll find **Cabrillo National Monument** (Map p220; admission per car/person $5/3; ☺ 9am-5pm, to 6pm in summer; bus 26 from downtown), offering fine views across the bay to San Diego's downtown. It's also the best place in San Diego to see the gray-whale migration (January to March) from land. The 1854 **Old Point Loma Lighthouse**, dramatically built at the top of the hill, was so prone to fog-in that a new, lower lighthouse took over duty 36 years later. On the ocean side of the point, you can drive or walk down to the **tide pools** to look for anemones, starfish, crabs, limpets and 'dead man's fingers'.

Ocean Beach

Ocean Beach, San Diego's most bohemian seaside community, is the Santa Cruz of the south, with OBecians proudly flouting the conservatism of inland San Diego – when they can find the time between waves and joints, that is. Newport Ave, which runs perpendicular from the beach, is a jumble of tattoo parlors, surf shops, secondhand furniture stores, coffee shops and no-shirt-no-shoes-no-problem bars. The street ends a block from the half-mile-long **Ocean Beach Pier**.

The real action, of course, lies on the sands. Just north of the pier is the headquarters for the beach scene, with volleyball courts and sunset BBQ. Further up you'll reach **Dog Beach** (Map p224), where pooches can run unleashed around the marshy area. A few blocks south of the pier, you'll find **Sunset Cliffs Park**, a great spot to watch the sun dipping below the horizon.

If you're here on Wednesday afternoon, stop by the **Ocean Beach farmers market** (Map p224, from 4pm to 7pm, and until 8pm June to September) to see street performers and sample fresh food.

Mission Bay

In the 18th century, the mouth of the San Diego River formed a shallow bay when the river flowed, and a marshy swamp when it didn't – the Spanish called it False Bay. After WWII, a rare combination of civic vision and coastal engineering turned the swamp into a 7-sq-mile playground, with 27 miles of shoreline and 90 acres of public parks. The river was channeled to the sea, the bay was dredged and millions of tons of sludge were used to build islands, coves and peninsulas.

The attractions of Mission Bay run the gamut, from luxurious resort hotels to free outdoor activities. Kite flying is popular in Mission Bay Park, beach volleyball is big on Fiesta Island, and there's delightful cycling and in-line skating on the miles of smooth bike paths. Sailing, windsurfing and kayaking dominate the waters in northwest Mission Bay, while water-skiers zip around Fiesta Island. For equipment-rental information, see Activities, p233.

Along with the zoo, **SeaWorld** (Map p220; ☎ 619-226-3901; www.seaworld.com; adult/child 3-9 $54/44; ☺ 9am-11pm summer, shorter hr rest of year; (P) (♿)) is one of San Diego's most popular attractions. There's no denying that SeaWorld has an overtly commercial feel, with corporate logos slapped on every available surface, but it's entertaining and, if you concentrate, it can even be educational.

SeaWorld's claim to fame is its live shows, which feature trained dolphins, seals, sea lions and killer whales. **Shamu Adventure** is the most visually spectacular program. Throughout the 30-minute show, the three star performers – Shamu, Baby Shamu and Namu – glide, leap, dive and flip through the water.

There are installations where you can see underwater creatures up close, as well as petting pools where you can touch the slippery surface of a dolphin or manta ray. Come face to face with sharks at the **Shark Encounter**.

By car, take Sea World Dr off I-5 less than a mile north of where it intersects with I-8. Take bus 9 from downtown.

Mission Beach & Pacific Beach

Between the South Mission Jetty and Pacific Beach Point stretch 3 miles of pure, unadulterated SoCal beach scene. **Ocean Front Walk** (Map p224) bristles with joggers, in-line skaters and cyclists – the perfect place for scantily clad pretty people-watching. Back from the beach, Mission Blvd consists of block after block of surf shops, burger joints and beer busts. Down at the Mission Beach end, beach bums pool their resources to rent small houses and apartments for the summer season.

The surf is a beach break, good for beginners, bodyboarders and bodysurfers.

The family-style **Belmont Park** (Map p224; ☎ 858-488-0668; www.belmontpark.com; admission free) has been on Mission Beach since 1925. One of the highlights is the classic wooden **Giant Dipper roller coaster** (admission $5; ☺ operates from 11am).

Up in Pacific Beach (or PB) the activity spreads further inland, especially along **Garnet Ave** (Map p224), with bars, restaurants and vintage clothing stores. At the ocean end of Garnet Ave, **Crystal Pier** is worth a gander. Built in the 1920s, it's still home to a cluster of rustic cabins (p236) built out over the waves.

Tourmaline Surfing Park (Map p220), at the far northern end of the beach, is particularly popular with longboarders. For information on equipment rentals, see p233.

To get around, consider renting a bike or in-line skates (see p239). **Cheap Rentals** (Map p224; ☎ 800-941-7761, 858-488-2453; www.cheap-rentals.com; 3221 Mission Blvd; ☺ 9am-7pm daily Mar-Aug, to 5pm Mon-Fri Sep-Feb) has low prices and rents everything from bikes and skates to baby joggers; it also accepts advance reservations.

La Jolla

Though technically part of San Diego, La Jolla feels a world apart, both because of its conspicuous wealth as well as its location above San Diego's most photogenic stretch of coast. With upscale boutiques, immaculate parks, sandy coves and turquoise waters, you can understand why locals say La Jolla is Spanish for 'the jewel.' But some challenge this claim, saying that the indigenous peoples who inhabited the area until the mid-19th century called it 'Mut la Hoya, la Hoya' – the place of many caves. Either way, it's pronounced 'la hoy-ya.'

Bus 34 connects La Jolla to downtown via the Old Town Transit Center. The **La Jolla Visitors Center** (☎ 619-236-1212; Ste A, 7966 Herschel Ave; ☺ 11am-4pm) is in the center of town.

DOWNTOWN LA JOLLA

The compact downtown sits atop a bluff lapped by ocean waves. Regrettably, there's little interaction between downtown and the sea, though you can catch lovely glimpses of the Pacific between buildings. The main thoroughfares, Prospect St and Girard Ave, are San Diego's favorite places for high-end shopping.

The **Athenaeum Music & Arts Library** (Map p231; ☎ 858-454-5872; www.ljathenaeum.org; 1008 Wall St; ☺ 10am-

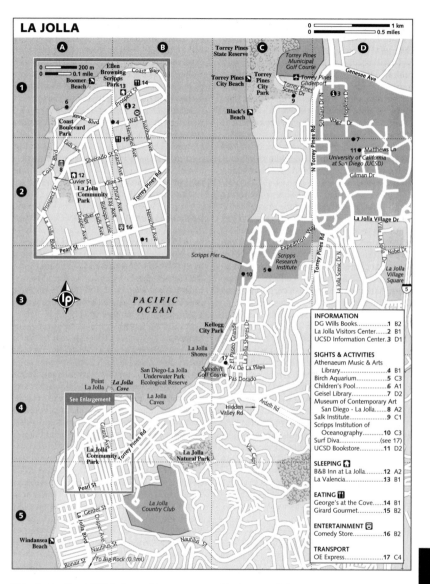

LA JOLLA

5:30pm Tue-Sat, 10am-8:30 Wed), housed in a graceful Spanish renaissance structure, is devoted exclusively to art and music. You can read daily newspapers here from around the globe.

The small but excellent **Museum of Contemporary Art San Diego – La Jolla** (MCASD; Map p231; ☎ 858-454-3541; www.mcasd.org; 700 Prospect St; adult/student & senior $6/2, 3rd Tue of month free; ⏱ 11am-5pm Mon, Tue & Fri-Sun, to 7pm Thu) supports a permanent post-1950s collection especially strong in minimalist, pop and California art.

THE COAST

Private property along the coast of La Jolla restricts coastal access, and parking is very limited in places, but there is a wonderful walking path that skirts the shoreline for half a mile. The path's western end begins at the **Children's Pool** (Map p231), where a jetty protects the beach from big waves. Originally intended to give La Jolla's youth a safe place to frolic, the beach is now more popular with sea lions, which you can view up close as they lounge on the shore. Atop Point La Jolla, at the path's eastern end, **Ellen Browning Scripps Park** (Map p231) is a tidy expanse of green lawns and palm trees, with views of **La Jolla Cove** to the north. The cove's gem of a beach provides access to some of the best snorkeling around.

If you like to surf and know what you're doing, head to **Windansea Beach** (Map p231), 2 miles south of downtown (take La Jolla Blvd south and turn west on Nautilus St). If you can brave the ire of the locals, you'll find that the surf's consistent peak (a powerful reef break not for beginners) works best at medium to low tide. You'll find a more civilized welcome immediately south at **Big Rock**, California's version of Hawaii's Pipeline.

LA JOLLA SHORES

Called 'the Shores,' this area northeast of La Jolla Cove is where La Jolla's cliffs meet the wide, sandy beaches that stretch north to Del Mar. To reach the **beach** (Map p231), take La Jolla Shores Dr north from Torrey Pines Rd and turn west onto Ave de la Playa. The waves here are gentle enough for beginner surfers, and kayakers can launch from the shore without much problem.

LOCAL VOICES

- The favorite surf spot of Pam 'Palen' Lehr, meteorologist, is the north side of Scripps pier, in North County. At dawn, naturally.

- Architect and native San Diegan Andy Crocker likes going to the Stratford Court Cafe in Del Mar on Sunday morning for the outdoor-garden coffee experience.

- Garrett Lee, college student, puts off studying by browsing the dusty stacks at La Jolla's DG Wills' Books.

- Artist and mom Sherry Geisler loves to take her kids to Mission Bay to swim and make sand castles.

Some of the best beaches in the county are north of the Shores in **Torrey Pines City Park** (Map p231), which covers the coastline from the Salk Institute up to the Torrey Pines State Reserve. The **Torrey Pines Gliderport** (Map p231), at the end of Torrey Pines Scenic Dr, is the place for hang gliders and paragliders to launch themselves into the sea breezes that rise over the high cliffs. Tandem flights are available if you can't resist trying it (p234). Down below – there's a path to the south from the parking lot – is the predominantly gay **Black's Beach** (Map p231), where bathing suits are technically required, but in practice are thin on the ground.

BIRCH AQUARIUM AT SCRIPPS

Marine scientists were working here as early as 1910 and it has grown to one of the world's largest marine-research institutions. It is now part of UCSD, and its pier is a landmark on the La Jolla coast.

Birch Aquarium (Map p231; ☎ 858-534-3474; www .aquarium.ucsd.edu; 2300 Expedition Way; adult/child/student 3-17 $11/7.50/8; ☼ 9am-5pm; ℗ ♿), off N Torrey Pines Rd, isn't as blatantly razzle-dazzle – or immense – as those other aquariums you'll find in Monterey or Long Beach, but this top-notch educational and research institution has brilliant displays on marine life. The staff has the time and the inclination to answer any underwatery question you can throw at it. Check out the touch tide pool overlooking the ocean, and don't leave without glimpsing the diminutive weedy sea dragons, in the Art of Deception hall.

SALK INSTITUTE

In 1960 Jonas Salk, the pioneer of polio prevention, founded the **Salk Institute** (Map p231; ☎ 858-453-4100; www.salk.edu; 10010 N Torrey Pines Rd) for biological and biomedical research. Louis Kahn designed the building, completed in 1965, as a masterpiece of modern architecture, with a classically proportioned plaza made of travertine (aka immature) marble and cubist, mirror-glass laboratory blocks framing a perfect view of the Pacific. Stand on the plaza's east end let your eye follow the 'river of life', representing knowledge, as it 'connects' with the ocean. There are three floors of laboratories, and above each of them is an entire floor used to house the necessary utilities. You can tour the Salk Institute for free with a guide on Monday, Wednesday and Friday at noon. Call (ext 1287) for reservations.

TORREY PINES STATE RESERVE
Encompassing the land between N Torrey Pines Rd and the ocean from the Torrey Pines Gliderport to Del Mar, this **reserve** (Map p231; ☎ 858-755-2063; www.torreypine.org; ⏰ 9am-sunset) preserves the last mainland stands of the Torrey pine *(Pinus torreyana)*, a species adapted to sparse rainfall and sandy, stony soils. The views over the ocean and north to Oceanside are superb.

Parking costs $6 per car ($8 on weekends), but admission is free if you enter on foot. Several walking trails wind through the reserve and down to the beach. If you want to hike, park near the driving range on N Torrey Pines Rd and take the paved path northwest until you reach a box of trail maps at the beginning of the Broken Arrow Trail.

UNIVERSITY OF CALIFORNIA SAN DIEGO
The University of California San Diego's 26,000 lucky students live and study amongst the campus' rolling coastal hills that are covered in fragrant eucalyptus trees. By far its most distinctive structure is the **Geisel Library** (Map p231), an upside-down multileveled pyramid of glass and concrete whose namesake, Theodor Geisel, is better known as Dr Seuss, creator of the Cat in the Hat. He and his wife contributed substantially to the library, and there is a collection of his drawings and books on the ground level.

From the eastern side of the library's 2nd level, an allegorical snake created by artist Alexis Smith winds around a native California plant garden, past an enormous marble copy of John Milton's *Paradise Lost*. The piece is part of the **Stuart Collection** of outdoor sculptures spread around campus. Most installations are near the Geisel Library, and details are available from the Visual Arts Building or the Price Center, where the **UCSD bookstore** (Map p231; ☎ 858-534-7323) has excellent stock and helpful staff.

The best access to campus is off of La Jolla Village Dr or N Torrey Pines Rd (buses 41 and 301 from downtown); parking is free on weekends. At other times, the meters are $1 per hour.

ACTIVITIES
If you love surf and sky, you'll go nuts in coastal San Diego. For information on biking, see p239.

Surfing
In general, San Diego is a great place for surfers of any skill level, though the water can get crowded and several spots, particularly Sunset Cliffs and Windansea, are somewhat 'owned' by locals – which means they'll heckle you to death unless you're an awesome surfer.

Fall brings the strong swells and offshore Santa Ana winds. In summer swells come from the south and southwest, and in winter from the west and northwest. Spring brings more frequent onshore winds, but the surfing can still be good. For the latest beach, weather and surf reports, call **City Lifeguard** (☎ 619-221-8824).

Beginners looking to rent equipment should head to Mission or Pacific Beaches, where the waves are gentle. North of the Crystal Pier, Tourmaline Surfing Park is an especially good place to take your first strokes. **Pacific Beach Surf Shop** (Map p224; ☎ 858-373-1138; www.pacific beachsurfshop.com; Ste 161, 4150 Mission Blvd, Pacific Beach) provides instruction as well as rents wet suits and both soft (foam) and hard (fiberglass)

BEST SURF BREAKS

The best San Diego County surf breaks, from south to north, are at Imperial Beach (especially in winter); Point Loma (reef breaks, which are less accessible but less crowded; best during winter); Sunset Cliffs in Ocean Beach; Pacific Beach; Big Rock (California's Pipeline); Windansea (hot reef break, best at medium to low tide); La Jolla Shores (beach break, best in winter); and Black's Beach (a fast, powerful wave). In North County (Map p241), there are breaks at Cardiff State Beach, San Elijo State Beach, Swami's, Carlsbad State Beach and Oceanside.

The bodysurfing is good at Coronado, Pacific Beach, Boomer Beach near La Jolla Cove (for the experienced only, best with a big swell) and La Jolla Shores. To get into the whomp (the forceful tubes that break directly onshore), know what you're doing and head to Windansea or the beach at the end of Sea Lane (both in La Jolla).

boards. Also check out **Bob's Mission Surf Shop** (Map p224; ☎ 858-483-8837; www.missionsurf.com; 4320 Mission Blvd, Pacific Beach). Rental rates at both vary depending on the quality of the equipment, but generally soft boards cost about $10 to $16 per half-day, $15 to $25 per full day; wet suits cost $5 per hour, $10 per half-day. For 90-minute lessons expect to pay at least $60 (including equipment) for one person, with discounts for additional people.

In La Jolla the women at **Surf Diva** (Map p231; ☎ 858-454-8273; www.surfdiva.com; 2160 Av de la Playa) offer two-day weekend workshops for gals of all ages for around $150. Due to popular demand, guys can take private lessons, too.

Diving & Snorkeling

Off the coast of San Diego County, divers will find kelp beds, shipwrecks and canyons deep enough to host bat rays, octopus and squid. For current conditions, call ☎ 619-221-8824. You'll find some of California's best and most accessible (no boat needed) diving in the **San Diego–La Jolla Underwater Park Ecological Reserve** (Map p231), accessible from La Jolla Cove. With an average depth of 20ft, the 6000 acres of look-but-don't-touch underwater real estate are great for snorkeling, too. Ever-present are the spectacular, bright orange garibaldi fish, a protected species. Further out, you'll see forests of giant California kelp (which can increase its length by up to 3ft per day) and the 100ft-deep La Jolla Canyon.

A number of commercial outfits conduct scuba courses, sell or rent equipment, fill tanks and run boat trips to nearby wrecks and islands. A snorkel and fins cost around $10; scuba-gear rental packages cost about $65; and certification and open-water dives run at about $375 for the first person, with discounts for additional people. Closest to the water, **OE Express** (Map p231; ☎ 858-454-6195; www.oe express.com; 2158 Av de la Playa) is a full-service PADI dive shop in La Jolla Shores that provides rentals and instruction.

Kayaking

You can rent kayaks and canoes on Mission Bay. Try **Mission Bay Sportcenter** (Map p224; ☎ 858-488-1004; www.missionbaysportcenter.com; 1010 Santa Clara Pl), which has single/tandem kayaks for $13/18 per hour.

Ocean kayaking is a great way to see marine life and explore cliffs and caves inaccessible from land. **Family Kayak** (☎ 619-282-3520; www.family

kayak.com) has guided single- and multiday trips and classes, both from $55 for three hours. It's easy to explore the caves and cliffs around La Jolla from the boat launch of **OE Express** (Map p231; ☎ 858-454-6195; www.oeexpress.com; 2158 Av de la Playa; 2hr kayak rental single/double $28/45) in La Jolla Shores.

Whale-Watching

Gray whales pass San Diego between mid-December and late February on their way south to Baja California and again in mid-March on their way back to Alaskan waters. Their 12,000-mile round-trip journey is the longest migration of any mammal on earth.

Cabrillo National Monument (p229) is the best place to see the whales from land, where you'll also find exhibits, whale-related ranger programs and a shelter from which to watch the whales breach (bring binoculars).

Half-day whale-watching boat trips generally cost $20 to $30 for adults and $15 for children for a three-hour excursion, and most companies give you a free pass to return again if you don't spot any whales. From late December through late March **San Diego Harbor Excursion** (Map p221; ☎ 619-234-4111; www.sdhe.com) offers 3½-hour trips guided by Birch Aquarium naturalists.

Hang Gliding & Paragliding

For a memorable fly-like-a-bird experience – and perhaps the most expensive 20 minutes of your life – head to **Torrey Pines Gliderport** (Map p231; ☎ 858-452-9858; www.flytorrey.com; 2800 Torrey Pines Scenic Dr; tandem hang-gliding flights per person per 20min $175, paragliding tandem $150) in La Jolla, a world-famous gliding location and one of the best gliding schools in the country. Even if you have no intention of going up, swing by and watch the fun. FYI, paragliding is to hang gliding as a plane is to a hot-air balloon, roughly speaking.

TOURS

We highly recommend getting the lay of the land with a tour, then going back to the sights that interest you most.

Old Town Trolley Tours (☎ 619-298-8687, 800-868-7482; per day adult/child 4-12 $30/15; ⏱ 9am-7pm) makes a loop around the main attractions near downtown and in Coronado inside an open-air trolley. Best of all, tickets are good for unlimited all-day travel – you get on or off at any number of stops, staying to look

SAN DIEGO AREA

around as long as you wish. The Old Town Trolley is a green and orange bus styled after an old-fashioned streetcar. You can start at any trolley stop – they're marked in orange and are usually next to a regular San Diego Transit bus stop.

Hornblower Cruises (Map p221; ☎ 888-467-6256; www.hornblower.com) operate boat tours of San Diego Harbor. One- and two-hour sightseeing tours (adult $15 to $20, child $7.50 to $10) leave from the Embarcadero (near the *Star of India*).

FESTIVALS & EVENTS

San Diego County Fair (☎ 858-755-1161; www.sd fair.com) Huge county fair held from mid-June to July 4; features headline acts and hundreds of carnival rides and shows at the Del Mar Fairgrounds in Del Mar.

US Open Sandcastle Competition (☎ 619-424-6663; www.usopensandcastle.com) You won't believe what can be made out of sand at the amazing sandcastle-building competition held mid-July in Imperial Beach, south of Coronado.

Del Mar Horse Racing (☎ 858-755-1141; www.dmtc .com) The well-heeled bet on the horses, 'where the turf meets the sea,' at Del Mar Fairgrounds, from mid-July to early September.

Old Globe Festival (☎ 619-239-2255; www.oldglobe .org) Renowned Shakespeare festival at the Old Globe Theatre in Balboa Park during August.

Fleet Week (☎ 800-353-3793; www.fleetweeksan diego.org) The US military shows its might in a parade of ships and the signature Blue Angels air show from mid- to late September.

SLEEPING

Downtown has the ritziest lodgings, but some good deals can be found. Ocean Beach (OB) is under the outbound flight path of jets departing from San Diego airport; pack earplugs. Pacific Beach (PB) has most of the beachside accommodations.

Budget

Ocean Beach International Hostel (Map p224; ☎ 619-223-7873, 800-339-7263; www.californiahostels.com; 4961 Newport Ave, Ocean Beach; dm from $20, r from $22; 🖳) OBI Hostel is a friendly, laid-back place popular with Europeans, and only a couple of blocks from the water. It's lousy with perks, like complimentary transport from the airport or bus and train stations and free BBQ dinners twice a week. Bus 35 from downtown passes Newport Ave a block east of the hostel.

HI San Diego Downtown Hostel (Map p221; ☎ 619-525-1531; www.sandiegohostels.org; 521 Market St; dm/d/tr $26/55/74; 🖳) Centrally located in the Gaslamp Quarter, this HI facility is handy to public transportation and nightlife and has a wide range of rooms. It provides a make-your-own pancake breakfast and has 24-hour access.

our pick 500 West Hotel (Map p221; ☎ 619-234-5252, 866-500-7533; www.500westhotel.com; 500 W Broadway, downtown; s/d $70/80; 🖳 🖳) Inside the elegant beaux arts building that was once the YMCA (the Y gym is still in the basement; guests pay $5 per day for access), this place is almost too good to be true, especially for the price – rooms are decked out with playful modern furniture, flat-screen TVs and platform beds. The catch is that bathrooms are shared, though they're private once you get inside, and they are cleaned fastidiously, 'round the clock The mission revival lobby has been lovingly restored and invites lingering with its soft lighting and chilled-out bar. Discounts can be had by reserving online. Because the hotel gets so much conference traffic, July in particular can be booked out a year in advance.

La Pensione Hotel (Map p221; ☎ 619-236-8000, 800-232-4683; www.lapensionehotel.com; 606 W Date St; r from $80; 🅿 🖳) All 75 rooms at this four-story, dramatically lit hotel in the heart of Little Italy have a queen-size bed, a fridge and charming black-and-white photos of the neighborhood. You'll feel like you're in the Old Country as you take your morning coffee in the courtyard. Parking is free, but there are only 24 spaces.

Midrange

Little Italy Inn (Map p221; ☎ 619-230-1600, 800-518-9930; www.littleitalyinn.com; 505 E Grape St; r $89-199; 🅿 🔀) It may lie in the shadow of the I-5, but this utterly charming boutique hotel manages to pull off 'urban getaway', regardless. Staff go out of their way to make you feel at home, and the 23 uniquely decorated rooms are all tastefully appointed, with luxuries like plush bathrobes. Most rooms have private bathrooms, and others boast indulgent in-room spa bathrooms. Stylish continental breakfast included.

Hillcrest Inn (Map pp222-3; ☎ 619-293-7078, 800-258-2280; www.hillcrestinn.net; 3754 5th Ave; r from $89; 🅿) This primarily gay hotel is smack-dab in the heart of Hillcrest. Its motel rooms – some smoking, some non, all with the fridge-microwave-wet-bar trifecta – surround a central courtyard. Request a balcony room. The six-person Jacuzzi sees its share of partying, thus the no-children policy. Continental breakfast on weekends.

Casa Granada (off Map pp222-3; ☎ 619-501-5911, 866-524-2312; www.casa-granada.com; 1720 Granada Ave; r $101-139) Casa Granada is just about the perfect B&B, minus the breakfast. This house in a residential area on the eastern edge of Balboa Park comprises three suites, all with private bathroom and full kitchen or kitchenette, and each lovely in its own way. The El Rojo Suite is a crimson-walled, hardwood-floored beaut. The house's deck – with a BBQ that guests are encouraged to use – overlooks a jungley backyard. Highly recommended.

Inn at Sunset Cliffs (Map p224; ☎ 619-222-7901, 866-786-2543; www.innatsunsetcliffs.com; 1370 Sunset Cliffs Blvd, Ocean Beach; r from $150; P 🖥 🐾) Hidden away from the hustle and bustle and right on the ocean (though with no beach access), this child-friendly motel has a courtyard terrace with great ocean views. Some rooms are small and look tired, but are clean. Ask about rooms with full kitchens. The free computer in the lobby is a welcome perk.

Bed & Breakfast Inn at La Jolla (Map p231; ☎ 858-456-2066; www.innlajolla.com; 7753 Draper Ave; r $179-400; P 🈳) An exuberant bougainvillea frames the gate as you enter the grounds of this chi-chi (candlelight with breakfast!) and historic B&B; the house was designed by Irving Gill and the original gardens by Kate Sessions (see p225). Throughout the 1920s John Philip Sousa and his family lived here. Now, guests unwind in the 15 antiqued rooms which vary greatly on their floral pattern quotient. Peacock Salon is a cozy option with garden-view balcony.

Surfer Beach Hotel (Map p224; ☎ 800-787-3373; www.surferbeachhotel.com; 711 Pacific Beach Dr, Pacific Beach; r from $239; P 🈳 🐾) Location doesn't get better than this medium-sized renovated 1960s motel right on the beach. All rooms have comfy pillow-top beds and slick bedspreads, and most have ocean view balconies. There is a wide range of rooms available, including family suites with kitchenettes.

Top End

Hotel del Coronado (Map p220; ☎ 619-435-6611, 800-468-3533; www.hoteldel.com; 1500 Orange Ave, Coronado; r $280-505; P 🈳 🖥 🐾) San Diego's iconic hotel, the 'Del' combines history (p229), luxury and access to the city's most stunning beach. It's flush with all the high-end ameni-

ties you'd expect, including tennis courts and full-service spa, but there have been recent complaints of laurel resting, indifferent staff and hidden fees. Half the accommodations are in an adjacent seven-story building, so if you stay at the Del, be sure to book a room in the Victorian main building.

La Valencia (Map p231; ☎ 858-454-0771, 800-451-0772; www.lavalencia.com; 1132 Prospect St; r $275-525, villas $695; P 🈳 🖥 🐾) This salmon-colored Mediterranean palace spills down the hillside toward the ocean. Guest rooms reflect a vaguely '70s beige carpeting/ficus-plant/mirrored closet sensibility, but hey, if that's your bag, go for it. If you don't stay, consider a lifting a toast – and a pinkie – to the sunset from its Spanish revival lounge.

Crystal Pier Hotel (Map p224; ☎ 858-483-6983, 800-748-5894; www.crystalpier.com; 4500 Ocean Blvd, Pacific Beach; 1-bedroom cottage $300-350, 2-bedroom cottage $500; P) The cottages at Crystal Pier fulfill all your old-fashioned notions of a quaint beach getaway, only these trim white-and-blue cottages are built right on the pier above the water. All have more-than-full ocean views and kitchens, but the original 1936 clapboard units are the best – though the newer, larger ones sleep more people. For stays between July and December, book on the morning of January 1; for January to June, book on November 15.

EATING

Hillcrest is one of the best neighborhoods to hit both for excellent international restaurants and hipster cafes. Because of the proximity to the convention center, the restaurants in downtown cater to an expense-account crowd and can be overpriced. Most Old Town eateries serve unexciting Mexican fare in contrived digs, although copious amounts of food, strong margaritas and outdoor seating can add up to a pleasant evening. The beach towns are it for cheap, plentiful grub.

Budget

Bread & Cie (Map pp222-3; ☎ 619-683-9322; 350 University Ave, Hillcrest; pastries $2.50-5, sandwiches $7-8; 🕑 7am-7pm Mon-Fri, to 6pm Sat, 8am-6pm Sun; P) This clattery, chattery cafeteria-sized bakery-deli makes the best bread around (with flavors like lemon sage ciabatta, anise and fig, and caramelized onion), and carries a limited assortment of gourmet sandwiches. Plus, it's got the best idea I've heard in a while: customized panini.

It's an excellent spot to eavesdrop on locals, especially in the mornings. And 'cie' is pronounced 'sea'.

Girard Gourmet (Map p231; ☎ 858-454-3321; 7837 Girard Ave, La Jolla; mains $5-7; ☷ 7am-8pm Mon-Sat, to 7pm Sun) Fresh, affordable no-nonsense quiches, soups and sandwiches, plus daily hot plate specials like salmon penne pasta. If you bring the kids, don't expect to escape without buying one of the huge clownfish cookies.

Big Kitchen (off Map pp222-3; ☎ 619-234-5789; 3003 Grape St, South Park; mains $5-8; ☷ 8am-3pm; 👶) The heart and soul of funky South Park, just to the east of Balboa Park at 30th Ave, Big Kitchen welcomes all to its enclave of food, art, music and civic bonhomie (though ardent Bush supporters may get a slightly frosty reception). The omelettes are stupendous, as is the challah French toast, and there's a whole page of breakfast combos named after regulars. It's many locals' vote for best brunch in town.

our pick **Cafe 976** (Map p224; ☎ 858-272-0976; 976 Felspar St at Cass St, Pacific Beach; mains $6-8; ☷ 7am-11pm; ▣) PB denizens of all shapes and colors flock to this mellow, yellow converted 1920s beach house for the magnolia-shaded gardens, the wraparound porch studded with colorful chairs, and eclectic comfort food like Indian tuna curry (limited menu at night) and vegetarian chili. There's local art on the walls and

often more being produced right at the tables. Kids will be spoiled by options like grilled cheese with the crusts cut off. You're all set if you need some wi-fi vibes to go with all the groovy ones here.

Waters Cafe (Map pp222-3; ☎ 619-237-0675; 1450 El Prado, Balboa Park; mains $6-10; ☷ 11am-3pm Tue-Fri, 9am-3pm Sat & Sun) Here's a rarity: well-prepared, good-value food at a museum café! Homemade soups and baguette sandwiches are some of the offerings at the elegant Waters Cafe, nestled in a courtyard overlooking the sculpture garden of the San Diego Museum of Art.

Hob Nob Hill (Map pp222-3; ☎ 619-239-8176; 2271 1st Ave, Bankers Hill; breakfast & lunch $7-14, dinner $11-16; ☷ 7am-9pm) Slinging down-home, midscale diner fare since 1944, this San Diego institution is a favorite with locals – elderly couples at breakfast, middle-management types and hung-over 20-somethings at lunch – who come as much for the uniformed, been-around-the-block waitresses as for the food. Vegetarians will starve.

Midrange

Kung Food (Map pp222-3; ☎ 619-298-7302; 2949 5th Ave, downtown; mains $8-16; ☷ lunch & dinner; Ⓥ) This eatery is a catch-all for the vegan community – you can get a sit-down meal of dishes like

---

IN-N-OUT BURGER

Even – or perhaps especially – to those who eschew fast food and all its concomitant evils, In-N-Out Burger stands as a bright, shining beacon. It's been privately owned since the first restaurant opened in 1948 in Baldwin Park, 18 miles east of Downtown LA, and was also California's first drive-thru hamburger stand. Today more than 150 locations dot the landscape from San Francisco to San Diego, and they're spreading eastward into Nevada and Arizona at a rapid clip. What makes this place so special? For starters, the menu is refreshingly basic – hamburger, cheeseburger, fries, shakes – and one size fits all, which helps keep prices as low as they are. If you're in the know, however, the menu is much bigger. In-N-Out's cult-status 'secret menu' allows Atkins dieters to order a patty wrapped in lettuce (a 'Protein Burger') or two patties and two slices of cheese (a 'Flying Dutchman'), a vegetarian to satisfy their Big Mac cravings (a 'Grilled Cheese') and for everyone to do up their order 'Animal Style', which adds pickles, grilled onions and an extra dollop of sauce.

And fast food doesn't get any fresher. Microwaves, heat lamps and freezers are anathema, and only real ice cream goes into the shakes. Watch as the freshly peeled potatoes are sliced and dropped into a vat of 100% vegetable oil in one stroke. Not only that, but In-N-Out employees earn the highest wages in the industry and participate in an employee profit-sharing plan, both of which help account for the almost unnervingly chipper service and remarkably low turnover rate.

The Bible verse numbers printed discreetly on the bottom of much of the packaging may be off-putting to some, but few can deny that In-N-Out's food – and business model – are heavenly.

tequila lime 'chicken' ($14), grab a bite to go from the deli or just sip on a bottle of organic beer while lounging on the umbrella-shaded brick patio. There's even a drive-thru! Free wi-fi, too.

Saska's (Map p224; ☎ 858-488-7311; 3768 Mission Blvd, Mission Beach; mains $10-20; ⏲ lunch & dinner; ♿) Joe Saska opened Saska's in 1955, and it's been family-run and locally loved ever since for its honest, unpretentious take on steak and seafood. Saska Sushi is a few doors down.

Gaslamp Strip Club (Map p221; ☎ 619-231-3140; 340 5th Ave; mains $14-20; ⏲ dinner) No, not that kind of strip…the New York strip steak kind, despite the restaurant's policy of refusing entry to anyone under 21. Maybe it's because the waitresses flash fishnet stockings, or simply because of the restaurant's three open flame grills. See, it's grill-your-own here, which contributes greatly to the festive atmosphere.

Mona Lisa (Map p221; ☎ 619-234-4893; 2061 India St; mains $9-16; ⏲ lunch Mon-Sat, dinner daily) Aside from delicious, hearty meals, Mona Lisa also makes some of the best sandwiches in town ($5.75 to $7), and sells imported Italian specialty foods. Linger in front of the deli counter and you're certain to be offered a tissue-thin sample of sausage. We recommend the spicy *sopressata*.

Top End

Parallel 33 (Map pp222-3; ☎ 619-260-0033; 741 W Washington St; mains $19-29; ⏲ dinner Mon-Sat) The cuisines of the 33°N latitude, which include Morocco, Lebanon, India, China, Japan, are masterfully fused and fancifully presented at this convivial neighborhood spot. Round off your meal (and start the after party) with a jolt of Turkish coffee. The elephant-headed sculpture in the altar is the Hindu deity Ganesha.

George's at the Cove (Map p231; ☎ 858-454-4244; 1250 Prospect St; mains $26-40; ⏲ dinner) George's proves the exception to the maxim that the better the view, the worse the food. Chef-proprietor Trey Foshee holds firm the helm at one of the city's top special-occasion eateries, placing local, natural ingredients like meats from hormone-free Niman Ranch in the starring roles in his acclaimed Cal-Med production. The tasting menu, including wine, goes for $86. Upstairs, the less expensive (mains $13 to $20) outdoor bistro is open for lunch and dinner and boasts the same view.

Modus (Map pp222-3; ☎ 619-236-8516; www.modusbarlounge.com; 2202 4th Ave, Banker's Hill; ⏲ from 5pm) From the ambient lighting and flickering fireplace to its red accent wall, everything at Modus is meticulously orchestrated for an evening of easygoing sophistication. This supper club slash lounge is justifiably proud of its clutch of organic, 'modern European' dishes like confit de canard, which are served until 1am. Spinmeisters like DJ Sergio work their magic on weekends and some Tuesdays.

DRINKING

Most of the bars in Hillcrest are gay. For a complete list, check out *Buzz* and the *Gay & Lesbian Times*, both widely available in the neighborhood. Downtown, the center of the city's straight nightlife, the line between restaurant, bar and club often gets blurry after 10pm.

Café Bassam (Map p221; ☎ 619-557-0173; 401 Market St; ⏲ 10am-3am, more or less) No alcohol is served at this European-style, humidor-licensed corner cafe, but you *can* smoke a cigar while sipping on your espresso or cup of tea (more than 100 varieties). Sit inside and soak in the singular decor, or pose at one of the sidewalk tables instead.

Wine Steals (Map pp222-3; ☎ 619-295-1188; 1243 University Ave, Hillcrest; cheese & charcuterie boards $10-13; ⏲ 2-10pm Mon-Thu, to midnight Fri & Sat; ℗) A convivial neighborhood place that specializes in fine but inexpensive wines (half a pour $1.50 to $2.50, glass $3 to $8, a 'splash' for a quarter), which you can pair with cheese-charcuterie boards.

Cass Street Bar & Grill (Map p224; ☎ 858-270-1320; 4612 Cass St, Pacific Beach) This PB institution attracts teasers and geezers alike with its 16 beers on tap and complete lack of attitude.

Vine (Map p224; ☎ 619-222-8463; 1851 Bacon St, Ocean Beach; ⏲ from 4pm Tue-Sun) For when you need a reprieve from the flip-flops-and-anklet set. This relative newcomer exudes zero pretension and caters to the beer and wine aficionado with more than 50 bottled Belgians of the former and the same number of wines by the glass. The small plates accompany the liquids perfectly.

ENTERTAINMENT

The free weekly *San Diego Reader* and *San Diego Union Tribune*'s Night & Day section have comprehensive listings.

Comedy Store (Map p231; ☎ 858-454-9176; 916 Pearl St, La Jolla) One of the area's most established comedy venues.

Landmark Hillcrest (Map pp222-3; ☎ 619-819-0236; 3965 5th Ave) Regularly shows new art and foreign films as well as classics.

Times Arts Tix (Map p221; ☎ 619-497-5000; www .sandiegoperforms.com; cnr 3rd Ave & Broadway) Sells half-price tickets for same-day evening or next-day matinee performances in theater, music and dance.

SHOPPING

Little Italy (www.littleitalysd.com) is the de facto design district, heaped high with browse-worthy home furnishings shops, from antiques and architectural salvage to cutting-edge modern ware. La Jolla is the place to go for jewels and couture, particularly along Girard Ave and Prospect St. For bikinis and surfboards, head to Garnet Ave in Pacific Beach or Newport Ave in Ocean Beach. They also have good thrift and vintage shops, but the best are along Hillcrest's 5th Ave.

GETTING THERE & AWAY

Air

Most flights into **San Diego International Airport** (SAN; Map p220; ☎ 619-231-2100; www.san.org), about 3 miles west of downtown, are domestic. Coming in from overseas, you'll most likely change flights – and clear US Customs – at one of the major US gateway airports, such as LA, Chicago or Miami.

The flight from LA takes about 35 minutes; the drive is around two hours.

If you're flying to/from other US cities, it's almost as cheap to fly to/from San Diego as it is to LA. Airlines serving San Diego include Aeromexico, America West, American, Continental, Delta, Northwest, Southwest and US Airways. For contact details see p259.

Bus

Greyhound (Map p221; ☎ 800-231-2222, 619-239-3266; 120 W Broadway) serves San Diego from cities all over North America.

To and from LA (one way/round-trip $16.50/28, 2¼ to four hours, almost every half hour) trip times vary depending on the number of stops en route. There is a bus to Anaheim, the home of Disneyland, which runs nine times per day for the same price.

Services between San Francisco and San Diego (one way/round-trip $63/124, 11 hours, nine daily) usually require a transfer in LA.

Greyhound also has direct services from San Diego to Tijuana, across the border in Mexico (one way/round-trip $12/24, one hour, hourly on the half hour).

Train

Amtrak (☎ 800-872-7245; www.amtrak.com) trains arrive at and depart from the lovely **Santa Fe train depot** (Map p221; 1050 Kettner Blvd) at the western end of C St. The *Pacific Surfliner* makes trips to LA ($28 each way, 2½ hours); as many as five trains continue on to Santa Barbara ($30 each way, 5½ hours).

GETTING AROUND

Many people get around by car, but you can reach most places on public transportation. Metropolitan buses and the trolley lines are run by Metropolitan Transit Service (MTS), and several other bus companies serve surrounding areas. All sorts of local public-transportation tickets, maps and information are available from the **Transit Store** (Map p221; ☎ 619-234-1060; 102 Broadway at 1st Ave; ☉ 9am-5pm Mon-Fri). It sells the Day Tripper Transit Pass (one day/four consecutive days $5/15), which is good for unlimited travel on local buses, the trolley and bay ferry.

To/From the Airport

Bus 992 – nicknamed the *Flyer* – operates at 10- to 15-minute intervals between the airport and downtown (adult/senior $2.25/1). Buses leave between 5am and 1am and make several stops along Broadway before heading north on Harbor Dr to the airport.

Several companies operate door-to-door shuttles from all three airport terminals. Per-person fares depend on the distance traveled; figure on about $12 to downtown and $18 to La Jolla.

If you're going *to* the airport, call the shuttle company a day or so ahead. **Cloud 9 Shuttle** (☎ 619-505-4950, 800-974-8885) is the most established company. Others include **Airport Shuttle** (☎ 619-234-4403).

Bicycle

Coastal San Diego has wonderful areas for biking. All public buses are equipped with bike racks and will transport two-wheelers free. Inform the driver before boarding, then stow your bike on the rack on the back of the bus. For more information phone ☎ 619-685-4900.

The following are just two companies that rent various types of bicycles, from mountain and road bikes to kids' bikes and cruisers. In general, expect to pay about $5 per hour, $10 to $14 per half-day (four hours) and $20 to $30 per day.

Cheap Rentals (Map p224; ☎ 800-941-7761; www .cheap-rentals.com; 3221 Mission Blvd, Mission Beach)
Holland's Bicycles (Map p220; ☎ 619-435-3153; 977 Orange Ave, Coronado)

Boat

A regular **ferry** (☎ 619-234-4111; one way $3) runs hourly between Broadway Pier and Coronado. An on-call **water taxi** (☎ 619-235-8294; per person $7) connects Coronado, Shelter Island and Harbor Island. The service runs 2pm to 10pm Monday to Friday and 11am to 11pm Saturday and Sunday.

Bus

MTS covers most of the metropolitan area, North County, La Jolla and the beaches and is most convenient if you're going to/from downtown and not staying out late. Get the free Regional Transit Map from the Transit Store (p239).

For route and fare information, call **MTS** (☎ 619-233-3004, 800-266-6883, 24hr recorded info 619-685-4900; ☼ 5:30am-8:30pm Mon-Fri, 8am-5pm Sat & Sun). For route planning via the internet, go to www.sdcommute.com.

Tickets cost $1.75 for most trips, including a transfer that is good for up to two hours; on express routes it's $2.50. Exact fare is required. A one-day pass is $5 and a three-day pass is $12.

Car

All the big-name rental companies have convenient desks at the airport, but lesser-known ones can be cheaper. The western terminal at the airport has free direct phones to a number of car-rental companies – you can call several and then get a courtesy bus to the company of your choice.

For contact details of the big-name rental companies, including Avis, Budget and Hertz, see p263. Some of the smaller, independent companies – such as **West Coast Rent a Car** (Map p221; ☎ 619-544-0606; 834 W Grape St) in Little Italy – may have lower rates and offer more relaxed conditions.

Taxi

Some established companies:
San Diego Cab (☎ 619-226-8294)
Yellow Cab (☎ 619-234-6161)

Train

A commuter train service, the *Coaster*, leaves the Santa Fe train depot (Map p221) and runs up the coast to North County, with stops in Solana Beach, Encinitas, Carlsbad and Oceanside. (You can bring your bike on the *Coaster*.) In the metropolitan area, it stops at the Sorrento Valley station (where there's a connecting shuttle to UCSD) and Old Town. Tickets are available from vending machines at stations and must be validated prior to boarding. Fares range from $4 to $5.50. There are 11 daily trains in each direction Monday to Friday. On Saturday, there are only four.

For information, contact **Regional Transit** (☎ 619-233-3004, from North County 800-266-6883; www.sd commute.com).

Trolley

Two trolley lines run to/from the downtown terminal near the Santa Fe train depot (see Map p221). Trolleys run between 4:20am and 2:20am daily at 15-minute intervals during the day, and every 30 minutes in the evening. The Blue Line continues running all night on Saturday.

Fares vary with distance ($1.25 to $3). Tickets are dispensed from vending machines on the station platforms and are valid for two hours from the time of validation. For information, contact **Regional Transit** (☎ 619-233-3004, from North County 800-266-6883; www.sdcom mute.com).

NORTH COUNTY COAST

A little north of La Jolla, the coastal cliffs shrink quickly, making way for a series of wide, inviting beaches that stretch nearly unbroken all the way to Camp Pendleton, the hulking military base that takes up the northwest corner of the county.

Known simply as 'North County,' this region resembles the San Diego of 40 years ago, though more and more development, especially east of I-5, has turned much of it into a giant bedroom community. Stick close to the water for the best ambience.

Information

The **San Diego North County Convention & Visitors Bureau** (☎ 760-745-4741, 800-848-3336; www.sandiego north.com; 360 N Escondido Blvd), in Escondido, is an

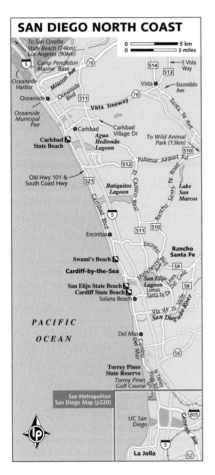

SAN DIEGO NORTH COAST

See Metropolitan San Diego Map (p220)

North County Transit District (NCTD; ☎ 760-966-6500; www.gonctd.com). The NCTD also operates the *Coaster* commuter train, which originates in San Diego, and makes stops in Solana Beach, Encinitas, Carlsbad and Oceanside. All NCTD buses and trains have bike racks. Greyhound buses stop at Oceanside and San Diego, but nowhere in between.

DEL MAR
pop 4400

Though Del Mar is the ritziest of North County's seaside suburbs, this doesn't translate into much apparent curb appeal, unless you're a surfer. 'Downtown' extends for about a mile along Camino del Mar, but the closest thing to a town center is the artificial-feeling yet not unpleasant Del Mar Plaza, which boasts expensive restaurants, boutiques and terraces that look out to sea – as well as a market where you can stock up on sandwiches for the beach. On the north end of town is where you'll find Del Mar's fabled horse-racing track, which is also the site of the annual county fair in June.

At the beach end of 15th St, **Seagrove Park** overlooks the ocean. This little stretch of well-groomed beachfront lawn has a great playground.

The **Del Mar Racetrack & Fairgrounds** (☎ 858-755-1141; www.dmtc.com; admission $3-8) was founded in 1937 by a number of Hollywood luminaries, including Bing Crosby. The lush gardens and pink, Mediterranean-style architecture are a delight. The racing season runs from mid-July to mid-September.

You can hardly see the **Les Artistes Inn** (☎ 858-755-4646, 800-223-8449; www.lesartistesinn.com; 944 Camino del Mar; r $150-195) for all the creeping vines, gurgling fountains and creatively placed tiles fronting it. Each room is devoted to an early-20th-century artist – except for Zen, which is catch-all Asian. The bright and airy Monet room overlooks the backyard goldfish pond through its French doors.

Visit the **Fish Market** (☎ 858-755-2277; 640 Via De La Valle; mains $12-22; ☽ lunch & dinner; ☖) and slide into a seat at one of the solid wood tables at this spacious, boisterous eatery just north of the fairgrounds. And as for what to order, just check the 'fresh today' list and go from there – unless you're a shellfish fan, in which case head straight to the oyster bar. A good spot to schlep the tykes.

excellent source for information on all of North County, including inland locations.

Getting There & Around
From the south, take N Torrey Pines Rd to Del Mar for the most scenic approach to North County. Continue along the coast on S21 (which changes its name from Camino del Mar to Pacific Coast Hwy to Old Hwy 101, going north). The I-5 is quicker and continues to LA. If possible, avoid driving during rush hour (7am to 10am and 3pm to 7pm Monday to Friday).

Bus 101 departs from University Towne Centre near La Jolla and follows the coastal road to Oceanside, while bus 310 operates an express service up I-5; for information call the

SOLANA BEACH
pop 13,400

Solana Beach has a more homey, walkabout feel than Del Mar, with good beaches as well as the **Cedros Design District** (Cedros Ave), which has a glut of home-furnishing stores, architecture studios, antiques shops and clothing boutiques.

Vegetarians visit **Zinc Café** (☎ 858-793-5436; 132 S Cedros Ave; mains $7-8; ⊙ 7am-5pm; **V**) and either order at the counter or sit outside. It serves a gourmet, Cal-Ital menu with precious dishes like potato arugula pizzette.

The crowd at the converted warehouse and bar **Belly Up Tavern** (☎ 858-481-9022, 858-481-8140; 143 S Cedros Ave) gets down to folks like Neko Case, Blackalicious and Calexico.

ENCINITAS
pop 62,700

Since Paramahansa Yoganada founded his **Self-Realization Fellowship Retreat & Hermitage** here in 1937, the town has been a magnet for healers and seekers. The gold lotus domes of the hermitage – conspicuous on Old Hwy 101 (S21) – mark the southern end of Encinitas, as well as the turnout for **Swami's**, a powerful reef break favored by territorial locals. Parking is free.

Sights

A highlight is the hermitage's **Meditation Garden** (☎ 760-753-2888; 215 K St; ⊙ 9am-5pm Tue-Sat, 11am-5pm Sun), with magical ocean vistas, multitiered koi ponds, and a palpable tranquility. The entrance is west of Old Hwy 101 (S21).

The heart of Encinitas lies north of the hermitage between E and D Sts. Apart from the outdoor cafés, bars, restaurants and surf shops, the town's main attraction is **La Paloma Theater** (☎ 760-436-7469; 471 S Coast Hwy 101), built in 1928.

The 35-acre **Quail Botanical Gardens** (☎ 760-436-3036; www.qbgardens.org; 230 Quail Gardens Dr; adult/child 3-12 $10/5; ⊙ 9am-5pm; ⑤) nurtures the largest variety of bamboo plants in North America. Its interactive garden for kids, Seeds of Wonder, is an award-winning romp. To get there, take the Leucadia Blvd exit from I-5 and head east for 0.5 miles.

Sleeping & Eating

our pick **Leucadia Beach Inn** (☎ 760-943-7461; www.leucadiabeachinn.org; 1322 N Coast Hwy; r $85-145; ⑤ ⊠) Manager Dolly Graciano treats this utterly charming 1920s motel like her own home, which is a good thing, as she's a neat freak (and knock-down friendly, to boot). Bedspreads get laundered after *every* stay, especially important since both kids and pets are welcome. All 21 rooms have Spanish tile floors and many have full kitchenettes. Room 1 is a favorite, with chipper pink walls and a bed partially recessed into the wall. The motel has free wi-fi, and whenever the spirit moves her (which is often), Dolly will throw a BBQ for staff and guests right in the courtyard. The beach is a few blocks' walk. The secret's out about Leucadia, so book early for a summer visit.

Swami's Café (☎ 760-944-0612; 1163 S Coast Hwy; mains $4-8; ⊙ breakfast & lunch) For breakfast burritos, salads and smoothies, you can't beat Swami's. Not surprisingly, there's lots for vegetarians.

Yu Me Ya (☎ 760-633-4288; 1246 N Coast Hwy; mains $3-7; ⊙ dinner Tue-Sun) If you've been to Japan, you already know all about *izakaya* fare, the small plates served at local watering holes. For the rest of you, we could call it Japanese tapas. Family-run Yu Me Ya pulls off a large menu crammed with mostly traditional takes on bites like barbecued beef salad, handmade udon, vegetable tempura with green tea salt, as well as a handful of sushi rolls. It's the perfect chance to try some Japanese food more adventurous than a cream cheese and asparagus roll without paying through the nose for it.

CARLSBAD
pop 95,100

Besides fine beaches, the town is home to the kitschy but fun Legoland. Carlsbad got its start when the train service arrived in the 1880s. As a result, it has a solid downtown of four square blocks rather than stretching along the highway like most North County towns. Homesteader John Frazier claimed his well water had identical mineral content to the spa water of Karlsbad (now in the Czech Republic), hence the name.

Modeled loosely after – but not quite as cool as – the original in Denmark, **Legoland California** (☎ 760-918-5346; www.legoland.com; ⊙ 10am-5pm daily summer, to 8pm daily mid-Jun–late-Aug, Thu-Mon fall-spring; adult/child 3-12 $57/44; **P**) is a fantasy environment built entirely of those little colored plastic building blocks that many of us grew up with. Highlights include **Miniland**, in which the sky-

DRIVING TOUR: ESCONDIDO VIA RANCHO SANTA FE

What to See

Here's a nice, meandering route to reach the Wild Animal Park (p227), or give the brutes a miss and come for the small, slightly quirk-filled city of Escondido itself, via a drive through the second-richest zip code in the nation. From Del Mar, head east on CR-S9/Via de la Valle, where your first stop, about 6 miles down, must be **Chino Ranch Vegetable Shop** (☎ 858-756-3184; 6123 Calzada del Bosque; ☉ Tue-Sun), which is just a roadside produce stand the way that wine is just a beverage. The Chino family has been selling heirloom varieties and creating hybrid cultivars since 1972, and the produce's quality and unbelievable variety (60 types of lettuces!) has earned the rabid loyalty of chefs like Alice Waters and George's at the Cove's (p238) Trey Foshee. One more mile to **Rancho Santa Fe** proper, where you'll find yourself winding up and down rolling hills, past homes inhabited by folks with a median income of $200,000. You'll see fancy landscaping framing impermeable gates, but not much of the mansions themselves. Soon you're in **Escondido** (Spanish for 'hidden'), lacking in both pretension and tourists. First stop, especially if you're towing kids, should be **Queen Califia's Magical Circle** (☎ 760-839-4691; 3333 Bear Valley Pkwy, Kit Carson Park; admission free), a whimsical sculpture garden that doubles as a playground, peopled by the colorfully mosaiced figures from the imagination of French-American artist Niki de Saint Phalle. Downtown, take a peek, or a swing, at the grapevine-shaped jungle gym in **Grape Day Park** (Valley Pkwy & Pennsylvania Ave). For copious amounts of Mexican finger food and a mind-boggling array of stuff (remember to bargain!), head to the outdoor **swap meet** (☎ 760-745-3100; 635 W Mission Ave; admission depending on day free-$1.75; ☉ 7am-5pm Wed, Thu, Sat & Sun, 3-9:30pm Fri), where Spanish is the default language.

The Route

It's 7 miles from Del Mar to Rancho Santa Fe on CR-S9. Then you'll take CR-S6 slightly north 19 miles towards Escondido. To get to Queen Califia, take a right onto W Via Rancho Pkwy, which becomes Bear Valley Parkway after crossing over I-15. To get into downtown Escondido, backtrack and jump onto I-15N for 5 miles. From Escondido, you can head back to the coast via the way you came, or take I-78 the 21 miles to Oceanside.

Time & Mileage

It's about a 50-mile round-trip, and can take from two hours to half a day.

lines of major metropolitan cities have been re-created entirely of Lego, complete with moving cars and Lego-folk. 'New York's' 25ft Freedom Tower was built according to the real Freedom Tower's winning design, years before the actual building will be complete. There are also lots of low-thrill activities like face painting and fire truck 'driving'. The roller-coaster rides are more mild than wild.

Take the Legoland/Cannon Rd exit off I-5 and follow the signs. From downtown Carlsbad or downtown San Diego, take the *Coaster* to the Carlsbad Village Station; from here bus 344 goes to the park.

The 86-room boutique hotel **West Inn & Suites** (☎ 866-375-4705, 760-208-4929; 4970 Av Encinas; r incl breakfast from $169; ☉ ☒ ☐ ☒) caters in equal parts to business folk (note the computer and fitness centers) and vacationing families (note the sparkling pool and the shuttle service – including car seats – to the beach and Legoland). It's not dirt-cheap, but as you enjoy your king-size bed, fresh orchids, Aveda bath products and 30in flat-screen TV, you'd think you'd be paying a lot more.

In an unassuming shopping center just off I-5, **French Pastry Cafe** (☎ 760-729-2241; 1005 Carlsbad Village Dr; mains $6; ☉ 7am-6pm) is the real-deal place for croissants and brioches baked daily and kick-start espresso, plus omelettes, salads and sandwiches until 2:30pm.

OCEANSIDE

pop 175,000

The preponderance of barber shops, surplus stores and 'no sniveling' bumper stickers immediately clue you in to the heavy military presence in Oceanside, which lies just outside

SAN DIEGO AREA

the Camp Pendleton Marine Base. It lacks the effervescence of its coastal neighbors, unless you're keen for some Saturday-night soldier love, but hey, the surf is great, and the streets sure are safe.

The wooden **Oceanside Pier**, which extends more than 1900ft out to sea, is so long that an **electric shuttle** transports people to the end ($0.50).

Displays at the **California Surf Museum** (☎ 760-721-6876; www.surfmuseum.org; 223 N Coast Hwy at Pier View; admission free; ☺ 10am-4pm) include the 8ft-long, 85lb redwood board that once belonged to Faye Baird Fraser, who, in the 1920s, became one of SoCal's first great female surfers.

Find a spot of peacenik in hawkish Oceanside at **Hill Street Coffee House** (☎ 760-966-0985; 524 S Coast Hwy; mains $5-18; ☺ breakfast, lunch & dinner) Housed in a yellow Victorian, this dog-friendly restaurant and espresso bar sources only organic meats, poultry, fish, and veggies for its gourmet-but-not-too-gourmet concoctions. Tons of vegetarian options, natch. Often there are bags of surplus produce you can buy off the porch. Next door is a cute sushi place that shares Hill Street's crunchy sensibility.

TIJUANA, MEXICO

pop 2 million

No one's pretending that a jaunt to Tijuana is going to instill any deep insights into Mexican culture. It's not 'real' Mexico by a long shot, but you're definitely not in San Diego anymore, Dorothy. Americans have long used Tijuana (pronounced tee-*hwah*-na and sometimes called 'TJ' north of the border) as a quick escape from moral norms, and SoCal teens, like their predecessors during Prohibition, still pour across the border for booze and boobs. These days storefronts proffering dirt-cheap prescription drugs are almost as much of a draw.

The Avenida (Av) Revolución – aka La Revo – is still one of the wildest streets in North America, its stores overflowing with kitschy souvenirs while strip-club touts, cab drivers and white-coated 'pharmacists' bark, hiss and purr at every passerby. All the while, the long-suffering, street-corner Mexican zebras (sombrero-wearing burros painted with stripes) look on, waiting to be photographed under guffawing gringos.

INFORMATION

Downtown Tijuana (also called Zona Centro) is a 10- to 15-minute walk southwest of the San Ysidro border crossing and consists of a grid pattern of north–south *avenidas* (avenues) and east–west *calles* (streets).

Worldnet (Calle 2a 8174) and **Matrix** (La Revo 1543) are good spots to surf the Net for about $1.50 per hour.

Everyone accepts (even prefers) US dollars. It's best to carry small bills; otherwise you may end up receiving change in Mexican currency at a poor exchange rate. There's a branch of the **Tijuana Convention & Visitors Bureau** (☎ 664-683-1405; ☺ 8am-5pm Mon-Thu, to 7pm Fri & Sat, to 3pm Sun) just south of the pedestrian border crossing.

See p260 for information on crossing the border.

DANGERS & ANNOYANCES

Theft, pickpocketing, short-changing, bill-padding and the addition of 'gringo-tax' are not uncommon in Tijuana. Keep your wallet close, your wits sharp and at least one member of your group relatively sober, and you should be fine. Don't leave anything valuable-looking in your car, and park in a guarded garage or lot.

Tijuana has a central number for all kinds of emergencies (☎ 066). The **central police station** (Av Constitución 1616) is at the corner of Calle 8a (Hidalgo) in the Zona Centro. If you are the victim of a crime, call the state government's **tourist assistance number** (☎ 078).

SIGHTS & ACTIVITIES

Every visitor has to experience at least a stroll up raucous **Av Revolución**, also known as 'La Revo'. The structure reminiscent of the St Louis Arch marks the street's north end. La Revo's a cacophony of nightclubs, seedy strip bars, American fast-food chains and tacky souvenir stores. As you head south, you'll pass **Hotel Caesar** (Av Revolución 827), where the Caesar salad was born.

An oddly baroque version of art deco, the grand **Frontón Palacio Jai Alai** hosted the fast-moving ball game of jai-alai for decades before morphing into a venue for the arts.

The centerpiece of the **cultural center** (☎ 664-687-9695; www.cecut.gob.mx; Paseo de los Héroes at Av Independencia) is a huge spherical structure that locals have dubbed La Bola (the ball). In the same complex is the **Museo de las Californias** (☎ 664-687-9641/42; admission US$1; ☺ 10am-6pm Tue-

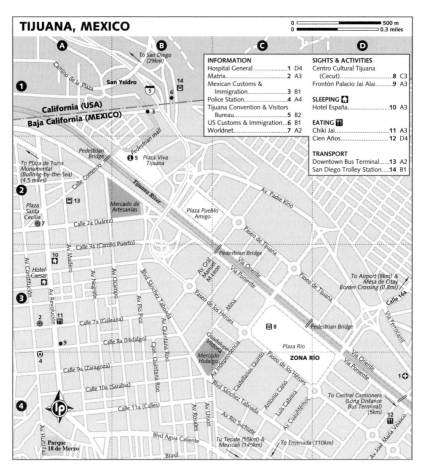

TIJUANA, MEXICO

INFORMATION	
Hospital General	1 D4
Matrix	2 A3
Mexican Customs & Immigration	3 B1
Police Station	4 A4
Tijuana Convention & Visitors Bureau	5 B2
US Customs & Immigration	6 B1
Worldnet	7 A2

SIGHTS & ACTIVITIES	
Centro Cultural Tijuana (Cecut)	8 C3
Frontón Palacio Jai Alai	9 A3

SLEEPING	
Hotel España	10 A3

EATING	
Chiki Jai	11 A3
Cien Años	12 D4

TRANSPORT	
Downtown Bus Terminal	13 A2
San Diego Trolley Station	14 B1

Fri, to 7pm Sat & Sun), which provides an excellent history of Baja California, with placards in commendable English.

Bullfights (*corridas*) take place on Sunday afternoons every two or three weeks from June through September. For information, see www.tjbullfight.com. Of the town's two bullrings, the more spectacular venue is the **Plaza de Toros Monumental**, the renowned bull-ring-by-the-sea in Playas de Tijuana, only a short distance from the border fence.

SLEEPING & EATING

Hotel España (☎ 664-685-7777; Av Revolución 968; r from US$45; P) This bright and airy option in the middle of La Revo has 30 rooms with cable TV (though your back can sometimes make out mattress springs), and continental breakfast is included. Rooms over the strip have balconies but are noisy.

Chiki Jai (☎ 664-685-4955; Av Revolución 1388; mains US$9; ☽ 11am-9pm) Thanks to its Spanish/Basque seafood (we recommend the *trucha al ajillo*, trout with garlic and olive oil), the pint-sized, tile-lined Chiki Jai has been packed with patrons since 1947. Pesos preferred, and no credit cards accepted.

Cien Años (☎ 664-634-3039; Av José María Velasco 1407; mains US$12-21; P) At this high temples of *alta cocina*, the chefs have dug deep into a box of ancient and exotic Mexican recipes (wanna take a stab at stingray taco?), some going back to the Aztecs and Mayans. Reservations recommended.

GETTING THERE & AWAY

The trolley is a great way to get to Tijuana from San Diego. It runs from downtown to San Ysidro ($5 round-trip, about 30 minutes) every 15 minutes from about 5am to midnight. From the San Ysidro stop, take the pedestrian bridge over the road and go through the turnstile into Mexico.

Your second-best option is to drive to San Ysidro. Get off I-5 at the Camino de la Plaza exit (1A), leave your car in a day parking lot ($7 to $9, cash only) and cross the border on foot.

On the other side of the border, most sites are within a 20-minute walk from the crossing. Follow the blue and white signs reading 'Centro Downtown' through Plaza Viva Tijuana, take another pedestrian bridge across Río Tijuana and walk a further couple of blocks to the northern end of Av Revolución. If you take a taxi, establish a price before hopping in.

If you do take your car into Tijuana, be aware that Mexican law recognizes only Mexican car insurance, so a US or Canadian policy won't suffice. Driving in Mexico without Mexican insurance can land you in jail.

Directory

CONTENTS

PRACTICALITIES

- California lies within the Pacific Time Zone: Greenwich Mean Time minus eight hours.

- The US uses the imperial system of weights and measures, but you'll sometimes see roadside mileage signs written in both kilometers and miles.

- If your portable electrical appliances have adjustable current-selector switches, set them to 110V for US travel.

- Video systems use the NTSC color TV standard that is not compatible with PAL or Secam.

- Six corporations own America's major media outlets. Listen instead to PRI (Public Radio International), Alternative Radio or more conservative NPR (National Public Radio) on the FM dial; for behind-the-corporate-veil news, see www.alternet.org or www.fair.com.

ACCOMMODATIONS

Accommodations in this book fall into one of three categories: budget (less than $100); midrange ($100 to $175); and top end (more than $175). We have marked our top picks within the lists. However, just because something isn't a top pick doesn't mean it's not good. On the contrary. Each property we recommend meets a certain baseline standard for quality within its class.

Lodging in Coastal California is expensive. In some regions, such as San Francisco, barebones budget lodgings start at $75 a night. Prices listed reflect *published, high-season rates* for rooms. You can almost always do better, particularly midweek or during the offseason, which along the coast means winter. Rates are generally highest in summer but they spike even higher around major holidays such as Memorial Day, Independence Day and Labor Day, when you should expect two-

and three-night minimum stays. Always ask about discounts, packages and promotional rates. Also check the web; some lodgings give better rates if you book online.

More and more properties are providing wireless-internet access (wi-fi), handy if you travel with a laptop, useless if you don't. Accommodations listed in this book that provide internet access for travelers without their own computers are indicated with an internet icon (🖳).

If you smoke, be sure to ask about the availability of smoking rooms. Many lodgings in California are exclusively nonsmoking. In Southern California, nearly all lodgings have air-conditioning, but in Northern California, where it rarely gets hot, the opposite is true. If it matters, inquire when you book.

If you book a reservation on the phone with a motel or hotel, get a confirmation number, and *always ask about the cancellation policy* before you give your credit-card number. If you plan to arrive late in the evening, call to confirm on the day of arrival. Hotels overbook, but if you've guaranteed the reservation with a credit card,

DIRECTORY

they will accommodate you somewhere else and pick up the tab for the first night's stay as a way of apologizing. If they don't, squawk.

Where available, we have listed a property's toll-free information and reservation number in this book. If you're having trouble finding accommodations, consider using a hotel-reservation service such as the **Hotel Reservations Network** (☎ 800-715-7666; www.hoteldiscount.com) or the big players such as www.orbitz.com, www.travelocity.com, www.expedia.com and www.hotels.com.

Camping

Campgrounds abound in California, and most along the coast are open all year round. Facilities vary widely. Basic campsites usually have toilets, fire pits, picnic benches and drinking water, and are most common in national forests and on Bureau of Land Management (BLM) land. The state- and national-park campgrounds tend to be the best equipped, featuring flush toilets, sometimes hot showers and RV hookups.

You can camp in national forests and on BLM land in any area where you can safely park your vehicle next to a road without blocking traffic. You are not allowed to park off undesignated roads (ie roads not shown on maps and that do not have signs that show the road number). Dispersed camping is not permitted in national parks, except for backpackers holding the appropriate permit. Check with a ranger station if you're unsure about where you can camp. Rangers also issue required fire permits (usually free).

Hostels

There are currently 21 hostels in California affiliated with **Hostelling International-American Youth Hostels** (HI-AYH; ☎ 301-495-1240; www.hiayh .org); check respective destination chapters throughout this book. Reservations are advised during peak season.

Independent hostels have no curfew and more relaxed rules. Often these hostels are convivial places with regular guest parties and other events. Some include a light breakfast or other meals in their rates, arrange local tours and pick up guests at transportation hubs. Some hostels say they accept only international travelers, basically to keep out destitute locals – American travelers who look like they'll fit in with other guests are usually admitted. A passport, HI-AYH card or international plane ticket should help establish your credentials.

B&Bs

If you want a comfortable, atmospheric alternative to impersonal motel or hotel rooms, stay at a B&B. They're typically in restored old houses with floral wallpaper and antique furnishings; they charge more than $120 per couple. Rates include breakfast, but rooms with TV and telephone are the exception, not the rule; some may share bathroom facilities. Most B&Bs require advance reservations, though some will accommodate the occasional drop-in guest. Smoking is prohibited.

Many places belong to the **California Association of Bed & Breakfast Inns** (☎ 800-373-9251; www .cabbi.com).

Motels & Hotels

Motels surround a parking lot and usually have some sort of a lobby. Hotels may provide extra services such as laundry, but these amenities are expensive. If you walk in without reservations, always ask to see a room before paying for it, especially at motels.

Rooms are often priced by the size and number of beds in a room, rather than the number of occupants. A room with one double or queen-size bed usually costs the same for one or two people, while a room with a king-size bed or two beds costs more. There is often a surcharge for a third or fourth person. Many places advertise that kids stay free, but sometimes you'll have to pay extra for a crib or 'rollaway' bed.

Room location may affect price; recently renovated or larger rooms, or those with a view, are likely to cost more. Hotels facing a noisy street may charge more for quieter rooms.

As a rule, motels offer the best lodging value for the money. Rooms won't often win design awards, but they're usually comfortably furnished and clean. Amenities vary, but expect telephone, TV, private bathroom,

DIRECTORY

heating, air-conditioning, and an alarm clock. More and more places now offer a small refrigerator, coffeemaker and microwave. Many have swimming pools and spas, coin laundry and free local telephone calls.

Make reservations at chain hotels by calling their central reservation lines, but to learn about specific amenities and possible local promotions, call the property directly. Every listing in this book includes local direct numbers.

Luxury Hotels & Resorts

Luxury hotels provide every imaginable amenity. Expect very comfortable, attractive furnishings, a bathrobe, iron, ironing board, hair dryer, thick terry-cloth towels, firm mattress, high-thread-count sheets and both down and foam pillows on the bed. If there's something missing, pick up the phone and call the concierge or front desk (see Tipping, p257). Higher-end properties offer more services, such as in-room massage and evening turndown. Some amenities cost extra. On the premises expect a restaurant of excellent caliber, serving three meals a day.

ACTIVITIES

Coastal California offers a bevy of activities for outdoor enthusiasts, from kayaking and kiteboarding to whale-watching and deep-sea fishing. Check the Outdoors chapter (p36) for ideas and inspiration; for specific outfitters, check the destination chapters. Most outfitters provide instruction and hand-holding for newbies, or they'll simply rent equipment for do-it-yourselfers.

BUSINESS HOURS

In large cities, several supermarkets and restaurants remain open 24 hours. Shops open from 10am to 5pm or 6pm (often until 9pm in shopping malls), except Sunday when hours are noon to 5pm (malls to 6pm). Post offices open 8am to 4pm or 5:30pm weekdays, and some are open 8am to 2pm on Saturday. Banks usually open from 9am or 10am to 5pm or 6pm weekdays; some also open until 1pm or 2pm on Saturday. Check with individual businesses for precise hours.

CHILDREN

Successful travel with young children requires planning and effort. Don't overbook your day! Cramming too many activities into a 12-hour day inevitably causes problems.

Ensure that the activities you choose include something for the kids as well – balance that morning at the art museum with a visit to the zoo or the beach. Include the kids in the trip planning; if they've helped figure out where you are going, they'll be much more interested when they get there. For more information, advice and anecdotes, read Lonely Planet's *Travel with Children,* by Cathy Lanigan.

Practicalities

Children's discounts are widely available for everything from museum admissions to bus fares and motel stays. The definition of a child varies – in some places anyone under 18 is eligible, while others only include children under six. Unless specified, prices quoted for children in this book refer to those aged three to 12.

Most hotels and motels allow children to share a room with their parents for free or for a modest fee, however, this practice is rare in B&Bs, and many don't allow children at all. Larger hotels often have a babysitting service, and other hotels may be able to help you make arrangements. Alternatively, look in the *Yellow Pages* for local agencies. Be sure to ask whether sitters are licensed and bonded, what they charge per hour, whether there's a minimum fee and whether they charge extra for meals and transportation. Always tip.

Most car-rental firms have children's safety seats for rent at a nominal cost, but be sure to book them in advance. The same goes for highchairs and cribs; they're common in many restaurants and hotels, but numbers are limited. The choice of baby food, infant formulas, soy and cows milk, disposable diapers (nappies) and other necessities is great in supermarkets throughout California. Diaper-changing stations can be found in many public toilets in malls, department stores, some gas stations, major airports and even some restaurants.

It's perfectly fine to bring your kids, even toddlers, along to casual restaurants (though not to upscale places at dinnertime). Children are generally welcome at daytime events.

Sights & Activities

Throughout this book you'll find family-friendly activities – Coastal California offers lots for kids to do. Aside from the many lighthouses along the shore, kids love **Fisherman's**

Wharf (p57) in San Francisco, **Legoland** (p242) in San Diego and **Disneyland** (p207) and **Universal Studios** (☎ 310-979-0114; 100 Universal City Plaza, Los Angeles) in Los Angeles, just to name a few. At national parks be sure to inquire at visitors centers for 'Junior Ranger' programs, in which kids complete specified activities and receive a badge or patch and certificate to take home. There's usually a nominal charge (less than $5) for the activity book. Many outdoor-activity tour operators have specially tailored gear for kids, depending on how little they are. Good activities along the coast include horseback riding, kayaking, bicycling and fishing. Check individual chapters for specific outfitters.

CLIMATE CHARTS

Coastal California has a diversity of climates, with the cool, foggy North Coast (including San Francisco) and year-round temperate regions further south. Summer months run from June to August. For more climate information, see p12.

COURSES

J World Sailing (☎ 619-224-4774; www.jworld-sailing.com) Sailing in San Diego.
Mendocino Art Center (☎ 707-937-5818, 800-653-3328; www.mendocinoartcenter.org) Art classes in Mendocino.
Old Mill Farm School of Country Living (☎ 707-937-0244, 707-937-3047; www.oldmillfarm.org) Organic farming workshops in Mendocino.
Surf Diva (☎ 858-454-8273; www.surfdiva.com) Women- and girls-only surfing school in La Jolla.
Torrey Pines Beginner Paraglider Program (☎ 858-452-9858; www.flytorrey.com) Flying in La Jolla.
World of Suzi Long (☎ 707-937-5664; 611 Albion St; Mendocino) Using a pocket-sized watercolor kit, wonderful Suzi teaches landscape drawing, helping you create a travel journal of the things you'll see during your trip. Ninety-minute classes cost $35; add another $35 for sketchbook and watercolors. Call ahead.

DANGERS & ANNOYANCES

By and large, California is not a dangerous place. The most publicized problem is violent crime, but this is confined to areas few visitors would go. Wildlife may pose some danger, and of course there is the dramatic, albeit unlikely, possibility of a natural disaster, such as an earthquake. Prepare for the worst, but expect the best.

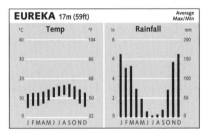

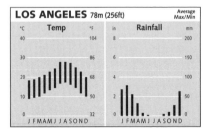

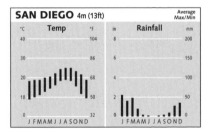

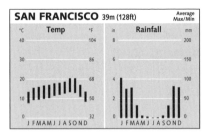

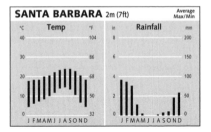

Crime

Tourists will rarely get tricked, cheated or conned simply because they're tourists. Potential violence is a problem for all, but there's really no need to worry. The Dangers & Annoyances sections in the destination chapters provide some details, but if you're worried, quiz hotel staff, locals and police about no-go zones.

If you find yourself in a neighborhood where you'd rather not be, look confident. Don't stop every few minutes to look at your map, and hail a taxi if you can. If you're accosted by a mugger, there's no 100% recommended plan of action, but handing over whatever the mugger wants is better than getting attacked. Don't carry valuables or an excess of cash, and don't put it all in the same pocket or wallet. Keep some money separate, and hand it over fast. Muggers are not too happy to find their victims penniless.

That said, don't meditate on crime. Protect yourself as best you can, then focus your awareness on having a great trip.

Panhandlers & Homeless People

If you visit a city you're sure to encounter beggars. Many suffer from medical or psychiatric problems, or the effects of alcohol and drug abuse; some are scammers. Most of them are harmless. It's an individual judgment call whether to offer them anything – you might just offer food if you have it. If you want to contribute toward a long-term solution, consider donating to a reputable charity that cares for the homeless.

Wildlife Dangers

Drivers should watch for stock or deer on highways. Hitting a large animal at 55mph will total your car, kill the animal and perhaps seriously injure you as well.

Bears are attracted to campgrounds, where they may find accessible food in bags, tents, cars or picnic baskets. Follow posted instructions at campgrounds. If a bear becomes habituated to human food, it will be shot by rangers. Use bear boxes when they're provided.

Mountain lions – also called cougars or pumas – are most common in the lower western Sierra, and the mountains and forests east of Los Angeles and San Diego, especially in areas with lots of deer. This includes some inland areas near the coast. Attacks on humans are rare.

Stay calm if you encounter a mountain lion, pick up small children, stand your ground – unless you've cornered the animal, in which case give it an escape route – and appear as large (and confident) as possible by raising your arms or grabbing a stick. If the lion gets aggressive or attacks, fight back, shout and throw objects at it.

Snakes and spiders are found throughout California, and not just in wilderness areas, but they prefer warmer inland areas. Attacks or fatalities are exceedingly rare; the following descriptions are necessarily general. If you get bitten, seek medical attention.

Watch your step when hiking, especially on hot summer afternoons in the inland hills and in the evenings, when rattlesnakes may bask in the middle of the trail. Most rattlesnakes have roughly diamond-shaped patterns along their backs and vary in length from 2ft to 6ft. Bites are rare (an average of 800 per year, ending fatally once or twice). Antivenin is available in most hospitals. Always wear hiking boots, and if you're worried, stomp your feet and stay out of thick underbrush and tall grass.

In Southern California, scorpions spend days under rocks or woodpiles. The long stinger curving up and around the back is characteristic of these animals. The stings can be very painful but are almost never fatal; however, bear in mind that small children are at highest risk.

The most dangerous spider in the area is the black widow. The female has a small, round body marked with a red hourglass shape under its abdomen. She makes very messy webs, so avoid these, as the normally shy widow will bite only if harassed. The bite emits neurotoxins; they're painful but very rarely fatal.

The large (up to 6in in diameter) and hairy tarantula looks much worse than it is – it very rarely bites and then usually only when it is roughly handled. The bite is not very serious, although it is temporarily quite painful.

Earthquakes

Earthquakes happen frequently in Coastal California, but most are so tiny they can only be detected by sensitive seismological instruments (see p32). If you're caught in a serious earthquake, get under a desk or table. Alternatively head to an inside doorway. Protect your head and stay clear of windows, mirrors or anything that might fall. Don't head for elevators or go running into the street. If you're in a shopping mall or large public building, expect the alarm and/or sprinkler systems to come on.

If outdoors, get away from buildings, trees and power lines. If you are driving, pull over to the side of the road away from bridges, overpasses and power lines. Stay inside the car until the shaking stops. If you are on a sidewalk near buildings, duck into a doorway to protect yourself from falling bricks, glass and debris. Prepare for aftershocks. Use the telephone only if absolutely necessary. Turn on the radio and listen for bulletins.

Riptides

The biggest hazards along the coast are riptides and dangerous ocean currents. Obey all posted signs on beaches. If you get caught in a riptide, which pulls you away from shore, don't fight it or you'll get exhausted and drown. Instead, swim parallel to the shoreline, and once the current stops pulling you out, swim back to shore.

DISCOUNT CARDS

Many hostels in California are members of **HI-AYH** (☎ 301-495-1240; www.hiayh.org), which is affiliated with the International Youth Hostel Federation (IYHF). You don't need an HI-AYH card in order to stay at these hostels, but having one saves you $3 a night. You can also buy one at the hostel when checking in.

If you're a student, bring along an International Student Identity Card (ISIC), which is a plastic ID with your photograph. These are usually available at your university or at student-oriented travel agencies and often entitle you to discounts on transportation and admission to sights and attractions. If you're a US student, carry your school or university ID card. Students can also buy the **Student Advantage Card** (☎ 877-256-4672; www.studentadvantage .com) for $22.50 for discounts on trains, buses, air fares and merchandise.

People over the age of 65 (sometimes 55, 60 or 62) often qualify for the same discounts as students; any identification showing your birth date should suffice as proof of age. Contact the **American Association of Retired Persons** (AARP; ☎ 800-424-3410; www.aarp.org), an advocacy group for Americans 50 years and older and a good resource for travel bargains. AARP offers membership cards for even greater discounts and extends its coverage to citizens

over 50 years and those of other countries. A one-year membership is $12.50.

FESTIVALS & EVENTS

Local celebrations occur frequently in California. The following list is representative only. Check with local visitors bureaus or chambers of commerce, or contact the California Division of Tourism (see p257) for more extensive listings.

January & February

Tournament of Roses Parade (☎ 626-449-4100; www.tournamentofroses.com) The famous New Year's Day parade of flower-coated floats, marching bands and equestrians held in the Los Angeles suburb of Pasadena.

Chinese New Year (San Francisco ☎ 415-982-3000, Los Angeles ☎ 213-617-0396) Held in late January/early February, Chinese New Year brings festivities, firecrackers, parades and lots of food, with the biggest celebrations in San Francisco and Los Angeles.

March & April

San Diego Latino Film Festival (☎ 619-230-1938; www.sdlatinofilm.com) Screens films from throughout Latin America and the US in mid-March.

Toyota Grand Prix of Long Beach (☎ 888-827-7333; www.longbeachgp.com) This week-long auto racing spectacle through city streets draws world-class drivers. Held in mid-April.

San Francisco International Film Festival (☎ 415-561-5000; www.sffs.org) The country's oldest film festival, held in late April to early May.

May

Bay to Breakers (☎ 415-359-2800; www.bayto breakers.com) The largest and craziest footrace in the world; it's a mob of costumed runners, world-class athletes and weekend warriors. Held in San Francisco in mid-May.

Kinetic Sculpture Race (www.kineticsculpturerace.org) On Memorial Day weekend, nonmotorized contraptions of all sorts ride from Arcata to Ferndale in the North Coast's wackiest, most famous event.

June

San Francisco Pride (☎ 415-864-3733; www.sfpride .org) Lesbian, gay, bisexual and transgender pride parade, in late June, attracts thousands of people to San Francisco.

July

Festival of the Arts & Pageant of the Masters (☎ 800-487-3378; www.foapom.com) Features exhibits by hundreds of artists and a pageant of art masterpieces 're-created' using real people; runs from early July to mid-August in Laguna Beach.

Annual US Open Sandcastle Competition (☎ 619-424-6663; www.usopensandcastle.com) Amazing sandcastle competition held mid-July at Imperial Beach, San Diego.
Carmel Bach Festival (☎ 831-624-2046; www.bach festival.com) If you love baroque music, make it a point of being in Carmel in mid-July or early August for the many recitals, lectures and performances.

August
Old Spanish Days Fiesta (☎ 805-962-8101; www.old spanishdays-fiesta.org) A celebration of early rancho culture with parades, rodeo, crafts exhibits and shows; runs in Santa Barbara in early August.
Steinbeck Festival (☎ 831-796-3833; www.steinbeck .org) Celebrates California's Nobel laureate with films, theater and lectures on John Steinbeck; in Salinas in mid-August.
Concours D'Elegance (☎ 831-622-1700; www.pebble beachconcours.net) Presents vintage vehicles to modern concept cars in a world-class parade in Pebble Beach in mid-August.
African Marketplace & Cultural Faire (☎ 323-293-1612; www.africanmarketplace.org) Celebrates African-American culture with traditional food, art and entertainment on three weekends in late August and early September in Los Angeles.

September
Fringe Festival (☎ 415-931-1094; www.sffringe.org) This theater marathon in mid-September brings a variety of performers from around the world to San Francisco.
Monterey Jazz Festival (☎ 831-373-3366; www .montereyjazzfestival.org) Held in mid-September, this is a long-running, big-name festival of traditional and modern styles of jazz, with workshops and exhibitions.
Simon Rodia Watts Towers Jazz Festival (☎ 213-847-4646) Features jazz, gospel, R&B and other sounds in the shadow of the Watts Towers; runs on the last weekend of September in Los Angeles.

October
World Championship Pumpkin Weigh-Off (☎ 650-726-4485; www.miramarevents.com) In Half Moon Bay, this is a competition of West Coast pumpkin growers, run in mid-October.
San Francisco Jazz Festival (☎ 415-788-7353, 800-850-7353; www.sfjazz.com) Features live music from top and new artists throughout the city from late October to early November.

November
Christmas Tree Lighting In late November many communities kick off the Christmas season by lighting up a large tree in a public place.
Hollywood Christmas Parade (☎ 323-469-2337; www.hollywoodchristmasparade.org) Features celebrities waving at fans lining Hollywood Blvd, classic cars, floats and marching bands.

December
Christmas Boat Parade (☎ 949-729-4400) A parade of 150 or so brightly illuminated boats floating in Newport Beach harbor.
First Night Santa Cruz Alcohol-free New Year's Eve street festival, with dance, theater and music, suitable for families. Santa Rosa and Monterey also have First Night celebrations. Call the respective visitors bureaus for details.

FOOD
Restaurants in Coastal California run the gamut from plain and simple to fabulous and stunning. Listings are presented in three general categories: budget (dishes $10 and under), midrange (dishes $10 to $20) and top-end (dishes $20 and over). As with accommodations, we list our top pick in each list. Remember, simply because a restaurant isn't our top pick doesn't mean it's not good. Indeed, there are several places where everything listed is equally good. For more on food, see p42.

GAY & LESBIAN TRAVELERS
San Francisco and Los Angeles have by far the most established gay and lesbian communities. In 2002 the *New York Times* started printing announcements of 'commitment ceremonies' on its highly prestigious Sunday Style pages. The next year, the Supreme Court overturned sodomy laws. The mayor of San Francisco declared gay marriage legal in 2004 (though the state overturned this). Such major advances clearly indicate a new cultural direction for America, but make no mistake, bigotry persists. Californians tend to be tolerant – especially along the coast – although there have been cases of bashings even in metropolitan areas. In small towns 'tolerance' sometimes comes down to a don't-ask-don't-tell policy.

San Francisco has its famed Castro District; San Diego's primary gay neighborhood is Hillcrest; and in LA it's West Hollywood and Silver Lake. All three cities have gay and alternative newspapers that list what's happening and provide phone numbers for local organizations.

Damron (www.damron.com) publishes the classic gay travel guides, including *Women's Traveler* and *Men's Travel Guide*, but they're advertiser driven and sometimes the information is out of date. Damron also publishes *Damron Accommodations,* with lists of gay-owned and gay-friendly hotels, B&Bs and guesthouses nationwide. On the web check out http://gay.com for loads of information – though some subscription-only. If you're looking for a gay mechanic or florist, see the **Gay & Lesbian Yellow Pages** (www.glyp.com).

Several important national and worldwide organizations also have a web presence; these include the **National Gay/Lesbian Task Force** (NGLTF; www.ngltf.org), **Gay and Lesbian Alliance Against Defamation** (GLAAD; www.glaad.org) and the **Lambda Legal Defense Fund** (www.lambdalegal.org), which provides legal counsel on gay-specific matters.

HOLIDAYS

Holiday travel can be very expensive and difficult, or cheap and easy. Thanksgiving weekend is America's biggest travel weekend, and you'll pay through the nose for a flight on either side of the holiday and be squeezed onto an overbooked flight – the same goes for Christmas. On the upside, people spend these holidays with their families, so city hotels stand nearly empty and consequently offer fantastic room rates.

On the following national holidays, banks, schools and government offices (including post offices) all close, and transportation, museums and other services operate on a Sunday schedule. Holidays falling on a weekend are usually observed the following Monday.

New Year's Day January 1
Martin Luther King Jr Day 3rd Monday in January
Presidents' Day 3rd Monday in February
Memorial Day last Monday in May
Independence Day July 4 (also called the Fourth of July)
Labor Day 1st Monday in September
Columbus Day 2nd Monday in October
Veterans' Day November 11
Thanksgiving Day 4th Thursday in November
Christmas Day December 25

INSURANCE

No matter how you're traveling, take out travel insurance. Read and understand your policy. Seek coverage that not only includes medical expenses and luggage theft or loss, but covers you in case of cancellations or delays in your travel arrangements. The best policies are those that also extend to the worst possible scenario, such as an accident that requires hospitalization and a return flight home. Check your medical policy at home, since you may already have worldwide coverage.

Ask both your insurer and your ticket-issuing agency to explain the finer points, especially what supporting documentation you need to file a claim. Buy travel insurance as early as possible – if you buy it the week before you leave, for instance, you may find that you're not covered for delays to your flight caused by strikes or other industrial action that may have been in force before you took out the insurance.

Wide varieties of policies are available and your travel agent should have recommendations. Some policies specifically exclude 'dangerous activities' such as scuba diving, motorcycling and even trekking. If these activities are on your itinerary, search for policies that include them.

While you may find a policy that pays doctors or hospitals directly, be aware that many health-care professionals still demand payment at the time of service, especially from out-of-towners – but they're legally bound to help you in an emergency. Except in emergencies, call around for a doctor willing to accept your insurance. Be sure to keep all receipts and documentation. Some policies ask you to call (reverse charges) a center in your home country for an immediate assessment of your problem.

INTERNATIONAL VISITORS
Entering the Country

Getting into the United States can be a bureaucratic nightmare, depending on your country of origin, as the rules keep changing. For up-to-date information about visas and immigration, check the website of the **US Department of State** (www.unitedstatesvisas.gov) and the travel section of the **US Customs & Border Protection** (www.cbp.gov).

In 2004 the US Department of Homeland Security introduced a new set of security measures called US-VISIT. Upon arrival in the US, all visitors will be photographed and have their index fingers scanned. Eventually, this biometric data will be matched when you leave the US. This is to ensure that the person who entered the country is the same one leaving it, and also to catch people who've overstayed their visas. For full details about US-VISIT, check with a US consulate or www.dhs.gov/us-visit.

Passports & Visas

Canadian nationals can enter the US with proof of Canadian citizenship. Visitors from other countries must have a valid passport, and many must also obtain a visa from a US consulate or embassy in their own country. In most countries this process can be done by mail or through a travel agent.

Under the Visa Waiver Program, citizens of certain countries may enter the US without a visa for stays of 90 days or less (no extensions allowed), as long as they have a machine-readable passport (MRP); if not, you'll need a visa. Under this program you *must* have a round-trip or onward ticket to any foreign destination, other than a territory bordering on the US (ie Mexico and Canada); the ticket must be nonrefundable in the US.

Your passport must be valid for at least six months longer than your intended stay. You'll need to submit a recent 2in-square (50.8mm x 50.8mm) photo with the visa application (plus a fee of $100). Documents of financial stability and/or guarantees from a US resident are sometimes required, particularly for those from developing countries. In addition, it may be necessary to 'demonstrate binding obligations' that will ensure your return back home. Because of this requirement, those planning to travel through other countries before arriving in the US are generally better off applying for their US visa while they are still in their home country, rather than on the road.

If you want, need or hope to stay in the US longer than the date stamped on your passport, go to the local **USCIS office** (☎ 800-375-5283 for the nearest branch; www.uscis.gov) *before* the stamped date to apply for an extension.

Immigration law is complex and ever-changing so always check with federal agencies for the latest.

Customs

US customs allows each person over the age of 21 to bring 1L of liquor, 100 cigars and 200 cigarettes duty free into the country. US citizens and permanent residents are allowed to import, duty free, $400 worth of gifts from abroad, while non-US citizens are allowed to bring in $100 worth. US law permits you to bring in, or take out, up to $10,000 (cash, travelers checks etc); greater amounts must be declared to customs.

California is an important agricultural state. To prevent the spread of pests, fungi and other diseases, most food products – especially fresh, dried and canned meat, fruit, vegetables and plants – may not be brought into the state. Bakery items and cured cheeses are admissible.

If you drive into California across the border from Mexico or the neighboring states of Oregon, Nevada or Arizona, you may have to stop for a quick inspection and questioning by officials of the California Department of Food & Agriculture.

Embassies & Consulates
US EMBASSIES & CONSULATES

Visas and other documents are usually handled by consulates, not embassies. While embassies are in a country's capital, the US also maintains consulates in many other major cities. To find the US consulate nearest to you, contact the US embassy in your country.

Australia (☎ 02-6214 5600; Moonah Pl, Yarralumla, ACT 2600)

Canada (☎ 613-238 5335; 4900 Sussex Dr, Ottawa, Ontario K1N 1G8)

France (☎ 01 43 12 22 22; 2 Ave Gabriel, 75008 Paris)

Germany (☎ 030 2385 174; Neustädtische Kirchstrasse 4-5, 10117 Berlin)

Ireland (☎ 01-668 8777; 42 Elgin Rd, Dublin 4)

Israel (☎ 03-519 7575; 71 Hayarkon St, Tel Aviv)

Italy (☎ 06-467 41; Via Vittorio Veneto 121, 00187 Rome)

Japan (☎ 03-3224 5000; 1-10-5 Akasaka, Minato-ku, Tokyo)

Netherlands (☎ 070-310 2209; Lange Voorhout 102, 2514 EJ The Hague)

New Zealand (☎ 04-462 6000; 29 Fitzherbert Tce, Thorndon, Wellington)

UK (☎ 020-7499 9000; 24 Grosvenor Sq, London W1A 1AE)

EMBASSIES & CONSULATES IN COASTAL CALIFORNIA

Most foreign embassies are in Washington, DC, but many countries, including the following, have consular offices in Los Angeles and San Francisco.

To get in touch with an embassy in Washington, DC, call that city's directory assistance (☎ 202-555-1212).

Australia Los Angeles (☎ 310-229-4800; 19th fl, 2049 Century Park E); San Francisco (☎ 415-536-1970; 625 Market St)

Canada Los Angeles (☎ 213-346-2700; 9th fl, 550 S Hope St)

France Los Angeles (☎ 310-235-3200; Suite 300, 10990 Wilshire Blvd); San Francisco (☎ 415-397-4330; 540 Bush St)

Germany Los Angeles (☎ 323-930-2703; Suite 500, 6222 Wilshire Blvd); San Francisco (☎ 415-775-1061; 1960 Jackson St)

Ireland San Francisco (☎ 415-392-4214; 100 Pine St)

Italy Los Angeles (☎ 310-820-0622; Suite 300, 12400 Wilshire Blvd); San Francisco (☎ 415-931-4924; 2590 Webster St)

Japan Los Angeles (☎ 213-617-6700; Suite 1700, 350 S Grand Ave); San Francisco (☎ 415-777-3533; Suite 2300, 50 Fremont St)

Netherlands Los Angeles (☎ 310-268-1598; Suite 1150, 11766 Wilshire Blvd); San Francisco (☎ 415-981-6454; Suite 1500, 275 Battery St)

New Zealand Los Angeles (☎ 310-207-1605; 11th fl, 12400 Wilshire Blvd)

South Africa Los Angeles (☎ 310-651-5902; Suite 600, 6300 Wilshire Blvd)

UK Los Angeles (☎ 310-481-0031; Suite 1200, 11766 Wilshire Blvd); San Francisco (☎ 415-617-1300; 1 Sansome St)

It's important to realize what the embassy of the country of which you are a citizen can and can't do. Generally speaking, it won't be much help in emergencies if the trouble you're in is remotely your own fault. Remember, you're bound by the laws of the country you're visiting and embassy officials won't be sympathetic if you've committed a crime locally, even if such actions are legal in your own country.

You might get some assistance in genuine emergencies, but only if other channels have been exhausted. For example, if you need to get home urgently, a free ticket home is exceedingly unlikely – the embassy would expect you to have insurance. If you have all your money and documents stolen, it will assist you in getting a new passport, but forget about a loan for onward travel.

INTERNET ACCESS

California leads the world in technology, so it's be pretty easy to check your email for the most part. There are internet cafés in cities large and small, and most hotels provide guests wi-fi and/or a place to log onto the internet. But in smaller towns, if you must stay connected, carry a laptop, a phone cord and your internet service provider's local dial-up numbers. Be sure to find out how to configure your modem before you leave home, and practice before you hit the road. But don't worry if you don't have a laptop: computer terminals are everywhere in the Golden State, and you'll never be too far away from your e-world.

LEGAL MATTERS

If you are stopped by the police for any reason, there is no system of paying fines on the spot. Attempting to pay the fine to the officer may lead to a charge of attempted bribery. There is usually a 30-day period to pay a fine. For traffic offenses, the police officer will explain the options to you. Most matters can be handled by mail.

If you are arrested for more serious offenses, you have the right to remain silent and are presumed innocent until proven guilty. There is no legal reason to speak to a police officer if you don't wish. Don't be cowed. All persons who are arrested are legally allowed the right to make one phone call. If you don't have a lawyer, friend or family member to help you, call your embassy. The police will give you the number upon request. If you don't have a lawyer, one will be appointed to you free of charge.

The legal drinking age is 21, and you can be asked for photo ID to prove your age. Stiff fines, jail time and other penalties can be incurred for driving under the influence (DUI) of alcohol or drugs. A blood-alcohol content of 0.08% or higher is illegal.

Police can give roadside sobriety checks to assess if you've been drinking or using drugs. If you fail, they'll require you to take a breath, urine or blood test to determine the level of alcohol in your body. Refusing to be tested is treated the same as taking and failing the test. Penalties for DUI range from license suspension and fines to jail time. If you're in a group, choose a 'designated driver' who agrees not to consume alcohol or drugs.

It is also illegal to carry open containers of alcohol inside a vehicle even if they are empty. Containers that are full and sealed may be carried, but if they have ever been opened, they must be stored in the trunk.

During festive holidays and special events, roadblocks are sometimes set up to deter drunk drivers.

In California, possession of less than 1oz of marijuana is a misdemeanor, and though

---

MAY I SEE YOUR ID, PLEASE?

Legal Minimum Age in California to…

- Drive a car – 16
- Fly a plane – 17
- Buy a shotgun – 18
- Vote in an election – 18
- Go to war – 18
- Drink a pint of beer – 21

it is punishable by up to one year in jail, a fine is more likely. Possession of any other drug including cocaine, ecstasy, LSD, heroin, hashish or more than an ounce of weed is a felony, punishable by lengthy jail sentences, depending on the circumstances. Conviction of any drug offense is grounds for deportation of a foreigner.

MAPS

Visitors centers and chambers of commerce often have good local maps, free or at low cost. For detailed state- and national-park trail and topographical maps, stop by park visitors centers or the forest ranger's station. The best are those published by the US Geological Survey (USGS), usually available at camping supply stores and travel bookshops. Many convenience stores and most gas stations sell detailed folding maps of local areas that include a street-name index for about $3.50. For a map atlas, the gold standard is the *California Road & Recreation Atlas,* by Benchmark Maps ($25; www.benchmarkmaps .com), which includes *every* road in the state, as well as topographic details, campgrounds and land features.

MEDICAL SERVICES

You'll pay through the nose for emergency care anywhere; expect bills from $100 to $500 – and up.

Always check with your insurance provider before you leave home to learn about your out-of-town coverage; or take out comprehensive travel insurance if you're traveling from overseas (see p254).

SOLO TRAVELERS

Traveling up and down the California coast alone can be meditative and peaceful, and there are no special cautions for solo travelers. Women should not fear journeying alone, but would be wise to remain aware of their surroundings as a matter of course.

TIPPING

Gratuities are not really optional in the US, since most people in service industries receive minimum wage and rely on tips as their primary source of income. However, if service is truly appalling, don't tip. There are customary tipping amounts.

Bartenders – 15% of the bill.
Bellhops, skycaps in airports – $1 to $2 per bag.

Concierges – nothing for simple information (like directions); $2 to $20 for securing restaurant reservations, concert tickets or providing unusual service.
Housekeeping staff – $2 daily, left on the pillow each day; more if you're messy.
Parking valets – $1 to $2 unless posted signs call for more when you retrieve your car.
Restaurant servers – 15% to 20% of the pretax bill.
Taxi drivers – 10% to 15% of metered fare.

TOURIST INFORMATION

The **California Division of Tourism** (☎ 800-463-2543; www.visitcalifornia.com) operates an excellent website packed with useful pretrip planning information. The office will mail you a free *Official State Visitors Guide,* but the website has just about all the same information, without all the paper.

The state government also maintains several **California Welcome Centers** (www.visitcwc.com) in various regions. Staff dispense maps and brochures and can help find accommodations. Look for them at Arcata (p124) on the North Coast, Los Angeles, and San Francisco (p49).

TOURS

Backroads (☎ 510-527-1555, 800-462-2848; www.back roads.com) Active guided and self-guided deluxe tours of the California coast, via bicycle and foot. Week-long tours cost $1000 to $2500.
California Dreamin' (☎ 626-533-5529, 866-440-4440; www.caldreamin.com) One-/two-week van tours ($540/1055) from LA to the blockbuster stops in California, such as Big Sur & Yosemite. Camp or sleep in hostels; meals included.
Elderhostel (☎ 877-426-8056; www.elderhostel.org) Nonprofit organization that offers learning trips throughout the world, including California, for active people over 55.
Incredible Adventures (☎ 415-642-7378, 800-777-8464; www.incadventures.com) One- & two-day trips ($75 to $229) from San Francisco – wine-tasting, river-rafting & hiking – in vans that run on biodiesel.

TRAVELERS WITH DISABILITIES

If you have a physical disability, there's no better place for travel within the US than California. The Americans with Disabilities Act (ADA) requires that all public buildings (including hotels, restaurants, theaters and museums) be wheelchair accessible. Buses and trains must have wheelchair lifts and telephone companies are required to provide relay operators (available via TTY numbers) for the hearing impaired. Many banks now provide ATM instructions in braille, and you'll find curb cuts at most intersections and sometimes audible crossing signals as well.

DIRECTORY

Larger private and chain hotels have suites for disabled guests. If you're worried about stairs, be sure to ask about the availability of an elevator. Major car-rental agencies offer hand-controlled vehicles and vans with wheelchair lifts at no extra charge, but you *must* reserve them well in advance.

All major airlines, Greyhound buses and Amtrak trains allow service animals (such as guide dogs) to accompany passengers, but you must have documentation. Airlines must accept wheelchairs as checked baggage and have an onboard chair available, though you should always call in advance. Airlines will also provide assistance for connecting, boarding and disembarking flights; request assistance when making your reservation.

Most national and state parks and recreation areas have paved or boardwalk-style nature trails. For free admission to national parks, blind or permanently disabled US citizens and permanent residents can get a Golden Access Passport. Books worth checking out include California Parks Access, by Linda and Allen Mitchell, and Easy Access to National Parks, by Wendy Roth and Michael Tompane. The Coastal Conservancy (☎ 510-286-1015; www.scc.ca.gov) publishes the free Wheelchair Rider's Guide: San Francisco Bay and the Nearby Coast, with details about access to coastal parks.

Organizations & Resources

A number of organizations and tour providers specialize in serving disabled travelers:
Access-Able Travel Source (☎ 303-232-2979; fax 303-239-8486; www.access-able.com) Excellent website with many good links.

Mobility International USA (☎ 541-343-1284; www .miusa.org) Advises travelers with disabilities on mobility issues; runs educational exchange programs.
Moss Rehabilitation Hospital's Travel Information Service (☎ 215-456-9600, TTY 215-456-9602; www.mossresourcenet.org/travel.htm) Lists extensive web contacts.
New Directions (☎ 805-967-2841, 888-967-2841; www.newdirectionstravel.com) Specializes in developmentally challenged travelers.
Society for Accessible Travel & Hospitality (☎ 212-447-7284; www.sath.org) Useful links and info specifically about travel.

WOMEN TRAVELERS

California is a relatively safe place to travel, even for women alone. Use the same common sense as you would at home.

The website www.journeywoman.com facilitates women exchanging travel tips and includes links to other sites. Another good source is **Her Own Way** (www.voyage.gc.ca/main/pubs /PDF/her_own_way-en.pdf), an online booklet published by the Canadian government and filled with lots of good general travel advice for women.

Though assault is unlikely, if you are assaulted, call the **police** (☎ 911). In some rural areas where ☎ 911 is not active, just dial ☎ 0 for the operator. Cities and larger towns have rape-crisis centers and women's shelters that provide help and support. Services include the **LA Rape Crisis Center** (☎ 310-392-8381) and the **San Francisco Rape Crisis Center** (☎ 415-647-7273). For other crisis centers and support services, contact the 24-hour **National Sexual Assault Hotline** (☎ 800-656-4673; www.rainn.org).

Transportation

TRANSPORTATION

THINGS CHANGE...

The information in this chapter is particularly vulnerable to change. Check directly with the airline or a travel agent to make sure you understand how a fare (and ticket you may buy) works and be aware of the security requirements for international travel. Shop carefully. The details given in this chapter should be regarded as pointers and are not a substitute for your own careful, up-to-date research.

GETTING THERE & AWAY

AIR

Domestic airfares fluctuate hugely depending on the season, day of the week, length of stay and flexibility of the ticket for changes and refunds. Still, nothing determines fares more than demand, and when business is slow, airlines lower fares to fill seats. Airlines are competitive and at any given time any one of them could have the cheapest fare. Expect less fluctuation with international fares.

International passengers to LA disembark at the Tom Bradley International Terminal of the **Los Angeles International Airport** (LAX; ☎ 310-646-5252; www.lawa.org).

Most international flights to the Bay Area land at **San Francisco International Airport** (SFO; ☎ 650-821-8211; www.flysfo.com), 15 miles south of downtown.

The airports in **Oakland** (OAK; ☎ 510-577-4000; www.flyoakland.com) and **San Jose** (SJC; ☎ 408-501-7600; www.sjc.org) are important domestic gateways with limited international services.

There are several smaller area airports, mostly for domestic travel:
Burbank-Glendale-Pasadena (BUR; ☎ 818-840-8847; www.burbankairport.com)
John Wayne-Orange County (SNA; ☎ 949-252-5200; www.ocair.com)
Long Beach (LGB; ☎ 562-570-2600; www.lgb.org)
Monterey Peninsula Airport (MRY; ☎ 831-648-7000; www.montereyairport.com)
Ontario/San Bernardino County (ONT; ☎ 909-937-2700; www.lawa.org/ont)
San Diego International Airport (SAN; ☎ 619-686-6200; www.san.org)
San Luis Obispo (SBP; ☎ 805-781-5205; www.sloairport.com)

The following major domestic airlines serve California:
Alaska (☎ 800-426-0333; www.alaskaair.com)
American Airlines (☎ 800-433-7300; www.aa.com)
Continental (☎ 800-525-0280; www.continental.com)
Delta (☎ 800-221-1212, 800-241-4141; www.delta.com)
Jet Blue (☎ 800-538-2583; www.jetblue.com)
Northwest (☎ 800-225-2525; www.nwa.com)
Southwest (☎ 800-435-9792; www.southwest.com)
United Airlines (☎ 800-241-6522, 800-538-2929; www.united.com)
US Airways (☎ 800-428-4322; www.usairways.com)

Major international airlines include the following:
Aeromexico (☎ 800-237-6639; www.aeromexico.com)
Air Canada (☎ 888-247-2262; www.aircanada.com)
Air France (☎ 800-237-2747; www.airfrance.com)
Air New Zealand (☎ 800-262-1234; www.airnewzealand.com)
Alitalia (☎ 800-223-5730; www.alitaliausa.com)
British Airways (☎ 800-247-9297; www.britishairways.com)
Cathay Pacific (☎ 800-233-2742; www.cathaypacific.com)
Japan Airlines (☎ 800-525-3663; www.japanair.com)
KLM (☎ 800-225-2525; www.klm.com)
Lufthansa (☎ 800-645-3880; www.lufthansa.com)
Mexicana (☎ 800-531-7921; www.mexicana.com)
Qantas (☎ 800-227-4500; www.qantas.com)

TRANSPORTATION

CLIMATE CHANGE & TRAVEL

Climate change is a serious threat to the ecosystems that humans rely upon, and air travel is the fastest-growing contributor to the problem. Lonely Planet regards travel, overall, as a global benefit, but believes we all have a responsibility to limit our personal impact on global warming.

Flying & Climate Change

Pretty much every form of motor transport generates CO_2 (the main cause of human-induced climate change) but planes are far and away the worst offenders, not just because of the sheer distances they allow us to travel, but because they release greenhouse gases high into the atmosphere. The statistics are frightening: two people taking a return flight between Europe and the US will contribute as much to climate change as an average household's gas and electricity consumption over a whole year.

Carbon Offset Schemes

Climatecare.org and other websites use 'carbon calculators' that allow travellers to offset the greenhouse gases they are responsible for with contributions to energy-saving projects and other climate-friendly initiatives in the developing world – including projects in India, Honduras, Kazakhstan and Uganda.

Lonely Planet, together with Rough Guides and other concerned partners in the travel industry, supports the carbon-offset scheme run by climatecare.org. Lonely Planet offsets all of its staff and author travel.

For more information check out our website: www.lonelyplanet.com.

Singapore Airlines (☎ 800-742-3333; www.singapore air.com)

Virgin Atlantic (☎ 800-862-8621; www.virgin-atlantic .com)

LAND
Border Crossings

Mexico and California share a border; Tijuana is the closest Mexican city, accessible via San Ysidro. Every day an average of 226,000 people and 82,000 cars cross the US–Mexican border here, making it the world's busiest border crossing. Open 24 hours a day, the border is about 20 miles south of downtown San Diego and about a 10-minute walk from Tijuana. You can cross the San Ysidro border on foot, by car or by bus from either side. The alternative crossing at Mesa de Otay, 5 miles east of San Ysidro, is open 6am to 10pm. There is no public transportation to Mesa de Otay.

US citizens or permanent residents not intending to go past the border zone (in other words, beyond Ensenada), or to stay in the border zone for more than 72 hours, don't need a visa to enter Tijuana. However, due to increased security, US citizens are required to carry proof of citizenship. Take a passport; or a certified copy of a birth certificate and photo ID; or US naturalization papers and photo ID. A drivers license is no longer proof enough, but a valid license can serve as photo ID. Non-Americans can be subject to a full immigration interrogation upon returning to the US, so bring your passport and US visa (if you need one).

For information on driving to Mexico, see 'Driving to Mexico,' p263.

Bus

Greyhound (☎ 800-231-2222, passes 888-454-7277; www .greyhound.com) is the main national bus carrier and operates to major and minor cities in California and the rest of the US. See p262 for information and details about fares and reservations.

If California is part of a wider US itinerary, you might save money by purchasing one of Greyhound's unlimited travel passes (called a Discovery Pass or an Ameripass), available for periods of seven, 10, 15, 21, 30, 45 or 60 consecutive days; average prices are $283 to $645. If you're coming from overseas, you can get a slight discount by buying in your home country; check the Greyhound website for overseas offices. You can only buy tickets online from within Canada and the US.

On regular tickets, students as well as seniors over 62 qualify for a 10% discount, and children get 50% off.

ROAD DISTANCE CHART (MILES)

Distances (miles) are approximated values, due to variations in route direction and selection.

	Crescent City	Eureka	Los Angeles	Mendocino	Monterey	San Diego	San Francisco	San Luis Obispo	Santa Barbara
Crescent City	---								
Eureka	81	---							
Los Angeles	727	644	---						
Mendocino	202	121	526	---					
Monterey	468	387	321	266	---				
San Diego	848	765	121	647	442	---			
San Francisco	356	275	380	154	112	505	---		
San Luis Obispo	526	443	201	325	120	322	230	---	
Santa Barbara	630	547	97	429	224	218	337	104	---

Car & Motorcycle

For information and advice on driving, see p263. Though each state legislates its own rules of the road, there's little variation from state to state.

If you're interested in driving someone else's car to save money on transportation, consider a drive-away car. To find an agency, check the *Yellow Pages* under 'Automotive Transportation & Drive-Away Companies;' also check the website, www.movecars.com.

Train

Amtrak (☎ 800-872-7245; www.amtrak.com) operates a fairly extensive rail system throughout the US. Trains are comfortable, if slow, and equipped with dining and lounge cars on long-distance routes. See p265 for details about intra-California routes, tickets and reservations.

Four interstate trains pass through California:

California Zephyr Daily service between Chicago and Emeryville (near San Francisco), via Omaha, Denver and Salt Lake City.

Coast Starlight Goes up the West Coast daily between Los Angeles and Seattle, with stops in Oakland, Sacramento and Portland.

Southwest Chief Daily departures between Chicago and Los Angeles via Kansas City, Albuquerque and Flagstaff.

Sunset Limited Thrice-weekly service between Los Angeles and Orlando via Tucson, El Paso and New Orleans.

Amtrak also offers passes for exploring other parts of the US. Children pay half price on all passes.

The USA Rail Pass is available to non-US or Canadian citizens only and is sold by travel agents outside North America as well as Amtrak offices in the US (show your passport). The pass offers unlimited coach-class travel within a specific US region for either 15 or 30 consecutive days; price depends on the region, number of days, peak or off-peak travel and the season. Average prices for the West Rail Pass (valid for travel anywhere west of Chicago and New Orleans) are $335/415 for 15-/30-day periods between June and early September and $215/280 the rest of the year.

Amtrak's North America Rail Pass, available to anyone, offers unlimited travel on Amtrak and Canada's **VIA Rail** (www.viarail.ca) for 30 consecutive days. Prices are $999 for travel between June and mid-October and $709 at other times of the year.

GETTING AROUND

AIR

If you have limited time and want to cover great distances quickly, consider flying. Depending on the departure airport, destination, time of year and booking date, air travel can be less expensive than bus, train or rental car. California airports are listed on p259.

Flights between the Bay Area and Southern California take off every hour from 6am to 10pm from OAK and SFO. It's possible to show up at the airport, buy your ticket and hop on, though good fares require advance

TRANSPORTATION

purchase, and you'll have set aside time to contend with security lines. You'll get discounts for booking seven, 14 and 21 days in advance; within a week of departure you'll pay full price.

Airlines offering flights within California include American Airlines, Continental, Delta, Southwest, United Airlines and US Airways (see p259 for airline contact information).

BICYCLE

Bicycling Coastal California requires a high level of fitness and focused awareness. Coastal highways climb up and down wind-blown bluffs above the sea and along narrow stretches of winding road with fast-moving traffic. Nonetheless, bicyclists are fairly common. Cars pose the greatest hazard.

You can rent bikes by the hour, day, week or month. Buy them new at sporting-goods stores and discount-warehouse stores, or used at flea markets and from notice boards at hostels. Also check the newspaper classified ads or online bulletin boards such as www.craigslist.org.

Bicycling is permitted on all roads and highways – even along freeways if there's no suitable alternative, like a smaller parallel route; all mandatory exits are marked. It's possible to bicycle on I-5 all the way from the Oregon border to just north of Los Angeles (but who would want to?). With few exceptions, you may not mountain bike in wilderness areas or in national parks, but you may cycle on their main roads. Bicycles, including mountain bikes, are allowed on national forest and Bureau of Land Management (BLM) single-track trails. Inquire locally about regulations. Yield to hikers and stock animals.

The **California Department of Transportation** (Caltrans; ☎ 916-653-0036, 614-688-2597, 510-286-5598; www.dot.ca.gov) publishes bicycle maps of Northern and Central (but not Southern) California and will mail them to you free of charge. Also try the **Adventure Cycling Association** (☎ 406-721-1776, 800-775-2453; www.adv-cycling.org), which is an excellent source for maps, bike routes and gadgets.

If you tire of pedaling, some local bus companies operate buses equipped with bike racks; for details, call the companies' telephone numbers provided throughout this book. For more on transporting bikes on Greyhound buses, Amtrak trains and on airplanes, contact the respective company for

details on whether or not you need to disassemble the bike and box it.

Wear a helmet – they're mandatory for kids under 18. Ensure you have proper lights and reflective clothing if you're pedaling at night. Carry water and a repair kit for flats.

To avoid all-too-common occurrences of theft, use a heavy-duty bicycle lock; some include theft insurance. Etch your driver's license number or other ID number onto the frame of your bike. Most police stations have etching equipment on hand, and it's easy to do. Then register your bicycle with the police.

BUS

Greyhound (☎ 800-231-2222, ticket sales 800-229-9424; www.greyhound.com) runs several daily buses along highways between cities, stopping at some smaller towns along the way. Frequency of service varies. Buses to more popular routes operate every hour or so, sometimes around the clock.

The cheapest way to get around, Greyhound serves the less-affluent strata of American society, but by international standards service is quite good. Sit toward the front, away from the bathroom.

Generally, buses are clean, comfortable and reliable. Amenities include onboard lavatories, air-conditioning and slightly reclining seats; smoking is not permitted. Buses break for meals every three to four hours, usually at fast-food restaurants or caféteria-style truck stops.

Bus stations are dreary places, often in sketchy urban areas. In small towns, where there is no station, buses stop in front of a specific business – know exactly where and when the bus arrives, be obvious as you flag it down and be prepared to pay with exact change.

Buy tickets either at the terminal, through an agent, over the phone or online with a major credit card (in the US or Canada only). You can receive tickets by mail if you order at least 10 days in advance, or show proper identification and pick them up at the ticket counter.

Children under 12 pay half-price; and seniors over 62 qualify for 5% discounts. Students with a Student Advantage Card (see p252) receive 15% off regular fares; otherwise, students receive 10% off by showing valid student ID.

For lower fares, buy tickets at least seven days in advance; also check the Greyhound website for special promotions. For information about Greyhound's multiday passes, see above.

CAR & MOTORCYCLE

Roads in California are excellent, and cars provide the most effective means to explore Coastal California. Neither buses nor trains access large swaths of the coast, so plan on driving if you want to visit small towns, rural areas, isolated beaches or far-flung forests.

Driving Routes

MAJOR ROUTES

Three major north–south routes run the length of California. Hwy 1 is the most scenic, but the slowest.

US Hwy 101, a mostly four-lane highway, and State Hwy 1 are the primary roads along California's North and Central Coasts. In the far north, Hwy 1 merges with Hwy 101 at Leggett, where Hwy 101 continues the rest of the way to Oregon.

In Southern California, Hwy 101 ends in Los Angeles; Hwy 1 merges with I-5, which hugs the coastline to San Diego.

Hwy 1, also called the Pacific Coast Highway (PCH) in Southern California, runs along high bluffs on much of its serpentine course between Los Angeles and the Far North. If winding roads make you carsick, take Hwy 101.

Los Angeles' tangled freeways can be confusing. The most important thing to note is that freeways in the LA Basin go by names *and* numbers. Hwy 101, for example, is called the Ventura Freeway northbound, but the Hollywood Freeway southbound. Pay attention and take your time.

From Los Angeles to San Francisco, the trip takes nine hours via Hwy 101, but 12 hours via Hwy 1. The fastest route, inland I-5, takes six hours; if you must travel up or down California quickly, take I-5, but beware dangerous wintertime ground fog.

DRIVING TO MEXICO

Unless you're planning an extended stay or thorough exploration of Tijuana, taking a car across the border is probably more hassle than it's worth. If you do decide to take one, though, the most important thing you must do is get Mexican car insurance either beforehand or at the border crossing (available in numerous offices right at the Via de San Ysidro and Camino de la Plaza exits of I-5; about $8 per day). Expect to wait, as US security has tightened in recent years. The alternative crossing at Mesa de Otay is much

less congested, but further from town. No car insurance is available at Mesa de Otay.

You may also leave your car on the US side of the border and either walk or take a shuttle across. Several parking lots are located just off the Camino de la Plaza exit (the last US exit) off I-5. A popular lot is **Border Station Parking** (4570 Camino de la Plaza; per day $7). Also here is a small tourist-information kiosk with maps and pamphlets.

If you're renting a car or motorcycle, find out if the agency's insurance policy covers driving to Mexico. Chances are it doesn't. If that's the case, don't risk it: if anything happens to the car, your insurance will be nullified and you'll be responsible for all damages or loss. Better to park and walk. For more on visiting Tijuana, see p244.

Hire

Most of the big international rental companies have desks at airports, in all major cities and some smaller towns. For rates and reservations, check the internet or call toll-free:

Alamo (☎ 800-327-9633; www.alamo.com)
Avis (☎ 800-831-2847; www.avis.com)
Budget (☎ 800-527-0700; www.budget.com)
Dollar (☎ 800-800-4000; www.dollar.com)
Enterprise (☎ 800-325-8007; www.enterprise.com)
Hertz (☎ 800-654-3131; www.hertz.com)
National (☎ 800-328-4567; www.nationalcar.com)
Rent-A-Wreck (☎ 800-535-1391; www.rent-a-wreck.com)
Thrifty (☎ 800-367-2277; www.thrifty.com)

You must have a driver's license to rent a car; most also require that you have a major credit card, *not* a debit or check card. Prices vary widely, depending on the type of car, rental location, drop-off location, number of drivers etc. Costs are highest in summer and around major holiday periods, when demand increases. In general expect to pay from $30 to $50 per day and $150 to $250 per week for a midsize car, more in peak season and for larger cars. Most rental agencies require that drivers be at least 21; drivers under 25 must normally pay a surcharge of $5 to $20 per day. Rates usually include unlimited mileage, but not sales tax or insurance.

You may be able to get better rates by pre-booking from your home country. If you get a fly-drive package, local taxes come as an extra charge when you collect the car. Several online travel reservation networks have up-to-the-minute information on car-rental rates at all the main airports. Compare their rates with any fly-drive package you're considering.

Liability insurance is required by law, but it's not automatically included in California rental contracts because many Americans are covered for rental cars under their personal car-insurance policies. Check your own policy carefully and don't pay extra if you're already covered. If you're not, expect to pay about $15 per day. Foreign visitors should check their travel-insurance policies to see if they cover rental cars.

Insurance against damage to the car itself, called Collision Damage Waiver (CDW) or Loss Damage Waiver (LDW), costs about $15 per day; it may require that you pay the first $100 to $500 for any repairs.

Some credit cards, such as American Express or gold and platinum MasterCard and Visa, cover CDW for rentals up to 15 days, provided you charge the entire cost of the rental to the card. Check with your credit-card company to determine the extent of coverage. It doesn't apply to all rentals; find out in advance.

Motorcycles

With a heritage that predates *Easy Rider* and *The Wild One,* motorcycling in America is an almost mythic experience. When the Golden Gate Bridge opened in 1937, the San Francisco Motorcycle Club crossed it first, ahead of the cars.

If you want to ride up and down the coast, you'll need a valid motorcycle license. An International Driving Permit endorsed for motorcycles will simplify the rental process. The free *California Motorcycle Handbook* details the road rules for motorcyclists. Pick one up free at any DMV office or online at www.dmv.ca.gov. Riders must wear helmets or face stiff penalties. To drive on freeways, you must have at least a 150cc engine.

Motorcycle rentals and insurance are not cheap, especially if you've got your eye on a Harley-Davidson or BMW. **Eagle Rider** (☎ 310-536-6777, 888-900-9901; www.eaglerider.com) has rental outlets in San Francisco, Los Angeles, San Diego, San Jose, Palm Springs and Las Vegas. It charges $75 to $150 per day, depending on the rental location, size of the bike and length of the rental. Rates include helmets, unlimited miles and liability insurance; collision insurance (CDW) costs extra. You can rent in one city and return in another for an extra $100.

Also consider **Dubbelju Motorcycle Rentals** (☎ 415-495-2774; www.dubbelju.com; 698 Bryant St. San Francisco) for BMW, Triumph and Harley-Davidson.

Recreational Vehicles

You can drive, eat and sleep in a recreational vehicle (RV). RVs remain popular for travel in California despite high fuel prices. It's easy to find campgrounds with hookups for electricity and water, but in big cities RVs are a nuisance, since there are few places to park or plug them in. They're cumbersome to navigate and they burn fuel at an alarming rate, but they solve transportation, accommodation and cooking needs in one fell swoop.

You can rent RVs and campervans from **Cruise America** (☎ 800-327-7799; www.cruiseamerica.com) and LA-based **Happy Travel Camper Rental & Sales** (☎ 310-675-1335, ☎ 800-370-1262; www.camperusa.com).

Road Conditions

Hwy 1 hugs the coastal bluffs along dramatic stretches of coastline, particularly between San Luis Obispo and Big Sur, and north of Jenner. Not for the faint of heart, Hwy 1 twists and turns on precarious cliffsides that often wash out in winter. The highway department always seems to be repairing it, and every couple of years, stretches close for months at a time and you can only reach certain communities by helicopter (it's rare, but it happens).

Further north along Hwy 101, just past Leggett (where Hwy 1 ends), the road runs between the Eel River gorge and unstable hillsides that regularly slide. When you see signs that read, 'Expect long delays 40 miles ahead,' or 'Hwy 1 closed north of Jenner,' heed their warnings, but don't panic. They sometimes overstate the situation to deter unnecessary travel. If you have hotel reservations, call the innkeeper. Folks north of Leggett *always* know precisely what's happening with Hwy 101: it's their only connection to the outside world.

For road conditions statewide, check with **Caltrans** (☎ 800-427-7623; www.dot.ca.gov).

Road Rules

The *California Driver Handbook* explains everything you need to know about California's driving laws. It's available free at any office of the Department of Motor Vehicles (DMV), or you can access it (as well as the motorcycle handbook) on the internet at www.dmv.ca.gov.

You must wear a seatbelt at all times. Children under four years old, or those weighing less than 40lb, must ride in approved child safety seats.

In winter months along the coast, avoid high-mountain inland routes unless you have a 4WD vehicle. If it's raining on the coast in January, chances are it's snowing above 5000ft in the mountains. Chains may be required at any time. Take note of weather forecasts.

Unless otherwise posted, you may turn right on red after stopping, so long as you don't impede intersecting traffic, which has the right of way. You may also make a left on red at two intersecting one-way streets.

At four-way stop signs, cars proceed in the order in which they arrived. If two cars arrive simultaneously, the one on the right has the right of way. This can be an iffy situation, and it's polite to wave the other person ahead.

On freeways, you may pass slower cars on either the left or the right lane, but try to pass on the left. If two cars are trying to get into the same central lane, the one on the right has priority. Some freeways and highways have lanes marked with a diamond symbol and the words 'car pool.' These lanes are reserved for cars with multiple passengers. Fines for driving in this lane without the minimum number of people are prohibitively stiff. Read the signs.

When emergency vehicles (ie police, fire or ambulance) approach, pull over and get out of their way.

For details about penalties for drinking and driving, see p256.

Speed limits range from 35mph (56km/h) on city streets to 55mph (89km/h) on two-lane highways and sometimes 65mph (105km/h) or even 75mph (120km/h) on interstates, freeways and rural highways. California has a 'Basic Speed Law' that says you may never drive faster than is safe for the present conditions, regardless of the posted speed limit. You can get a ticket for driving too slowly as well as for speeding, based on the police officer's assessment of the safe speed.

In cities and residential areas, watch for school zones, where limits can be as low as 15mph (24km/h) when children are present. These speeds are strictly enforced. *Never* pass a school bus from either direction when its red lights are flashing: it means that children are getting off the bus.

California has an aggressive campaign against littering. If you are seen throwing anything from a vehicle onto the roadway, you can be fined as much as $1000. Littering convictions are shown on your driving record the same as other driving violations. Gas stations always have garbage pails.

When parking, read all posted regulations and pay attention to colored curbs, or you may be towed.

LOCAL TRANSPORTATION

Cities, larger towns and counties along the coast operate local commuter-bus systems; some provide evening and weekend service. Check specific geographical chapters for coverage of local transportation.

TRAIN

Amtrak (☎ 800-872-7245; www.amtrak.com) operates train services throughout California, with bus services providing connections to some rural towns. Sometimes you'll only spend an hour on the train, then four hours on a bus, but it's more civilized than Greyhound.

The sleek, double-decker *Pacific Surfliner* operates a two-class train service between San Luis Obispo (SLO) and San Diego. All seats have laptop computer outlets, and there's a café car. A dozen daily trains ply the San Diego–LA route (via Anaheim), with four trains continuing north to Santa Barbara and four more continuing to SLO. Tracks hug the coastline for beautiful vistas.

Coast Starlight travels daily between LA and Seattle, stopping along the coast at SLO, Paso Robles and Oakland. Despite its romantic name, it travels on inland rails north of Santa Barbara but provides a comfortable alternative to flying, driving or taking the bus between San Francisco and Los Angeles.

Check with Amtrak for fares, promotional offers, information on California rail passes and details on inland routes.

Four interstate trains (see above) serve California. From LA to San Francisco the *Coast Starlight* costs around $70 (11½ hours); San Diego to Santa Barbara on the *Pacific Surfliner* costs $32 (5½ hours).

Seniors receive a 15% discount, children (two to 15) get 50% off and students with a Student Advantage Card (see p252) get a 15% discount. Fares are generally lower from January to May and September to mid-December.

Reserve as far in advance as possible to ensure a seat and a good fare.

Behind the Scenes

THIS BOOK

This 2nd edition of Coastal California was researched and written by John A Vlahides (coordinator) and Alex Hershey. Amy Balfour wrote the 'What to Do If You See a Star' boxed text in the Los Angeles & Orange County chapter, Josh Krist wrote the Windsurfing & Kiteboarding section of the Outdoors chapter, and Heather Dickson wrote the 'Woodies on the Wharf' boxed text in the Central Coast chapter. The last edition was written by John A Vlahides and Tullan Spitz. This guidebook was commissioned in Lonely Planet's Oakland office and produced by the following:

Commissioning Editor Suki Gear, Heather Dickson
Coordinating Editor Shawn Low
Coordinating Cartographer Owen Eszeki
Coordinating Layout Designer Katie Thuy Bui
Managing Editor Liz Heynes
Managing Cartographer Alison Lyall
Assisting Editors Helen Yeates, Monique Choy
Assisting Cartographers Anneka Imkamp
Cover Designer Candice Jacobus
Project Manager Sarah Sloane

Thanks to Sin Choo, Sally Darmody, Laura Jane, Celia Wood, Raphael Richards

THANKS
JOHN A VLAHIDES

My father passed away suddenly during the writing of this book, and though it initially feels too personal to state that in text, I am compelled to do so to emphasize the gravitas of my gratitude for the following people at Lonely Planet: Suki

Gear and Brice Gosnell for their compassion and generosity of spirit, and for encouraging me to do whatever I needed to regain my footing; Melanie Dankel and Alison Lyall for their wisdom and support; Shawn Low for his patience and sunny disposition; Heather Dickson for mapping out the book; and my coauthor Alex Hershey for her damn good work.

On the road, I am indebted to Christine Murray, John Rossell and Cora Clementine for their help finding an angle on wacky Santa Cruz, and to Eliot Busse for creating distraction. Thanks also to Debra Stegman and Tony Smithers for their wonderful insights. At home, I owe serious props to the best writing group in the world: Karl Soehnlein, Catherine Brady, Elizabeth Costello and David Booth. I'd be lost without you.

Mom, Barb and Tere: thanks for helping me through. I love you. Come to California and use this book.

I dedicate this book to the memory of my father, George D Vlahides, a great dad and an even better hematologist.

ALEX HERSHEY

Enormous tip o' the hat goes to my coordinating author John A Vlahides. Someone get this man a drink! Commissioning Editors Heather Dickson and Suki Gear started this ball rolling and kept it on track, respectively. Elaine Simer and Buster at Hostel Obispo win my generosity-of-spirit award. Bottom-of-the-heart gratitude to all who supported me emotionally, financially, calorically and every-other-ally during this adventure, especially

---

THE LONELY PLANET STORY

The story begins with a classic travel adventure: Tony and Maureen Wheeler's 1972 journey across Europe and Asia to Australia. There was no useful information about the overland trail then, so Tony and Maureen published the first Lonely Planet guidebook to meet a growing need.

From a kitchen table, Lonely Planet has grown to become the largest independent travel publisher in the world, with offices in Melbourne (Australia), Oakland (USA) and London (UK). Today Lonely Planet guidebooks cover the globe. There is an ever-growing list of books and information in a variety of media. Some things haven't changed. The main aim is still to make it possible for adventurous travelers to get out there – to explore and better understand the world.

At Lonely Planet we believe travelers can make a positive contribution to the countries they visit – if they respect their host communities and spend their money wisely. Every year 5% of company profit is donated to charities around the world.

after The Theft: Brice Gosnell, Sean Brandt, Ann and Roger Young, Meg Schaefer, Kryst Muroya (whether he likes it or not), Melissa Bolger, Jesse Fankushen, Mychal Mitchell, Robin Stark and Andy La Fond, Pam 'Palen' Lehr, Stacey Miller and Matt Wester. Love y'all!

OUR READERS

Many thanks to the travelers who used the last edition and wrote to us with helpful hints, useful advice and interesting anecdotes:

Norm Dandurand, Paul Kotz, Stan Kynsh, Cathy Larson, Celine Lescaut, Michelle Moore, Rachel Morrison, Arabella Richards, Joanne Thomson, Stewart Thomson, Aisla Van Dijk, Robin Vermoesen, Deb Wyatt

SEND US YOUR FEEDBACK

We love to hear from travelers – your comments keep us on our toes and help make our books better. Our well-traveled team reads every word on what you loved or loathed about this book. Although we cannot reply individually to postal submissions, we always guarantee that your feedback goes straight to the appropriate authors, in time for the next edition. Each person who sends us information is thanked in the next edition – and the most useful submissions are rewarded with a free book.

To send us your updates – and find out about Lonely Planet events, newsletters and travel news – visit our award-winning website: **www.lonelyplanet.com/contact**.

Note: we may edit, reproduce and incorporate your comments in Lonely Planet products such as guidebooks, websites and digital products, so let us know if you don't want your comments reproduced or your name acknowledged. For a copy of our privacy policy visit www.lonelyplanet.com/privacy.

Index

000 Map pages
000 Photograph pages

INDEX

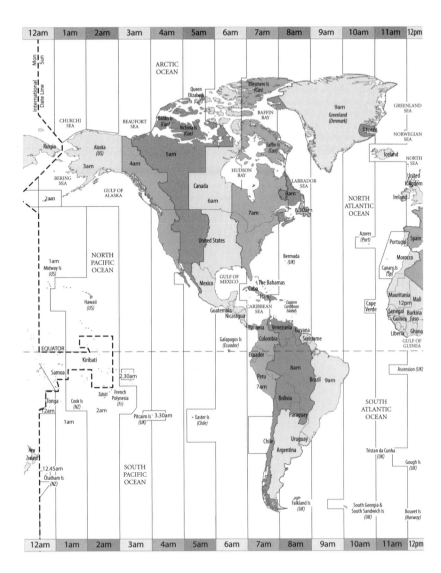

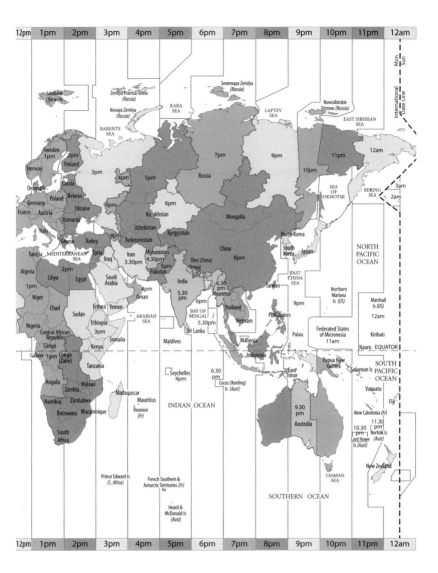

| 12pm | 1pm | 2pm | 3pm | 4pm | 5pm | 6pm | 7pm | 8pm | 9pm | 10pm | 11pm | 12am |

Mon
Sun

International Date Line

Svalbard
(Norway)

Zemlya Frantsa-Iosifa
(Russia)

Severnaya Zemlya
(Russia)

Novaya Zemlya
(Russia)

KARA
SEA

LAPTEV
SEA

Novosibirskie
Ostrovo (Russia)

EAST SIBERIAN
SEA

BARENTS
SEA

Sweden
1pm

Norway

Finland

2pm

3pm

7pm

9pm

11pm

12am

3am

Denmark

Latvia

4pm

5pm

Russia

10pm

SEA
OF
OKHOTSK

BERING
SEA

2am

Germany
France

Poland
Austria

Belarus

Ukraine

4pm

Kazakhstan

6pm

Mongolia

Italy

Romania

Uzbekistan

Kyrgyzstan

China

North Korea

NORTH
PACIFIC
OCEAN

Tunisia

Greece
MEDITERRANEAN
SEA

Turkey

Syria
Iraq

4pm

Turkmenistan

Afghanistan
4.30pm

8pm

South
Korea

Japan

Algeria

Libya

Egypt

Iran
3.30pm

Tibet (China)

Nepal
5.45
pm

Taiwan

EAST
CHINA
SEA

Northern
Mariana
Is (US)

Marshall
Is (US)

Niger

Saudi
Arabia

5pm

Pakistan

India

6.30
pm

9pm

12am

Chad

Sudan

Eritrea Yemen

4pm

Oman

5.30
pm

Myanmar

Nigeria

Ethiopia

ARABIAN
SEA

BAY OF
BENGAL

6pm

Thailand

Philippines

Federated States
of Micronesia
11am

Kiribati

Central African
Republic

3pm

Somalia

5.30pm

Vietnam

Palau

Nauru EQUATOR

Congo

Kenya

Sri Lanka

Malaysia

Gabon 1pm

Congo
(Zaire)

Tanzania

Maldives

Indonesia

Papua New
Guinea

Solomon Is

SOUTH
PACIFIC
OCEAN

Angola

Malawi

East
Timor

Vanuatu

Zambia

Madagascar

Seychelles
4pm

6.30
pm

Namibia

Zimbabwe

Mauritius

Cocos (Keeling)
Is (Aust)

Fiji

Botswana

Mozambique

Reunion
(Fr)

INDIAN OCEAN

New Caledonia (Fr)

11.30
pm

South
Africa

9.30
pm

Australia

10.30
pm

Norfolk Is
(Aust)

Lord Howe
Is (Aust)

New Zealand

Prince Edward Is
(S. Africa)

French Southern &
Antarctic Territories (Fr)

TASMAN
SEA

Heard &
McDonald Is
(Aust)

SOUTHERN OCEAN

| 12pm | 1pm | 2pm | 3pm | 4pm | 5pm | 6pm | 7pm | 8pm | 9pm | 10pm | 11pm | 12am |

MAP LEGEND

ROUTES

Tollway	One-Way Street
Freeway	Mall/Steps
Primary	Tunnel
Secondary	Pedestrian Overpass
Tertiary	Walking Trail
Lane	Walking Path
Under Construction	Track
Unsealed Road	

TRANSPORT

Ferry	Rail (Underground)
Metro	Tram
Bus Route	Cable Car, Funicular
Rail	Rail (Fast Track)

HYDROGRAPHY

River, Creek	Water
Intermittent River	Lake (Dry)
Canal	Lake (Salt)
Swamp	

BOUNDARIES

International	Regional, Suburb
State, Provincial	Cliff
Marine Park	

AREA FEATURES

Airport	Land
Area of Interest	Mall
Beach, Desert	Market
Building	Park
Campus	Reservation
Cemetery, Christian	Rocks
Forest	Sports

POPULATION

● CAPITAL (NATIONAL)	◉ CAPITAL (STATE)
● Large City	● Medium City
● Small City	○ Town, Village

SYMBOLS

Sights/Activities
- Beach
- Buddhist
- Castle, Fortress
- Christian
- Diving, Snorkeling
- Monument
- Museum, Gallery
- Point of Interest
- Pool
- Ruin
- Surfing, Surf Beach
- Trail Head
- Winery, Vineyard
- Zoo, Bird Sanctuary

Eating
- Eating

Drinking
- Drinking
- Café

Entertainment
- Entertainment

Shopping
- Shopping

Sleeping
- Sleeping
- Camping

Transport
- Airport, Airfield
- Border Crossing
- Bus Station
- Cycling, Bicycle Path
- General Transport
- Parking Area
- Petrol Station
- Taxi Rank

Information
- Bank, ATM
- Embassy/Consulate
- Hospital, Medical
- Information
- Internet Facilities
- Police Station
- Post Office, GPO
- Telephone
- Toilets

Geographic
- Lighthouse
- Lookout
- Mountain, Volcano
- National Park
- Pass, Canyon
- Picnic Area
- River Flow
- Shelter, Hut
- Waterfall

LONELY PLANET OFFICES

Australia
Head Office
Locked Bag 1, Footscray, Victoria 3011
☎ 03 8379 8000, fax 03 8379 8111
talk2us@lonelyplanet.com.au

USA
150 Linden St, Oakland, CA 94607
☎ 510 893 8555, toll free 800 275 8555
fax 510 893 8572
info@lonelyplanet.com

UK
72–82 Rosebery Ave,
Clerkenwell, London EC1R 4RW
☎ 020 7841 9000, fax 020 7841 9001
go@lonelyplanet.co.uk

Published by Lonely Planet Publications Pty Ltd
ABN 36 005 607 983

Driving Coastal California

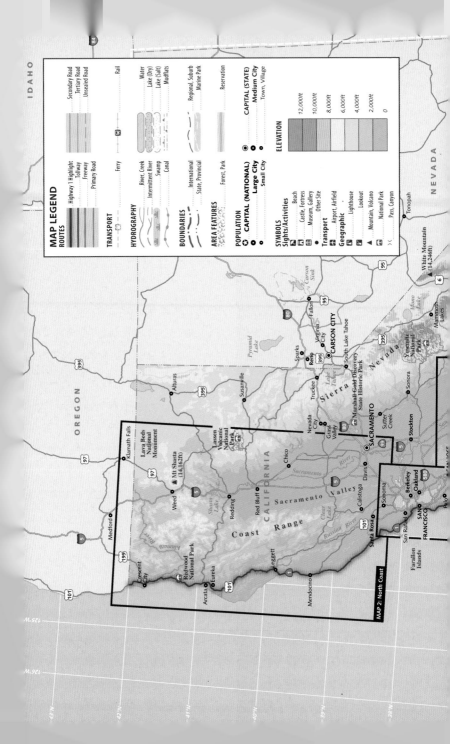

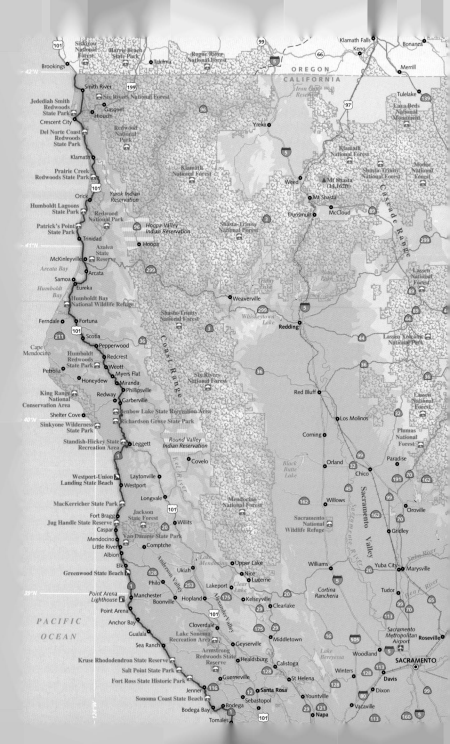